EXPERIENTIAL LEARNING

in

Schools and Higher Education

Edited by

RICHARD J. KRAFT

Professor of Education
University of Colorado, Boulder, CO----USA
Past Executive Director, AEE

JAMES KIELSMEIER

President
National Youth Leadership Council, St. Paul, MN----USA
Past President, AEE

ASS
2305 Ca

Cover photographs courtesy of (clockwise from left):
Tracy Silberman; Evelyn McLaughlin—The Montessori School in
Lutherville, MD; and Garth Lewis—Eagle Rock School, Estes Park, CO.

Contents

Preface

In this book, we have attempted to include a broad range of articles from the *Journal of Experiential Education.* Not everything that we wanted to place in this volume could be included due to space limitations, and because many excellent articles are in our companion volume, *The Theory of Experiential Education,* edited by Karen Warren of Hampshire College, Dr. Mitchell Sakofs of Outward Bound USA, and Dr. Jasper Hunt of Mankato State University

A majority of these articles are from the past five years, but a few older ones have also been included for historical and contextual reasons. While some readers have suggested that these older articles be edited to use more inclusive language, we have left them as the writers wrote them, asking the reader to recognize the period of time in which they were written.

Since this is a publication of the Association for Experiential Education, we have limited the document to articles from the Association's *Journal* and to speeches given at regional or national AEE conventions. We fully recognize that there are many additional excellent sources of information on experiential learning, adventure education, alternative schools, special populations, and the wide range of other topics covered in this and similar volumes. We do not claim that this is a complete compendium of knowledge on the topics, but do believe that it adds significantly to the growing body of literature which informs schools and higher education as they seek to put experiential learning into practice.

Dr. Richard J. Kraft, Professor of Education
University of Colorado-Boulder, CO
Past Executive Director, AEE

Dr. James Kielsmeier, President
National Youth Leadership Council
St. Paul, MN
Past President, AEE

A Century of Experiential Learning

Richard J. Kraft
Professor of Education
University of Colorado-Boulder
Past Executive Director, AEE

While some might suggest that experiential learning has been the dominant mode of learning since humans first set foot on this earth, experiential educators generally look to the French philosopher Rousseau in the early 19th century or to John Dewey, the American philosopher who began his educational writing almost one hundred years ago, as the "founders" of the movement. While Dewey's earlier writings dealt with a wide range of educational topics, it was in his *Experience and Education,* published in 1938, that he grappled in depth with the role of experience in learning.

> I assume that amid all uncertainties there is one permanent frame of reference: namely the organic connection between education and personal experience; or some kind of empirical and experimental philosophy.... The belief that all genuine education comes about through experience does not mean that all experiences are genuinely or equally educative...some experiences are mis-educative...any that has the effect of arresting or distorting the growth of further experience...engenders callousness...produces lack of sensitivity or responsiveness.... Everything depends upon the quality of the experience which is had. (Dewey, pp. 225–26)

Dewey goes on to emphasize that experience does not take place strictly within the individual learner, but has an active side which changes the objective conditions under which experiences are had. Experiences always involve a transaction between the individual and what constitutes his or her environment. Dewey juxtaposes traditional education with experiential education in the following manner.

> To imposition from above is opposed expression and cultivation of individuality; to external discipline is opposed free activity; to learning from texts and teachers, learning through experience; to acquisition of isolated skills and techniques by drill, is opposed acquisition of them as means of attaining ends which make direct vital appeal; to preparation for a more or less remote future is opposed making the most of the opportunities of present life; to static aims and materials is opposed acquaintance with a changing world. (Dewey, p. 20)

Progressive educators in the 1930s and radical reformers in the 1960s took up Dewey's call, but it is generally conceded that they failed to impact mainstream American education. With the founding of the Outward Bound movement in the 1940s in Great Britain and the formation of Outward Bound schools in the United States in the 1960s and 1970s, the "adventure" wing of experiential education was formed. Foxfire burst on the national scene with its creative approach to the teaching of a range of communication skills. In this same period of time, national organizations such as the Association for Experiential Education (AEE), the National Society for Internships and Experiential Education (NSEE), and the Council for the Advancement of Experiential Learning (CAEL) were formed with, among others, the purpose of reforming public and higher education in this country.

While John Dewey laid the philosophical framework for experiential learning a century ago and the progressives attempted reform education a half-century ago, it has been in the past quarter-century that the AEE and its allied organizations have attempted to bring American public education back to the fundamental proposition that all "genuine education comes through experience." Genuine learning must involve the individual in a social learning context, be carried out in a range of learning environments, and be of perceived relevance to the learner. One look at the continuing crisis in American education tells us that we have not succeeded in changing our schools toward Dewey's vision.

Experiential education has had an increasingly profound impact, however, on the therapeutic community, business organizations, the environmental movement, and the justice system, and there are glimmers of hope on the horizon for experiential learning taking its proper place in the schools and colleges of the U.S. What are some of the signs that give one hope for the turn of the century, after our failure to make major impact to this point.

1) The national goals of education for the year 2000, while containing many traditional and back-to-the-basics statements, also recognize the importance of active learning, citizenship education, service to the community, and other topics of importance to experiential educators.

2) The New American Schools Development Corporation is funding many experimental schools that have strong experiential learning components, including Outward Bound's Expeditionary Learning Schools. These are to serve as national models for dissemination and replication throughout the U.S. in the coming decade.

3) The near collapse of many inner-city schools has led school systems to start countless alternative schools and to permit new Charter Schools, started by parents, teachers, and the community to come into existence. The vast majority of these new institutions are utilizing the range of experiential learning techniques developed by experiential educators over the past three decades.

4) The National Service Act and the formation of the Corporation for National and Community Service has brought this important form of experiential learning to national attention and spawned literally thousands of service learning programs from preschool through higher education and in almost every community in the United States. The Americorps program is utilizing trained experiential educators to administer its programs and train corps members throughout the country. The state and national campus compacts have begun to bring service learning into thousands of college classrooms.

5) While never at the forefront of higher education, experiential learning programs of one form or another can now be found in Schools and Colleges of Education, Departments of Physical Education, Colleges of Business, Recreation programs, and other sites in our institutions of higher education.

6) Private corporations have begun to fund experiential school-based programs from short weekend programs to full schools such as the American Honda Educational Foundation's Eagle Rock School.

7) The Middle School movement has adopted many things for which experiential educators have always stood as part of its approach to working with early adolescents.

8) In the international arena, experiential learning has a solid base throughout Europe and is expanding to Russia and other parts of the former Soviet Union. Third World countries have found its philosophy and approach to be adaptable to the poorest and most rural settings, in addition to changing schools and teachers in their more developed urban settings.

9) Mainstream educational researchers have begun to take a serious and sustained look at what we as experiential educators claim to accomplish with our students in schools or in nonformal educational settings in the wilderness, urban settings, or other locations where learning can and does occur.

The Association for Experiential Education has been on the cutting edge of educational reform for a quarter of a century and continues its commitment to make schools better places for children, teachers, and administrators. This book is one part of our attempt to help professional educators, school board members, administrators, professors, and researchers improve education for all our children, young people, and adults. It is also based on the century-old belief of John Dewey, that "all genuine education comes through experience."

Section

1

Theoretical Underpinnings of Experiential Learning

Experiential Educational Theory

Growing with the Times: A Challenge For Experiential Education

by James Kielsmeier

"Like the Hopi vase on the museum shelf which cries for water, the youth of our society cry for useful work." —Marge Pearcey

Kurt Hahn's central youth development principle was the idea that young people need to know that they are useful. Hahn's Gordonstoun School in Scotland was founded in that part of the United Kingdom because there were ample community needs for young people from the school to address. Mountain rescue and lifesaving service were in short supply in the 1930s when the school was founded, and shortly thereafter, there was a need for military-type service on that northern coast because of the activities of German U-Boats. The adventure training that Hahn built into the Gordonstoun curriculum was not intended to teach outdoor skills in isolation; rather, the adventure experience was seen as preparation for rescue,

lifesaving service, and coast watching. Adventure activities were clearly a means to an end.

A key to understanding Hahn, the roots of Outward Bound, and the roots of adventure-based experiential education, involves understanding the climate within which young people in the West were nurtured at the time. In the 1930s, a young person on the farm in the United States, or in Britain, was worth a considerable amount of money to the family economic unit. In similar fashion, as apprentices working side-by-side with family members, young people in the 1930s and 1940s made a significant contribution to their families. Their work meant not only a paycheck, but skills that led to a livelihood.

Times have changed. The transition to adulthood today rarely involves a transitional work experience that prepares a young person for life-long work. Young people still do work, but the work itself has meaning only because of the paycheck, not the learning aspect associated with the job. The key element for most young people in the dead-end jobs that they are relegated to, is money. Even with the positive reinforcement that money offers, many American youth find little meaning in life and little reinforcement of self by the adults around them. In 1985, the Center for Youth Development and Research at the University of Minnesota asked young people what they felt was the perception that adults had of them. The survey included over 2,000 young people throughout the state of Minnesota and was later replicated in the Chicago area. The study found that over two-thirds of the young people felt that adults had a negative perception of them. A striking statistic! Especially when we recognize the effect on behavior which results from low self-worth.

The context in Great Britain or the United States during Hahn's time offers a sharp contrast to the context today. Once a young person was energized through the kinds of adventure experiences offered at Gordonstoun and later in the Outward Bound Schools, there was a natural context for them to apply their new skills and values. Not only did young people train in an adventurous environment where for a period of days and weeks they were necessary, but when they came home, they went on to public service, or professions or jobs that reinforced their self-images as necessary citizens of a community.

Over the past several decades, we have grown more sophisticated in our adventure skills, but the societies to which young people return have undergone major transformations. No longer are there clear pathways to what E. F. Schumacher called "Good Work." Roles which offer meaning, adventure, and challenge, comparable to the outdoor adventure experience, are few and far between for the American adolescent once she or he graduates from high school or from the adventure program. No longer is there a major national defense effort that requires every person, no longer is there a rapidly expanding economy filled with entry-level positions for people with only the most basic educational skills. Does this mean our experiential education methods are without worth for the broad spectrum of Western youth? Are adventure activities only needed by those who use the methods as adjunct therapies, to "cure" at-risk youth, or to reawaken stagnant business executives? My answer is a clear no and my suggestion is that the times in fact call for an even clearer application of Hahn's principals with modifications based on the reality of growing up in the last decade of the twentieth century.

Young people in the 1930s with basic skills who were motivated by adventure programs, had places to work and serve, clear roles that led to a secure niche in society. Experiential learning needed to emphasize the essential intervention or motivational experience. The community and labor market defined the next step. We have continued to operate our experiential programs, with a few exceptions, in the same manner. We assume that once motivated, "treated," or inspired, there are infinite possibilities for youth to find meaningful roles. But the intervention fades quickly as a metaphor if there is no reinforcing context to apply new skills, values, and energy. The assumption is no longer appropriate. We must go beyond the intervention to an emphasis on the setting to which people return and the creation of contexts where youth can be genuinely useful. Service learning is an experiential education model which creates useful roles for youth.

Creative and Useful Youth Roles

Hahn was right. Young people do respond remarkably when asked to do something real, to engage in something where they are needed. I recall my St. Louis experience in Youth Experiencing Success (YES), a program that engaged economically poor, high school young people as leaders. Organized by the St. Louis Public Schools, Project Stream, and the American Youth Foundation, we worked together to train three hundred high school young people to mentor three thousand middle school students, five days a week, ten weeks of the summer. The high school students' roles as mentors were far more challenging than the make-work, youth employment jobs which were common at that time.

The young people took those roles very seriously. For example, during the training of the high school leaders, there was a warm-up activity every morning, a takeoff on aerobic exercises. It involved music and movement, and the older students in training would eventually lead the exercises for the young people. Derek Jackson, a sharp, young, African-American, was always there on time and with it during all the training activities. He looked as if he could be a tight end on the football team, six feet, two inches tall, physically strong and determined. One

day at aerobics, I noticed Derek suddenly leave the elementary school gymnasium where we were training. He came outside and sat down on the curb. I went over and asked him, "What's gong on?" Derek was not the type of person who would walk out of training without a reason. He said that while he was doing aerobics, he was accidentally kicked. I said, "Look Derek, that's not the kind of excuse that I can relate to." He stood up and said, "My leg really does hurt," and he rolled up his pants leg. There was a bullet hole in his leg and it was bleeding.

Derek had taken a bus for an hour-and-a-half that morning from his home in north St. Louis to get to the training session. He had been through almost an hour of exercise before he confessed that his leg hurt. As we got him to the hospital, Derek told me he had been shot at a party the night before. He was afraid to say anything about the bullet wound because he really wanted the job, not because of the pay, as there were a lot of other minimum-wage jobs around. He really wanted the job because he knew that he would be making a contribution to the lives of kids he cared about. Derek's leg healed and he went on to be an outstanding leader.

There are dozens of examples I could give of young people in service situations where they began to see themselves as needed and of worth. In Blooming Prairie, Minnesota, a very small town, the high school principal learned that the ambulance rescue service did not have enough emergency medical technicians (EMTs), and the ones they did have were scattered all over the county. The head of the rescue service and the principal, working together, decided to build the training of young people into the curriculum so that when they became eighteen, they could qualify as EMTs and help run the rescue unit. Their idea became a reality as it has in several small towns in Minnesota. These students carry beepers to class because they are regularly called out on ambulance runs.

Service learning is beneficial to the community as well as to the young people. There are many things happening in our society that are never going to be fixed unless young people are involved in fixing them. For example, right now we are working with the Department of Natural Resources on a potential survey of all the lakes and waterways of Minnesota in cooperation with the high schools to measure where acid rain is affecting the natural environment. This project can work, not because of a massive pool of professionals, but because science teachers and high school students can work together to bring in information that will influence public policy.

We do not have a compelling, heroic time like Hahn encountered with World War II. But we have other needs and it is time to start thinking about how young people can become involved in addressing these needs. The major limiting factor to engaging more youth in experiential service learning is not an absence of need; I see it as an absence of creativity on our part.

The Multicultural Challenge

There is a second major difference between Hahn's context and conditions today in the West. The statistics I mention are from the United States, but I am told that they are also closely mirrored by statistics in Canada. We all know that the cohort of young people is dropping rapidly and in fact, by the year 2000, we will have twenty percent less young people under the age of 18. Even as the number of young people is going down, the character of that smaller group of young people will be changing very dramatically. For example, for the children in first grade right now (the class of 2000), one in four are poor. Young people of color are increasing while the birth rates for European-American children decrease. In California and Texas, the term "minority" in schools means absolutely nothing since over fifty percent of the young people in those schools are now people of color. We cannot call "them" minorities anymore in these states; they are the majority, and that is going to happen across the country. We are not in a situation like Hahn's when there was a relatively homogeneous population. Young people in our programs will be more diverse, if they can be attracted.

Most of us have worked on the issue of increasing racial and cultural diversity in our organizations. How do we recruit "them"? How do we get "them" to join us? I say these are the wrong questions. Instead, why not ask the question, How can our organization adapt, or better yet, recreate itself to become culturally diverse? How can we change first? Other questions I think we should be asking ourselves, given we are predominantly a group of European-Americans, include: How much power am I willing to share with people of color? How willing am I to encourage spin-off organizations owned and operated by people of color who may turn out to be competitors? You say, this might put my program in jeopardy. I identify with that, I run a non-profit organization, I worry about a payroll, I worry about a balance sheet, I worry about competition, I go after the grants just like you do. Is this going to damage my organization if I begin to share power like this? I say on the contrary, from my own experience, the engagement and collaboration with the rich cultural diversity of this society has been incredibly beneficial to me and the National Youth Leadership Council.

A specific example may help illustrate the strength and richness in this diversity: Anne Bancroft's presentation last night took us on a beautiful journey, an adventure. There are a lot of other rich adventures experienced by recent immigrants from Southeast Asia who, unlike Anne's group, did not have the benefit of the National Geographic Society, or other forms of acknowledgment of their journey. In fact, there is a young man here today, Born Chea, who at the age of eight in 1975, was separated permanently from his parents. For four years, he worked in a labor camp not far from Phnom Penh, Cambodia. At the age of twelve, he began his escape with nine other children. Over a three-month period, he walked barefoot until he reached the Thai border. Of the nine members of the party, he was one of two that made it to Thailand alive. He has been in this country five years, is fluent in English, has graduated from high school, and is already a college sophomore. Along with four colleagues, all unattached minors who came to the United States under the same conditions, he has formed the Khmer Youth Leadership Program and raised over thirty thousand dollars to put on a special youth leadership camp for the purpose of helping young people, like himself, deal with the horror of the Cambodian holocaust.

The cultural diversity of the participants in our programs is not reflected in the leadership of our programs and organizations. This is not a new revelation. In 1979 I was part of a group of people who offered a resolution to AEE around this very same issue of increasing cultural diversity. There are people here who have watched this brought up and discussed and then have seen it die off and go nowhere. One of those people is Arthur Conquest, the first black instructor in Outward Bound, who rocked the International Outward Bound Conference in Cooperstown, New York, last month. Arthur said at the conference, "The social and political structures that allow organizations like Outward Bound to use black children to make money and create jobs for themselves is built upon the false assumption that blacks are inferior and unqualified and should remain servile by doing as we are told." I bring this up not to give Outward Bound a hard time—Outward Bound has worked hard in this area. But results are few. I hope that work from this day forward represents a new solid step forward. We simply cannot retreat from this issue!

Finding the Strength to Promote Change

Finally, I would like to challenge you as individuals. James Coleman says in his indictment of Western education that young people who grow up in this society are information rich but experience poor. Following Coleman's logic, people are deprived if they are experience poor. But who are you? You are the experience rich. It is unsettling to be giving this speech but not nearly as unsettling as it was last winter before the Minnesota Legislature. In the past six years, I have grown tired of sitting by and seeing good programs go down the drain due to inadequate financial support. Last winter, I stood before a Minnesota State Committee and defined experiential education and helped nurture a bill which eventually passed. This was the personal equivalent of doing a 5.9 rock-climbing move at the age of forty-six, and I was very scared. But I learned from it, I grew from it, and my base of personal experience bolstered my resolve as I took on the daunting assignment of working on public policy.

Do you care about the earth, poor children, conflict among nations, or issues of race and gender? My point is that your life experience means something and is a building block for getting things done in many arenas—even public policy. I would say as well, to think hard on your own wellness as a practitioner, and to reflect deeply and nurture your own foundations as a person. Somebody said to me the other day, "If we are going to teach risk taking as experiential educators, we also have to teach convalescence." If you are are doing genuine risk taking, sometimes you fail, and you crash and burn. So where do you get the stuff to put yourself back together? Nurture your foundations, especially your spiritual foun-

dations. I can not tell you the number of times I have reached for my spiritual roots and gone to the book of Isaiah, where the passage in the fortieth chapter reads, "Even youths shall faint and be weary and young men shall fall exhausted, but they who wait for the Lord shall renew their strength and they shall rise up with wings like eagles." There are lots of other people who have gone to sources like this to shore themselves up.

Generative Themes

The philosopher and educator Paulo Freire said that every period of history has a generative theme, a signal characteristic that organizes our thinking about the time. For Hahn it was the period of the pre-war challenge to England and Europe, and then the war itself, followed by the post-war expansion. That context and those themes shaped adventure-based experiential education. The questions for me and for you are, What are today's generative themes? Are our professional and personal tools honed for the task of creatively engaging our context? We are people mostly of action. Dealing effectively with these questions requires disciplined reflection. This is a challenge we need to accept.

What Constitutes Experience? Rethinking Theoretical Assumptions

by Martha Bell

There is a need in our professional discourse for more thinking about how the central concepts that direct what we do are organized. In trying to respond to this need, I find myself in a strange place. Reading and writing theory are not thought to be concrete enough activities to count as experientially exciting, or practical enough to engage the focus of practitioners who would rather be out there "just doing it."[1]

I find reading and writing theory challenging, risky, and nerve-wracking. I find facing big rapids on a river the same. Sometimes I am drained, physically, by the tension of concentrating, of experimenting, and of experiencing adrenalin highs on a breakthrough. I feel it in my mind, but I also feel it profoundly in and with my body, just as with paddling the big rapid. I decided to try to persevere with the thinking that I have been doing around the theoretical perspectives in our field, because reading, thinking, and writing have given me an embodied location in which to begin such reflecting, just as I would have for any other "concrete" experience. And this embodied location is also the very site for me of the contradiction in terms which I experience in the field's theories.

When I have worked with groups, I have always thought that actually touching the rock (or the wind, water, sand, snow) is an important, concrete experience of something powerful. The theory organizes the learning process, however, around facilitated, abstract, conceptual, "objective" reflection on that quite subjective, embodied experience. Experiential learning is group-based, a social experience, and yet our traditions call it "personal growth" and "character building," individual changes. Theories of group process acknowledge that there is a group identity or culture (e.g., Mitten, 1986; Phipps, 1991), but there is still no clear sociological analysis informing our theorizing. I am looking for understandings of how social subjectivities are formed through embodied knowing, and I think that what happens in experiential learning could help illustrate this.

I will focus on two important aspects of learning through experience which have not been addressed adequately in the theory: the embodied location of experience and the social organization of the process. In this article, I explore more of the reading behind my critical "rethinking" of these two aspects of my practice in the field. I start with a brief reference to Dewey's theory of experience. Part of my aim is to contest the neatness of theories that present all the answers, so I try to work with partial, sometimes convoluted, attempts at thinking about some of these issues. I find it a challenging, but impelling experience.

Theorizing is a Social Practice

John Dewey cautions that "any theory and set of practices is dogmatic which is not based upon critical examination of its own underlying principles" (p.22). Ideally, critical examination is not destructive, but works to expose everything that defines and directs a situation, to be assessed by all. Often those who were not involved in defining the terms of the situation can then identify what is not useful for them (Henderson, 1989, relates this to recreation programming). Changing what we do as practitioners is hard work when we aim to find new strategies that will be as effective as those we had thought to be "tried and true." Furthermore, being critical of the very principles underlying such strategies in our practice may seem suicidal.

And yet, when theories become so well-established that their premises become "common sense," they are rarely examined critically. They organize our thinking to the extent that we do not even think that they exist. Things known to be common sense are taken for granted as part of "the nature of things." Aspects of theories come to be accepted uncritically as "natural," rather than understood as the result of social forces: certain thinking, meeting certain interests, at a particular time in history, and in a specific context.

As an example, I do not find it useful to think in terms of experience in general. *All* experience does not relate to, or even clarify, *my* experience. We talk about concrete experience, but I do not know what this means. To me experience "exists" through interpretation. It is produced through the meanings given it. Interpretations of lived experiences are always contextual and specific. Experiences are contingent; interpretations can change. There is no generic clone for "the experience" which applies to everyone. This could only happen if experience was an ab-

solute principle, or if people were clones of each other, without personal situations, social contexts, or historical places in time. In reality people have very different experiences. And yet discussions of experience in this journal commonly take this for granted, as if experience has fixed, inherent meaning.

Just recently this occurred in the theme issue on Theory and Practice. Michael Gass writes in the editorial that "one of the best functions of experience is that it validates all of the processes that theories support" (p.7). The process of theorizing which this approach illustrates abstracts real experiences into *a concept of experience* which then does not relate to a context. Experience becomes "it" and is treated like an object that can be expected to do the same thing to us every time. The theory of what experience does then bears no resemblance to the experiences actually occurring in local settings. In fact, the theory is used to shape and direct, or constitute, what does happen, so that it resembles what the theory says is happening. Such theories of experience leave little room for more than one explanation of what is happening. They quickly legitimate the single, linear view as a "model" for others to follow.

This is not new. It is "common" practice in theorizing, and is a tool of the Western European intellectual tradition. Abstract thinking is privileged over embodied knowing. Dewey's own writing employs a model for the logical steps of inquiry which he thought were essential to the experience of learning (McDermott, 1973/1981, pp. 160–240). Dewey does not take it for granted that experience has fixed, inherent meaning; he specifically theorizes that this is so. It has become common sense to us. His model has been simplified for discussions of the process of experiential education, such as David Kolb's (1984, p.23).

Laura Joplin's five-stage model is another good example of this approach, and one to which many people point when asked for definitions of our field (1981, pp. 17–20). We can then say, "This is what happens in experiential learning!" Experience becomes accepted as a social form through abstract models, and is no longer known as a personally and socially lived reality given contextual meanings. The *concept* in turn informs social relations (Smith, 1984, offers an excellent analysis of how the abstraction of specific activities makes them into social rituals). The social concept of gender also refers to a social relation, an experience of becoming feminine or becoming masculine, and yet now the concept actually serves to inform social behaviors. Sociologists are interested in the ways in which gender is specifically experienced and replicated, rather than just accepting it as a conceptual label.

Theorizing is constructing a set of concepts which are deemed a universally applicable and replicable explanation for what is happening. It is, itself, therefore a social practice used to organize social relations. Standardized social rituals can be replicated so that we come to expect certain practices to symbolize social meanings. In *Experience and Education,* Dewey gives two examples of this: sport and manners. He refers to the social control exerted by common expectations that there are unspoken "rules of the game" which prevail over all. He also refers to the code of social conduct which manners represent. Specific manners may change or differ among people, but "the existence of some form of convention...is a uniform

attendant of all social relationships," he writes (p. 59). From these examples, we might refer to social practices in everyday terms, then, as rules and etiquette, which we come to expect as "natural."

Experience, according to Dewey, is also a social relationship. He sees experience as a relationship between the individual and their environment, a replicable interaction in which meanings are found. He explores the social aspects of experience in the context of a natural harmony of social consensus. In his time, it was radical enough to propose that experience was separate from an absolute ideal of knowledge and engaged in by an active individual. He would not have thought to question the existence of a social harmony.

In our time, we cannot take for granted a social order governed by natural principles, such as fair play or just desserts. These are socially constructed conventions constituting social relations. As such, they represent the interests of those responsible for their construction, those with the power to define them. Thus theory is constructed, as well, to make sense from a certain perspective. An acknowledgment of this is missing from theorizing about experience today.

Having set up the problem that I see with current theorizing in our field, I will go a bit deeper into some of the areas which have serious limitations for me. First, I will take some time to outline how a critical perspective helps to unravel some of these unaddressed issues. They are present in constituting experiences and knowledges for our students, even though "unstated." Then I will look at some of the assumptions on which our practice might rest.

The most important point to start with is that what were radical ideas in another time are resting on assumptions which are inadequate now to help us understand the complexities of experiential learning situations today.

Being Critical

An obvious question for practitioners and theorists, then, is that if we already think the basic assumptions of our profession make common sense, then what would motivate us to question them? If the principles ground the practice, indeed are validated in concrete practice, as Gass suggests above, then why the need for constant critical examination?

The significance of such questions rests on the invisibility of the person doing the asking. The universality of Western traditions of language and knowledge pivots on an invisible, central "we" that treats everything around it from its own perspective. But "we" are not in the picture.

It helps to go back to the underlying principles of the very structure of knowledge, the ways meaning is constructed though ways of defining reality. Theorists like Dewey, who set out principles of experiential education, based their assumptions upon taken-for-granted tenets about thinking and knowing, which organized their approach to forming theories. Logic, rationality, scientific method, and the discovery of intrinsic meanings were essential to Dewey. In his day, these were not seen to be connected to learning, and so it was radical to suggest that there were clear, practical, "scientific" steps making up a learning process. It had been common sense in his time that learning happened when the proper information to be known was imposed on students from above.

However, today his promotion of scientific logic can be seen to reinforce linear, cause-effect, "either-or" terms of facts and knowledge. This gives us a false sense of the unity of knowledge, its objective nature, and the ability to "discover" reality. With enough personal effort, we can assure our students, they will "discover" who they really are. Or they can "discover" that they can go past their limits. Humanistic definitions of identity involve a firm belief in the perfectibility of humans though their lifespan. Dewey refers to learning as having the same continuity as growth and development (1938, p. 36). Knowledge, identity, and meaning in this perspective are intrinsic to the world and human beings. Yet how often is life straightforward or lived on one level? How often do we find ourselves experiencing, and living, contradictions? Is growth cumulative and developmental, as theorists claim? A critical perspective does not accept the liberal humanistic perspective, such as Dewey promotes, as the *only* overarching explanation for reality.

Constructions of knowledge have also structured our language as a meaning-making system by setting up dichotomies in which the world is categorized. If something is not one, it is "the other." Starting with the self, known internally, the other term juxtaposed in the dichotomy can only be known externally. "The other" is always objectified. If the self is the center, the subject of all experience, then the other is experienced, and denied subjectivity. Western theory of knowledge privileges objectivity as the prerogative of the subject. Dewey's theory of experience also privileges objectivity. His steps to inquiry are based on rational, logical problem solving that takes the central position of the subject for granted. The subjects, or authors, of Western definitions of rationality were always those with access to the texts and their transmission: masculine, Caucasian, well-educated, and heterosexual. Those not involved in defining the dominant terms can only be objectified, such as women, "other" classes, races, ethnicities, sexual identity groups, and so on. This is not a tangential point. This is where being critical becomes important.

It becomes more apparent that something requires a critical examination when the accepted definitions do not match the lived experiences of "others," when they do not "make sense" to those whose experience is denied by the dominant norm. Those who do not experience "reality" the way "everyone else" does cannot take it for granted. And, when the dissonance is not experienced by "us," it is easier for "us" to take things for granted as "natural," suppressing calls for change.

To go back to Gass's premise above, I would contest his statement by suggesting that one of the best functions of experiences is that they are diverse, cannot be fixed or determined, and may *invalidate* the assumptions that theories rely on. My belief in this comes from my own experience. In this way, experiences of dissonance constantly provide us with the location for critical examination. They put "us" in the picture. However, our own or our students' lived experiences are rarely interpreted as useful in cracking open accepted interpretations or theories when they are not consistent. More often, if they do not fit, they are seen to be abnormal, "unique," or otherwise rationalized, while the overarching theory is unchanged.

The Body

One of the reasons that I am active in the outdoors and deliberately choose to take other women into the outdoors is to encourage them to feel strong in their bodies. This may seem like a small point or a self-evident goal. I take into account the way norms of femininity are lived by women in white Western society, so that our bodies become a site of expressing heterosexual attractiveness, and our soft, gentle, and nurturing "nature." I see my desire to allow women to experience a different way to feel in their bodies—harder, alert, and effective in initiative and action—as being a form of resistance to a social code that shapes and directs our bodies, and our embodied experiences. And yet, becoming fit and healthy is still sexualized for women so that there are also dominant definitions for an attractive "active woman" (as studies of "feminized" aerobics classes have shown; see MacNeill, 1988). Paradoxically, I may be participating in reinforcing standards of strength and capability for women which again subject us to masculine definitions. What assumptions am I operating from about "ideal" body size and image which limit large or "fat" women?

Bodies seem like unique, personal possessions, or perhaps attributes, and yet there are social expectations and regulations around all of our bodies. As experiential educators, we must be aware of these social forces. We often treat experiential learning as a neutral space, a "leveler." It is common sense that women can do anything that men can do in the outdoors (see Knapp's, 1985, and Friedrich and Priest's, 1992, calls for a theory of androgyny). And yet this is an argument of human "nature," meant to neutralize gender roles, which are a social code. If we really question this assumption, we would see that women bring with them to the outdoors, or their learning experiences, social practices which shape them and their experiences, no matter how much personal achievement they gain (see Warren, 1985).

I notice that I am writing of all women as if all women experience their physical bodies as socially regulated in the same way as I do. I speak here from conversations with women in groups in the outdoors; I cannot speak for all lesbian women, Maori women, women of color, women with disabilities. Where are they in "our" picture of experiential education?

What I am suggesting is not new; yet my body, as the site of my socially learned practices of (and resistances to) femininity—a large part of my identity—has been invisible in the theory. It is not left out, but remains present as the oppositional term in the mind-body dichotomy. The mind is privileged in the process of reflection. As long as experience is understood through abstract, rational, objective reflection, then, in order to participate, I must also use my mind and ignore my body. Yet my experience happens in the very site of my social identity, the site of the rules and etiquette which define me as a woman (and the site of my training in race, class, and heterosexual practices). If I reflect on it from this "feminized" location of knowing, I risk being objectified as "a body." If I remain distant and detached from it, I cannot question the social assumptions that place restraints on what I am capable of experiencing.

Rethinking the Practice

In seeking to expand a theoretical analysis of experience as socially produced for our students, I think we must make spaces to invite and explore different representations of experience.

This challenges many of the most common aspects of the way this profession is practiced. For example, Ewert reports that the psychological perspective is "the most widely used viewpoint" in the research in outdoor adventure (1987, p. 25). This tradition starts with the assumption that the individual is an autonomous being, in rational control of their choices and following developmental patterns of growth, as if every individual will experience the same things in certain predicted situations. In short, the psychologized view of the individual decontextualizes our behavior, seeking to produce generalizable knowledge. Critical approaches uncover different and contextual *knowledges*.

One example of this is a consideration of the use of ice breakers and initiative problems with a new group. I find it problematic to treat "the group" as if it were homogeneous, and there are many ice breakers/initiatives that require too much intimacy and more stress than particular participants may be willing to share at that time. It has been reported that in some women's groups the participants waited until well into the expedition before they disclosed more personal information and built trusting relationships; ice breakers such as Trust Falls created more anxiety and not necessarily trust (Mitten, 1986, pp. 25–26). A critical view of this might reflect a rethinking of the lived experiences of different women (or members of "other" dominant social categories of identity, such as class, race, age, ability, sexual orientation) and an invitation to a group to openly question social assumptions about consent.

Another example might be a rethinking of the use of debriefing or processing. This component is based on an assumption that the reflection which is integral to Deweyian and other models of the experiential learning cycle actually enables participants to remember and so learn from their experiences. Reflection tends to be treated as memory work, a biological function, in models such as Joplin's (1981)—in which it is taken for granted that an experience can be remembered as it was and learning can be taken away from it—rather than as a social practice. Giroux writes that it is the "memory of the oppressed" that keeps the struggle against relations of power alive, and calls for a broader notion of learning that would "include how the body learns tacitly, how habit translates into sedimented history, and how knowledge itself may block the development of certain subjectivities and ways of experiencing the world" (in Freire, 1985, pp. xix–xx). When I sit down with a group to "go around the circle," am I really offering a space for the tensions and contradictions of lived experience, the memories of pain and pleasure, and the confusions in knowing to be expressed?

Memory work can surface "body memories," which, painful in the remembering, bring back to consciousness parts of the body that were risked or abandoned for survival. In outdoor "survival" situations, it is important to understand that representations of experience may come in partial forms because of this history, expressed not in one telling but in many, as participants become the subjects of their own embodied knowledge.

How can memory frame identity, contributing to self-awareness and self-knowledge, in ways that affirm, resist, or challenge externally accepted meanings? Perhaps remembering an experience recomposes it so that its meaning changes. This remembering might contest the dis-remembering, or fragmentation, of much of the psychological definitions of the self. Whose memories are privileged in the discourse of "the group," and how am I complicit in this in my practice as facilitator?

One last example: facilitating opportunities for participants to "overcome their fear" may be working against the needs of those participants who want to learn to feel their fear, physically, when appropriate, and respond in a way that does not put them at risk, but allows them to act to protect themselves. If the metaphor for overcoming resistance and taking risks is not questioned, it may be used to eliminate resistance which may be essential to struggle against disempowerment. Again, what are the particular and subjective needs of my different participants?

If we take Dewey's philosophy of experience and apply it today, out of the historical moment and social context in which it was theorized, we are limiting the possibilities for lived experience of social relations to emerge described in dissonant, contradictory ways. A critical perspective would allow our students, and each of us, to seek meanings in contexts which intersect at different social moments. Experience might be best remembered in the first telling, the collective telling, the re-telling, and the re-remembering of our bodies, not simply our minds.

We have yet to theorize adequately *how* many of the experiences which we facilitate actually operate to organize who speaks, who remembers, who trusts, who fears, and how they operate in certain interests. These are important questions for exposing the ways in which experience is theoretically constituted, and then dislodging it from the dominant definitions which organize it in practice.[2]

NOTES

1. A note about style: words or phrases with common-sense meanings often have other meanings embedded within them, and I use quotation marks to indicate that I question the taken-for-granted use of such words.

2. I want to acknowledge with appreciation the comments, critique, and support through the many versions of this article from Alan Warner, Daniel Vokey, Karen Warren, and Barbara Williams. Thanks to Chuck Luckmann for helping me to separate the jargon from the ideas.

Experiential Education: A Search For Common Roots

by Greg Druian, Tom Owens, and Sharon Owen

Do experiential programs have any common elements? A comparison of some successful programs indicates that there are some essential similarities.

Do experiential education programs have more in common than coincidental resemblances? There are compelling reasons for starting to look at common features. As long as programs operate in isolation from one another, they will be vulnerable to the chipping away that accompanies economic hard times. In order to overcome their isolation, they need to learn more about the purposes, outcomes, and techniques of similar programs. In this way, good programs will be able to present a stronger front and will be more likely to sustain the momentum generated over the past decade. An understanding of features held in common by successful programs could strengthen the case that any specific program might make for continuance; it could lead the way to standards for quality in experiential education; it could help in the adaptation of programs by assuring that site-specific conditions and needs are attended to; and it could facilitate the integration of new elements into an ongoing program, thereby offering an alternative to the establishment of new programs.

The main purpose of this article is to offer a framework for identifying essential elements of three experiential education programs: Experience-Based Career Education, Foxfire, and Outward Bound. A second purpose is to select elements that we believe to be essential to effective experiential education. After review of pertinent literature and

our discussions with staff in the three programs, we chose the following nine categories as most likely to contain essential program elements: purposes; setting; characteristics of participants; learning strategies; student roles; instructor roles; product of learning activities; management and support; and program outcomes. Experience-Based Career Education, Foxfire, and Outward Bound were chosen because they have been around long enough to have become stable, each was developed in response to a different set of needs, all three have separate and clear identities, they have reasonably clear and well-articulated principles and procedures, and each has been widely imitated and adapted.

Experience-Based Career Education (EBCE) is a program that began in 1971 for high school juniors and seniors, and has since been adapted to many other groups of people, including adults. It provides students with a comprehensive, fully accredited education that emphasizes community-based learning. EBCE staff are learning managers and facilitators; no classes in the traditional sense are offered, although seminars are frequently used. The learning managers help students design and follow individualized learning plans that incorporate basic skills, life competencies, and career development. Students profit from the chance to explore various careers of interest in the community; many are helped to prepare for adulthood and economic self-sufficiency as well as to interact with adults in natural work settings. EBCE was developed by four regional educational laboratories with funding from the National Institute of Education, and EBCE projects are now operating in over 200 school districts throughout the country.

Foxfire, by contrast, began with one man's effort to design a curriculum that would draw upon the unique resources of the local community. Eliot Wigginton, faced with a class totally turned off to the traditional approaches to learning English, one day simply asked his students in Rabun Gap, Georgia, whether they wanted to write a magazine. Today there are programs similar to Foxfire operating in approximately 145 schools across the nation. Most cultural journalism programs engage students in developing and publishing a journal that reflects the cultural pluralism of the community in which they live. Many related activities may be pursued in conjunction with the journal. For example, in some cases videotapes replace the journal as a project. Students do most of the work associated with whatever project they happen to be working on. Thus, Foxfire tends to be comprehensive in the kinds of activities it offers students. It has been implemented in colleges, high schools, junior high schools, even elementary schools.

Like Foxfire, the Outward Bound program may be implemented for practically any age group. Typically a wilderness experience, Outward Bound is an educational process in which students find meaning through group and individual encounters with unfamiliar environments that provide physical stress. The focus of Outward Bound is on building self-confidence, trust, and acceptance of personal responsibility. Since

1962 when the Outward Bound movement began in this country, having been imported from Great Britain where it was started in 1941, Outward Bound has expanded to six schools, a center based at Dartmouth College, and a national organization based in Greenwich, Connecticut. Outward Bound has also been implemented in conjunction with school programs at the high school and college levels, as well as outside the educational system with people of various ages. In a typical Outward Bound course, participants might spend the first few days together coping with relatively unfamiliar tasks, learning new skills, and developing greater physical stamina. Next, they might spend two to three days on a "solo," alone with few resources and no responsibilities except to reflect on their experience. Finally, participants might spend the remaining time on an expedition they carry out themselves without instructors. Characteristic of the Outward Bound experience is a powerful sense of accomplishment—often preceded by extreme frustration. Having experienced and successfully coped with one's physical limitations, and with limitations of self-awareness and of group responsibility and identity, participants emerge with new confidence in their abilities.

In the remainder of this article, we will describe what we believe to be common elements of these three programs, following the nine categories listed above. Then in Table 1, we distill the elements we hypothesize as essential for experiential education.

1. Purpose

Successful experiential education programs have clearly articulated purposes that are interpreted similarly by program participants. It is reasonable to suppose that stated program purposes both reflect needs of a group of learners and imply a certain program content. In successful programs, the relationship of program purposes to educational need and program content are demonstrable.

2. Setting

Setting refers to the physical and psychological environment in which the learning takes place. If more than one environment is involved, setting also refers to the manner in which the environments are controlled so as to maximize learning. Characteristic of experiential settings are four essential factors: realism; challenge; an appropriate level of risk; and diversity. A setting has *realism* when the learner thinks it is not contrived. A realistic setting may be either natural (e.g., wilderness) or man-made (e.g., the workplace or a person's home). In both cases, the setting is not artifically developed as a place for student learning. The setting is viewed as *challenging* because there are adults there who are engaged in dynamic activities. The presence of psychological or physical *risk* often motivates the learner to maximum performance. In Outward Bound, the natural environment provides physical risk, which is kept at a manageable level by the presence of a highly trained leader. In EBCE or Foxfire, the anticipation of first voyage into the community to meet an unknown adult is a psychological risk for an adolescent. Finally, in cases where a *diversity* of settings is part of an experiential education program, activities within these settings are integrated. In Foxfire and EBCE, in-school

activities are integrated with community activities through a process of analyzing which academic skills are needed for task accomplishment. A major purpose of these programs is to combine learning activities inside and outside the school into a balanced, comprehensive, and individualized program to help high school students prepare for the demands of adulthood. Outward Bound, on the other hand, is not generally geared to combining in-school with out-of-school activities. A main purpose of Outward Bound is to use the outdoors to help participants develop personal skills such as self-confidence, team work, and self-understanding, which will contribute to success in adulthood.

The learner in Experience-Based Career Education spends time in a least three settings. First is the workplace, where the student may either be performing real work or learning about a job through observation or "shadowing." The second is a learning resource center where students work with a learning manager to plan, monitor, and assess their activities. At the learning center, skills can be practiced and developed; it is also a place where seminars may be held to discuss issues. The third setting is the classroom. Some programs offer a part-time EBCE program, with students attending regular classes the rest of the time. The EBCE learning manager is able to help the student coordinate the activities in each setting by helping to develop a learning plan that specifies objectives appropriate for the student.

In Foxfire, there are two settings that relate to the program. One is the community. In Foxfire this means anywhere in the community where something is going on that the learner thinks is important. Frequently this means going to meet people and interview them in their homes. In other cases, it may mean visiting their places of business. The second setting is the in-school location where the information gathered in the community is processed and turned into a written, taped, or printed product that can be shared with others.

Outward Bound programs use learning settings in still a different way. The setting, normally in the outdoors or wilderness, is treated as a challenge to be overcome. In the overcoming of challenges, the learner's self-image, sense of responsibility, and will to achieve develop steadily. It is expected that there will be a carry-over effect; a learner who sees how to overcome an obstacle during a rock climb will use similar strategies to solve problems encountered in the classroom—or, for that matter, in life. The outdoors and the wilderness are treated as a metaphor, standing for something that can be anticipated to occur after the program is over. At the same time, the immediate sensory appeal of the outdoors is exploited in the Outward Bound program. Intense experience over a short time-period is the goal. Unlike the other two programs, there are usually no multiple learning settings to be integrated during the time period of the program. Outward Bound does, however, concern itself strongly with the question of how learning during the wilderness experience can be transferred back home and how learning relates to the individual's own development.

3. Characteristics of Participants

We are referring to the types of students involved in experiential education programs, particularly to learner characteristics such as sex, age, ethnic background, economic status, preferred learning style, level of academic, moral, and psychosocial development, and reasons for joining the program. Elements hypothesized as essential are voluntary participation and diversity of participants. The fact that experiential learning strategies may be effective for some students does not imply that they would work best for all students. Foxfire, EBCE, and Outward Bound involve only students who voluntarily join the program. In each case, participants reflect all segments of the population from gifted and talented students to mentally retarded youth. Often a program will try to establish a diversity of students so that those less advanced in some areas can profit from the help of their peers.

4. Learning Strategies

"Learning strategies" has to do with the sequence and interrelationship of learner activities. There is greater congruence of approach among the three programs in this category than in any other. The common sequence of the learning process characteristic of these programs is:

- Assessment and goal setting;
- Negotiation and planning;
- Engaging and experiencing;
- Reflecting and evaluating;
- Sharing and publishing;
- Application and generalizing.

Though the names of the steps may differ, each program uses a version of the above steps. All three programs begin with an assessment of student needs, along with some kind of determination of where the student would like to go. A set of activities is planned or negotiated that both student and instructor believe is likely to lead to the desired goal. All three programs involve the student in the negotiation and planning step, although the degree of implementation of this step varies.

The next step is engaging in the experience itself. Following engagement, the learner reflects on the activity through a personal journal, group discussion, discussion with the instructor, or by other means. This step often merges with the next, which involves transforming the raw material of the experience through reproducing it in a form that can be shared by others. This is a crucial step of experiential education programs and what differentiates experiential learning from the mere having of experiences. Both immediate and delayed transformations occur. As part of the program, EBCE students transform their experience into a project portfolio or journal; in Foxfire, raw material of interviews and photography is transformed into a magazine; in Outward Bound groups, rap sessions and personal journals are used. Finally, this "thing" created out of the experience is tried out in a new situation. This last step may not be part of the experiential education program itself— although it certainly is in Foxfire as the magazine gets marketed, people purchase it, students receive feedback, and ideas for new projects are generated.

All three programs provide an opportunity for students to renegotiate their learning plans and to learn from unplanned experiences. The latter is important since all three programs operate in the real world where the environment cannot be entirely predicted or controlled. The strength of all three approaches is linked with certain assumptions about how people learn. Without documenting fully, it seems safe to list the following assumptions about learning as among those shared by EBCE, Foxfire, and Outward Bound. First, people learn best from doing real tasks. Second, young people carry serious consequences. Third, everyone learns best by following a systematic process that leads them from where they are to where they want to go. Fourth, adolescents can learn or reinforce basic skills as effectively out of class as in class.

5. Student Roles

Student roles are extremely important in experiential learning programs. The key questions here are what roles are played by students and with whom does the student interact in each role. In experiential learning programs, it is worth investigating when students are learning primarily alone, in interaction with one adult, with peers, or with a diverse group of people. It is also important to know whether students are learning from people with backgrounds similar to or different from their own, since the latter provides greater opportunity for growth in empathy with others possessing different values. Furthermore, experiential learning programs may show important differences and similarities in the extent and the conditions under which learners are expected to play the roles of leader, tutor, active learner, observer, employee, advocate, and entrepreneur.

The elements of this category that we consider essential are an active student role in planning and carrying out activities; a chance to experience various roles; the assumption of responsibility for one's own actions; and the opportunity to interact with

Table 1. Essential Elements of Experiential Education

Program Categories		Essential Elements
Purpose	1.	Purposes reflect learner needs
	2.	Purposes imply program content
	3.	Clearly shared and understood purposes
Setting	4.	Setting considered realistic by the learners
	5.	A physical or psychological challenge is provided by the setting
	6.	An appropriate degree of risk exists
	7.	Diverse settings are integrated
Participants' Characteristics	8.	Voluntary participation
	9.	Diversity of participants
Learning Strategies	10.	Based on an explicit theory of learning
	11.	Encourage young people to perform tasks normally given to adults in our society
	12.	Emphasize a balance of action, reflection, application
	13.	Provide learning experiences that are individualized, sequential, developmental
	14.	Involve frequent structured interaction between student and instructor
	15.	Provide opportunities for unplanned learning from new experiences
Student Roles	16.	Active student role in planning and carrying out activities
	17.	Chance to experience various roles—leader, team member, employee, tutor, etc.
	18.	Assuming responsibilities for one's own actions
	19.	Opportunity to interact with various adults as well as with peers
Instructor Roles	20.	Help students plan and carry out their activities
	21.	Provide role model as participant in the learning process
	22.	Monitor progress, assess and feed back information to students
	23.	Provide motivation and encouragement
	24.	Model skills in planning, empathy, communications, and resource sharing
Outcomes of Learning Activities	25.	Outcomes of learner activities are perceived as real and important by students and others
	26.	Students feel ownership for the outcomes
Management and Support	27.	Locating community resources for student learning
	28.	Forming positive relationships with external agencies (such as may be needed in awarding regular school credit for program participation)
	29.	Obtaining funding and community support
	30.	Recruitment and selection of staff who are committed to using experiential learning strategies
Program Outcomes	31.	Increased student self-confidence and ability to relate to others
	32.	Staff and students are involved in assessing effectiveness of program
	33.	Openness to looking at both positive and negative outcomes and in examining areas for program improvement

adults as well as with a variety of peers. In the three programs described here, students' roles are different from those they play in the traditional classroom. In Foxfire, students may serve as reporters, photographers, or local historians. To the extent that some students instruct less experienced ones in darkroom techniques, they also share the role of teacher. Outward Bound participants have the opportunity to serve as team members and leaders during certain phases of their program. In EBCE, students often take on the role of employee and have responsibilities similar to other employees in the organization. They sometimes serve customers, handle money or equipment, or coordinate the activities of others.

6. Instructor Roles

Effective instructors help students plan and carry out their activities while also serving as role models of active, involved learners. They monitor student progress; they assess and feed back information to students. Effective instructors motivate and encourage students, demonstrating skills in planning, empathy, communications, and resource sharing. Instructional roles in the programs under discussion require similar skills, knowledge, and attitudes. The instructor functions as a facilitator of learning, rather than primarily as a dispenser of knowledge. This attitude is a mixture of sensitivity to individual needs and of conviction that engagement with unfamiliar but feasible activities can meet those needs. The instructor must have imagination to use the immediate environment as a learning resource to provide that unfamiliar but feasible task. In EBCE, the learning manager needs to show

the same kind of skills in helping students formulate individual learning plans. In Foxfire, it is crucial to have students do things for themselves, showing each other how to accomplish tasks that have been mastered by others before. And Outward Bound instructors must not only be sensitive to the needs of the individual; they must also know how to guide the development of a group of individuals engaged in their common wilderness task and how to implement the safety requirements.

Interpersonal skill is required of instructors in these programs. Empathy, individual and group communication, and the ability to elicit response are skills that instructors in these programs use regularly. A further characteristic is the ability to function as a resource person able to link the student with appropriate people, things, or pieces of information. This ability may be described in terms of the instructor having knowledge about knowledge—how it is obtained, how to gain access to it—rather than simply having knowledge about one subject matter area.

7. Products of Learning Activities

In successful experiential learning programs, students exhibit a high level of ownership of their products. Similarly, successful programs exhibit a high degree of student responsibility for the consequence of activities undertaken by the student. The Foxfire magazine or videotape is the group product of the program; Foxfire as a concept or a project is a product of student energy and group decision making. In fact, the responsibility for managing the project makes for unique kinds of student involvement.

With EBCE, the products usually reflect individual rather than group effort and consist of written reports or other presentations for which individual academic credit is awarded. In Outward Bound, there is more engagement and commitment to process outcomes than to a tangible product; in this respect, it differs from Foxfire and EBCE.

8. Management and Support

Management and support contribute to the climate of the program: sponsorship, program image, support services, relationship to other aspects of the school system, staffing patterns, funding, and community support. We consider four elements to be essential within this category: locating community resources for student learning; forming positive relationships with external agents (such as may be needed in awarding regular school credit for program participation); obtaining funding and community support; and recruitment and selection of staff committed to using experiential learning strategies.

Successful EBCE programs usually have a strong program identity that is manifested in a distinctive name and the evolution of unique habits and routines that convey the message, "This is how we do it." The same characteristics may be seen in Foxfire. Foxfire-like programs have been adapted in numberless ways, but one of the surest ways of identifying them is by a name that refers to a forgotten folkway, artifact, or custom of the region. The concentrated nature of the Outward Bound program appears to result in students identifying closely with the group that develops over the course of the program.

Each of the three programs is sponsored and financed differently. Foxfire receives much of its funding from sales of its publications. Outward Bound generally charges a tuition, offers scholarships to those without funds, or is subsidized by special project funds, such as those for helping to rehabilitate youth offenders. EBCE programs are usually funded by the school districts adopting them, often using state or federal support for career education, vocational education, CETA funds, or categorical aid (as for the gifted or handicapped).

9. Program Outcomes

Although Foxfire, EBCE, and Outward Bound have developed independently of each other, they contain some common program outcomes. Each develops self-confidence in young people and an increased ability to relate to others. Each is concerned about both the short- and long-term effects on students. In each, some short-term effects are seen as instrumental for longer term effects. In EBCE, the students' exploration of a particular career is intended not only to learn about that one job, but also to gain a broader perspective for looking at other occupations. Outward Bound students use initiative groups, climbing exercises, and other experiences to examine how they react to metaphorically similar situations in their lives. Foxfire students learn camera and darkroom techniques that can be used to produce a magazine and also to promote social and cultural values. Foxfire and EBCE share a characteristic of being broader than a single subject area. Thus, the experiences learned may be translated by school staff into academic credit in language arts, social studies, or elective credit. In Fox-fire and EBCE, the mode of experiential learning is sometimes used as a vehicle for broader curriculum reform. Both provide a model of integration of separate subject content to blend in with the interests of the students. The final essential element hypothesized for this category is that students and staff are involved in assessing the effectiveness of their program, using both positive and negative outcomes for program improvement. Because EBCE programs are often publicly funded, the evaluation process is more formal than that of Foxfire or Outward Bound. Comprehensive summaries of EBCE evaluations have been done by Bucknam (1976) and Crowe and Adams (1979), while Shore (1977) has analyzed numerous evaluations of Outward Bound.

Summary

In this article, we have suggested essential elements of three experiential learning programs. We grouped these elements in nine categories that can be used to describe programs. Thirty-three elements were hypothesized within these nine categories, as shown in Table 1. While these essential elements represent a beginning in the task of building bridges between experiential learning programs, much remains to be done. The nine categories may need to be refined. The number of essential elements probably needs to be reduced to be useful to practitioners. Before these refinements can take place, other experiential learning programs should be studied. The categories and essential elements listed here will, no doubt, be tried out on selected programs over the next several years. Out of these studies we expect not only to refine our findings, but also to collect practical examples of ways in which essential elements are made manifest in successful programs. Ultimately, these examples will serve as point of reference for any interested in experiential education, whether in developing new programs or in improving those that already exist.

Designing Experiential Curricula

by Jed Williamson

Public schools can involve students, parents, community, and school board in the design of experience-based learning. The author describes one such program, The Mt. Cardigan Environmental Unit.

The purposes of this article are first to provide a framework which contains what I believe are some essential understandings for allowing one to think experientially, and second to suggest some strategies for implementing activity-centered and community-based curricula within a typical public school context.

The Framework

Among the goal statements in every school district with which I have come in contact can be found tenets upon which the experiential process is based. These goals include the following, usually stated in this format:

- to provide students with the skills necessary for coping with a changing world;
- to teach students how to solve problems;
- to provide students with challenging and real learning experiences;
- to meet the individual needs of students;
- to help students learn how to communicate effectively with each other;
- to prepare students for living in a society founded upon democratic principles.

It is not essential for the purposes of this article to list those goals which specifically pertain to "demonstrated competence" in basic skill areas, although they must be addressed through the curricula. Keeping all of these goals in mind, I will state the framework for learning experientially, be it for a 40-minute class, an eight-week unit, or an entire year. First, (1) the learners must be placed in a problem situation which calls for individual or cooperative actions; these actions and their attending consequences are then (2) observed and reflected upon, and from these reflections, the learners (3) review the appropriateness of their actions and attitudes and postulate what changes might be desirable in a similar problem-solving situation. Then, (4) learners are placed in a new problem-solving situation in which to test any desirable changes.

Diagrammatically, this cycle can be represented as follows:[1]

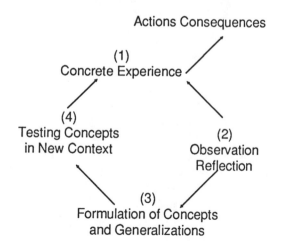

Actions Consequences

(1) Concrete Experience

(4) Testing Concepts in New Context

(2) Observation Reflection

(3) Formulation of Concepts and Generalizations

To foster this process in any school setting, certain preconditions are desirable. Generally, the faculty would view the school building as primarily the place where Steps Two and Three occur. The direct, concrete learning experiences would take place as much outside of school as inside school. Additionally, the faculty would view the role of the teacher as being the problem poser rather than the problem solver, as someone who establishes clear objectives which focus as much on what is happening, and how, as on content. In short, the teacher is a process expert as well as a subject matter expert. The concern is to help learners achieve a personal high standard of comprehension and perception of their outside world and inward lives. The school curriculum would have an emphasis on integrating disciplines, and, thereby, on collaborative teaching. With interdisciplinary units and a core of faculty working with one grade or one group of students, the 45- or 50-minute class period could be shortened or lengthened, and class sizes could vary according to need. Learning situations would stress involving students physically, mentally, and socially in direct, active experiences.

Designing Experiential Units

Whether one teacher wants to devote fifteen minutes a week to experiential learning, or a team of teachers wants to develop a ten-week interdisciplinary unit using an experiential approach, the process for design and implementation is the same. The following three tables are illustrative of how this process is accomplished in the Live, Learn, and Teach program. Table A, "A Checklist of Factors in Planning for Experiential Learn-ing—A Planning Format," is a fairly typical lesson-planning format, while Table B is a very specific and detailed expansion of Step IV, "The Planning Process," from Table A. Table C is but one method of determining if a given unit meets the criteria for experiential learning. In keeping with the goal of involving learners, all three tables should be viewed as instruments to be used by both teachers and students.

Table A: A Checklist of Factors in Planning for Experiential Learning — A Planning Format

   I. Theme of the plan
      Rationale including overall purpose
      Desired results
         Cognitive
         Affective
         Behavioral
  II. Resources and needs
      Personnel
      Materials and geographic locations
      Budget
 III. Logistics
      Dates and places
      Transportation
      Emergency procedures
      Permission/medical requirements
 IV. Planning process (See Table B for detail)
  V. Assessment procedures for student learning (consider pre- and post-test/assessment).
 VI. Journal observations and conclusions

As an example of what is possible in a typical American public school, I will describe how an eight-week interdisciplinary unit, the Mt. Cardigan Environmental Unit, emphasizing a study of the natural environment, has been developed over the past six years at the McKelvie Middle School in Bedford, New Hampshire. As a supervisor of

Table B: This is a sample of how the Planning Process in Table A, Item IV, might appear for a beginning lesson on orienteering

IV. PLANNING PROCESS

OVERALL PURPOSE: A growing sense of
competence in dealing with
the environment

ACTIVITY: Orienteering
DATE:
NAME:

RESULTS	PROCESS	PROCESS CHECK
What the learner-centered teacher seeks to accomplish. Think in terms of affective, cognitive, and behavioral growth.	What actions the learner-centered teacher takes to achieve the desired results. Consider also resources, logistics, and budget.	What behaviors during the PROCESS will verify if the activity is succeeding or if any adjustments in actions are needed.
1. -reduce potential threat -remove mysterious aspects -create a sense of comfort/ease -gain attention of learners 2. -provide sense of all learners becoming involved -provide initial success experience -provide acquisition of skill in reading compass, setting compass dial	1. Introduce activity by: (10–15 min.) -Holding up grapefruit as representation of world -Describe where poles and magnetic pole are located. -Describe characteristics of compass while handing out compass (one for every five) -Break into small groups (4–5 each group) 2. Go to point from which prearranged sightings have been made and: -Have groups together -Have them turn dial to 42˚ and sight most significant object in distance -Have them turn dial to 203˚ and do same -Continue above process until learners have "got it" 3. Pacing and distance 4. Short course 5. Larger course 6. Post-activity discussion	1. Are learners exhibiting ease, understanding? (Look for relaxed facial expressions, physical proximity, minimal movement. Listen for relatedness of questions and conversation.) 2. -Are learners in small groups with friends of strangers? -Are all individuals involved with task? -Are learners sighting correctly?

EVALUATION

How many of the desired RESULTS were attained? How much of the OVERALL PURPOSE was achieved? Which teacher actions must be changed to achieve the desired RESULTS?

graduate interns in that school for the past several years, my firsthand experience has shown that the usual roadblocks and constraints, such as lack of money, community involvement, or support, can be surmounted.

In its current stage of development, the unit works in the following manner. During the late spring, parents of seventh-grade students and the students themselves are given a presentation and description of the unit. This occurs at an evening meeting, with teachers and administrators present, and includes videotape and slide presentations, a question-and-answer session, and information handouts. Over the summer, the eighth-grade teachers finish the current year's

Table C: Sample of an Experiential Class Assessment Format

1. This class had the following experiential components (on a scale of 1 to 10):

    ___ students actively involved — physically
    ___ students actively involved — mentally
    ___ students actively involved — socially
    ___ teachers actively involved
    ___ teachers set up problem
    ___ others

2. The teachers (on a scale of 1 to 10):

    ___ were well organized
    ___ were aware of students' abilities
    ___ were aware of students' concerns
    ___ made good use of resources
    ___ made good use of time
    ___ communicated well with students
    ___ were enthusiastic about what they were doing
    ___ did not get between the students and the learning situation
    ___ other

3. The students (on a scale of 1 to 10):

    ___ liked the lesson
    ___ understood the lesson
    ___ were fair to the teachers
    ___ cooperated with each other
    ___ learned something
    ___ other

4. The things I liked most about this class:

5. Something which could be improved:

6. Something I did not like or which made me uncomfortable:

revision of the Field Study Manual, which becomes the guide book for each student throughout the unit. This guide book contains a great variety of problems to be solved, with considerable latitude for each student to identify his or her own particular area of inquiry. The manual is meant to serve as a journal, as a guide to inquiry, as a means to record observations, and as an aid to posing and solving problems.

For the first six weeks of school, all eighth-grade students (the number has ranged from 125 to 160) and their teachers prepare for a week of investigation and exploration on and around a mountain in northern New Hampshire. The skills which the youngsters learn prior to the trip include water testing, soils testing, flora and fauna identification, mapping, orienteering, archaeology, camping, first aid, weather observation and prediction, food preparation, and photography. All of these skills are taught through actual field problems set up in the school, on school grounds, and in the community. Steps One, Two, and Three of the experiential process are engaged in daily, with Step Four presenting a real and immediate prospect in mind. From the first day of school, students work in groups of twelve with at least one adult in each group. School subjects such as physical training, writing, and social studies are integrated as a result of the kinds of problems that must be solved throughout the unit.

By the time students embark on their trip to the mountain, they have encountered in a direct and personal manner the problems they will be solving in the new setting. Although the students are structured into activities such as a beaver pond study, a plant succession observation, an archaeological dig in an old farm house cellar hole, and a stream flow study, there is also an individual focus which each student has chosen, and which will result in a culminating project synthesized during the final week, then presented to parents and the community. Such projects have included making scale models of the 25-square-mile study area, picture displays, written and pictorial reconstruction of farm life 200 years ago, a videotape production depicting the entire unit, flora and fauna guides for the area, and a booklet designed to help other teachers and students start such a unit. All but a few students choose to work on these projects collaboratively. Teachers and students assess whether learning goals have been met both by the projects and the continuing work in the Field Study Manual.

It is hoped this brief sketch of a fairly complex unit will give the reader one indication of the kind of experiential approaches possible. In addition to the pre-conditions stated at the end of the first section, some specific details need attention. These details are revealed through the following interview which Greg Kniseley, a graduate student intern, conducted with the school principal, Robert Little:

> The science Curriculum Coordinator had the task of reviewing and revising our science curriculum five years ago (1973). Ray Landry, and the other science teacher, Dick Janelle, wanted to provide an exciting "hands on" experience for the eighth grade class. In a brainstorming session during an eighth grade team planning period, the teachers conceived the idea of involving students, parents, and community leaders in developing an interdisciplinary unit of instruction, which has now come to be known as the Mt. Cardigan Environmental Unit. Ray also involved the Assistant Superintendent, Rod Mansfield, in the preliminary stages, and this proved to be an important step in gaining support for the idea. During the summer, Ray, with input from his peers, used the vehicle of the summer Curriculum Development Committee to have the program come far enough along in its design that first year so that it was included as part of school district policy. As principal, I directed as much funding as I could towards the project.

> As is the case in most innovative or new projects, one person really has to get turned on to an idea and then develop the plan. In this case, Ray Landry was the person. In addition to the steps mentioned, he built an evaluation model and kept the right people involved and informed throughout.[2]

Implicit in his statement are some important factors essential to the success of such a venture:

1) The project began with a few dedicated teachers, low-key in their approach, and a principal, willing but thorough in matters of an exploratory nature, spending the time in and out of school to launch the project, taking care to involve all of the necessary people.

2) The teachers began with modest, step-by-step experiments. At first, the unit focused entirely on science and math, and did not include all teachers in the eighth grade. Year by year, the unit expanded to include the other subject areas. The current level of complexity is a healthy indication of the support and involvement of many adults in the community and of agency participation.

3) The teachers' primary motive was to create an interesting set of learning

experiences from which observable and measurable skills would generate. Like their students, these teachers have developed a keen sense of ownership of the teaching materials and the learning experiences—which is not a typical response when using prepared texts.

4) Teachers ensured that lines of communication remained open with all the people concerned. Written information to parents, presentations to school board and community, slide and videotape documentations, student projects, parents' meetings, and continual program evaluations are among the essentials.

During my five-year tenure, I have observed some positive changes in attitude and involvement on the part of staff, and I believe this is attributable to the fact that the learning experience has been so obviously successful, as determined both by academic achievement and by student and teacher attitude. At this point, not only are the academic subject matter teachers involved; the nurse, secretary, home economics teacher, and physical education teachers have joined the effort. All staff have galvanized—in spite of obvious and expected differences in style and approach—around the task of preparing for the week in the mountains. It is a time they enjoy, as do the students.

Although some of the students feel that the Field Study Manual is really just another workbook to be completed, most students use it for what it is—a guide to give substance to their observations and discoveries. The blend of experiential and pencil/paper learning is achieved through necessity and natural inquiry. This is not to say that students can choose to do nothing. Rather, it is

to say that there are more options than might be found if they were pursuing a curriculum in a more traditional manner. As to student/teacher relationships, it would be apparent to an observer that a positive tone for the school year is generated through the shared learning and living experiences.

It is encouraging to see the many schools which have developed units of a similar scope. The message which comes through from each of them is that the development of experiential approaches is limited only by temporary constraints, most of which are within the people doing the developing. As the network of teachers who are currently able to use these approaches becomes more sophisticated and as more articles on this topic are written, it is hoped there will follow a substantive increase in the use of experiential curricula.

NOTES

1. This diagram is a combination of ideas taken from models of experiential learning by James Coleman, et al., in "The Hopkins Game Program: Conclusions from Seven Years of Research," *Education Researchers,* August 1973, and David Kolb, et al., in *Organizational Psychology,* Englewood Cliffs, NJ: Prentice-Hall, 1974. The groundwork was done by John Dewey, as stated in his *Experience and Education,* New York: Collier Books, 1963, and by Kurt Lewin, in *Field Theory and Social Science,* New York: Harper, 1951.

2. *Autumn Adventure—An Eighth Grade Environmental Experience,* Greg Kniseley, et al. Published by McKelvie Middle School, Bedford, New Hampshire, 1978.

The Future of Experiential Education as a Profession

by Paul Michalec

The present is a time of reassessment of dominant ideas across the human sciences (a designation broader than and inclusive of the conventional social sciences), extending to law, art, architecture, philosophy, literature, and even the natural sciences. This reassessment is more salient in some disciplines than in others, but its presence is pervasive (Marcus & Fischer, 1986, p.7).

The periodic reorganization of knowledge is not a new phenomenon. Thomas Khun (1962) argued that science communities periodically pass through paradigm revolutions. These are not peaceful and ordered transitions but rather abrupt and jarring movements from one set of organizing principles to another.

In 1978, Norman Denzin wrote *The Research Act.* His main thesis was that the three elements of sociology—theory, research methods, and area of researcher interest—had become separated and were no longer a coherent unit. For Denzin, this was a dangerous situation; he argued that these pieces of the research act should be reunited under a discipline-wide commitment to one theoretical framework.

A final example of reorganization is the reworking of the term "researcher collaboration" by Margaret Eisenhart (an educational anthropologist) and Hilda Borko (a cognitive psychologist). They characterize historic attempts at collaboration as additive; research questions would be answered from the isolated perspective of each academic discipline and then added together in the final document. Their book, *Designing Classroom Research: Themes, Issues, and Struggles,* is an elaboration of Eisenhart and Borko's struggle to achieve a new form of collaboration, the synthesis of educational anthropology and cognitive psychology (Eisenhart & Borko, 1993).

Is experiential education going through a similar period of redefinition? I believe that current discussions concerning professionalism mirror transformations that have occurred in other fields of inquiry. In the last few years this concept (professionalism) has increasingly become a regular part of Association discourse.

I started to ask questions such as: Is experiential education a profession or a discipline? Would the critical dialogue associated with academic disciplines be a useful tool for defining experiential education? Who or what forces within the field are striving to create a workable definition of experiential education? To answer these questions, I decided to investigate professionalism and an allied term, academic discipline, and to conduct a study featuring the views and ideas of the Board of Directors for the Association for Experiential Education (AEE).

Academic Discipline

What are some of the accepted definitions and hallmarks of an academic discipline? In answering this question, I will draw on two works: Tony Becher's *Academic Tribes and Territories* (1989) and Stephen Toulmin's *Human Understanding* (1972). Toulmin focuses primarily on paradigm changes within disciplines while Becher constructs an ethnographic tale of the culture of academia.

Becher (1989) uses the cultural metaphor of tribes and inter-tribal relations to describe disciplines. He points out that academic disciplines are separated into distinct tribes which have their own myths, language, symbols, icons, and initiation ceremonies. The territorial markings between disciplines are methodological differences in terms of how problems are stated and resolved. To understand what a discipline is entails knowing both the social context in which critical dialogue occurs as well as the ideas, techniques, and conceptual frameworks that direct inquiry. For Becher, disciplines are defined by the existence of large academic social structures.

Toulmin (1972) uses the metaphor of evolutionary change to capture the essence of how disciplines move from one intellectual paradigm to another. As Darwin saw species developing in response to environmental stimuli, Toulmin sees disciplines evolving out of their intellectual history in response to pressure from new ideas. As in evolutionary theory, new disciplines can form as intellectual mutations from established branches of knowledge, or become extinct when they do not respond to changing environmental/social conditions. Toulmin's main concern is with disciplines as repositories of changing theories on how the world operates.

Both authors share commonalties in their characterizations of academic disciplines.

Toulmin, like Becher, claims that disciplines can be defined by the existence of socially constructed boundaries that mark off what is and what is not acceptable information within a discipline. Becher uses language similar to Toulmin's when he acknowledges the impact conceptual change has on the cultural structure of a discipline.

For the purpose of this paper, I will define a discipline as the relationship between knowledge and its academic social arrangements. By knowledge I mean the intellectual markers that separate engineering from education, and sociology from high-energy physics. Knowledge is distinct from ideas: individuals are the source of ideas, but knowledge is communal (Toulmin, 1972). It is the product of the intellectual re-working of a community of scholars. In a true discipline, knowledge occupies the intellectual guard posts of the citadel. Any new concept seeking admission to the discipline must first present its credentials to the sentry. If the credentials are not recognizable, the concept is barred access to the citadel; which, if this is the case, then 1) the conceptual framework must be reformulated, or 2) it must seek admittance into a different discipline, or 3) become a subdiscipline that sets up camp outside the protective walls of the parent discipline.

The social component of disciplinary knowledge refers to the way members of a discipline relate to each other: How are conflicts resolved? What are the standards for acceptable arguments? Who are the cultural heroes? And, how are new members initiated into the tribe? Social arrangements also influence the changing dynamic quality of disciplines. As new people with new ideas enter the critical dialogue which shapes academic knowledge, new paradigms are formed. When this occurs, forms of knowledge that were once outside the discipline may suddenly find acceptance inside. Conversely, old cherished maxims and ways of thinking may be cast out and denied disciplinary citizenship.

Types of Disciplines

Becher (1989) develops a typography of disciplines which is responsive to the relationship between knowledge and its social arrangements. He divides disciplines horizontally along a hard/soft line and vertically along a pure/applied continuum. In addition to this gross pairing, he also inserts finer separations as to whether or not the core concepts of a discipline are divergent or convergent. Physics and math are examples of hard/pure disciplines with central concepts that tend to be convergent. Disciplinary growth in these fields can be classified as crystalline. The humanities and social sciences, by contrast, fit within a soft/pure quadrant. Switching to the applied side, one finds mechanical engineering in the hard/applied category and education, social work, and law as tribes in the soft/applied realm. The latter forms of knowledge have divergent concepts and meander intellectually like a braided river.

Becher clearly states that his typography is not meant to be exclusive and dogmatic. There are a number of disciplines that cross over the boundaries, as well as forms of knowledge that defy categorization. His proposed typography is simply a way to begin exploring the intricacy of disciplinary knowledge.

Profession

How does a profession differ from a discipline? What is the relationship between these two terms? Can a profession become a discipline? Since both disciplines and professions are human constructs, they share a social context. Disciplines are socially constructed around university life while professions are socially ordered around professional organizations and trade unions. Professions are collections of practice-oriented individuals who are guided in their actions by theory and professional standards of conduct. The main area of divergence is the source of central concepts: professional knowledge is informed by practice while disciplinary knowledge is informed by theory.

The Relationship between Professions and Academic Disciplines

Experiential educators have a long-standing tradition of anti-intellectualism, a habit of valuing practice over theory (Gass, 1992). At first blush, this seems like a reasonable relationship. After all, everyone knows that it is only through action that problems are solved. You cannot sit around all day talking about minimum-impact camping while the woods are trampled down around you.

Stephen Toulmin (1972) argues against the assumed validity of this relationship. He claims that theories can thrive without the support of a profession, while the opposite is not true. In other words, professional practice is dependent on an academic discipline for its vigor; thus, by definition, professionalism means connection to a discipline. Toulmin argues that when professions abandon the theoretical frameworks provided by a discipline, they lose professional status and collapse into rogue ideologies.

Support for this position, as well as a new twist to the debate, can be found in the work of John Dewey (1938). "The Need of a Theory of Experience" is a main chapter title in his book, *Experience and Education*. In that chapter, Dewey lays out an argument concerning the relationship between theory and practice. He claims that progressive educators will escape the imperialism of traditional models of education only when they have developed a coherent theory of experience to guide their practice. However, rather than falling into the either/or trap, Dewey urged the educators of his time to seek a both/and perspective that synthesizes the theory/practice split.

In a recent *Journal* article, Mike Gass called for an Association-wide integration of the theory/practice split. "Experiential education must integrate theory and practice together in a synergistic and appropriate manner to be a powerful and effective process in today's world" (Gass, 1992). It is my belief that Gass's vision is a valuable one and worth the pain, trouble, and uncertainty associated with pursuing it. There are not many models for this sort of endeavor, but who ever said experiential educators were followers of the status quo? I believe that as an organization, we have the tools and ability to redefine the relationship between professionalism and academic discipline in such a way that they can support and enhance the objectives of the Association.

The Board's Views on Professionalism and Academic Discipline

In the fall of 1991, as part of a class project, I had the opportunity to conduct telephone interviews with all members of the Board of Directors for the Association for Experiential Education. I asked each member the same set of questions related to definitions of professionalism and academic discipline. The five questions were: Compare and contrast the terms "profession" and "academic discipline." Is experiential education a discipline or a profession? How can experiential education become more of a profession or an academic discipline? What are your goals for the Association? And, What is the role of conflict in the Association?

Question #1: Compare and contrast the terms "profession" and "academic discipline."

The Board's Response

A profession is:

- An application of techniques
- More general of the two
- A body of fellow professionals practicing a similar craft and guided by similar ideas and practices
- An acknowledged body of knowledge
- A code of ethics
- Accepted peer practices
- A strong research base, a body of knowledge
- Healthy debate around ideas that are important to a profession
- Where the ideas of a discipline are applied
- Always changing

An academic discipline is:

- Strict and principled, focused on something for a short period of time
- Individuals working in isolation; searching through closed, particular sets of ideas

- Static
- Focused
- Certain theoretical aspects
- A significant body of knowledge
- A variety of disciplines inside the rubric of profession
- Research

One way to make sense of these two lists is to compare them to the definitions of professionalism and academic discipline that I developed earlier in the paper (profession as practice and academic discipline as theory). Based on this quick sketch, it is possible to say that the Board generally identifies a profession with practice and an academic discipline with theory.

Other frames of analysis could include: which term incorporates community themes; which is more individualistic; which appears to be more responsive to open debate and dialogue; or, which term fits experiential education? An interesting question to ponder, in relation to Mike Gass's statement, is: What concept or idea synthesizes the two terms?

Question #2: Is experiential education a profession or discipline?

The Board's Response

- AEE is a profession not a discipline.
- AEE is an umbrella professional organization for its various members.
- It is not a separate profession; it fits under the general profession of education.
- Experiential education is a tool that can be used by professionals.
- As a profession, it is well substantiated by safety records, peer practices, and a code of ethics.

- As a discipline, we have a weak body of knowledge which could be improved.
- Experiential education should not try to become a separate discipline, but rather part of an existing one, such as education.
- It is a theoretically new discipline.

The above answers can be summarized into three major trends: 1) the Board favored labeling experiential education as a profession; 2) because of its weakly organized body of knowledge, experiential education falls short of disciplinary status; and 3), of all the disciplines, experiential education fits best with education.

Question #3: How can experiential education become more of a profession or discipline?

The Board's Response

- Continue expanding the work of Jasper Hunt and the adventure alternative special interest group in the area of ethics
- Become more of a profession by moving away from a broad nebulous term and toward a systematic entity
- Get out into the broad educational arena and participate in other educational conferences
- Become more mainstream in its orientation; a regular part of academic settings
- Do more research building on established ideas and arguments
- Publish, especially in journals other than the *Journal of Experiential Education*
- Bring the debate on what is experiential education into other academic settings.

Imbedded in this set of statements is a call for increased efforts toward consolidating the research, ideas, and definitions of experiential education. This can be accomplished through the work of special interest groups and research grounded in existing theories of experience.

Question #4: What are your goals for the Association of Experiential Education?

The Board's Response

- To create a support network for a wide range of practitioners
- To influence mainstream education through increased professionalism
- To promote experiential education at both a national and international level
- To make experiential education more than rock climbing
- To push the edges of where and how experiential education is known, so that we begin to have broader name recognition
- To create a stronger organization through the diversity initiative
- To secure grant money so that we can support research and stabilize the intellectual and practical base of experiential education
- To define the mission of the organization

Many of the themes common to previous answers come through in this question: consolidation of experiential theory, inserting experiential education into mainstream settings, and increasing the professional status of the Association.

Question #5: What is the role of conflict in the Association of Experiential Education?

The Board's Response

- It can be a very positive force if handled correctly.
- It can both validate and question various points of view.
- The process of conflict resolution will become more difficult before it gets easier, as the organization grows and becomes more professional.
- Historically there has been some in-fighting within the organization between those who have power (outdoor educators) and those seeking power.
- Conflict is disagreement with someone while still giving them support.
- We need to trust each other more. We are fearful of what each other is doing as well as who has the biggest piece of pie.

What is striking about the answers to this question is the willingness of the Board to embrace conflict and view it as a positive force for change. This dovetails nicely with the Board's goals for the Association, many of which entail a change in the way the organization has historically operated.

What are the Potential Consequences of Using the Frameworks of Profession and Academic Discipline?

Theory and practice tension

As I have mentioned earlier, there has been a long-standing history of tension between educators who feel that the essence of education can be found in theory and those who believe in the preeminence of practice

(Clifford & Guthrie, 1988, and Feiman-Nemser, 1990). These contested boundaries can, among other things, mark out the territory between academia and the public school system. As Mike Gass has pointed out, experiential educators tend to perpetuate this dichotomy.

The Association for Experiential Education is currently a loose collection of academics and practitioners: outdoor instructors, public school teachers, adventure therapists, academics, and corporate trainers. It is deeply immersed in the arguments of practice. If and when the Association begins to consolidate its theoretical grounding (a likely direction given the Board's responses and other internal pressures), the historical tension between these terms is sure to arise. Some key questions to ponder are: How is the Association going to deal with the cry from members who believe in the preeminence of practice; Is it possible to redefine the relationship between theory and practice such that the historical tension is bridged; and, Are there frameworks, beyond theory and practice, that more accurately define the terrain of experiential education?

Change in membership

During a classroom discussion concerning the identity of the Association for Experiential Education, I was asked: "Is the Association a haven for alternative educators, a serious agent of change in mainstream education, both, or something else?" In addition to raising questions of identity, this question also brings to my mind the diversity of educators who call themselves experiential educators. Participants at a recent conference included: outdoor educators, classroom teachers, public officials, health workers, academics, and program administrators.

There is currently enough wiggle room in the definition of experiential education to encompass a vast array of educators. If and when the Association moves toward either a clearer definition of experiential practice and/or a more coherent theory of experience, some current members may be excluded. Their definitions of experiential education may no longer fit within the new paradigm. Again, the Board's willingness to embrace an inclusive form of conflict is comforting. Thus, discussions about definition and identity can be both rather than either/or.

Reformatted journal

The current format of the *Journal of Experiential Education* reflects the wide ranging tastes of its membership. In the pages of the *Journal* can be found articles that would appeal to practitioners, public school teachers, adventure therapists, and academics. If a new definition of experiential education changes the profile of Association membership, then the format of the *Journal* may also have to be updated. For instance, if the Association chooses to strengthen its theoretical and academic status, the *Journal* would have to keep pace and adopt a style consistent with other academic journals.

Conclusion

In an earlier section of this essay, I claimed that the Association's practitioners embodied an alternative framing of knowledge that could bridge some of the historical pitfalls associated with professionalism and academic discipline. Jean Lave and Etienne Wenger (1993) in *Situated Learning:*

Legitimate Peripheral Participation write about two distinct values of knowledge: exchange and use. Students participating in an education system that promotes the exchange value of knowledge learn that the value of knowledge is equated with what it can be exchanged for (e.g., power, money, prestige). Students in an education system committed to the promotion of the use value of knowledge learn that the purpose of knowledge is to advance the goals of their working community through the shared use of knowledge.

Lave and Wenger go on to elaborate a theory of learning that embraces the use value of knowledge, a theory they call legitimate peripheral participation. One key to their theory is that all learning is social, that it occurs within a community of practice. Their learning theory is a challenge to educators and academics who believe that learning occurs within the heads of individuals and is not influenced by the social context.

It is my belief that what Lave and Wenger describe is what experiential practitioners do best. Educators using experiential techniques tend to be more concerned with the use value of knowledge than its exchange value. For evidence, I point to the common refrain, "I am an experiential educator because I love what I am doing, not for the money." Moreover, consider the fact that a student's growth is valued for what it contributes to the overall strength of the learning community, as much as it is valued for the student's personal development. In essence, many experiential programs are creating mini-communities of practice that emphasize the use value of knowledge.

If it is indeed the case that practitioners have a strong history of embracing the use value of knowledge, then perhaps the Association can tap into this energy as it moves toward increased alliance with academia and professionalism. Much of the current tension in other fields between theory and practice can be tied to a commitment to the exchange value of knowledge. If the Association focuses on its historic commitment to the use value of knowledge, however, it may be able to transcend this tension and find a creative synthesis of theory and practice.

The National Reports and Educational Reform: A Contemporary and Historical View

School Reform for the Nineties: Opportunities and Obstacles for Experiential Educators

by Joel Westheimer, Joseph Kahne, and Amy Gerstein

Over the course of the last decade, there has been growing awareness of the need to radically re-shape American education. By 1985, more than twenty national commissions had issued reports describing the nation's ailing high schools and over two hundred state commissions had been created to arrest the decline of public education (Kirst, 1984). These investigations and the resulting policy recommendations have generated powerful and diverse agenda for restructuring schools. The dialogue about reform has included teachers, administrators, policy makers, government officials, business groups, and concerned community members.

Experiential educators have much to contribute to this conversation. By engaging students in active learning experiences, these strategies offer powerful responses to problems surrounding student motivation and performance (Hamilton, 1980; Kielsmeier, 1989; Shore 1977). Research demonstrates that experiential programs can profoundly affect participating students and the school community (Conrad & Hedin, 1981; Shore, 1977). However, despite the potential contribution to both affective and cognitive student development, experiential strategies remain marginal to mainstream educational reform efforts. Advocates of these strategies struggle to convey to school personnel that their programs offer more than enjoyable field trips.

In this article, we highlight the links between experiential approaches to education and those espoused by authors of the recent school reform literature. The current compatibility between experiential strategies and mainstream educational reform provides experiential educators with a timely opportunity to further their own agendas while forging stronger links with mainstream public schools.

The Unused Resource

Experiential education has a rich history at the center of educational theory and practice. Experiential learning "place[s] participants in responsible roles and engage[s] them in cooperative, goal-directed activities with other youth, with adults, or both" (Hamilton, 1980, p. 180). Broadly used to denote active or participatory education, these strategies draw from students' own experience and the experience of their peers rather than exclusively from instructors and textbooks.

Many teachers in mainstream school settings employ experiential education strategies in their instruction. However, these efforts—field trips, community service projects, wilderness trips—are frequently viewed as "add-ons" and often rely upon transient funding, time, and energy. The vast majority of programs exist independently of schools, working with children in the afternoons, on weekends, or during school vacations (Shore, 1977). Experiential programs remain distinct from both the standard curriculum and the normal school day, are rarely institutionalized, and are more often linked to affective than cognitive development.

To date, policy analysts and school reformers have written much about the need for increased "active learning," "relevance," and "personalization" (i.e., Sizer, 1984; Goodlad, 1984). But little has been written about the merits of including experiential education in school reform efforts. In what follows, we identify three areas in which the goals of experiential education and those of the current reform movement are well-matched. Specifically, we examine reforms designed to 1) unify a highly fragmented curriculum, 2) promote pedagogical techniques which engage students as active participants in learning, and 3) better serve at-risk student populations. In addition, we suggest that a prominent element of the reform movement—the recent push to hold schools and school systems accountable to standardized state and national goals—conflicts with the principles of experiential education. These goals and accountability measures present formidable obstacles for educators interested in bringing experiential techniques to the classroom. By examining these major themes in school reform, we assess the opportunities and obstacles for experiential education in the 1990s.

Restructuring the School Day

The fragmented curriculum is frequently cited as an impediment to more dynamic, holistic, and engaging education (Sizer, 1984, 1992; Goodlad, 1984). Nonetheless, little has changed this century in the organization of a typical high school student's day (Sarason, 1971, 1990) or in the manner of teaching used to implement a highly compartmentalized curriculum (Cuban, 1984). Students move from one subject to another with little or no connection between disciplines. Each period is generally fifty minutes long, allowing as many as six or seven in one day. Fragmentation exists within disciplines as well. Teachers are often compelled to follow detailed and lengthy curricula that emphasize memorization of isolated facts over understanding concepts. Moreover, standard student assessment practices perpetuate the splintering of subject matter by emphasizing the recall of factual information. This emphasis on basic skills and isolated facts renders students passive participants in activities as disconnected from each other as they are from students' concerns and experiences. As Ted Sizer (1984) writes,

> So I know that Franklin Roosevelt launched the New Deal; so what? These data may make good sense to the curriculum planner or to a teacher in a discipline, but they often appear inchoate to even the eager student and senseless to the docile student, save as grist for the examinations that ultimately provide credit toward a diploma. (p. 93)

In response, many curriculum reforms emphasize the development of critical thinking, in-depth study on fewer topics rather than broad surveys, and integration of subject matter across disciplines (Powell, Farrar, & Cohen, 1985; Sizer, 1984). Rather than teaching "Plato to NATO" in a Western Civilization course, these reformers suggest that teachers focus on a few important themes characteristic of particular historical time periods. Larger blocks of time and program flexibility would allow projects that span several disciplines, utilize innovative resources, and engage students through the application of newly acquired knowledge.

Revitalized Pedagogy

Reformers also worry that teacher-centered instruction dominates classroom practice, preventing the adoption of more effective strategies. John Goodlad, in one of the largest and most comprehensive studies of American schools to date, found that more than 70% of talk in classrooms was teacher talk. Further, most of the student talk did not reflect critical thinking (Goodlad, 1984). Students have little opportunity for active involvement in the learning process. Too often they simply regurgitate facts on tests. Rather than engaging in critical evaluation of the subject matter, students make "silent treaties" with teachers, agreements that trade a passing grade for docile behavior (Powell, Farrar, & Cohen, 1985).

In response to student passivity, educators hope to engage students in more active learning. They are looking for ways to align curricular objectives and pedagogical techniques with student experience and to engage students in the active discovery of knowledge. Perhaps no other element of the current reform agenda aligns as well with the strengths of experiential education. For example, a field study in physical geography demands that students utilize multiple senses and call on a variety of disciplines to explore the world around them. Whereas traditional approaches to this subject rely on abstraction and result in student passivity, experiential approaches encourage active participation in meaningful, task-oriented activities.

Students might be asked to draw a topographic map of the school grounds or a nearby park. To accurately portray the area, students would need not only geographic knowledge (longitude, latitude, land forms, etc.) but also math and drafting skills. If, in addition, students were asked to develop a proposal for redesigning their school or park, they would conduct interviews, write persuasive editorials, and formulate economic assessments. They would also confront environmental and political issues surrounding their proposal. In short, experiential education can reduce disciplinary fragmentation and foster instruction which is interactive, varied, and engaging.

Increasing Attention to At-Risk Students

Just as experiential strategies can help to meet the goals of current pedagogical and curricular reform efforts, they are similarly well suited to meet the educational challenges posed by poverty and an increasingly diverse student body. Adolescents, particularly those from minority backgrounds and in urban settings, are often poorly served in

schools (Fine, 1991; Kozol, 1991). As a result, dropout rates in some of America's largest school systems exceed fifty percent. Measures of scholastic achievement, whether in literacy, mathematics, history, or science, demonstrate alarming shortcomings in the way we school our children (National Commission for Excellence in Education, 1983).

Recent research indicates that student alienation is a particularly salient factor contributing to these worrisome statistics (Wehlage et al., 1988; Fine, 1991; Sizer, 1992). Studies show that students in underserved areas find themselves disconnected from the purpose of schooling. A lack of motivation stems, in part, from academic goals which seem irrelevant.

Recent studies of students' affective and social development paint an equally disconcerting picture (Dryfoos, 1990; Ianni, 1989). In many urban and rural settings, the inability of authorities to respond effectively to poverty, homelessness, and crime creates a sense of hopelessness which promotes alienation from mainstream institutions. Students' estrangement from school, in turn, creates barriers hindering both personal and academic growth.

Reform efforts of the past decade have noted the deleterious effects of student alienation and have recommended that educators adopt strategies which personalize the school setting and foster stronger school communities. As McLaughlin and Talbert (1990) write, "For students of all degrees of academic involvement [and particularly for at-risk students] personal bonds with adults in the school have a greater capacity to motivate and engage than do forms of social control that emphasize obedience to authority and conformity to rules" (also see Wehlage et al., 1988; Swidler, 1979). In addition, sensitivity to various learning styles is seen as an important component of new pedagogical strategies which seek to reach a diverse student population (Gardner, 1989).

Experiential programs offer a means of responding to the problems facing at-risk youth. They can help make school more relevant, personal, and flexible, and less alienating through cooperative, hands-on learning experiences. For example, initiative activities, which are used in many experiential education programs, encourage students to understand and meet the challenge of a group working together toward a common goal. Outdoor education programs are particularly well suited to the establishment of a strong sense of community. Facing the challenge of round-the-clock living with peers and teachers, students are drawn together, developing an increased sense of commitment and attachment to the group.

The positive effects of these educational strategies need not be limited to the outdoors. The interpersonal and group skills cultivated on outings is reflected in positive relationships in the classroom (Taini, 1992). Alienation—a reform concern—is thus diminished. Furthermore, educators can learn from these strategies and apply them to a variety of experiential activities in the classroom. For example, New York City Outward Bound instructors have collaborated with teachers from the city's public school system to create *Lessons From Our Classrooms: A Guide For Experiential Educators* (Udall, 1991). With lessons on writing which use students' timelines, and literature exercises which use music, this three-year effort to integrate the tenets of experiential

teaching into the classroom holds much promise for future classroom-based experiential programs.

In short, experiential strategies can help educators respond to the needs of at-risk students. These strategies promote interpersonal interaction and curb alienation; teachers have more time with students in both formal and informal settings; and students feel a part of a community of learners.

Despite the promise of experiential strategies, those designing programs intended to support at-risk student populations face significant challenges. Experiential programs must be infused with a greater sensibility toward minority populations. Jim Kielsmeier (1989) worries that leaders of experiential education programs, when trying to increase diversity within their ranks, have too often asked "How do we get 'them' to join us?" Kielsmeier asserts that organizations such as Outward Bound must "adapt, or better yet, re-create [themselves] to become culturally diverse" (Kielsmeier, 1989). At the very least, such adaptation requires a staff which reflects the diversity of the student population. At best, experiential educators need to work with community educators to design new curricula and teaching techniques which demonstrate sensitivity to the particular needs of diverse student populations.

Adequately serving at-risk students requires changes beyond modifications in method and staffing. Evidence indicates that though students benefit from participation in out-of-school experiential activities, particularly adventure education programs, the lasting effects of these programs on school-related measures such as attendance and standardized test scores is uncertain (Sakofs et al., 1988; Smith, 1976). To effectively serve these populations, experiential programs need to coordinate their efforts with the schools these students attend. By bringing students, teachers, and even administrators together on outings and in preparatory activities, the experiences are more likely to have a notable effect on students' commitment to academics and the school community.

Unfortunately, many experiential educators lack both professional knowledge of mainstream school settings and a desire to work in heavily bureaucratized environments. This exacerbates the difficulty of implementing alternative methods and curricula. Successful coordination may well require a willingness on the part of experiential educators to learn about and accommodate and adjust to the organizational and cultural constraints of mainstream schools (Gerstein, Kahne, & Westheimer, 1992).

Numerous challenges await experiential educators as they prepare to serve at-risk student populations: first, normative questions regarding programmatic form and content must be resolved; second, program staff must be representative of and sensitized to the multicultural diversity of the students they serve; and finally, barriers to successful implementation in schools must be overcome.

School Accountability and the Common Core Curriculum

Rather than focusing on the classroom or on a particular segment of the student population, many reformers have attempted to influence educational practice through critiques of national and state education policy. *A Nation at Risk* (1983) focused on the desperate state of American schools and on the poor performance of students relative to other nations. Citing a "rising tide of mediocrity," the report warned that America was in danger of losing its place as the leader in the world economy. *A Nation at Risk* recommended raising standards for academic performance and eliminating "distractions" from the standard curriculum.

Supported by this "back to basics" philosophy, many reformers advocate longer school days, a return to a more traditional curriculum with fewer electives, and higher standards. These efforts have been fueled by the contributions of noted academics who fault educational institutions in the United States for moving away from a common core curriculum (Ravitch & Finn, 1987; Hirsch, 1987; Bloom, 1987). Ravitch and Finn, for example, in their book *What Do Our 17-Year-Olds Know?*, discuss the need to provide all students with a shared body of knowledge. Hirsch makes a similar argument. Having completed his "dictionary" of cultural literacy, he is currently designing a curriculum aimed at providing all students with the knowledge he believes every "culturally literate" American student should know.

In May of 1991, President Bush issued his report *America 2000* which supported the agenda of those who emphasize the need to develop a common set of curricular goals and national standards. Some of those reformers emphasize the need to promote cultural literacy and foster among the youngest generation a shared understanding of American culture. Others argue that common curriculum goals will promote equity by ensuring that expectations remain high for all students. In addition, many believe that specification of a set of goals will improve the assessment of educational quality. Clear articulation of goals permits quantifiable studies which can hold both schools and policy makers accountable for the results of their efforts (Shepard, 1991).

As a part of his "New American Schools" agenda, President Bush called for the establishment of a national exam. He capitalized on state-level reform initiatives which have attempted to guide the curriculum used in classrooms through the creation of curricular frameworks and state-level exams, as well as on efforts by the state governors to establish national goals and a system of nationwide accountability.

This particular set of reforms presents experiential educators with formidable obstacles which are likely to hamper collaboration with mainstream public schools. Implicitly, the commitment to national goals and standards reflects the belief that relevant knowledge is determined by experts. Experiential educators, building on the work of Dewey (1916, 1938), reject the notion that experts can specify a common set of learning goals suitable for all students in all situations. The notion of teaching to and learning from experience grants primacy to the relationship between teacher and student.

Eliot Wigginton, the Rabun Gap, Georgia, teacher who created the student-run publication, *Foxfire,* asserts that the pursuit of meaningful education must grow out of student/teacher collaboration and that the ends of such interaction can not be specified in advance (Wigginton, 1986). In practice, as tests become the ultimate measure of students,' teachers', and schools' performance,

educators will feel increased pressure to "cover" mandated material rather than challenge students to engage in the type of active learning which emerges when teachers draw on the experiences and interests of the particular students with whom they work. Experiential education programs which do not directly align with standardized measures of success may come to be viewed as unnecessary frills and as an inappropriate use of scarce resources.

Ironically, the reforms which emphasize a common core curriculum and national standards conflict with other reform efforts mentioned above—those that align well with the values and methods underlying experiential education. Calls for tailoring curriculum to the interests and experiences of students make contextualized learning a priority. For schooling to be relevant, these reformers argue, multiple curricular goals must reflect the many perspectives of an increasingly diverse student population.

Despite the conflict between standardized assessment measures and experiential strategies, some experiential educators might be tempted to argue that their programs promise to satisfy national achievement goals. While experiential education may motivate students to achieve and increase their self-esteem, emphasizing the possible impact of these programs on standardized cognitive measures of achievement leaves educators vulnerable by holding them accountable to goals which do not represent their true mission. A highly successful experiential program may not raise test scores. At the same time, tests typically fail to emphasize the kinds of critical thinking and concrete problem-solving skills that are inherent in experiential learning.

Thus, the current enthusiasm at the state and federal level for a standardized accountability system will add to the difficulty faced by those who seek to integrate experiential education strategies into mainstream school settings.

Opportunities and Obstacles

John Dewey (1916, 1938) calls the notion of experiential education redundant. All learning, he asserts, is rooted in experience. While experiential educators may find it easy to agree, the conceptual framework which Dewey promoted and the pedagogical techniques derived from it continue to remain marginal in a vast majority of public schools. Teachers, administrators, and policy makers are striving to unify a fragmented curriculum, foster teaching methods which engage students as active participants in the learning process, and respond to the needs of at-risk students. These efforts call for experiential educators to enter the national discourse on educational reform.

There are, however, substantial obstacles. Experiential educators' lack of familiarity with traditional school organization and practice has left many programs peripheral to the curriculum and an easy target for budget cuts. Furthermore, reform efforts aimed at standardization and more formal-

ized national assessment practices conflict with experiential strategies. Tests based on predetermined material ignore and may compromise the benefits of drawing on student experience.

Recently, organizations well known for their experiential techniques have renewed an effort to work closely with school systems, particularly those serving at-risk students. Rather than offering add-on "enrichment" programs distinct from the regular school day, new programs initiated by Outward Bound, for example, seek to become an integral part of the school curriculum. Joe Nold, Director of the Pacific Crest Outward Bound Bay Area Urban Youth Program, sees experiential programs as having potential as major contributors to the future of education. As he told us, "We know how to run programs for kids, but we need to learn how to link our efforts more effectively with schools. The potential benefits are enormous."

The moment seems right for these efforts. By forming partnerships with schools and remaining sensitive to the directions of school change, practitioners in the field of experiential education can become players in mainstream efforts to reform the educational system.

A Conversation with Theodore Sizer

Interviewed by Peggy Walker Stevens

Horace's Compromise: The Dilemma of the American High School, by Theodore R. Sizer, was published by the Houghton Mifflin Company. It is the first of three reports based on a five-year study of American high schools co-sponsored by the National Association of Secondary School Principals and the National Association of Independent Schools.

Theodore Sizer, director of the study, is a former dean of the Harvard Graduate School of Education and former headmaster of Phillips Academy in Andover, Massachusetts. As part of the study, he visited 80 schools in the United States and Australia in an attempt to get "the essential 'feel' of high schools." The book presents his findings and recommendations for reforming the schools.

Stevens: Why did you title the book *Horace's Compromise*?

Sizer: The book is about 40% stories because some of the subtler things I wanted to say about teachers and teaching are easier said with word pictures than with expository prose. Furthermore, books about education are terribly dull and story books are a little more fun. All of the portraits are real people, but some are composites; that is, I invented a 53-year-old English teacher at a suburban public high school whose name is Horace Smith, a bad joke on Horace Mann. I describe at length how this composite character spends his day. Pieces of the day are all real classes taught by different people, but I've strung them all together in a kind of fiction/non-fiction way. The lesson which comes out of the extended anecdote of how Horace spends his day is that he has to make a whole lot of compromises. I mean, all of us have to make compromises in life. It's just that the ones he's forced to make by the system are really intolerable, and he knows

that in the pit of his stomach although he doesn't like to express it.

Stevens: How does your report differ from the others?

Sizer: It's much narrower. The focus is just on high schools and primarily on the insides of high schools—teachers and kids. So it doesn't deal with a whole lot of other issues like teacher education, school finance, state role, and all those other things, except by inference. It rests very heavily on a lot of listening to teachers and kids. The priorities for change are different in our case than those in many of the other reports. To oversimplify, I find the structure of the school not only remarkably pervasive across the country but also getting in the way. It's forcing Horace to make compromises that he shouldn't have to make. If you have 150 kids a day, 5 classes of 20, 30, 40 kids, there's no way you can get to know them. And if you can't get to know them, how can you figure out how their minds work? And if you don't know how each kid's mind works, how do you get them to think clearly? It doesn't need an awful lot of research—you just have to be able to add and multiply. The typical city high school teacher has, by contract, 5 classes a day, 35 kids each. Now, if you spend 5 minutes a day, even 5 minutes a week just reading the homework or talking outside of class to each of those students, you're talking a dozen or more hours. That system is the problem. Not the only problem, but certainly a fundamental problem, and you're not going to change the schools until you change the compromises that are made in the school. That's our message and it's not the message you're hearing from some other quarters. It is the message we're getting from John Goodlad. And it is not for nothing that his research and ours, although quite different in the way we proceeded, are heavily field-based rather than holding hearings and that sort of thing.

Stevens: You would say, then, that all these reforms about increased teacher pay, increased graduation requirements, etc., are beside the point?

Sizer: They're not beside the point—teachers need to be paid more. Some of the diploma requirement improvements make some sense, but why add 20 days to the school year when the teachers are already incapable of doing the job in 180 days? why make it 200? If you have 180 days of low quality, you're just adding 20 more low-quality days. It's missing the point.

Stevens: You say that your ideas will require new teacher behaviors. What are the types of roles that teachers will have to learn?

Sizer: Less talking and lecturing. Much more coaching where kids will be expected to do the work and the teacher will support that. This is where John Goodlad's research is so devastating. A large percentage of the time in classrooms that he and his army of people observed with their little stopwatches was spent in teacher talk, not surprisingly. If you have 5 classes a day, 175 kids, you don't have time to do anything else but talk. But people don't learn by being told things. I can lecture to you about how to write, but until you write, you're not going to learn how to do it. So much more coaching is necessary and it's hard. For many teachers it's a new kind of pedagogy, and in many ways a very boring pedagogy.

Stevens: Why do you say it's boring?

Sizer: Well, you get 100 papers every other day—misspelled and silly prose—and you write all over it, trying to get kids to do better the next time. You give the papers back to them and two days later get another 100 papers. It can be pretty devastating. But important! It's tough work. A lot of people like to stand up and talk about Marie Antoinette and they think that's teaching. You can tell about Marie Antoinette a little bit, but if you do nothing but tell stories.... Some people get a kick out of pretending they're Herr Doktor Professor, lecturing. I think it will be really hard to shift teachers to coaching.

Stevens: What kinds of things would help teachers to make the shift?

Sizer: On-the-job training—teachers helping teachers. The best kind of thing is workshops using real kids, the real youngsters you're teaching, the department you're working with—that's the way to do it. It's going to be slow.

Also, people say, "Well, let's cut the teacher's load by 5%." Forget it. You have to cut it in half. Then you'd get somewhere. And the only way you can do that is by making some compromises on the other side. You can't double your teaching force. People aren't going to pay for that. So you have to give up some things. Right now, we're compromising the wrong things. We're compromising on teacher load in order to provide a whole raft of good [subject] specialties and we can't afford to do that any more.

Stevens: In your article, you state that you found students to be docile and compliant.

Sizer: If you're being talked at all the time, you can just sit there. [The teachers] have to start saying, "I'm not telling you the answer. You've got to find it and I won't even tell you the answer once you show me the work. I'll ask you a whole lot of questions about the steps you went through and ultimately, you've got to tell me 'By God, *that's* the right answer' and then you have to figure out how to prove it."

Stevens: What kinds of activities do you see students doing in this ideal school?

Sizer: There'd be a lot more hands-on kind of work. The easiest to describe is science and the most difficult is history. History is my own subject and, in many ways, the hardest to teach in school because it deals with this abstraction called time past. For a kid to get a sense of abstraction of what time is, you get them writing their autobiographies and the biographies of other people and then they begin to realize that history is nothing more than a collective biography. I think we can waste an awful lot of time thrashing around tying to make them pseudo-historians. There are certain kinds of "play" history and you can go too far in that direction, spending all

of your time on some little local thing. You have to have balance. There is an awful lot of information out there that the kids ultimately should and will want to know and you can just tell them. The point I'm making is that we need a lot more balance. The example that I've always found telling is in teaching the Civil War—Pickett's charge. Pickett's Brigade had a lot of teenagers in it the same age as the students. And yet, knowing full well that they were going to charge across an open field into an absolute hail of gunfire from well-protected Yankee soldiers, they still did it. You ask the kids "Would you do it?" "Oh, no, I wouldn't do it. No way!" "Well Pickett's men all charged." "They all charged?" "Yes, they did." " Did they get killed?" "Yes, they did." "Why do you think they charged? What is about a 19-year-old in Pickett's Brigade that made him fix his bayonet and run right to certain death?" You try to create a sense of empathy for the values of the time. And that's history. That's really history. You have to give some sense of what it was like to be 18 or 19 in 1863.

Stevens: I've always found in teaching literature and history that it is more difficult to make experiential because in both subjects, you are vicariously experiencing someone else's life. Subjects like science and government lend themselves more readily to experiential education.

Sizer: Yes, it's like the advanced sciences. There is an abstraction and, in many ways, the abstractions of science are more difficult to emphathize with than the 19-year-olds in Pickett's Brigade. That's why narrowly defined experiential education has suffered at the senior high school level. Much of the important work at the senior high level is, necessarily, abstract. You just can't *do* it very well. At least it's not obvious. The hands-on exercises are not obvious, or if they appear to be obvious, they're spurious. When you set up a mini-government in your school and play United States Congress, it's a joke. And the kids know it's a joke.

Stevens: That's also one of the reasons why people often only let you do experiential programs with the non-college-bound students. There's a sense that anything you do with them is more than they were doing before.

Sizer: That's right. And isn't that a sad commentary? We call them the "unspecial" majority.

Stevens: Do you see a role for experiential education in high schools?

Sizer: It depends on definitions. As John Dewey says, "All learning is experience," so the experience of thinking hard about some knotty problem is a form of experiential education, as all good education is experiential at one level. Without experience, there wouldn't be learning. But that's not what you mean. It's narrower. My view is that a lot of what we now try to and often succeed at organizing as experiential education in fact is exploding in acceptance outside of the schools; the most important of that being work. One of the least expected facts that we are now confronted with in our work is the percentage of kids who work regularly for pay for strangers. The Coleman *High School and Beyond* data show that 60% of high school kids have jobs or are seriously looking for them. We've been in high schools where, particularly among twelfth graders, the kid who doesn't have a job is considered some kind of freak. Well, those kids are getting a lot of "experience," some of it quite

demanding, much of it totally undermining the athletic and activities programs of the schools. A lot of schools essentially shut up at 2:30 and everybody, teachers and kids, go to work. That is a relatively new phenomenon; it wasn't that case in the sixties. There's not much demand for some kind of organized connection between that youngster [who works] and the real world—that youngster is deep into the real world.... There may be stronger arguments for more organized, off-campus, experiential education at the middle school level than in the senior high school because many of those [older] kids are already out there.

To me, the trick in experiential education is not to let them get over their heads where they have some experiential assignment quite beyond their competence and they either end up faking it or making fools of themselves. You never want to exceed the kid's grasp. And to come up with a problem that the kids can solve in a legitimate way, not a fake way—that's hard to do. That's why the kid's own employment is probably the richest soil for careful experiential education.... If a student has a demanding job, we can ask, "How can we extend your knowledge in general by using the material you have to use in order to master your job?"

Stevens: But most kids don't have those kinds of demanding jobs.

Sizer: No, they don't. Most have jobs at check-out counters, but there's a lot even in those jobs. All you have to do is watch them. Go to a mall after school and watch the kids. There's a lot of engagement there. There's a lot of things to work with. I mean, just dipping ice cream and putting it on ice cream cones for the people who come up involves a lot of facing of humanity. You deal with all kinds of people. You might be able to do very interesting things in the humanitites with kids who have to see the public all the time. How do you deal with the making of an ice cream cone for the terribly crippled person? How do you help a person who is semi-senile make up her mind what flavor she wants? We've all seen people who can't make up their minds. What do you do? Yell at them? What do you do? And what does it mean? What is the paralysis, the inability to select an ice cream cone? What is it like for the person to be in a place in life where he can't do that? Oh, there are all kinds of things you can do to get kids thinking, reflecting.

Stevens: In your study, did you find that the kids who work don't value learning but want to have the diploma in case they need to get a job someday?

Sizer: That's why we think the diploma's so important. Get the diploma connected to kids actually showing they know something, rather than serving time. Then you get everything lined up right. Now a kid can work the 3-to-11 shift and do virtually no homework, show up regularly, be relatively orderly, and get a diploma even if that youngster's semi-literate. And that's too bad, that's cheating kids.

Stevens: How would a diploma based on achievement work?

Sizer: There would be what we call an exhibition. When a lot of people hear that they say, "Oh, great. We'll just give them machine-graded exams, a three-hour exam, and that's it." That's too narrow. To pass a test tells you something, but not everything. I think there ought to be a variety of ways that the kids can exhibit their mastery of the

work. Some people display their knowledge better orally than in writing. People have to be able to lead with their strongest suit. There ought to be a variety of ways of showing off. There ought to be a limited amount of specific subject matter and a maximum amount of demonstrated skills. Subject matter you forget; skills are what you retain. It's a matter of indifference to me whether a youngster studies Modern European History or Modern Asian History. What I'm more concerned about is whether he can deal with some historical phenomenon that doesn't relate to his immediate American past. So I can see quite flexible areas set up where kids can show in a variety of ways how they do well in each of those areas. Complicated. Very complicated, but time spent setting up those exhibitions would be well spent. It would force a lot of issues and would give the kids a sense of what they needed to do. Then if they didn't do any homework and sat like munching cows in class, they would suddenly realize that the only loser was themselves. Kids want the diploma. If you set up incentives so they have to work to get it, they'll work. If you set up the incentives so they can just sit and be entertained, they'll sit and be entertained just like we would.

Stevens: In your study, you talk about making the curriculum more simple and reducing the number of subjects studied. Could you explain your ideas about this?

Sizer: There are many ways of making the curriculum more simple, and the idea I've been fussing with is only one. The point is to say you have to simplify; you have to take our best understanding of different modes of inquiry or subjects or disciplines [and see how they] can be grouped in useful ways. For instance, literature and the arts [the art of language, the art of the visual realm, the art of music] have a great deal in common. They are the aesthetic realm. Right now, we teach them in separate little specialized boxes: English, art, music, drama, public speaking. We fractionate them, split them up, and I'm suggesting that we put them all together. The same with the forms of expression of which writing and speaking are obviously important, but there are other forms of expression—gesture, use of a foreign tongue, painting, drawing, music. They're all aspects of expression and the sensible way to help a person who is learning how to express himself or herself, is to give them these various forms of expression in a connected way, not a disconnected way. So I approve of a curriculum which would consist of four areas: forms of expression and inquiry, math and science, history and philosophy, literature and the arts. Basically, it's going back and thinking through the relationships of areas of knowledge with the imperative always behind you that you have to simplify. You no longer have the luxury of breaking things into further and further little pieces. You're going to have to go the other way. You're going to have to find what is important, what's at the core.

Stevens: What would you envision students doing in an inquiry and expression class?

Sizer: That has to be heavily, if you will, experiential. The only important thing is how the student uses her mind, not how I tell her to use her mind. You have to get the kid to [solve problems] and the problem may be an abstraction: "I want you to describe for me and define for me the concept and the word called cruelty. I want you to write me a paragraph, I want you to write me two bars of music, I want you to draw me a

picture." The kid is dealing with an abstraction, but that's the kid's work. I just don't lecture, "Write after me: cruelty is..." and read the Webster's dictionary to the student.

Stevens: Doing something like that would be good for students. I know that I can feel a little panic in my gut at the thought that someone might ask me to draw my concept of cruelty, when my idea of myself is that I couldn't possibly draw anything.

Sizer: Just think of the kid who can draw but can't write. That kid has been humiliated every day in every school. Ours is a culture of words. It would be good education [for teachers to try things they aren't good at] because every teacher is going to be a klutz somewhere and it would be good for kids to see that teachers can be klutzes and aren't afraid to exhibit klutziness, if that's a word.

Stevens: One of your statements, that we must stop thinking of how to present materials to kids, struck me hard because when planning my teaching, I often think "How can I best present this material?" and I've never questioned using those words.

Sizer: Well, if you want to tell somebody something, that's a good question. If the person wants to be presented the material and the person understands the context in which I'm making the presentation, then it's a good question to ask, "How do I present it?" But, if the kid doesn't understand the context or if the kid doesn't want to be lectured at, you've got a prior job to do. The context is important because any one of us has to know why something is important before there's any energy to learn it.

Stevens: You see the teacher, then, as a problem-poser.

Sizer: That's right. Coach, critic, cajoler, supporter, harasser, lover, all of that. But the kid has to be the worker. We have to stop thinking of the schools as a deliverer of instructional services. That's nonsense. Nobody ever learned by being delivered knowledge on a platter. They have to experience it.

A Summary of the Educational Reform Reports in the 1980s

by Richard J. Kraft

In 1978, Richard Zajchowski examined five major reports on education for the *Journal of Experiential Education*. Those reports, almost without exception, were supportive of experiential education in its many forms. They advocated improved transition to adulthood, service learning, work-study, internships, flexible scheduling, consideration for student interests and needs, alternative paths to graduation, action-learning, a reduction in compulsory attendance rules, and a host of other "progressive" ideas. The educational critics of the 1970s recognized that much of education, particularly at the secondary level, was not functioning, and that the solutions lay not in a return to the past, but rather to a major restructuring in what happens to children and adolescents, both in and out of school.

In 1983, the "Year of the Public Schools," educational critics once again were out in full force, but this time most of the voices were raised in favor of traditional educational ideas. In this article, we shall summarize the major recommendations from the various studies. Few recommendations from the 1970s Task Forces were ever implemented on a large scale, and many of those that were tried were destroyed in budget cutbacks and the cries of "back to the basics." Ignoring this fact that the "crisis" in which we find ourselves is due to the old

ways in which we have been doing things, and not to "progressive" ideas which have never been implemented, many of the national and state reports call on us to return to the way we imagine things used to be.

The concern for education should be welcomed by all of us, as it contains the greatest possibility for change than at any time in the past quarter-century. Those of us committed to experiential education can ill afford to remain on the sideline, while legislatures, governors, and state and local boards of education mandate major reforms. Political activism in 1984 is mandatory, if we are to move forward rather than backwards in our educational systems. An important place to start is with the national reports themselves.

A Nation at Risk

Without question, the most highly publicized educational report of 1983 was *A Nation at Risk*. This document was the result of a task force appointed by President Reagan and Secretary of Education Bell, and was the first of the major reports. The document defines the crisis in extremely powerful terms.

> If an unfriendly foreign power had attempted to impose on America the mediocre educational performance that exists today, we might well have viewed

it as an act of war. (National Commission, 1983, p. 5)

Each generation of Americans has outstripped its parents in education, in literacy, and in economic attainment. For the first time in the history of our country, the educational skills of one generation will not surpass, will not equal, will not even approach, those of their parents. (National Commission, 1983, p. 11)

Such rhetoric captured the headlines of newspapers and the attention of educational decision-makers at all levels. Although the accuracy of some of the statistics given in the report has been questioned, the following "indicators of risk" have served as a major impetus for new legislation rules and regulations.

1) On an international comparison of achievement, American students were never first or second, and ranked last seven times.

2) Twenty-three million American adults are functionally illiterate.

3) Thirteen percent of all 17-year-olds are illiterate, and among minority youth, illiteracy is as high as 40 percent.

4) Test score have been dropping for two decades.

5) Remediation is costing universities, businesses, industry, and the military millions of dollars.

6) Gifted students are not being challenged, and science and mathematics achievement continues to drop.

To deal with these and other problems, the National Commission on Excellence made the following recommendations.

Recommendations

1. Strengthen high school graduation requirements through 4 years of English, 3 years of mathematics, 3 years of science, 3 years of social studies, and a 1/2 year of computer science, along with 2 years of foreign language for the college-bound.

2. Schools, colleges, and universities need to adopt more rigorous and measurable standards as well as higher expectations for academic performance and student conduct.

3. More time needs to be given to learning the "New Basics" though better use of the school day, a longer school day, or a lengthened school year.

4. The schools need brighter, better educated, and better paid teachers and administrators.

5. The schools need better leadership from principals and superintendents, and the local, state, and Federal governments must provide the leadership, fiscal support, and stability to bring about the reforms.

The Commission on Excellence conducted hearings throughout the country and commissioned many studies, but appears to have ignored what it heard and read, in favor of a more politically palatable attack on public education, with a call to do more of the same. The report has done a major service in laying out the problems, but is the most conservative of the national reports in its recommended solutions. Experiential educators can use the statistics and powerful rhetoric to help build the case for needed educational reforms, but will find little support for its underlying philosophy or educational methods.

The Commission comes down squarely on the side of learning taking place within the formal educational institutions of the society, rather than through informal or nonformal experiences. Interdisciplinary studies are hardly mentioned in the recommendations to require more of each of the "Basics." Acquisition of measurable content is the major, if not only, mechanism for measuring achievement, and little value is placed on the needs or interests of the students. The authoritative and authoritarian role of the teacher and principal underlie much of the report, rather than an emphasis upon all participants being both learners and teachers. Vocational education, work-study, internships, and other experiential modes of learning are hardly mentioned, and certainly do not play a prominent role in what the Commission sees as necessary for the reform of education in this country.

High School

While the President's National Committee on Excellence has received the most publicity and has served as the major impetus for reform, the Carnegie Commission report, *High School,* is likely to turn out to be the most influential of the year. In addition to a careful diagnosis of the various problems facing secondary education, Ernest Boyer and his staff have produced a document filled with positive suggestions for change. While the President's Commission tended to ignore the research and reports of the past decade, the Carnegie Commission built on those studies, and added careful observation of its own. Rather than producing a political diatribe, Boyer and his staff conducted a

careful field study of 15 high schools, using knowledgeable observers and researchers.

After a description of the research leading up to its conclusions, the Commission concludes with the following recommendations.

Recommendations

1) High Schools must have a clear and vital mission. Goals must be clearly stated and shared by teachers, students, administrators, and parents.

2) Language, oral and written, is central to the success of all students.

3) A core of common learning is essential. This core should be expanded to include up to 2/3 of the required units, and should contain work on literature, U.S. history, Western civilization, non-Western civilization, science and the natural world, technology, mathematics, foreign language, the arts, civics, health, and work.

4) High schools must help young people make the transition from school to the world of work or higher education. The last two years of schooling should contain an elective cluster helping students to explore a career option or do further study in selected academic subjects.

5) A new Carnegie unit in SERVICE should be part of all high school student requirements, to help students meet their social and civic obligations.

6) Working conditions for teachers must improve, with a better reward structure, recruitment incentives, and better training programs to attract better qualified persons.

7) Instruction must be improved through the use of a variety of teaching styles. There

The Same Course of Study for All

	COLUMN ONE	COLUMN TWO	COLUMN THREE
Goals	ACQUISITION OF ORGANIZED KNOWLEDGE	DEVELOPMENT OF INTELLECTUAL SKILLS—SKILLS OF LEARNING	ENLARGED UNDERSTANDING OF IDEAS AND VALUES
	by means of	by means of	by means of
Means	DIDACTIC INSTRUCTION LECTURES AND RESPONSES TEXTBOOKS AND OTHER AIDS	COACHING, EXERCISES, AND SUPERVISED PRACTICE	MAIEUTIC OR SOCRATIC QUESTIONING AND ACTIVE PARTICIPATION
	in three areas of subject matter	in the operations of	in the
Areas, Operations, and Activities	LANGUAGE, LITERATURE, AND THE FINE ARTS MATHEMATICS AND NATURAL SCIENCE HISTORY, GEOGRAPHY, AND SOCIAL STUDIES	READING, WRITING, SPEAKING, LISTENING CALCULATING, PROBLEM SOLVING, OBSERVING, MEASURING, ESTIMATING EXERCISING CRITICAL JUDGMENT	DISCUSSION OF BOOKS (NOT TEXTBOOKS) AND OTHER WORKS OF ART AND INVOLVEMENT IN ARTISTIC ACTIVITIES e.g., MUSIC, DRAMA, VISUAL ARTS

The three columns do not correspond to separate courses, nor is one kind of teaching and learning necessarily confined to any one class

should be a particular emphasis upon the active participation of the students.

8) Technology, particularly computers, should be used to enrich instruction and extend the teacher's reach.

9) Flexibility in schedules, size of classes, size of schools, and types of programs should characterize secondary education in this country.

10) Principals must be more than administrators. They should be the educational leaders of their schools.

11) Connections to lower and higher education, business, and industry must be strengthened.

12) Support for the schools must be strengthened at the local, state, and national levels.

The Carnegie Commission is not just making recommendations, but is allocating millions of dollars over the coming years to help implement them. Recognizing that education reform is best done at the local level, it is providing initial seed money for hundreds of secondary schools to explore ways of bringing about one or more of the reforms.

For experiential educators, the Carnegie report is like a breath of fresh air in its call for community involvement, oral and written literacy programs, the importance of a transition to the world of work, the formation of a service ethic in our youth, an experiential base for teacher training, the active participation of the student in his/her learning, and the need for flexibility in schedules, class sizes, and programs. The report is based on the real world of adolescents, rather than the mythical past or technocratic future, and experiential educators would do well to use it in bringing about reforms in their local schools.

The Paideia Proposal

For over half a century, Mortimer Adler has been an advocate of a classical education for all young people. As chairman of the Paideia Project, a group made up of university scholars and public school administrators, Adler has authored the most scholarly of the numerous educational reports. Some basic assumptions underlie the *Paideia Proposal:* the tracking system is inherently unequal and must be abolished in favor of quality education for all young people; all children are capable of learning, regardless of background or ability; and schools must help to create lifelong learners who have the ability to learn on their own.

Education should have three basic goals:

1) Every child should be able to look forward to a lifetime of personal growth or self-improvement—mental, moral, and spiritual.

2) The schools should cultivate appropriate civic virtues and an understanding of the framework of our government and of its fundamental principles.

3) Young people should be prepared to earn a living, not by training for a particular job, but by possession of the basic skills common to all work.

To achieve these goals, Adler and the Paideia Group advocate the same course of study for all children for 12 grades, with only one exception—the choice of a second language. The proposed curriculum depicts in three columns three distinct modes of teaching and learning. The three columns are integrated and rise in complexity and difficulty throughout the twelve years of schooling.

Like the ancient Greek model on which this proposal rests, all students would be required to take physical education and participate in intramural sports. Manual activities such as typing, cooking, auto repair, and maintenance of household equipment would also be required for part of the time, along with career exploration.

As if speaking directly to experiential educators, Adler clarifies Dewey's oft-quoted maxim that "learning is by doing."

What John Dewey had in mind was not exclusively physical doing or even social doing, but engagement in practical project of one kind or another. The most important kind of doing, so far as learning is concerned, is intellectual or mental doing. In other words, one can learn to read or write well only by reading and writing....To learn how to do any of these things well, one must not only engage in doing them, but one must be guided in doing them by someone more expert in doing them than oneself. (Paideia, 1982, p. 52)

Like the other reports, the *Paideia Proposal* also speaks to the training of teachers, the role of the principal, and the better use of school time. It is the least specific, however, on how reforms should be implemented. It is perhaps best seen as a plea for the liberal arts and the passing on of the intellectual and aesthetic heritage to all children, regardless of ability, social class, race, or other differences which have traditionally separated them. Such a goal is admirable, but when considering how feasible it will be to implement such a system, this report sounds utopian compared to the others.

A Place Called School

The most carefully researched of the 1983 reports on education is John Goodlad's *A Place Called School*. The research on which the book was based involved 38 schools in 7 states, and included 1,350 teachers in 1,000 classrooms. Over 17,000 students participated in the study and 8,600 parents were surveyed and interviewed. Unlike the Carnegie report, Goodlad's study covered education from kindergarten through grade 12. This book is by far the most detailed of any of the reform documents due to the extensive research which went into it. Unlike most of the reports, however, the recommendations for reform are scattered throughout the four hundred-page report, and are so numerous that the following listing is limited to the major and most provocative reforms.

As an educator, Goodlad recognizes the difficulty in bringing about rapid educational reform, and continually cautions against quick fixes mandated by the state or federal government. He also recognizes that most meaningful reform must come at the local school level and must involve all the participants, or it is doomed to almost certain failure. *A Place Called School* is unique among the various reports in giving a detailed description of what actually occurs in the schools and individual classrooms throughout the United States, and it does an excellent job of pointing up the failures and weaknesses of traditional education today. Rather than making global prescriptions for more mathematics, foreign language, or other subjects, it speaks in great detail about how the total educational environment or ecosystem can be improved to meet social, civic, personal, and cultural goals.

Recommendations

1) More time needs to be spent on teaching higher order skills, rather than the current emphasis on factual information.

2) Too much time is spent on "teacher talk." Other teaching methods more actively involving the students must be used. Specifically, discussion, writing, problem solving, and analysis are recommended.

3) A core curriculum made up of a common set of concepts, principles, skills, and ways of knowing should be developed. This is not a core of topics or subjects, as most other reports have recommended.

4) Mastery learning, which can significantly improve achievement and cut down on failure, can be a valuable tool in improving the schools.

5) Vocational education which does not train for work should be eliminated, and hands-on experiences should be more extensively used.

6) Tracking and minority over-representation in vocational programs must be eliminated. The best education for the world of work is still a general education.

7) A better use of instructional time is critical in improving the schools. Too much time in many schools and classrooms is spent on housekeeping chores, discipline, getting the class started, etc. All schools should aim for a minimum of 25 hours of actual instructional time per week. The concept of "engaged" time is of critical importance, rather than just spending time in a classroom.

8) The curriculum should aim for:

   a) 18% of student's time on literature and language

   b) 18% on mathematics and science

   c) 15% on social studies and society

   d) 15 % on the arts

   e) 15% on vocational education and career preparation

   f) 10% on electives of the student's choice

9) Most of the top-rated schools in the study were small. Where small schools are impractical, schools-within-schools should be created. Non-graded minischools with four teachers and 100 students should be developed.

10) Teachers need a career ladder to provide an incentive for excellence (head teachers, residents, interns).

11) Schooling should occur in four phases: Ages 4–7, primary; 8–11, elementary; 12–15, secondary; and 16–18, service and work/study. Compulsory education should start earlier and end earlier than is currently the case.

12) Better use of technology should improve education, and partnerships and networks with business, industry, and the community must be developed.

Experiential educators would do well to make Goodlad's book required reading. Not only does it detail the significant problems to be found in our schools, and the failure of the traditional ways of teaching, but it makes countless suggestions for the teacher or administrator on how to change and improve. The book is short on political rhetoric and long on research-based reform, and as such should be welcomed by all who are committed to improving the ways that children and adults learn.

Other Major Educational Reports

Space does not permit us to go into detail on the other national and state reports, but all agree with Governor Hunt of North Carolina, who chaired the Educational Commission of the States Task Force on *Education for Economic Growth:*

> We have heard now from many directions about the problems of our schools. We have had an abundance of research, a plentiful supply of analysis and an impressive piling up of reports. Public concern is rising. What is needed now is action:

action for excellence. (Education for Economic Growth, 1983)

His task force concentrated on ways that governors, legislators, educators, and business and industry can collaborate to improve education at the state level. Governors concerned about balancing their budgets made up a large number of the Task Force participants, so it is not surprising that the emphasis of the report is on mathematics, sciences, and technology. Improvements in these areas are seen as a way out of economic stagnation and will lead to a more competitive position in the international marketplace.

The *Business-Higher Education Forum* document was prepared at President Reagan's request and focuses attention on industrial competitiveness. Like the Economic Growth Task Force, it focuses on science, mathematics, engineering, and collaboration between business, industry, and education. It calls for retraining through a national displaced workers program using educational vouchers, and individual training accounts (ITAs) to give incentives to individuals to save for their training and retraining needs. Tax incentives, scholarship programs, and other economic incentives form the basis for much of the report.

The *Twentieth Century Fund* report calls for a new federal policy on elementary and secondary education. While many of the other reports concentrate on what can be done at the state and local level, this report concentrates on federal policy, and calls on the federal government to meet the special needs of the poor, the immigrants, the bilingual, and handicapped populations. It calls for a core curriculum of reading, writing, calculating, computers, science, foreign languages, and civics, with a strong emphasis on mastery of oral and written English.

The National Science Foundation report entitled, *Educating Americans for the 21st Century,* concentrates its recommendations on the improvement of science and mathematics instruction from kindergarten through higher education. All students should take three years of mathematics and science and technology in high school, and schools should emphasize higher level problem-solving skills. The report spends a good deal of time on teacher recruitment, training, and compensation, and calls for higher pay for math and science teachers, career ladders for teachers, raising standards to enter the profession, and many other related ideas. It also calls for massive federal intervention in K–12 and higher education to improve the quality and quantity of science and mathematics training in this country.

Other Reports Completed or Due in Early 1984

The College Board

The Southern Regional Education Board

The Association for Supervision and Curriculum Development

The Northwest Regional Laboratory

The National Association of Secondary School Principals and the National Association of Independent Schools

The National Academy of Education

The Congressional Office of Technology Assessment

The National Institute of Education and the Ford Foundation

Stanford University

Summary and Conclusions

Many themes appear throughout the various reports. On the subject of teachers, they call for recruitment incentives to attract higher quality personnel, better pay, career ladders, revision of tenure laws, improved teacher training, and better working conditions. On curricular matters, most call for a diminution in the number of courses offered, a required core curriculum, better use of technology, particularly computers, a clarity of goals, greater variety in instructional procedures, and vocational education more closely tied to the real world of work. The school principal is singled out in most of the reports as the key individual, and most call for an expanded instructional leadership role. While some call for an extended school year and school day, most agree that better use of school time is essential. The role of the federal, state, and local governments in school reform differs in the various reports, but all call for greater connections between the schools and business, industry, higher education, and the community.

More good and harm for education is possible in the next year than at any time in the past twenty-five. The American schools have been dramatically successful in educating millions of students, but their failures are all too evident, and we must continue to speak out on the role of experiential learning, both in and out of school.

Section

2

Experiential Learning in the Community, Environment, and Cross-Cultural Settings

Chapter 3 Service Learning

The Sleeping Giant of School Reform

By Joe Nathan and James Kielsmeier

Brisk winds blowing across the American political landscape are now converging behind national proposals for youth service, and their force has stirred a sleeping giant in the school reform movement. Combining classroom work with service/social action projects can help produce dramatic improvements in student attitudes, motivation, and achievement. Moreover, this strategy is not a "one size fits all" change imposed from above but builds on local circumstances and teacher insights.

Before going any further, let's get specific. Barbara Lewis is a Salt Lake City teacher whose fourth- through sixth-grade students have been responsible for the cleanup of a hazardous waste site, the passage of two new environmental laws, the

planting of hundreds of trees, and the completion of a number of other neighborhood improvements. The families of the students in Lewis's school have the lowest per-capita income in Salt Lake City, and the students themselves aren't unusually gifted or articulate. However, according to Lewis, "One thing they do have is courage. They believe that the future depends on them. They're not afraid to attack things that other people say can't be done."[1] And Lewis's students are not alone.

- Students at Bronx Regional High School in the South Bronx are working with a local community organization to restore a building near their school that will then provide housing

Reprinted with permission of Phi Delta Kappan.

- Middle schoolers in Chicopee, Massachusetts, saved their town $119,500 while helping to solve a sewage problem.
- High school students in Brooks County, Georgia, conducted a needs assessment of their county and determined that day care was a major need. The students and their teacher established a day-care center that is still operating today—10 years after its founding.[2]

One of us taught a class in an inner-city public school in which 14- to 18-year-old students learned about consumers' rights and responsibilities. The youngsters read a variety of materials and listened to outside speakers. In addition, they worked on real consumer problems referred to them by adults. Over the course of several years, the students successfully resolved more than 75% of the 350 cases adults had turned over to them.

A group of 5- to 9-year-old students at the same school designed, obtained permission to build, gathered materials for, and then created a new playground. They had to make 20 phone calls before finding someone who would donate six truckloads of sand. The arrival of that sand was a big event in the students' lives.

The youngsters at this inner-city school learned important skills in research, thinking, writing, public speaking, and problem solving—the very outcomes that many school critics demand. The students also learned that they could make a difference.

As one youngster noted after his picture appeared in a local newspaper story about the consumer action class, "I often thought I might have my name in the newspaper. I even thought I might have my picture in the paper. But I never thought that it would be for something good."[3]

The idea that students can learn from community action and from performing a variety of services is not new. But in the wake of largely unsuccessful reform proposals and daunting new societal challenges, the political/educational climate has become more open to the kinds of school change demanded by learning that derives from service and social action. We now have the opportunity to expand and improve service/social action projects, to help many more youngsters learn important skills, and to help them realize that they have the power to make changes.

Much recent discussion of school reform has focused on rules, regulations, and decision-making processes. While these are important matters, we think it is also critical to change the way we view young people.

Ernest Boyer recalls a young person's description of his summer job: "Last summer I got a job working at McDonald's. It didn't pay too well, but at least I felt needed for a while." Boyer then commented, "There's something unhealthy about a youth culture where feeling needed is pushing Big Macs at McDonald's."[4]

Young people used to assume increased levels of responsibility gradually as they grew into adulthood. Over time, however, the classic agrarian models of apprenticeship with and mentoring by adults have given way to the isolation of young people in youth-only educational, social, and employment groupings.

Young people have become a distinct subculture that is unique in modern history, and their adjustment to this phenomenon has been uneven. In a University of Minnesota their adjustment to this phenomenon has been uneven. In a University of Minnesota poll conducted in 1985, 66% of the young Minnesotans polled said they believed that adults have a negative view of youths.[5]

Though they may be in high demand for entry-level employment at fast-food restaurants and all-night gas stations, many young people are alienated from the society. They are heavy users of drugs and alcohol, they consistently maintain the lowest voting rates of any age group, and the teen pregnancy rate has been described as epidemic.

We believe that these problems stem in part from the way adults treat young people. Unlike earlier generations, which viewed young people as active, productive, and needed members of the household and community, adults today tend too treat them as objects, as problems, or as the recipients (not the deliverers) of services. Young people are treated as objects when they are routinely classified as a separate group, isolated in age-based institutions, and beset on all sides by advertising—though not otherwise recognized or treated with respect. They are treated as problems when they are feared, criticized, and made the focus of preventive and remedial programs. They are treated as recipients of services when they are viewed as creatures to be pitied, "fixed," and "controlled."

We need to change our views of the young. We need to see youths as citizens: as resources and producers who are valued, needed, respected, and acknowledged. Ken Nelson, a Minnesota state representative and a strong advocate of learning from service, believes that much of the concern in this country about youths "at risk" should be refocused on "youth potential, youth strengths, youth participation, and contributions."[6] The Children's Defense Fund agrees, noting that "the experience gained through service can make a lasting difference, giving young people a sense of purpose and a reason to remain in school, strive to learn, and avoid too-early pregnancy."[7]

Both of us have worked with angry, alienated, and violent students. We readily acknowledge that no single curriculum or strategy will solve every problem, transform every student, regenerate every school. However, each of us has experienced and heard about situations in which acting on a new view of students produced dramatic improvements.

When teachers integrate service and social action into their academic programs, students learn to communicate, to solve problems, to think critically, and to exercise other higher-order skills. They learn these things because they are deeply immersed in a consequential activity—not a metaphor, not a simulation, not a vicarious experience mediated by print, sound, or machine. A task force of the Minnesota State Department of Education explained that service learning occurs when youths, "involved in planning and providing," render "significant and valuable service to meet genuine needs in their community."[8]

The point merits emphasis: learning is furthered when students play an active role in selecting and developing their own service projects. For example, students who attend Gig Harbor High School in Washington State make decisions about how their newly acquired science, social studies, and English skills will be applied in addressing environmental issues in and around Puget Sound. And the students can feel the importance of a teacher at Gig Harbor High, who explains: "For the first time, students become central and valued." Also in this special section, John Briscoe, the director of Pennsylvania's PennSERVE program, describes this shift in our perspective on youth as "profound."

In the best youth service programs, students have a chance to reflect as well as to serve. Their reflections often lead to new attitudes toward school and academics. Seventeen-year-old Quinn Hammond of Waseca, Minnesota, describes the impact of his tutoring third- and fourth-graders: "The little kids look up to you so much. This taught me to have a lot more patience and gave me a real good feeling. Before, I was kind of a class clown. Volunteering gave me a lot of respect for teachers."[9]

The most effective service/social action projects are developed at the local school site, rather than in the district office or in the state education department. This means that real authority to design programs must be vested in the school and its staff. It's no mystery that the teachers most involved in service projects are those who feel personally responsible and empowered to tackle important issues. And teachers derive enormous satisfaction from seeing youngsters become more motivated and eager. As Waseca teacher Don Zwach comments, "This is the most enthusiastic class I've had in 30 years. You hear a lot about the problems of motivating students in the 1990s. But there's absolutely no problem motivating these young people."[10]

The most effective service/social action programs are integrated into a school's curriculum. The entire range of courses—math, English, social studies, home economics, science, art, physical education, and so on—

can be modified to include some form of service or social action. Handled correctly, these changes enable youngsters to apply classroom lessons to the world beyond the classroom and so make it much more likely that teachers' academic goals for their students will be attained. For example, Eliot Wigginton, founder of the Foxfire project, reports that students become much better writers as they help produce a magazine (originally intended just for a few people in Rabun Gap, Georgia, but now read throughout the world).[11]

A vast array of service/social action learning programs now operate in the nation's schools. However, research and experience lead us to conclude that the most effective programs are drawn from criteria used for the Governor's Youth Service Recognition Program in Minnesota:

- significant, necessary, and measurable service is accomplished;
- youths are directly involved in planning and implementation;
- clear institutional commitment to the service program is reflected in goals or mission statements;
- community support for and involvement in the program are strong;
- learner outcomes for the program are well articulated;
- a well-designed and articulated curriculum for service exists that includes preparation, supervision, and active reflection on the experience; and
- regular and significant recognition of the youths and adults who participate takes place.[12]

Combining classroom work with service and social action means learning by doing

Combining classroom work with service and social action means learning by doing and giving. And it's the *giving* that answers the "why" questions students so often raise about school. Students and teachers trained to address issues of environmental quality in Puget Sound have a clear purpose for learning principles and skills in science, sociology, and English. Students in St. Paul who solved consumer problems learned the importance of carefully reading and understanding in advance any paper they are asked to sign; they also learned to value clear writing. Students in Folsom, Pennsylvania, discovered the importance of basic principles of physics as they helped families weigh different options for making their homes more energy efficient. Philadelphia high school students who tutor their peers or teach a health lesson in a junior high school see a clear application for their knowledge and a larger purpose for schooling.

We reject the often-stated assertion that *the* fundamental task of school is to prepare students for the work force. In a democratic society, one of the basic purposes of public schools is to prepare students for active, informed citizenship. Part of being a responsible citizen is knowing how to get and keep a job, but an equally important part of citizenship is working to build a better world. Moreover, a thoughtful citizen will sometimes question what's happening in the work place. For example, one's employer might be discriminating against certain people or polluting the air or ignoring basic safety principles. Today, more than ever, schools must help youngsters develop the skills and attitudes needed to work for justice—not just the skills needed to pass an examination or to work on a high-tech assembly line.

Unlike most school reform initiatives, the new interest in learning through service is arriving on the scene without the impetus of top-down pronouncements from high-level committees. While the National and Community Service Act of 1990 and parts of the national goals for education do endorse and provide incentives for youth service, the growing acceptance of this idea is largely a product of successful efforts by small national and state-level organizations that provide networking, materials, and technical assistance to interested educators.

Teacher creativity is central to this effort. Teachers dreamed up and developed the environmental service programs at Philadelphia's Lincoln High School. Teachers in Springfield, Massachusetts, initiated programs that provide services to the elderly—not by replicating someone else's model, but by responding to local needs and interests. Teachers in Ortonville, Minnesota, didn't follow a statewide curriculum when they showed students how to use computers to help their parents run more efficient farms.

Learning through service is an idea that is bubbling up, rather than trickling down. Fueled by a fresh infusion of energy during the 1980s, it rekindles an idea brought to life by John Dewey in the 1930s: that schools should be democratic laboratories of learning, closely linked to community needs. These learning labs create new roles for students and teachers, make use of action-based instructional methods, and lead to the learning of meaningful, real-world content.

Salt Lake City teacher Barbara Lewis points out that "the real world is chock-full of real problems to solve: real letters to write, real laws waiting to be made, real surveys to analyze, real streams needing monitoring, scraggly

Solving social problems will bring excitement and suspense into your life. Instead of reading textbooks and memorizing what other people have done, you'll create your own history with the actions you take. And here's a promise: As you reach out to solve problems in your community, you will not only design a better future. You'll also learn to take charge of your personal life. You'll become more confident in yourself because you'll prove to yourself that you can do almost anything.[13]

What wonderful gifts to pass on to young people. What wonderful gifts to our communities, our country, and our world.

NOTES

1. Barbara Lewis, *The Kids' Guide to Social Action* (Minneapolis: Free Spirit Publishing, 1991), p. 11.

2. For information on school-based economic development programs, contact Paul DeLargy, Georgia REAL Enterprises, P.O. Box 1643, Athens, GA 30603. DeLargy has worked closely with Jonathan Sher, who originally developed this concept.

3. Joe Nathan, *Free to Teach: Achieving Equity and Excellence in Schools* (New York: Pilgrim Press, 1991), p. 38.

4. Ernest Boyer, "Foreword," in Charles H. Harrison, *Student Service: The New Carnegie Unit* (Princeton, N.J.: Carnegie Foundation for the Advancement of Teaching, 1987), p. vii.

5. Diane Hedin, *Minnesota Youth Poll* (Minneapolis: University of Minnesota Agricultural Station, 1985).

6. Ken Nelson, "Minnesota's Youth Development Initiative: Building on Strengths," *Community Education Journal*, October 1988, p. 5.

7. Children's Defense Fund, *Service Opportunities for Youths* (Washington, D.C.: Adolescent Pregnancy Prevention Clearinghouse of CDF, May 1989), p. 3.

8. *Model Learner Outcomes for Service Learning* (St. Paul, Minnesota Department of Education, September 1990).

9. Joe Nathan, "Youth Service Class Helps Kids and Community," *St. Paul Pioneer Press*, 26 November 1990, p. 5-C.

10. Ibid.

11. Eliot Wigginton, *Sometimes a Shining Moment: Twenty Years at Foxfire* (Garden City, N.Y.: Anchor Press/Doubleday, 1985).

12. Jim Kielsmeier and Rich Cairn, "Minnesota Governor's Youth Service Recognition," program guidelines, May 1988.

13. Lewis, p. 2.

School-Based Community Service:
What We Know from Research and Theory

by Dan Conrad and Diane Hedin

In November 1990, President George Bush signed into law the National and Community Service Act of 1990, the most significant community service legislation in many decades. The act provides funding for community service programs in schools and colleges and support for full-time service corps that students can enter after high school. In a period when every issue in education becomes more and more politicized, this legislation stands out as a cause championed by both outspoken liberals and staunch conservatives. Even more remarkable, the law was passed in a time of severe federal austerity.

Yet there has been almost no mention of Congress's action in the public media or in education publications. In fact, when the subject of youth service was featured in the press a few weeks after the legislation passed, it was in the context of the possible renewal of the military draft in light of events in the Persian Gulf.

Youth service seems to be one of those ideas that many people view as "good" but not of critical importance to education or to the wider society. Only time will tell whether the current interest among politicians and educators in strengthening the service ethic of our nation's youth will be sustained or whether new priorities or the same old pressures for higher test scores and improved basic skills will keep youth service on the fringes of the political and educational agenda. We hope that decisions about whether to make service a regular feature of school practice will be informed by evidence about its value to young people. And in that hope we present the "evidence"—both the arguments for including community service in the educational programs of elementary and secondary schools and the research findings on the impact of service.

The Idea of Service in the Educational Literature

While much of the initiative for school-based service currently comes from policy makers and politicians—not from educators—this has not always been the case. Recommendations that service be a part of the school experience have reappeared in cycles throughout this century and have been a consistent, if less than dominant, feature of educational reports and reform proposals for the last 15 or 20 years.

Proponents of service who stress its power as a tool for teaching and learning typically link their ideas to the educational

Reprinted with permission of Phi Delta Kappan.

philosophy of John Dewey. It is not so much that he directly advocated service as an educational method as that his ideas on how learning takes place and for what purpose suggest the possibility of stimulating academic and social development through actions directed toward the welfare of others.[1]

Probably the earliest proponent of school-based community was William Kilpatrick, who, in the waning years of World War I, urged the adoption of the "project method" as the central tool of education.[2] He argues that learning should take place in settings outside the school and involve efforts to meet real community needs. Throughout the 1930s, the idea was echoed by Progressives, who believed that schools should inculcate the values of social reform and teach the attitudes, knowledge, and skills necessary to accomplish it. Such books as *Dare the Schools Build a New Social Order?* and *Youth Serves the Community* exemplify the passion of that time for using education for social transformation.[3]

Curiously, it was in the more cautious and passive fifties that the idea reemerged, most prominently in the Citizenship Education Project initiated by Columbia University's Teachers College. Launched with great fanfare and prestigious endorsement (President Eisenhower was the honorary chair), the project stressed participation and direct community involvement. Its famous "Brown Box" of teaching ideas contained (and still does if you can find one) hundreds of detailed guides to social investigation and social/political action. Suffice it to say, its timing could hardly have been worse. And by the time community activism became the rage, in the sixties, the project was but a dim and dusty memory.

The next wave of emphasis on school-based community service arose in the 1970s and was propelled by several major reports that bemoaned the passivity of life in the schools and the separation of young people from the life of the community. Reports by the National Committee on Secondary Education, the Panel on Youth of the President's Science Advisory Committee, and the National Panel on High School and Adolescent Education were among those urging that young people be reintegrated into the community, encouraged to interact with a wider range of people, involved in real and meaningful tasks, and afforded more responsibility through a variety of direct experiences that included, but were not limited to, service activities.[4] The National Commission on Resources for Youth worked on many fronts throughout the 1970s to promote youth participation programs, such as those described in the commission's report, *New Roles for Youth*.[5] In *Education for Citizen Action*, Fred Newmann outlined the most comprehensive and sophisticated curriculum proposal we have had to date for using community service as a stimulus for developing in students the attitudes, skills, and knowledge required for influencing social policy.[6]

The value of service experiences for young people has been the topic of more recent educational literature as well. In *Sometimes a Shining Moment*, Eliot Wigginton describes his work with the Foxfire project in a way that offers inspiration, theoretical grounding, and practical assistance to teachers working with youth service programs.[7] In *A Place Called School*, John Goodlad includes community service among suggested practices to improve education.[8]

The same is true of *Reconnecting Youth*, a 1985 report of the Education Commission of the States,[9] and of a series of reports sponsored by the Carnegie Foundation, including Ernest Boyer's *High School*, in which he recommends that high schools require 120 hours of community service for graduation.[10] The latter idea was further developed in Charles Harrison's *Student Service: The New Carnegie Unit*[11] and in another Carnegie report, *Turning Points*, which focuses on the educational needs of junior high and middle school students.[12] A report of the William T. Grant Foundation, *The Forgotten Half*, makes a strong plea for non-college-bound youth to perform community service, arguing for the "creation of quality student service opportunities as central to the fundamental educational program of every public school."[13]

Rationale and Possible Outcomes

Our brief historical review suggests some of the arguments for the role of service in an educational program—as a way to stimulate learning and social development, as a means of reforming society and preserving a democracy, and as an antidote to the separation of youth from the wider community. The term *youth community service* represents a wide array of programs operating under an equally wide array of assumptions about their impact. While advocates of youth service agree at least superficially on a general rationale for its adoption, there are differences in what they emphasize, and these differences carry over to the types of service programs they advocate. At the risk of oversimplification, advocates can be divided into those who stress the reform of youth and those who stress the reform of education.

The heart of the case put forth by those who would reform youth is that there is a crying need for young people to become engaged in democracy. Those making this argument produce statistics showing that youths vote less frequently than any other age group, that they are less likely to volunteer than older citizens (and the rate is dropping steadily), and that their values have shifted dramatically in the last 15 or 20 years in a direction that is dangerous for democracy. Data on participation are commonly accompanied by statistics on crime, pregnancy, suicide, and drug use—and, nearly always, by data from the annual survey of incoming college freshmen conducted by the American Council on Education. These survey results do seem to indicate a change in the attitudes of young people over the years: between 1970 and 1987 the percentage of students choosing "being well-off financially" as their most important goal rose from 29% to 76% (the highest percentage accorded any goal). In contrast, "developing a meaningful philosophy of life" moved from being the students' top-ranked goal in 1967 (chosen by 83% of the respondents) to being the 13th-ranked goal in 1987 (chosen by 39%).[14]

From this base, it is argued that service provides a potent antidote to young people's ills and should be added to their experience through requirements—or opportunities—for participation: a national service program, state or local youth service corps, a revitalized service ethic in traditional youth organizations, school-based service clubs, and service requirements for high school and/or college graduation.

The other dominant strain in the advocacy of youth service is a focus on the reform of education. With a longer history but less current fanfare, this approach stresses the power of service to meet the basic objectives of schools: promoting the personal, social, and intellectual development of young people and preparing them to become involved and effective citizens. Those who make education reform their chief concern are more likely to emphasize service as a part of the academic curriculum and to urge its integration into the regular activity of schools.

Since our emphasis in this article is on school-based community service, we shall discuss this second perspective in more detail. Community service as a means of education can be viewed as a particular manifestation of a still broader method labeled "experiential education." Rooted in the developmental theories of John Dewey, Jean Piaget, and others who stress learning as an interaction with the environment, this approach holds that development occurs as individuals strive to come up with more satisfying and complex ways to understand and act on their world.

James Coleman contrasts this experiential approach to learning with what he terms the "information-assimilation model" used in most classroom instruction.[15] The latter model consists of receiving information that has been presented through symbolic media, organizing the information into principles, inferring a particular application from the general principle, and applying the principle in a non-classroom situation. The experiential approach essentially turns this model on its head. Information is not introduced symbolically but is generated and assimilated through an entirely different sequence of steps. First, a student performs an action in a particular situation; then he or she observes its effects, understands these effects in a particular instance, understands the general principle in operation, and applies the principle in new circumstances.

Both approaches have strengths and weaknesses. The strength of the information-assimilation model is that it can impart large amounts of information and systematically develop principles and generalizations from that information. Its concomitant weaknesses are that instruction may bog down in the presentation stage and that the information may never be applied in practice—and thus not really learned.

The strengths and weaknesses of the experiential approach are just the reverse. The weaknesses are the less efficient presentation of information and the danger that students will not draw out principles and generalizations from practice. The strengths are that it counters the distancing abstraction of much classroom instruction by placing information in context, with the real-life nuances and applications that any fact or principle must have if it is to carry genuine and useful meaning; that it motivates the learner by providing connections between academic content and the problems of real life; and that it aids in retention of knowledge, as learning is made personal and applied in action. A 16-year-old member of an ambulance crew put it more succinctly: "In school you learn chemistry and biology and stuff and then forget it as soon as the test is over. Here you've got to remember because somebody's life depends on it."

The Impact of Service

Very little, if anything, has been "proved" by educational research. Advocates of almost any practice—be it cooperative learning, team teaching, computer-assisted instruction, or the lecture method—can find research evidence in its favor. Detractors and empirical purists can likewise find reasons for discounting the results of almost any study. Moreover, it is doubtful that substantiation by research is the prime reason for the adoption of any educational method—even those most commonly practiced. Educational research is a difficult and complex business—and particularly so when service is the target of investigation.

The analysis of community service programs presents unique problems to researchers, problems that go beyond the usual assortment of methodological snares. The fundamental difficulty is that service is not a single, easily definable activity like taking notes at a lecture. An act of service may be visiting an elderly person in a nursing home, clearing brush from a mountain trail, conducting a survey of attitudes about recycling, or participating in any of a vast array of other activities—each with different potential effects.

Not only is the independent variable—service—difficult to define, but any service activity has a wide range of plausible outcomes. This situation makes it hard to determine the appropriate dependent variables to study. Newmann laid out nine possible benefits that could accrue to a person from one act of direct civic involvement, and he did not even touch on how that involvement could affect one's political efficacy, later civic participation, factual recall, or self-esteem![16]

Sound research into the effects of community service is difficult, but not impossible. Many solid and inventive studies have been

undertaken, and, while none are without flaws, they provide useful information on the impact of service. Some of these findings are reviewed below.

There are two types of research evidence on the effects of community service. The first is qualitative, drawing on researchers' observations of community service programs, reports from participants, journals, interviews, testimonials, and the like. Often these sources of data are dismissed as "soft"—not serious or objective enough to count as evidence. In the eyes of some educational evaluators and policy analysts, the only evidence that counts is quantitative—with numbers derived from standardized instruments administered before and after, with control groups, random assignment of participants, sophisticated statistical analysis, and so on.

We have both kinds of evidence regarding the impact of community service, and both can be informative. Evidence from quantitative methodologies is somewhat limited, though a body of research does exist that tends to show that social, personal, and academic development are fostered by community service. Evidence from qualitative, anecdotal studies suggests even more strongly and consistently that community service can be a worthwhile, useful, enjoyable, and powerful learning experience.

Quantitative Findings

Academic learning. Many proponents have claimed that community service is an effective way to improve academic learning. The evidence for this relationship is strongest for service in the form of peer tutoring or teaching younger students. Using the technique of meta-analysis, researchers have combined the findings of many tutoring studies and have consistently found increases in reading and math achievement scores for tutors and tutees.[17] The gains in reading and math tend to be modest, but such is the case with most learning and growth. Changes in curriculum and instruction rarely, if ever, produce dramatic results. Yet the gains achieved through tutoring are consistently positive—most particularly for the tutors.

It may be that, when we seek to determine whether community service influences academic outcomes, we find a positive correlation most frequently when we look at tutoring because it is the form of service that is most "school-like" and because the knowledge and skills in question are most like the ones the tutors have already been using. In the few cases when students in other forms of service have been tested for gains in factual knowledge, the results have been less conclusive. When the measuring instrument is a general test of knowledge, there is usually no difference at all between students in service programs and those in unconventional classrooms—which may establish that at least nothing is lost by time spent out of school. Consistent gains in factual knowledge have been found, however, when researchers have used tests designed to measure the specific kinds of information that students were likely to encounter in their field experiences.[18]

Some researchers have focused on the effect of service experiences on such basic processes of thinking as solving problems, being open-minded, and thinking critically. Thomas Wilson found that students who participated in political and social action in the school or wider community became more open-minded.[19] In a study that we conducted in 1982, we found that problem-solving ability, as measured by reactions to a series of real-life situations, increased more for students in community service (and other experience-based programs) than for those in comparison groups. Furthermore, students' ability to analyze problems improved the most when they had encountered problems similar to those presented in the test and when the program deliberately focused on problem solving. Students who had neither discussed their experiences with others nor encountered problems similar to those in the test showed no more change than students in conventional classrooms.[20]

Social/psychological development. Well-run, well-conceptualized community service programs can also influence social development and psychological development. Our study looked at 27 school-sponsored programs featuring direct participation in the community, including programs of community service, community study, career internships, and outdoor adventure. We found that students in participatory programs, including service programs, gained in social and personal responsibility.[21] Stephen Hamilton and Mickey Fenzel reported similar gains in social responsibility with groups of 4-H members engaged in various forms of service: child care, community improvement efforts, and the like.[22] Fred Newmann and Robert Rutter found less dramatic and less consistent differences between service and classroom programs but concluded that community service appeared to affect students' sense of social responsibility and personal competence more positively than did regular classroom instruction.[23]

Researchers have investigated several other dimensions of social development as well. In our work, we found that students in service programs and in other experiential programs developed more favorable attitudes toward adults and also toward the types of organizations and people with whom they were involved.[24] Kathy Luchs reported that students involved in community service gained more positive attitudes toward others, a greater sense of efficacy, and higher self-esteem than nonparticipating comparison students.[25] Raymond Calabrese and Harry Schumer reported that a program that assigned junior high students with behavioral difficulties to service activities resulted in lower levels of alienation and isolation and fewer disciplinary problems.[26] Studies that have examined political efficacy and inclination toward subsequent civic participation as a result of service activities have had mixed results. About an equal number of studies find increases and no increases on these factors.

The effect of community service on self-esteem has been the psychological outcome most commonly investigated. Increases in self-esteem have been found for students who play the role of tutor, who provide for the mentally disabled, and who fill more general helping roles. Newmann and Rutter reported that students involved in community service projects gained a better sense of social competence in the performance of such tasks as communicating effectively to groups, starting conversations with strangers, persuading adults to take their views seriously, and the like.[27]

A number of studies have used the developmental theories of Lawrence Kohlberg and of Jane Loevinger to frame their assessment of the impact of service experiences (usually those involving work as a peer counselor, interviewer, or teacher) on moral and ego development. The typical, though not universal, outcome is that students gain in both moral and ego development.[28] Reviewing the research on developmental education, Ralph Mosher concluded that moral and ego development can be enhanced by educational programs, the most powerful of which combine discussion of moral issues with the exercise of empathy and action on behalf of moral and social goals.[29]

The value of combining action and discussion has been noted by other researchers as well. Rutter and Newmann, in examining the potential of service to enhance civic responsibility, concluded that the presence of a reflective seminar was probably the key to achieving that goal.[30] In our own study, we examined the impact of several program variables (e.g., length, intensity, type of community action) on student outcomes and found that the presence of a reflective seminar was the one program feature that made a clear difference — particularly with respect to intellectual and social dimensions of development.[31]

Effect on those served. In assessing the impact of service programs, researchers have mainly been concerned about the effect on the volunteer and have seldom taken into account what young people accomplish for others. There are two significant exceptions—assessments of tutoring and peer-helping programs. Researchers have consistently found tutoring to be an effective mode of instruction. In one comparative study, for example, tutoring was found to be a more effective tool for raising academic outcomes than computer-assisted instruction.[32] With regard to peer helping, a meta-analysis of studies of 143 drug prevention programs for adolescents concluded that, of five approaches examined, peer programs were the most effective on all outcome measures and stood out most on the criterion of reducing actual drug use.[33]

In summary, quantitative research on the impact of community service suggests that it can and often does have a positive effect on the intellectual and social/psychological development of participants. Researchers consistently report a heightened sense of personal and social responsibility, more positive attitudes toward adults and others, more active exploration of careers, enhanced self-esteem, growth in moral and ego development, more complex patterns of thought, and greater mastery of skills and content that are directly related to the experiences of participants. Furthermore, when the impact of service on others has been examined, young people have proved to be effective in raising mathematics and reading scores and in reducing drug use among peers.

Findings from quantitative studies are mixed on whether community service increases one's political efficacy and later involvement in civic affairs. Only rarely does participation result in higher scores on tests of general knowledge, with the clear exception of academic achievement scores for students in the role of teacher or tutor.

Qualitative Findings

While quantitative research yields reasonably consistent evidence on the positive impact of community service, the methodological problems mentioned earlier stand in the way of establishing a clear causal connection. Yet anyone who has worked with or evaluated community service programs cannot help but be struck by the universally high regard in which the programs are held by those associated with them. Students, teachers, community supervisors, parents, and those being served consistently attest to the benefits of community service.

The gap between what quantitative and qualitative methodologies uncover about community service suggests that a practice so varied and complex demands equally complex and varied types of assessment. Sometimes the rigid reliance on paper-and-pencil surveys and tests can obscure the most obvious and meaningful data of all. In an inquiry into the impact of service on social responsibility, for example, the fact that participants are willingly and consistently acting in a socially responsible manner (volunteering in a nursing home or petitioning city hall to crack down on polluters) is at least as relevant to the issue as how they score on a test of attitudes about being socially responsible.

The spontaneous comments of participants in interviews and in journals are a rich source of qualitative data, revealing not only the general effect of a service experience but its particular and peculiar impact on each individual. The more the analysis is grounded in theories of how growth and development take place, the more useful these data can be. Below, we offer an example of how qualitative analysis can reveal the dimensions of learning and intellectual development that can accrue from service experiences.

A qualitative analysis of what is learned from service. A consistent finding of research into service and other kinds of experiential programs is the high degree to which participants report that they have learned a great deal from their experiences. In a nationwide survey we conducted of nearly 4,000 students involved in service and other experiential programs, about 75% reported learning "more" or "much more" in their participation program than in their regular classes.[34] Similar findings are regularly reported in other studies. When people feel strongly that they have learned a great deal, they probably have done so. But it is not always possible for them or others to articulate just what they have learned.

To probe this issue more deeply, we analyzed the journals of high school students whose social studies curriculum included time spent working as volunteers four days a week in schools and social agencies.[35] The journals were a valuable tool for qualitative analysis in that they revealed what the students learned *specifically* from their service experiences (95% of them had indicated that they learned more or much more from those experiences than from their regular classes).

Many students commented on the power of being in a new role, as in this excerpt from one student's journal:

> As I walked through the hallway [of the elementary school on my first day of leading elementary children in theater experiences], I realized what I had gotten myself into...a challenge. But as I step through the door I transform from student to person....The first day went extremely well, but I'm glad I don't have to go through it again. Now I return to school and become student again.

In another entry, a student suggests that a relationship with a child is a more compelling incentive to act responsibly than are the demands and sanctions of school authorities.

As I entered St. D's it was my joy to see Adam, wearing a smock covered with paint, washing his hands at the sink. "Hi," I said.

> "Did you go to school yesterday?" he replied shortly.
> "Yes," I said guiltily [having skipped my service assignment].
> "Why didn't you come?" he demanded.
> "I didn't have a ride to get back from here," I explained, thinking as fast as I could. When I started to touch his shoulder, he jerked away and said, "Don't." So I left him alone....I felt like a criminal.

Another dimension of the service experience is that it gives students a sense of connection with a wider range of people, places, and problems, In this report, a student recounts how her world was broadened:

> I have come a long way, though. I remember my first few days at Oak Terrace Nursing Home. I was scared to touch people, or the doorknobs even. And I used to wash my hands after I left there every single day! Can you believe it? Now I go and get big hugs and kisses from everyone. Get this—I even eat there! That's a horror story for some people.

Unfamiliar settings, new experiences, and wider associations can lead to new knowledge and understanding, as they did for this girl, who volunteered in a soup kitchen:

> I feel bad when they're called bums. I kinda understand why they're there. People end up on the street because of depression mostly. They have a divorce, or they lose the right to see their kids, or lose their job or their housing, and they get depressed. One guy I regularly talked to said suddenly one day, "I don't want to talk to you—you're a kid." I was hurt. But I found

out his wife had just denied him the right to see his kids. He was lashing out at me as a kid and as a woman.

Some journal entries reveal insights even more profound that these—something akin to a new way of knowing, a new process of thinking. Consider the words of a young woman volunteering in a nursing home who discovers a new pathway to knowledge and understanding:

> As the [first] morning came to an end I began to deeply ponder the reason for my parents telling me to respect my elders. Honestly, I thought, I doubt if I can respect these people that wear diapers, drool gallons of saliva a day, speak totally incoherently and [are] totally dependent on a youth. But finally the first week passed. I became very attached to the residents. I think those insecurities you feel when you start working with elderly people disappear when you begin to really *love* them.

The writer of the journal went on to describe the beauty of the residents as she came to really "know" and relate to them. Her observations about them—especially about what they knew and could do—changed dramatically. But the turning point, the new perspective, was her insight that love precedes knowledge—not the other way around. It is precisely the point that the philosopher George Santayana made in 1925 about knowing the truth about another person.[36]

Through comments such as these, the "more" or "much more" that these students had said they learned from their service experience began to take on meaning. The "more" turned out to be a reference not so much to *amount* as to *significance,* not so much to new information as to more important and more personal knowledge and un-

derstanding. The students were probing the fundamental questions of life: Who am I? Where am I going? Is there any point to it all? They were thinking and writing about the basic issues of adolescence and beyond: relationships, significance, connection, suffering, meaning, hope, love, and attachment.

In summary, the case for community service as a legitimate educational practice receives provisional support from quantitative, quasi-experimental studies and even more consistent affirmation from the reports and testimony of participants and practitioners. Whether the current interest in youth service represents the wave of the future or a passing fancy cannot, of course, be known. Whether service as a school practice merits the serious consideration of practitioners and policy makers seems to be beyond question.

NOTES

1. John Dewey, *Experience and Education* (New York: Collier Books, 1938); and idem, *Democracy and Education* (New York: Free Press, 1916).

2. William H. Kilpatrick, "The Project Method," *Teachers College Record,* September 1918, pp. 319–35.

3. George S. Counts, *Dare the Schools Build a New Social Order?* (New York: John Day, 1932); and Paul R. Hanna, *Youth Serves the Community* (New York: D. Appleton Century, 1937).

4. National Committee on Secondary Education, *American Youth in the Mid-Seventies* (Reston, VA.: National Association of Secondary School Principals, 1972); James S. Coleman, *Youth: Transition to Adulthood* (Chicago: Report of the Panel on Youth of the President's Science Advisory Committee, University of Chicago Press, 1974); and John

Henry Martin, *The Education of Adolescents* (Washington, DC: National Panel on High School and Adolescent Education, 1976).

5. National Commission on Resources for Youth, *New Roles for Youth: In the School and the Community* (New York: Citation Press, 1974).

6. Fred M. Newmann, *Education for Citizen Action: Challenge for Secondary Curriculum* (Berkeley, CA: McCutchan, 1975).

7. Eliot Wigginton, *Sometimes a Shining Moment: Twenty Years at Foxfire* (Garden City, NY: Anchor Press/Doubleday, 1985).

8. John I. Goodlad, *A Place Called School* (New York: McGraw-Hill, 1984).

9. *Reconnecting Youth: The Next Stage of Reform* (Denver: Education Commission of the States, 1985).

10. Ernest L. Boyer, *High School: A Report on Secondary Education in America* (New York: Harper & Row, 1983).

11. Charles Harrison, *Student Service: The New Carnegie Unit* (Princeton, NJ: Carnegie Foundation for the Advancement of Teaching, 1987).

12. Carnegie Task Force on Education of Young Adolescents, *Turning Points: Preparing American Youth for the 21st Century* (New York: Carnegie Council on Adolescent Development of the Carnegie Corporation, 1989).

13. William T. Grant Foundation Commission on Work, Family and Citizenship, *The Forgotten Half: Pathways to Success for America's Youth and Young Families* (Washington, DC: William T. Grant Foundation, 1988), p. 90.

14. "Freshmen Found Stressing Wealth," *New York Times,* 14 January 1988, p. A-14.

15. James S. Coleman, "Differences Between Experiential and Classroom Learning," in Morris T. Keaton, ed., *Experiential Learning: Rationale, Characteristics, and Assessment* (San Francisco: Jossey-Bass, 1977), pp. 49-61.

16. Newmann, pp. 9-10.

17. Diane Hedin, "Students as Teachers: A Tool for Improving School Cimate and Productivity," *Social Policy,* vol. 17, 1987, pp. 42-47.

18. Stephen F. Hamilton and R. Shepherd Zeldin, "Learning Civics in Community," *Curriculum Inquiry,* vol. 17, 1987, pp. 407- 20.

19. Thomas C. Wilson, "An Alternative Community-Based Secondary School Education Program and Student Political Development" (Doctoral dissertation, University of Southern California, 1974).

20. Dan Conrad and Diane Hedin, "The Impact of Experiential Education on Adolescent Development," *Child & Youth Services,* vol. 4, 1982, pp. 57-76.

21. Ibid.

22. Stephen F. Hamilton and L. Mickey Frenzel, "The Impact of Volunteer Experience on Adolescent Social Development: Evidence of Program Effects," *Journal of Adolescent Research,* vol. 3, 1988, pp. 65-80.

23. Fred M. Newmann and Robert A. Rutter, *The Effects of High School Community Service Programs on Students' Social Development* (Madison: Wisconsin Center for Education Research, University of Wisconsin, 1983).

24. Conrad and Hedin, op. cit.

25. Kathy P. Luchs, "Selected Changes in Urban High School Students After Participation in Community-Based Learning and Service Activities" (Doctoral dissertation, University of Maryland, 1981).

26. Raymond L. Calabrese and Harry Schumer, "The Effects of Service Activities on Adolescent Alienation," *Adolescence,* vol. 21, 1986, pp. 675-87.

27. Newmann and Rutter, op. cit.

28. Philip V. Cognetta and Norman A. Sprinthall, "Students as Teachers: Role Taking as a Means of Promoting Psychological and Ethical Development During Adolescence," in Norman A. Sprinthall and Ralph L. Mosher, eds. *Value Development as the Aim of Education* (Schenectady, NY: Character Research Press, 1978), pp. 53-68.

29. Ralph L. Mosher, "Theory and Practice: A New E.R.A.?," *Theory Into Practice,* vol. 16, 1977, pp. 81-88.

30. Robert A. Rutter and Fred M. Newmann, "The Potential of Community Service to Enhance Civic Responsibility," *Social Education,* October 1989, pp. 371-74.

31. Conrad and Hedin, op. cit.

32. Hedin, op. cit.

33. Nancy S. Tobler, "Meta-analysis of 143 Adolescent Drug Prevention Programs: Quantitative Outcome Results of Program Participants Compared to a Control or Comparison Group," *Journal of Drug Issues,* vol. 16, 1986, pp. 537-67.

34. Conrad and Hedin, op. cit.

35. Diane Hedin and Dan Conrad, "Service: A Pathway to Knowledge," *Community Education Journal,* vol. 15, 1987, pp. 10-14.

36. George Santayana, "Philanthropy," in David L. Norton and Mary T. Kille, eds. *Philosophies of Love* (Totowa, NJ: Rowman & Allanheld, 1983), pp. 128-38.

Developing a Service Ethic

by Anthony Richards

The notion of service learning may be seen in a variety of programs which range from caring and sharing in an elementary school to residential national service programs such as the Peace Corps and VISTA. While each program requires its own specific curricula, management, and participants, this article will describe the common elements of service learning that have emerged as a result of some specific case studies (Richards, 1987).

The ideal outcome of any service learning program is that the participant has developed a service ethic. This service ethic has also been a long-time goal of most traditional education programs. However, in traditional programs, most of the learning has been vicarious and as a result of strong role models or specific environments. It is only recently that such courses as "community-service" and programs like "We Care and Share" (Richards & Scrutton, 1980) have deliberately set out to have a service ethic as a major goal of the program. Even well-known national service programs such as the California Conservation Corps have the work ethic as paramount rather than the service ethic.

The two case studies which will be considered in this paper are "We Care and Share," a program designed for elementary school children, and the KKN, a National Service Program which serves the country of Indonesia.

Case Study: We Care and Share

Ethics and values are generally established over time. The pervasive environment will have an influence over the kinds of values and ethics which will either be promoted or accepted. The traditional education system and elementary schools in particular would all claim that they promote and nurture caring behaviors in their students. However, seldom do schools deliberately include caring and sharing as a curriculum topic, although some elementary schools or elementary classes will become involved in service projects. The problem with these with respect to developing a service ethic is that they are generally short, on/off projects that are isolated from the ongoing curriculum.

An elementary school in Nova Scotia, Canada, was selected as a suitable place for a demonstration project called "We Care and Share." It was important that *all* the students and staff were simultaneously part of the project. The reason for this was that caring and sharing for each other and the school needed to be pervasive and perceived as the normal behavior by the entire school community.

During meetings with the teachers, it was determined that the syllabus would not be violated with respect to content in order to accommodate the demonstration project. However, the approach, teaching techniques, and methods would change to promote the service ethic. For example, the art class for Grade III was scheduled to paint patterns on paper with the purpose of decorating the outside of a box. To utilize this required aspect of the syllabus in a caring and sharing context, the students each interviewed one teacher and asked for their favorite colors and designs. Upon returning to the art room, they created patterns and decorated an AJAX container for use as a pencil holder. When completed, the children presented the teachers with a personalized pencil holder which had a use and was displayed on the teacher's desk. Because the children felt good about creating something for a specific use and for a specific person, the children were excited and worked with much greater skill and care. The teachers were genuinely touched and grateful for the gift.

This kind of activity was replicated in all of the subject areas and promoted by all the teachers. The effect was that students' caring and sharing for each other increased, the school building had less garbage, and reports from parents suggested that willingness to help at home also improved.

The Concept of National Service

National service is a term which has a variety of interpretations. In the U.K. following World War II, it meant two years of conscripted military service designed primarily to train men who would be prepared to serve their country as soldiers. This form of national service still exists in some European countries. Since the decline of wars in Europe and the recognition of human rights and responsibilities, some countries have provided options. For example, all West German 18-year-olds without criminal records and of sound mind and body must choose one of four national service options: Military Service; Zivildienst (national civilian service for conscientious objectors); Technical Aid Service (emergency services); and Overseas Development Service.

Other forms of national service range from 6-month voluntary training and employment programs which combine literacy, civic, and technical skills (Kenya), to Conservation Corps work which has minimum financial benefits but serves environmental needs of the country (CCC California). The Canadian National Service program (Katimavik) attempted to utilize the best of all programs and place young people in a 9-month residential setting where they provided a community service and lived a strong environmental ethic. In addition, they developed job skills for themselves.

Another area of national service which has probably more potential than most is the concept of Study Service. This utilizes the skills, expertise, and education of young people to serve a community, at the same time using the service experience to support and consolidate their own educational process. The programs can operate with school children or university students. The aim of the National Youth Service Corps of Nigeria is to promote a work ethic, ensure national unity, bridge cultural gaps among tribes, and integrate service learning into educational institutions. The Hong Kong Polytechnic has included a service project for all students related to their field of study. For example, engineering students might be challenged to design products which make life easier for the handicapped.

Case Study: KKN

Dr. Koesnodi Hardjasoemantri pioneered a study service program for Indonesia. At the time (1973), he was the Director of Higher Education of the Ministry of Education and Culture. This program was named Kuliah Kenja Nyata (KKN), which literally translated means learning through real work. One of the important features of this program is that it was developed by an Indonesian specifically for Indonesian needs. It drew ideas from many international experts, but it represents one of the best service learning concepts in the world today.

The KKN is now required of all university students. That is, in order to graduate from a university program, each student spends 3–6 months in the villages performing a community service. This KKN experience has the potential to develop committed, young, educated leaders who will be better able to lead their lives committed to service and the development of Indonesia.

The aims of the KKN are:

1) To enable the institution of higher learning to produce graduates who will promote development because they have experienced the very complex problems faced by the community, and studied practical and interdisciplinary ways of tackling these problems;

2) To bring the institution of higher learning closer to the community and to adapt higher education to the demands of development;

3) To help the Government to accelerate the development process and form development cadres in the villages. (KKN Guidelines, 1978)

The aims of the program are commendable, but in practice there are results and outcomes that go far beyond the three aims established by Hardjasoemantri. For example, the training and preparation of the students became the responsibility of the faculty. The result was that the approach to teaching was adapted to reflect a service ethic. This was quite subtle and was not necessarily deliberately planned by the professors.

There is a deliberate attempt to place students in villages and projects which do not specifically relate to their major field of study. Even though a student majors in medicine, law, or engineering, it does not necessarily follow that the village project will reflect that particular expertise. In fact, there is much to be said for an engineering student becoming involved in a community administrative issue rather than becoming overtechnical and too sophisticated with an engineering problem. The qualities and skills that the KKN students offer should be generic and simple enough for the village people to learn, continue, and follow-up on their own after the student has returned to the university.

A simple measure of whether the program is successful would be to observe the degree of empowerment of the village people after the student has left. This can be achieved if the KKN students motivate the young people into "village development cadres." There is a need to unearth hitherto unknown or concealed local resources and expertise. The village head can be assisted in creating a kind of village planning board which involves community members. Most important will be the student's ability to create a sense of ownership for the project.

When the students have completed their KKN experience, they return to the university for their final year. This experience then helps them to consolidate their learning as well as broaden their concept of the human needs of the nation. KKN gives them a sense of responsibility toward rural communities so that after they graduate, they will be willing to work in any place that needs them.

Principles of Service Learning

There appear to be some common principles which emerge from these two service learning programs. These commonalities may help to create strategies which are essential to the development of service learning programs.

1. Selection of Participants

In both cases, the students are required to participate in the program. One advantage of this is that the number of students involved is much greater. Another is the fact that involving the entire school (as in We Care and Share), or the entire university population (as in KKN), leads to service becoming a pervasive activity and part of the normal behavior and attitude of the group.

Other service learning programs may be elective. The chance of these volunteers being highly committed initially is much greater. However, it is only those who are predisposed to service who serve and it becomes an activity of the elite or privileged. This is seen in the elementary school where children refer to helpers or volunteers as "goody goodies." Among their peers, this is often perceived as a negative reaction which could stifle volunteerism and the willingness to serve.

This pervasiveness within the community of school or university seems to indicate that service, caring, and sharing will become a normal and accepted behavior. This, in turn, suggests that there is a greater chance of developing a service ethic.

With highly committed volunteers, the chance of the quality of service may increase. This notion of "a few volunteers being better than an army of pressed men" has some merit if the only goal is to get the job done. A service learning program is generally designed to develop a service ethic within the participants which is transferable to other settings and aspects of their lives, rather than to be merely project oriented.

It was evident in the elementary children who continued to care and share at home and in settings outside of the classroom. Similarly, upon graduation, the university students often take up positions in remote villages that need help rather than confine their aspirations to the safe, affluent cities.

2. Sequential Development

So often it is presumed that if a community service component is included in a school or university curriculum, then the students will benefit and develop a service ethic. This is far from the truth. The formation of the ethic takes time and is generally based on sequential development from simple to more complex issues. When children are learning to read, they are not expected to pick up the works of Shakespeare and comprehend them at the age of seven or eight. As with most subjects, the syllabus starts with simple things and simple concepts and slowly develops before the student approaches some sort of mastery.

Service learning as a subject is no different and therefore, there should be a sequential development. Community service experiences should be given to young people based on their age, aptitude, and ability. In addition, the development of a service ethic is also a function of time and variety of experiences. The KKN program might do well to look at introducing the concept of service to freshmen students. This would enable a slower and more integrated approach to the development of students who would be well equipped to take on a larger and more complex challenge of service in the villages.

This concept of a developmental approach to service learning is one that has been greatly overlooked in the education literature. If service is indeed an ethic, then it needs to pervade all aspects of a person's life at all stages. Therefore, a program of caring and sharing for each other in elementary school could lead to a strong commitment to national service beyond high school.

3. Fiscal Considerations

The We Care and Share program operated with minimal extra costs. However, the KKN is necessarily very expensive because of the travel and living expenses of the students. One of the key principles which emerges from fiscal considerations is that the costs should be shared by all parties in the process. Both those serving and those being served need to share in the financial responsibility. The result is that they share the ownership of the project. The majority of the costs can be met with in-kind donations of time, accommodation, meals, etc. It is this process of sharing in the project which helps to empower the recipient of the service to help themselves. Whereas this is more evident in the KKN program, the support from parents, teachers, and community in the We Care and Share program was vital to the success of the project.

4. Project versus Process

When the KKN students are placed in a village, their task is to help the community to plan and carry out development projects, improve the attitude of the community and their ways of thinking and behaving, help needed modernization to take place, and form development cadres to guarantee the continuation of the development process and self-reliance (Guidelines, 1978). Unfortunately, these ideals require some sophisticated skills in interpersonal relationships and leadership. If the students are having difficulty, they will often revert to the easiest and most objective route, which is that of the physical project. In other words, they see the project (water pump, W.C., irrigation, etc.) as their sole contribution and service to the community. Instead, they could use the project as a means whereby they can communicate, relate, and influence the members of the community on a level that goes beyond the physical.

Similarly, the children's involvement in the We Care and Share program went beyond the physical nature of the service projects. It was the process of making someone else feel good that became significant. It was this sensation that caused the children to go on and do other similar caring and sharing activities.

In creating service learning programs, it is important to look beyond the activity or project. The physical activity becomes the means only to the development of a service ethic. However, the process cannot be left to chance. There should be as much deliberation and energy in developing the process as there is to securing a suitable and exciting project.

Conclusion

This paper has looked at an elementary school program and the model of the KKN Study/Service program in Indonesia. These programs have demonstrated that the theoretical and conceptual aspects of the models are at the cutting edge of service learning programs throughout the world. It is important that the mere descriptions of these programs are not used as prescriptions. In other words, the best concepts and processes should be teased out, then adapted and applied to a new setting. It is through the shortcomings of some of the programs as well as the strengths that generic strategies can be developed. It behooves experiential educators to do what they do best, which is to engage the learner in action and reflection. By injecting this experiential learning philosophy and methodology into the mainstream of education and social programs through the medium of service, it should be possible to strengthen the service ethic around the world.

The Social, Psychological, Moral, and Cognitive Effects of Service Learning

by Richard J. Kraft

Introduction

While service learning, community service, and volunteer programs have been a part of schools and colleges in the United States for decades and there has been a range of research and evaluation studies, there is a general lack of solid evidence on its effects. One of the major difficulties in evaluating or researching service learning programs is the lack of agreement on what is meant by the term and exactly what it is meant to accomplish. While some programs emphasize social growth, character development, or civic responsibility, others attempt to study psychological development and effects of programs on self-concept. Moral judgment studies have sought to evaluate the effects of service on moral and ego development, and others have attempted to measure the effects of service on the broader community. Perhaps the most difficult arena has been in the area of intellectual, cognitive, and academic effects. It has been difficult to design tight experiments to isolate the effects of service on specific academic achievements. A recent experimental study (Markus, Howard, & King, 1993) of students in a university political science course provides some of the first strong evidence of the positive "academic" effects of service learning.

As indicated, an additional problem with evaluation and research on service learning has been the lack of an accepted definition. Voluntary service, volunteerism, national service, community service, peer helping, community-based learning, study service, and youth service, are all terms which have been and continue to be used. With the formation of the Commission on National and Community Service and the passage by Congress of two major acts on service learning (1990 and 1993), we shall accept the definition of programs being funded under rules from the Commission.

A service learning program provides educational experiences:

a. *Under which students learn and develop through active participation in thoughtfully organized service experiences that meet actual community needs and that are coordinated in collaboration with school and community;*

b. *That is integrated into the students' academic curriculum or provides structured time for a student to think, talk, or write about what the student did and saw during the actual service activity;*

c. *That provides a student with opportunities to use newly acquired skills and knowledge in real-life situations in their own communities; and*

d. *That enhances what is taught in school by extending student learning beyond the classroom and into the community and helps to foster the development of a sense of caring for others.*

A challenge for evaluators and researchers in the field is the dramatically different nature and duration of the programs that go under the guise of service learning. For evaluators and researchers, it is difficult to compare one-term service events for a group of eight-year-olds in an elementary classroom with full-time, paid programs for young adults in conservation corps. In-depth, semester-long academic courses in international settings for college students differ greatly from once-a-week volunteer visits to a senior center. Yet all of these can and do meet basic criteria for service learning.

Krug (1991). The following cursory review is taken from the Literature Review on Service Learning conducted by Dr. James Krug (1991) at the University of Colorado. Krug's research was on the effects of service learning on four groups of high school young people: at-risk youth in a special program, student assistants (primarily minority) within the school, nature guides, and tutors at a primary school. Preliminary results indicate that, while all the experimental groups gained on measures of potency, activity involvement in the community, self-concept, and other factors, the statistically significant growth at the .01 and .05 levels was found almost exclusively with the at-risk and minority young people. The control group, as predicted, did not change on the pre/post instruments.

General Surveys

Newmann and Rutter (1986). The authors estimated that in 1984, approximately 27% of all high schools offered some form of service program, involving 900,000 students in 5,400 schools. Service took on the form of 1) school clubs or co-curricular organizations; 2) service learning credit or requirement; 3) a laboratory for an existing course; 4) a service learning class; or 5) a schoolwide focus. Non-public schools were most likely to offer service, and suburban and large schools more often than urban, rural, or small schools. An estimated 6.6% of all high school students were involved in 1984, with 2.3% tied to the curriculum. This compared with 52% of seniors involved in team sports and 34% in the performing arts. Time spent was an average of four hours per week across all programs, and six hours in elective programs. Those with high school graduation requirements spent one hour per week. Schools where a majority of students were non-white were more likely to offer programs than white majority schools, and three times as likely to offer community service as an elective course and award academic credit. Programs involve students in near equal proportion from the college prep., general, and vocational tracks. At-risk students and those with behavioral problems were found to be non-existent in service programs. Thirty-four percent of programs were in schools, not in the community.

Harrison (1987). Harrison reports that among voluntary programs, most (61%) involved less than 10% of the student body. Ninety percent of students put in less than 200 hours, about half the time required by one season of high school football. Sixty-five percent of service programs were within the school itself.

Whatever the actual numbers of students involved in service learning might be, the surest conclusion that can be drawn is that school-based service learning is an educational concept that has endured throughout this century, but has not become an integral part of the high school experience for more than a small group of students. In addition, few programs involve participation by at-risk and minority youth, and a majority of school-sponsored programs are focused on college-bound white students.

Social Growth Investigations

Riecken (1952). Riecken studied college students involved in two months of intensive, full-time summer experiences designed to strengthen humanitarian ideals by having youths participate in physically useful labor in an economically deprived community. Using a questionnaire, he discovered participants became less prejudiced, more democratic, less authoritarian, more service oriented, and developed greater ego strength.

Smith (1966). Smith, in a study of forty-four Peace Corps volunteers who taught in Ghana during a period of two years, discovered that after the first year in which the volunteers displayed initial and perhaps naive optimism, a more reasoned but no less committed moralistic philosophy emerged. They demonstrated more realism, autonomy, independence, and significantly increased levels of self-worth and insight. In addition, they became more service oriented in terms of their own career aspirations.

Hunt and Hardt (1969). Students in a Project Upward Bound, pre-college enrichment program for high school students from poor families were involved in communal living. Both white and black groups achieved nearly identical increases in motivation, self-esteem, and academic achievement. Other researchers have indicated positive results in social growth from less intensive school service programs.

Marsh (1973) concluded that participation in community affairs as part of a high school experimental course increased, as did interest in political activities and a desire to support political issues.

Using a model based on Mosher's moral education, Newmann's citizen education, and Hampden-Turner's psycho-social development, **Bourgeois** (1978) concluded that democratic values were accepted by young teenagers, an urgency for personal competence existed, and community activities helped to develop civic competence.

Wilson (1974) examined open-mindedness and a sense of political efficacy in a community-based, alternative education program. Wilson concluded that because the learning environment became one of openness, changed authority relationships between students and teachers, and student self-selection of the subject matter and process of curriculum, the findings of greater open-mindedness and political efficacy on the part of participants were able to occur.

Corbett (1977) studied the effects of high school students' participation in a year-long community program which aimed to develop student commitment to the solution of social problems. He found that during the first year when the program was teacher centered and directed, student moral and psycho-social development was nonsignificant, but in the second year, when it became student centered and reflective in nature, significant gains on personality measures and emotional and task competence were found. He concluded that students who worked with individuals in providing service developed more commitment to the solution of social problems than did the students whose volunteer work was focused upon group situations.

Stockhaus (1976) sought to determine if twenty hours of helping in social service agencies would positively affect self-esteem, political efficacy, social responsibility, and community responsibility in high school seniors. Stockhaus found that participants in one school developed greater senses of social responsibility, community responsibility, and altruism, than did nonparticipants and controls, but that strong support for community involvement programs to bring about positive changes in citizenship attitudes was lacking. Changes were too small to be of practical significance.

Broudy (1977) delineated problems which limited the effective development of moral/citizenship, experiential, and service learning programs in the public schools. They included heterogeneity of values and lifestyles, discrepancies between educational objectives and community behaviors, discrepancies between structured classroom teaching and students' informal community learning, and community experiences of differing intensity and quality.

Conrad and Hedin (1982) found that students in service and other experiential programs developed more favorable attitudes toward adults and also toward the type of organizations and people with whom they were involved.

Luchs (1981) reported that high school students involved in community service gained a more positive attitude toward others, a grater sense of efficacy, and higher self-esteem than nonparticipating comparison students.

Calbrese and Schumer (1986) reported lower levels of alienation and isolation, and fewer disciplinary problems among junior high school youth involved in service as part of a program for students with behavioral difficulties.

In summary, the literature findings on social outcomes as a result of students' involvement in experiential and service learning programs are mixed. Intensive, full-time, communal living programs have generally proven to be more successful in changing attitudes; these programs, also, have usually included older students who may have already committed themselves to achieving program objectives, primarily because they entered the programs in a voluntary mode. Too many of the studies suffer from small sample size, lack of strict controls, previous volunteer experiences on the part of students, and uneven quality of students' experiences in the program.

Psychological Development Investigations

A number of research studies have concentrated upon the study of a student's psychological development as a result of participation in experiential education and service learning programs. Taking full responsibility for one's own actions, developing a sense of self-esteem and ego strength, reaching a high level of moral reasoning, and becoming psychologically mature were seen to be key determinants for success in school and for active involvement in positive citizenship (Shockhaus, 1976). Unfortunately, traditional school curricula frequently not only do not promote these aims, but conversely, appear to negatively affect them (Goodlad & Klein, 1990; Martin, 1975; Cusick, 1973; Silberman, 1972; Bidwell, 1965; Jackson, 1968; Surges, 1979; Coleman, 1961).

Advocates of experiential education and service learning programs believe that development of psychological strength will occur more strongly in such programs than in traditional school programs (Conrad, 1982; Coleman, 1974; Dewey, 1938; Frankena, 1965; Piaget, 1970; Schwebel & Ralph, 1973; Rogers, 1969; Rich, 1962; Kohlberg, 1970; Erikson, 1968).

Bontempo (1979) conducted field interviews with students and coordinators, and studied program documents from the various schools. Her conclusions were that this type of learning was clearly grounded in consistent philosophies of learning and was making valuable and extensive use of community resources in students' education. Students enrolled in the programs demonstrated positive self-concepts and an increase in feelings of self-worth.

Kazungu (1978) concluded that voluntary, youth helping experiences promoted a more positive self-concept among youth and significantly helped to improve the community.

Sager (1973) studied twenty-two high school seniors who volunteered for nine weeks during their summer vacations at state hospitals. Young people increased their self-esteem and self-confidence significantly on 30 or 34 sub-scales on seven personality inventories. In addition, they were more self-accepting, felt more adequate and worthwhile in human interactions with their peers and with the persons they were helping.

Kelly (1973) found that therapeutic helping behavior generated positive changes in self-concept and other self-perceptive dimensions on the part of the helper. He found that students who helped on a one-to-one personal level underwent significantly greater positive changes in self-concept and other related measures than did those in more general types of service activities.

In order to determine whether self-concept of students who had experienced school behavioral problems of apathy, vandalism, and delinquency would be improved by enrollment in a voluntary curriculum with a traditional school setting, Martin (1977) employed a case-study approach to a year-long study of thirty male and female high school students. By the end of the year, student behavior had positively changed as measured by teacher interviews and by students' own self-reflections as reported to the research. Both teachers and students believed that students had also developed more positive self-concepts as their former negative behaviors became socially unacceptable.

Exum (1978), in addition to investigating interpersonal behaviors and ego-development, also studied the results of systematic reflective discussions of college students' helping experiences upon the development of self-concept. Conclusions indicated that a combination of actual experiences and systematic reflective discussions were the most important components in the curriculum and that participants showed significant growth in self-concept and ego-development.

Rutter and Newmann (1989) found that the potential of service to enhance social responsibility was dependent on the presence of a reflection seminar. The opportunity to discuss their experiences with teachers in small, peer-group settings greatly impacted whether they reported a positive interaction with the community.

Saunders (1976) investigated whether or not junior and senior high school student tutors would demonstrate a positive attitude change in self-concept, in reading, and toward school when compared to student non-tutors. While no significant difference was found, Saunders concluded that the program had an effect on maintaining positive attitudes.

Soat (1974) examined college students in an introductory psychology course as to whether one's cognitive style and self-concept were related to expressed willingness to help others. He found no significant relationships.

In summary, the research evidence does give some indication that experiential and service learning programs may have a positive effect upon the development of a positive self-concept in those students involved in such a program. More research must be done in order for that evidence to be definitive.

Moral Judgment Studies

Alexander (1977) investigated whether or not moral thinking, ego development, and the lessening of prejudice in youth could be changed by an alternative education curriculum. Significant changes were discovered in moral reasoning, ego development, and lessening of prejudice.

Edwards (1974) studied experiential education as it relates to moral development, and explored the influence of environment upon moral reasoning development. Studying 103 high school and university students in Kenya, she confirmed the following hypotheses relating to the effects of intellectual and social experiences. 1) Students who attended multicultural secondary schools displayed higher levels of moral judgment than did students who attended ethnically homogeneous schools. 2) An atmosphere of mutual trust and cooperation stimulated students in preconventional (Stages One and Two) reasoning postures to develop toward more adult postures (Stages Three and Four). 3) Students who resided at boarding schools displayed more Stages Three and Four moral reasoning than did students living at home. 4) Students who studied law and social sciences displayed more Stages Three, Four, and Five moral reasoning development than did students who studied primarily science and engineering.

Reck (1978) attempted to determine whether or not participation in a school service learning program was positively related to moral development, whether the amount of time given to service was related to students' positive moral development, and whether students with little experience in service activities experienced more moral development than students with more prior experience. On only two of sixteen variables was there significant difference between experimental and control groups. 1) Students who pretested low in moral development demonstrated greatest gains in the post-test. 2) Students who served only during the program in their assigned tasks showed significant growth.

Mosher (1977) concluded that moral and ego development can be enhanced by service learning programs, with the most powerful being those that combine discussion of moral issues with the experiences.

Although the research results in the area of moral judgment are mixed, they do tend to indicate that experiential and service learning programs may have an impact upon the development of moral judgment. What have not been answered are the questions of what are consistently effective ways in which moral judgment may be developed; what types of students will benefit from what programs; and what formats will be most successful.

Intellectual Learning Investigations

Houser (1979) recorded significant gains in an experimental group versus a control group in the development of both reading skills and self-concept at the seventh- and eighth-grade level. Students participated in a student-aide program involving elementary school students.

Lewis (1977) recorded significant gains in his investigation of whether learning by doing (experiential learning) was as effective a method of teaching subject matter concepts to adolescents and adults as was expository learning. Although, in a number of situations, expository learning was effective, learning by doing coupled with receipt of procedural knowledge learned both by declarative and procedural knowledge was more effective.

Hedin (1987), in a comprehensive meta-analysis on peer tutoring by high school students involved in service, found increases in reading and math achievement scores both on the part of the tutor and tutee. Although the achievement score increases in reading and math were modest, the author defends

the analyses on the basis that small increases are evident with most learning and growth in general.

Hamilton and Zeldin (1987) found that when the measuring instrument is a general test of knowledge, there is usually no difference between students in service programs and those in conventional classrooms who do not participate. Consistent gains in factual knowledge have been found, however, when researchers have used tests designed to measure the kinds of information students were most likely to encounter in their field experiences (Hamilton, 1987).

Braza (1974) studied fifteen experimental and eight control group students in an attempt to discover significant gains in knowledge, behavior, and attitudes recorded as a result of a community-based, service learning procedure. Control group students received traditional classroom instruction in health problems of disadvantaged groups, while the experimental group students were given intensive community experiences. Post-test results demonstrated that both methods were equally effective in promoting knowledge gains; in addition, both groups expressed essentially identical increased commitment to the study of health problems of disadvantaged persons.

Markus, Howard, and King (1993). The authors report results of an experiment in integrating service learning into a large, undergraduate political science course. Students in service learning sections of the course were significantly more likely than those in the traditional discussion sections to report that they had performed up to their potential in the course, had learned to apply principles from the course to new situations, and had developed a greater awareness of societal problems. Classroom learning and course grades also increased significantly as a result of students' participation in course-relevant community service. Finally, pre- and post-survey data revealed significant effects of participation in community service upon students' personal values and orientations. The experiential learning acquired through service appears to compensate for some pedagogical weaknesses of classroom instruction.

Thus, the findings on intellectual learning and participation in experiential and service learning programs are mixed. It may be that positive intellectual outcomes are found most frequently for tutoring because it is the form of service learning that is most "school like," and the knowledge and skills examined are most like those the tutors have been using. In the instances when students in other forms of experiential and service learning have been tested for gains in factual knowledge, the results have been less conclusive. In most cases, the test instruments used to measure intellectual gain were developed by the same individual responsible for the service learning program, therefore raising questions of researcher bias and lack of test validity.

Community Impact and Effects on Those Served

Ellington (1978) studied the effects of contact with and education about the elderly in three experimental classes of high school seniors. Although no differences were discovered between students who received only contact with the seniors and the control group, and none were discovered between the attitudes of the two groups receiving inductive and deductive teaching, the study did find that a combination of contact with the seniors and learning about their problems appeared to positively change young peoples' attitudes.

Glass and Trent (1989) concluded that adolescents' attitudes toward the elderly can be changed through classroom experiences.

Owens (1979) sought to determine whether or not student attitude toward academic and vocational goals would change in a positive direction after involvement in a year-long, service learning program. He concluded that students in the experimental group experienced significantly larger attitudinal changes than did the control group in the areas of more positive self-confidence and more clarity in educational direction and career paths.

Shroup (1978) sees service learning as a viable alternative to the set secondary curriculum, and as a valuable method for expanding the traditional classroom experiences to promote citizenship attitudes.

Clayman (1968) in a study of training pre-service teachers to become familiar with community resources discovered that although student teachers were committed to using the community as a resource, supervision of their activities was complex and difficult.

Conrad (1979) chose eleven experiential and service learning programs from various cities for intensive study. The eleven programs from nine schools involved more than six hundred students in nine experimental and four control groups; foci included community service, outdoor adventure, career exploration, and community action. The overall conclusions of the study were that experiential education and service learning programs can promote social, psychological, and intellectual development, that they appear to do so more effectively than classroom-based programs, and that the key factors in promoting growth are: 1) that the experiences be significant and provide for the exercise of autonomy; 2) that there be opportunity for active reflection on the experience.

Keene (1975) examined whether students involved in an elective, high school sociology course, where classroom instruction was coupled with five hours of volunteer, direct experience per week for one semester at various social agencies, would have a more positive attitude change toward poverty and minority problems than students who took only a required political science and economics course. She found no significant difference in the groups, but the experience was perceived as positive by parents, students, and the community, so was continued.

Newmann (1978) found negative results on attitudes when elementary students were placed in contact with severely emotionally disturbed children, as compared to those who received classroom instruction on working with handicapped children.

Tobler (1986) conducted a meta-analysis of 143 studies on drug prevention programs and found that peer-helping programs were identified as the most effective on all outcome measures.

Sprinthall and Sprinthall (1987), reporting on a series of studies of high school students engaged as teachers, tutors, and peer counselors, observed that in addition to other gains, many students had developed higher-level counseling skills than those achieved by graduate students in counseling.

The findings on community impact and the effects on those served are primarily positive, indicating that young people enrolled in experiential education and service learning programs which focus upon making a difference in terms of community do, in fact, positively affect community members. In addition, the attitudes of young people frequently are significantly changed in the process of helping others.

Evaluation of Colorado Service Learning Programs

Kraft, Goldwasser, Swadener, and Timmons (1993). The evaluation of Service Learning Colorado was conducted by a team of researchers from the University of Colorado at Boulder. It looked at all K–12 Serve-America, the Youth and Conservation Corps, and the Higher Education programs funded from grants made by the Commission on National and Community Service to the Colorado State Commission. In order to give the readers a sense of the wide range of possible outcomes of service learning, the following table indicates the impact domains, participant and teacher attitudes, participant behaviors, and institutional and community impacts which were looked at in the Colorado research.

Legend:

   I = Interviews
   O = Observation
   PP = Pre/Post Instruments
   D = Documentary Evidence (Journal, videos, tapes, photos, news articles, student records)
   S = Surveys

Impact Domains	Serve America	Higher Education	Youth/Cons. Corps
Participant Attitudes			
Civic/Social Responsibility...........	O/I/PP	PP	O/I/P
Self-Esteem.......................	O/I/PP	PP	O/I/P
Leadership........................	O/I/PP	PP	O/I/P
Poverty...........................	O/I/PP	PP	O/I/P
Career Aspirations	O/I/PP	PP	O/I/P
Moral Development	O/I	PP	O/I/P
Empowerment.....................	O/I/PP	PP	O/I/P
Service/Community	O/I/PP/D	PP/D	O/I/D/P
Gender	O/I/PP	PP	O/I/P
Alienation	O/I/PP	PP	O/I/P
Social Justice......................	O/I/PP	PP	O/I/P
Race	O/I/PP	PP	O/I/P
Efficacy	O/I/PP	PP	O/I/P
Environment	O/I/PP	PP	O/I/P
Peers.............................	O/I/PP	PP	O/I/P
Elderly	O/I/PP	PP	O/I/P
Younger Children...................	O/I/PP	PP	O/I/P
Handicapped	O/I/PP	PP	O/I/P
Family	O/I/PP	PP	O/I/P
Reflection	O/I/PP	PP	O/I/P
Cross-Cultural Exp.	O/I/PP	PP	O/I/P
Teacher/Professor/Director Attitudes			
Above List of Attitudes Plus			
Relationship to Academic Learning....	O/I/PP	PP	O/I/P
Rewards for Service Learning.........	O/I/PP	PP	O/I/P
Students	O/I/PP	PP	O/I/P
Time Spent	O/I/PP	PP	O/I/P
Caring and Compassion..............	O/I/PP	PP	O/I/P

Participant Behaviors

Attendance........................	D	—	—
Grade Point Average	D	PP	—
Basic Skills Scores.................	D	—	D
Service Performed	O/D	O/D	O/D
Interpersonal Relationships..........	PP/S	PP/S	O/I/S
Group Interaction	O/D	O/D	O/I/D

Institutional and Community Impacts

Connections to Curriculum	O/I/D	D	—
Institutionalization	O/I/D	D	—
Teacher/Professor/Director Behaviors....	O/I/D	D	O/I/D
Services Delivered	D	D	D
Community Awareness	D/S	D/S	O/D/S
Reflection	D/S/I	D/S	O/D/S

Over 2,000 students and staff from middle school through higher education responded to the pre- and post-attitude survey which follows. The survey instrument was developed by the researchers and based on previous research on the effects on service learning. Among the results of the pre/post attitude survey were the following.

1. There were few items on which the students made statistically significant gains in positive attitudes toward service, possibly due to the short time frame of most of the programs, often only once a week for 6–8 weeks.

2. Teachers, all of whom had received grants to administer service learning programs, were significantly more committed on almost all items to the goals of service learning than were their student participants.

3. There were few statistically significant differences between middle school service learning participants and those in high school as far as their attitudes toward items on the service learning instrument. This could be seen as a surprising finding as research by the Search Institute (1993) found that high school students were significantly less committed to serving others than younger students in grades 6–8.

4. Students in higher education tended to be more positive in their attitudes toward service learning than students at the younger grades.

5. Short-term service learning experiences did not have a statistically significant effect either way on attitudes of students.

6. On almost all attitudinal items, girls were significantly more positive in their attitudes to service and related values than were boys.

Attitude Survey of Students and Staff

Legend:
    1 = SA = Strongly Agree
    2 = A = Agree
    3 = N = Neutral
    4 = D = Disagree
    5 = SD = Strongly Disagree

Item	Student Pre-test Mean	Student Post-test Mean	Staff Post-test Mean
1. People are poor because of lack of effort.	3.22	3.12*	*3.76*
2. Individuals have a responsibility to help solve our social problems.	2.48	2.54	*1.57*
3. People have little control over being poor.	3.25	3.31	*2.95*
4. The problems of unemployment and poverty are largely the fault of society rather than the fault of individuals.	2.91	2.98	*2.70*
5. It is important to help others even if you don't get paid for it.	1.86	1.83	*1.57*
6. People should only help people they know, such as close friends and relatives.	3.85	3.90	*4.27*
7. It is the responsibility of the community to take care of people who can't take care of themselves.	2.67	2.80*	*2.16**
8. It is my responsibility to do something about problems in our community.	2.59	2.59	*1.72**
9. I feel uncomfortable around people with handicaps.	3.67	3.67	*3.91*
10. Success in life is not really dependent on how hard I work.	3.72	3.83*	*3.87*
11. I decide what to buy because of what a product does (or does not do) to the environment.	2.82	2.90*	*2.32*
12. I am happy with who I am.	1.79	1.79	—
13. I don't worry much about others less fortunate than myself.	3.71	3.79	*4.17*
14. I try to stay in good physical shape.	1.93	1.92	1.98

15.	We should preserve our environment even though there is pressure to develop it.	1.94	2.00	*1.56*
16.	I think I can make a contribution to solving some of the problems our nation faces today.	2.41	2.37	*1.83*
17	Using land for parks and wilderness is a waste of valuable land.	4.22	4.17	*4.65*
18.	Maybe some people do not get treated fairly, but that is not my concern.	3.89	3.83	*4.37*
19.	It takes too much time to recycle newspapers, cans, and bottles.	4.28	4.22	4.33
20.	I don't think or worry much about what's going on in the world because I can't do anything about it.	3.91	3.88	*4.36*
21.	People should give some of their time for the good of other people.	1.97	2.00	*1.64*
22.	My involvement in the community improves the lives of others.	2.40	2.30*	*1.81*
23.	I have helped out on special projects in my community.	3.05	2.49*	2.02
24.	I feel comfortable around people who are from different races than me.	1.90	1.85	1.72
25.	People from other cultures should try to fit in to American culture.	3.14	3.10	2.91
26.	My family supports my involvement in community service.	2.38	2.23*	—
27.	Being around elderly people makes me uncomfortable.	3.85	3.84	*4.10*
28.	Women need an education just as much as men do.	1.46	1.49	1.13
29.	Adults don't give kids credit for being as capable as they are.	2.71	2.76	*1.98*
30.	Reflecting on my experiences makes them more meaningful.	2.37	2.39	*1.62*
31.	Getting an education will help me get the job I want.	1.46	1.43	—
32.	I enjoy learning in school.	2.30	2.36	—

33.	I value being the member of a team.	2.01	1.98	*1.63*
34.	Learning to work alone is more important than learning to work in a group.	3.30	3.35	*3.83*
35.	I feel that my teachers care about me.	2.37	2.49*	—
36.	What I learn from my teachers means a lot to me.	2.26	2.29	—
37.	When I work on group projects in school, I only like working with my friends.	2.91	2.91	—

Questions on Staff Questionnaire only.

a	I feel that the students I work with care about me.	—	—	1.95
b.	I don't mind spending the extra time to structure service learning programs in the community.	—	—	1.99
c.	It is important for students to develop a sense of caring and compassion for others.	—	—	1.36
d.	Service should be closely tied into the curriculum.	—	—	2.04
e.	My fellow teachers or co-workers support my service learning activities for students.	—	—	1.99
f.	I enjoy teaching and/or being around students.	—	—	1.30

*   *Statistically significant difference at the .05 level between pre- and post-survey for students.*

**   *Statistically significant difference at the .05 level between pre- and post-survey for staff. Pre-test means not listed.*

Bold/Italicized: Statistically significant difference at the .01 level between the post-survey for students and the post-survey for staff. Items 4, 5, 6, and 27 are significant at the .05 level.

Self-Concept Inventory
Read the following sentences and circle that which best describes you.

Legend:
1 = A = Always
2 = AL = A Lot
3 = S = Sometimes
4 = SE = Seldom
5 = N = Never

Item		Pre-Survey Mean	Post-Survey Mean
1.	People feel good when they are around me.	2.40	2.32*
2.	I talk with people who may feel left out.	2.54	2.49
3.	I help people see that things can change.	2.65	2.63
4.	I help people talk to each other.	2.81	2.78
5.	People try to copy how I act.	3.42	3.33
6.	I listen to and understand people around me.	2.17	2.21
7.	I like to help others meet their goals.	2.51	2.52
8.	I complete things that I start.	2.26	2.25
9.	I try new things.	1.93	1.93

*   *Statistically significant at the .05 level between the pre- and post-surveys*

Chapter 4 Outdoor and Environmental Education

Tasting the Berries:
Deep Ecology and Experiential Education

by Bert Horwood

Gary Synder (1977) dedicates his little book, *The Old Ways,* to Alan Watts with the remarkable words:

> *tasting the berries*
> *greeting the bluejays*
> *learning and loving the whole terrain*

This poem is, at the very least, an account of education at its simplest and best. Direct experience is central. The complete world, including one's self, is the arena. Learning and loving are linked together with a kind of easy light-heartedness. If such thinking and feeling were to be taken seriously (but not too seriously), what sort of education might result?

One of the problems inherent in experiential education is that its modalities are mor-

ally flexible. They have no clear intrinsic moral value. This argument has been developed elsewhere (Horwood & Raffan, 1988a), and here I'll only assert the claim that an adventure event (for example) like a ropes course, could as easily train powerful terrorist teams, as it trains high-performance management teams or promotes healing in a wounded personality. The special excitement in linking deep ecology with experiential education is to see what happens when the values of one are attached to the instructional methods of the other.

Joseph Meeker (1980) says that tragedies end in funerals, but comedies end in weddings. The path of survival with joy is through the comic. This article attempts to "taste the berries and greet the bluejays" by examining the synergy when ideas from deep ecology and experiential education are brought together. I will compare the two movements and offer some guiding principles which will enable the people in any program to learn and love "the whole terrain."

Deep ecology and experiential education have much in common. Both are products of the late twentieth century. Both take the form of a modern rediscovery and recreation of ancient ideals gradually lost in the materialism and alienation of Western culture. The two movements have experienced an increasingly powerful impact from the work of women. Both have uncomfortable relations with their respective mainstreams; they are somewhat radical and touched with a distinctly disreputable air.

These similarities spring from the fact that both movements present a critical shift in central values. In the case of deep ecology, it parts from mainstream thought by shifting the centre of its concern from human beings to the biosphere. In big words, it moves from anthropocentrism to biocentrism. Deep ecology also goes beyond science as the best, or only, way of knowing. Thought is taken to include feelings and spirituality, the entire range of mentality. Experiential education, likewise, shifts concern from what teachers can teach from their experiences to what the students could learn from their experiences; in short, a shift in the centre of concern from teacher to student. Like deep ecology, experiential education tries to see things whole.

Just as the experiential education movement seeks to eliminate those discriminations which exclude people from its processes, so the deep ecology movement seeks to remove discriminations which would put one species of life above another in terms of value and importance. Respect is the key attitude. Henley (1989, 1991) shows how students, living in primitive conditions with experienced elders, gain respect for their knowledge. That respect for the person, in turn, generates respect for the place and important general learning results.

There are numerous accounts of deep ecology as a system of thought and as a way of life. The best of them are cited by Dolores LaChapelle (1991). Her article is an excellent primer, well suited for experiential educators.

The deep ecology literature is strong in its philosophical development. Its ends and values are clearly and powerfully stated. It lacks a matching educational framework for the transmission and inculation of those values. Conversely, experiential education possesses powerful instructional methods which can be bent to a variety of ends. Most experiential education has served progressive social purposes, but its literature and practice reveal a variable and relatively undeveloped moral framework.

The methodological implications of deep ecology are highly compatible with experiential methods, and the value implications of experiential education are close to the values of deep ecology, although more restricted to the human species. The logical end for progressive value-based experiential education is the adoption of deep ecology values. Together, there would emerge a more powerful way to influence the transformation of the world toward some set of comprehensive, biospherically benign principles.

There are two reasons for believing that such a transformation is critically needed. First, the principles are right because they

Bert Horwood

include virtues such as respect, wholeness, justice, and community, among others. Second, the world, and our place in it, will not survive if we do not undergo such a transformation.

What would experiential programs look like if they were to include the values of deep ecology? There are such programs already in existence. Dolores LaChapelle describes one. The Institute for Earth Education programs, such as Sunship Earth and Earthkeepers (Van Matre, 1990), are other examples. Rather than provide a specific program description here, I will give a set of general guiding principles which any such program must have. It is important to note that I mean to include all forms of experiential education, including adventure, therapy, work experience, and so on, because the synergy is general.

I have chosen five principles that are convenient and useful, but I do not claim they are absolute. The many connections among them invite other patterns of organization. The principles are: place, wholeness, identity, integrity, and wildness.

Place includes both knowledge and feeling about one's place, in this case the program site. Whatever the special goals of the program, participants should know something about the other inhabitants of the place, where they come from and go to. What plants and animals are there? How is the land formed? Where is the North Star? The sunrise? Where does the drinking water come from and where does it go after it has been drunk? Similar questions apply to the food, shelter, and materials in use.

Dolores LaChapelle (1991) speaks of the use she and Rick Medrick make of the concept of "affordances." Self-propelled expeditions in remote country invariably teach people that the terrain affords people certain opportunities and denies others. For example, strong headwinds make paddling impossible on an arctic lake, and the open tundra offers no shelter for pitching tents. But a short distance away, there is a grove of shin-high willow. Here travellers are afforded shelter and a place to rest. They gratefully recline under the willows among musk ox scat and learn to see the sky through a different screen.

Experiences like this teach participants that the world affords people opportunities to climb, to sleep, to eat. When participants look for what the place affords, and use the affordances, they live and work in the place harmoniously. They force things less. Place also becomes more personified and less objectified. We become a little like Schultz's cartoon character, Sally Brown, who knows that her school building is a person and talks to it regularly.

Such knowledge should promote feelings of belonging to the place, of experiencing its hospitality, first as a guest and later as a full member of the household in that place. To feel like a guest leads to different behaviour than to feel like an invader. To feel owned by the place has very different consequences than to feel like an owner. For example, travellers who feel like guests feel less guilt for being in the place. They also take care due to motives of profound gratitude and respect rather than from duty, which is more likely to fail. There is more to be said about hospitality as an analogy for the principle of place, but I will reserve it for another occasion.

In my dream program, there would be no water on tap. Participants would, as a matter of routine, need to pump or haul it to meet their daily needs. If I could, I'd extend that to all the ordinary aspects of everyday life,

including shelter and food supply. Participants would routinely kill their own food, whether animal or vegetable. The principle of place, whether the program was therapeutic, recreational, or environmental, would require participants to be able to live their lives harmoniously within the affordances which the place offered.

The principle of *wholeness* is meant to be comprehensive. It refers to wholeness within each individual and to wholeness in the context of the place. It also implies a healthy balance among factors of risk and safety; intellect and spirit; giving and getting; sacred and profane. Wholeness means that there would be moments of profound solemnity and moments of total hilarity. Demands on muscles would be matched by the demands on brains. The community of participants would be matched by times of solitude and independence. Planning would be larded with spontaneity.

The principle of *identity* is an antidote for the alienation which most of us carry to some degree. The malaise of our dominant Western culture is alienation from self, society, and our fellow creatures. Arne Naess (1985) provides a full development of the concept of identification in deep ecology. When persons move from alienation to identity they begin to know themselves and to recognize that they share a common identity with other beings, human and nonhuman. It is the difference between a person trying to protect a wild river from a dam and feeling that one is the wild river protecting itself. This is an advanced stage of identification known to be achieved by aboriginal people but reached in the present Western culture by only a few.

There was a countrywoman driving into town who noticed a neighbor holding a small

Ottawa Valley 1969 28

Bert Horwood

pig up into an apple tree to reach the apples. On her late return, he was still there with the pig. She stopped and observed that he had been holding the pig up for a long time. He replied, "What's time to a pig?" That's identification.

It will take continued exploration to learn how to do the hard work needed to increase identity within participants. Certainly there must be ceremonial and celebratory events because they emphasize relationships and kinships. There needs to be sensitive and respectful living in the place, not accidentally, but with deliberate intention to know it in a new way. One example is to experience a place alone for the purpose of coming to know it rather than for the purpose of personal trial or vision-questing. For LaChapelle and Medrick, tai chi is an essential ingredient in the mix. In other programs, paying close attention to the world with all the senses is a means to increase identity. It is impossible to do this fully without the presence of poetry, chanting, drumming, and dance because they arouse sensory acuity and permit expression of it beyond the limits of rationality.

There are also things that need to be avoided. One is any programmatic tendency to promote ideas of domination. No one can develop identity when one is trying to dominate, predict, and control. Rather, program operation should be accepting of times and events. Searching for affordances and enjoying them is the way to set aside our desire to dominate everything around us.

The principle of *integrity* refers to the congruence between the values espoused by a program and those actually driving practice. There is a strong tendency in Western culture for organizations to become self-serving while claiming to serve others. In attempting the radical shift to deep ecological values, any person or group may easily fall into shallow lip service by making superficial changes on a fundamentally unchanged perspective. Walter Raleigh was asked by his executioner whether he wished to face east. He replied that it mattered not which way the face was, so long as the heart was right. The principle of integrity requires that both heart and face be right.

One difficult example is the practice of no-trace camping. It is fatally easy to adapt a kind of doctrinaire self-righteousness that leads participants to believe that they can travel and live in a wilderness area without impact. It is possible to go lightly, but even shadows have impact. Furthermore, the advanced technologies which make low-impact camping possible invariably have very large impacts elsewhere in our earth home. It is not clear why one region should enjoy low impact at the expense of another. Integrity requires that a program practice, to the fullest extent, what it claims to teach.

This example also raises the point that, as abundant mammals on the earth, human beings are bound, even entitled, to have an impact. Just as I assert the right of skunks and mosquitoes to be here in harmony, I assert the right of my fellow humans to live out their lives likewise.

The principle of *wildness* comprehends all the others. It calls for high value to be placed on the cultural and technological power of the primitive (Horwood, 1988b). By primitive, I mean that state of things which people can do entirely with their own personal resources and energy. The word is not meant to have any negative context nor to imply any sort of deficiency. Here, primitive is the cultured counterpart of citified (civilized).

Wildness also refers to the ultimate in freedom to be: to be oneself; to be in rela-

tionship and community with one's fellow beings; to live and die as a full-fledged, mature animal. To accomplish that kind of wildness, there must be appropriate initiation leading persons to know themselves and to know their respective paths. Wildness is both serious and comic, rich and frugal, but it never includes license and irresponsibility because there are always dire, inescapable consequences.

The primitive quality of wildness also provides for simplicity in everyday acts and materials. Bannock baked on a stick is wilder than when baked in a reflector oven. Labrador tea is much wilder than instant coffee. This is not to oppose technology, but rather to choose, always, those techniques which are simplest and most direct.

Robert Bly (1990) presents a vivid account of the potential within humans to be wild, to find the low, the wet, and the simple. "Little dances are helpful in the middle of an argument as are completely incomprehensible haikus spoken while in church or buying furniture" (p. 223).

I have tried to show that there is a good match between experiential education and deep ecology. From the latter come principles which are recognizable, even friendly, to experiential educators. To integrate the two is to reverse the mainstream and to embrace a very long-term view of things. It is like the very old woman who wanted to plant a black walnut tree in her garden and was advised against it "because they take a hundred years to mature." She insisted, "That was all the more reason to plant the tree today." I think that woman knew the taste of berries and how to greet the bluejays.

Wilderness Keeping by Wilderness Educators

by John C. Miles

Twenty-five years ago, Joshua Miner, a founder of Outward Bound USA, wrote that "We train *through* the mountains and not *for* them..." (Miner, 1964). Outward Bound aimed to use a wilderness experience to help its students grow in confidence and personal competence. Whether they learned anything about mountains or wilderness was incidental. The quarter-century since Miner wrote these words has witnessed a large growth in the use of mountains and other wildlands for such education. Tens of thousands of people enter the wilds in organized schools searching for insights into themselves.

While Miner and his colleagues were building their school, conservationists were battling for legislative protection for the "mountains" so important as a resource for education. They achieved a measure of this protection in 1964 with passage of the Wilderness Act in the U.S. As of 1990, there are more than ninety million acres of official wilderness in the U.S., yet even as these acres are protected from mining, logging, and other development, there is concern for the wilderness values such as naturalness and solitude for which these lands are protected (Cordell & Hendee, 1980).

Wilderness lands are, in many places, being used and degraded by people who love and value them. Fragile vegetation is trampled by too many lug-soled boots. Limbs are stripped from trees to fuel campfires. Trails widen in moist meadows until they become large, ugly brown scars. Water pollution increases, and solitude is often impossible because of too many noisy and thoughtless wilderness neighbors. Some users even want a tame wilderness. In Washington's North Cascades, for instance, an argument rages over whether to encourage the return of the grizzly to a large block of grizzly habitat from which they were driven decades ago. The debate is fueled by concerns of some wilderness travelers that grizzlies in "their" wilderness will increase danger and reduce their ability to enjoy themselves. Such threats to the integrity, beauty, and wildness of wilderness indicate that this scarce and limited resource cannot be protected only by laws and boundaries.

Management agencies like the U.S. Forest Service are responding to the problems created by too much use and ill-behaved users. Fires are increasingly being banned, numbers of users limited, and permits required. Recently, for instance, the author arrived at a trailhead only to be greeted by a prominent sign informing him that *day use* permits were required. Elaborate signs are increasing in size and number at trailheads as managers try to send people where they want them and to educate them about good backcountry behavior. Managers call this the "indirect" approach to management of wilderness users—inform and educate rather than control and direct. Increasingly, though, control and direction occur, and

David Gross/Public Image

home to do their part to assure sustainability of nature and civilization. Education in wilderness can help build ever greater appreciation of the values preserved in wild nature, such as biological diversity, ecological stability, and the wonder and excitement that come with encounters with "vast and titanic" nature, as Henry Thoreau called it in *Walden*. Such education can provide perspective on how humans can and should relate to the underlying nature which nurtures them. Students can learn the meaning of conservation, stewardship, and sustainability, and all of this can be done while pursuing the personal knowledge that Miner viewed as the primary purpose of the Outward Bound experience (Miles, 1987).

Educators who use wild places for teaching can do much to assure that such places remain wild and beautiful, healthy natural systems which support plants and animals threatened nearly everywhere else by human activity. They can and must educate themselves, their students, and land managers on how to use wilderness while nurturing wildness there. Offered here are suggestions gleaned from the author's personal experience and from the growing literature devoted to this problem.

casualties of this situation are not only the accessible beauty spots of wilderness and the experiences of silence and solitude, but also the very "freedom of the hills" which so many seek there.

Experiential educators are a large, important and growing wilderness user group, and the time has come for them to teach *for* the mountains as well as *through* them. They must teach responsibility for nature and wildland values. They must help their clients learn the special lessons about nature and human nature which may be revealed in wild places, lessons which may help them back

Basic Principles of Teaching For Wilderness

1. Wilderness is a finite resource requiring constant care and stewardship by all who go there. As Will Rogers said of land, "They

ain't making any more of it." The National Wilderness Preservation System is growing, but the actual wilderness acreage is declining. There will likely never be more than at present.

2. The opportunity to teach in wilderness is a privilege, a rare gift, and thus carries with it great responsibility. Those who travel in wildlands must care for them. If they do not, then who will?

3. Wilderness should be used for education only when the lessons to be taught can best be learned there. Programs must be matched to places.

4. The ultimate salvation of wilderness lies in caring for earth generally. Students must learn that their actions on the environment at home bear directly on the future of wilderness. Islands of naturalness surrounded by degraded environments cannot endure.

5. Use of a wild place inevitably creates an impact upon that place. This impact, even when the user consciously tries to minimize it, is a small increment in the long-term change and degradation of wild places. One solution to this it to consciously seek ways to mitigate these incremental impacts through good works for wilderness, such as restoration, clean-up, and similar positive actions in the field. Wilderness educators must teach the mitigation and "no net-loss" approaches to wilderness use (Miles, 1988).

Another necessary part of the solution involves political action, for forces are at work to reduce wilderness, to convert the wild to the "useful" (read, "economically beneficial"). Political action has been critical to protecting wilderness up to the present, and may be even more crucial in the future. The

political story can be told and students urged to use their growing personal power (such as the empowerment gained from their wilderness experience) to work in political arenas on behalf of wilderness and the environment in general, as well as on other important political issues.

Preserving Wildness and Minimizing Impact

After the boundary is drawn around a piece of wilderness, the paradoxical enterprise of wilderness "management" must begin. The managers are usually government people, and their aim is to allow use of the wilderness while maintaining the values for which the wilderness area was established. Their greatest challenge is to do this management without reducing the quality of the experience for the wilderness user, who often goes to the wildlands to escape management.

Wilderness educators can and must work with these managers. Education is, in fact, one of the major tools of management, and a very desirable one (Fazio, 1979). In theory, the more users understand what they must do to maintain wilderness values, the more likely they will be to voluntarily care for them and the less managers will have to resort to active regulation. A goal of both users and managers is self-regulation.

The following are suggestions as to how wilderness educators might work with managers:

1. Adopt self-regulation as an organizational goal. This involves learning what managing agencies think are the best practices for responsible wilderness travel. A wilderness program might, for instance, adopt a policy of no campfires in sub-alpine

regions under any but the most dire emergency situations. Discussion with managers and constructive criticism of their programs, as well as thorough organizational self-examination, may be part of this self-regulation. The educational organization and the agency must see themselves as partners in using and maintaining the scarce wilderness resource.

2. Insist on consistency of management between agencies and throughout the Wilderness Preservation System. The National Park Service and Forest Service, for instance, should be consistent in the requirements for visitors, especially in areas where wilderness units under their management are adjacent to each other. Different wilderness environments (lakes, deserts, seashores, mountains) require measures specific to them, and users and managers must work together to understand the special requirements of each place and establish fair and effective approaches (Hampton & Cole, 1988). Users need consistent and predictable approaches and must work with managers to achieve them. Educators can assist agencies in developing consistent *educational* approaches throughout the system.

3. Knowledge of wilderness problems and solutions to them is at an early stage of development. Managers need help in acquiring resources to do research necessary to identify the most effective ways to avoid and to mitigate degradation of wilderness. Wilderness educators must work together to assure that more resources are allocated to wilderness research. At the same time, they should insist that wilderness management agencies raise wilderness research in their list of research priorities.

4. Training of staff for wilderness schools should include an extensive element about how to travel responsibly in wilderness and how to teach students about doing so. Agencies should require such training as a condition of issuing special-use permits, and should devise ways to assess the effectiveness of staff training about responsible wilderness use.

5. Many of the most experienced wilderness travelers are instructors for wilderness schools. They know from experience what needs to be done to reduce and mitigate impacts. The National Outdoor Leadership School has taken the lead in developing and disseminating information about how to travel responsibly in wilderness. *Soft Paths* (Hampton & Cole, 1989) is an excellent example of such work. Wilderness schools should go a step further and work with agencies to develop guidelines on how users might work to mitigate their inevitable impacts. These guidelines should be published and distributed by the agencies when they issue permits.

6. Wilderness educators might work with managers to develop regional wilderness education teams to tailor training schemes to the particular challenges of specific regions. Such teams might include representatives from management agencies as well as resource people from outside agencies. Experienced educators from wilderness schools should serve on these teams. This service function is a direct way schools can work toward the reduction of their impacts. The teams should work with schools, youth groups, outdoor recreation clubs, and other organizations who use wilderness.

David Goss/Public Image

Finding the Lesson in the Field

The educator training *through* the mountains can educate *for* them without sacrificing the program's personal growth goals. Incorporating this goal into the program mission is the first step. Once this goal is affirmed, many opportunities will present themselves. Effective education for wilderness is always a combination of planned and serendipitous programming. No comprehensive list of techniques for accomplishing the goal can be presented here, but several general suggestions are offered:

1. A central lesson to teach is that wilderness is not just a "resource" for humans but a living community with its own needs. What animals and plants live here, and why are they here rather than somewhere else? What do they need to survive? There is the possibility, for instance, that grizzly bear

and gray wolf populations might be restored to the wilderness areas of the North Cascade mountains of Washington State. Should this be encouraged? Why or why not? Nearly every wild area sustains species which depend on the naturalness of the place. These can be described as a way of pointing out that wild places serve purposes other than the satisfaction of purely human needs.

2. Another lesson which can be taught effectively in wilderness is that humans are an integral part of, dependent upon, and responsible for the welfare of the biotic community. The wilderness experience involves briefly stepping out of the human-built and -dominated environment where people believe they are separate from and in control of nature. In wilderness, new views of nature can be examined. Native peoples at one time lived in many of today's wild areas. How did

they view nature? How did their view differ from ours today? What part of their view might be usefully adopted today so as to assure the "beauty, integrity and stability" of the environment. What does this last phrase, used by Aldo Leopold to describe the goal of lands ethics, mean to us? Emphasis must be placed on transferring these ideas back home so that students have a changed view of the human relationship to the natural world. Wilderness experience can thus be a powerful element of a person's overall environmental education.

3. Once students have been introduced to the idea that they are citizens of the biotic community, they must be helped to understand the responsibility that goes with such citizenship. This can be explored in terms of their responsibility in this unusual setting—wild nature—in which they find themselves. Practicing minimum-impact techniques for camping and travel in wildlands is being responsible there. The idea of minimizing impact upon the environment in general is a simple and powerful one. Students can learn that minimum-impact behavior is no less important outside the wilderness boundary, and can be helped to explore its meaning in all aspects of their lifestyle.

4. Reflection is a powerful tool used to address many of the primary goals of experiential education. So, too, with wilderness education. As many teachers have discovered, wilderness is an especially good place for reflection. The solo experience is the most commonly used vehicle. Students may be urged to observe their environment and reflect upon what they find there. They may be given tasks to focus their observation, such as inventories of natural creatures they see (perhaps using field guides and keys),

writing assignments aimed at challenging them to focus their awareness on specific elements of their environment, or philosophical prompts such as quotations which may focus their thoughts on particular problems or ideas. Educators sometimes think the place is the teacher, and often it is, but there is still a need for a program to set up experiences which force students to reflect (Stremba, 1989).

5. Wilderness educators can and should be models of curiosity and caring while in the field. They should go into the field knowing as much as they can about the natural and human history of the wild place they are visiting. Leaders should be hired not only for their technical and interpersonal skills, but also for their desire to learn about and knowledge of place. When the students wonder about a plant, tree, cloud, or animal track, etc., the leader may share what she knows. Or, she may say "I don't know, but I want to find out. How might we do it?" People often take their natural setting for granted. A wilderness education experience can be a powerful reminder that nature can be an infinite source of wonder and discovery. A teacher interested in this wonder and discovery is essential to awakening these processes in students.

6. Nature is full of surprises. Leaders go out with plans, with carefully developed learning programs, only to encounter many unexpected circumstances which upset the schedule. One of the virtues of wilderness is its unpredictability. The challenge is to make this into an asset. Understanding the virtues of the "teachable moment" is particularly useful to wilderness educators, simply because more such moments seem to appear out there than in other learning settings.

A classic case in the author's personal experience was the eruption of Mount St. Helens in May 1980. Students were in the middle of a wilderness field trip, two hundred miles north of the mountain, when it erupted. At first there was uncertainty about what the series of concussive explosions that broke the morning silence might be. No jets in sight. No clouds. The group knew the mountain was acting up—"Could it be the mountain?" they asked. Most went on solo that day and watched the sky turn gray as the ash cloud spread overhead. The leader confirmed, from a Forest Service person who hiked in bringing the big news, that the mountain had indeed erupted, and left word at solo checks that this colossal natural event had occurred. Reflect on it, he urged them. They did, and when the solos were over, there was exciting processing of their experience of this unusual natural event. The group gazed south off toward the mountain, over tens of thousands of wilderness acres from their discussion site high on a ridge, and reflected on the nature of nature and their experience of it. They were humbled and impressed by the scale of the event, struck by the fact that while humans generally feel in control of nature, here was a clear indicator of the limitations of that control. This is an exceptional example of an unplanned opportunity for teaching, but multitudes of less dramatic teachable moments have occurred during the author's twenty years of teaching in wilderness settings. The importance of being flexible and alert to the spontaneous learning opportunity has been revealed time after time.

Wilderness education can and should be the vehicle for an educator to humbly share himself or herself to a degree unusual in conventional teaching. It is an opportunity to serve as a Socratic midwife, working with an environment of great power to help learners bring forth their potential as persons. If the importance of wilderness education as a complement to conventional schooling is recognized, and if wilderness places are respected and cared for, as they must be to survive, then teaching and learning in wilderness will continue to play an important role in educating responsible biotic citizens of the future.

The Failed Curriculum

by James Raffan

Nature lessons have been taught as long as there have been schools and teachers. However, the term "environmental education" only began turning up frequently after the 1972 United Nations Conference on the Human Environment. Environmental education encompasses activities designed to instill knowledge and values for and about the non-built world. But is it working?

First, let me narrow the scope of activities under consideration for the purpose of answering this question. While environmental education occurs in many places, I wish to confine use of the term to include only environmental lessons in schools and environmental education centres. Some points will be generalizable, but most are derived from Canadian experience. In this paper, I examine environmental education's main goal, decide if it's being met, and offer a personal perspective for re-orientation.

Is it Working?

Hines et al. (1987) conducted a meta-analysis of research into environmental education and concluded, "It can now be said that the development of environmentally responsible and active citizens [is] the ultimate goal of environmental education" (1987, p. 1).

Responsible environmental behaviour ranges from picking up litter to conscientious civil disobedience. Sia et al. (1986) surveyed environmentalists and isolated eight predictors of such behaviour including environmental sensitivity, knowledge of action strategies, practice in implementing environmental action strategies, knowledge of sex role classification, and a healthy attitude about pollution. Surprisingly, school experience was not listed as a predictor of environmentally responsible behaviour in this study.

School *was* mentioned in a 1989 environmental poll conducted by the Angus Reid Group in Canada. Surveying over three thousand adults and grade-eight students, they learned that only *one percent* of Canadians credit school as the most important source of information on environmental issues (results can be generalized to all Canadians to within 2.5 percentage points, nineteen times out of twenty; Ludlow, 1989).

So here is the situation: environmental education's ultimate goal is to develop environmentally responsible citizens. Evidence reveals that environmental education is not a predictor of such behaviour; one in one hundred people say school is the most important source of information on environmental issues. Conclusion? Environmental education is failing in a grand way!

As an environmental educator, I want to cry out "They're wrong!", but I fear that some of what the researchers have found is true.

In my own study into the backgrounds of environmentalists, school is never credited as a driving force. These people—a fighter for old growth timber in Oregon, a citizen struggling to keep a toxic waste incinerator out of his county, a Texan forester who has set aside his comfortable government salary to take people into the wilderness on ecologically sensitive trips—have fire in their eyes that I rarely see in schools. They are emotionally involved! Perhaps we are too clinical in our lessons. It is plausible that we are doing something wrong.

What is Wrong?

In a recent column, environmental guru David Suzuki wrote: "Science is a powerful way of knowing. It is based on the replacement of subjective, emotional experience with objective observation, free of distortions of personality and replicable anywhere and any time." Strange that Suzuki's throwaway "subjective, emotional experience" is what seems to drive effective environmental action. Biographies of environmental award recipients confirm a common *subjective and emotional* bond between activist and action (McDonald, 1990; Caldicott, 1990; Outdoor Canada, 1990).

Winners of the 1990 Goldman Environmental Prize "for men and women of vision and courage who take great risks for the environment" illustrate just how little conventional science has to do with making a difference. Prize-winning physician Bob Brown, for example, became Australia's most notorious environmentalist by being robbed, shot at, and set upon by thugs in his battle to save the Franklin River in Tasmania (Time 1990). Clearly there is more to Brown's quest than facts and figures!

Scientifically derived knowledge is important, but it is not the only way of knowing. Bloom (1956) defines cognitive, affective, and psychomotor domains of learning. Howard Gardner (1983) details at least five types of knowledge in his theory of multiple intelligences. M.I.T. researcher Marvin Minsky (1985) suggests an infinite number of ways of knowing in his book, *The Society of Mind*. Whatever the number, like Suzuki, I suspect environmental education is guilty of selectively highlighting cognition and of undervaluing—or ignoring— other ways of knowing.

The spin-off of this in day-to-day terms in environmental education centres is a preponderance of sheets (pieces of paper for students to fill in while they are outdoors) that give the *illusion of science* to outdoor lessons. On the basis of a year-long study of two outdoor teachers (Raffan, 1986), I concluded that there may even be practiced deception in environmental education on the part of teachers who disguise noncognitive outcomes of learning (cooperation, leadership, communication, commitment, expression of emotion, etc.)—to which the natural environment is so well suited—in favour of the trapping of natural science. Only in therapeutic outdoor settings—where science can in good conscience be left out—can the subjective and emotional outcomes of learning be addressed and even celebrated in the open.

Allegiance to science affects environmental education's place in the school system. In 1988, the Ontario Ministry of Education released new guidelines for environmental science, giving teachers detailed curricula for five courses in Grades Ten through Twelve. This prompted just over a quarter of Ontario's secondary schools to offer their students one or more courses in environmental education (Cundiff, 1989). While this initiative represented a significant increase in the amount of environmental education activity in Ontario schools, two serious problems remain: 1) the guidelines do not call for *action* on the part of the students; and 2) as a subject, environmental science is not a prerequisite for any university program, nor, under the Ontario's guidelines, can it be taught at the university-entrance level. A disgruntled Toronto teacher is quoted as saying, "I've always fought the Ministry of Education's attitude that environmental education should be an alternative for students who are unsuccessful in the 'real' sciences" (Cundiff, 1989). Second-class science will never save the world.

A low priority on environmental education is also evident in the United States government, which spent $3.5 million dollars in a recent fiscal year on the Office of Environmental Education, about half the amount spent on helicopter and limousine service for the executive branch (Williams, 1979).

Enterprising classroom teachers still manage to get students outside for environmental education lessons, but it is a chore that requires tenacity. Occasional field trips are not enough. I underline the words of another Ontario teacher who cried: "Environmental Science [read outdoor lessons] should not be part of the academic roster. It's disruptive to the status quo. It doesn't fit in. They miss time in other subjects." It's okay to skip school to play football or basketball, but it's not okay to skip school to learn about the environment (Cundiff, 1989).

Other teachers, who themselves may feel insufficiently qualified to conduct environmental education lessons, are left with the opportunity of arranging a visit to a nature centre where students are exposed to the wisdom of experts away from their home turf. Who knows how much learning transfers back to the kids' sphere of personal action? More insidious perhaps is the fact that while instruction at environmental education centres is *supposed* to buttress study in class, connections between nature centre studies and in-class curriculum are tenuous at best. In reality, most of what occurs at outdoor centres is throw-away schooling—it may have an impact on the students who visit, but it is never catalogued, evaluated, or valued by the curriculum planners.

Other writers contend that environmental education itself is the problem. In a scathing attack on what he calls "the new environmentalism," A.T. Williams (1979) says environmental education is meaningless because it "integrates many different disciplines but often seems to be taught partially and incoherently, with virtually no thought to its organization, philosophy or design." Rudy Schafer, by contrast, says that environmental education is suffering from "The dung-heap syndrome." This is a destructive condition in which environmental education practitioners stress a holistic view of the environment and yet live without action in a world divided into independent patches of curricular turf, each competing for attention and resources (Schafer, 1979). Ted Williams says simply, "We have replaced good, old-fashioned nature study of Liberty Hyde Bailey and Rachel Carson with Environmental Education.... Rather than nurturing the natural sense of wonder in our children, we lecture them [on subjects] that bore even the lecturers" (Williams, 1988).

Some of the most exciting initiatives in environmental action are occurring in schools, but *not* as a planned result of instruction. Environmental clubs, recycling groups, student action committees are leading whole communities—and often teachers—into new forms of responsible environmental behaviour. Almost in spite of environmental education, change is occurring, driven by industry, television, and other forms of mass media.

It is time we paid attention to what *is* working. It is time we worked to rectify wrongs and to get environmental education a passing grade! We must work to integrate problems, settings, and solution finding across subject disciplines and eradicate the paralytic effects of the dung-heap syndrome. We must start paying attention to research and the ways of knowing that really drive environmental action. We must start acting, close to home, outside, in city hall, on local issues, and beyond the curricular cover of scientific respectability. We must educate ourselves first.

Earth Education: Learning to Live More Lightly on the Earth

by Bruce Johnson

Like the first Earth Day in 1970, Earth Day 1990 focused our attention on our planet's environmental problems. Almost overnight, rain forest destruction, ozone depletion, acid rain, and species extinction have become topics of everyday discussion. People are concerned about the quality of life on earth. The concern of 1970 was followed by the apathy of the '80s. Will the same thing happen today?

Once again, more and more people are calling for the education of young people as the long-term solution to the environmental crisis. It seems clear that children need to be taught at a deep level that the earth is our home, how life on this planet functions, that we are a part of those systems of life, and that how we live affects life as a whole. Equally important, they need to experience the natural systems and communities of life, to form direct, personal connections with the earth. And in the end, they need to learn how to lessen their impact on the natural world.

In 1970, the educational response in North America was something called "environmental education." Based on the belief that teachers were already overwhelmed by what they were expected to teach and could not handle another new curriculum area, it set out to infuse environmental messages into the existing school curriculum, mainly through collections of activities that were mass produced and distributed to the teachers.

The infusion approach has not worked. Dozens of collections of activities were produced in the 1970s, mainly with government or corporate money. Most went out of print when the money dried up in the 1980s, and those still around are mostly collecting dust on teachers' shelves. Most of these activities were to be used in isolation or at random; the activity guides do not even suggest to the teachers that they need to come up with a way to tie them together or that there are certain fundamental ecological concepts that are crucial for understanding how life works.

Another problem with environmental education is that it ended up being something different to everyone who did it. To some, it was performing acidity tests in streams or identifying the trees; to others, it was orienteering or picking up litter; to a few, it was lecturing about the causes of species extinction. But to most, it was nothing, because they did not do it.

Educators need to do much better in the '90s. We need to take seriously the renewed call for education. Overworked teachers do not need another supplemental collection of activities to put on their shelves. Children do not need a few isolated lessons sprinkled here and there throughout their years in school.

In most cases, environmental education is seen as fluff, something that is fun to do if the time and resources are there; it is usually

Model Earth Education Programs

Earthlings™ — 4- to 5-year-olds — building a sense of wonder and place. Designed for pre-schools and day care centers, this program is being developed now. The first pilots will be starting soon.

Nature's Family™ — 6- to 7-year-olds — dealing with the characteristics and the needs of life. We are getting ready to begin major piloting.

Lost Treasures™ — 8- to 9-year-olds — emphasizing the characteristics of plants, animals, and minerals, and the natural communities they share. There are components that take place both in the classroom and on excursions to museums, zoos, arboreta, and several natural areas throughout two full school years. We are piloting the program now.

Earth Rangers™ — 10- to 11-year-olds — based on one day away from school initially, with another day later in the year. A trash can that arrives in the classroom with messages and a riddle from the two "rangers" sets the stage for the program, while ongoing notes from the rangers and another riddle keep up the excitement and help the participants keep track of their progress.

Earthkeepers™ — 10- to 12-year-olds — pre-trip activities, a three-day magical outdoor experience, and follow-through activities at home and school. Now published and in operation at numerous places across three continents.

Sunship Earth™ — 10- to 12-year-olds — an intense, action- packed, five-day experience that includes crawling inside a giant leaf to learn about photosynthesis, searching for a missing passenger to learn about the ways living things interact with each other and their surroundings, becoming bloodhounds to sniff out natural scents, and venturing into the shady side of the planet with the old "nightwatcher" to get immersed in the world of darkness. It includes pre-trip activities in the classroom, the five-day outdoor experience to assimilate the concepts and experience the natural world, and follow-through back in the classroom to transfer the understandings and feelings into personal action.

SUNSHIP III™ — 13- to 15-year-olds — revealing the hidden ways we use energy in our lives. A dynamic program, it challenges early adolescents to see that there are different ways to view the world and different choices to make about how they live on the earth. Every waking moment of this three-day program is an integral part of the learning, from journeying to the "Solarville Pizza Parlor" to discover the many hidden energy costs in our everyday lives, to working in the "Cycle Factory" to get the air, water, and soil cycles operating smoothly; from witnessing a rendezvous between endangered species and the figure of death, to wearing permits to use energy and materials for everything from washing hands to wearing clothes. It is now being prepared for publication after nine years of piloting.

Earthways™ — 16- to 18-year-olds — helping each other gain personal responsibility while exploring the richness of the planet. Nearly ready for piloting.

For information please contact
The Institute for Earth Education
Cedar Cove
Greenville, West Virginia 24945, USA
(304) 832-6404.

the first thing cut in a school's budget. Much of that is due to the fact that it is presented as supplemental and superficial. Our society has never approached any kind of education that was felt to be important in such a random way.

The 1990s may be our last chance to adopt a serious response to the environmental crisis.

Earth Education

Earth education is the process of living more harmoniously and joyously with the natural world. With earth education, we take a different approach from that followed by environmental education. Our focus is on carefully crafted, sequential and cumulative programs rather than random, isolated activities. Earth education programs are exciting, fun-filled adventures that go from the head to the heart to the hands, from understandings to feelings to processing.

The understandings focus on basic ecological concepts. The four major concepts that are vital to understanding how life works are: the flow of energy, the cycling of materials, the interrelating of life, and the changing of form. Rather than getting caught up in the minutiae and details, the facts and figures, the big picture concepts are presented. It is far more important to understand how sunlight energy is captured by green plants and turned into food for all life than it is to memorize the names of wildflowers.

Earth education programs are based on the belief that people learn best by doing. They bring abstract ecological concepts into the concrete by using hands-on and minds-on activities that include all the participants and which are an obvious and integral part of a whole program. Rather than just being

an isolated piece, the "doing" fits into an overall learning model.

Understanding: the I-A-A Learning Model

People learn by taking something in, doing something with it, and using it. For example, in the Earthkeepers™ program for upper elementary students, the participants each have a training manual. To learn about the flow of energy from the sun through a food chain, they first read a description of how this works in the training manual (inform-I) They then take part in the "Munch Line Monitors" activity (assimilate-A). After a brief demonstration of a "munch line" or food chain, they head out with "munch counters" (tally counters) to find and count evidence of munching, including green leaves capturing sunlight, insect holes in tree bark, and so on. They then gather evidence of different kinds of munchers on "munch trays," which have separate compartments for "sun-munchers" (green plants), "plant-munchers" (animals that eat plants), and "animal-munchers" (animals that eat other animals). Finally, they sort out the contents of brown paper munch bags containing evidence or pictures of several munchers. They put them into the proper compartments of the trays and find out that often a top predator is at the end of several food chains. Afterwards, the participants find an example of a food chain in the natural world and draw or describe it in writing on an example page in their training manuals (apply-A).

The Feelings

The feelings are *just* as important as the understandings. The four major feelings earth education programs address are: a joy at being in touch with the elements of life, a kinship with living things, a reverence for natural communities, and a love for the earth. Developing these feelings requires firsthand contact with natural places.

In Earthkeepers, one of the activities that helps build these feelings is "E.M.'s Diary." Introduced at the beginning of the program, E.M. (pronounced em) is a mysterious, unseen character who loves to share the marvels and mysteries of the natural world. E.M. often explores new areas and keeps track of those times in a diary. Using E.M.'s diary and an accompanying map, the students explore one of those places and re-live the adventures E.M. had, finding the "miniature world" and using hand lenses to explore it, sitting silently at a "listening post," and building a wonderful sense of discovery.

Processing

The processing components in each program ensure that the learning transfers back to the participants' lives and that they actually change some of their habits in order to live more in harmony with the earth. The processing components are: internalizing understandings for how life works on the earth, enhancing feelings for the earth and its life, crafting more harmonious lifestyles, and participating in environmental planning and action.

At the end of the three days at the Earthkeepers Training Centre, participants in the Earthkeepers program choose tasks to work on back at home and school to complete their training. They choose one way each of using less energy and fewer materials, two experiences in the natural world

near their home or school, and four ways of sharing their knowledge and experiences with others. Rather than being the entire program, the initial three-day experience away from school serves as a springboard for what happens for the rest of the school year.

Creating a magical learning adventure, though, requires more than just the understandings, feelings, and processing components. "Hookers" pull the participants into the learning and "organizers" help them hold on to what they experience in a meaningful way. For example, in the Earthkeepers program, the learners visit "E.M.'s lab," a special room set up as a nature lover's nook, when they first arrive at the Earthkeepers Training Centre for their three-day visit. The mystery of the room along with its unseen character, E.M., "hook" the learners, motivating them to become Earthkeepers. E.M. also serves as an "organizer" for the program; the letters stand for key components of the program. In Earthkeepers, there is another hooker and organizer, KEYS. The learners earn four keys during the program, and the letters in KEYS also organize the parts of the program for the learners— Knowledge, Experience, Yourself, and Sharing. Each of the four keys the participants earn unlocks a special box and reveals one of the secret meanings of E.M.

In The Institute for Earth Education[1], we develop model earth education programs that others can use (see Table), or help them build their own programs for their own settings and situations. We are designing model programs for every age, from Earthborn™ for infants to Earthbound™ for adults. Some of our model programs are published and are already running in a number of places around the world. Others are still in the developmental and piloting stages. What all earth education programs have in common is an underlying structure based on beliefs about how people learn and interact with the natural world. Steve Van Matre's new book, *Earth Education... A New Beginning,* describes in detail what earth education is and how to go about designing an earth education program.

All earth education programs are magical learning adventures that aid participants in forming some good environmental habits and breaking some bad ones. They offer a serious educational response to the increasing human impact on our home and the life that shares this planet with us. We at the Institute for Earth Education are convinced that there is no more important task in the world today.

NOTES

1. The Institute for Earth Education is an international, non-profit educational organization whose purpose is to develop and disseminate earth education programs. Founded in 1974, the Institute offers training workshops and members' conferences, and publishes a seasonal journal, *Talking Leaves.* There are active branches of the Institute operating in Australia, Britain, Canada, France, and the United States. For more information on becoming a member, purchasing materials, taking part in a workshop or conference, finding out about becoming a pilot site for one of our model programs, or obtaining a copy of our free sourcebook, contact the Institute at:

The Institute for Earth Education,
Cedar Cove,
Greenville, WV 24945, USA,
(304) 832-6404.

The Experience of Place:

Exploring Land as Teacher

by James Raffan

During the last decade, powerful images of people in conflict over land have slowly burned themselves into the consciousness of people around the world. In Canada, for example, emotion-charged blockades have become symbols of land use disagreements amongst people of different traditions. The Innu in Labrador, James Bay Cree, Algonquin of Barriere Lake, the Teme-Auama Anishinabai in Ontario, Alubicon in Alberta, Haida of the Queen Charlotte Islands, and the Dene/Metis of the Mackenzie River valley have all fought in one way or another with governments over land. Perhaps best known in Canada are the Mohawks of Kanesatake near Oka, Quebec. At the height of that conflict, in the midst of barbed wire, tear gas, guns, and assault uniforms, stood Mohawk Ellen Gabriel, who asked quietly, "Why should someone die for nine holes of golf? This is crazy?"

The struggles of Canadian aboriginals are mirrored around the globe in the lives of the Yanomami in northern Brazil, the Mbuti of the Ituri forest in Zaire, the Suma of the Honduran Mosquitia, the Kuna of Panama, and the Pehuenche of Chile. Fights between indigenous peoples and dominant cultures are symptomatic of a global problem, which is while growth continues in every sector of almost every economy, the total amount of land available for use remains about the same. Competition for resources—land particularly—can only increase.

If the conflict at Oka is in any way an example, these conflicts are not so much fights about land use, per se, as they are dramatic differences in points of view about what land means. To the developer, land may be a commodity that can be bought and sold; to the recreationist, land can be a place of haven from technology; to the industrialist, land may represent timber, ore, or energy potential; to the aboriginal, land, in all its dimensions, may be an integral part of a god-centered universe. So while a land conflict may focus on functional issues like timber rights or golf, the fight itself is more likely rooted in the deep-seated emotional bonds that tie people to places. To say that a Quebec Police corporal's death at Oka was "for nine holes of golf" was a gross oversimplification. Unfortunately, in the case of the Mohawks of Kanesatake and the town council of Oka, there was nothing available, no words or literature or existing understandings previously articulated to help others comprehend these two very different interpretations of what the disputed land means. Unfortunately, there is very little empirical research having to do with *how* people of specific cultures are attached to specific pieces of land, except to say that, by

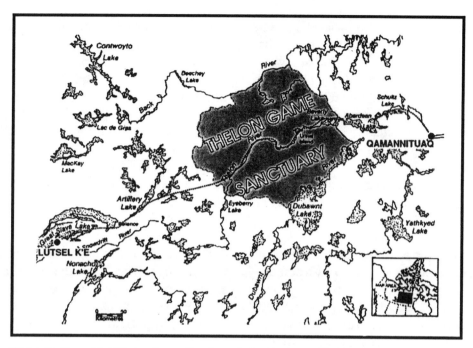

Figure 1: Map of the Thelon Game Sanctuary in the Northwest Territories, Canada.

and large, people who are closest to the land are prepared to die for it.

As an outdoor educator, I have been increasingly disturbed by this gap between knowledge and understanding. Like many of my colleagues, I assume that spending time outdoors will make a difference, somehow, in acquainting my students with land, with nature. But when it comes time to assess or to prove what students have learned outdoors, efforts always come down to functional, testable knowledge—the names, the facts, the figures. The rest of the outdoor experience, the part that lingers in the heart, that goes home in story form, the part that touches the world—these are almost always eclipsed by the need to appropriate, commodify, and quantify what is learned. We seem to know very little about the affective bonds to place—the very outcomes of learn-

ing that may well drive land conflicts around the world. This article reports on a study of people's attachments to place.

The central organizing idea of the project was land-as-teacher. Having travelled extensively in the wilderness and served as an outdoor educator of one kind or another for 20 years, I acknowledge the cognitive aspect of these experiences—the names, the facts, the figures—but I also must acknowledge my love for the natural world, and the role these wild places have had in shaping who I am.

The piece of land I chose to investigate was the Thelon Game Sanctuary, a large nature preserve in the barrenlands in Canada's Northwest Territories, set aside in 1927 to protect musk oxen. I had travelled through the region in the early 1980s for six weeks by canoe and had been moved by its sheer presence as a location—barren, beautiful, powerful, austere, wildlife rich. The research idea was to collect for analysis: every available impression of this place, including those found in archival and library sources; impressions gleaned through solo travel inside the sanctuary; and conversations and time spent with the Chipewyan Dene from Lutsel K'e (Snowdrift) and the Caribou Inuit from Qamanittuaq (Baker Lake), who have both historic and contemporary knowledge of the area.

The intellectual context of this inquiry was shaped by the writings and traditions of cultural geography having to do with perceptions of environment, landscape, agency, and sense of place; with the growing and sometimes scattered literature of environmental issues and concerns, especially in the areas of deep ecology, bioregionalism, and spirituality; aspects of discourse in ethnology and anthropology, in particular writings about so-called "new ethnography"; and, of course, by the literature of Canada and the land. (Selected readings are noted in the bibliography following this article.)

Perhaps the most penetrating works about people/place relationships were written in the last two decades and have to do with symbolic representations of landscape as found in regional novels and other fiction. Dansereau (1975) was among the first to pick up on Hopkins' theme of symbolic *inscape,* writing not about physical settings but about landscapes of the imagination. The most creative and interesting investigations of people's symbolic understandings of place arise from writers who have gone beyond literature into the lived worlds, art, popular culture, language, and iconography of everyday interactions between people and place (e.g., Cosgrove & Daniels, 1988; Jackson, 1989; Moss, 1990; Porteous, 1990; and Tuan, 1990). This literature points to the possibility that the information I was seeking was internal, as impressions and intuitions often are, as opposed to external types of knowing which have to do with conscious observation, reflection, and analysis, the kind of knowledge that typically fills the reportage on land disputes. Early on, in the absence of an abundance of literature about the Thelon Game Sanctuary, it became clear that I would have to visit the land and to attempt, at least, to enter what Porteous calls the *paysage interieur*—the interior landscapes—of the people who know it best.

Yi Fu Tuan, in many respects leading the writers in this field, points to the existence of something called sense of place, but even he has resisted the temptation to take the concept into the field to attempt to empirically derive a value or values for group X's sense of place. Hay (1988) attempts to pin down a definition for sense of place but in the end, all he can say is this: "How place...is constituted in everyday life, especially the assumptions in modern people's thought...is largely unknown. People's emotive bonds to place...have seldom been studied" (p. 159).

If I were to begin to understand emotive bonds to place, beyond the facts and figures, literature indicated that I would have to go to that place and feel the experience it had to offer; but more importantly, one would be obliged to contextualize what people say and know about land in the land itself. The need to explore sense of place *experientially* was clear.

The study was founded on five assumptions: 1) that place knowledge is not exclusively determined by culture; 2) that experience on land plays an important role in shaping sense of place; 3) that place knowledge cannot be expressed easily in words; 4) that one should not expect to advance and build upon ideas about sense of place by continuing to use only written sources of data; and 5) that interacting with people using a variety of capture devices in the field would allow some of these other ways of knowing to be included in discourse about place.

The formal findings of the investigation are detailed elsewhere (Raffan, 1992); however, in this article I wish to focus on the role of primary field experience and the experiential learning process in exploring the notion of land-as-teacher.

I went initially to the Chipewyan settlement of Lutsel K'e, on Great Slave Lake, to establish the collaborative context for the work and to secure permission from the band to proceed. Later that winter, I returned and spent several weeks speaking with elders and other community members about the Thelon. Conversations in people's home were interspersed with day and overnight trips out on the land to hunt and fish with people as they told me about their land. Lutsel K'e highlights included community festivals, prayer gatherings, lots of wonderful conversation, and an extended journey by snow machine onto the barren lands to hunt for musk oxen and caribou.

More or less the same pattern of interaction was used in Qamanittuaq in the summer months to learn about the Inuit perspective on the Thelon. The experiential cornerstone of my efforts to understand the Euro-Canadian perspective of the Thelon was a three-week, solo canoe journey though the heart of the sanctuary.

Three types of findings—or texts—emerged from each cultural experience: written texts came from available literature; spoken text came from interviews with key consultants in each of the three groups; and experiential texts were written from time spent on the land in the communities as recorded in photographs, audio tapes, and personal journals. After spending a total of 20 months on the project—9 weeks and 1,200 km on the land, 6 weeks and 33 interviews in the communities, and 25,000 km in chartered bush planes and commercial flights—the experience was reduced to 574 pages of transcripts, 45 hours of audio tape, 960 pages of journal entries, and 3,500 photographs. All that needed doing when the information field experiences were complete was some kind of massive debriefing to complete the experiential learning cycle.

The main processing technique I employed was writing, capitalizing on current anthropological trends (Barnes & Duncan, 1992; Geertz, 1988; Clifford & Marcus, 1986) and Tuan's (1991) narrative-descriptive approach. Tuan's main point is that language itself has built into it interpretive and explanatory categories delineated by the prose itself. He discourages undue reliance on theoretical constructs to make sense of human experience because:

> theory, by its clarity and weight, tends to drive rival and complementary interpretations and explanatory sketches out of mind, with the result that the object of the study—a human experience, which is almost always ambitious and complex—turns into something schematic and etiolated. By contrast in the narrative descriptive approach, theories hover supportively in the background while the complex

phenomena themselves occupy the front stage. For this reason, the approach is favoured by...scholars who are predisposed to appreciate the range and color of the life and world. (p. 686)

I chose to narrate a path through the available written texts; to create visual and verbal portraits of consultants which were followed by blocks of their spoken texts; and finally to draft a story, based on my journals, of what it was like to live and travel alone and with Dene and Inuit people in the vicinity of the sanctuary.

Several scholars, including Tuan and Porteous, have suggested in passing that to access other ways of knowing, researchers should try other ways of thinking about human phenomena. Porteous (1990) writes:

Despite recent humanistic revolutions in psychology, sociology, and geography, society continues, as yet, to revere technical science and remains skeptical of the insights to be derived from poetry, introspection, free-association, and other 'unscientific' forms of knowing. This is ill advised.... It is my contention that literary and artistic expression, whether ours or that of others, is essential in helping us to experience the world around us in a richer, more authentic way. (p. 283)

With that in mind, I set out to augment what I was learning about people's attachments to the sanctuary through writing, with attempts at verse and visual art.

The following poem, after the Inuktitut word meaning "land," was written in response to experiences with the Inuit in Qamanittuaq:

NUNA

Nu Nun Nuna Nunavut
Sastrugi
Parallel ridges of snow

Mark here, and there
And the line that joins yesterday
with tomorrow
Nu Nun Nuna Nunasila
Here is a good place for wolf
the caribou cross here in summer
Where is here?
Where is there?
There is here.
We went there when I was young.

Nu Nun Nuna Nunaissaqanituq
Ajurnarmat
It can't be helped
We are equally thankful
for all that the land provides
People live. People talk. People die.
What frequency do you need
to link with a Tapir-i-sat?

Sa San Sanct Sanctuary
An invisible line
that tethers meat from hungry mouths
The stranger with the striped pants
flies in the air
Could he be God?

Nu Nun Nuna Nunatsiaq
People live. People hunt.
People go to the Bay.
People talk
of times gone by
of times yet to come
in a beautiful land
Moving—always moving
Across invisible landscapes
Until the game runs out,
and they begin again.

Uu Kanata saalagijauqunak . . .

The exercise of writing the verses allowed ideas to crystallize from the mass of data and

Figure 2: "Learning from Lutsel K'e" by James Raffan.

sensory impressions generated by the study. In itself, the poem becomes a sketch of Inuit perceptions of place for a reader, but in addition it embodies perhaps something of Inuit land sensibility, and mine, both derived of the Thelon Game Sanctuary.

"Learning from Lutsel K'e" (see Figure 2) is one of several interpretive drawings that attempts to capture themes implicit in the lessons of life, travel, and conversation in Lutsel K'e. Although it is difficult to say whether the ideas in the image came before, after, or as a result of producing this image, I'm convinced that drawing it did play a significant role in making sense of the study data.

One of the main motifs in the image is the way in which land comes between people and the creator: in fact, it was described by several people as being the connection to the creator, represented by the bright light in the sky. Other elements in the drawing are the right road, the red road, the four quadrants of knowledge, the fire of life, the old ways represented by the tipi, the circle of life represented by the incomplete wreath of smoke that takes prayers from the land to the creator. The break in the smoke indicates that times have not always been good in Lutsel K'e, connections to the land have been broken in the modern era, but the old ways are still there if people choose to find them again. An outside viewer may see other symbols and pertinent iconography in this image, and I suppose that is both one of the strengths and shortcomings of going beyond words in analysis of this kind. The beauty of any visual image, created in response to experience, is that it provides stimulus for further conversation, further writing, further processing of the experience; alternatively, it can be left to stand without further comment, likewise with poetry.

Using the narrative-descriptive approach, in concert with poetry and visual art, four principle components to sense of place emerged, four ways in which people in the study were attached to place, four types of knowledge invoked and celebrated by the land as teacher.

First, there is the *toponymic* component having to do with place names and with the process of naming places. The Chipewyan and Inuit have a much more fully developed and finely tuned system for place naming (and a more developed sense of the sanctuary) than most Euro-Canadians, but I think it is interesting that the historical and contemporary Euro-Canadian figures with the most detailed knowledge of the sanctuary all had their own names for places in the Thelon area, and this I take as an indication of their rich knowledge of the local area but also as an indication of their attachment to the place. The interesting thing for me was that most of the names used by people were not to be found on any published map. They were names derived from personal or family or prior-community experience on the land.

Secondly, there exists a *narrative* component to sense of place. There were stories about how the land came to be (i.e., "in the beginning"), or how things used to be (i.e., "long ago"), and tales of current travel on the land (i.e., our snow machine trip from Lutsel K'e to the sanctuary in the spring), and even gossip in Lutsel K'e about Inuit posturing and inflated claims, and vice versa, to support argument that the other was trying to curry favour with federal land negotiators. All of these types of narrative demonstrate the connections to land of the teller, the listener(s), and of the cultures in which the dialogians are immersed. What sets apart Inuit and Dene narrative from most Euro-Canadian stories of place, is that the native narrative is integrated into the mix of place names and personal experience that has been used for many years by the elders to teach young people about land and survival.

The third form of connection of people to place is what might be called an *experiential* link to the land. One can learn names of places from a map or from listening to stories told by an elder, or one can read about the place in a magazine or see slide shows, but without any kind of *personal* experience on the land itself, any sense of a place, any emotional bond to land, appears limited. I must add, however, that it appears that not every experience in the sanctuary leads to a deepening of sense of place. Trip reports indicated that it was possible for a person to paddle through the sanctuary and return with no appreciable new insights or observations of what the land was like or what the land had to offer. Listening to many returning canoeists in conversation confirmed this possibility.

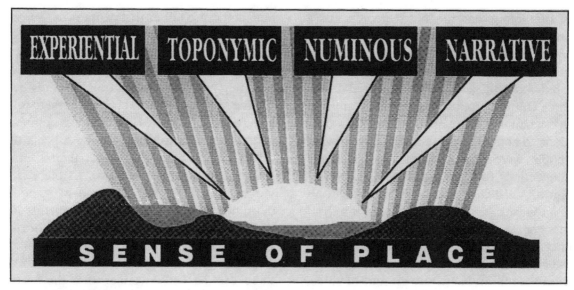

Figure 3: Four types of knowledge invoked by the land.

One very significant type of experience with place that emerged was *dependence* on the land. I was struck by the difference in detail and substance between the comments of people (of any culture) who trap or hunt for survival, or people who were dependent on the land for survival, and people who merely visited the sanctuary on a self-contained canoe trip. The trapper or hunter knows the land in intimate detail, while the canoeist often has a hard time conjuring up images of even places where camps were set, to say nothing about which way the water flows, which way the prevailing wind blows, where the game feeds, or when the winter comes. The only time when a canoeist's depth of land knowledge would approach that of a hunter or trapper was when the canoeist became—willingly or serendipitously—dependent (or helpless) through starvation or need for wood heat or shelter. From the moment of dependence, the knowledge of a person about a place can make an

almost exponential jump in magnitude, perhaps because at this point the land experience becomes a defining feature of that person's character.

The final people/land connection revealed by this study is a *numinous* attachment, the spiritual bond between people and place. There can be no doubt that for my Inuit and Dene consultants, and for a small number of Euro-Canadian contributors, there was in their thinking a sense of divine presence in their encounters with the land. People in Lutsel K'e spoke of the land as an embodiment of the great works of the creator, and as such a link to the creator, a link to understanding. The omnipresent aura of the creator was to be recognized through payments of tobacco or matches or of other considerations of value to the land, for safety's sake and for the sake of honoring the force behind all life. For the Inuit, the times of demons and fears of shamanic beliefs have passed from common cultural practice to the realm of mythology and art, but there remains a powerful belief in the sanctity of land and all connected to it that can't be explained. In the most profound bonds to place I encountered—and these were encountered in all three cultural groups—there was an at times overwhelming sense of inadequacy in words alone to convey the essential nature of what people were trying to convey. Numinous connections to place are all that is awe-inspiring, all that transcends the rational, all that touches the heart more than the mind, all that goes beyond names, stories, and experience and yet still plays a significant role in the bond that links people and place. I saw this in the faces, heard it in the tone of voice, felt it when on the land, and almost never heard about it directly in conversation.

In many ways, the processing of these land experiences is ongoing. Research and common sense tell us that people who act on behalf of the environment are usually first emotionally attached to it. I wonder now, having conducted this study, if I should be spending more time on getting kids outside, to give names to their favorite places, to tell and re-tell the stories of their adventures, and allow them to celebrate the aspects of outdoor encounters that touch their souls. Because it appears that sense of place, in varying degrees, constitutes an existential definition of self. For many consultants to this study, you take away the land or break the connection to land, you prevent them from being who they are. In light of this, there can be little wonder that there are assault rifles on the barricades. Perhaps land negotiations would be different if the people involved, on both sides, shared more of their sense of the place at stake.

A People-to-People Environmental Program in Russia: Experiential Service Learning in Novgorod, Russia

by Harry C. Silcox and Shawn Sweeney

A group of 26 American students, teachers, and environmentalists left the United States on June 20, 1992, to pursue an environmental, community service learning project in Russia. They were part of a people-to-people exchange that had as a theme, the environmental monitoring of Novgorod, Russia, a city with a population of 300,000.

The joint American and Russian environmental service project to the city had three basic goals: 1) to set up a Russian-American environmental learning center; 2) to introduce and provide training in the use of environmental laboratory equipment; and 3) to encourage civic spirit and democracy in Novgorod. The environmental theme also masked an underlying effort to improve relationships between Russians and Americans, which was as important as the environmental theme, especially when viewed from a service learning perspective.

The vision of an independent environmental learning center was

conceived in 1990 by Dr. Harry C. Silcox, Director of the Pennsylvania Institute for Environmental and Community Service Learning in Philadelphia, and Dr. Alexander Popov, a medical doctor who was elected People's Deputy for the City of Novgorod on an environmental platform. Dr. Popov and the city were to provide building space and basic laboratory equipment, and the Americans were to provide the portable monitoring equipment, as well as training in its use. Although construction of the environmental

Using portable environmental measuring equipment, American and Russian students and teachers measure metal content of a small stream that empties into the Volkhov River.

learning center began in November 1991, unbeknown to the Americans, it was stopped in early 1992, which left the project without a laboratory in which to set up the environmental equipment. The Americans, however, arrived with $10,000 worth of donated portable monitoring equipment that they expected to give to the new environmental learning center.

When the Americans arrived in St. Petersburg, they learned that besides lacking a finished laboratory, the Russian hosts had not arranged for Russian families to house the American students. Despite these initial unforeseen difficulties (housing was later arranged for the Americans), the project began to take shape. A room in the city's High School #30 was set up as the environmental learning laboratory.

Although many of the Russian students volunteered for the project solely to have "American tourists" in their homes, this did not interfere with the direction of the project. The dynamics of cultural exchange that emerged from living in Russian homes provided the Americans with ample experience to reflect upon, while the environmental theme gave the students a daily routine.

Despite many obstacles and frustrations, the American and Russian students conducted fourteen experiments on the city's air, water, and soil (see Figure 1). The students traveled on their own throughout the city to get samples, and returned to School #30 to do their testing with the environmental monitoring equipment. The testing procedures used by the American students and demonstrated to the Russian students clearly brought to the forefront the need to improve the environment in other Russian communities as well. In addition,

1. Lead levels in the public water supply
2. Cyanide levels in the Volkhov River
3. Ammonia levels in the Volkhov River
4. Comparison of total iron in the public water supply
5. Ozone levels in the Volkhov River
6. Copper levels in the public water supply
7. Cobalt and nickel levels in the river water
8. Detergent levels in the Volkhov River
9. Soil radioactivity levels in Novgorod
10. Atmospheric lead levels in Novgorod
11. Aluminum levels in the Volkhov River
12. Chromium levels in the Volkhov River
13. Nitrate and nitrate levels in the Volkhov River
14. Conductivity, pH, and total dissolved solids levels in the Volkhov River

Figure 1: List of Environmental Monitoring Projects Completed in Novgorod

reports were written in English and translated into Russian for presentation in both languages during the Novgorod International Environmental Conference from July 6–7, 1992. Additionally, the Russian reports were published in the local newspapers.

The Environmental Conference heightened environment awareness in the community; moreover, noted scientists from Moscow, England, and Norway were also present at the conference. The event was unusual for a city the size of Novgorod and for one so far removed from Moscow. Undoubtedly, the environmental equipment and the monitoring project attracted the attention of Moscow and promoted the attendance of Russians from across the republic.

All of this excitement led to an effort by various groups in the city to "capture" the environmental monitoring equipment for themselves. Jealousies also exacerbated internal disputes between the city's environmental groups. The lack of a finished laboratory for the monitoring equipment further complicated the situation. In order to reduce conflict and encourage cooperation, the feuding scientists and environmentalists were informed that the chemical reagents necessary for continual use of the equipment would be forthcoming only if the environmental learning center was completed and functioning as planned.

In the interim, it was decided that the environmental laboratory would be set up in the Regional Hospital and that it would be run by Ury Pavlovich, a technician at the hospital, who had spent every day at School #30 learning how the equipment worked. This decision was based in part on the fact that Victor Veinstein, a member of the Supreme Soviet and the Committee on Health Protection, Social Security, and Physical Culture, controlled the operation of the city's hospital and requested that the environmental center be placed there to help train doctors to better understand the impact of environmental conditions on health. The decision was also based on the hospital's willingness to provide environmental workshops for teachers, doctors, and students, as well as to establish regular monitoring of the city's environmental conditions. It was clear from the experience that Americans who wish to work jointly with the Russians must be flexible and able to adapt daily. Clearly the Russians are willing and able to pursue joint Russian/American environmental projects if given the opportunity.

Experiential Learning

In addition to the scientific and environmental scope of this project, another object of this program was to use experiential education approaches to promote transfer of knowledge from one cultural group to another. On previous visits to Russia, Dr. Silcox had witnessed attempts by American college professors to provide information about science and business practices. They often failed to promote understanding, however, because of their reliance upon the lecture method and printed documents. (A single word in a translation often took minutes to clarify, and translations often proved futile.)

The Novgorod Environmental Student-to-Student Project, on the other hand, focused on field-based experiential learning with interpersonal connections that extended to the homes of the participating Russians. Neither the Russian students (ages 12-18) nor the American students (ages 14-17) spoke the other's language. Nevertheless, they came to understand one another through the necessities of daily living, games, and the use of the environmental monitoring equipment.

This international experience raised a number of questions: Of what value is community service/experiential learning in transmitting knowledge between cultures? What attitudinal changes were fostered in the minds of American and Russian students? It was clear from the start of the environmental monitoring that to develop and test hypotheses, and to publish the results, were new ideas to the Russian students. The American students found themselves in the position of having to do most of the early scientific work, with some of the Russians (especially the girls) eventually becoming full partners in the project. The Russian boys, however, were particularly difficult to motivate; they exhibited the traditional Russian male attitude that translated into them "knowing best" and refusing female peer guidance. For example, the American girls were especially alarmed at the treatment they received from the Russian boys. "Respecting their culture is one thing," said one girl, "but I'm tried of their treating me as an inferior and not answering me when I speak to them." The American girls had difficulty understanding how Russian girls willingly accepted their passive role.

Despite these cultural conflicts, the American students remained focused on their projects. Special praise must go to Lena Tzvetzinskaya, Russian interpreter and geographer from Moscow University, who acted as translator for the students and teachers. She patiently worked with each Russian student during the experiments, enabling them to complete a written report that formed the basis for the information released to the city. The value of this service was crucial since the city itself had no interpreters with the scientific background to translate the complicated, environmental testing terminology. With the help of local Novgorod scientists, technicians, and teachers, Ms. Tzvetzinskaya also helped the American teachers establish the sites for environmental testing.

The importance of this type of experiential learning to the success of the project reflected itself everyday in the conduct and behavior of the students. Few American students complained about the hardships, such as the lack of food or sanitary conditions. The Russian students became increasingly interested in the environmental results. In their reports, the Russian students unanimously proclaimed a willingness to work on environmental issues and to actively seek solutions to their country's environmental problems. The following examples demonstrate this change:

> I have always tried to contribute useful things to this important work. But before I didn't know exactly what had to be done and who to address. Now that I know, I hope that I shall be able to try myself in this field [environmental activism]. I now feel that I owe more to nature.

> I perceive myself differently because I have communicated with American students, have worked with the environmental equipment, and have understood more things. I must do something to change the ways of my country.

In addition, the Americans theorized that if a Russian boy will not listen to an American girl (even if what she has to say is important), then how could Russian leaders, all of whom are male, be sensitized to environmental issues when they were so insensitive to women? One female student asked, "How are they ever going to learn if they won't listen?"

The above reaction notwithstanding, the farewell exchanges between the American and Russian students were uplifting. The Russians got up early and walked miles to watch the Americans depart at 6 AM. Watching this farewell, one would never have suspected the underlying differences between the two groups. Respect and affection were obvious, but cultural misunderstanding remained an unresolved issue.

Nevertheless, the experiential educational opportunities that placed the American and Russian students together during the project promoted a spirit of public concern and activism. The Russian students escorted their American guests around the city, and openly analyzed and discussed the data gathered at each monitoring site. For the first time in their lives, they were able to measure the damage done to their city by the unsound environmental practices used by the former communist government. This, in turn, resulted in some attitudinal changes on their part, of which the most visible focused on social responsibility. A prevalent view exists among young Russians that "nothing will change," so why try. This attitude is encouraged by the seeming hopelessness of a world that lacks opportunity for self-actualization. Immoderate drinking, smoking, and sexual escapades are to most young Russians far more inviting than any thought of improving the world around them. The authors, however, observed a change in the social attitudes of the Russian students, who began to see their environmental work as a catalyst for positive social change.

Chapter 5

Internships and Apprenticeships

Internship Education: Past Achievements/Future Challenges

by Tim Stanton

Alice laughed. "There's no use trying," she said, "one can't believe impossible things."
"I dare say you haven't had much practice," said the Queen. "When I was your age I always did it for half an hour a day. Why sometimes I've believed as many as six impossible things — before breakfast."

Lewis Carroll

Would you believe that almost every college and university, and many, if not most, high schools offer internships or other experiential learning opportunities to their students? Would you believe that in many institutions these experiences are now required of all students and that nationally, one in seven students is involved in field experience education? That's the "conservative estimate" of the National Society for Internships and Experiential Education, extrapolated from data developed in statewide surveys in Ken-

tucky and Michigan, and from their experience of more than 10 years' service to practitioners of this form of education.

What is internship education? It is a form of learning as old as our civilization, which has recently been rediscovered and reintegrated into modern educational practice. It includes all experiences wherein students learn by taking on responsible roles as participants in organizations, observing and reflecting while they are there. Expected outcomes of such experiences include increased self-esteem and personal growth derived from successfully meeting new interpersonal and intellectual challenges, acquisition of particular skills and knowledge, exposure to various work roles and career choices, and service to a particular community or group.

Internship experiences are found in every sort of organization — non-profit agencies, corporations, government, policy institutes, neighborhood centers, etc. They are open to high school students (and recently even junior high students), undergraduate and graduate students, continuing education students, faculty, executives, unemployed youth. There are internship opportunities for everyone.

Internships can be paid or volunteer, part-time, or full-time. They last anywhere from a few weeks to a year or more. They may be arranged and sponsored by educational institutions (for credit, career awareness, etc.), by work organizations (for personnel recruitment, professional advancement, etc.), by independent organizations and government agencies (to enable students to explore issue areas, policy making, etc.), or simply to provide extra hands for needed tasks. Name an activity and there's probably an internship related to it.

Long before the creation of schools and universities, learning-by-doing was the only way to learn. Craft guilds, apprenticeships, and the continued, informal passing-on of wisdom, skills, and lore were the essential means of teaching. Distinctions between learning and doing, between scholarship and work, arose with the creation of the first universities. Only then did education evolve toward the theoretical, abstract, removed-from-the-practicalities-of-life model, which became paramount by the mid-point of this century.

Early colleges in the United States, patterning themselves after their European sisters, developed curricula which were widely separated from the needs of a newly established nation. It was not until the founding of Rensselaer Polytechnic Institute, in 1824, that field experience learning was organized and sponsored by an educational institution. In this case, students made field trips to factories and coal mines to examine first-hand their subject of study.

Passage of the Morrill Act (1862) represented the first national mandate for systematic application of knowledge. In each state, the "agricultural and mechanical arts" were to be studied and shared with those on the farm who needed and would use them. "Field" work became a natural and integral part of "land grant" students' curricula.

The Settlement House movement of the late nineteenth century added to the trend toward practicality in education and the connection between it and the needs of society. Colleges and universities sponsored human service centers through which students served individuals and groups adjusting to the disruptions of migration and industrial urbanization, an early form of "service learning."

With the inception of professional education, the traditional internship was born. William Osler, Professor of Medicine at Johns Hopkins University, required his medical students to perform autopsies and observe his treatment of patients, a revolution in medical education at the time. Eventually, other professions followed the doctor's lead, developing "practice teaching," "moot court," "social work practica," etc.

Starting in 1906, a few, scattered undergraduate colleges, such as Northeastern, Antioch, and Benoit, began experimenting with "cooperative education," requiring their students to supplement their liberal arts learning with alternative semesters of work or service. Internships and field experience education had developed a small, but firm toe hold in U.S. education, which it maintained into the early 1960s.

What accounts for the recent, exponential growth in internship education? As in so many aspects of life in the United States since 1960, educators were suddenly forced by events, by changing technologies and cultural mores, to shake loose from their traditions. True believers among them began to identify "learning-by-doing" as an answer to a variety of social concerns and educational problems.

In response to the call, "If you're not part of the solution, you're part of the problem," students and faculty rejected the notion of a removed, cloistered curriculum, and worked to combine community service with learning. In the social sciences particularly, internships and practica were developed to relate studies directly to the social problems they were meant to address. Students exercised their social commitment and compassion through volunteer work in neighborhoods and communities surrounding their campuses. Faculty found a means to support their activities with seminars and credit.

Field experience education was seized by other educators and students as a means of reducing the Grand Canyon-like gap that traditional education had erected between learning and career development. Internships were developed to enable students to take on adult roles in a society that was establishing ever-increasing education and professional certification prerequisites for joining the work force.

Not to be left in the dust, liberal arts faculty began to perceive internship experiences as important to both their disciplines and their students' rising clamor for relevance in the curriculum. Through "field studies" and internships, the students were offered opportunities to develop critical thinking, problem solving, communication, and learning-to-learn skills, which faculty grudgingly admitted could be more effectively acquired and practiced in the field than in the classroom.

Then there were the educational critics and reformers. Inspired by the philosophies of Dewey, Goodman, Whitehead, etc., and armed with the theories and findings of Coleman, Rogers, Freire, Kohlberg, Kolb, etc., they saw the purpose of education as holistic, developmental, and political: to enable students to become whole and complete persons, equipped with both "critical consciousness" of themselves and their place in society and the tools, knowledge, motivation, and roles with which to effectively participate in the world and improve it. For these people, linking theory and practice through field experience and critical reflection was the only means of effective, progressive education.

Finally, and most recently, field experience education has been utilized by those working to provide equal access to education and career advancement for such groups as adult learners, women, racial minorities, handicapped students, and unemployed youth. Internships and assessment and crediting of experiential learning have become a means of recognition and certification of the skills and knowledge possessed by individuals previously underserved by and underrepresented in traditional education.

Thus, we find ourselves today surrounded by a large and expanding variety of field experience-based learning opportunities. Whether labeled service learning, cooperative education, field study, or internships, (just to list a few of the names currently in use), these experiences have transformed our thinking about learning and doing and the relationship between the two, and fundamentally changed curriculum and instruction in our educational institutions.

Given this considerable achievement, what are the next challenges to be faced by practitioners of this form of education and training? How can programs become fully institutionalized and available to every interested learner? How can coherence and professional discipline be brought to a "field" as dynamic, diverse, pioneering, and fragmented as experiential education? The contributors to the Fall 1983 issue of the *Journal of Experiential Education* suggest at least a few directions for our attention.

Jon Wagner describes a program model which effectively integrated three traditions of experiential education—group process, simulation, and field experience—into academic, university-sponsored field studies. He notes the importance of combining these traditions to enhance and ensure student learning from experience. His article reminds us of the breadth of the field we call experiential education, its differing and often separate traditions and strands, and the potential benefits available to us through combination and integration of our differences.

Dennis Pataniczek and Carol Johansen examine the new roles internship education

requires for both students and faculty, and the need to better understand these differences in order to maximize benefits to all concerned. Joan Chan, supervisor of interns at New York's Downstate Medical Center, describes the role interns take in her program and the significant contributions they make to patient care, noting the means she utilizes for providing training and supportive supervision. Samuel Mungo describes an internship program designed to combat later "burnout," a common problem of those in the helping professions. Gale Warner, ex-intern, eloquently outlines her internship with the Hidden Villa Environmental Project, and articulates many feelings, problems, and benefits she derived from her experience.

Each of these writers touches upon another serious challenge to field experience educators—our need to develop more complex and more accurate methods with which to define and describe what interns, faculty, and field supervisors do to ensure learning for the student and service for the host organization. A first step may be simply to examine field experience itself. David Thornton Moore describes two dimensions of interns' experiences that contribute to learning: the substantive knowledge gained and the social relationships experienced on the job. He suggests that increased understandings of these categories of experiential learning would enable field experience educators to both better articulate what interns actually learn and begin to break down the troublesome dichotomy between classroom and field learning. Judith Kleinfeld, in *The Idea Notebook* (published in the *Journal of Experiential Education*), offers a helpful suggestion for discovering the content and extent of student learning without undertaking an ambitious research project.

And there are still other serious challenges before us. Perhaps later issues of the *Journal* and other publications should address some of the following issues.

- When are learners ready for field experience education? More specifically, how do we determine which particular program model and strategy is most appropriate for an individual learner at any particular individual stage of personal development? What type of program best serves adult learners? Underprepared learners? Adolescent learners? Primary school learners?

- What is the most appropriate relationship between field experience learning and traditional, disciplinary learning? Should one dominate the other? Can they serve and support each other?

- Can we define and develop professional development tracks for practitioners of field experience education, internship coordinators, etc.? How and where may they effectively sharpen their skills and extend their abilities to apply their experientially gained skills and knowledge?

- Finally, and perhaps most importantly, what is the ultimate purpose and value of this form of learning and teaching? What sort of citizens do we hope to develop as a result of an internship program? Were field experience learning to become a dominant pedagogy in U.S. education, what sort of schools would we have, or would we have any? What sort of society, and what values do we wish to promote as a result of our effort?

The next two decades of development in field experience education should be no less critical, nor less difficult than the last two. I believe they will also be equally productive and rewarding for all concerned. How many impossible things can you believe before breakfast on December 31, 1999?

Overview of the Youth/Adult Partnership Issue

by Kathryn Ramsey Chandross

Introduction

How often have we heard the admonition that our nation's schools do not prepare our young people for the "real" world? The mere fact that so many members of our society believe that there is a "real" world, a separate entity apart from our schools, is a danger signal. If education is to be responsive to the needs of society, then young people, as members of society, must share in the creation, management, and evaluation of education or any other service that affects their lives. Adolescents must be provided with opportunities to interact with adults. They must be given increased responsibility and encouraged to develop the skills and abilities needed to make informed and considered decisions.

We will look at ways of involving young people not only as participants in programs and schools, but also as partners with adults.

Those of us with an experiential philosophy of education demand the active participation of young people every day, usually in programs and activities we have designed *for* them. I hope that this will cause you to reflect on the role of youth in your organization.

Why Form Youth/Adult Partnerships?

Joan Schine, Director of the Early Adolescent Helper Program in New York City, has been the inspiration for several programs that have brought young people and adults together in an effective working relationship. She points out that,

> Young people need to learn how to make wise decisions in much the same way they learn other skills—by starting gradually, testing their strength, increasing the complexity and the urgency of the decisions they are called upon to make—until they can apply those skills as thoughtful, responsible adults. In making the transition from the role of child to that of an adult, the young person needs opportunities to acquire decision-making skills through practicing them. Talking about the Australian crawl is interesting; reading about buoyancy and water displacement may be informative; but the only way to learn to swim is to be in the water.

Since young people lack the life experience that adults have, their knowledge of the systems behind youth services and the need for being political is understandably less than that of adults. Without such knowledge, they can be more idealistic than adults, who are all too well acquainted with the pressures and conflicts caused by those systems. On the other hand, teenagers are more aware of the conflicts and pressures that affect them. They are closer to youth issues such as employment, education, substance abuse, and sexuality. They bring vitality, new ideas, and new talents to youth services, while adults provide stability, experience, and technical know-how. Both contributions are valuable in the design, implementation, and evaluation of schools and other youth-serving organizations.

An example of a successful partnership program is the Nassau County (New York) Youth Board's Youth Participation Project which has, for the past seven years, trained and helped others to train adolescents to serve as effective members of the boards and committees of youth-serving agencies.

While the primary goal of the Youth Participation Project is to involve adolescents in the design and implementation of youth-serving programs, as director of the program I have found that there are secondary benefits that result from participation in the project. The participants achieve personal growth and development. They acquire self-understanding, insight, and self-worth. Often, they improve their academic skills and become more aware of community, social, and global problems. They grow socially, learning to work as part of a team.

Many of the skills that they learn are universal in nature, such as leadership skills, communication skills, and assertiveness. Some are particular, such as Robert's Rules of Order. There is benefit to society as well as YPP develops more productive, informed, compassionate citizens. The pool of potential community leaders is substantially expanded as YPP graduates a new crop of young people each year.

Finally, the most important benefit of the Youth Participation Project is that it has strengthened the sense of purpose of the Nassau County Youth Board. The hard work and dedication of the young people reflect the vested interest they have in the decision-making process.

The Necessary Ingredients

Adults in schools and other youth-serving agencies must develop the wisdom to know how and when to let young people experience automony. Putting theory into practice requires a conviction that young people have a valuable contribution to make to their own learning, to the learning of others, and to the success of the organizations that serve them.

Because of my work with the Youth Participation Project (YPP), I am well aware of the fact that an authentic partnership between young people and adults is not easily achieved. Adults are accustomed to making decisions for young people, and young people have been brought up to accept that adults make decisions for them. These two habits are hard to break. It is difficult for adults to accept that there are occasions when their ideas and opinions should not necessarily prevail. And young people, who have not dealt with adults as partners, often lack the confidence to work at their sides without feeling inferior. A tremendous amount of time and energy must go into reorganizing the structure of the school or agency and into changing the attitudes of people so that the young people can have legitimate power and responsibility within the organization. Equal time and energy must be put into training and supporting the young people if they are to be prepared to take on more and more responsibility.

The Youth Participation Project was designed to test whether or not it was possible to involve adolescents fourteen to twenty years of age in the planning, implementation, and evaluation of services in an agency as complex as the Youth Board. From our experience, it seems that the following ingredients are necessary to forge an effective youth/adult partnership:

- the conviction that adolescents are capable of making a valuable contribution to the agency
- a commitment to the project being long-term rather than short-term
- the restructuring of the organization so that adolescents have a definite role based upon the concept of youth/adult partnership

Long-Term Commitment

There are several kinds of activities that involve young people but which are not youth empowerment programs. Short-term, one-shot service events such as a car wash, a Christmas party, or a clothing drive are worthwhile events, but they are not the kind of programs being focused on in this issue.

Also, much of the volunteer work traditionally reserved for young people does not meet the aforementioned criteria. An example would be work in a hospital in which young people simply carry out menial and unchallenging tasks assigned by a supervisor, with no provision for critical reflection or for making independent decisions.

Experience alone does not automatically produce learning. There is a need to link theory with practice. Deliberate learning requires an ongoing, long-term commitment in which participants are given the opportunity to be engaged in significant tasks with real consequences, where the emphasis is on learning by doing with ongoing reflection and evaluation. It is equally important that the agency and its staff understand that the process of changing attitudes, restructuring

the organization, and learning to share power takes time. It cannot be rushed.

Definite Role in the Organization

Once a school or agency determines that it wants to involve young people in its organization, it must establish which decisions can be shared with the young people, and which decisions must remain the responsibility of the adults. This gives clear-cut definition to the role of the youngsters in the organizational structure of the agency and reinforces the concept of youth/adult partnership.

Current management theory talks about involving all the players in a shared goal. Just as in "real" life where some people have more power than others, young people and adults do not have equal power. There are many instances when the bottom line reflects the legal responsibility of adults. This is especially true of financial matters in which age is a barrier and young people under eighteen years of age are prohibited from certain activities.

In designing a youth/adult partnership, the adults should establish a set of realistic goals that encourage the involvement of the young people in their attainment. At the same time, if there are going to be limitations placed on the role of the young people in decision making, such limitations must be clearly established from the start. Communication is the key. It is of prime importance if the partnership is to succeed. With this clear understanding, young people and adults can sit down together and design a program which is based on the goals of the organization and on the needs and concerns of the young people. The beauty of this kind of program is that it is custom tailored to its environment.

Once the role of the young people has been clearly established, the school or agency must make a commitment to provide the much needed moral and financial support. The adults who have administrative responsibility must communicate to their youthful partners that they value their opinions and, whenever possible, provide them with opportunities to exercise legitimate power. There must be an understanding among all involved as to when decision making rests exclusively with the adult members, when it can be shared by the adults and the young people, and when the young people can make decisions on their own.

In the seven years that the Youth Participation Project has been in existence, the participation of the teenagers has been so successful that the project has received ongoing support from the Nassau County Youth Board through increased funding and staffing. Also, YPP participants have consistently been given more responsibility in the decision-making processes of the Youth Board. Three YPP members now serve as full voting members of the policy-making board of the NCYB. In addition, they represent the Youth Board at state and national conferences, where they conduct workshops and training seminars.

Conclusion

Youth/adult partnerships exist all around us. They can be found in schools, churches, synagogues, and a wide variety of formal and informal organizations. However, it must be remembered that young people cannot exercise power unless adults agree to share power with them. In order for teenagers to gain power, adults must give some up. Very often, when adults give power to adolescents, they do so with specific expectations. They expect that the young people will use their power to achieve results that are substantially those that would have been achieved by adults wielding that power. When the expected results are not achieved—or if the young people aim at a different set of results—the adults often feel betrayed. This scenario does damage to the partnership. Adults must understand that when they give up power, they give up control—that the expectation should be that young people will learn to make decisions, but that the decisions will not necessarily coincide with those that the adults would make.

Programs in which young people and adults work together, whether formal or informal, publicly supported or privately funded, school related or not affiliated with our schools, should be viewed as a sound investment in our society's future. As John Dewey stated:

> The idea of using the present simply to get ready for the future contradicts itself. It omits, and even shuts out, the very conditions by which a person can be prepared for his future. We always live at the time we live and not at some other time, and only by extracting at each present time the full meaning of each present experience are we prepared for doing the same thing in the future. This is the only preparation which in the long run amounts to anything. (*Experience and Education*)

The most important thing that adults can do is to look for situations in which they can share power with the younger generation.

School administrators and directors of youth-serving agencies should actively seek opportunities to involve young people in the design, implementation, and evaluation of the services that affect their lives. If they follow that path, the resulting trust between generations will become the rule rather than the exception and youth/adult partnership will become a way of life.

I would like to thank Edward M. Krinsky, Director of Guidance, Westbury Public Schools, in Westbury, New York, for helping to clarify the ideas in this article. It could not have been written without his assistance.

Chapter 6   Cross-Cultural Settings

Closed Classrooms, High Mountains, and Strange Lands: An Inquiry into Culture and Caring

by Richard J. Kraft

Even as I write, presidents and prime ministers from 160 nations are meeting at the Rio International Conference on the Environment. In the same city, private hit squads, many made up of policemen, kidnap, torture, or kill scores of street children each year in order to "clean up the streets" and make the city safe for the rich, living on the beach at Ipanema. In Africa, rain forests are being destroyed, and a predicted five million children will be orphaned by the year 2000 due to the AIDS epidemic sweeping that continent. Each year, several million children worldwide die of malnutrition or easily preventable childhood diseases. In the United States, thousands of children and adolescents, most with little hope of a decent future, take to the streets of Los Angeles to protest the injustice of the Rodney King verdict and proceed to pillage and

burn to the tune of hundreds of millions of dollars' damage.

While the consciousness of children, political leaders, and the general public throughout much of the world has been raised on issues of the environment, the United Nations Year of the Child went almost unnoticed. When an individual child in the United States falls into a well, is trapped in a cave, or needs a bone marrow transplant, we as people respond with an outpouring of caring. When 25% of U.S. children under age six live below the poverty line and millions of children and young people are trapped in our inner city, rural, and reservation ghettoes, the public and political response is one of yawning indifference. My formal and informal education has led me into an inquiry about what educational practices and experiences really make a difference in my own life, the lives of my students, and to the world in which we find ourselves.

Forty-four years as a student, teacher, and professor force me to agree with the literally hundreds of national, state, and local reports about the failure of American formal education systems (*A Nation at Risk*, 1983; Goodlad, 1984). "Closed classrooms" are not sufficiently powerful to reform the educational institutions of ours or any society, much less to begin to solve the broad political, social, and environmental issues facing us today. In my search for a pedagogy that would change lives, I turned to the "high mountains," adventure and environmental education. While addressing personal and environmental issues in a considerably more powerful manner than the closed classroom, they failed to provide for me the moral imperative to address our world's problems. The service learning movement shows real promise of helping the young find personal meaning, while bringing greater justice to their communities and the world. However, as I look at the learning experiences which have most profoundly affected my own life, they are overwhelmingly found in the cross-cultural and international arenas, which I have titled "strange lands." It is in war-torn Central America, South Africa, U.S. ghettoes and barrios, current and former Communist regimes, and the slums of Calcutta that I find the exemplars of moral courage that challenge my most fundamental beliefs. This article is an inquiry into the failures of mainstream schooling, the successes and limitations of environmental and adventure education, and the power of cross-cultural experience as a learning environment.

Closed Classrooms

While experiential or adventure education is far from being accepted as a mainstream teaching/learning process, one indication of a possible pendulum swing is the growing interest on the part of the educational research, evaluation, and assessment establishment on what is learned "in school and out" and how to assess that learning through performance outcomes, not just pencil-and-paper tests. Lauren Resnick (1987), in her 1987 Presidential Address to the prestigious American Education Research Association, explicated some of the differences between "practical and formal intelligence." Using research by anthropologists and psychologists in such disparate settings as navigation practice on U.S. Navy ships, black market lottery bookmaking in Brazil, mathematics knowledge among dairy workers, and arithmetic performance by people in a Weight Watcher's program, Resnick (1987) concludes that school learning differs from other learning in four basic ways:

a) *individual cognition* in school <u>versus</u> *shared cognition* outside;

b) *pure experimentation* in school <u>versus</u> *tool manipulation* outside;

c) *symbol manipulation* in school <u>versus</u> *contextualized reasoning* outside school; and

d) *generalized learning* in school <u>versus</u> *situation-specific competencies* outside.

Resnick suggests that school learning often becomes a matter of manipulating symbols rather than connecting with the real world. It often becomes the learning of rules disconnected from real life. She concludes that:

...there is growing evidence, then that not only may schooling not contribute in a direct and obvious way to performance outside school, but also that knowledge acquired outside school is not always used to support in-school learning. Schooling is coming to look increasingly isolated from the rest of what we do.

Experiential educators and any thoughtful classroom teacher could have told Resnick and her colleagues this decades ago, as could almost any child in school today. It is, however, refreshing to hear a major researcher indicate the irrelevance of much, if not most, of what goes on in schooling. Dewey made the same point almost a century ago, and regrettably, it will probably be made a century from now. Somehow the closed, traditional classroom remains almost impenetrable.

Resnick (1987) concludes that we need to help students gain skills even when optimum conditions do not exist. We need learners who can transfer skills from one setting to another and who are adaptive learners. The discontinuity between the worlds of school and work suggest that we should not focus so much on "symbols correctly manipulated but divorced from experience." Successful schooling must involve socially shared mental work and more direct engagement with the referents of symbols. Schooling should begin to look more like out-of-school functioning and include greater use of reflection and reasoning.

One would think that the renowned researcher was speaking to the Association for Experiential Education rather than to a group of educational statisticians, anthropologists, and historians. Experiential educators and their predecessors in the Progressive Education Association have been preaching for years the need to tie schooling to the "real" world; the need to work cooperatively in the solution of real problems; the importance of immediate feedback; the use of concrete tools and experiences, not just abstract symbols; and the application of what is learned to life.

As Marshal McLuhan (1966) wrote over two decades ago, children in the twentieth century intuitively know that going to school is interrupting their education. With television, radio, libraries, educated parents and neighbors, and countless other educating agencies in modern society, the school itself has in many ways become an anachronism. Research from the Third World would appear to confirm McLuhan's observation, as we now know that up to ninety percent of the variance in school achievement in many Third World countries is the result of what happens to the child in school. Only fifteen to thirty percent of the variance can be explained by the activities of school in First World settings (Fuller, 1989).

If the closed classrooms of this society are failing as meaningful learning environments, and the educational establishment is apparently incapable of changing course, then we must look to other settings as possible sites in which meaningful learning can occur. I now turn to the mountain or wilderness environment to look at what there is in those settings which might hold out the possibility of being not only a learning, but possibly a "life changing," environment.

High Mountains

Having been born and raised in the Himalayas of west China, I was inexorably drawn as an adult to the mountains of Colorado, where I have lived for the past twenty-four years. Much of my sabbatical time from my role as Professor of Education has been spent in the Andes, in Ecuador and Chile, and more recently, in visits to mountainous regions of Africa. In addition to living, researching, and teaching in mountain settings, I have spent a fair amount of time hiking, camping, and climbing in those environments. It was perhaps inevitable that I would be attracted to the work of Outward Bound and the Association for Experiential Education, and spend much of the past two decades inquiring into the effects of adventure education, particularly in the mountain environment.

I have often pondered what there is about the mountain environment, or I could add the ocean, desert, or other wilderness setting, which has so profoundly influenced several generations of young people and adults in Outward Bound, the National Outdoor Leadership School, and the countless other outdoor programs with which experiential educators are connected. Why is it that we can study "about" the environment for thirteen to seventeen years of school, but that for most of us, it isn't until we taste, touch, and feel it that we truly come to "know" it? I believe with Barry Lopez (1989) that education or knowledge must be "intimate, not encyclopedic; human, but not necessarily scholarly. It must ring with the concrete details of experience."

I admit to having little memorized knowledge of the names of rocks, trees, birds, and animals, or much formal knowledge of geology, biology, zoology, or other natural sciences. It is as if somehow my training in the social sciences precludes my ability to learn information and facts in the natural sciences. However, on the Mesa Trail in front of my home in south Boulder, I have an intimate, twenty-four-year knowledge of every bush, rock, and stream in that environment, based on hundreds of hikes and jogs through my local landscape. Do I "know" the environment in the way that our world-class scientists know it? No, of course not! On another level, however, I would suggest that I know the trail better and in greater depth than any laboratory scientist, who has not spent time to become intimately involved with it. Knowledge is so much more than the memorization of chemical tables, species lists, or geographic boundaries. It is that which comes from touching, tasting, smelling, and feeling a "loved" environment over an extended period of time. It is not studying "about" something, it is falling in love "with" something. I believe that many in experiential education have learned this, while much of mainstream education has not.

I have already indicated how the high mountain environment has imprinted itself on my mind since birth. In a more formal learning sense, however, I became attracted to the power of the mountains as a learning environment back in 1971, when I kept meeting teachers who said their "lives had been changed" by going on something called Outward Bound. Having already spent several years in the public schools and at the university level, and having observed, even during the radical sixties, the general quiescence, if not boredom, induced in the formal classroom setting, I was immediately attracted to any learning tool or environment that could "change lives." As a researcher, I have been trained to be skeptical of such statements, but when so many claim to have "seen God on the mountain top," who am I to say otherwise.

In an attempt to explicate what happened in the process of using the outdoor, wilderness, mountain environment, Vic Walsh and Jerry Golins, both of whom went on to head Outward Bound Schools, attempted to define what happens in this seemingly "miraculous" process. Figure 1 is a shortened version of their attempt to explicate the Outward Bound Process.

Looking at Figure 1, it becomes apparent that there are several ways in which the adventure learning process differs from that of the classroom. As adventure educators, we are spoiled by the general motivational readiness of most of our learners. Classroom teachers have bemoaned the lack of motivation of their students, with each generation seemingly less interested and motivated than the last. The physical environment of the classroom, while generally attractive at the preschool and primary levels, soon becomes a drab and unattractive place in which to learn. Social interaction becomes much more difficult in a class of thirty bored or unruly students, than with an intimate group of six to ten in the wilderness setting or environmental program. Problem solving

becomes the preferred and dominant mode of instruction in wilderness settings, replacing the lecture-recitation, teacher-talk which still dominates the schools. Real problems replace the "you will need it when you grow up," argument so common to us as teachers and parents. Adventure, uncertainty, risk, and danger lead to the state of adaptive dissonance, and with success the learner experiences mastery, rather than failing grades. With "new and improved" self-esteem, the learner reorganizes the meaning and direction of his or her experience.

Resnick has pointed out the failure of traditional education to help learners understand mathematics or other abstract, symbolic concepts. Adventure and environmental educators learned long ago of the importance of involving children and young people in hands-on, active learning about the environment. Over the past two decades, even while mathematics scores continued to plummet and illiteracy rose to alarming levels, a whole generation of young people was turned on to "saving the earth." Whether environmental education was a cause or an effect of this changing consciousness, there is little doubt that environmental and adventure educators were among the first and only groups to recognize the critical importance

The Learner—
motivationally ready

is placed into a ⇨

Unique Physical Environment—
contrasting, novel, outdoors

and into a   *then given a*

Unique Social Environment—
ten-person primary group

Figure 1: The Outward Bound Process

of actively involving the young in improving their world.

These educators were not content with the abstract study of ecology, but rather took children and young people to outdoor education centers, formed recycling programs in schools, built wetlands and nature parks on school grounds, adopted streams and roads for litter control, bought pieces of the Amazonian rain forest, planted millions of trees, monitored local pollution sources, designed and wrote letters to national and local politicians and officials, to mention but a few of the more obvious examples. These many projects reflect beautifully what Resnick suggests is missing in the regular classroom setting: shared cognition, tool manipulation, contextualized reasoning, and situation-specific competencies.

Service learning, perhaps the most powerful, contemporary, experience-based movement in the United States today, has also learned these important lessons, and emphasizes the active over the passive, the student as producer rather than consumer, and youth as actors, change-agents, and

solvers of problems rather than as at-risk or problems themselves. Service learning is an attempt to help our children to not only "hug a tree," but learn to "do justice." Just as it was necessary for environmental education to move out of the classroom and into the real world, so it is that service learning programs have now moved English, social studies, mathematics, science, art, and music out of the school and into changing the lives of children and the broader community. It is the hope and promise of service learning that the next generation of children will learn citizenship by actively politicking in their local communities, learn sociology through active involvement with the homeless and unemployed, learn mathematics by helping senior citizens with their taxes, learn healthy habits through working with drug addicts and alcoholics, and learn caring and compassion in Head Start and daycare centers.

Adventure programs, environmental education, and service learning have transformed and will continue to transform the lives of individuals, the classrooms and

---

Characteristic Set of Problem-Solving Tasks—
prescriptive, organized, incremental, sequential, concrete, solvable, consequential

and a   ***to which one adapts by***   *which*

State of Adaptive Dissonance is Created—
succumbing, coping, thriving

Mastery—
motivationally ready, alert in a new environment, bolstered by supportive group

Reorganizes the Meaning and Direction of the Learner's Experience

---

Adapted from Walsh and Golins (1972)

schools, and slowly, but surely, the broader societies in which we live. Much more could be said about all these topics, but readers of the *Journal of Experiential Education* are generally well acquainted with them and their use as settings for learning. What we have not generally considered, however, is the international or cross-cultural settings as experiential learning environments. As the aging process sets in and my own physical condition deteriorates, I have become more interested in study abroad, international travel, and living and working overseas as powerful tools for learning and changing behavior. I have entitled the next section "Strange Lands," recognizing that they are only strange to the "stranger" and not to those who are native to it.

Strange Lands

Perhaps it is due to my childhood in China or perhaps my lifelong interest in the social sciences, particularly the history, geography, and culture of other countries, but I have found that my life and work in other countries now far surpasses the wilderness setting as the most powerful learning environment for me. As we look back at Walsh and Golins's explanation of the Outward Bound process, it becomes evident that the international setting has many of the same characteristics: motivated learners, a unique social environment, endless problem-solving tasks, a state of adaptive dissonance, possible mastery, and a reorganization of meaning and direction of the learner's experience.

Having lived in fifteen different countries, traveled in over fifty, and led groups of students and adults all over the world, I am convinced that properly designed interna-

tional experiences can be and are among the most powerful "life-changing" experiences that we as learners can have. While the wilderness environment takes away many of the traditional environmental cues for city dwellers and suburbanites, "strange lands" change not only the environmental setting, but take away most of the linguistic, cultural, religious, political, and other cues with which we have become accustomed.

The effect of such a new environment is almost always some level of culture shock, and whether learning or disintegration is the dominant response appears to depend on the reasons for going to the international setting, preparation for the experience, understanding what is happening around and within oneself, and the ability to adapt to the new environment. Among the various major groups of persons in cross-cultural contact are tourists, overseas students, immigrants, traders, experts, missionaries, and diplomats (Bochner, 1982). The individual and group responses to other cultures is not limited to those who travel "overseas," but is an important part of everyday life for millions of North Americans and others who live in multicultural settings. The purpose of this article is not to deal with how immigrants adapt to their new culture or how the dominant cultures react to sojourners in their midst, but to specifically look at how tourists, students, and professionals react to "foreign" environments.

A key to understanding the power of the international, cross-cultural environment is the concept of culture shock, first used by the anthropologist Oberg (1960), who hypothesized that it was precipitated by the anxiety resulting from a loss of all our familiar signs and symbols of social intercourse.

The daily cues of life change; words, gestures, facial expressions, customs, and norms no longer have the same meaning. He suggests at least six aspects of culture shock (see Figure 2).

---

1. *Strain* due to the effort required to make necessary psychological adaptations.

2. A *sense of loss* and *feelings of deprivation* in regard to friends, status, profession, and possessions.

3. Being *rejected* by and/or rejecting members of the new culture.

4. *Confusion* in role expectations, values, feelings, and self-identity.

5. *Surprise, anxiety*, and even *disgust* and *indignation* after becoming aware of cultural differences.

6. *Feelings of impotence* due to not being able to cope with the new environment.

Adapted from Oberg (1960)

Figure 2. Aspects of Culture Shock

While the wilderness environment can bring about many of the same shock symptoms, the effect of cross-cultural settings tends to be even greater. In the wilderness, while we may not be used to sleeping under the stars, living with strangers, or putting our physical beings at risk, we can still count on being able to communicate with other members of the group and the fact that we will be able to "read" the reality around us. Cross-cultural settings on the other hand can, and often do, destroy our very sense of selfhood, and put everything we are into question. Oberg

(1960, p. 176) graphically describes the symptoms of many persons in culture shock:

> ...excessive washing of the hands; excessive concern over drinking water, food, dishes and bedding; fear of physical contact with attendants or servants; the absent-minded, far-away stare...a feeling of helplessness and a desire for dependence on long term residents of one's own nationality; fits of anger over delays and other minor frustrations; delay and outright refusal to learn the language of the host country; excessive fear of being cheated, robbed or injured; great concern over minor pains and irruptions of the skin; and finally that terrible longing to be back home, to be able to have a good cup of coffee and a piece of apple pie, to walk in to that corner drugstore, to visit one's relatives, and, in general, to talk to people who really make sense.

Even as experiential educators have observed the stages of growth and learning to adapt to the wilderness setting, researchers on culture shock have posited four (Oberg, 1960) to nine (Jacobson, 1963) stages. Adler's (1975) five-stage theory (see Figure 3) is perhaps the most widely accepted, although as with any stage theory, questions are raised about whether everyone passes through all stages, for how long, and in what order. The universality of the stages across cultures has also been questioned. My own experience and observations of hundreds of fellow travelers and sojourners provides evidence not only of the reality of culture shock, but some steps or stages through which most of us pass.

Just as some students in wilderness settings never adjust to the new physical and social environment, so personal experience and research indicate that a significant percentage of people never go through the five stages to become autonomous, independently functioning people in the new culture. Time is one factor in adjustment to the wilderness and also affects one's ability to adapt to the cross-cultural environment. Tourists, who are generally in such a setting for a few days or weeks at the most, generally only get into "contact" or Stage One. At this stage, they are still excited and even euphoric, even while complaining about the bad service, water, or other inconveniences.

In my own Study Abroad research, I have found, as have other researchers, (Bochner, Lin, & McLeod, 1980; Church, 1982; and Torbiorn, 1982), that there appears to be an adjustment profile of culture learners and travelers. A flat "curve," a U curve, and a W curve have all been found in the research, with the low points of disintegration occurring several weeks into the intensive long-term program. In my early work overseas, I experienced the U curve in almost every international context in which I found myself. Depression and disintegration would strike about four to six weeks into the experience, and I would then begin to dig myself out, so that by the time I returned to the United States, I would be well into the independence stage. With countless international sojourns now under my belt, I have moved from being a "cultural learner" to being an experienced "cultural traveler" (Furnham & Bochner, 1986), and I now evidence a flat "curve." It has taken me a lifetime, however, to be able to move comfortably into almost any cross-cultural setting and function at a full professional level almost immediately.

Perhaps the most studied group of international travelers and sojourners are Peace

Corps Volunteers. One would expect that with the extremely tight screening, extensive language and culture training, and overseas support personnel, this group would have a very high success rate. Harris (1973) and other researchers have found that the worldwide attrition rate has often exceeded forty percent, and that the real figure might actually be over fifty percent. Initially, the Peace Corps attempted to select their candidates based on personality characteristics, but that proved to be unsuccessful. Guthrie (1975, 1981) rejected the selection approach to reducing culture stress in favor of the view that in unfamiliar cultural settings, situational determinants assume a far greater significance than they do in more familiar surroundings. He recommended that greater emphasis be given to training and social support during the early stages of a foreign sojourn. His work is based on the premise that external, environmental, and situational determinants of behavior are more important than internal ones in coping with second-culture stress.

My purpose here is not to go into great depth on the causes and effects of culture shock, but rather to suggest that like the wilderness, cross-cultural and international settings are very powerful learning environments in which life-changing learning experiences can and do occur. Using Resnick's basic points once again, I would hold that successful cross-cultural experiences are very dependent on shared cognition. Isolated individuals in an international setting have little chance of success, unless they have had a long background of history and training in such settings. Personal experience would indicate that this explanation alone accounts for much of our inability to learn foreign languages in the isolation of the

Stage	Perception	Emotional Range	Behavior
Contact	Differences are intriguing Perceptions are screened and selected	Excitement Stimulation Euphoria Playfulness Discovery	Curiosity Interest Assured Impressionistic
Disintegration	Differences are impactful Contrasted cultural reality cannot be screened out	Confusion Disorientation Loss Apathy	Depression Withdrawal
Reintegration	Differences are rejected	Anger Rage Nervousness Anxiety Frustration	Rebellion Suspicion Rejection Hostility Exclusive Opinionated
Autonomy	Differences and similarities are legitimized	Self-assured Relaxed Warm Empathic	Assured Controlled Independent "Old hand" Confident
Independence	Similarities are valued and significant	Trust Humor Love Full range of previous emotions	Expressive Creative Actualizing

Figure 3. Adler's Five-Stage Theory of Culture-Shock Development   Adapted from Adler (1975)

classroom or language laboratory. Tool manipulation in the cross-cultural sense is the ability to just survive in another culture, whether it is finding the bathroom, renting a room, buying groceries, or the thousand other tasks of living. These are not purely abstract concepts, but rather survival tools which we must learn. Language and cultural traits are not the pure manipulation of symbols, which they tended to be in our foreign language and culture classes, but rather learning which becomes critical within a specific cultural context. Finally, the lessons of cross-cultural living are not abstract concepts of the classroom, but rather situation-specific, in which making change in pesos is necessary for survival, and not just a general mathematical abstraction.

Cross-Cultural Settings and Moral Courage

It is in cross-cultural settings within our own society and internationally that the most powerful, life-changing experiential learning can, and often does, occur. We may be shattered by culture shock, but if we persevere, the lessons can be overwhelmingly powerful and life-changing. I believe it is only when all of the cues which prop up our racial, gender, ethnic, religious, and cultural biases are knocked out from under us, that we can begin the process of becoming caring and compassionate people who can reach beyond the individual child in our own culture who is in distress, and begin to reach out to a world filled with millions of suffering and dying people.

Our schools and communities are as segregated as ever along class, racial, and ethnic lines. Experiential education, particularly in the cross-cultural sense, is one extremely powerful tool for helping us bridge those gaps which continue to lead to rioting in East Central Los Angeles, starvation in Ethiopia, the spread of AIDS around the world, and all the other horrors from which we too often turn our faces.

I believe there is a connection between "Strange Lands" and the issue raised in the introduction as to why the great moral courage and leadership of our time appears to rise from the oppressed of the world. I fear that those of us in the privileged minority in the world are perhaps incapable of moral courage or even moral outrage. Each of us can name our own heroes or exemplars of moral courage. A few of those who have greatly influenced me are Vaclav Havel, Mother Theresa, Nelson Mandela, Martin Luther King, Jr., Bishop Tutu, Archbishop Romero, Mahatma Gandhi, Wang Ming Dao, and Malcolm X. Almost all are people of color. Most spent time in prison for their beliefs. Several were assassinated for threatening the power systems which kept them and their people oppressed. Paulo Freire suggests that it is only the oppressed who can free the oppressors. Perhaps this is why the moral leadership of the world is so seldom found in the United States, Western Europe, or Japan, and particularly from the privileged white, Anglo populations of Western societies.

In my work in Third World settings, both in the United States and abroad, I catch regular glimpses of moral courage. For that reason, I now believe that it is cross-cultural programs that are perhaps our most powerful experiential learning environments, certainly not the failed classrooms of our schools and universities, and not the wilderness environments to which so many of us have committed years of our lives. For me, cognitive development, self-esteem, and environmental awareness are not sufficient reasons for living. Moral courage in the face of social injustice is perhaps a powerful enough ideal to capture the minds and hearts of the next generation, even if it is too late for mine.

Education for International Competence

by Ward Heneveld

Senator William Fulbright, in reflecting on the scholarly exchange program that bears his name, has commented that the world's problems are not technological, but human. Unless learners obtain not only the knowledge, but also the experience and skills required to interact constructively with people from cultures and countries other than their own, the world's future will be bleak. For fifty years, the Experiment in International Living has responded to the need for people to have a global perspective by sending Americans abroad, hosting visitors to the United States, teaching languages and cross-cultural skills to Peace Corps Volunteers and refugees, and offering management and technical assistance for the development of human resources in the Third World. In addition, since 1964, the School for International Training (SIT), the academic arm of The Experiment in International Living, has prepared students at the undergraduate and graduate levels for careers in international affairs, Third World development, student exchange, and language teaching. The challenge for the School for International Training has been to combine the philosophy of experiential learning of the Experiment's founder, Donald Watt, with the traditional expectations of an academic institution.

The "SIT" Model

The programs at the School for International Training reflect The Experiment in International Living's mission of helping individu-als develop their knowledge about world issues, skills in cross-cultural communication and problem solving, positive attitudes toward all people and toward the world's problems, and high levels of self-awareness and responsibility for one's own learning. SIT's contribution to this mission is to help learners develop these attributes in an academic setting. Over the years, the School has sought to improve the academic content of offerings without sacrificing those program elements that encourage personal growth. Today, SIT's undergraduate and graduate programs, its College Semester Abroad program, and other short professional courses, all reflect a commitment to education that effectively combines high intellectual standards, concern for the whole person, and practical pre-professional and professional content to produce internationally competent individuals.

The "SIT Educational Model" has four sequential elements (see the accompanying diagram). All programs start with a period of formal academic study. This is followed by a field experience in which students try out what has been learned during the first period. The students then come together again to share their experience and reflect on and share what those experiences have added to their classroom learning. Finally, students are expected to complete a significant project that builds on what has gone before. In all the programs, this combination of formal study, experience, reflection, and a project creates graduates who have the intellectual and personal characteristics necessary to contribute to creating a better world.

Introductory Phase

The more traditional introductory phase of each program is defined by a scope and sequence of academic content that the faculty has decided is appropriate for the purpose of the program. The content mixes traditional subject matter, including language and analytic theories, with an introduction to practical methods in the world. In the undergraduate World Issues Program (WIP), the

---

SUMMARY OF THE EDUCATIONAL APPROACH BY STAGE AND COMPONENTS

STAGE 1 — FORMAL STUDY

Community building
Coursework
Field experience preparation
Field experience placement

↓

STAGE II — FIELD EXPERIENCE (INTERNSHIP)

Learning contract/work plans
Student reports
"Distance advising"

↓

STAGE III — REFLECTION

Evaluation of field experience
Synthesis of theory and practice
Additional formal study
Preparation of/for project

↓

STAGE IV — PRODUCT (THESIS or PROJECT)

Research
Written report
Presentation

---

curriculum is built around the five world issues identified by U Thant, former Secretary General of the U.N.: the environment, social development, cross-cultural communication, the world economy, and peace. In the Master of Arts in Teaching Program, linguistics and culture courses complement what is covered in the Approaches to Teaching Languages course. In the Master's Program for Intercultural Management, organizational behavior, social change, and economic development are studied along with project design, generic training methodology, and financial management. The initial coursework on the College Semester Abroad program is organized around traditional disciplines with lectures and reading on the country in which the students are studying. Also, during the academic phase of each program, links between theory and practice are strengthened by assigning practical projects which students carry out. For example, this past year, undergraduate students put on an exhibition with lectures on textiles from the Third World, and a group of graduate students organized a series of lectures and discussions on issues related to human rights. Other students prepared and presented complete project proposals in the Project Design course, and participated in the selection and planning of the workshops presented during the final three weeks of their program.

Despite the practical activities during this period of formal study, SIT's approach would be much like that of other institutions were it not for the time built into the curriculum for community-building and community-maintenance activities. All programs are characterized by significant faculty attention to individual student needs and by frequent group social and intellectual events throughout the program. World Issue Program students start the semester with nine days at a wilderness camp, which also includes a "drop-off" exercise. Each student is left in a New England village for 24 hours with an assignment to "make-do" on $5 and a roll of life savers and to find out about and fit into the local culture. The graduate Program in Intercultural Management begins with a week-long orientation which includes group-building activities. College Semester Abroad groups have a brief but intense orientation together and then study together during the coursework period abroad. The degree programs have weekly community meetings which all faculty and students attend. Indicative of the importance attached to community in each program is the faculty members' and students' reluctance to let outsiders join the weekly, "family" meeting.

Field Experience

During the period of formal coursework, projects, and community building, students are expected to choose and secure a field placement for themselves. In the degree programs, this next phase in the SIT education is an internship (or series of internships) of at least six months' duration. To help them find places, SIT's Professional Development Resource Center provides a data bank of over 2,000 organizations, assists in preparation of resumes and in development of interviewing skills, and advertises possible placements.

In the Master of Arts in Teaching Program, students spend eight to ten weeks teaching, many of them going abroad for this experience. In the College Semester Abroad

program, homestays and independent study projects immerse the student in action-oriented situations and thus serve a purpose commensurate to that of an internship. Even in six-week management courses on campus, participants plan a follow-up activity during the course, and, whenever possible, course instructors visit the participants in the field to see how these post-course "internships" are going.

The field experiences are organized around a work plan defined beforehand by the student in consultation with one or more faculty members. Undergraduates prepare detailed learning contracts and carry them out primarily on their own; graduate students prepare work plans before starting their internships and receive supervision in writing and/or through visitation. Having gotten to know the student while he or she is on campus, there is a strong collective responsibility among faculty for each student, although one of them takes the lead in assisting each individual. Since the student's activities and study needs often change while they are on their internships, adjustments can be made in consultation with faculty. "Distance advising" is the most difficult part of the faulty job as each instructor tries to balance the student's operational needs in the field setting with the academic expectations of an institution of higher education. There is a continual effort to improve the mechanisms whereby students make conscious connections between theory and practice as they learn about and act on the world.

Final Phases

All SIT degree students return to the school, which is located in Brattleboro, Vermont, after their field experience. The follow-up programs range from only two weeks for the graduate-level Program for Intercultural Management to a full additional year for the World Studies Program undergraduates. In all programs, this final period of residential interaction with faculty emphasizes reflection and evaluation of what has been learned, and students are required to continue to explore the connections between theory and practice.

As a final step after their study, internship experience, and reflection, all degree students must produce a major paper, project, or presentation before their degrees are awarded. For example, World Studies Program students spend their senior year after their internship following their personal plan of concentration which results in a major research paper, a project, or a presentation. Semester Abroad students conclude their semester by presenting, orally and in writing, their independent study projects. Graduate students in both language teaching and intercultural management are required to submit a thesis. Having emphasized academic work at the start of our programs, SIT expects students to demonstrate both their academic competence and its practical application at the end of the program.

The SIT model is not for all students. In fact, SIT students tend to share a number of characteristics that set them apart from other college and graduate students. Almost all of them have lived abroad before, or they come from another country. Because of their international background, they share The Experiment and SIT's interest in international and cross-cultural issues and our concern for peace, social justice, and the alleviation of poverty. They are more interested in acting on the world than in learning about it, though they have recognized the importance of additional formal study or they wouldn't enroll at SIT. Because of this desire for action and their previous experiences, students tend to have only an average inclination toward traditional forms of academic study. Most have already assumed the primary responsibly for their own learning. Finally, we find that SIT students usually possess only moderate financial resources and are not overly concerned that their SIT education significantly change this situation. Rather, they expect SIT to help them pursue more effectively their life's work. People with these characteristics have high expectations of the School, which is as it should be. Our challenge is to provide each of them with an effective mix of academic and experiential education so that they can make a contribution to improving the state of the world.

The SIT education approach has evolved over the School's 25-year history. Our offerings have moved beyond the emphasis on experiences that characterized The Experiment's original exchanges. Demands of students and accrediting agencies as well as professional integrity have led to more program structure and increases in course requirements and electives. In this process, SIT has maintained its commitment to and delivery of The Experiment's traditional mission of educating the whole person for international competence by providing experiential opportunities for practical learning. The SIT approach to education provides an effective framework within which to educate the head, heart, and hands of those world citizens that will be needed if we are to survive into the next century.

How Inclusive Are You? Ten Ways to Limit or Empower Members of Oppressed Groups

by Mary McClintock

Every day, educators who are members of privileged social groups act in ways that are disempowering of clients and co-workers who are members of oppressed social groups.[1] The following is a list of actions that are based on traditional, stereotypical assumptions about people who are members of oppressed groups.[2] Although unintentional or unconscious, these behaviors have the effect of being disempowering to the people to whom they are addressed. This list does not include the many intentionally hurtful or oppressive actions directed toward members of oppressed groups.

Many educators are members of both privileged and oppressed groups. Please read this list from the perspective of one of your privileged group identities. For example, if you are a Jewish man or a heterosexual woman, consider the list in light of your experience as a man or as a heterosexual.

At first, reading this list, you may think that any one of these actions is not very harmful. What is harmful or disempowering is the pattern, the constant experience of these "little" things that members of oppressed groups face—daily, weekly, continuously.

Think of your goals as an educator. If, as educators, we have goals of fostering personal development in our clients and of creating positive, supportive relationships with our co-workers, we must find ways to stop our disabling behaviors and promote atti-

tudes and behaviors which are enabling and empowering of all people.

Excluding, Avoiding, Ignoring, Forgetting

Ignoring the concerns, ideas, opinions, culture, or experiences of a person; planning a program that is for a group of people without including them in decision making (for example, outdoor programs for people with disabilities); assuming everyone is heterosexual; assuming everyone celebrates the same holidays, then scheduling events/programs on oppressed groups' holidays; not being accessible to people with a variety of disabilities; avoiding certain groups or individuals whom you feel uncomfortable around because of stereotypes and fears; using exclusive language—such as "two man" tents, using male pronouns to refer to all people.

To be empowering, include and acknowledge the concerns of all people, include members of oppressed groups in making decisions that impact on them, learn about the cultures of groups other than your own and about the ways oppression affects them, examine ways to make your program accessible to people with disabilities.

Loyalty Tests

Only approving of members of oppressed groups who try to be like members of privileged groups (such as, "Suzy is all right, she swears just like one of the guys"); making jokes or derogatory comments about, for example, gay men, Jews, or Asians, and expecting the gay man, Jew, or Asian person to appreciate the joke; telling someone that s/he is not like other African Americans, deaf people, etc. (such as s/he is unusual, special); baiting or teasing someone and then complaining about her/his lack of sense of humor when s/he reacts.

To be empowering, acknowledge and validate difference rather than trying to force people to be the same, conform to your group's norm, or fit into your expectations.

Stereotyping/Role-typing

Making assumptions about the physical abilities, interests, traits, qualities, preferences, and habits of a group or individual (such as, "The Latino kids in the group will abuse the equipment"); asking people to do tasks or take on roles that are based on stereotypes; for example, assuming a Jew will want to take on financial tasks, expecting women to cook a meal while men set up tents or gather firewood.

To be empowering, dispel myths and stereotypes by seeing the whole person, rather than making assumptions based on stereotypes. Learn about the lives of real people rather than believing and reinforcing myths and stereotypes.

Generalizing

Viewing one person as representative of a whole group (such as, "The last blind kid we had on the ropes course didn't do well, so we should plan a different activity"); asking someone to speak for all members of a group

(such as, "What kind of food do you people like to eat?"); expecting the staff person who is a member of an oppressed group to take care of all the concerns of his/her group (such as expecting an African American person to run the trips for African American kids).

To be empowering, individualize by treating people as individuals rather than representatives of a social group. If you wish to know about the concerns of a particular social group, ask many members of that social group for input.

Staying "One Up"

Doing something for someone rather than helping him/her learn how to do it for him/herself; trivializing someone's concerns (i.e., "Bob says that the staff insurance program discriminates against him and his lover, Steve, but we have more important things to discuss with the Board of Directors"); using expensive clothes/equipment as status symbols; lavishing praise on relatively ordinary accomplishments; assuming someone is in a job because s/he is a "minority" or a woman.

To be empowering, value difference by acknowledging that your way or your social group's way of thinking and behaving are not necessarily the only or best way of thinking and behaving.

Inappropriate Sexualization

Believing stereotypes about sexuality such as: assuming that African American or Latino adolescents are more likely to be sexually active on trips than White adolescents; assuming that all gay men and lesbians want to get sexually involved with heterosexuals; assuming that gay and lesbian relationships are sexually motivated only; assuming that people with disabilities are asexual; turning neutral topics into sexually suggestive ones; touching women or girls in sexually suggestive ways.

To be empowering, avoid assumptions about sexuality by viewing people as individuals in regards to how they express themselves sexually. Don't believe or reinforce stereotypes about the sexuality of people who belong to specific social groups. Examine the cultural values inherent in your view towards sexuality.

Over-protecting/Self-protection

Making assumptions about the abilities of individuals based on their social group memberships ("This would be a good route for the women's trip, there aren't many miles to paddle or many portages"); not encouraging people to try difficult tasks; not giving negative feedback to an individual for fear of being perceived as prejudiced; making decisions for others; expecting credit for being "liberal"; trying so hard to avoid the other behaviors listed here that you seem stiff, distant, and not genuine.

To be empowering, enable and empower by giving people credit for knowing about their own needs and abilities and being able to make decisions for themselves. Ask if someone needs help, rather than assume it. Offer help, but allow it to be refused without taking offense. If help is requested, follow the direction of the person asking for help, rather than assuming you know how to give help.

Forced Integration

Making an issue of the fact that some African Americans, gays, women, etc., sit to-

gether, socialize, have their own programs; perceiving that "they" are segregating themselves, while not acknowledging that members of privileged groups sit together, socialize together, etc.; splitting up the clients into groups so that the women, African Americans, Latinos, etc. are isolated in predominantly privileged groups, in the interest of being "integrated," "diverse"; not recognizing that such isolation can set up tokenism and its disempowering dynamics.

To be empowering, acknowledge the power of numbers by learning about the dynamics of tokenism (where there is one or a few members of one social group and many members of another social group). Avoid the negative dynamics related to tokenism by working to have groups with balanced memberships. Respect the wishes of oppressed social groups to have separate time and space within which to work on healing from hurts of oppression or to celebrate their own culture.

Privileged Group Solidarity

Backing up another member of a privileged group when s/he says or does something racist, sexist, homophobic, etc.; excusing another person's oppressive behavior by saying that "s/he is a great person, only a little prejudiced"; laughing at or remaining silent when someone says sexist, ableist, or anti-Semitic jokes; telling the victim of oppressive behavior that s/he is overreacting or being too sensitive when s/he gets upset.

To be empowering, interrupt oppressive behavior by not telling jokes or making statements based on stereotypes and assumed superiority. Talk to co-workers, clients, or friends who make sexist, ableist, or other kinds of oppressive statements or jokes. Ask them to stop such behavior and tell them why (such jokes reinforce hurtful stereotypes, etc.)

Expecting to Be Taught

Expecting co-workers and clients who are members of oppressed social groups to teach you about their group's culture (such as, assuming a lesbian staff member is willing, able, and interested in presenting a staff training session on homophobia, in addition to her other tasks); asking women, Jews, African Americans, etc., to keep you on your toes about your language or actions that may be oppressive; ignoring/not seeking out other means of learning about groups other than your own; not taking responsibility for yourself and about how you may be hurting others.

To be empowering, be an ally by doing the rest of the things on this list. Educate yourself and other members of your privileged social groups. Identify and work to change discriminatory practices and policies.

Reading this list may feel overwhelming. Experiencing these behaviors on a regular basis as a member of an oppressed group can also have that effect. Here is a suggestion for sorting out those overwhelmed feelings: read through this list and the enabling/empowering behaviors and plan ways you can be more empowering of your co-workers and clients. Then, check yourself against the list periodically. You may also want to use this list as the basis for a discussion with your co-workers on how you can work toward being more empowering of all people.

NOTES

1. By privileged social groups, I mean those groups which have traditionally been privileged by North American society, including men, heterosexuals, Gentiles, whites, able-bodied/minded people and upper middle-class people. By oppressed social groups, I mean those groups which have traditionally been oppressed in North American society, including women, lesbians, gays, bisexuals, Jews, Asians, Africans, Latinos, Native Americans, people with disabilities and people from working-class and low-income backgrounds.

2. I have taken these categories from the unpublished articles that I have documented in the reference section and adapted and applied them to educational settings.

Integrating Work and Learning with Multicultural Inner City Youth

by Robert Burkhardt, Jr.

How can we integrate labor and learning for youth so that their passage to adulthood makes educational, technical, social, and cultural sense? What is the best way to teach the interdependent dignity of work and education? Is it possible to choreograph the rituals, conventions, and procedures of a curriculum so that young adults will internalize habits which in turn become the tools of lifelong learning, without stifling their individuality? These questions are at the heart of the sixty service and conservation corps programs in states and cities across America, and their answers have intriguing implications for the structuring of educational activities in public and private schools. Here is how one program, the San Francisco Conservation Corps (SFCC), currently answers these questions through its activities.

It was Crew 10's turn, so their representative Craig walked to the blackboard, wrote, turned, and announced, "La palabra de la semana es 'strategia.' Who's got a definition?"

We had done our daily exercise at 7:30 sharp: stretching, 120 jumping jacks, 60 pushups, 160 situps, trunk rotations, cherry pickers, and a brisk run. The staff and corpsmembers of the SFCC had come in from the Great Meadow at Fort Mason for our Monday community meeting which, after a brief silence for focus, and "hello" in a dozen languages, always begins with "Word of the Week."

"Plan?" offered a hesitant voice, followed by an uncomfortable silence as many of the one hundred corpsmembers studied their workbooks. "Strategy" is not a frequent flyer in the street vocabulary of high-risk, inner-city youth. Craig, who was himself uneasy teaching his peers, turned and

quickly printed a definition on the blackboard. Others put the word of the week up in Spanish, Chinese, and French.

"It is corps strategy," I reminded them, "that you write about the word of the week at least once in your journal. And we look forward to Crew 10's 'strategic' skit this Friday." Craig sat down to applause, and the meeting moved on to announcements and issues before the crews left the center for their work sites, where they are currently, among other tasks, removing graffiti, landscaping a park, recycling cans and bottles, teaching literacy in a summer program for Latino youngsters, doing home repair for the frail elderly, installing play structures in child care centers, completing a mural, and removing fish from a pond they are draining to repair.

Three years ago, I personally selected the weekly words and led the discussion in search of definitions. You can hear the need to control (disguised as a search for virtue) in the words I chose: service, quality, production, character, learning, competence, etc. One day a corpsmember walked up and asked, "How come you always get to pick the Word of the Week?" Since that date, on a rotating basis, the crews have picked the words, and while there have been some doozies, corpsmembers hid paydirt repeatedly: crack, minimum wage, electoral college, poetry, violence, contract, music, colors, responsibility, culture, racism, to name but a few.

The Friday skits amplifying and reinforcing the word of the week began several years ago as brief, wooden productions watched by a disinterested, uncomprehending crowd. The initial perfunctory performances evolved into two- and three-scene scripted playlets with props, confronting the issues and sub-themes of daily life in the Corps, presented to an audience of critics. "You call that art? Hell, wait till you see what we have planned for next week!" The corpsmember-produced, word-of-the-week skits normally focus on work relations (especially the injustice of having to take orders from a supervisor who doesn't know anything), but onstage we have seen babies delivered, death by crack overdose, a revolution in the streets after a "stolen" presidential election, ethnic dance, muggings, weddings, gay-baiting, family violence, theft, a rap on the virtue of recycling, and more. Crew 1 once selected "imitate" as w.o.w., and corpsmembers *became* administrative staff, mirroring our pontifications, our foibles, our mannerisms, and our twitches. It was hilarious, particularly during the Spanish translations (we ask bilingual corpsmembers to serve as translators at community meetings, strengthening a variety of their skills). Brief program announcements became long discourses about the Golden Gate Bridge; complex statements were translated monosyllabically, delivered deadpan by polished bilingual actors, secure enough in their surroundings to lovingly and skillfully bite us. The staff was bent over in tears of laughter.

The Friday skit always follows crew reports, in which the 18- to 23-year-old corpsmembers summarize the projects on which their crews are working. These reports are a conscious attempt to develop leadership through public speaking, and include the corpsmember's name and crew, what the crew "stands for," the nature of the project and the reason for doing it, tools used, safety hazards encountered, when intelligence was most used, when the crew worked best as a team, where they will be next week, and the most important thing the corpsmember learned during the week (which frequently is to listen to her/his supervisor). Reports may be in English or Spanish, and corpsmembers are encouraged to give reports in a language different from their native tongue, fostering cross-cultural appreciation. We regularly ask American-born corpsmembers to imagine themselves obligated to give a crew report one year from now in Tagalog, Chinese, Polish, or Arabic; we then ask them to find a way outside community meeting to thank Arminda, Juan, or Mauro for having mustered the bravery and skill to present a crew report in English.

Since most young people are going to watch television, why not educate their eyes? Eighteen months ago, I taped a piece off the evening news about the South African singing group, Ladysmith Black Mambazo. Ladysmith was up for a Grammy

Award (which it won), and the four-minute segment hauntingly interwove apartheid, injustice, creating culture, and popular music. I showed it to the SFCC corpsmembers, who watched silently and attentively, breaking into spontaneous, enthusiastic applause at the end. Thus was born the SFCC Video News.

As a result, several nights a week, I tape anything which might provoke discussion and expand minds. In that community meeting where Craig named "strategy" as the w.o.w., I later wrote on the board, "What is the purpose of art?" Ideas flew in from all over the room: "For beauty." "To use the imagination." "To show truth." "To offend." "To give hope." I asked if movies qualify as art, and most corpsmembers assented. After framing the discussion, we watched the "Person of the Week" story on Spike Lee's "Do the Right Thing," and we talked for a few minutes about imagination, offense, truth, and hope.

Whether the topic is orphans overcoming adversity, Kiowa dancers, competing environmental interests, stroke victims who play the piano, Latino youth who make the Olympics, or Black singers who perform in Japanese, there is an immediacy to the visuals which piques interest as it expands world views. Corpsmembers are asked to express and defend their opinions about the stories. We believe that SFCC Video and the related discussions will bear cumulative fruit. Combined with the speaking, listening, reading, and writing experiences already mentioned, they help to foster an environment where opinions are sought, questions are useful, minds are engaged, and ideas are honored.

Less than half the SFCC corpsmembers have high school diplomas, and one-third

did not grow up speaking English. These factors reinforce our decision to provide a daily program of reading and writing. All corpsmembers keep journals, and their work supervisors write responsive comments in an ongoing dialogue. We do not care so much what corpsmembers write as *that* they write, every day. Four days a week, out on the work sites, corpsmembers use breaks, down time, or the lunch hour to record their feelings and frustrations, aspirations and achievements, as well as the technical aspects of the deck they are building or the fence they are constructing.

After thirty-two hours of paid labor, Monday through Thursday, Friday is education day. Each corpsmember has had at least one 4-6 P.M. class earlier in the week: English as a second language, G.E.D. preparation, Spanish for Anglos, etc. On Friday mornings, immediately after our Chinese fitness exercises, writing circles start the day. All staff members lead a group of five or six corpsmembers, and no two writing groups approach the forty minutes in the same way, except that everyone writes, and everyone shares her/his writing. We once considered having a weekly topic for all groups, but staff overwhelmingly insisted on personalizing the writing for the individual groups.,

My own section is probably representative: Lynell, who is very bright and prefers drawing cartoons or performing rap to writing; Demian, enthusiastic and quick with words, though terse in prose; Cesar, who doesn't even like to write in Spanish; Robert, who writes methodical, painstaking, scholarly responses; Sylvia, whose mind is always off somewhere, usually with her three-year-old; Mike, hearty and cheerful when with us, but currently in jail for two months; Andres, serious and careful, who helps translate for Sylvia and Cesar; and Carmen, new to the SFCC and slowly figuring out our system. Each week we reveal a little more of ourselves: family problems, aspirations, past failures and successes. Each week the corpsmembers grow more able to contradict me and assert their own opinions. Each week, the written word is somehow less threatening and more of a tool for living. It is a slow, but palpable process.

We started "The Reading" two years ago when we determined that a daily reading/thinking/speaking exercise would promote critical thinking, improve morale, and increase production. Each work supervisor gets a packet every morning with ten copies of the day's reading, which fits on one side of a page and is prefaced by a provocative question: What do you say to someone who has lost a loved one? What if your daughter were a lesbian? How would you solve the crack problem? What is fear? Who were the freedom riders? What makes a good worker? What is a Catch-22? We have developed some three hundred and fifty such readings. Below the question is text. For example, one reading asks, "How did the world begin?" Below are a passage from Genesis, a paragraph on the Big Bang, and a Native American creation myth.

In the van on the way to the worksite, the supervisor asks the question of the day and elicits responses from the crew. The supervisor's ability as a facilitator plays no small role in the success of the discussion, since many corpsmembers prefer Walkmans to Wordsworth. There are benefits to this discussion which go beyond preparing the crew for the day's reading. Corpsmembers may now experience their supervisors as curious, vulnerable, questioning human beings, rather than as martinets who simply issue orders and enforce discipline. Further, illiteracy is no barrier to opinions, and the discussion can become sufficiently lively to engage corpsmembers emotionally, which can in turn fuel the desire to read. Many SFCC corpsmembers have less than happy memories of "school," yet are full of insights and awareness. In the safety of a small, supportive group of non judgmental peers, reading aloud and animated discussion become the building blocks of improved literacy.

At the worksite, having framed the reading with oral discussion, the group takes a few minutes to read aloud and discuss the day's selection. Sometimes it works, sometimes it doesn't. There are days when one can hear the thump of lead balloons hitting the ground all over San Francisco. Less frequently (ah, but when it happens!), the crews have returned to the center so deeply caught up in the day's question and reading that debate rages during tool storage, van cleaning, and—que milagro!—continues as they depart for home. What do the other passengers on the 49 Van Ness think when they see a group of young Latino, Black, Asian, Pacific Island, and White workers, their uniforms spattered with paint, concrete, sawdust, or mud, climb on the bus energetically arguing ethical and moral questions? It seems to me that they see the future of their city.

Certainly a daily diet of labor-intensive, hands-on, hard physical work can offer opportunities which challenge young women and men to grow in skills and abilities: reading blueprints, installing community gardens, sharpening tools, mixing concrete, operating chain saws, framing walls, or painting senior centers, are all activities where inspired adults can help foster thinking workers. One supervisor in the SFCC, for example, is famous for holding blueprints upside down, scratching his head, and asking his crew to assume a leadership role in building the play structure. It rarely fails to produce the desired response. His belief is that production schedules are more easily met when workers "own" the project, even if it takes an investment of time at the beginning.

However, cerebral skills such as curiosity, deduction, articulation, making connections, and synthesis must be practiced regularly by the young if they are to become healthy life habits in maturity, and labor alone is an insufficient instructor. The appropriate role of the "teacher" is to maintain a high level of intensity, demanding the engagement displayed by minds at work, whether on the job site or in a "class." "Students" need a variety of ways to link learning and life, in which growing minds are challenged by new information, situations, and questions which impel response.

There is no best way to do this. What are the conditions? How capable are the "teachers?" Who are the "students?" How much time is available? What goals are realistic? The answers to these and other questions shape a curriculum. Adults do not necessarily know which experiences are the best teachers, but in an era when illiteracy, drugs, and sexually transmitted diseases among youth are a plague, adults must act to save lives and society. In a time when technology has essentially eliminated geopolitical borders, adults must develop global consciousness and teach multiculturalism. In an age when the disappearance of species and natural resources is accelerating, survival for any depends on all of us becoming environmentalists.

I have recently begun teaching a class entitled "Origins of Ethics." Too many young people I meet act as though they are outside of and unaffected by history; they do not have a context to understand the caves we have come from nor the uncertain future toward which we are headed. So a group of eight corpsmembers and I spend two hours every Friday morning looking at the ethical questions posed by the lives, actions, and writings of people like Gandhi, King, Mother Teresa, Moses, Miyamoto Musashi, Lao-Tzu, Mohammed, Crashing Thunder, John Stuart Mill, Jesus, Hammurabi, and more. We move chronologically from creation to the formation of societies, and use the ideas raised by the minds we encounter as a backdrop to examine our own lives. The impact of the ideas we discuss helps the corpsmembers see themselves as part of the continuum of people inside history, building and creating, rather than as hapless spectators or victims. We talk about justice, and love, and service, and tolerance, and we look at events in the corps and the world around us to measure our own awareness and values. There is much shouting and laughter, and regularly I marvel that the discussion is swirling noisily without my leadership. The eagerness with which the class devours material suggests to me that Bertrand Russell was correct to assert that we make moral progress only when we are happy.

The apparent contradiction on which the corps is created finds expression in the tension between rigid production schedules and our desire to nurture growth in corpsmembers. The SFCC $3.1 million budget is constructed on a planned number of hours to install the irrigation system or plant the dune grass, and youth's personal needs frequently have to wait until the end of the day, lest the enterprise become enfeebled through cost over-runs. Good judgment by the supervisor is essential here; there are problems which can't wait until four P.M. We believe the activities, exercises, and practices described above promote in corpsmembers the capability and resilience to unify our dual mission.

Youth empower themselves for leadership through the hard task of production; the corps produces quality work in the public interest because corpsmembers have internalized the discipline of self-direction. This integrated approach to work and learning in the SFCC has helped us evolve as an organization during our first five years. In the next five, we will build on the base, continuing to seek ways to assist youth in the difficult transition to active, responsible citizenship.

The Power of Stories:

Learning from the Lives of Young People

by Denis Udall

Chanrithy Ouk steps up to the microphone. "Thank you for inviting me here," he begins nervously. He looks out at two hundred Brooklyn high school students sitting patiently in their seats. "I want to tell you my story," he continues, searching for words. "I want to tell the whole world my story because I don't want you or anyone else to go through what happened to me. I hope that by telling my story to others I can help make a safer world for all young people." Chanrithy, 18 years old, begins a haunting tale of his life in Cambodia under the murderous Pol Pot regime and his flight to a Thai refugee camp during the subsequent occupation of his country by Vietnamese troops.

Chanrithy is one of seven young people on a youth "speak-out tour" that visited five New York City high schools. The tour was co-sponsored by the New York City Outward Bound Center and the Children of War, a youth leadership training program which organizes national tours of young people from around the world who share their experiences of growing up in war-torn countries. The tour's New York City youth came from three public high schools where Outward Bound staff work to integrate experience-based education into English and social studies classes. Two of the three refugee youth (one each from Nicaragua, Afghanistan, Cambodia) attend International High School, a small alternative school which attracts recently immigrated refugees.

The tour offered these young people, all of whom had suffered violence and mistreatment, a chance to speak about their experiences in a community of peers. As they shared their feelings, they and their audiences became deeply connected with one another. In recognizing the universality of their experiences, they begin to develop a commitment to the struggles of others and the vision to see themselves as leaders, teachers, and healers who can make a difference in the world.

Chanrithy continues his story:

At the time I was born in 1971, everything was mixed up because a war had started between the Khmer Rouge and the former government of Cambodia. In 1975, the Khmer Rouge won the war. Any family that had been involved with the government was to be killed. My father had been a policeman. He lied and told them he was a farmer. When I was 6, the government separated my family and put us to work. They put me in a child labor camp. There was no house and we had to sleep on the ground. I had no idea where my parents were or what they were going to do with us. I cried most of the time. During that time my mom and her newborn baby died of starvation. There was no milk and no one could take care of them. In 1979, the government found out that my father had worked for the former government, so they brought us together to kill us. We were guarded with guns and they didn't give us any food at all. We escaped and met up with Vietnamese troops in a forest. They tried to take care of us. But one night there was bad fighting. It was very dark. I ran to get away from the bombs, and I got lost from my father and stepmother. I didn't know if they were alive or dead. I just cried and cried. My grandmother finally found me. I stayed with her for a little while, and then she died. Then I stayed with my aunts and uncles. By then I had grown up a little bit and I started to think about freedom. I had heard about a refugee camp along the border of Thailand and Cambodia and I decided to go. I went alone, walking with a group of people I didn't know who were going there too. It took me a month to get there. It was very hard. We walked at night and hid during the day. At the camp, the United Nations gave out food and tents. I stayed there for three years. I talked to the Red Cross about how I got separated from my father. They gave me hope that he was still alive. I also heard about America. Refugees talked about the Statue of Liberty as a symbol of freedom. Eventually, the Red Cross found out that my father was living in New York City. I came to the U.S. on April 29, 1988. I was 16 years old. I hadn't seen my father since 1979. When I got off the plane, three men were walking toward me. I didn't know which one was my father. I started sobbing. Then I saw one of the men cry, and I knew that he was my father. I'm going to college next year. I'll probably study international law because I really believe in peace. I don't want anyone to suffer from war and violence the way I did. I don't want the next generation of kids to see the things I saw.

Jesus Goyco, the next speaker, is visibly shaken by Chanrithy's story, yet he finds in it the strength to tell his own. "The war I went through wasn't like Chanrithy's—it wasn't fought on a battlefield—but in other ways it had a lot in common with what he went through. You see, my war took place in my house and in my own head." As the audience listens, Jesus unravels a dark period in his family's history.

My father and mother got divorced because my father used to abuse my mother. I would watch and I wanted to do something but I couldn't disrespect my father. All those years it hurt me a lot to see my mother getting beat up. It started when I was seven. When she finally threw him out I was going crazy because I couldn't control my feelings. All those years I had that pain locked up inside of me and I'd take it out on other people. I went out robbing. I did a lot of crazy things. I was also heavy into smoking marijuana and drinking. The brothers I used to run with, we'd rush anyone we saw for no good reason. That's how I took my anger out, because I thought if I cried I'd have been weak. I was taught that a strong man is one who doesn't cry, but it's really the opposite. The years past [sic] and when I was about 15 my mother became addicted to crack. It hurt me a lot because I saw it coming, but I couldn't do anything about it. I tried to give her advice but she would blow-up and start beating on me saying that she was older and knew better. She got so bad that she turned the house into a crack house. She and some friends were pulling in money and making crack. Some other drug dealers saw how much money they were making and they rushed the house. I was a hostage in my house for three months. It's still very painful to think about it...being locked up in your own house. Getting beat up on. Sometimes I would try to get away and they would strap me down. I'm the oldest and every night I had to live with my brothers and sisters crying to me to help them. But

I really didn't want to leave them there. Once I offended one of the drug dealers and they took out a gun and played Russian roulette, taking turns pulling the trigger. I heard the clicks and each time I thought: any moment now, any moment. Thank God one of them had forgotten to put a bullet in the gun. Finally I did get out and I went to the cops and they got my family out. After that we were split up. My mom went into rehab. I went to a place to get help for my problems and that's where I learned to cry for the first time. I realized that I wasn't the tough guy I really thought I was. I even went so far as to find all those people who I wronged and asked them to forgive me. Now I just want to tell my story so you can learn from what happened to me. So you don't have to go through it yourself.

Lately I have been listening closely to the stories of young people like Chanrithy and Jesus. I have also been watching how they teach one another by speaking openly about their lives. Two related observations emerge from what I've seen and heard. One has to do with what young people's stories have taught me about my own work as a teacher; the second concerns what young people have to teach one another.

Learning From Young People

It's not always easy to listen to young people's stories. Many are painful to hear and painful to tell. But if I allow myself to see into their lives through the window of their stories, it changes me and the way I think about my work as a teacher. Their words guide me to see how I can be an ally in their struggles.

Listening to young people helps me to see them in their own terms through what they tell me. It allows me to get inside their lived experience and walk around. I become less inclined to treat them as recipients of my services, as clients, or as passive individuals who need me to develop their character through "value-forming experiences" I initiate. Listening helps me to see them as intelligent, caring, compassionate, creative human beings. Chanrithy's and Jesus's tales are especially compelling, dramatic, but during the week-long speak-out, I was equally impressed by young people in the audience who responded with their own inspiring narratives. As they stood up and spoke, I was moved by the insights and values that animated their stories. The depth of their responses and their willingness to share showed that they were strongly motivated by many of the same values and qualities that teachers often assume are lacking in their students.

Most teachers know the age-old adage that our assumptions about students' intellectual abilities can have a profound affect on their academic performance. Similarly, our expectations and assumptions of how young people behave or what motivates them can work powerfully to influence their self-image. For example, stereotyping young people as unmotivated, needy, and violence-prone can lead them to live down to those expectations. If, on the other hand, we allow ourselves to listen to what young people have to tell us about their lives, about their dreams and fears, our expectations of them can't help but become more positive and nurturing.

What I learn from young peoples' stories affects me personally as well as professionally. Indeed, the two are inextricable. I shouldn't be surprised that a teacher like myself can learn profound lessons about compassion, trust, and hope from his students, yet I am always astonished at the things they teach me and how I grow as a result of knowing and caring for them. I discover in their words a piece of my story; my life is echoed in their own. For instance, I see in their lives my own despair at watching high school friends destroy their lives through drug addiction. And like many young people, I found passive academic seatwork to be unrelated to my true concerns and needs. Finally, listening to Chanrithy's story helps me to understand (though not reconcile) my own moral quandary in being a citizen of a country that could visit mass destruction and death on Iraqi non-combatants. When I show young people that I care about their lives by listening carefully to their stories and reaching inside myself to respond genuinely to their fears, hopes, and pain, I find it a deeply healing experience for them as well as me.

I've found that to shed an abstract notion of what it means to grow up in the inner city takes me deeper into my own history to examine experiences that could help me grasp what urban youth confront daily. I'm convinced that this perspective is essential for those of us who devote our lives to working with inner-city youth. Especially those, like me, who aren't people of color, those who come as strangers to this life experience. We need to know. We need to open ourselves to what young people have to teach us about themselves, about their aspirations, fears, and dilemmas. To be a teacher in a place like the South Bronx means to be forever the student.

Young People as Healers

Through their stories, young people have taught me a great deal about moral knowl-edge, theirs and my own. I've developed a new appreciation for Carol Gilligan, who sees moral development through the lens of interpersonal relationships and the experience of caring and being cared for by another person. Gilligan's ethic of care "emphasizes seeing people in their own terms, seeing problems in a narrative context, a concern for non-violent resolutions of problems, and non-exclusiveness...it eschews hierarchical relationships in favor of a web, a network of concerns" (Garrod & Howard, 1991).

When I really listen to what young people have to tell me, I am struck by their depth of understanding about ethical issues and the many ways in which they live out an ethic of care. In places like New York City, countless youth are in a perpetual state of crisis. Faced with a never-ending array of difficult choices, some literally matters of life and death, many develop a keen sense of moral judgment. If given a chance, they can teach one another.

For an appalling number of young people from our inner cities, violence, mistreatment, and negative influences envelop their lives, making survival a full-time occupation. The despair, anger, and hurt that they carry with them is emotionally incapacitating. Not long ago, a young man was killed at gun point outside South Bronx High School where Outward Bound has a program. This was a devastating incident for the school community. A wave of fear, depression, and anxiety swept over the students, enveloping not only those who knew the young man, but many others for whom the event conjured up other suppressed, equally horrifying events that they had heard about or witnessed.

The third leg of the tour took place at South Bronx High School. As each speaker told his or her story, the pain caused by the shooting and other experiences with violence came suddenly to the surface. Walter Calderon, a member of the speak-out tour and a student at South Bronx, spoke after Chanrithy and Jesus. After telling about his experiences of fighting as a 13-year-old Nicaraguan Contra and watching his 11-year-old brother killed in combat, he ends by telling his audience, "You know, I hear a lot of people around here saying how they're going to get a gun and hurt someone because they did them wrong. They just don't understand. I have to live with what happened to me. They just don't know what they're doing. They don't know what it means to kill someone."

After the speakers finish, they gather in a tight knot around the mike and invite the audience to come up and share their stories. No one budges. Virginia Sache, an Outward Bound alumni from Washington Heights, grabs the mike, "Don't be afraid. We know what you have to say is important. We'll support you." Finally, José, a twelfth-grader, steps up to the applause of his classmates. "You know these projects across the street. They may look all nice and new but life in them is hell. My brother is a leader of one of the worst posses in the Bronx. There's nothing that's beneath these guys—stealing, selling drugs to kids, even murder. It hurts to see what my older brother has become. It's all I can do just to keep out of it. I'm constantly getting dragged in when I don't want to be. I'm lucky I'm still here. This is the way it should be. All of us together. Being here for each other." More applause. Someone is overheard telling Walter, "I never knew that about you. I've known you all this time and I didn't know what you've

been through. I didn't think it was okay to talk about this stuff. We just come and go and everybody pretends like it's not going on all around us. We ignore it because it's too hard to look at."

As the event comes to an end, the speakers call the audience up on stage. Without talking, a hundred young people organize themselves into three tight circles, each embedded in the other. Daniel Rivera, one of the adult coordinators, addresses the group, "Look at what you've started here! Who would think that in the middle of the South Bronx there'd be such a strong pocket of caring and generosity. I have tremendous hope for this community because of what I've seen here today. I think what you're discovering is that you don't have to survive by denying what's going on around you. That'll just make you cynical and emotionally hard. What you're finding is that you can begin to heal those wounds by finding strength in each other. You're beginning to turn things around by what you're doing here today."

In a world that crowds out their ability to react humanely to events, these young people are working to form a kinship with their peers, one that serves as a foundation for acting on the world in deep and lasting ways. By telling of their own oppression or mistreatment, experiences which once hindered their personal growth and ability to respond to the needs of others, their words become sources of healing for others as well as themselves. Looking within to find ways of communicating, they encourage their listeners to see their own lived experience reflected in the life of another. A hurtful experience, empty of meaning in its cruelty or disregard for human life, is transformed into a life-affirming message containing hope, courage, and heroism. Together they recognize in each other a portion of their own lives and in doing so, develop a deep bond and a common purpose to confront the struggles they face.

Acknowledgements

The author would like to thank Judith Thompson, John Bell, and Daniel Rivera from the Children of War, and the members of the speak-out tour: Chanrithy Ouk, Jesus Goyco, Michele Bynoe, Virginia Sache, Donovan McCoy, Walter Calderon, and Kahlillulah Ayubi.

Youth Take the Lead:

Cherokee Nation's Approach to Leadership

by McClellan Hall and James Kielsmeier

"An Indian leader is very important in these times."

"An Indian leader should help in taking care of our environment and be a leader for non-Indians as well as Indians."

—Cherokee 8th graders
(Conrad, 1983, p. 23)

Introduction

The Education Department of the Cherokee Nation of Oklahoma had its hands full in early 1984. The second 30-member class of the high school Youth Leadership Program concluded its year-long series of meetings and projects, while a new group was recruited for the 10-day National Leadership Conference in Minnesota. Fifteen graduates of last year's Leadership Program prepared for 1,500-mile bike trip retracing the Trail of Tears from North Carolina to Oklahoma, at the same time that a team of high school and college students planned for the Second Annual Indian Youth Leadership Conference (for one hundred 7th- and 8th-graders) in June.

From modest beginnings, a spark is brightening into a flame in Oklahoma—some would say analogous to the sacred Cherokee fire that has burned throughout the history of the people. Not only is there heated activity emanating from this unusual youth program, but illumination on the issue of modern Indian leadership as it affects both Indian and non-Indian people and how it can be nurtured in tribally controlled set-

tings. Our purpose in this paper is to tell the story of the Cherokee Nation Youth Leadership Program, emphasizing how this experience relates to a more general understanding of Indian leadership.

Background

In 1982, discussions among Cherokee Nation Education Department members centered on the dysfunctional relationship between Indian young people and the Oklahoma public schools. In Adair County, which has the highest concentration of Cherokee youth in the tribal area, 70% drop out before high school graduation. It's not much better in other counties. The development of a program to deal with the school failure rate would require a bold undertaking. Success, based on past experience, would be problematic, because of historical obstacles.

With roots in a unique set of circumstances that can be traced to the forced removal from Georgia, Tennessee, North Carolina, and the surrounding area, the Cherokee Nation in Oklahoma today includes all or part of 14 counties. Some

Cherokees live as many as 200 miles apart, at opposite ends of the traditional boundaries. In addition to geographical separation, the tribe has been fractionalized by religious conflict (Christian vs. Traditional), and cultural loss brought about by intermarriage with non-Indians. A constitution which provides for election of 15 council members at large, rather than as representatives of geographical districts adds further political dissensions. Finally, for nearly 50 years, from 1907 to the 1950s, they were without formal tribal leadership. These factors have combined to fragment and disperse the tribe to the point where a tribal community spirit is difficult to recognize, and programs that effectively engage Cherokees from all 14 counties are rare.

Cherokee Nation Youth Leadership Program (CNYLP) began with the vision of drawing elements of the tribe together through an innovative youth program. Initially, thirty Cherokee high school students were selected from within the 14-county area and spent one year in a program designed to install self-confidence, positive regard for Cherokee identity, and a sense of community spirit through service to others. From this first step, other directions and programs have developed to bring the vision closer to a reality. The program marks the first attempt since Oklahoma statehood in 1907 to bring young Cherokee people from the entire Nation together to work and learn as a group, addressing directly the issue of leadership. A key element has been the service-oriented approach to leadership. This has proved to be the catalyst that unified the group, and it has had a profound impact on individual young people.

I feel great about being one of the Cherokee Nation's first leadership students. I consider it a privilege and success in itself. I felt successful because I was looked up to by the kids this week. I hope I was a good example to them.
—Cherokee High School Student Staff
    Member
Indian Youth Leadership Conference
(Conrad, 1983, p. 35)

Program Development

Countless high school and college graduating classes have been exhorted to recognize that the future is theirs to create. Seemingly, a magical role change is expected to take place as a student crosses the stage to receive a diploma. Formerly a diligent absorber of knowledge and member of a social/academic community, the young person symbolically receives the key to not only unlock the door to his or her career path, but also the larger door leading to solutions to their communities' and the world's major ills. This is, of course, absurd. But is it not what is asked of the best and brightest of Indian youth?

Cherokee Nation recognized that this was too much to require without the addition of guided preparation and training and appropriate attempts at leadership development. However, before they could train and educate the young, the staff needed to be clear themselves about what they were educating for, and what the curriculum of the program would be. Borrowing from another group's cultural experience was not appropriate, nor were there clear outlines available in other Indian programs. There was, however, a multicultural, youth leadership development program created by the National Youth Leadership Council (NYLC) that held promise as a foundation on which to develop a distinctively Cherokee model. In broad outline, the program involved training selected Cherokee Nation high school youth in a challenging multicultural setting—the National Leadership Conferences—then creating ways of "bringing back" the high motivation generated there and applying it to useful service projects in home communities.

Cherokee traditional religion teaches that the creator made the four races of people and gave them their original instructions. The Cherokee once believed that all races are to be respected equally, and all are mentioned in some of the ancient songs of prayer and healing. However, most Cherokee people today, especially the younger ones, are products of the broader American culture in which they have grown up and have strong racial attitudes, often borrowed from their non-Indian neighbors. There is a certain amount of distrust and uncertainty regarding whites and a great deal of prejudice toward blacks held by Cherokee people. The Cherokee students who attended the first NYLC experience were apprehensive about spending 10 days in close contact with complete strangers, many from racial groups with which they were not familiar. Further contributing to their anxiety, was the uncertain self-image the Cherokee young people had of themselves.

The multicultural experience at the 10-day National Leadership Conferences had positive consequences for individual Indian youth and the Cherokees as a whole. The insecurity experienced by the Cherokee students rapidly gave way to a feeling of new-found importance. For the majority of the non-Indian participants, this was their first contact with contemporary Indian people and they were very respectful. Numerous questions were asked which reflected their lack of knowledge of Indian culture. "Do you live in a teepee?" "Where are your feathers," etc. As the students experienced challenges together and became better acquainted, the racial barriers dissolved and good friendships developed. It was apparent that Cherokee students grew to respect themselves as well as others in the process.

It was a powerful experience for the Cherokee students and the non-Indian participants to discover that there were many more commonalities than differences that surfaced at the NLC. During the 6-hour drive to the camp, the Cherokee leadership students had plotted ways to stay in the same cabins and to stick together as much as possible, since they had heard that they would be separated once they reached the camp. But the separation of the group and contact with other people of different races, in spite of initial apprehension, proved a key element in the success of the camp. It was important to Indian youth to know that there were members of the Cherokee Nation staff nearby to provide support but also to know that they would have to deal with many of their problems personally.

It was clear to the Cherokee staff that a significant change in self-image occurred as a result of the camp experience. (This was borne out by the evaluation data to be discussed later.) Not only did students feel better about themselves as individuals, but a distinct pride in being Cherokee developed as well. For example, during many hours spent preparing for a cultural presentation to the entire camp, the Cherokee youth came to realize how little they really knew about their heritage, and they needed to work hard to pull it together. Their presentation on contemporary Cherokee life in Oklahoma received a standing ovation that lasted several minutes. This performance proved critical in the formation of the bond that developed among the group.

The NLC Design: Creating a Multicultural Community

The National Leadership Conference by design includes participants from a diversity of cultures (50% of the students attending each of the 9 conferences since 1978 have been people of color). The program is planned to create a neutral setting for every group represented. Activities, therefore, are geared not to a single culture nor just to the outdoor athletically inclined, but also to young people more comfortable in artistic or other less physically demanding settings.

The National Leadership Conference is a distinct model—unique among structured outdoor, leadership, or camping experiences. From its base in a semi-primitive residential camp, it uses the wilderness, but also nearby cities and town as its campus. Combining action and reflection, outdoor adventure challenges with formal lectures and discussions, the curriculum focuses on a unifying theme, such as justice or youth participation. It emphasizes a particular model of leadership, the "servant leader": one who leads by serving and empowering others. It allows, even demands, the exercise of such leadership in all phases of the Conference.

Participants, who come from a wide variety of backgrounds and parts of the country, are initially thrown together in highly intensive Seminar experiences which combine physical, intellectual, and moral challenges.

These are followed by choice experiences, both on and off ground, called Pursuits of Excellence, in which smaller groups develop and apply the concepts and skills introduced in seminars. Following these, the participants reunite to reflect on and to synthesize these experiences. Together, each sub-group forms the compact through which they will apply their new and strengthened leadership skills in their home schools and community.

All of this takes place within the crucible of community building, the very real and difficult task of developing a multicultural community of love, respect, trust, and caring by young people who had not experienced such diversity before. As one student commented, "It was the working together of 200 people from all cultures and races that really made it work—and us work. This was 'real world' democracy and equality."

Another summarized what they had learned most clearly:

> Wow, this is feasible! All races of people can get along, trust each other and be great friends no matter if they're Black, White, Indian or Mexican-American. We must bring this message to others—no matter if it takes 10, 20, 50 or 100 years. (Conrad, 1982, pp i–ii)

Evaluating Self-Esteem at the NLC

Dominant groups in American society have been slow in recognizing the achievements of ethnic minorities. Typically, this has left the minority group with a sense of collective inadequacy which is translated into low self-esteem for the individual young person growing up in such a group. It is one of the aims of the National Youth Leadership Conference to break into this destructive cycle to raise the self-esteem of the individual participants, and further, to help them apply their new perspectives on themselves to the groups with which they identify.

The NLC finds the raw materials of raised self-esteem in building positive relationships with others, and in carrying through challenges successfully. When the various groups arrive at camp, their baggage generally includes many cultural stereotypes—both about themselves and about the other groups they find in the multicultural community which they suddenly must enter. As they move through the program, the young people are confronted with a series of demands which carry a certain amount of risk—whether it be interpersonal, social, intellectual, or physical. It is hoped that as they proceed through these activities, they will come to see themselves as capable risk-takers—as able as any of the others to undertake and meet a variety of challenges. This sense of accomplishment, of being on a par with others whom they may have either held in awe or have disparaged, is a key factor in the strong sense of community which develops in the course of the 10-day experience. The NLC leadership is hopeful that in the surmounting of obstacles, including their stereotypes of themselves and others, and in the building of a trusting and caring community, more positive self-images will emerge. The data from evaluation studies conducted in 1982 and 1983 (Tables 1 and 2) indicate that they are meeting these goals.

Using the Janis-Field Self-Esteem Scale, scores were obtained for the participants at the beginning and the end of the camp periods. The data for both years consistently show two important outcomes. First, the NLC program had a universally positive impact upon the self-esteem of all groups participating, regardless of race or ethnicity. Second, in both years, while the mean pre-camp score of Cherokee Nation youth was the lowest for all groups, the gain in the mean score at the end of the camp experience exceeded that for all groups combined. In both years, the gains in self-esteem scores attain statistical significance. Thus, not only was it found that the Cherokee youth responded to the NLC camp in a manner comparable to that of other groups, but the score gains suggest that they may have benefited from it to a greater degree than most of the others.

The evaluation data are consistent with the informal assessment made by Cherokee Nation staff who felt that the young people returned to Oklahoma with a stronger collective sense of self. They left Oklahoma as individual representatives from the 14-county area, but after excelling in an intense experience with people of many other backgrounds, were able to return home with new pride in themselves and their Cherokee heritage.

> A good leader is not marked with a sign that says 'leader.' Anyone can be one if they really want to. A leader, though, has to be willing to help others and to serve.
> —Cherokee Nation 8th-grader
> June, 1983

Leadership in Oklahoma

Standing by themselves, these test results could be dismissed as artifacts of the evaluation process; however, in the two years of the program there has been activity in Oklahoma which is far more indicative of actual leadership development.

Returning home after the summer, the Cherokee Nation Youth Leadership Program focuses attention on home communities. During the year following the camp experience, monthly sessions are planned and conducted with a great deal of input from youth participants. A "curriculum" of applied leadership development is being built—staff and students defining together what it means to be an Indian leader through the projects and programs created. Actual accomplishments speak loudly to the substance of the dormant leadership that is now blooming:

- Renovation of the Cherokee Artists' Association building

- Service projects involving visits to senior citizens and nursing homes

- A nearly 70% participation rate in the follow-up programs by high school students

- Creation of a ropes challenge course that can be used by young people from throughout the tribal area

- Creation of a leadership training camp in Oklahoma for 7th- and 8th-graders (to be discussed more fully below)

- 1,500-mile bike expedition along the route of the Trail of Tears completed in 1984 and repeated in 1985

- In addition, there have been numerous individual accomplishments by the high school students beyond previous expectations, such as President of the Indian Club, Homecoming Queen, President of the Senior Class, All-State Basketball, improved grades, high rate of college entrance, etc.

Impact on the Community

Direct results include a significant number of parents and school personnel who have rediscovered the concept and the value of the experiential approach to education. The traditional Native American educational model has always been experientially based. Traditionally, Indian young people became adults through a natural process of working with and emulating adults, gradually assuming their roles within tribal societies. The idea of bringing young people into direct contact with the subject matter to be learned—experiential education—is the heart of the teaching method at the National Leadership Conferences and its back-home programs. Enlarging the classroom to include the rivers, hills, forests, towns, and cities, brings life to learning. In the case of the leadership training, people learn leadership by "doing leadership." Realizing the benefits of this approach, the Cherokee Nation staff structured their entire program in order to place participants in responsible, decision-making activities. Young people not only wielded paint brushes at the renovation of the Artists' Association building, but helped organize the project. They have played key roles in the operation of the 7th- and 8th-grade leadership camps and have been asked to provide leadership in other community projects initiated through the program.

Service learning—engaging young people in community service projects for the purpose of developing responsible citizens—is a method of experiential education used extensively by the CNYLP. Based on the premise that one develops elements of character such as honesty, a sense of fairness, and compassion by doing acts that call

**Table 1.   Janis-Field Self-Esteem Scale
1982 National Leadership Conferences**

	(N)	Pre-test Mean Score	Post-test Mean Score	Mean Gain
Combined	(259)	33.98	35.43	1.44
REGIONS				
Omaha	(24)	35.21	36.46	1.25
St. Louis	(58)	34.48	35.31	.83
Kansas City	(18)	35.00	36.67	1.67
Cherokee	(32)	31.59	33.63	2.03
Indianapolis	(51)	32.94	34.82	1.88
Gary	(14)	36.14	38.07	1.93
Des Moines	(14)	33.36	33.86	.50
Flint	(7)	34.57	34.14	.43
Robbins	(8)	36.75	37.38	.63
Oak Park	(7)	37.71	37.86	.14

*Highest mean possible is 50.

**Table 2.   Janis-Field Self-Esteem Scale
1983 National Leadership Conferences**

	(N)	Pre-test Mean Score	Post-test Mean Score	Mean Gain
Combined	(137)	31.01	32.46	2.45
REGIONS				
Indianapolis	(40)	30.15	33.23	3.08
Evans	(28)	30.71	33.32	3.08
Gary	(16)	29.56	32.31	2.61
Oak Park	(11)	36.00	37.27	1.27
NY	(8)	31.00	32.50	1.50
Minn	(6)	31.33	34.83	3.50
Cherokee	(11)	29.55	32.09	2.55
Nova S	(6)	35.00	36.00	1.00
Indiana	(6)	31.00	32.67	1.67
IYA	(5)	31.20	32.00	.80

*Highest mean possible is 50.
Tables taken from *Evaluations of National Leadership Conference 1982, 1983* Dan Conrad

on these capacities, programs committed to the development of service-oriented youth leaders had adopted service learning approaches. The open demonstration of the service ideal through the many projects operated by staff and students has had an important impact on participants and community alike.

Indian Youth Leadership Conference: A New Model

The Cherokee Nation Department had a dual concern: they needed more creative outlets for the able, young, high school leaders finishing their training, and they wished to design a program for 7th- and 8th-grade youth. School retention studies have identified this age as a critical period. The decision was made to operate a leadership camp in Oklahoma using elements of the National Leadership Conference model but directed specifically toward the needs of Indian youth. The junior high-level-camp would be staffed in part by the high school leadership students after they received intensive training in small-group skills and experiential education methods.

Funded by the Johnson-O'Malley program, the camp focused on the theme, "Today's Indian Youth—Living in Two Worlds." The curriculum guide, written by Richard Allen, outlines the camp's purposes:

The underlying goals and objectives of this curriculum are to develop a cadre of Indian youth knowledgeable about life-experiences and influences from both an Indian and non-Indian perspective in an effort to better prepare them for the existing world. Therefore, it is important to create and reinforce a positive experience in both

worlds for positive self-image, self-awareness and self-actualization.

Allen goes on to emphasize the need to include an Indian environmental approach:

...It will be necessary to employ an Indian resource person schooled in tradition and who also has the ability to relate not only to the use of the plant, but can also relate specific lore associated with that plant. In this manner, we will shed light on and provide a better understanding of why nature is held in such high esteem and with such a deep-felt religious respect by Indian traditionalists. (Allen & Bread, 1983, pp. 4–6)

Sixty-five 7th- and 8th-graders attended the first Indian Youth Leadership Conference at Camp Lutherhoma on the banks of the Illinois River. Student leaders and younger students worked together on service projects, were engaged in seminars related to self-worth and environmental education, and were exposed regularly to elders who spoke to the group. Dan Conrad from the University of Minnesota served as the external evaluator and summarized the major outcomes of the camp as follows:

...For the young participants [there] were, first of all, a new sense of personal confidence and competence, and, secondly and relatedly, increased pride in being Indian and stronger identification as such. Other outcomes reported by participants were a resolve and a commitment to try harder in life, to persevere in the face of difficulty; a strong belief in the power of cooperative effort and the value of sharing; and new ideas about what it means to be a leader — particularly that a leader is one who serves his/her followers. Not the least of the outcomes was the very real accomplishment of saving the life of a drowning man on the Illinois River.

The major outcomes for adult staff members were gaining insight into and skill in working with junior high youth; development and testing of a leadership training model; and building their own skills in leading the same. (Conrad, 1983, p. 2)

Students rated the program very highly, 60% giving it an excellent score and 30% very good.

I got this new idea: I can do anything I want to if I set a mind to.

I'm just as good as anyone else, and I should be proud of my heritage and not be afraid to let people know I'm Indian.
—Cherokee 8th-graders
Indian Youth Leadership Conference
(Conrad, 1983, p. 19)

Key to the success of the week was the effectiveness of the high school leaders. They were assigned significant responsibility and worked very hard serving as teachers, counselors, role models, and friends to the 7th- and 8th-graders. Clearly the Conference could not have functioned without high school student leadership and, in return, the Conference gave them the opportunity to test and apply the leadership skills learned throughout the year.

Implications of the Cherokee Nation Experience for Indian Leadership

Youth are a window to the future. Through them we can anticipate the shape of the world to come. Often, as Indian children grow older, their interest and success in school diminishes. The future for the majority of Indian youth who struggle in this fail-

ure-laced setting is not encouraging. Seeking to arrest present trends through youth leadership and education, the Education Department of the Cherokee Nation has synthesized a powerful new model which offers a different vision of the future. Strong young people, proud and knowledgeable of their past, yet self-confident and comfortable in multicultural settings, are the "products" of these efforts. Such young people embody a future for Indian and non-Indian people where dialogue, mutual respect, and shared learning are possible. It is also a future where Indian traditions are retained and passed on in a non-threatening way to Indian people employed and living in a predominantly non-Indian world. It suggests the possibilities of comfortable coexistence between peoples without the suggestion of acculturation. This is a new vision clearly articulated by the Cherokee Nation experience.

Robert (not his real name), a young Indian man, was on the edge of serious trouble two years ago. He was in an uncertain home situation, failing in school, and the local police were keeping an eye on him. Robert's Oklahoma schooling experiences caused him to be placed in Stillwell Academy, the first tribal school to be operated by the Cherokee Nation since 1907. He was picked to join the first leadership program group and traveled to the leadership camps in Missouri and Michigan. Prior to going, he had difficulty standing in front of a camera—he was very shy.

Something happened while Robert was away because he returned with new drive and direction. Becoming the president of a school club, the respected head of his leadership group, and successfully completing a month-long Outward Bound course have been his achievements since. Robert was a key staff member at the 1983 and 1984 Indian Youth Leadership Conferences and was named by the younger students in their evaluations as the student staff person who expressed the most caring attitude toward them. Robert was also asked to be a staff member at the multicultural National Leadership Conferences where he was responsible for some of the high-risk challenge activities. There he was a leader for whites, blacks, as well as Indian young people, and his performance was rated outstanding.

Robert has come full circle and his route symbolizes hope for all Indian people on this continent. A product of racism and inappropriate educational methods combined with a stressful home situation that can be traced to discriminatory policies, Robert was sinking into a cycle of self-destruction. Encouraged to test himself in a multicultural setting, he, along with his peers, returned home with a new-found sense of personal and collective worth. He was urged to apply his skills and

share with other people—Indian and non-Indian—and through this experience, is finding a place for himself as an Indian person, effective and comfortable in two worlds.

Cultural rootedness, confidence in a multicultural world, ideals of compassion and service to others combined with a strong sense of self and personal competence are the key aims of the Cherokee Nation Youth Leadership Program. They are the personal characteristics that Robert and many other Cherokee Nation young people have already begun to demonstrate with their behavior. We believe they are important characteristics of the effective Indian leader—for today and for the next generation.

Editor's Note:

The model described in this article is now being used as a community development model by four tribal groups in New Mexico. McClellan Hall is directing the project in cooperation with the Santa Fe Mountain Center.

Cross-Cultural Learning with the Navajo

by Charles Luckmann

In the *Souls of Black Folk,* William E. Dubois prophesied that the dominant issue of the twentieth century would be one of race. As we approach the twenty-first century, out of the array of problems we now face, it has been suggested that a prominent issue will be understanding cultural differences. With this in mind, I offered a year-long, high school anthropology course as a history elective.

For the final segment of the course, I took nine Seattle juniors and seniors in the spring of 1988 to live for four weeks with two traditional communities on the Navajo Reservation at Big Mountain and Rock Point, Arizona. The purpose of the trip was to learn firsthand as much as we could about the Navajo. I wanted to get my students out of the classroom to experience another way of life in the backyard of our own country. As part of the preparation, in addition to my anthropology class, we studied the Navajo language for three months with a linguist and Navajo speaker from the University of Washington.

It was an experiment in cross-culutral living. I was not sure at the time if high school students could successfully integrate a fundamental difference in values and way of life. I was surprised at how quickly they discarded their rigidly held opinions when confronted with the Navajo way of seeing the world. They grappled with the differences between them and the Navajo in a mature and thoughtful way.

The first Navajo phrase that my students learned was the usual greeting "yá át ééh" (it is good). With the response being "Aoó" (yes, it is good). A very positive greeting in comparison with the usual American greeting of "how ya doing," followed by "not bad," "pretty good," or "not so good," with the focus on individual feelings and one often expecting the worst.

My students found the Navajo people surprisingly positive. They expected, I guess, the stereotypical view of the disillusioned Indian. The Navajo seemed to look for beauty and goodness in all things. The Navajo word hózhó expresses this fundamental outlook. Hózhó is generally translated as beauty, harmony, happiness, and everything that is positive. The Seattle students found hózhó a refreshing contrast to the cynicism and fear in their own lives. The tables were turned, they were the disillusioned ones.

A Different Set of Values

We attended school for two weeks in the Rock Point community. The first hour at school was, for my students, an episode they will never forget. At breakfast, two Seattle girls sat down next to a couple of Rock Point students who promptly got up and left. Though I had tried to prepare my students for this, they wanted to run back to Seattle. It was their first lesson in coping with cross-cultural misunderstanding.

During the first week at Rock Point, the Navajo students found it difficult to speak with my students. This prevailed mostly at school, however, and loosened up considerably in the home environment when the students could talk to each other one on one. The social pressure at school made it difficult for the Navajo students to approach their non-Indian visitors comfortably. For my students, this was a valuable lesson in feeling what it is like to be a minority and an outsider in a school community. Initially, my students misinterpreted the Navajo shyness or silence as a lack of genuine interest in them, instead of what it really was—a natural fear of strangers. Two Seattle students, Ben and Bob, were fortunate to find a crack in this barrier because of their basketball skills. Shortly after arriving, they were invited to join the Rock Point basketball team in a weekend tournament, which also gave them invitations to stay at the homes of two Rock Point players.

Back in the classroom, the lack of motivation or "drive" (as Ben called it) among the Navajo students was disturbing to him and forced him to think about the situation carefully. He knew it was not a lack of intelligence, but something to do with a fundamental difference in values. Rock Point students did not want to achieve in the same way he had been taught. Ben related how one of the Navajo students had asked the teacher to lower his grade because he felt uncomfortable with an "A." Ben was thunderstruck. He had never before heard a student ask for a lower grade. Eventually, Ben became aware of a Navajo trait of not wanting to be better than others. Ben discovered that, especially to the Navajo parents, treating everyone as a kinsman is the golden rule

to follow, and that community cooperation is better and healthier than individual competition. Navajo students do not feel compelled "to succeed" in a way that Ben took for granted.

To these white teenagers, anyone outside their nuclear family is usually treated as a potential competitor. They erect symbolic fences saying "this is mine," "keep out," "no trespassing," excluding almost everyone except their immediate family. To the Navajo, extending k'e (kindness, love, peacefulness, and a congenial social environment) to neighbors outside their own clan and even to non-Navajos, is fundamental to their social universe. They chastise someone by saying "doo k'e nizin da," meaning that person does not think toward k'e (treating everyone as a kinsman). This emphasizes how positive thinking can mean the difference between friend or enemy, extending good will or bad. At Rock Point, we experienced a strong sense of clan, community, and k'e (especially when they invited us into their homes).

Furthermore, contrary to the normal social atmosphere in Seattle of feeling alienation between neighborhoods and communities, the Navajo celebrate reaching out and forming alliances with other communities. This is demonstrated by the Anaají Ndáá or Alien Way ceremony where two communities are joined in solidarity to exorcise evil from a patient. They symbolically assert power over one's enemies by mutual help and felicitation, which is represented by the sharing of food and assistance as well as all-night dancing. Family mobility in the lives of my students from one city to the next emphasizes to them that people are essentially strangers and not to be trusted outside the four walls of their homes. As viewed by my students, this was probably the least understood aspect of Navajo life. They have been conditioned to think and act as individuals, to look out for themselves at all costs.

Humor is not usually mentioned when speaking about Native Americans. The mirthless Indian is another common stereotype. At Rock Point Community School, my students were initially confronted by the stereotypically stoic Indian; however, whenever we were not present, laughter usually filled a room. At first my students felt they were probably being laughed at, or talked about, because their presence would shut down laughter. After a week or so, the laughter did not stop after my students entered a room, thus helping them to relax and feel less self-conscious. It became apparent after a while that the humor often revolved around the Navajo children teasing each other. The Navajo "first laugh" ceremony, a unique ritual that celebrates a child's very first laugh, eloquently expresses the importance of laughter in Navajo life. Navajo humor seems to attach emphasis on keeping one's humility, in affirming a communal spirit, and in coping with a legacy of suffering.

A Reverence for the Earth

Our stay at Big Mountain was the most exciting for my students, and where they learned the most from an extended family of four generations, led by a seventy-two-year-old grandmother (shimá sani). At Big Mountain, my students experienced hózhó incorporated into everyday life. Even though the family we stayed with was threatened by removal from land their ancestors had lived on for over two hundred years, and had witnessed the removal of thousands of their neighbors, their outlook on life remained positive and inspiring to all of us.

First and foremost was their respect for the land, reflected in their daily life. Grandmother instructed the high schoolers on the proper way to collect firewood—leaving the root in the earth. "It's not good to take all of the tree," she said. Talking about the strip mining nearby at Black Mesa, she said, "You wouldn't cut the heart and liver from your mother." Her home or hogan was built from all natural materials. It is octagonal shaped and made of vertically placed cedar posts chinked with adobe. The roof is a mud dome, laced underneath with piñon. The hogan interior is the world in microcosm: earth floor and sky dome. The cardinal directions are also reflected in the hogan: door facing east, grandmother's loom on the west wall, her bed at the south wall, and dried goods stored on the north wall. When we entered her hogan, she told us to walk as the sun moves across the sky, from east to south to west, which was clockwise around the handmade wood stove in the center of the one-room hogan. To the nine juniors and seniors, this practice was refreshing, perhaps because it fit their romantic notions of Indian life; but regardless, they were deeply attracted to this reverence for the earth. Everything which gave the family nourishment and sustenance—the sheep, the land, the garden—grandmother referred to as mother (shimá). At first we took this in a metaphorical way, but later we understood that, like hózhó, it was at the core of Navajo cosmology. The reproductive and regenerating power of the mother's womb is the same as the reproductive and regenerating power of the earth, and since we are the earth's children—sustained and nourished by the fecundity of the land—the land is our mother too, not just metaphorically, but as a result of the role she plays. The same can be said of the sheep herd from which the family derived most of its sustenance and a lot of its pleasure. My students resonated with the integrity and rightness of this view. In their daily lives, they had grown cynical with the common, every-day abuse of the earth—acid rain, nuclear waste, water and air pollution, to name a few. They came to the reservation feeling out of touch with the natural world—cars, money, and television entertainment seemed to be most important. The "rituals" they practiced at home were not based on any awareness of the celestial dance, but were socially and economically oriented to help them "get ahead" in life.

Grandmother often referred to the Long Walk when Kit Carson rounded up most of the Navajo in 1864 and marched them to Bosque Redondo in eastern New Mexico where they were kept in captivity at Fort Sumner until 1868. Her great-great-grandmother, she said, returned from the Long Walk to reestablish the family's home where it is today. "The umbilical cords of our children are buried in the corral," she said. "This land is sacred because our ancestors are buried here." This feeling of place awed my students. They realized in astonishment that Native people love their home because they have always lived there—not for economic reasons, but for reasons of identity. Some of Grandmother's children live off the reservation, but they return every summer and at ceremony time because it is their home and will always be their home.

Confronting Romanticism and Stereotypes

It was interesting that the Seattle students much preferred the traditional Navajos over the more assimilated and modern ones. The fact that some families did not have a traditional hogan, and had all the latest compact disc and VCR equipment, shattered their romantic notions about the Navajo formulated at Big Mountain. My students were initially critical of those Navajo families who had all the same manifestations of "civilization" as their families had in Seattle. However, their thoughts were challenged by a field trip to the Black Mesa coal mine where Walter, a strapping and handsome Navajo in his mid-thirties, gave us a tour of the strip mines and coal sluicing operations of the Peabody Coal Company.

The day was cold with intermittent snow flurries. And since strip mines tend to look alike after awhile, my students became more interested in our Navajo guide and driver than the ravaged landscape. Walter described himself as an "ambitious" Navajo. He lived outside of Flagstaff in a modern ranch style house on several hundred acres. He commuted every day by plane from Flagstaff to Black Mesa, roughly two hundred and fifty miles. He said that several of his brothers and sisters also worked for Peabody, at over thirty thousand dollars a year. Walter said that his parents still lived a traditional life outside of Kayenta, but he openly desired to have everything that American society offered. When one of my students asked him why he did not build his house on the family land outside of Kayenta, since it would be a closer commute to work (thirty miles), Walter explained that you cannot really own property on the Reservation, and besides, he said, the equity in his one hundred-thousand-dollar-house, if it were built on the Reservation, would only be a fraction of what it is in Flagstaff. Since he based most of his major decisions on financial reasoning, he explained, it would be illogical to live on the Reservation. My students sat mute, dumbfounded by Walter's reasoning. However, among the Navajo we had met so far, Walter clearly thought and acted closer to the way their own parents made major decisions, and to the ways the students themselves presumably will make their decisions in the future. Walter buried once and for all the stereotype of the simple Indian. He taught us that what motivates the individual Navajo cannot easily be generalized.

My students sensed at the end of our month on the reservation that the Navajo culture was not dying, but evolving in response to change. It was not a sense of tradition versus progress, of choosing one over the other, but a creative synthesis of them both. Since the arrival of Europeans in the Southwest four hundred years ago, the Navajo have grown from a small tribe of 1,500 to a nation of over 200,000, and their collective land holdings continue to grow as well. The Navajo have shown a wonderful and uncanny ability to strengthen their culture with the borrowings from others, without losing their language or cultural identity. My students realized that it is easy to be rigid in your romantic ideas or misconceptions about Indians, feeling that progress destroys tradition. The history of the Navajo has displayed a successful synthesis of the two.

It is not possible in this short article to illuminate the numerous subtle shifts in perception that my students underwent during our stay at Rock Point, but they came away with a profound glimpse into another world. Grandmother referred constantly to the hogan as the center of her life because "that is where the ceremonies are held." We discovered that her home was also her temple, so to speak. My students deeply respected Grandmother—acknowledging a respect for elderly wisdom that I seldom see nowadays at a typical high school. To my students, who have little knowledge of their own myths or accept the myth of American materialism, Grandmother's poverty was only superficial, her spiritual depth exorcised the nihilism and cynicism from their minds. They came to understand the richness of Navajo spiritual wealth, and its positive effect on one's life, even when surrounded by injustice and cultural insensitivity. All of my students spoke of how difficult the experience was, but also of how essential it was to their shedding layers of ignorance and misunderstanding. They now appreciate that to be in conflict culturally is uncomfortable, but also the quickest way to learn.

Integrating the Experience

There is one last ingredient to our trip that is important to share. I presumed, as did everyone else, that the greatest learning would take place on the trip. Returning to Seattle, I learned otherwise. In establishing the timetable for the program, I had decided to return two weeks before graduation to emphasize our sharing of our experience with the rest of the school. When we returned, the nine students launched themselves into putting together a slide show with music and preparing individual presentations on an area of interest which they had chosen before we left Seattle, and which they had investigated throughout the field trip. I had made this a requirement for academic credit. Later, the presentations were typed, copied, and bound into softcover books.

The process of putting together the presentations and preparing the book helped us in ways I had not imagined. It helped us to integrate and articulate the full meaning of our experience. It helped us to cope with reverse culture shock—perhaps the most difficult part of the field trip for most of the students was the reentry to Seattle. They found themselves questioning the fast-paced and materially centered way of life, preferring the slower-paced and land-oriented Navajo way. It also gave us a process through which we could gain group support as we tried to assimilate ourselves back into our families and school.

Rigidity in their values, and rigidity in their thinking, typifies most high school teenagers that I know. Before leaving Seattle, I wondered if my students could have their self-centered values reformulated by the alchemy of a cross-cultural experience. I can truthfully say that our stay with the Navajo changed them in a profound way. They learned to distinguish between material poverty and spiritual poverty. They learned the value of language as a creator of a unique world. Probably the most important things they learned, however, were about themselves. The harmony, beauty, and goodness of the Navajo walk on the earth will now be a part of their walk as well.

Section

3

Experiential Learning in the Classroom

Chapter 7

Experiential Learning

Experiential Learning: A Teacher's Perspective

By Tom Herbert

While on sabbatical during the fall semester of 1980, I have struggled to find answers to several questions that have plagued me about experiential learning. The two questions that I started with were: "What is experiential learning?" and "How can the experiential process be applied to the classroom?" What follows are some of my findings and conclusions.

What is Experiential Learning?

When I first started to deal with this question, I tended to view experiential learning in an either/or framework: either a teaching/learning strategy is experiential or it is not. The more I studied and learned, the more I realized that this is incorrect. It is more accurate to look at it as a continuum or sliding scale. On the one end of this scale is the transmission or command approach (Sheffler, 1980, p. 61) to learning, and somewhere on the other end is the experiential process.

In the transmission or command model, the learner is a passive recipient of second-hand information. It is assumed that the student will listen and absorb information from the teacher, who, it is thought, is more experienced and knowledgeable. The teacher is the decision maker and creates the structure within the classroom. The responses sought and the stimuli used to produce the responses are the result of the decisions made by the teacher.

In the experiential model, the learner is actively involved in his/her education. Decisions are made by the learner that have a direct bearing on what is learned and how it is learned. The teacher's role is that of guide, resource person, clarifier. Their attention is on both the content of what is being learned, as well as the process of learning that is taking place.

Some of the variables that affect where the style of learning is on the continuum are reality, risk, responsibility, predictability, and analysis or reflection. They deserve a closer look.

Reality of the Experience

How long the learning lasts is dependent on the amount of reality involved, the directness of the experience, and the number of senses involved. Interviewing a former P.O.W. in person is going to result in longer-lasting learning than reading the same interview that was conducted by someone else.

Dr. C. Christian Jernstedt, an associate professor of psychology at Dartmouth, has done research on the use of experience in academic courses. He points out that "active learning is more efficient than passive or highly directed learning" (Jernstedt, 1980, pp. 12–13). He also states that "students who use information they are trying to learn, who challenge and grapple with their new knowledge, or who use it to solve new problems, tend to learn more effectively than students who passively read, memorize, or merely absorb that to which they have been exposed" (p. 12). He cites other research that shows that "learners remember not what they encounter while learning so much as what they do while learning" (p. 12).

Although primary experiences are better, indirect experiences aid in learning. Vicarious experiences, such as examples, stories, or movies help to secure the learning. Jernstedt states that "tying information to be learned to experience, even when the experience is purely hypothetical, can preserve the learning within the mind and prime the mind for new learning more effectively than other techniques" (Jernstedt, 1980, p. 13).

In his article on academics and experiential components, Dr. Jernstedt shared some of his research conclusions on the benefits of vicarious experiences in the classroom. Among these conclusions were:

- instructor supplied, class-wide experiences, such as from a movie, novel, or trip, are better than individual experiences because they have been shared and can be validated;
- printed handouts or examples drawn from real life [were] remembered more accurately and longer than those taught without them;
- demonstrations, remembered the best and for the longest period of time, should be chosen for their intellectual value and not simply as motivational aids;
- modeling, in which the instructor actually engages in the behavior which the students are trying to learn, has a powerful effect on learning. (Jernstedt, p. 15)

Level of Risk

There needs to be a sense of uncertainty for the learner and that is a part of the sense of reality stated above. In *Experience and Education,* John Dewey states that "...growth depends upon the presence of difficulty to be overcome by the exercise of intelligence" (Dewey, 1938, p. 79). The difficulty Dewey refers to can be either physical, emotional, social, or intellectual. It could be the result of having to make a speech on a personally important issue, finding oneself in what is perceived to be a dangerous situation, or being relied upon by other class members to successfully complete a task.

In utilizing this discordant atmosphere, the teacher must also take care to create an environment of trust and support, without which the learner will not risk anything. For example, in a recent sociology class at our high school, we discussed different types of risk in class participation. The class concluded that being called on by a teacher was of little risk because your opinion was being solicited. You were not being given the choice of sharing it or not. To volunteer an opinion involved a lot of risk because what you said had to have some value to you because you were offering it. Class discussions and opinion sharing are important to our class. Therefore, we do not allow "killer statements" or put-downs. We disagree, but disagree without value-laden judgments. To do otherwise would be to foster an environment where only a few would be willing to risk.

This concept of risk has been defined as a "vigorous environment," which is "...any place in which you are uncomfortable, or any place in which you have not learned to behave" (King, 1980). Thus there is personal risk involved on the dance floor or on a rock wall, spending time alone or standing in front of a group, or working in a day care center or old age home. Vigorous environments vary for the individual.

The greater the level of risk, the more real one perceives the consequences of one's actions. The sense of reality of those consequences helps to involve the entire person into the experience. It is no longer simply a physical or intellectual exercise. The reality of the consequences that arises from the uncertainty is the glue that cements the learning for the individual.

Sense of Responsibility

In experiential learning, a sense of personal commitment or investment by the learner in what is being undertaken is required. The learner is involved in decisions leading up to the experience. He or she chooses the course, the assignment, or method of presentation; helps in the construction of the test; participates in the decision of what should be covered in the unit of study. This establishes a certain level of responsibility and expectation on the part of the student.

Once the student has been involved in the decision making, he or she also has a responsibility to help carry it through. Instead of remaining on the sidelines as a recipient of someone else's decisions, the learner is now responsible for helping to implement them. Eliot Wigginton once advised staff members of a basic belief at Foxfire. Simply stated it was: "Before you start to do anything related to your work with this organization, ask yourself first why a student is not doing it instead. If you don't have a good reason, then go and find a student—preferably one who has never done it before" (Wigginton, 1978, p. 30). In experiential learning, teachers are not responsible for their students' learning so much as they are responsible to their students to help them learn.

Students involved in experiential learning make decisions that affect their learning. A teacher committed to experiential learning must be willing to accept the consequences of those student activities. (The only exceptions to this are decisions that affect the safety of an individual or the group. In these cases, student decisions must be carefully monitored by the teacher and may be occasionally overruled.)

Perhaps two examples will help establish this point. Before we left on a March trip to a mountain pond with the ROPE class (a modified, Outward Bound course at Concord

High), one of the students asked if he could bring along his fishing pole. As long as he had the proper licenses, it was not a problem…except for the thick layer of ice on the pond that we expected to discover. When we arrived, he went down to the pond with a small borrowed hatchet to chop a hole in the ice. Just before we left the next day, he was still chopping in the hole, visible only from the waist up.

The point here is that the staff expected the pond would be covered by an impossibly thick layer of ice. Yet we allowed him to learn this for himself in a far more meaningful way than if we had told him. (He ended up bringing his fishing gear on every future trip, as a matter of pride I suspect. On the last trip, a bike trip, he finally managed to hook something—his hand—while riding his bike!)

The second example is from a different class. "Homegrown" was an oral history class that we had at CHS. As a part of the class, we took a field trip of 12 days to another part of the country. The trip was designed to provide us with the opportunity to learn from local people rather than simply sightsee. One year, the class had set up a seminar with a local resource person from a college. He was an extremely easygoing and humorous person, until he got in front of a group. In that formalized situation, he became very boring, reading virtually verbatim from his notes. True to form, this trip he had roughly 40% of the class nodding off within 20 minutes. When we went out for a break, I asked the class if everyone had liked the first half of his presentation. After a few initial grumbles and foot shuffles, someone, in a bit of understatement, said, "Uh, I think he's a bit dry." I then asked if there was any way they could change his method of presentation to make him feel more comfortable. After talking for a few minutes, they decided to ask him questions and to get him telling stories. The second half was much more interesting, and even the resource person enjoyed it more because he could sense the students' interest through their questions.

In this example, I asked a question, seeking to determine if the students were dissatisfied with the presentation. If they had all been content, I would have let the issue drop. I would not interject my opinion, at that point. After the session was complete and we were back at camp, I would have posed questions to determine if the students perceived the same boredom as I did. If they did not, I would have left it alone. If they did, then another question could follow about how they would deal with a boring or uncomfortable resource person at another time.

In these examples, the carrying of the fishing pole and the lack of initiative in dealing with the boredom in the first half of the presentation, are not "mistakes." The only true mistakes are experiences that one doesn't learn from or that don't lead to further learning. What is ordinarily perceived as a mistake is an acceptable part of experiential learning because the focus of learning is on the process of achieving the goal, as well as on the goal itself.

Note in the second example that it was the students who determined that the speaker's presentation was boring. It was not my imposing my value structure on the students. This is not to say that the teacher must never offer his or her opinions. On the contrary, the teacher must be responsible to the group to share his or her observations. In fact in that same example, I would still share my feelings that night, but only as observations. However, one must be aware of the weight one's opinion carries and how easily one can affect decisions, simply because of one's role as "teacher."

Predictability

In experiential learning, the specific outcome is not always predictable. This is a result of the students' involvement in decision making and the teacher's role being that of clarifier, rather than leader, and the overall process versus product approach. The range of student options requires the teacher to determine the possible outcomes of the student choices. The teacher must plan for each of those possibilities. The student choices should not be limited by ineffective teacher planning. At the same time, teacher enthusiasm should not be tempered by overplanning.

Anticipating every possible outcome and planning for it removes some of the adventure and discovery for the teacher. Nothing can replace that genuine shared enthusiasm between teacher and students. This is a fine line for the teacher to walk, and how much to pre-plan and how much to allow to develop is dependent on both the teacher's experience in this area as well as his or her confidence in being able to adjust to the moment.

It is very tempting for the teacher to try and manipulate the students to select the one plan for which the teacher is ready. It can also be frustrating for the teacher to plan for five possibilities, knowing full well that only one may be selected. It is important for the teacher to appreciate the significance of choice in experiential learning in order to

keep this possible frustration at manageable levels.

An example of this planning might be the teacher who has decided that the students should determine what format their reports will take. Thinking about it, the teacher anticipates that some students will write as usual. What other options are there? Tape record it! Are tape recorders available for student use in the media center? Videotape it! Is there someone available to instruct the students in its use? Are blank tapes available? A photographic essay! Is there film available and can students borrow the camera from the photography class? Once answers to these and other questions are determined, the teacher knows it is possible. It is important for the teacher to know if the options are feasible. If not, then it is really no choice at all. This information is not passed on to the student. It is up to the student to discover this information on his or her own. If he or she does get stymied, then the teacher can guide with some hints or possibilities, while not robbing the student of that experience.

Occasionally a student will propose an option that has not been planned for. Rather than rejecting it as unrealistic, the teacher should encourage the student to develop the idea more. Perhaps the student will discover that it is truly unrealistic. On the other hand, perhaps the teacher will learn that it is possible.

Reflection and Analysis

In experiential learning, the student decides what he or she learned from the different experiences that were encountered. One method of determining this is through reflection, or thinking about what has taken place and one's position within that process. This reflection can be verbal or nonverbal, alone or as a group, or alone with the instructor, or with the class and the instructor. There is no single correct way. It should also be understood that this analysis and reflection does not just take place after the conclusion of the planned activity. It takes place when it is needed during the activity, not only when it is convenient. The goal of education is learning. If that learning takes place at the beginning, in the midst, or at the conclusion of the activity, the goal is met. The experience is simply the vehicle to achieve the learning. An experience by itself is just that—an experience. It was John Dewey who said "Learning is thinking about experience" (Dewey, 1938).

To be an effective facilitator of this type of reflection and analysis, the teacher must be a good observer of what is happening. He or she needs to observe not only the learners' actions and nonactions toward the activity, but also vis à vis each other. Then, at appropriate times, observations could be offered, questions asked, feelings explored.

The teacher must also be able to vary his or her approach in helping the students analyze what has taken place. The methods are dependent on the personalities and situations involved. At times, it might be necessary to be blunt and honest with feedback. At other times, questions, discussions, or a gentle approach help the students discover for themselves what they have done and how they are perceived. Sometimes nothing needs to be said. It is difficult to know the approach to use with each individual in each situation. Experience is a good teacher.

Another stimulus for analysis and reflection in experiential learning is the application of the newly learned skills in another demanding situation. The re-application of the learning helps to ensure that the students know the skills. The fact that it is in a different situation helps the students understand that the learning is not in isolation; there are other applications. Without this "bridge building," what is learned in the woods will stay in the woods, what is learned in science will stay in science, what is learned in school will stay in school.

For example, in a geometry class, if a student learns about angles and degrees and then is given a compass and asked how it could be used and how one could find one's way with it, the student can begin not only to understand some of the applications but also appreciate the principles involved. The teacher could then go on and have the students determine other possible applications of the principles.

A second example is the speech requirement we have in the ROPE class at Concord High School. The question is often asked, "Why a five-minute prepared speech in an outdoor class?" The reasons are two-fold. First, it helps the students realize that fear is fear, whether it is on a rock face or in front of a class. If you can use your inner strength to overcome it in the former, that same inner strength can be drawn on to help you in the latter. And why stop tapping that strength there? The second reason is so that those students who felt little or no fear on the rock face can understand something about those people who did, when the roles are exchanged, and they stand alone in front of the class, sharing a part of themselves.

The interrelationship of these five factors is complex. It is impossible to withdraw or modify one without affecting the others. The level of risk is at least partially determined by the reality of the experience and vice versa. The students' sense of ownership and responsibility for what is being learned influences the outcome and makes it less predictable. The students' analysis of what has been learned is influenced by all of the others.

The first three of these factors are each on their own continuum. The greater the reality of the experience, the higher the level of risk, and the more responsibility the students sense, then the more experiential the process. Movement on any of these scales affects the overall predictability of the experience. They will vary and shift depending on the situation. The type of reflection and analysis utilized will be dependent upon the above four factors. In order to be able to deal with this ebb and flow, the teacher must have a good understanding of the experiential learning process.

Successful experiential learning might appear to simply be a series of unconnected and haphazard events that students are doing, if the observer has little or no understanding of the learning process involved. In fact, there have been several attempts to explain this process. One of the earliest is the model by Ron Gager (Gager, 1977, pp. 4–5).

In this representation, the learner should be impelled (rather than compelled) into the "demanding reality context." This is accomplished through encouragement, reasoning humor, gentle pressure, or other techniques. The point is to make it the student's choice

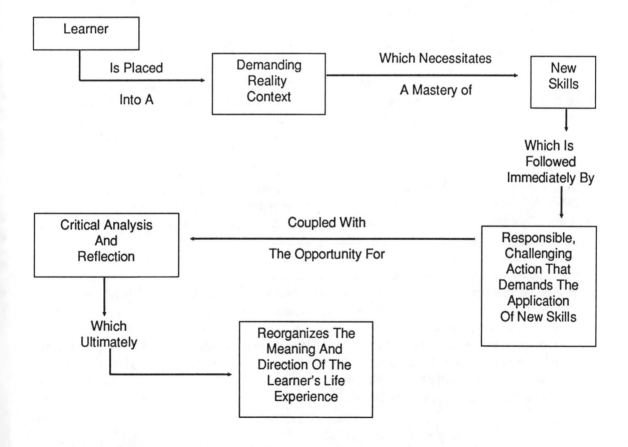

to partake in the experience. The "demanding reality context" is a situation that can cause people to act and to be responsible for themselves and others. It requires decisions to be made and immediate feedback will result. The "new skills" are taught in sequence and as building blocks. These skills are necessary to function effectively in the new environment and they show tangible evidence of growth in the learner's abilities. The "responsible challenging action" that follows the learning of the new skills is one in which others are dependent on what one does, and the consequences are examined directly by the learner and others. These acts need to be meaningful to the learner and beyond his previous level of experience. The "critical analysis and reflection" is related to the action undertaken and leads to further action. It provides a sense of closure on the one hand, but also suggests ways to transfer the learning to other aspects of one's life (James, 1980, p. 12; please see Appendix 1 at the end of this chapter for suggestions on where and how teachers can learn these principles).

How Can Experiential Learning Be Applied in a Classroom Setting?

The problem here is not only the physical limitations of the classroom. Rather, it is the other restrictions that go along with it as a part of a school program: noise level, time constraints, student and teacher responsibilities in other classes, and transportation, to name a few. Also involved in this is the problem of how to create a "vigorous environment" in a place where students already know how to behave. Finally, it must be remembered that students generally have little choice over whether to be in school or not. Since student choice is an important part of experiential learning, this is almost an impossible problem to overcome.

There are several ways of dealing with these restrictions. Here are some of mine. Students have to be in school. It isn't a choice they have. Without getting into the pros and cons of that issue in this paper, I deal with this law in my classes by accepting it as a given that I have to work with. It is not a pure and perfect world with all students choosing to be in school or in my class.

I tend to view the problems of noise, time, outside commitments, and transportation as just that—problems. They are difficult to deal with, but not insurmountable. They can be overcome. By remaining flexible, keeping a sense of humor, being reasonable in what I do, and not impinging too much or too often on other teachers, I can generally do what I want to do. The classic example is the seats-in-the-row problem. I like moving desks around to fit what the class does. Other teachers with whom I share the rooms (and the desks) don't. Instead of a cold war, we have established the "Concord High Compromise": they put them in a circle for me and I put them in rows for them or vice versa. The point is, different people learn in different ways. My way is not the only way. My way is only one way.

The problem of creating "vigorous environments" where students are generally comfortable can also be solved. First, the teacher must determine in what ways the students are used to behaving. Once those have been determined, then the expectations or environment can begin to be changed. A student who is used to a teacher-centered classroom will find a student-centered classroom creates a "vigorous environment." Students used to only individual tests will find group tests challenge their accepted ways of acting. Since there is usually more than one student in a class and what is a "vigorous environment" for one might not be for another, then the environment needs to be changed on an irregular and unpredictable basis.

The concept of "an adventure" is also helpful when one is faced with these restrictions. In the book, *Teaching Through Adventure,* the authors identify four elements that comprise "adventure education" (Lentz, Smith, Sentowski, & Seidman, 1976). One of these is the idea of having "an adventure," which is different from the stereotype of adventure programs, which were, and still are, thought of as wilderness programs. Many people have not been adventurers in the wilderness-traveler sense of the word. Yet they have been on "an adventure" at different times. These adventures could have been the development of the first photograph, reading one's own poem to a class, the writing of a book review and then the sending of it to the book's author, or the discovery of a possible solution to a difficult problem confronted by a social agency in one's town. One doesn't have to go to the top of a mountain to have "an adventure."

There appear to be some elements common to all adventures, and I believe all three must be present in some degree for "an adventure" to take place. Called the "Three Rs," they relate back to the description of experiential learning. Reality—There is a sense that what is being encountered is real. Risk—The adventure creates some uncertainty or discomfort. Responsibility—The learner has a sense of ownership for what is being undertaken. For each student, his or her sense of what is real, the risk involved, and his or her responsibility to the outcome will vary.

One of the easiest ways to create the idea of "an adventure" within a school is for the class to go on an extended field trip. This is one of three different types of experiential curricula that exist in the schools. The extended field trip could be for the weekend or over several weeks. It could be a trip to the mountains to study ecology, a sociological study in an urban area, or a history class re-enacting a march across the state. Activities and preparations within the classroom focus on the trip and become part of the adventure. Fund raising, development of the areas of study, logistics, relations with the rest of the school, and media contacts are only a few of the activities that can be utilized.

The second type of curriculum is planned around the short adventure of a few hours. This is different because the time constraints limit not only what can be done, but also where. Field trips to a funeral home or a prison are examples of "vigorous environments" that can be utilized in experiential lessons. A class studying Shakespeare can stage one-act presentations for the school or nursing homes in town. French classes can make use of the Home Economics facilities and bake French pastries, speaking only in French while cooking...and eating. The possibilities are limited only by one's imagination.

The third type of curriculum is what can be done in a classroom period. This is even more limited by the constraints noted in the short adventure. As a result of these constraints, the levels of risk and reality in the adventure are reduced. This should not deter the experiential teacher, for experiences in the day-in-and-day-out schedule are critical.

Too often, teachers will become discouraged because they can't seem to pull off the "big adventure." While important, in the long run the "big adventure" is no more important than what the teacher does in the other 160 days of the year.

Within the classroom period, adventures can be undertaken that involve direct experience. A lesson on trust can be underscored with a blindfolded Trust Walk. A study of prisons can be augmented with a period of sensory deprivation. An important decision in history can be brought more clearly into focus by a difficult problem-solving situation with which students must grapple. An English teacher at our high school uses obscure facts and little known people in a mystery-like format to introduce his students to the resource section of the library. Classes can be split in half with each half making up a test for the other group. Then the test can be given to either group. In sociology, a recent project was for students to become experts on one of the many social agencies in town. They had to contact the agency, spend ten hours of volunteer time there, and learn the social problem that the agency was trying to deal with. They were also asked to determine what difficulties that agency faced in trying to solve that social problem and to pose some practical solutions for those problems. Members of the agency were asked to read and comment on the students' reports. Other small-group or individual projects can be structured that utilize reality, risk, and responsibility, and incorporate student decision making and analysis.

Conclusion

I have tried to answer two specific questions in this paper. On the way to those answers, I have learned a great deal more and have tried to pass some of that along to you, the reader. In answering those questions, I have reached two conclusions that are extremely important. These are:

1. Understanding the flow and process of experiential learning is critical to its implementation. Too often, practitioners will latch onto the outward visible manifestations of an educational concept without really understanding the underlying philosophy. Without an adequate grounding in the principles, they can only repeat what others have done before. They cannot transfer the principles to new learning situations because they only know the symbols of those principles, be it a ropes course or cultural journalism magazine, and not the principles themselves.

2. Experiential learning can take place anywhere there are interested people. The adventure doesn't have to be of monumental proportions. Leo Buerman, a man born with severe birth defects and sheltered for most of his life, wrote that "Courage is a factor in many things that are seemingly insignificant" (Buerman). It is one of the jobs of the teacher to find some of those "things" that appear insignificant and to let students learn from them.

For the teacher, experiential learning is "an adventure" in and of itself. It carries with it those elements of risk, reality, and responsibility. Although it is hard to plan for the various options, to deal with the unexpected, and to remain flexible to student needs, the results can be worth it. Note that I didn't say "will be worth it," in the previous sentence.

In experiential learning there are few guarantees, for to have them would reduce these same "Three Rs." The teacher, then, becomes a student as well.

END NOTES

Israel Shefler's discussion of the transmission-style of teaching is quoted in an unpublished paper by Sherrod Reynolds, "A proposal for marriage: competency based education and experiential learning," December 16, 1980. The command-style of teaching is from Muska Mosston, *Teaching Physical Education*.

Buerman, L. In a movie made by Coronet Films.

Dewey, J. (1938). Experience and education. New York.

Gager, R. (1977). Experiential learning process flow. Voyageur Reports, 1(1).

James, T. (1980). Education at the edge: The Colorado Outward Bound School. Denver.

Jernstedt, G. C. (1980). Experiential components in academic courses. Journal of Experiential Education. 3(2).

King, K. V. (1980–81). Operation LIVE Bulletin, Vol. 2, No. 3, (second semester), side 1.

Lentz, R., Smith, M., Sentowski, A., & Seidman, M. (1976). Teaching through adventure: A practical approach. Hamilton, MA: Project Adventure.

Wigginton, E. (1978). Beyond Foxfire. Journal of Experiential Education, 1(2).

Appendix 1

What follows is a list of written and human resources that I found useful and relevant:

1. The Association for Experiential Education publishes a professional journal and has many other services. The address is 2885 Aurora Ave. #28, Boulder, CO 80303.

2. Project Adventure has several curriculum guides that are useful for classroom teachers. One of the best is *Teaching Through Adventure: A Practical Approach*. Their address is P.O. Box 100, Hamilton, MA 01936.

3. *Moments: The Foxfire Experience*, by Eliot Wigginton provides a good philosophical background for experiential learning as well as a practical introduction to culture.

4. *Experience and Education*, by John Dewey, is a very small book that is packed with ideas. An excellent resource that needs to be re-read occasionally.

The Midwife Teacher: Engaging Students in the Experiential Education Process

by Karen Warren

Uncritical advocates of experiential education might say that students are so naturally impelled into an absorbing experience that it just cannot help being richly educational. Yet, is creating a dramatic unknown enough to engage tentative participants in activities? I suggest that the skilled experiential educator must do more than create an activity and hope that students will embrace it with willingness. A major role of the teacher in the experiential education process is provide a safe space for learning to occur and to encourage students to recognize the opportunities for growth available to them. How to create both safe and educationally nurturing programs is the focus of this article.

Teacher as Midwife

> Midwife teachers are the opposite of banker teachers. While the bankers deposit knowledge in the learner's head, the midwives draw it out. They assist the students in giving birth to their own ideas, in making their own tacit knowledge explicit and elaborating it. (Belenky, Clinchy, Goldberger, & Tarule, 1986, p. 217)

The experiential educator as midwife is a useful metaphor in describing how to engage students. This idea is based on the notion that the group or class collectively holds all the information, experience, or knowledge necessary for learning to occur. The role of the midwife instructor is similar to the traditional midwife whose job is to guide and to guard birth (Willis, 1991). She/he assists in the birth of new ideas by: 1) drawing from the resources of the group of learners (*guiding*), and 2) securing the safety of the learning environment (*guarding*). (See Table 1.)

While I have used a midwife teaching style to work with college students in experiential classroom settings for Hampshire College and Lesley College's National Audubon Expedition Institute, applications of these ideas are possible with other student populations or in other classroom, outdoor, or community situations.

When acting as a midwife, the teacher creates a safe learning atmosphere, both physically and psychologically, where learners are not afraid to take risks. A student in an educationally safe space more fully bonds with the group, maintains self-esteem, and embraces all learning potentials. As Rogers (1969) points out, learning that is perceived as threatening is much more easily assimilated when the environment is safe.

Methods of Educational Midwifery

The traditional midwife guides the pregnant woman along the journey toward birth, stepping aside when the mother's ability to give birth naturally occurs. The teacher midwife steps aside when the student is engaged in the learning process, yet continues to guard the learning environment to allow a blossoming of the student's curiosity and quest for knowledge. In a sense, the teacher vacillates between guiding the students to solve the barriers to learning they often encounter, and guarding the intensity and safety of their engagement.

Table 1. Parallels Between the Traditional Midwife and the Teacher Midwife

Traditional Midwife
(adapted from Willis, 1991, and Solomon & McLean, 1991)

1. Provides a quality of care and uses available resources effectively
2. Guards the birth environment
3. Displays an attitude of undiscriminating nurturance
4. Does not place instruments between herself and the mother and baby
5. Is able to see the whole picture of the woman and child
6. Remains an apprentice to the birth process with a capability to cycle, change, and grow
7. Believes that women and babies are the true experts in giving birth and being born
8. Is not afraid of death, rather sees it as a natural process

Experiential Educator Midwife

1. Manages logistics
2. Guards the learning environment by using ground rules and naming fears
3. Serves as nurturer
4. Establishes an accessible relationship with students
5. Acknowledges commonalities and recognizes differences
6. Remains a learner/participant
7. Creates student-centered learning by using dialogic teaching, student decision making, and real choices
8. Assists with closure

Based on definition, the traditional midwife is with the mother and child at birth (Kramarae & Treichler, 1991); accordingly, the midwife experiential educator is with the student in their learning cycle—guiding and nurturing the experience from whatever role seems necessary at the time.

The following eight responsibilities are essential for teachers who hope to utilize methods of educational midwifery in experiential education settings.

1. Manage Logistics

It is the job of the midwife teacher to handle logistics, to allow students full attention to the lessons possible in the situation. Shoddy logistical management often gives rise to focus on minutiae rather than substantive experiential learning. For example, if the experience I have chosen is a blindfold walk in a local woods to build group unity and awareness, certain logistical supports will enhance the event. If I ignore the transportation arrangements, forget the blindfolds, get lost because I'm not familiar with the environment, or neglect to tell the students what to wear, then I am detracting from the intended experience. Of course, I could use the "teachable moment" to transform my mistakes into something educational (i.e., that getting lost shows students' self-reliance). However, the original goals of the activity have been compromised. The activity had been chosen to glean results from the original intention of the experience, not its serendipitous transformation.

Equipment that doesn't work, areas that are unfamiliar to the instructor, and lack of suitable contingency plans all impede the smooth development of a learning experience. Experiential education has enough distracting moments without neglected logistical details adding to the chaos. Time is valuable in teaching; therefore, having the props, as well as a finely crafted progression of presentation, is imperative.

2. Guard the Initial Learning Environment

The creation of safe space in teaching geared to using experiences cannot be underestimated. Both physical and emotional safety are imperative; they also don't just happen. In fact, they are often overlooked due to what I call the tyranny of experience. Often in their belief in the value of the activity and the subsequent follow-up, instructors bypass the initial psychological safety building in an effort to get right to the heart of the experience. Such instructors have students out swinging in the treetops before they are even comfortable in a group of their own peers.

Taking small incremental steps in culturing safe space pays tremendous dividends later on in the experience. Illustrative of this concept is a statement a student once made after a particularly intense class. She said that when there were unknowns in class she did what was most familiar to her, but when she felt comfortable she was able to branch into the unknown. She could risk only when she was emotionally protected.

Sometimes I'm tempted to pass over steps in the development of a safe space because it appears that the students are already at ease. I remind myself that adaptation to a situation is not the same as true engagement; and the appearance of comfort displayed by the group should be tempered by an awareness that, in our culture, people are often not taught to be responsible for their emotional safety.

The following methods are ways for an instructor to set the stage for enhanced student engagement in an experience. They are hallmarks of an educational midwifery process that values a psychological safety net.

Table 2. Examples of Ground Rules Set by Students

- Confidentiality—whatever is said in the group stays within the membership.
- Each person has the freedom to say no or to pass.
- There is no right answer or way of doing something.
- Everything is negotiable
- Use communication enhancers:
  - Allow people to say complete sentences without interruption.
  - Leave a pause after someone speaks to allow less vocal people a chance to enter the conversation.
  - Allow brief moments of silence to assimilate what a person has said.
- Use inclusive language whenever possible.
- Each person's experience is valid—you don't have to be politically correct.
- Disallow "put downs."
- Respect people's different backgrounds and learning styles.
- It's okay to listen and not have to talk.
- Speak only for yourself—use "I" statements.
- Stick to commitments made.
- Respect people's ideas and where they are on the "path."
- Both feelings and logical ideas are important.
- Be honest to both self and others.

a. Ground rule setting. Ground rules, or ways of relating to each other in class, provide a consistent set of operational standards for the learning community. Students help set these standards and are responsible for ensuring that they are upheld. I usually start a course by facilitating a brainstorm of the ground rules, so students have an initial sense of security they can control (See Table 2). An immense degree of trust and potential for risk taking emerges when the students voice to their peers how they envision the class can be made safer for them.

b. Naming of fears. Each student carries to an experience a certain hesitancy which they sometimes are not able to share with the rest of the group. A common assumption, that if fears are ignored they will be dispelled, can invalidate the student's experience. Bringing fears to the awareness of the entire group is a method for diffusing their impact and an opportunity for the group to problem-solve solutions before they potentially occur.

At Hampshire College, we often use a game called "Fear in a Hat." Group members anonymously write a fear they have about the impending experience on a slip of paper which goes into a hat. A fear is then drawn from the hat by each student, who makes sure not to choose his/her own. Each person in succession then acts out the fear as if it were their own, ad libbing to clarify and truly "own" the fear. Other group members offer support for the person's fear and suggest ways to resolve it. The advantage of this exercise is that it allows people to voice fears anonymously and experience a compassionate response from the group. Many times the fears in the hat are similar and students express relief that others in the group share their apprehension.

3. Serve as Nurturer

Students come to classes with years of very intense schooling in ways that are far from experiential. They are bursting with hopes of an educational panacea, yet at the same time they are caught by routinized constructs of learning. They are ineffective and clumsy in their attempts to question and dismantle stilted educational methods because they have been trained so well in what to expect from a class. They have been indoctrinated in what to give and receive, while being mystified about how much they can claim of their own learning and how much they must wait to be fed. Therefore, the teacher's first challenge is to deprogram the students' dependence on spoonfed learning and to inspire curiosity.

Many times I see experiential educators who are wary of structuring an experience, believing that rigidity and loss of creativity might result. Yet if structure is reframed as nurturing and respectful guidance, its value is obvious. Dewey (1938) maintains that guidance given by the teacher is an aid to freedom, not a restriction. So those times when I expect the students to dive right into an exciting activity, yet they seem to be holding back, I should consider that they might need a compassionate boost.

The Foxfire program is an excellent example of this concept of educational midwifery. When the Foxfire staff started using cultural journalism, they didn't just cast students out into the mountains of Georgia to find a good story. Teachers nurtured students by instilling confidence and, with student input, set up a structured experience (Wigginton, 1986). Conducting an interview and writing a proper sentence were just a few of the skills students were taught to guide their endeavors. Foxfire teachers took the background and heritage students brought to the program and cultivated it to draw forth new skills and knowledge.

4. Establish Relationship

As any effective speaker knows, establishing a relationship with the audience is the foundation of a successful speech. The midwife teacher strives in the same vein to convey a sense of connection with the class so that trust and relationship sustain the budding learning collaboration. Because relevance of knowledge occurs when we can understand something in relationship to ourselves or the world, the model that the midwife teacher creates in building relationship is integral to constructing knowledge. Being vulnerable and accessible are primary avenues for the teacher to build relationship.

Analogous to the midwife, who places no instruments between herself and the mother and baby, is the midwife teacher who demonstrates no excessive reliance on power between themselves and the student. Their relationship is symbiotic with learning flowing in both directions. Power entrusted to the teacher in a midwifery model of education is based on "the concept of power as energy, capacity and potential rather than as domination" (Shrewsbury, 1987, p. 8).

5. Acknowledge Commonalities and Recognize Differences

When beginning a group experience, students need to feel that there are others like them ready to embark on the journey. Feeling alone is not conducive to engagement in an activity. Consequently, the midwife instructor's attention to discerning commonalities takes priority in the initial stages of the group. This is consistent with many group theorists' (Jensen, 1979; Weber, 1982) ideas about the cycle of group process.

"Common Ground " is a great exercise to achieve recognition of things potentially shared by group members. The group stands in a circle with one person in the center who invites anyone who, for example, was born on the East Coast, or likes avocados, or plays the guitar, etc., to come into the circle and share common ground. After a moment of acknowledgment, the game continues with a new person stepping to the center and announcing the commonality. Students begin to recognize their connections with other group members and use the feelings of belonging as support to take risks in new situations.

As with commonalities, when teachers ignore diversity, they lose a vital opportunity to promote a climate of psychological safety in their classes. If students are assimilated into a narrowly defined view of identity (i.e., the dominant social paradigm), teachers disallow students who are different to occupy a central place in the learning community. Some differences are obvious, but others are hidden, in part, due to the melting pot mentality of many societies. It might be useful for teachers to consider that composition of any group they work with might include students who have physical and learning disabilities, who are survivors of physical or sexual violence, who are gay/lesbian, whose subordinate religious or ethnic identity is not immediately obvious, or who have contact with some form of drug or alcohol abuse. Good midwife teachers cannot afford to imagine their classes as homogeneous units where they teach to a presumed common denominator.

After I've established some initial commonalities, I usually proceed with a "diversity rap." I name the significant differences that may be present in any group and state that each student brings the gift of their unique experience, even if that difference is considered silent or taboo in this society. I don't single people out or ask people to reveal any secrets, but I do acknowledge that we are vulnerable and have parts of ourselves that are difficult to share. I've had students tell me later on that the unconditional acceptance they experienced early in the group solidified their ability to participate as themselves.

6. Remain a Learner/Participant

Experiential education should not be something we do to our students. Passion must not be passé in teaching. Students benefit when they know what raises the teacher's creative energy level. Beidler (1986) suggests the best way to learn a new subject is to teach it.

The midwife experiential educator sees students as her/his primary teachers and listens to the students in order to retrieve the information essential to strengthen the teacher/learner synergy in the learning process.

While I'm not supposing that teachers will engage in each activity in the same manner as the students, teachers who model the joys and challenges of their own learning process can help students become comfortable with learning experientially. So if educators require students to read journal reflections, they should be prepared to share their own. If they use initiatives to build group unity, they should do the Trust Falls right along with the students.

7. Create Student-Centered Learning Experiences

Student-centered learning is essential to keep students passionately involved in the experiential education process. Students plunged into an experiential learning situation do not necessarily embrace a student-centered existence; it is through the conscious intention and skilled educational invitation of the midwife teacher that a student-centered milieu is created. Teachers, by virtue of their granted power of position, are continually engaged in guiding students to claim their own education (Rich, 1979). Similar to the traditional midwife who believes that the woman and baby innately understand birth, the midwife teacher respects the student's ability to discern a responsible learning path. Therefore, acting as a resource and facilitator of the student's chosen path is the role of the midwife teacher. Student responsibility for curriculum development is one way to achieve this (Warren, 1988), but there are other methods as well.

a. Dialogic teaching. The use of a dialogic technique, suggested by Freire (1984), is an excellent tool for the experiential educator. The teacher strives to engage the students by posing questions or problems to be solved, then cultures an interactive discussion rich in critical thinking. The goal is to decrease teacher "air time" and promote student involvement. As Shor (1986) points out, "dialogue is the art of intervention and the art of restraint, so that the verbal facility of a trained intellectual (the teacher) does not silence the verbal styles of unscholarly students." How experiential learning situations are processed could certainly be enhanced by the dialogic method. A midwife experiential educator can guide the reflection sessions by instigating a dialogue that builds on students' reactions to an experience, and then encourage students to engage in dialogic processing with each other.

b. Student-centered decision making.

There are many decisions that teachers make out of habit that can be the domain of the learners. Everything, from when to take a break to what to learn, can be the responsibility of the students to decide in a course taught with attention to educational midwifery.

The midwife teacher guides the students by teaching them how to make decisions consensually, by assisting with the development of new roles in the use of consensus, and by pointing out where other forms of decision making might be better employed (Warren & Tippett, 1988). They guard the students' newborn flash of power to determine their own destiny by firmly facilitating through the problem parts in early attempts to reach consensus. The teacher does this by protecting the consensual process from being subtly subverted or railroaded, and by picking up advocacy roles the group forgets to assume.

c. Real Choices.

Student choice is at the heart of student-empowered learning. Pioneered by women's programs, the "okay to pass" option in an activity has gained popularity over the "only failure is not to try" philosophy that has been the foundation of many adventure-based programs in the past. This trend evolved as program staff started to realize that empowerment came more from choice than subtle coercion. Certainly work by Hunt (1990) on ethical considerations of experiential education advanced the notion that a participant's informed consent extended to all elements of experiential programming.

I remember the days in outdoor adventure programs when pressuring students off rappels or onto ropes courses because it was "good for them" was the norm. Students either caved in to the peer pressure or abdicated their power to the instructor's "trust me." Fortunately, professional leaders have come to realize that giving learners the power to determine what will enhance their experience is an avenue of real growth. Students must have the ability to say "no" before they can ever strongly affirm a "yes."

The midwife teacher fosters student choices that can be supported no matter which they choose. They work to remove the subtle consequences and implications of failure that exist when a student says no to an experience.

8. Assist with Closure

The teacher midwife's role in a group which is ending is to provide guidance that will ease the transition. Closure is difficult for students; it brings up other endings in their lives that might not have been satisfactorily resolved. Students have not been taught in our society to productively reconcile losses such as death, divorce, and the breakup of friendships, so these losses have echoes haunting the closing of every group (Tippett, 1988).

Teacher-assisted endings are critical. there is a psychological satisfaction in tying things up, in reaching conclusions, in making connections between things learned. Sloppy closure robs importance from what might have been a poignant experience. The teacher assists with termination primarily by providing a safe space for feelings to exist. It helps to inform groups that intense emotions will arise, that tasks will take longer, and that expectations individuals have of themselves and others may need to be temporarily scaled down. It behooves the instructor to provide more structure than might be apparent at this stage of group development, mainly because the group is so engaged in feelings of mourning and transformation that group members don't have the same ability to attend to group needs that they had earlier in their process. Their detachment is the challenge confronted by the midwife teacher who attempts to deliver them safely to the next life experience by effectively facilitating the closure of the present experience.

The following are closure ideas I have used in teaching situations:

▪ Set a distinct time for closure with the group. It may be difficult but attempt to find some time when everyone can be present. Be clear about the starting and ending time of the closing session. People leaving early profoundly discounts the value of designated closure, so it is important to get each group member to agree to a workable ending time.

▪ Have a ceremony. Graduations are one possibility. Rituals are another. In a Hampshire College Outdoor Leadership class, I copied quotes from Heider's (1986) *The Tao of Leadership* onto certificates that I presented as part of an ending ritual. Each quote represented the path I saw the student taking in becoming an outdoor leader.

▪ Have a give-away where students present gifts to each other to symbolize the connections they had developed with other group members. I had one class in which the students drew names and each brought their person something they had made which represented what that person had contributed to the group.

▪ Use affirmations, either written or verbal, as ways of ending. The midwife teacher should set the tone appropriate to the level of the group. On some outdoor trips I've led, the group ends by writing affirmations of each person that they gain support from in starting the next chapter of their life.

▪ Make time for evaluation. Creative evaluation allows students to synthesize meaning from their experience. It also indicates that their opinion is valued. I make it a point to let students know I prize the constructive feedback they give me.

▪ Pay attention to the value of metaphoric transitions. Students from a National Audubon Expedition Institute course I taught designed a group project where they elaborately drew their semester together on a huge piece of paper and then convened outside to burn their collaborative work. Students took ashes away with them to symbolize the ending of their group as well as the transformative beginning of new opportunities.

Conclusion

An experiential educator has many opportunities to entice a student into learning activities. The attention given to promoting engagement enriches the ultimate learning of the student. Ignoring the element of emotional safety may cause incomplete immersion in an experience and an eventual loss of learning potential.

Most of the methods of engagement detailed in this article can be construed as simply good teaching, not just effective experiential education. Yet since the power of experience intensifies with the degree of involvement of the learner, methods to create more profound immersion levels can particularly benefit experiential educators.

Exploring the metaphor of the teacher as a midwife who guides and guards the learning environment may assist experiential educators in developing means to amplify learning. As it is based on a foundation of respect for what the student brings to any experience like traditional midwifery, this style can be seen as holistic and empowering.

Do Your Homework: A Guide For Starting An Experiential Program In A School

by Peggy Walker Stevens

A college graduate at his first job, a woman in a traditionally male-dominated field, or an architect watching the building of his radically new design all feel the pressure of doing something new. Everyone is watching. Small mistakes will be noted; large ones will confirm traditionalists' belief that they should have stayed with the proven person, idea, or way of operating.

As an educator who has introduced eight alternative programs into public high schools, I feel the constant tension as well as the rewards of being labeled an innovator. My mistakes have sometimes been conspicuous, but through them I have learned that an experiential program must be better planned and more comprehensive than the regular school curriculum in order to gain acceptance. Anything that bucks a school's normal way of operating will probably be resisted unless problems are anticipated and minimized. This fact is true especially when starting a program that extends more than one class period, crosses over subject boundaries, involves more than one teacher, or engages students in concrete experiences.

Despite the extra work involved, there is a great need for programs which do exactly these things. It takes time for students to explore, to problem-solve, to understand the interrelationships among things, to learn to become a constructive member in a group task. In a typical secondary school, students are lectured at and questioned by a random series of adults who specialize in certain subject areas. In a well-planned experiential program, academic knowledge in a variety of disciplines can be integrated with skills and experiences. This unified approach adds a rich dimension to the learning of all students. But such an approach should not be assembled haphazardly. Do your homework first.

1. Assess School and Student Needs

A look at the student needs that are not being met by present school programs will provide a good starting point for an experiential program. It is easier to get others to support your proposal if it is designed to help a group of students who obviously need additional motivation or an alternative approach. It isn't difficult to document your hunches about who this group might be, with statistics usually available from secretaries, the guidance office, or the administration.

In one school where I taught, absenteeism, discipline problems, and failing grades all increased for the freshmen class by the end of the year. Few freshmen were involved in extracurricular activities. For many students, this pattern continued throughout high school. I was able to document this problem and propose an experiential program that involved freshmen in a variety of activities, inside and outside of the classroom.

The needs were different in another school. Here, it seemed to me that the most uninvolved and troublesome students were enrolled in the school's "Level II" classes, designed for the "non-college-bound" student. They called themselves "the rats" and could usually be identified by their dislike of school, their faded denim clothes, and their proximity to the school's smoking area. Using the school's computerized grade records, I found that Level II students had substantially higher failure rates than "Level III" students in many required courses. One percent of the students enrolled in Level III biology failed the course whereas fifteen percent of the students enrolled in Level II biology failed the course. By documenting examples such as these, along with comparative rates of absenteeism and suspensions, I convinced the administration that an alternative was worth trying.

The students whose needs you identify and document do not have to be those with many problems in school. You may demonstrate the needs of gifted students who need leadership training, or of the senior class who generally get low grades during their last semester and who could benefit from concrete experiences in the community before graduation. If you want to avoid having your program labeled as one strictly for "troublemakers," you can combine students who cause a variety of problems in school with others who are more motivated and can serve as role models. Experiential programs often work well with students who are unsuccessful or difficult to handle in traditional school programs, but it would be unfortunate if those became the only students who are given opportunities to learn through experience.

2. Set Goals and Devise a Plan to Meet Them

Once you have chosen the student population for whom you will design your program, decide upon the major goals that you would like the programs to meet. These goals can relate to an improvement in student attitude and behavior or to growth in academic skills or knowledge. It is best to limit your goals to three or four and to state them so that you can measure what you have accomplished at the end of the year. "The absentee, suspension, and failure rates of the students will decline when compared to their previous year's records (or compared to a control group)" is better than "Students will do better in school." Combine data from school records with attitude surveys, student and parent comments, pre- and post-writing samples, and other, more subjective evaluations. Emphasize that you are willing to be held accountable for the results of your program. Evaluation can be an important selling point to the administration who will have a clearer picture of what was accomplished in your experiential program than is the case in a traditional history or science or physical education class.

Curriculum planning will be necessary if you are to meet your goals. It is not necessary to have the entire curriculum planned before your proposal is approved, but you should have an outline of the topics which will be taught and sample activities which indicate the nature of the experiences which you will incorporate into the program and the ways in which different disciplines will be related to one another. Perhaps you and another teacher already have a great idea for your classes or for an experiential program you'd like to start. If not, find teachers who experiment with new approaches and brainstorm what you could do together. Anything can fit into an interdisciplinary approach. Teachers have combined subjects as diverse as French and peace studies. In your school's curriculum guide, you can find courses or units that fit logically together. In one school, freshmen earth science teachers taught topographical map reading and so did the freshmen geography teachers. They were able to combine the two and teach the skills outdoors in an orienteering unit. In another school, a look through the course selection guide revealed separate courses in New Hampshire geology, New Hampshire history, and New Hampshire literature.

Department heads and others will have legitimate concerns over the academic aspects of your program. While it is often true that students will not learn if they are bored, hostile, on drugs, etc., changing attitudes and behavior is not enough. If your program does not improve students' ability to read, write, solve problems, and think critically, it probably won't last long and doesn't deserve to. This is true especially if your program is to be an alternative way of earning credit for required courses such as English rather than for physical education or general credit toward graduation. Bob Gillette of Fairfield, Connecticut, has had a successful experiential program in a public high school for twelve years. His students represent a cross-section of that school's population. They spend three periods each day in the program for both their freshmen and sophomore years. At the end of that time, his students are expected to do at least as well as their classmates in the traditional program on standardized achievement tests. Bob Gillette feels that not only do these standardized

scores help to validate his program in the eyes of the school and community, but also that if he is going to involve students in a long-range program, they must make academic progress.

3. Plan for the Necessary Resources

Another planning step is to determine what resources the program will need. You must first be realistic about your commitment of time and energy. Don't design a program where you promise to take students on one weekend trip each month, only to find that your family is resentful and you are exhausted. Taking twenty students backpacking, for example, requires hours of preparation. It is never relaxing because you are always alert and working to make the trip a safe, enjoyable, and effective learning experience. Experiential programs take more time than more traditional classes in a number of other ways. Adapting a course so that it includes more hands-on activities takes time, and developing a whole new curriculum for a course that has never existed before takes even more time. Keeping track of equipment, recruiting for the program, talking and writing about the program to maintain good public relations, and supervising student money-raising activities are just some of the things that take after-school and weekend time. Some teachers are reimbursed for this extra time by teaching half days or by being paid the equivalent of a coach's salary for after-school activities done with students. How much you are willing to do with and without compensation is an issue that should be addressed in your original proposal. Programs that take an unreasonable amount of time from a teacher's personal life often don't last more than a year or two. It is up to you to assess your limits from the beginning.

It is also important to be realistic about the amount of money which will be necessary to carry out the program. Outside funding (grants, etc.) are helpful for getting a program started and for the initial investment in equipment. However, beware of making your program dependent for its operating expenses on funds outside of the school or district. The funds often dry up, as many programs are finding in this budget-cutting era. Think about what you can study which is close by. In one school, the original curriculum called for a study of a mountain area about 40 miles from the school. Just before the start of the new school year, the school board cut the field trip budget to zero. Even if they had been able to keep the original funding, they had severely underestimated the cost of transporting students on afternoon and weekend trips. When the teachers were forced to revise the original curriculum, they took advantage of a river environment within walking distance of the school.

Find out ahead of time the price of the books, backpacking equipment, printing costs, ropes course hardware, or whatever you will need. One hidden cost which teachers often overlook but of which administrators are very aware is teacher time. If a teacher earns $15,000 and normally teaches 5 classes, the cost to the school district is $3,000 per class. If two teachers are to team-teach the same group of students during a period, the cost to that class becomes $6,000. Their team teaching may also burden other teachers with a larger class load and may cause scheduling problems.

You must consider not only how much money you will need, but also from whose budget it will come. Find out how your school budget works if you have not had experience with it before. Are field trips, books, equipment, and supplies all separate parts of the budget? Would it be better for your program to have its own budget or for it to be part of another department's budget? The budget for a program at one school came from the physical education, English, social studies, and science departments. This approach had the advantage of keeping a lot of people involved in the ongoing process of the program, but it had a distinct disadvantage: sometimes the money for the experiential program was lost in favor of earth science textbooks or a new goal post. On the other hand, a well-established program in Massachusetts with a yearly budget of its own of over $50,000 was recently eliminated completely from the budget by the school board which found it an "extra" that the town could no longer afford. Consider the alternatives carefully before making your program a highly visible and very vulnerable budget item.

4. Sell the Program

Not only will it be necessary to plan appropriately, but you must also sell your program effectively. Decide who will have to approve your program and figure out what the concerns of each decision-maker are. Is the superintendent worried because too many freshmen are opting to go to private school instead of public school? Is the principal concerned about the number of suspensions? You can design your proposal to meet some of the legitimate concerns of influential people in the school and this increases the probability of them approving your program. It is also crucial for you to discern the actual decision-making hierarchy. Who makes decisions is often different in reality than it is on paper.

Don't be deterred by your own or the administration's initial reaction that your interdisciplinary teaching idea will be too difficult to schedule. You can work out numerous arrangements if you plan far enough in advance. One possibility is to teach two related subjects yourself so that you can have the students for more than one period. A course which teaches the scientific and social aspects of environmental problems is a good example of this arrangement. If two teachers want to work together, plan to team-teach during the same period, occasionally or all the time, or plan the course together but teach the same students during different periods. Schedule your class at the end of the school day and require students to stay after school one day each week, giving them extra credit for their additional time. The key is to be both flexible and persistent when convincing the administration to adopt your proposal.

An alternative way of designing a program that you would like to teach is to develop it slowly, over a number of years, from activities you do with a particular class. One of the more famous examples of this is Eliot Wigginton's assignment to his English class to interview some of the older people in the community. The assignment evolved into the Foxfire magazines and books. Other teachers have involved their classes in career internships, investigations in cities, and environmental clean-up projects, and have seen the initial idea grow into a permanent part of the school's offerings. A program

which emerges slowly has the advantage of "proving" itself as it goes along. It may, therefore, be less controversial than an entirely new program. However, it sometimes takes a great deal of negotiating to make changes once a program is established. Institutions often take even a new idea and quickly become rigid about the way it operates and fits into the budget and schedule. There are times when a bold proposal is approved more quickly and without compromising your vision of what the program could be. Whether to start slowly or boldly is something that each person must decide by assessing the school climate.

Anticipate opposition because you will be sure to get it. Try to figure out who will oppose your idea. Will it be the central administration, a school board member, principals, department heads, certain teachers? Find ways to involve these people in the planning or at least to discuss your ideas with them. You will probably feel like avoiding your opposition, but don't give in to this natural tendency. Find out what their concerns are. A reservation expressed to you in a discussion over lunch is better than one stated vehemently at a faculty meeting. In discussion, you can clarify misunderstandings and consider making some changes if the person's concern is valid. If a skeptic comes to respect you and sees how well-planned the program is, he may be willing to let you give the idea a try. One of the advantages of planning a program which involves team-teaching is that the enthusiasm of several respected teachers will carry more weight than that of a single teacher when a program is being considered.

By listening to your opposition, you will also have a more valuable critique of potential problems than you can get from more enthusiastic colleagues. If both the vice-principal and the guidance counselor are worried about scheduling problems, maybe you need to revamp that part of your proposal. If that old-fashioned department head is concerned about basic skills, perhaps your program needs to be more specific about the ways in which students will be able to use and improve these skills.

Some teachers are uncomfortable with the idea of selling their program proposal. They see the process as "playing politics," something which they are reluctant to do. However, it is senseless to spend hours assessing student needs, deciding upon goals and curriculum, and finding the necessary resources if you don't spend an equal amount of time convincing others of the merit of your idea. An experiential program can be designed so that it fits almost any circumstances. Step-by-step planning at least a year in advance is the key to gaining approval for any experiential program.

Reflections on Reflection

by Bert Horwood

Reflection is hard mental work. The word itself means "bending back," and this has just the right connotations for our use of it. There is something importantly backwards about reflection. The thinking involved must scan memory of the past, seeking connections, discrepancies, meanings. The notion of bending or folding is also useful because events in memory acquire new meanings over time, especially as they may be molded and reframed by the reflective processes.

Our language provides other interesting and colorful words for the kinds of thinking that must be involved in reflection. These words show that remembering, comparing, and valuing is not all there is to it. The mental work of reflection includes deliberation (methodical and slow), rumination (thorough chewing), pondering (weighing or judging), and musing (aimless speculation). Forms of meditation which are focused on a specific goal rather than on a quiet mind are forms of mental work closely allied to reflection.

The goal of reflection is for students to construct meaning out of their experiences. The direct product of reflection is the discovery of new connections between the most recent experience and past ones, including past thought. It is the discovery of connections, the construction of nets and maps in our minds, that is the stuff of learning through reflection. These are the processes that integrate past experience into the present and allow its projection onto the future. These are the processes that rewrite our personal histories, keep us from being walking archives, and prepare us to find future insights. Mental work at this depth is needed if experiences are to be significant, memorable, and ultimately transforming.

Reflection should also include emotions. We cheat our students when reflection is confined to the levels of intellect and cognition. And yet it is as limiting to emphasize emotions alone. Reflection can yield refinement of both knowledge and feelings. I wonder if, in fact, we have reached a stage where the distinctions among the cognitive, affective, and spiritual aspects of mental work have outlived their usefulness. That is a new connection I am starting to make.

The demanding and difficult character of reflection is described with clarity and sensitivity in *Islands of Healing* (Schoel et al., 1988). The Project Adventure team shows the need and methods to take people beyond superficial talk about events to much deeper, authentic reflection. They capture the resistance put up by participants when asked to dig deeply and do the mental hard work of reflection. They emphasize preparation and good humor, and provide fair but tough mechanisms to impel people into reflection. *Islands of Healing* takes the adventure branch of experiential education a big step forward because it is the fruit of thoughtful practitioners reflecting on reflection. It is equally valuable as a contribution in other branches.

From a totally different perspective, Donald Schon's work is provocative and indicates serious current philosophical attention is being paid to reflection in professional practice (Schon, 1983, 1987). Schon's contribution has the tonic effect of putting practice at the center of professional concern. Professional knowledge and knowing comes much more from reflecting on practice than from applying theoretical ideas. Schon has validated for us the notion that theory should be constructed from practice by practitioners rather than the other way around.

Schon's work emphasizes reflection at the instructor level more than at the participant level, but refreshingly, it includes teachers and learners together in the process. A reflective leader in Schon's terms is one who has the tools and disposition to recognize problems, to examine them from alternative perspectives, and research solutions. For Schon, the reflective practitioner has power as an autonomous but interactive inquirer, disciplined by the bounds and demands of practice.

In his latest book, Schon (1987) draws examples from such diverse fields as architecture, music, psychoanalysis, and counseling to illustrate a complex reflective process he calls "coaching." Out of many professional training situations, Schon has distilled some essential features for educating reflective practitioners. Many outdoor and experiential educators will recognize in Schon's account of coaching some of the most effective learning experiences they ever received as part of their own professional preparation. The ideas are a boon for staff development and, in my opinion, have great promise for encouraging the kinds of thoughtful, autonomous instructors who will promote reflective learning among their students.

I have emphasized reflection as mental work because there seems to be a tendency to let reflection pass as a superficial retrospective of an experience, usually in a group context. On the contrary, the labour of reflection is solitary. Sooner or later, it must be done alone, in the privacy of one's own head. This makes demands on teachers, because no one can read minds. Reflection requires instructional organization which gives participants quiet time and support for their hard mental work. An apparent paradox is that experiential educators put high value on the social context of education. Somehow, instructors must find ways to combine adequate conditions of privacy for reflection with the social interactions of community in which the fruits of discovered connections are expressed. The social setting contributes stimulus to the reflective process by providing something more for a person to think about. A patient, caring, and trusting community is the context within which the best reflection can occur. But the thinking still needs to be done alone.

A second demand that reflection places on teachers is to provide the substantial amounts of time required. The kind of mental hard work involved cannot be rushed. There is no fast food in the reflection deli. Not only is time required, but the amount of time needed varies with participants and circumstances. Very subtle changes in instructions can change the reflective time requirements from one occasion to another. This makes planning difficult, because tight planning is based on an accurate prediction and control of parameters, of which time is the most difficult and inflexible.

The scope for practitioners to write about reflection in experiential education is large.

The methods of promoting reflection by participants are continually being tested and refined. Innovative techniques for group and private introspection on experience are being developed. There is growing recognition that instructors need to be systematically and authentically involved in personal reflection if they are to grow and if programs are to evolve and provide the best learning possible. Experiential educators who are doing these things have stories to tell and lessons to teach. In some cases, the best evidence of the process is given by the productivity and learning of students.

Leaders in the field are emerging with new tools and exciting new insights due, in part, to making their reflections public. This is especially valuable because serious matters such as the state of our planet home and the deteriorating state of people of the continent and the world must become more centrally our business. Reflection is one of the essential tools we need to make a difference.

8 Experiencing History

Experiencing History

by Adolf Crew, James Brown, and Joyce Lackie

An innovative graduate course in education devoted to the development of techniques utilizing direct experience in the history curriculum.

Introduction

In 1976, a private Washington-based organization took tentative steps toward creating an Experiential Learning Center for the State of Alabama. Some thirty interested Alabamians from a diverse geographical and institutional range were brought into contact, many for the first time, to listen to and talk with the creators of exciting educational programs, including cultural journalism, traditional crafts-apprenticing, and adventure-based programs.

While planning and funding were still in the early stages, the group assayed a pilot program based primarily on local resources. The pilot was an inter-university, interdisciplinary course entitled "A Workshop in Experiential Education" and is the subject of this article. The course was offered for six

hours' graduate or undergraduate credit (three in education from the University of Alabama, and three in History or Folklore from Samford University in Birmingham) and comprised six weekends over a six-month span during the summer and fall of 1977. Primary locale for the course was Tannehill Historical State Park, site of two impressive furnace structures of Civil War vintage and proposed site of the Learning Center.

The three themes pursued in the course were: 1) experiential learning techniques; 2) local cultural history; and 3) the local environment, in the ecological sense. Although the pilot in no way was a polished course, having been put together under time pressure and the uncertainties of new friendships, it developed a momentum that tended to leave its inventors behind. With some modification, it might be applicable any place on most any level of education. The following is a three-part presentation of the course from the perspectives of Jim Brown, a historian and sometime folklorist from Samford University; Adolph Crew, Head of the Department of Secondary Education at the University of Alabama; and Joyce Lackie, a participant.

Part I: The History Component

To show how ecological consciousness and a range of experiential learning techniques can be linked in the same course by cultural history.

As a historian, I naturally saw chronology as the key to a course structure and lobbied for that sort of organization with my colleagues in Education. The general idea was to 1) take a level of local cultural history on each weekend, 2) show how that culture related to and changed the land, and 3) whenever possible, communicate that with experiential learning techniques. Here is how it went, and on further reflection, how it might go again.

WEEKEND ONE—Wilderness: Alabama on the Eve of European Settlement

The first weekend, the local cultural level was *Amerind;* in historic times in Alabama that means mainly Creek, with Cherokee in the north and Choctaw in the west. The ecological horizon was the well-nigh incredible southeastern wilderness as it was when Michaux and William Bartram, the first naturalists to describe it, came through in the 1700s. The major experiential learning techniques were adventure-based, taking place on a two-day backpack in the Sipsey Wilderness Area of the Bankhead National Forest.

Doug Phillips, University of Alabama, was the instructor and, judging by evaluations, it may have been the best one of the course, creating an initial bond among students as well as a lasting feel for the natural environment. The Bee Branch area of the Wilderness is a small canyon with one of the most remarkable forests left in Alabama, including one of the largest tulip poplars east of the Rockies. Doug spent a lot of time explaining primeval botany there and having us experience it. An introduction to the forest by a slow single-file walk, keeping the person in front just out of sight; a blindfolded Trust Walk and a night hike; a map-and-compass exercise; a community bread bake the night before the trip; group packing and communal meals of natural foods— these were new and of real value to a class of twenty-five graduate students and active teachers.

In this instance, local cultural history was not necessary as a link between experiential techniques and ecological knowledge. Even here, though, thinking about the culture and its relationship to the environment is a good way to visualize that environment and begin seeing it in new ways. One of the many Indian statements on the relationship between a people and the land was read on a morning just after the group went down into Bee Branch; its message was clearer there than in a classroom. Another reading for the course was William Bartram's *Travels*. He cut across Alabama from central Georgia to Mobile, went a way up the Tombigbee and then back again to Georgia, in 1776 and 1777. The first naturalist to describe the interior of the state, Bartram ran out of superlatives. Despite the Latin lists of flora and fauna, his is a vivid, immediate look at the pre-European ecology and the Indian relation to it.

Finally, in Alabama as in much of the rest of the Western Hemisphere, Indian cultures were the foundation for the cultural evolution of the land, no matter how overwhelming later cultural invasions may have been in numbers. The natives' relation to the land was intimate, of thousands of years' accumulation. Some of their practices were necessary for the survival of all the early immigrant groups, even those of a higher technological level, and many are still visible in cultural survivals today. Controlled burning seems to have been the only major impact the Indians had on the local ecology, creating the extensive cane "meadows" and the first pasture lands hereabouts. There are many plants of known Indian usage and name; herb medicine as it survives in the remoter areas of the state has Indian overtones, as does folk cookery. Alabama place names are mostly Indian or translations of Indian names, especially rivers and other geographic features. Fortunately, a dictionary of those names exists. It can be used not only to illustrate the land as the Indians saw it, but as a tool to uncover usable information. "Choccolocco" in Creek means "big shoal"; there must be half a dozen of these on detailed maps of the state. If you like rapids to fish or gig or float or whatever, here is a geographical index that is rich even after all these years. Of primary importance in the area of cultural survivals plus experiential education—each of the three major tribes of Indians has a remaining center: the Creeks around Atmore, Alabama; the Cherokee around Cherokee, North Carolina; and the

Choctaw at Philadelphia, Mississippi. All three, for example, still keep alive their traditional versions of dyed rivercane basketry. That craft would make a nice vehicle for a hands-on history and ecology lesson.

WEEKENDS TWO AND THREE—The Iron Age: From Indian to European Settlement Patterns.

The local cultural level was rural settlement from pioneer times, which in Alabama amounts to the first two-thirds or so of the nineteenth century. The ecological horizon was the extensive European-style farming of the land. The major experiential learning techniques were oral history and cultural journalism for Weekend Two, and for Weekend Three, crafts apprenticing.

These weekends were back-to-back in early August at Tannehill Park. Sessions went from 9:00 a.m. Saturday to 2:30 p.m. Sunday, most of the class choosing to camp together at the park. We had the run of a Pioneer Inn just being finished, and a spring-fed creek for swimming—in all, a beautiful setting in a place historically connected with the period under discussion.

Eliot Wigginton came for Saturday of Weekend Two. We had in mind to listen to him for half the weekend and try to put out a small cultural journalism project in the other half. The Foxfire magazine and books had concentrated on the pioneer heritage of the Georgia mountain country, making it on the surface an ideal parallel for Alabama pioneer history. Wigginton's students had seemed to get interested in the present of their region through its past, and in its ecology through its people. True, Wig did come and talk about cultural journalism in particular and education in general in a powerful

way. Better, he and two local high school students conducted a remarkable interview in class with Mr. Ray Farabee, a retired engineer who presided over the refiring of the Tannehill Furnace 110 years after it was shut down by Union raiders. The major difficulty was that cultural journalism is only a small part of what is included in the word "Foxfire," and the mountain community only part of the potential of cultural journalism. Wig had to caution us not to see a magazine as the end-all of experiential learning. In fact, our high-pressure crash course in magazine production evolved into several gentler seminars on photography, oral history, layout, and such, and left some time for other things.

A minor part of the weekend was dealing with some oral cultural survivals from the pioneer period of Alabama history. I tried a class singalong and history lesson on the mountain ballad and fasola (Sacred Harp shaped note singing), the first a dying form and the second now resurgent. They are both of British origin and little-changed over the last hundred years. Essentially white forms, they are nice to pair with black shape note music, spirituals, and down home blues. In rural Alabama, all these nineteenth-century forms are still come by. Singing the music is a good way to experience the hopes and fears of a bygone era; Laurie Seidman and Tony Scott are preaching that gospel nationwide now, with considerable success. In the same vein is the narrative—classic, popular story-telling. Every region tucks its most powerful thoughts away in stories, of its strong men and women, tragic love affairs, and supernatural happenings. We discovered later that Alabama's premier collector of ghost stories and a fine teller of tales herself had heard of our course and come to crash it, only to be turned away by someone who didn't know what she had to offer. Too, if this part of the course were to be taught again, I would like to use Lyn Montell's Sage of Coe Ridge, a powerful oral history account of a small, black Kentucky settlement, and talk about, demonstrate, and have the class get involved in some Alabama parallels. The nineteenth-century settlement period is only a step or two back in folk memory.

Weekend Three featured Lance Lee, by general consensus the best teacher (and learner) most of us encountered in the course. Lance tried to communicate the mechanics and magic of apprenticing and the values associated with the old-time hand crafts. He not only discussed good and bad tools; we learned them by touch in carving models. A considerable historian and folklorist of the seafaring community of northern Europe and New England, Lance was quick to point out the Tannehill furnaces as the key to a nineteenth-century craft matrix. The iron and soft steel parts of woodcraft tools once came from here and similar places. Part of Lance's vision for the Learning Center is that Tannehill might produce them again, as part of an educational process, since the old-quality tools are gradually disappearing. The role of education in community and the folk technique of education through apprenticing were the big lessons he taught. Small fragments of that are encapsuled in hard-to-forget phrases, like "those intricate tricks of self-sufficiency" developed by people in any traditional lifestyle.

Lance Lee's message neatly fit the historical framework of the course, and called up all sorts of Alabama parallels. Regional folkcrafts are still alive in almost every Alabama county: split oak basketry, net tying, quilting, and blacksmithing among them. Some of the same beauty, economy, and strength of Maine wooden boat building can be found in a white-oak cotton basket from the Deep South. Folk crafts of any region are an eloquent introduction to the land and the people.

In retrospect, the fate of the land got short shrift these two weekends. We tried a field geology trip to explain why Tannehill came about and how it led to the future steel industry of Birmingham; we seined creeks to identify local darters, sampled wild peppermint, and such. But we did not document the extent of the change in the environment. The cotton lands of Alabama lost perhaps five feet of topsoil in the first forty years of farming. The fantastic population growth over the once-stable population of 25,000 or so Indians meant more extensive as well as intensive farming. Siltation of rivers probably wiped out many species of fish before any biologist sampled the rivers; at least one of these, the Harelip Sucker, supported a sizable fishery on the Tennessee River. The creeks at Tannehill, now blue-green, ran red as blood from the open ore pits that fed the furnaces, and the woods for miles around were cut down for charcoal. Early reports from the Geological Services of the State show that the great timber, pine and hardwood, fell to the saw by the turn of the century. The major predators were exterminated except in large swamps, and valuable game became more scarce as the century wore on. By 1920, beaver and deer were extirpated in most of the state. In north Alabama, the chestnut blight seems to have cut into the squirrel population, a usually reliable food source for the marginal farmer. These scattered facts outline a massive change in the ecosystem. It is a familiar story in every state: when the culture changes the land, the land in turn restricts the possibilities of the culture. The bad news is that you can't find this kind of history in an Alabama high school or college text; the good news is that a class can build one from game wardens, gardeners, farmers, and all the other people resources of the rural community.

WEEKEND FOUR—Urbanization & Industrialization: Alabama in Recent Times.

The local cultural level for this weekend was Twentieth Century Modern. The ecological horizon was the massive urbanization of the past century and the accompanying development of industry. The major experiential learning techniques developed in the context of a two-day adventure in downtown Birmingham, largest and most industrialized city of the state.

Ron Gager set this weekend up, with help from a part-time class member who lives in the city. On Saturday morning we left our cars on a manicured suburban campus, walked four blocks, and committed to mass transit for the weekend. There followed a morning-long cultural scavenger hunt in Southside, an old and ethnically varied neighborhood of the city. By early afternoon, we moved base camp to a downtown church where we were to spend the night. We drew a "human interest map" of the area and listened to a dedicated church worker and enthusiastic city dweller talk about mi-

nuses and pluses of city life. Ron took us through a series of New Games in the city, fondly remembered in course evaluations later. The class members were mostly suburban or rural in origin, with a built-in distrust of anybody's inner city; but by the end of the first day, a whole new attitude toward cities and city people was evident. The spark of city life that got struck several thousand years ago in the Near East is still very much alive in Birmingham. All of a sudden, the city was seen as responsible for civilization (museums, zoos, great libraries, etc.), and as a place of unparalleled social variety and excitement. Having seen the attractions of city life, one had a more balanced view of the social price of late: white flight and inner city collapse, street crime, and the like. The chief lesson learned was that the city is of fascinating potential as a setting for education.

We could and should have done the same thing with industrialization. Technology's attractions are powerful, in medicine, communications, luxuries, and sheer physical capabilities. From UAB Med School to the South Central Bell building, and from U.S. Steel to the new car dealerships, you can see it clearly in Birmingham. In this light, then, maybe the ecological change wrought upon the land by industrialization can be weighed as being either too expensive or a cheap price to pay. Because of the urbanization of the Birmingham area, the creek into which the Tannehill springs drain thirty miles away is often an open sewer; if the species of life in those springs are ever destroyed the way they were in the 1860s, they will not be restocked again from lower down the drainage. Because of the steel industry, part of the pure water that drains from the forest of the Sipsey Wilderness where we spent the first weekend goes into Village Creek in Birmingham in a state akin to liquid mothballs. The open waste, the underlying aquifers, the air, and the soil have been drastically changed by urbanization and industrialization. For all the attractions of the city and technology, nothing in them replaces the wilderness. Mental health indices reflect that fact almost as surely as the particulate count. Maybe the beginning of wisdom is that this is not an either/or proposition. As Schumacher says in *Small is Beautiful,* the manner of technology can be changed so that the extreme ecological price need not be paid. Again in retrospect, we certainly should have made time to visit the Recycling Center operated by the Alabama Conservancy, the same group that spearheaded the drive to protect the Sipsey Wilderness.

WEEKEND FIVE—Regional Planning: Awareness of What is to Come.

The cultural and ecological level under consideration was the foreseeable future. The experiential learning techniques were ways of community planning.

The second assigned text for the course was Ian McHarg's *Design With Nature,* read for this weekend. Professor McHarg approaches ecology and culture as units that are related, and he does it historically. On his faculty at the University of Pennsylvania, he has assembled geologists, biologists, ethnographers, and finally, political specialists. In approaching an area, he begins with basic geology and climate, moves through natural flora and fauna, traces early settlement patterns through to the present. This identifies the directions of a community's evolution and its effect on the environment. This approach then enables a planner to say: 1)

here's what you will look like in the year 2000 if you don't change your ways, and 2) tell us what you want to look like in 2000 and we'll tell you what you can do to achieve it, barring man-made catastrophes and acts of God. On Dauphin Island, where half the class spent a much-acclaimed optional weekend at the Sealab of the Marine Sciences Consortium, there was a perfect illustration of McHarg's introductory exercise on sand dunes. Some school keeper cut the beach grass to get a better view of the ocean or to tidy up, and the dunes are now covering the playground and threatening the building itself. Seining the marsh and noticing the beach erosion seemed to make several students appreciate the seriousness of McHarg's arguments.

Some of the tools of the planner should make great teaching techniques. McHarg makes use of the transparent overlay as a way to get social values into the planning process alongside purely physical and economic ones. If you are considering routes for a highway, make transparencies in suitable, marginal, and unsuitable shades for areas of sinkholes, flooding, slope, and other physical features. But don't stop there: consider recreational use, agricultural value, historic importance, and all the other important social variables. By stacking the transparencies together you might be able to identify the wisest route for the road. I wanted the class to have the chance to try this technique in helping plan a part of the Learning Center at Tannehill, but fell down on advance preparation.

This weekend, as special consultant, we had Ron Thomas of Attic & Cellar Studies in Washington, a planning and environmental collaborative. After the class ended, Ron did double duty by working with the steering committee of the Learning Center. From him we got a professional's view of participatory design and cognitive mapping. Most impressive were his slides and explanation of a series of community planning projects across the country. He also brought a valuable bibliography in the form of a suitcase of books dealing with the planning process and some aspect of education.

Course evaluations indicated that we spent too much time indoors and not enough time in hands-on learning. One of the purposes of this last substantive weekend was to show that culture is always limited by the parameters of ecology, and that the future is, to some extent, controllable if we are conscious of that fact. On reexamination of that statement of purpose, it now seems to me that this weekend more than any of the others could have benefited by in-the-field experience.

A CASE STUDY—Freshwater food fishing in Alabama.

This sort of integrated treatment of cultural levels, the environment, and experiential learning techniques can work with smaller, more manageable units as well; in this example, an occupational group.

Most of Alabama's rivers still support a population of commercial fishermen. Today they use nylon lines and chromium hooks, and those few who still tie nets use nylon needles and fiberglas hoops. They are a fascinating breed but vanishing fast because of social changes generally, perhaps, but more particularly because of siltation, chemical pollution in the form of oil, PCBs, heavy metals and insecticides, organic pollution from fertilizers and sewage, and new regulations for the benefit of sport fishermen.

So as a teacher you begin to time travel, first stop thirty years or so ago when the hoop nets were woven of cotton twine, put on white-oak splits made into hoops, and the whole dipped in tar. There are old-timers out on all the rivers who can teach you elementary net tying in an hour and how to make a functional net in a day or two. Better yet, bring one to the class and let him tell great fish stories while he teaches the craft. Visions of hundred-pound yellow catfish and blue cats that will twist your fingers off. Even the illegality of the net under construction is appealing. Two large balls of #15 cotton twine and 30 net-tying needles from Memphis Net & Twine's mail-order catalog will cost maybe $10.00. The white oak is free, growing in some second-growth woodlot behind school, perhaps. Knowledge of how to split it and shape it is free, too, but takes some looking for. And the questions ought to come naturally: What was the fishing like? What was the river like, and the people who lived by it?

Next stop, 1930, before they dammed the rivers. The people still fished long woven baskets like giant minnow traps, baiting with cotton seed meal or spoiled cheese. With a class or two of students looking, you might find one stored on the rafters of an old barn, or still in use in some private pond. The same fisherman who used hoop nets all his adult life probably learned to make these baskets as a youngster, and can do one for you or with your class. Best of all are the descriptions and the stories of the fish traps. Whole rivers, then running, were funneled down by wings into millraces ten feet wide or so, and when the water would color and rise after a rain, fish by the boatload would come sliding out on a series of inclined slats called fingers. Not just your everyday catfish and shad and the like, but fish long gone from the rivers like great sturgeon and twenty-pound eel as big around as your leg. On first frost in central Alabama, they had to mesh the traps to hold the eel on their annual downstream run. Why no more eel and sturgeon? The dams.... How'd you catch 'em? What'd you do with 'em? What'd you do when the river was too high to use the traps? Can you see where they were?

Then you go on back to 1800 or so when most Alabamians were still Creek Indians and the first naturalists described their fishing. Back way beyond the first netting laws, when pioneer communities still had huge summer fish fries, the young men swimming long nets down a mile of river to meet another net while the grown folks set up the fires and tables and got the skillets hot. And even before that. Last year field researchers with the Office of Archaeological Research in Tuscaloosa studied a river in Randolph County of East Alabama prior to impoundment. Aerial photos taken during the drought showed the stone structure of as many as sixty fish traps in a ten-mile stretch of river. Digging at the places where the trap wings touched the banks, they almost always found an Indian site. One yielded a Clovis, a paleo projectile point from sometime before the dawn of world history. Sometime in this process, it dawns on the more outdoor types in class that common methods of fishing—gigging, netting, trapping, driving, poisoning, noosing, jiggerpoling, and grappling, to use the local terms—in fact every fishing technique short of dynamiting and electric shock, is of Stone Age origin. Cultural transmission begins to take on tangibility at this point. A semi-retired commercial fisherman

I spent some time with over the past couple of years surprised me one day with some old-style whittled toys to take home to my children. Things that danced and flip-flopped and whirled, made of string and wood. One was a functional Indian pump drill, lacking only the stone point, but not recognized as being a drill at all by the fisherman, just a toy his grandfather had made. How is it that an Indian tool becomes a pioneer toy? This sort of history is visible and cumulative. That drill works as well in each year's class as it did the last.

The inescapable conclusion of such a history lesson is that commercial fishing on the rivers is an arduous but time-honored and rewarding lifestyle. Only an unconscious culture destroys traditional jobs like this and a valuable local food supply by turning a river into a waste disposal system. The impact of the culture on the ecology is always reflected back again on the culture.

This historical model is simple, seeing the culture and ecology as intertwined, and communicating that through as immediate and vivid ways as are at your disposal. I have used variations on that theme for two years now on the university level, and know it works; one of the reasons I was excited about this course is that I feel sure it will work on other levels of education, too. Unfortunately, I am no high school teacher, and this class of active or prospective teachers couldn't help but be aware of that. From them, especially the social studies teachers, I learned that enthusiasm and some fresh insights are not enough to make education work in the public schools: it takes a level of organization and preparation beyond that. It was a painful lesson, but I will profit by it. The other side of the coin, something I couldn't help but be aware of, as much as I liked the members of the class, was their strange attraction to canned units not of their making, experience, or personalities. I know there is a time pressure element involved; but this seemed to me more part of the "mortmain" of the system, Education with a capital "E." I hoped an experiential component could break through some of this. The value of taking students through an experience I have already had is that education becomes as personal as Thoreau's journal at Walden, and achieves a new level of honesty. If I really "know" something in the sense of being able to do it—as in singing mountain ballads, say—I find an immediacy in my teaching of it that helps bridge the credibility gap between teacher and student. From Doug Phillips in the Sipsey Wilderness to Ron Gager on Southside, I think that was the key to the successful part of every weekend.

This concludes my part of the article. In discussing this course I have surely exaggerated my component of it and slighted the other contributors. I leave it to Professor Crew to rectify that imbalance, and possibly to talk about History with a capital "H."

Part II: The Secondary Education Component

The primary objective of the education component of the weekend program was to instruct teachers in experiential learning and to help them see applications to their classes and school programs. The rationale was that the most effective way to learn about experiential education is to experience it, then analyze and draw implications from the experiences. This approach was used whenever feasible and whenever the instructors

would conceive ways to do so. The disciplines of history and folklore were used as the content through which experiential learning was primarily demonstrated, thereby avoiding the age-old problem of separating methodology and content.

To encourage students to engage in the reflective phase of experiential learning, class members were asked to keep a diary of reactions to their experiences. A limited amount of class time was used for students to interact and to discuss course experiences. "Free time" and "after hours" during the weekends also proved to be fruitful times for such discussions.

The overall theme of the first weekend, "Experiencing the Environment," was chosen for several reasons. Not only did this approach fit the chronology of the historical theme, as described by Professor Brown, but the more experiential thrust was to experience the natural environment, to have a wilderness experience. A part of the Outward Bound philosophy of experiential learning was implemented by placing teachers in a challenging situation through the backpacking, camping-out experience in the wilderness. Several teachers were not quite sure how well they would be able to cope, and after they found that they could, there was a tangible sense of personal achievement, and, since it was also a group effort, a unifying process.

The wilderness experience was also used as a base to inform and sensitize class members to the additional potentialities of school camping and outdoor education for elementary and secondary schools. Three staff members, Doug Phillips, Tracey Leiweike from IDEAS, and I, had been involved in programs of this nature, and we shared these experiences with the class.

Over the span of the first three weekends, as time permitted, the class was introduced to the nature and theory of experiential learning through presentations, through follow-up discussions of selected readings from the professional literature, and through the process of drawing implications from the ongoing activities during each weekend. This overview of experiential learning, albeit brief, ranged from the views of Carl Rogers to group process, from simulation and open-ended inquiry to experience-based or action learning processes.

During the second weekend, classroom applications were enhanced by interaction with sponsors of two Foxfire replicas in Alabama: Tommie Harrison, from the Shelby County Schools, and Bob England, from the Bibb County schools. An added dimension was the opportunity to talk with high school students from Bibb County who were involved in publishing *Sparrow Hawk*. Eliot Wigginton was there to inform and inspire; the replications were there to demonstrate that it can be done in Alabama, on limited budgets and by hard work.

The major theme of the third weekend, "Experiencing the World Through Work," was certainly highlighted by the presence of Lance Lee and the apprenticeship approach to experiential learning. It also provided the opportunity to share with the class my long-time interest in the values of productive work for adolescents, both in terms of its potential for experiential learning as well as an effective means for linking adolescence to adulthood. As part of this, the class read the current literature about the Walkabout model, sponsored by *Phi Delta Kappan*. The class was interested in the *Newsletter* from the Walkabout Task Force, especially the

description of various experience-based programs in operation.

A local person, Mary Dodd, presented information about the Executive Internship Program in operation in the Birmingham City Schools. The Executive Internship Program is a national program in which the secondary student works full-time as an intern with a local executive for a semester and receives academic credit.

For the weekend, "Experiencing the City," students were asked to read inquiry materials about cities from the High School Geography Project and the Sociological Resources for the Social Studies. The consultants for both the City and Regional Planning Weekends also brought excellent materials for examination by the class. Ron Marley's Regional Planning dealt extensively with urban areas. In retrospect, his information would have been excellent preparation for "Experiencing the City" and probably should precede the city weekend in any future course.

The final weekend was devoted to sharing experiential teaching units, analyzing and critiquing course experiences, and talking about future plans. At the beginning of the course, each class member was asked to develop an experiential teaching unit, to teach the unit during the fall semester, and to share the plan and the results of its implementation during the final weekend. Those who were not teaching were asked to develop an experiential unit that they would like to teach. Class members enjoyed this sharing of experiences, and the staff was impressed with the quality of the units, several of which were highly innovative.

Student evaluations of the course were very positive. Class members enjoyed and learned much from interaction with different consultants each weekend. Permanent friendships were formed among class members. There was a deep commitment to experiential learning and to the development of an experiential learning center at Tannehill Park. The group also wanted to continue this involvement beyond the end of the course, and a decision was reached to establish an informal association of experiential education and to have occasional meetings for interested participants.

Depending on one's perspective, each staff member saw areas for improvement. From my view, not enough attention was given to classroom applications, to appropriate materials, and to alternative school programs. At times, partly due to time constraints, instructors tended to become didactic and propagandistic, and probably too much was attempted in too short a time. Not enough time was allowed for class interaction. In some ways, having so many class instructors complicated coordination and continuity.

In spite of whatever shortcomings were perceived, the spontaneity and intensity of this initial venture in experiential education, both for the instructors and for the students, more than compensated for deficiencies in planning and implementation. In the final analysis, the course appeared to have an impact that few courses have.

Part III: A Student's Perspective

My perceptions of the experiential course are from the point of view of a student who found it to be one of the most stimulating educational experiences I have had in my program. There were secondary teachers of social science, English, biology, home eco-

nomics, business, and agribusiness; and also, an elementary school teacher, two college teachers, and a number of full-time graduate and undergraduate students, most of whom were pursuing degrees in some area of education.

Many of the participants in the course were interested in learning more about the natural environment, and two or three had taken wilderness education courses previously. Others had directed experiential learning projects in their schools and several were interested in folkcrafts, but most of the students had had little exposure to experiential or outdoor education. Only a few had participated in any backpacking and camping activities.

By the end of the experience, however, we had a strikingly altered clientele, and that is perhaps most evident in the types of projects the participants had carried out. Two groups of teachers had organized overnight camping trips with their pupils, one to Tannehill Park with emphasis on local history and English experiences, and the other to Talladega National Forest with development of the disciplines of science and creative writing. Both experiences were carefully structured by the teachers, who planned numerous group and individual activities, including tours of historical sites, scavenger hunts, nature sensitivity walks, storytelling sessions, and journal-writing periods. The pupils were also responsible for preparing their own meals and cleaning up afterwards. Once back in their schools, the pupils related their experiences to information they had been studying and finished developing such projects as short stories, poems, and written reports. The teachers reported both successful and unsuccessful aspects of the trips, noting precautions they could have taken, such as providing extra large amounts of food when feeding teenage boys, and the like. On the whole, however, the teachers involved felt that the trips were highly successful in achieving the goals they had set up.

Other teachers planned experiential units with one-day field trips as enrichment or central activities. One group of junior high pupils studied such aspects of their local natural environment as water supply and conservation, forest resources, wildlife, national parks and reserves, and local vegetation, following these efforts with a one-day trip to Tannehill State Park. The pupils were responsible for mapping out the area, directing the bus driver to the park, taking pictures, and pointing out historic sites, types of architecture, wildlife, vegetation, and signs of pollution. Another teacher's class in civics discussed different kinds of city governments, held a mock election, studied the many services rendered by a city, and then took a field trip to discover the services, sights, and sounds of their own town. They also mapped their town and then planned an ideal city.

A junior high teacher of gifted classes involved her pupils in short trips to several different interesting locations, including a cemetery, and showed them how to analyze one square foot of ground for its natural and man-made phenomena. She also developed a Learning Center packet of experiential materials for those of us in the class. The elementary school teacher took her boisterous youngsters on a carefully planned field trip to a nearby Indian burial ground and museum as part of a unit on Alabama history. These pupils referred to what they had seen

and done frequently in the daily discussions that followed, showing that they had gained a vital interest in the subject.

There were also internship and community service projects. An instructor in nursing set up a program whereby her student nurses helped to implement the federal handicapped children's law (P.L. 94–142) in the public school system. A high school social studies teacher set up what she called mini-internships in which her students spent one hour per day for one week working with such city officials as the sheriff, probate judge, tax assessor, and probation officer. A business class participated in a local Trade Day, deciding what they would sell and for how much, setting up the booth, taking turns with all the jobs, and closing the booth.

A teacher who was working with the culturally disadvantaged planned a sequence of three outdoor excursions to give the pupils insight into themselves and their natural environment. Her first excursion involved a Trust Walk in which blindfolded pupils were supposed to trust themselves to the guidance of others, but that project failed and led instead to a discussion of trust and the lack of it. The second trip found the pupils a little more helpful to one another as they tried to follow the course of a stream that flowed past the school and into a swampy area. These pupils seemed to have gained more than just an understanding of their physical surroundings.

In addition to the varied outdoor education projects, some teachers worked from the cultural journalism concept, one directing a student-written local history and another a "Roots" project in which students traced and wrote up their genealogies. A home economics teacher had her students research a craft, but their purpose was to recreate it rather than write about it. The class developed a resource file of community residents skilled in quilting, a file of terms, historical incidents, and patterns used in the art, and a list of materials needed, and in addition, they began making their own quilts. A science class did structured interviews with older relatives or adults to find out what lifestyles were like before our country depended on petroleum for so much of its energy needs.

One of the most elaborate service projects was carried out by several classes working together. An enterprising teacher used the combined efforts of his conservation, welding, and advanced agribusiness classes to convert two military surplus, four-wheel-drive weapons carriers into a cross-country, off-the-road fire truck and an equipment-and-manpower transport vehicle. The fire truck was compete with 500-gallon water tank, high pump, pressure hose, and fire fighting equipment when the students finished with it.

Some of the projects were difficult to classify but nonetheless exciting. A social studies teacher had his class make a large dugout canoe following the procedures used by Indians, and that class also planted and cultivated a small wheat field using the methods of the early pioneers. The following semester the class intended to harvest their wheat, take it to the Tannehill Gristmill for milling, and use the home economics facilities to bake bread with their home-grown flour. One park commission chairman submitted a plan for the development of an outdoor performing arts center which is actually going to be constructed.

These were just some of the imaginative projects that were created in response to the stimulating learning situation developed in this course. The many rich experiences afforded us, the dynamic speakers and guests, the harmony between what staff members "practiced" and what they "preached," all contributed to a positive atmosphere and a growing cohesiveness in the group. By the end of the course, we all felt a common bond, and we made commitments to try to keep the group alive and working toward the development of experiential education projects throughout the state.

Experiencing History

By Raymond H. Muessig

Introduction

"History is more or less bunk," Henry Ford observed. Said Carl Sandburg, "I tell you the past is a bucket of ashes."

As taught for decades in too many traditional classes throughout our nation, history has ranked high on the "Hate Parade" of innumerable people, both during and after their formal schooling. Frequently the content of history instruction has consisted of a potpourri of endless names, battles, and treaties. Many of the facts memorized by hapless students have been unimportant and even untrue. The customary method has followed a lecture-assign-read-study-recite-test-regurgitate-grade sequence. To a considerable extent, *learning* has meant a dreadfully small percentage of the happenings remembered, incompletely and often inaccurately at that.

A fundamental problem is that subject-centered history teaching has focused on the *product* (end result, outcome) of historical research and writing and not on the *process* (the way of working and thinking, the system of inquiring and analyzing). Although many historians are responsible for the emphasis of ends (answers) over means (questions), some of the brightest and the best servants of Clio (the Muse of history)—especially those interested in historiography (methods of historical investigation)—have championed a more balanced approach for some time. In 1956, for example, Fritz Stern made this observation:

...History is the cognitive expression of the deep-rooted human desire to know the past which, in a spontaneous untutored way, is born afresh with every child that searches the mystery of its being. History springs from a live concern, deals with life, serves life....[1]

In 1970, David Hackett Fischer wrote, "historians have a heavy responsibility not merely to teach people substantive historical truths but also to teach them how to think historically."[2] And in 1980, Robin W. Winks said that an "understanding of the past helps us to analyze our relationship to our environment today. If education ideally has a dual purpose—to provide joy in itself and to give the student the tools necessary to decipher his or her environment—the study of history serves that purpose well."[3]

Searching for Answers to Questions

Assuming that enlightened, dedicated contemporary teachers of social studies in general and history in particular would like to help their students to *experience history as a process,* to become active searchers and thinkers both today and throughout their lives, rather than being passive sponges just during their school years, how might they begin? Probably the last place for competent, motivated, creative teachers to start is by worrying about writing lists of behavioral objectives, referring to criterion-referenced and standardized tests, "covering" all of the content in adopted textbooks, adhering rigidly to mandated courses of study, and other such albatrosses that have been hung around their necks by various bureaucracies. Rather, taking into consideration the needs, interests, talents, problems, and aspirations of their students and the nature and potential experiential resources of the local community, teachers could encourage class members to frame appealing, challenging questions that learners—individually, in small groups and committees, and as a total class—could investigate as historical detectives.[4] Questions generated by students might be trivial or significant, humorous or serious, proximate or far-reaching, bland or controversial, just as long as they launch an active, purposeful, historical pursuit after defensible answers. Examples of some possible questions have been provided below to give teachers a feeling for the approach being recommended here. An attempt has been made to order the following questions from simple to complex, concrete to abstract, to demonstrate that different individual students, groups of learners, and classes can begin at different levels and advance their understandings, skills, appreciations, and values by tackling increasingly demanding questions. Additionally, comments have been inserted under questions for clarification and amplification purposes.

Where is the oldest grave marker in our city?

This is a down-to-earth (pun intended) question that could motivate students at various instructional levels to begin an active historical quest. If each individual student were to decide to try to answer this question on his or her own, in time, when experiences are compared, class members

might discover that there may be different ways of tracking down answers to a given historical question and that there may be different answers to the same question, depending on a historian's frame of reference, the accessibility of data to different researchers, the patience and thoroughness of an investigator, the way a sleuth "adds up" the facts, and so on.

But, let us briefly consider different techniques individual students might employ to locate the oldest grave marker and the extent to which they could take advantage of their environment. One person might rely on a kind of trial-and-error procedure, walk, hike, ride a bicycle, or take a bus; go to all of the oldest cemeteries, look around; and record the date of the oldest grave marker she or he finds. Using the "Yellow Pages" of a telephone directory, a second individual could call all of the cemeteries in the city for leads. Another student might talk with older people, including relatives and family friends, seeking advice with respect to where to look. Still another historical detective could visit a local, county, or state historical society to uncover clues. A fifth amateur researcher might spend some time in a public, college, or university library. And so on. Their investigations could bring class members into contact with a number of people and could take them to many parts of their community. Some budding scholars might even attempt to document their findings with rubbings, photographs, xerographic copies of records, etc., resulting in bulletin board displays, interest centers, and the like. Resource persons could be invited to class sessions, possibly including an archaeologist. Many rich and varied experiences could result from endeavors to respond to the first question suggested here. As a follow-up—for various reasons and with different possible experiential rewards—teachers might form committees to locate the city's oldest living person, standing building, operating business, and the like.

What was the most important event in our town's history?

Questions such as this could bring out the resourcefulness of students and encourage them to evaluate their data. Using the facilities of newspapers, historical societies, and various libraries, class members could learn to use, and to become more familiar with the use of, card catalogs, clipping files, photograph collections, microfilm, microfiche, computers, histories, biographies, diaries, memoirs, documents, maps, ad infinitum. Superlatives such as "worst" and "most" could fuel enthusiastic discussions often difficult to resolve. Considerable incidental learning might occur as students search for and exchange information.

What are some of the things that have attracted people to Courtesyburg?

For what reasons have people moved away from Courtesyburg?

What do you think are the most useful explanations for Courtesyburg's immigration and emigration?

"Multiple causation" is one of the key concepts in contemporary historiography. In their lectures, some traditional U.S. history teachers have told their classes that slavery was the cause of the Civil War. An approach more likely to stimulate students to think would be to ask, "How many causes can you identify that resulted in the Civil War?" Pressing class members to evaluate the importance of contributing factors further enriches learning.

What are some of the things that the people of Friendlyville used to do and/or believe that they no longer do and/or believe?

Heraclitus observed that change is the basic condition of life and that there is nothing permanent except change. Through their manifold experiences with history, students may discover that change has been an important part of the human condition and that the rate of change may differ from time to time, place to place, ingredient to ingredient.

In-depth, tape-recorded interviews with community residents of different ages in homes, schools, libraries, museums, churches and synagogues, places of employment, recreational sites, hospitals, convalescent facilities, retirement villages, and so on could contribute to experiential growth in many ways, but students' interactions with others are especially germane to a class study of changes over time in activities and beliefs. Having conversed with people in different settings, learners might write insights they have gained on a time line, drawn on unrolled butcher paper and taped on the walls around the classroom. During their discussion of entries on the time line, class members could observe that technological changes have occurred more rapidly than have those of an ideological nature, that the pace of change has accelerated in Friendlyville in more recent decades, and the like.

Has Happytown had an interdependent relationship with different nations of the world in the past? To what extent does Happytown have an interdependent relationship with various countries at the present time?

How likely is it that Happytown will have interdependent global relationships in the future?

What resources have been the most important to the residents of Helpful County in the past? What resources are the most important to the people of Helpful County at the present? What resources are likely to be the most important to the citizens of Helpful County in the future?

What are some of the most difficult problems that have faced the residents of Port Sunshine in the past? What are some of the most difficult problems facing the people of Port Sunshine today? What are some of the most difficult problems likely to face the citizens of Port Sunshine in the future? Are any of the past, present, and future problems related to each other? Why, or why not?

How might you describe the quality of life in Pleasant City in the past? How would you characterize the quality of life in Pleasant City today? What do you think the quality of life is likely to be in Pleasant City in the future? From past to present to future, have there been and may there be more gains or losses on the whole in the quality of life in Pleasant City? Why?

Historian Michael W. Curran has written that "history and historical understanding are essential if we are to make informed judgments about the present and act reasonably responsibly in trying to shape a world in which we want to live."[5] Committed, innovative history teachers can and should provide opportunities for experiences in which youth come to perceive past, present, and future relationships through real-life inquiry in the immediate community. By seeking their own answers to their own questions concerning interdependent relationships, the use of resources, personal/social problems troubling local citizens, the quality of life, etc., students can establish past-present-future connections that reinforce Shakespeare's line in *The Tempest:* "What's past is prologue." They may also identify some of history's limitations when they find certain possible future concerns for which the past and the present provide few or no precedents.

Conclusion

"Nothing ever becomes real till it is experienced...," wrote John Keats. Isadora Duncan said, "What one has not experienced one will never understand...." Experiencing history as a process, through active questioning and searching for meaningful answers—especially by tapping readily available and vivid resources in the immediate community—offers students "an arch to build upon," as Henry Brooks Adams put it.

NOTES

1. Stern, F. (Ed.). (1956). The varieties of history. Cleveland, OH: The World Publishing Company.

2. Fischer, D. H. (1970). Historians' fallacies: Toward a logic of historical thought. New York: Harper & Row, 316.

3. Winks, R. W. History. In V. Rogers and R. H. Muessig (Eds.), Social Studies: What is Basic? *Teacher 98*(3), 43.

4. For additional background and methodological ideas, please read: Muessig, R. H. (1980). Suggested methods for teachers. In H. S. Commager and R. H.

Muessig. The study and teaching of history. Columbus, OH: Charles E. Merrill, 104–119.

5. Curran, M. W. (1981). A historical perspective. In R. H. Muessig, and M. E. Gilliom (Eds.), Perspectives of global education: A sourcebook for classroom teachers. Columbus, OH: College of Education, The Ohio State University.

Chapter 9

Experiencing Mathematics and Science

Eureka! A Yurt! Integrating Mathematics, Cooperative Learning, and Community Service

by Jo Anna Woo Allen

The significance of "Eureka!" in the title derives from the exhilaration of discovery that took place through a project in which a class of sixth-graders built a Yurt.[1] There was a "Wow!" sense of awe and achievement akin to completing one's first rock climb or a thousand-piece puzzle. In the words of many of the sixth-graders who participated—"I can't believe we did it!" They built a scaled-down Yurt (see photo), a circular building having walls that slant upward and outward from a round base, with an overhanging cone-like roof. The roof has a skylight in the middle, capping the top of the walls. After a fresh four-inch snowfall, the Yurt looks like a frosted

The Yurt built by Class 6B of the Perry Hall Middle school in 1988.

cupcake. This wooden Yurt has a folded roof which resembles the folds in cupcake papers.

The main goal of the project, however, was not to build just a unique structure, but to teach mathematics experientially and to facilitate growth through service learning. The Yurt became part of the playground facilities of a special education school for severely and profoundly handicapped students.

The project was full of adventure and learning because, first of all, it had never been done before by such young students. One of them even said in her evaluation, "It was too difficult for sixth-graders, but not for us!" Secondly, in a large public school system there is always the suspense of whether someone will suddenly object to the project, or if red tape will undermine or throw off-schedule even the best laid plans. Finally, the project was begun without knowing exactly how the money for materials would be obtained.

Because of the many positive outcomes that are possible through this project, it is being shared in the hopes that others may adopt it and report back their findings. Some of the more general outcomes were direct application of mathematical principles, increased awareness of the benefits of doing community service, practical knowledge of carpentry, and leadership development. More specifically, over a span of three months during weekly class sessions, twenty-five sixth-grade math students at a middle school journeyed through these steps:

1) learned about the history and evolution of the modern Yurt,

2) designed eight different models of Yurts and learned the math needed to do it (three classes)

3) built Yurt models out of tagboard (three classes)

4) analyzed the structures and processed the design and building experiences (one class outdoors),

5) visited a special education school where they would build a wooden playground Yurt (field trip),

6) successfully solicited the building materials ($200 in wood and galvanized nails) themselves from a local business (the math office picked up the remaining $75 for costs of a skylight, hardware, cable, caulking, and engraved nameplates honoring the class and the donor),[2]

7) sawed by hand all the pieces needed for the wooden Yurt to make a kit for the big day (one class and two Saturdays),

8) and erected the Yurt in about four hours with the help of parents, teachers, and administrators (one final Saturday).

The project required vertical and horizontal collaboration of teachers and administrators. Even the special education school's PTA became involved and informed as they provided lunch on the day the Yurt was built. The special education principal was present that entire day.

The teachers at the middle school who were involved included the class's regular math teacher (who understood experiential education), their English teacher (who directed letter-writing to the lumber company and the reflection essays), and the industrial arts teacher (who supplied tools and advice). Parents helped to measure and saw, and assisted on the Yurt-raising day. Teachers and parents were learners along with students because none had ever built a structure having only one right angle amidst circles and slants and yet still put the Pythagorean theorem into use so frequently.

How Much Math?

Only very basic geometry is needed to design a Yurt. Trigonometry can also be used if the class is sufficiently advanced. The Pythagorean theorem ($c^2 = a^2 + b^2$), the formula for the circumference of a circle ($C = 2 \pi r$ or πd), and a basic calculator are the only mathematical tools needed for the design process. The starting dimensions given to each group were the diameter of the center roof skylight and the diameter of the base. The students were allowed to choose on their own, after group discussion and consensus, the number of wall pieces and the remaining dimensions such as the height of the walls and the height of the completed structure. On the data sheet (see Table 1), the dimensions needed to build the model are listed in the order in which they need to be calculated. An examination of the vertical cross-section (Figure 1) of the structure will show the relationships between the dimensions. The two given diameters are sufficient to get the students started and yet create a range of models. The letters (A, B, C, etc.) of each dimension in Table 1 are labeled to correspond with the sketches of the pieces in Figures 1 & 2.

Table 1 gives a description of how to calculate each dimension for a model posterboard Yurt. In designing a wooden Yurt, the width of the lumber must be taken into ac-

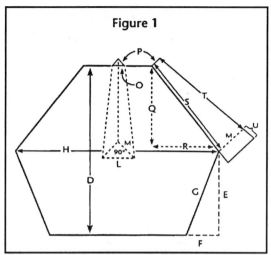

Figure 1

Cross-section of the dimensions of the Yurt with the letters corresponding to the dimensions labeled in Tables 1 & 2.

count and the sawing of the roof boards must be exact. In our Yurt, zeal in planing edges resulted in an error that multiplied to leave a gap in the roof. After a brief moment of disappointment, this was treated as a repairable error and part of the learning process. The sample calculations in the table are for a model Yurt having a base diameter of eight inches and a skylight diameter of three inches. Table 2 provides the step-by-step derivation of the sample numbers in Table 1 as a means to illustrate the calculation process for those who want to put it into practice.

Teaching the derivation of the structural dimensions from the two given numbers, plus the calculations for their own designs, required three class sessions for the group. Older students would take less time.

Using Cooperative Learning and An Experiential Approach

It does help to have somewhat of a spatial sense to facilitate the design process.

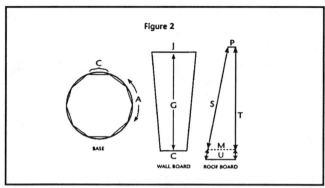

Dimensional diagrams of the base, wall board, and roof board of
the Yurt.

Table 1

This table lists the dimensions required for the calculations to design
a Yurt and corresponds to the lettered dimensions in Figures 1 & 2.
The process typically starts with the designation of the base diameter
and the skylight diameter. All of the other dimensions can either be
decided upon by the students (noted with a * below) or calculated.
Actual numbers in inches are filled in as a sample and as a means to
demonstrate the calculation process.

Base Diameter (BD) = 8   Skylight Diameter (SD) = 3

A.	Circumference of the base	A =	25.10
B.	Number of wall boards *	B =	24.00
C.	Bottom width of the wall boards	C =	1.05
D.	Height from floor to skylight *	D =	8.00
E.	Vertical height from floor to top of wall *	E =	5.00
F.	Smaller leg of wall triangle	F =	1.92
G.	Length of the wall board	G =	5.36
H.	Diameter of the top circle of the wall	H =	11.84
I.	Circumference of top circle of the wall	I =	37.20
J.	Top width of the wall board	J =	1.55
K.	Number of windows *	K =	8.00
L.	Base of triangular window	L =	4.65
M.	Leg of triangular window	M =	3.28
N.	Skylight circumference	N =	9.42
O.	Base of triangle at skylight	O =	1.18
P.	Leg of triangle at skylight	P =	0.83
Q.	Height from top of wall to skylight	Q =	3.00
R.	Segment of diameter of top circle of the wall	R =	4.42
S.	Length of the valley edge of the roof piece	S =	5.34
T.	Length of the peak edge of the roof piece	T =	6.27
U.	Overhang of the roof piece	U =	0.50
V.	Valley edge of the roof piece plus the overhang	V =	5.84
W.	Peak edge of the roof piece plus the overhang	W =	6.77

Student groups can be formed in accord with this ability or their computational skills. The cooperative learning technique of putting low-, medium-, and high-ability students together in groups of three or four is very effective. Designated duties may be assigned such as materials manager, recorder, and calculator operator. The highest ability student should not work the calculator or the likelihood is that s/he will come up with the figures without the others understanding their origins. This is analogous to an orienteering adventure in which the youngest child or the slowest-moving one is designated the compass-carrier. "Numbered heads together" (another cooperative learning structure) can be used to report on group progress so that the normally dominant student does not continually take the lead (Kagan, 1989). "Pairs check" can be used to double-check the figures within the group or even between groups.[3]

If the teacher happens to be unfamiliar with Yurt design, s/he can compensate by being one who likes to learn with the students and values the mistakes that will undoubtedly happen. The teacher should consider whether to allow the model-building to speak for the accuracy of the calculations, or to play it safe and check each and every number. My preference is to let the consequences teach the students, and use reflection and group debugging to decide how models can be improved or rescued. A wrong-sized roof can be given a new base and vice versa.

The teacher can also dive right into the project without making a test structure beforehand. I recommend starting from scratch with the students, and making your own Yurt model alongside the class. It is important to keep in mind that it is the process that teaches and not the product. The students in my group saw slides of various Yurts, but never saw a completed tagboard model except for their own. We did not want them to have preconceived ideas of a "correct" answer. This is not to say the teacher does not have to work out the mathematics ahead of time to understand where the pitfalls are for the students. One group capped off their wall base with the roof, only to have it fall inside, which resulted in peals of laughter and light-hearted jokes rather than tears of frustration.

The "correctness" of the results is a matter of aesthetics. Following the completion of the model building, we arranged for the class to meet outdoors in a grassy setting with the various Yurt models positioned in the center of the circle of students. (It is best not to do this on a windy day.) The sun, shining on the unique shapes with curved shadows, nicely set off the structures.

It became very clear to the students that some of the Yurts looked better than others. Their words included "too squatty," "too tall" or "has a better shape." Their observations were a perfect lead-in to a discussion of proportions and aesthetics, one of the goals of our school system's math program, but one which is difficult to address within the curriculum.

From this discussion, it was decided by the class that one particular model looked the best, and that became the basis for the wooden playground Yurt. To save time, I calculated those dimensions myself, taking into account the 3/4-inch thickness of the board lumber we would use. For the model-building, this was a factor that could be ignored. Although we used tagboard, I now

Table 2

This table describes the step-by-step process for designing a Yurt. The lettered dimensions correspond to the dimensions designated in Table 1 and Figure 1 & 2.

1. The circumference of the base (A) is found by using the formula for the circumference of a circle, c = πd, in which d is the diameter of the circle and π is 3.14. In this case, A = π(Base Diameter).

2. Decide by consensus how many wall boards (B) the Yurt is to have. The sample shows twenty-four. Students might sketch a circle and divide it with chords representing wallboards to help decide (see the sketch of the base in Figure 2).

3. The bottom width of the wall boards (C) is found by dividing the circumference (A) by the number of wall boards (B). Given a sufficient number of wall boards, the chord length is close enough to the actual arc length.

4. Decide on the height from the floor to the skylight (D). The sample shows 8 inches.

5. Also decide how high the top of the boards will be from the floor (E), i.e., the vertical height. Notice in Figure 1 that E is the longer leg of a right triangle and the wall board is the hypotenuse of the right triangle. In the sample, E was chosen as 5 inches.

6. Calculate the smaller leg of the wall triangle (F) using proportions so that E divided by F equals 13 divided by 5. With 5 substituted for E, the bottom leg of the wall triangle becomes 1.92 inches. This slope can be changed to whatever is aesthetically pleasing or practical. If the wall is to be a back rest for benches, a less steep slant might be desired such as 13/4 or 14/5.

7. The length of the wall board (G) is calculated using the Pythagorean theorem. In this project's playground Yurt, a standard four-foot board was used to determine the vertical height rather than vice versa.

8. The diameter of the top circle (H) is found by adding the base diameter (BD) to two times the F dimension (H = BD = 2F).

9. The circumference of the top circle of the wall (I) is calculated using the circumference formula (see step 1) with H being the diameter.

10. To get the width of the top of the wall board (J), divide the circumference of the top of the wall (I) by the number of wall boards (B), which is 24 in the example.

11. Decide how many windows (K) the Yurt will have. The windows are the triangular openings formed where the roof boards meet the top of the wall. In the sample, 8 windows were decided upon based on using three wall boards per triangular window.

12. The width of the base of the window (L) is determined by dividing dimension I (the circumference of the top wall) by K (the number of windows).

13. The legs of the window (M) have a 90-degree angle between them and are equal. Use the Pythagorean theorem once again, which in this case is, $L^2 = M^2 + M^2$. Solve for M.

14. To get the skylight circumference (N), use the skylight diameter (SD) given at the outset (3 inches) and the formula for circumference (see step 1).

15. Divide answer N by K (the number of windows) to obtain the base of the triangle at the skylight (O).

16. The leg of the triangle at the skylight (P) is calculated the same way M was in step thirteen, only using O as the hypotenuse rather than L ($O^2 = P^2 + P^2$).

17. The length of the valley edge of the roof piece (S) is the hypotenuse of a right triangle in which one leg (Q) is the vertical height from the top of the wall to the skylight and the other leg (R) is one segment of H, the diameter of the top circle of the wall. Q is calculated by subtracting E from D (the height from the floor to the skylight minus the vertical height from the floor to the top of the wall), or 8 minus 5 equals 3 in the example. R is calculated according to R = (H - SD)/2 (the diameter of the top of the wall minus the skylight diameter, all divided by 2). S is now calculated using the Pythagorean theorem as follows: $S^2 = Q^2 + R^2$, or 5.34 inches in the sample. Note that in a wooden Yurt, the grain of the wood should run parallel to this edge for maximum strength.

18. Ignore the P length and assume a right triangle in order to calculate the length of the peak edge of the roof piece (T), based on the lengths S and M. Use the Pythagorean theorem: $T^2 = S^2 + M^2$.

19. For overhang (U), .5 inch is sufficient, although a 1-inch overhang might ensure that the roof doesn't fall in.

20. Add the overhang (U) to S to get the actual valley length of the roof board (V).

21. Add the overhang (U) to T to get the actual peak length of the roof board (W). Eureka! A Yurt!

recommend using poster board which is thicker and can be bought in an assortment of colors. The "winning" Yurt was the largest and had to be strengthened with shoe strings woven into the walls because of the thinness of the tagboard, much like the cables that support a full-sized Yurt. This can be avoided by using heavier stock.

One of the comments by one group whose Yurt had many problems was, "I guess we could have worked more carefully." Calculating carefully and measuring, marking, and cutting exactly makes a tremendous difference. With twenty-four wall pieces, an error is multiplied by twenty-four.

Other mathematical concepts that were picked up experientially were the need to round off answers on the calculator, and the meaning of .45 feet which needed to be translated into inches, pointing out the advantage of the metric system. The idea of limits is actually inherent in the design because the more wall pieces there are, the closer the chords approximate the circle. Without prompting, students will probably come up with their own techniques for constructing the models. The fastest group actually chose the most labor-intensive method, cutting and taping individual wall and roof sections. Others found they could score and fold the tagboard and do less cutting. We tried to give no hints as to which way to proceed. Once the decision was made, groups worked oblivious to what other groups had chosen, convinced that their way would work just as well. Everyone was right.

How Big a Project?

There are all sorts of ramifications and extensions that can be tacked on to this initial phase. However, there is no need to go beyond the model-building in order to have a complete project or to learn mathematics experientially. But the growth and self-esteem component of the project was greatly enhanced by its extension into building a playground Yurt as a service project. So many of the essays that culminated the endeavor spoke of the feelings the students experienced from having contributed to the special education population. Repeatedly they expressed the disbelief they had felt on being told of the upcoming project, skeptical that as sixth-graders they would build a structure that they "could really walk into!" When they finished, the most repeated phrase was, "I can't believe we did it."

A drafting class, or an art class, or any group could be encouraged to be creative with the design. I chose the folded roof simply because of its beauty and uniqueness. There are many other possibilities for both the wall and roof which have been tried out in actual structures all over the world. If more time had been spent on scale drawings, it would have expanded the students' experience. We found the time needed to develop this skill was too great to fit into the original project timetable. Scale drawing is also a somewhat difficult task for sixth-graders. I am not sure at what point scale drawings can be used with ease for a two-dimensional preview of the aesthetics of the chosen designs.

A science class could delve into the heat efficiency aspects of insulating the structure, using their mathematical skills to calculate surface area versus volume. Because the space under the folded roof consists of diminishing equilateral triangles rising at an angle, the best way to calculate the volume is to use calculus. The volume of the base is most simply derived by using the formula for the volume of a cone, $V = (\pi r^2 h)/3$.

One extra variation of the project would be to have students use a computer spreadsheet to derive the figures for a multitude of Yurt sizes, not all of which may be aesthetically pleasing, but which would result in a data table that could be used to check student calculations. However, once devised, such a spreadsheet should not be allowed to take away from the sheer discovery and pleasure of calculating for oneself, and finding that the numbers one derives by hand can be translated into concrete results.

Anyone wishing to build a wooden Yurt would benefit from experience working with wood and doing carpentry.[4] Our Yurt's dimensions included a forty-four-inch-diameter base (from a cable reel) and a height of approximately six feet (see photo). The skylight was eighteen inches in diameter with a twenty-four-inch-diameter plexiglass skylight bolted on top. There is no door closing the Yurt but benches were added a week after the Yurt was built. The custodial staff of the special education school painted the structure orange and blue, inside and out, to match the other playground structures.

A standard-sized Yurt, seventeen feet in diameter at the eaves, makes an excellent classroom-in-the-round with benches built at a comfortable height against the wall (yes, only one wall!). It also can be built as housing for one or two persons.[5] Much larger, concentrically designed Yurts have been built as homes.

The possibilities are endless, starting with an understanding of the mathematics, or even better, not knowing the math. Where the class goes depends on the energy and creativity of both the teacher and students working together. It is a unique way of combining mathematics and hands-on experience with the lessons of service learning.

NOTES

1. The word Yurt is being capitalized to distinguish it from, and out of respect for, the Mongolian yurt, a portable shelter whose building principles inspired the modern version.

2. Class 6B of the Perry Hill Middle School built the Yurt for Ridge School in the Spring of 1988. Both schools are in Baltimore County, Maryland.

3. *Numbered Heads Together* originated with Spencer Kagan (see Kagan, 1989). It is useful for reviewing material and responding or reporting to the class. The students in each team are numbered (a team of four would have 1, 2, 3, 4). They do not know who is going to be called on. Once the teacher is ready for reports from groups or answers to a questions, (s)he calls out a number, all of whom answer taking turns, or simultaneously using hand signals, showing response cards, or even in chorus. In a project such as this, this reporting process allows the quieter student to be the spokesperson for the group. The student must also collaborate with the team to get a consensus on the report.

Pairs Check is another Kagan structure. Within each team of four, students can be paired to calculate the Yurt dimensions. One member of each pair solves the problem while being coached by the partner. They can then check with the other pair in the team to see whether that pair also obtained the same answer for the dimension. Both pairs are working with the same starting numbers for the base and skylight diameters. For this project, we used eight teams of three persons each in order to get eight different models. Groups of four would facilitate *pairs check* but would result in fewer models to study.

4. There are a variety of additional considerations when building a wooden Yurt. Attaching the wall boards to the floor can be tricky, but trial and error will probably suffice. It helps to see a building firsthand to understand the overlap of the wall boards to produce the slope. Yurts with larger diameters are built with a steel cable around the top of the wall, cinched up tightly and fastened in brackets or clinched nails, in order to help support the weight of the roof pressing out on the wall. The wall boards overlap more at the bottom than at the top, and are nailed the length of the overlapped area. In a small-sized Yurt such as this one, the cable is actually not necessary.

The roof boards converge around the skylight and in large Yurts, the skylight opening is strengthened through the use of a steel or wooden compression ring which maintains the shape of the round skylight and bears the weight of the roof forcing in. The small Yurt done by the students did not need a compression ring in the skylight, although we did put a steel cable around the top of the wall boards.

5. For more information on Yurts and Yurt workshops, contact Dr. Wm. S. Coperthwaite, Director, Yurt Foundation, Bucks Harbor, Maine 04618.

Experiential Mathematics

by Roger H. Marty

Consider $V = 4/3 \ \pi r^3$. To many people, a collection of symbols such as this, along with numbers, represents the totality of mathematics. That is why cartoonists frequently depict mathematics by displaying a smattering of symbols on a chalkboard.

Some people with greater mathematical knowledge may recognize this as the formula for computing the volume of a sphere of given radius, and their understanding is limited here to just this "formula" concept.

Other people with more understanding may recognize this as an equation relating two variables, the volume of a sphere and its radius. Some of these also understand that, generally, in an equation involving just two variables, knowing a specific value for one is often sufficient for computing the value of the other (some would even think in terms of "corresponding" value).

Still others with a fuller understanding recognize this equation as defining, implicitly, two distinct functions; one is the volume of a sphere in terms of its radius, and the other is the radius of a sphere in terms of its volume.

This article will illustrate how the concept of function, which is fundamental to all of mathematics, might be explored in a student-centered learning situation. The framework for the learning situation consists of finding a solution to a problem. The solution requires devising procedures for gaining intermediate information. The teacher's role is that of guide—permitting students at times to attempt methods that seem certain to fail as they explore and probe various approaches.

Posing the Problem

Students are presented the problem of determining various dimensions (of diameters, circumferences, etc.) of spheres (basketballs, soccer balls, bowling balls, etc.), cubes, cylindrical solids, etc., without using rulers or any other devices for measuring lengths. The students work in groups and are provided with water-tight containers (metal or plastic waste containers or buckets), calibrated beakers, a scale for determining weights, calculators, water, and of course, some appropriate formulas ($V = 4/3\pi r^3$, $V = \pi r^2 h$, $V = e^3$, $C = 2\pi r$, etc.).

The students are expected to devise various procedures, as needed, in solving the problems. These might include a method of determining the volume of water displaced by a submerged object, or of proving their conjectures such as that the diameter of a right circular cylinder is *not* a function of its volume.

The students write group reports on their findings and hypotheses and then compare their results with other groups. At this time, rulers are permitted for confirming (or rejecting) hypotheses.

Expected Outcomes

Methods of learning as described here not only reinforce and deepen the understanding of concepts already known, but also result in the introduction of new concepts in a special, personal way that is not easily forgotten. More importantly, having constructed productive procedures, students gain confidence in their own analytical powers and abilities in active inquiry.

More specific discoveries by students include the following:

(i)   the ability to solve mathematical equations for particular variables is useful and meaningful (the present mathematics curriculum is devoted extensively to developing various techniques for solving mathematical equations),

(ii) mathematics is a creative endeavor involving procedures actually devised by the students themselves, and thus, doing mathematics has great potential for satisfaction,

(iii) problem solving is more than an exercise in translating a specific problem into mathematical expressions, and

(iv) solutions to mathematical problems are human creations having various possible forms (rather than existing as a fixed sequence of rules).

Recycling with an Educational Purpose

by Tom Gerth and David A. Wilson

I. Overview: David A. Wilson

The ECO-ACT Environmental Leadership Program sponsored by Missouri Botanical Garden was selected by the National Science Teacher Association as an exemplary program in its 1983 Search for Excellence in Science Education. What follows is one example of a project conducted by students in that program.

Four high school students from St. Louis University High School taught environmental science once a week in Mrs. Velma McCall's fifth-grade class at Buder Elementary School in St. Louis. In December, they encouraged their class to bring in aluminum and steel cans for recycling as part of their study of resources and resource management.

Students spent three weeks collecting 30 lb of cans worth approximately $6. Based on this experience, the high school students involved the class in a program to establish a recycling competition throughout the school.

As the high school students met with teachers, the principal, the custodian, and laid plans for the project, they gained practical experience as organizers and leaders and taught the fifth-graders those skills as well.

The class was first divided into teams, with one group preparing speeches, the other posters. Students read contest announcements over the school P.A., and subsequently students announced weekly contest winners in similar fashion.

As the collection campaign began, one crew went around to the rooms each day to pick up the bags of metal cans, another crew smashed cans, and all weighed and recorded results by classroom. The collection, weighing, recording process took 40 minutes of class time each week. As they tallied each classroom's volume, they had an opportunity to use their mathematical skills. They prepared charts and graphs and weighed the cans by the metric system. Then they converted their figures to pounds to estimate the amount of cash they could expect to earn at the local recycling center.

In a five-week contest, the school collected over 500 lb of aluminum and steel worth about $135. The winning class received a field trip to Missouri Botanical Garden. Then Mrs. McCall's class decided how to spend the money for the school.

This recycling project was conducted with the assistance of several high school students working in an elementary classroom. The fifth-grade class became the true leaders in their school in the project. While every elementary teacher may not have some high school leaders to help, a project like this can be undertaken with minimum risk and maximum learning. It is an effective way of involving students in concrete action based on what they learn about the environment.

II. Our Project: Tom Gerth

Project Description and Objectives

Our project was one that involved beautifying and cleaning up the environment, while at the same time saving energy and natural resources. The project consisted of three phases: 1) collecting the beverage cans—both steel and aluminum, 2) saving and eventually recycling these cans, and 3) using the resulting cash to further beautify the environment—in our case, buying and planting trees.

The objectives of the project were many. Of course, the major thrust of the program was to allow the students to help improve their environment. By letting them take part (and actually operate) in the collection and recycling process, we taught them practical ways in which they can do their part, both in the project and eventually on their own. In addition, the students also learn organizational, public relations, and money management skills.

Pre-Project: How did we prepare?

The first thing we had to do was discuss our plan with the fifth-grade teacher, Mrs. McCall, and the principal, Mr. Eckols. They were both very receptive to the plan, so we went ahead to plan a small-scale, trial can drive. This drive included only the one fifth-grade class and lasted a total of three weeks. To plan this small drive, the only necessary preparations were to 1) explain the plan to the class, 2) give a crash course on recycling and its importance, and 3) ask for input. After three weeks, the one class collected almost 30 lb of cans, worth approximately $6. With these statistics, we figured that a 19-classroom school like Buder would recycle a lot of metal and make a lot of money.

The next step was to plan for the drive and work out the logistics. We had to discuss our plans with the different teachers, find a place to store the metal, organize a "pick-up" crew, and plan trips to the recycling center.

Perhaps most integral to our efforts was devising a way to maximize metal intake. To get maximum results, we decided to operate in competition style. Each classroom competed for a prize: a field trip to Missouri Botanical Garden.

With the logistical problems out of the way, the next step was to publicize the project. Since our fifth-graders were the ones running the project, we divided them into 2 groups—the speech group and the poster group. The poster group made big colorful contest posters, while the speech group submitted speeches, one of which was chosen to be read by its creator over the school P.A. system (we continued to use the P.A. for publicity, later announcing the weekly and contest winners). We, the ECO-ACT students, also attended a teachers' meeting where we announced the project plans to the entire faculty.

The Project Itself

Once the project was underway, the work was still far from done. We had a collection crew (which went around to the rooms each day and picked up the metal), a smashing crew (to maximize space efficiency), a weighing crew, and a recording crew (to keep track of which room was winning the contest). Idealistically, we planned on spending the initial 10 minutes of class doing this. In reality, however, it took about 30-40 minutes.

After five weeks of collecting aluminum and steel, the whole school had collected over 500 lb worth about $135. And with the first two phases of the program over, we went into the final stage: spending the money to help beautify the Buder School environment. After a lengthy class meeting, we decided on buying and planting trees. These trees not only taught the students the practical art of planting, but also added beauty by providing two living monuments to ECO-ACT, to the concept of conservation, and to the Buder School.

An In-depth Look at Planting a Tree

When our fifth-grade class decided to use its project money to buy and plant trees, we had to figure out the best ways for them to learn about planting a tree. What did we do? First we brought the tree into the schoolyard, placing it in a spot where the class would have to pass it on the way to the planting site. When we brought the students out, we let them examine the tree, showing them the parts, the function of the burlap-wrapped base, and the size. We let them discover the elements necessary to tree growth—sunlight, oxygen, rain. We then sat around the tree and planting site, and asked general discussion-type questions: What do the trees need for growth? What purpose do the wood chips and mulch serve? How big would the tree get? What good would it do for Buder? We had a nice discussion before planting.

To plant the tree, each student helped. Some took turns digging, others measuring the depth of the hole, others filling, watering, and mulching. Periodically, the depth of the hole, the diameter of the tree, and the circumference of the tree were measured. What did the students learn?

- practical art of planting a tree
- basic biology—plant parts
- basic Earth Science—elements necessary for plant (and animal) growth
- mathematics—measuring

- working together
- satisfaction of getting a job well done.

Problems we encountered

Surprisingly enough, we encountered very few problems. Just for the record, though, I'll relate the ones we did have, and how we attempted to solve them.

- MISSING STUDENTS!

Since some students would be busy working with their committees, sometimes several students would miss a class; and this can really throw off a lesson plan that relies on the previous class. To overcome this problem, we taught self-contained lessons—ones that taught a concept in one class.

- NOISE!

Several teachers complained about noise, both from the students and from the crashing and smashing of cans. To solve this we did two things—first, we warned the students about their noise, and second, we got permission for a new storage room, downstairs and away from the classrooms.

- BUGS!

Toward the end of the project, the janitors complained about cockroaches that were attracted to the empty soda and beer cans. The project was almost over, so we couldn't really do anything to solve the problem. In the future, though, more frequent pickups could help.

- ASSAULT!

Some of the kids were throwing cans at each other on the bus, and one of the drivers wouldn't allow cans on his bus anymore. What could we do? We had to take the loss.

Evaluation

In general, the project went exceptionally well. The students learned a lot about recycling, organizing a project, money management and use, and practical knowledge about improving the environment. More importantly, though, is the fact that the students did more than learn; they put their knowledge into use—they acted. And that's what ECO-ACT's all about.

The Gunpowder River Project: Experiential Education in a Large Public School System

by Jo Anna Woo Allen

Second graders aboard the *Lady Maryland* look at a chart of the Chesapeake Bay.

*"He won't catch anything, but we'll let him take his fishing gear anyway,"
were the high school teacher's thoughts upon the student's request. The class
had already become acquainted with the river near their end of the county
where it passed a sewage treatment plant and approached the Chesapeake
Bay. Now they were taking a field trip to the northern part of the county nearer
the source of the river to compare sites. Results? One good-sized rainbow trout
within minutes after students debarked off the bus and the hit of the day's
activities. Another teacher proven wrong!*

*"Hey, look at Nicky! He's doing it! He's in the water!" The huge smile on
Nicky's face flashes his accomplishment in collecting specimens just as well
as anyone else. Not bad for a kid in a primary "learning disabled" class who*

used to get picked on. (This was to begin a new respect for him by his classmates.)

"Yuk!" is the seventh-grader's response to looking closely in the menhaden's mouth. A fishmouth isopod! She and her gifted and talented science class are out on the Chesapeake Bay in an oyster boat. The afternoon half of the day would be spent in a rowboat exploring the ecology of a tributary creek.

*   *   *   *   *   *   *   *

What curriculum has students from first grade through senior year in high school, "Learning Disabled" to "Gifted and Talented," so turned on to rivers and salinity and buffer zones and grass shrimp and saving our stream?—The Gunpowder River School Action Project in Baltimore County, Maryland! This project so captured students, teachers, parents, and administrators alike in its pilot year ('85-'86) that the '87-'88 school year finds the project being adopted by neighboring school systems to study their rivers as part of their own curricula.

What captured this writer, who as a county teacher is only reporting what happened, was that the project exemplified experiential education without it having been planned as such. The great success in such a large public system where there is still no formal outdoor education program (and where conservatism generally prevails) fascinated me. What made it so successful? And can we keep it going and growing?

Background of the Project

In 1985, the Maryland legislature approved monies for a Chesapeake Bay Initiatives Program, geared to "Saving the Bay." Part of the money was earmarked for education. A state environmental education director was appointed and grant money for selected projects was made available.

Very little of Baltimore County actually touches the Chesapeake Bay, but its rivers and streams feed into the bay, plus all its farm runoff, sewage system output, sediment, etc. Thus, the Gunpowder Project was proposed and funded through the State Department of Education to involve students in studying the Gunpowder River which empties into the Chesapeake Bay.

The major county school departments involved were the Office of Science and the Office of Elementary Education, the grant application arising out of the former. In the pilot year, two elementary, two middle, and three high schools which were near the Gunpowder River were approached and invited to be "charter" members of what was to be a very special group. Primary responsibility for implementation of the project would lie with science teachers at the middle and high school levels and selected elementary teachers.

These nine teachers with the support of five administrators (vice principals and supervisors) met in the summer of 1985 for field instruction and development of the pilot curriculum. The guide they developed included "in school," "on site," and "community awareness" activities for each of the three levels of schools. The activities were science oriented and were designed to increase environmental awareness, particularly for

"Saving the Bay." Appendices included activities for assessing stream quality through physical/chemical techniques and aquatic and land flora and fauna. Each school "adopted" a site to be its own study environment.

Implementation in the Pilot Year

There was tremendous variation in what each teacher involved chose to do. Teacher interest and creativity, grade level, science curriculum parameters, and type of school and community all led to the diversity which became a strength of the project. Teachers getting together to share experiences were stimulated by and learned from each other. Elementary teachers were impressed by high school teachers who were "experts" in chemical analysis. High school teachers were in awe of elementary teachers who amazed them with their integration of reading, writing, math, art, music, vocabulary, and social studies into the Gunpowder curriculum. For example, at Oliver Beach elementary school, the whole fifth-grade curriculum found ties to the project. Ecosystems was the theme and Gary Gunpowder became the imaginary folk hero. Directions to the site, descriptions of the river, and depth measurements using math all related to the project.

Middle school science curricula that meshed best with the project were the seventh-grade "diversity of living things" unit and the "ecology" eighth-grade unit. The two middle schools involved pooled their funds and shared equipment. In addition to field trips to the river itself were trips to a tidal estuary (where fishmouth isopods and oyster toad fish were captured) and a day spent with the county naturalist.

At one high school near the mouth of the river, the Aquatics Biology classes became the natural home base for the Gunpowder curriculum. Out of one of their field trips arose the triumphant trout fisherman. Another field trip took students canoeing down one section of the river to observe changes in ecology. Students tested the water and collected species of fish using seine nets at sites ranging from forested areas to saltwater marshes. Other students chose to board a skipjack in Annapolis to study oystering.

The Aquatics II class took a whole-year approach, monitoring water quality on a monthly basis. They tested for carbon dioxide, dissolved oxygen, pH, larvae analysis, temperature, and plankton.

At the northernmost high school in the county the biology classes studied aquatic ecosystems—cycles, energy, food webs, etc., along with the aforementioned tests. A physical education teacher with a high interest in outdoor education set up a nature trail marked for study of the ecosystem. One Gunpowder teacher who also serves on a committee to develop writing across the curriculum has combined the two projects. Students submit drafts summarizing their findings on the analysis of the river and polish them into well-written reports.

Outcomes of the Pilot Year

With the enthusiasm generated and the careful planning that went into the project, achievement of objectives was accomplished at an excellent level. Students who participated have been educated to an environmental awareness of appreciation for the Gunpowder and rivers in general. The community has been very much involved through presentations at conferences and PTA meetings and displays at shopping malls by students of their work on the Gunpowder and its relationship to the community. Science was learned experientially with "real" applications. Through letter writing and dissemination of information on county agencies that monitor pollution, citizenship was promoted.

But the outcomes with which this writer is most fascinated are the spinoffs that were not written into the objectives. As I interviewed various pilot teachers, I was struck by their universal involvement and motivation. They expressed an enthusiasm that was contagious and perfect for tapping to train new second- and third-year teachers participating in the project. This same enthusiasm and dedication has spread to their students. As Gary Slavin said of his eighth-graders, "They were motivated to science for the rest of the year. It was good to do the field trip in the fall." Students discovered the Gunpowder River Project is fun learning!

The parental involvement at the elementary level sets an impressive standard. Parents are genuinely needed and the project has given them a unique opportunity to participate in their children's education.

With such positive results for all the hard work, teaching the Gunpowder curriculum has meant reaping those intangible rewards that keep a good teacher going in these days of budget cuts and increased workloads. Brian Migliarini stepped into a high school department headship from a middle school position only to find he inherited the Gunpowder project on top of all the strains of breaking in. When asked if participation in the project was worth it, he responded, "Unequivocally."

Maureen Savage, an elementary school teacher, found working with other teachers to develop curriculum from scratch was a tremendous growth experience for herself. She tested all her new materials and lessons on her family first. Seldom is there a project where elementary, middle, and high school teachers are collaborating and sharing from their respective perspectives. Their commitment has now widened to encompass the whole county as the project has grown and expanded. The magnitude of the project has taken them by surprise. The first Gunpowder Awareness Day had excellent media coverage and fourteen dignitaries were present, including the governor. Rarely do teachers get such acknowledgement and appreciation for their work.

In the fall of 1987, the project will have spread to the Patapsco River which is the southwest boundary of Baltimore County. A neighboring county will adopt the Patuxent River, and Baltimore City will use the Gwynns Falls River. All nine pilot teachers are involved in the training of these teachers, just as they assisted the eighteen new schools studying the Gunpowder in '86–'87. The word had gotten out so that schools which have so far not been involved are claiming proximity to the Gunpowder so as to participate. One principal, who is historically critical of the Office of Science, has admiringly admitted to the tremendous success of the program.

Why the Success?

Can the success be maintained and imitated? What are the critical factors?

Unquestionably, without the state funding, such a project would have been difficult to initiate. The monies paid for equipment, teacher workshop time, materials development, and bus rental for field trips. More importantly, it began a network of interest and support at the highest-level educational agency in the state. This was appropriate to the scope of efforts to save the Bay which affects the economy of all the states bordering the Bay. With the curriculum guide completed and start-up equipment in place, second-year funding was used for teacher training, transportation, and more materials. Hopefully, the curriculum can eventually be absorbed into normal curriculum budgets. The success of the program has captured the support of PTAs which may provide further financial support if necessary. The same state monies are available to any local education agency in the state.

A second large factor was the availability and cooperation of several resources in the area. Gunpowder State Park very generously freed rangers to give talks, visit classes, and coordinate the buffer-zone tree planting that was a large part of the second annual Gunpowder Awareness Day.

Oregon Ridge Nature Center, a Parks and Recreation facility, was the site of many meetings and training sessions. The county education naturalist there helped to train parent volunteers and acquainted teachers with much of the local ecology needed to study the river.

Many of the field trips on tributaries and in the Bay itself were sponsored and led by the Chesapeake Bay Foundation, a well-established nonprofit citizen's organization that supports efforts to help clean up the Bay.

Save Our Systems is another citizen's organization instrumental in getting more construction site inspectors funded to help safeguard against sedimentation flow into the rivers that feed into the Bay. Their Rivers and Streams Conference in the Fall of 1986 provided opportunity for spreading the word about the Gunpowder River Project.

The *Lady Maryland* is a sailing vessel completed last year and serves entirely as an education vehicle to bring students on to the Bay. The boat was built right at the downtown shore front in the vicinity of the Science Museum. Jennifer Pahl's second-graders, the youngest group ever taken on the ship, taught the crew a lesson in sophistication at an early age.

Finally, the Maryland Association of Environmental and Outdoor Educators was formed a few years ago and unites the efforts of state educators in a field closely related to the Project. Combined with all the education agencies and departments, these resources all help to expand and strengthen the network on which teachers can draw.

A third factor is simply the excitement generated when there is novelty and experimentation going on—akin to the Hawthorne effect. The newness and undeveloped waters of the Gunpowder curriculum served as wilderness for adventure for pilot-year teachers. The end of the pilot year proved the journey was worthwhile beyond expectations and produced enough synergy to propel the project into a second successful year. One teacher expressed concern that the novelty will wear off as elementary and middle schoolers move into the ranks of high school biology and state the words that make any teacher grit his/her teeth, "We studied that already." However, a middle school teacher expressed the opposite, that there is so much to do with the curriculum that every year is new and no student is really able to do it all. Besides, it's a new class, a different teacher, and a different approach and emphasis!

A fourth factor was the opportunity for personal growth and actualization on the part of the teachers. We teachers tend to work in our own little pockets, in our little assigned cubbyholes or homerooms, without sharing our personal achievements or being able to send out an SOS when we need a little helpful advice. The Project integrated teachers vertically and horizontally, and learning from each other became the theme. It was an open market for trying out new ideas. No one was an expert because there was no precedent. No one was wrong and no one was absolutely right.

Teachers were given "permission" to be creative and that they were. As in Maslow's Hierarchy of Needs, the curriculum was filling not security needs of salary, since that existed without participating in the project, but higher needs of esteem and recognition and expression of self and creativity.

There were communication and community within school buildings as art teachers helped design T-shirts, reading specialists made bulletin boards out of Gunpowder vocabulary, and a music teacher composed the Gunpowder Song for the whole county. The physical education instructor at Gunpowder Elementary tailored half-mile hikes to the Gunpowder River to each grade level's science curriculum. Stops were made to identify and talk about interesting plants found along the way. Pupils would hike the trail for physical fitness, stopping to take their pulses. Discussions would focus on the value of leisure activity and the relationship to resources such as the Gunpowder. Not often do varied curricula integrate so well,

nor do teachers team outside of their own specialties.

If the teachers were "permitted" to be creative then a very large fifth factor has to be administrators and supervisors who empowered them to be creative.

Administering the project was facilitated by the small scope of the initial efforts. Pilot-year implementation was wisely scaled to resources and manageability given the ground to be broken. As suggested in *In Search of Excellence,* supervisors were right where the action was—on the boats and in the water with the teachers. Teachers enjoyed autonomy and freedom yet always had ties to and support from the system.

Most of all, the Gunpowder River Project is *experiential learning* and that is what drew my attention to it. It is also *experiential education* according to Conrad and Hedin's definition because it is part of the formal school curriculum but much of it takes place outside the classroom with students applying themselves to an action study and participating in "Saving the Bay." Studies of food chains and causes of pollution show the Bay has real significance in their lives. Discussion following activities continually reflects on the responsibility we all have in caring about it. It fits very well into the county's values education program. In addition it utilizes writing across the curriculum better than any other curriculum I have seen.

In summary, here is an experience and curriculum that ought to be shared and is being shared in Maryland. Other school systems can adopt it as long as they have a river. Lo and behold, it developed in a *large, public school system!*

Of all the factors I have examined, I tend to return again and again to the actualization of the creative individual teacher as a critical component. The factors of funding and resources could change significantly, but not have as negative an impact on the final result as restricting or mismanaging the teachers would. It is my belief that as long as the flexibility and freedom are there, and the curriculum is allowed to change and grow with teacher input, the Project will continue to thrive.

For more specific information about the Gunpowder River Project (now Gunpowder/Patapsco River Project), contact Ronald Barnes, Science Supervisor, Baltimore County Public Schools, 6901 Charles St., Office of Science-ESS Bldg., Towson, MD 21204.

Chapter 10

Experiencing the Language Arts

Time, Place, and Community:
Ingredients for Good Writing

by Ian Sykes

When I have some time to myself, I like to daydream. I daydream about lots of things, for instance I dream about a horse running through a grove of flowers, or a bird flying through the clouds and sometimes I just sit there watching butterflies dance in the wind.

Ami (grade 3, age 8)

Reflection is the process of looking back. It devotes time to sorting the experiences of life and making connections among them. I have been an elementary teacher for many years, using a whole language approach with my young students (Goodman, 1986). In years past, allowing students to daydream or taking children up into the mountains was often regarded as a negligent waste of school time. In this article, I take you on a journey with my class into those fields and mountains to show how careful preparation and

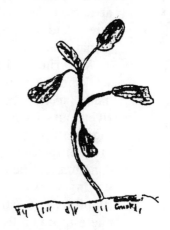

understanding of reflection in the experiential process are essential to the development of vivid writing.

My team partner, Anne Davies, and I think that children should be given a wide range of related experiences, time to reflect upon them, and time to write about them, all within a caring community of learners.

We work with grade-three and -four students in a mid-sized city, sixty minutes from the mountains. The school is surrounded by a large playing field and hill, partially preserved in a noncultivated state. We use all of these natural resources to support a strong program of reading literature and writing.

The program also integrates social studies and fine arts elements with language arts. It is part of the daily classroom routine for children to have time to sit quietly and think, discuss issues with peers, and to write about their thoughts. This is a flexible routine with each writing activity evolving from the connections teachers and students see in our classroom. Such opportunities arise from discussions, literature, field experiences, and human interactions.

We write as a group in a workshop style. We normally spend about four or five hours each week sharing, writing, and discussing in order to develop a trusting community. The essence of a writing workshop requires a supportive, trusting atmosphere based on the child's individual needs (Calkins, 1983, p. 114). The community of writers includes the adults working in the classroom. Anne and I write with the students or bring our writing to them. As well, we belong to a professional group that meets to compare reflective logs about daily classroom practice. The logs are often shared with our students as well. This gives children confidence in our abilities, windows on our fallibilities, and trust in our relationship with them, making the community healthy and genuine.

We plan our school year to include occasions for the class to move outside and experience the surrounding country. This in itself might be considered frivolous if we did not take the time for students to value the experience (Joplin, 1985, p. 117). The idea is to allow the experiences to build on each other so that each child is encouraged to make connections. John Dewey discussed the relationship between present and future knowing. He states, "The persons who should have some idea of the connection between the two [present and future] are those who have achieved maturity" (Dewey, 1963, p. 50). As teachers, we have reached the maturity to understand this process, not only for ourselves, but its importance for children as well. The following pieces demonstrate how children begin to make connections through reflecting on experience, and thus mature in their writing.

I think about these things and wonder. These flowers, branches and thorns are a bit of what it is going to be like. The beautiful nature of these objects touches everybody by the heart. I believe this will happen at Johnston's Canyon.

James (grade 4, age 9)

Never Lives Never Dies

Lifeless branch day and night
Lives not longer but is forever
Not alive save in the heart
Never lives never dies
A shadow in the sun
A highlight in the moon
Never lives never dies.

Andrew (grade 4, age 9)

Both of the boys express connections with their environment. James is making an esthetic prediction of future events and feelings. Andrew is using a poetic form to understand and put in perspective the existence of a branch.

These pieces were written on the hill behind our school. During the spring, we watched crocuses bloom, insects crawl, birds fly, and Chinook clouds form arches over the city. The childrens' writing showed the kinds of connections they were finding among themselves and the natural world. The students were becoming ready to experience a larger, less familiar, setting.

We discovered Grotto Canyon, a long, high-walled, narrow chasm with a stream in the center, a short drive from the school. On its walls are found Indian pictographs, and our discussion of the sacred significance of

the canyon to the neighboring Stony Indians was an important part of the overall preparation for the trip. The unique geographic formations created an eerie and imaginative place for the children to explore their feelings and the land. Their explorations led to more reflection and writing in this new environment.

The Giant's Dungeon

I feel as if I am stuck in a Giant's dungeon and I only have water to drink but nothing to eat. I also feel comfortable because the only sound is rushing water. If this was a dungeon, it would be the nicest one on earth.

Katherine (grade 4, age 9)

Katherine captures the romance of the place with her reference to dungeons. Her obvious exposure to fairy tales allowed this experience to have that romantic meaning. One experience, the literary, was enhanced by the other, the physical environment. In the same situation, Lauren's reflections led her in another direction.

Reflections

When I think back to Grotto Canyon, I think of the fun times had together. I think of the things we saw and how quiet we were. It was like being one big family because nobody got in a fight and everybody got along. I really enjoyed the trip there and back. I liked seeing the Indian Reserve. The waterfall at Grotto Canyon was very nice to see, but going up there was not too fun. I really liked the Indian pictographs, they were very interesting. One thing I really, really liked was all the way up the canyon you were in between two rock walls and while you were walking you had to walk side to side because there was a stream going down the middle. The place where we ate lunch was very nice too. I liked the fact that we ate on rocks. One thing that was really funny was when Carol dropped her clip board in the water. I will never forget the wonderful times we had together.

Lauren (grade 4, age 9)

Lauren clearly had good feelings about the togetherness she experienced. Were these connected to feelings she has within her own family experience?

The ultimate experience for which we had been working so hard to prepare our students was a hike up Johnston's Canyon. The hill behind the school prepared the students to accept learning in an outdoor setting. The skills of sketching, reflecting, and writing outside were introduced and polished. The work in Grotto Canyon made the jump from familiar to unfamiliar. It was a gentle but powerful experience in a real mountain canyon. Finally, we were to make the last step: a full day exploring a much larger canyon in the mountains of Banff National Park.

We always include parents in our field excursions. We had twenty adults, teachers and parents, as well as fifty-six students on this trip. Some of the parents were artists or naturalists. Others were simply interested in being with their children in this challenging environment.

Joy MacLeod, an artist and parent of two boys in our class, had spent time with the students over the year teaching sketching. Anne and I use sketching in conjunction with writing to develop observation skills and teach the children to look at the world with new perspective (the accompanying sketches provide examples of their work). The art, social studies, storytelling, writing, and reading all blend to develop broader esthetic understanding and literacy in our students (Harste, 1984, p. 38).

We provided advanced physical preparation for the twelve-kilometer hike in Johnston's Canyon and were confident that the students were ready, physically and mentally. This class walked the lower canyon in small groups with an interpreter. Time was given for rests, observation, and reflective writing. In the upper section of the canyon, the groups moved at their own pace, meetings as a whole class at the top. The canyon opens into a lovely meadow, in a valley complete with a rushing river and picnic tables. Here, we had lunch. Students took time after lunch for what I call "the silent sit." They scattered over the meadow, distanced so that they could not speak to each other. The instructions were to sit for a period of fifteen minutes. They could write, sketch, or just sit. We had done silent sits before, on our hill and at Grotto Canyon, but here, nestled in the majesty of this mountain valley, the full impact was realized. The following pieces are samples from that silent sit.

Taking Time

Sitting in a tuft of grass I see many things. I feel the warm earth beneath me and the cool air around me. I see a green plant behind me and the flowers are white with pink tips. It reminds me of a frosted window on a cold winter night. Now the sun begins to come out and then fades away behind the clouds. I look up at the mountains around me and see the steepness of them. I hear a bird sing a short friendly song and I wonder is it calling me?

Lisa (grade 3, age 8)

Sounds in the Meadow

The water comes down in a loud crashing sound, but it is a loud peaceful sound. As the wind blows my hair, I listen, I hear water. I feel the wind. I see bush, grass and little plants. I smell the fresh air. It is peaceful, wonderfully quiet. It is like another world compared to the city. A more decent more appropriate world. I feel the wind brush my cheek. I see a tree close by sway in the breeze. The water seems like liquid glass. The grass tingles. I stop for a moment. I think, "This is the place for me."

Harmony (grade 3, age 8)

Harmony compares her feelings in this place with her feelings about the world in which she lives on a daily basis. She makes a judgment about the two worlds.

Nature

I love the sweet smelling air and the little shrubs and plants growing in the moist ground. The streams around the field looked extraordinarily beautiful. Every time I look around the wilderness, it makes me feel closer and closer to nature than I ever did before. The mountains with the green trees and the sun peering through the cracks in the clouds and shining down on the water and making it glisten like crystal.

Little animals scurrying around the forest. As a slight breeze blows across the wilderness I feel a cool chill and I think that this is defiposilutely the place for me.

Ashley (grade 3, age 8)

Ashley echoes Harmony's sentiments. There is a pattern in the writing. Each of these students writes with innocence, but detail in their observations. Each questions their own existence relative to this setting. These are powerful and complex thoughts coming from young writers expressed in their own voices.

Donald Murray defines voice as "...the force which drives a piece of writing forward. It is what is between the words on the page, what glues the piece of writing together" (Murray, 1981, p. 70). The program has clearly made it possible for the students to find and tune their voices.

Anne and I work very hard to create an environment of trust, a community of writers who experience real-life situations and then reflect upon them. Only by providing time for reflection can meaning be made out of the experience. John Dewey says it best: "To reflect is to look back over what has been done so as to extract the net meanings which are the capital stock for intelligent dealing with further experiences. It is the heart of intellectual organization and of the disciplined mind" (Dewey, 1963, p. 87).

Our journey took us in progression from a caring classroom to a series of planned experiences outside the classroom in places of special power and impact. We teachers considered the future, devoted time to reflection and writing, and prepared students to accomplish both during the excursions. Each new outside experience served to prime students for the next. Each step allowed for more connections to be made. Time, place, and community, in combination and interaction, were the essential ingredients for success.

Storytelling Tips for Experiential Educators

by Lana S. Leonard

A storyteller is not a different kind of person—every person is a different kind of storyteller. We experience our lives from within the context of "our story," which is a composite of things like: genes, education, socio-economic status, and family and cultural "myths." By refining our storytelling skills, we can broaden the context of our life story and develop the ability to refine its meaning, purpose, and style.

The first element of becoming a good storyteller is *reading and listening to lots of stories*. If you read a broad selection of stories, you will have a good chance of finding those that you love. Discovering which stories are personally appealing is a good way to discover your sense of self, your style, and your own values.

The second element of good storytelling, then, is to *tell stories that you love*. Your belief in their value and your passion will help captivate the attention of your listeners. Discovering and sharing stories that have personal appeal, helps you create the experience that a good story, well told, can offer listeners. "Good" stories share certain qualities: they inspire a sense of wonder; they have action involving conflicts that demand resolution; they are puzzles that stimulate the imagination; they deal with values that transcend time and circumstance; and they invite reflection and discernment but do not preach or judge.

Once you have selected such a story, *become very familiar with it*. Understand the story, why it appeals to you, why you want

to share it, and with whom. Most storytellers agree that the easiest way to learn a story is to *divide it into sequences* of events, each with a main point. *Visualize each sequence* and/or make a sketch symbolizing them.

Learn but do not memorize each sequence by telling them out loud. Most tellers find that learning a couple of sequences at a time, not the whole thing at once, works best. *Practice* in front of a mirror and/or into a tape recorder and go back to see if you developed the details and key points you had in mind.

Once you can *tell the whole story*, try it out on a supportive friend or family member. *Relax and have fun*. Improvise if you make a mistake. Storytellers create some of their best refinements this way. You do not have to be a ham or a great actor to be a good storyteller. You improve by developing a style that suits you, that makes you comfortable and believable.

Voice and body language are major tools of articulation and expression. The key is to *find ways to project the images and feelings of the story using voice and body language that suits your style*. Experiment with special noises and sounds. Try variations of: pitch, rhythm, volume, inflection, emphasis, and tone, to project the emotions and character traits that will *make your story live*.

Combine vocal with facial and body expressions in ways that work for you and fit the characters and drama of the tale. If you experience genuine emotions and vivid mental pictures, you will be effective in projecting these images and feelings to your listeners. Enchant them to new heights of perception, awareness, and feeling by *engaging and enlivening your own senses*. Lick your lips as you "taste" the delicacies, wave or wiggle your nose as you "smell" the coming rain, cringe when you "feel" fear, glance up when you "see" the rain clouds, tilt your head as you "hear" the distant drummer. Empathic communication can create a powerful and delightful synergy—a oneness between the teller, the tale, and the listeners that is well worth the effort it requires.

Timing is a further refinement. *Coordinate your pace with the drama of the story*. Pauses are potent. They can create drama, heighten suspense, and emphasize points. Well-timed pauses give listeners time to consider and identify their feelings, speculate on meaning and outcome, and engage fully in the story.

The depth and meaning of *the story experience is enhanced through interaction between the teller and the listeners*. Direct eye contact can be made with many listeners as the storyteller's eyes meander through the audience. When pausing at critical moments—conditions of choice, decision, or crisis—storytellers may shrug their shoulders and turn palms up, as if to ask, "What will happen next?" or "What would you do?"

This moment in storytelling is a most powerful educational experience. If the listener's emotions and imagination are engaged, this moment can be an opportunity to be led out of one's personal context, to experience another life, adopt a new hero or role model, practice a new way of being without the usual risks, create previously unimaginable resolutions and options. Once listeners have moved into the story emotion-

ally, they are open and ripe for the changes and growth that often result.

After the storytelling is over, the story experience continues. Many storytellers find it appropriate to *let the group share their reactions and feelings*—how the story relates to their lives or changes their perspectives. Listeners often talk with each other to unravel mysteries still contained in the story and within themselves. Articulating these feelings and experiences helps us claim them for ourselves and use them in our lives.

The Benefits of Storytelling

Unintended outcomes unfold as teachers and students alike experience the surprise endings. Teachers may find students are more curious, doing unsolicited research, recalling previously unrelated information, more willing and able to analyze, compare, contrast, and develop opinions and ideas. Facts become educational tools rather than ends in themselves.

The serendipities of storytelling can also include internal rewards of: discovering new interests and motivation, enhanced empathy and compassion, and greater awareness of self and the authentic power that comes from within. We become more conscious of choosing our reactions to the events of our lives rather than being victimized by them. With the sharpened awareness of a story-nurtured mind, we can choose behavior from a wider context than the one into which we were born. Crises and transitions are viewed more as opportunities to choose the direction of our life story and allow us to use the new role models and behavior patterns we have adopted along the way. We consciously refine our personal theme. Our sense of adventure, style, depth of purpose and meaning, evolve through relevance and satisfaction as we learn to create our story. Simply put, how we live becomes more important than the pursuit of a happy ending.

NOTES

A valuable resource is the National Association of the Preservation and Perpetuation of Storytelling, NAPPS, P.O. Box 309, Jonesborough, TN 37659. NAPPS publishes *Stoytelling,* a monthly magazine, *Yarnspinner,* a newsletter eight times a year, and a yearly National Directory of Storytelling. NAPPS also sponsors The National Storytelling Institute as well as various festivals and conventions.

Putting Principles into Practice: Traveling the Foxfire Trail in Graduate School

by Clifford E. Knapp

The Foxfire approach was developed more than twenty-five years ago by Eliot Wigginton, a high school English teacher in Rabun Gap, Georgia. Early in his teaching career, he departed from traditional ways of teaching. Out of frustration over his students' disinterest and apathy, he recognized a need to engage his students in an experiential way of learning. He knew that he had to change his teaching methods if he was to survive as a teacher. In 1966, he asked his students to go into the community and interview relatives and local people about the Appalachian crafts and skills.

He and his ninth- and tenth-grade students produced the quarterly, *Foxfire Magazine*, based on what they discovered in the local communities. Later, articles from the magazine were incorporated into a nine-volume Foxfire book series and published by Doubleday. Over the years, Wigginton refined his approach to cultural journalism and developed a list of Foxfire Core Practices (Jennings, 1990, p.6). Some of these practices recognized the following educational principles:

- All work must flow from student desire and concerns.

- The work is characterized by student action.

- The work emphasizes peer teaching and team work.

- The work must be clearly connected to the real world outside the classroom.

- Students must take the time to reflect upon experiences.

Readers familiar with experiential education will recognize these principles as belonging to this approach to learning. The Foxfire approach is now a shining example of experiential education and provides evidence that it can work in a public school.

Since its beginning in 1966, the Foxfire approach has spread to other schools across the United States and to other countries. The scope has expanded to encompass the entire curriculum across all grade levels. A teacher outreach program provides a network for communication and staff development. Also, some colleges and universities offer graduate courses in the Foxfire approach for teachers. This article chronicles my attempt to apply the Foxfire approach to teaching educators at the graduate level.

Preparing to Teach the Course

The fact is some schools of education with which I am familiar are about as close to being worthless as I can imagine. The very way their professors teach contradicts everything we know about the forceful acquisition of knowledge. Most of them, quite simply, should not be allowed to graduate teachers at the present time. (Wigginton, 1986, p. 282)

Wigginton's book, *Sometimes a Shining Moment* (1986), which includes quotations such as the one above, inspired and motivated me to try my hand at using the Foxfire approach. Then, after meeting Eliot Wigginton face to face at our field campus during the summer of 1991 and interviewing him, I was convinced that I wanted to use this teaching method. During the fall semester, I was scheduled to teach a graduate course, "Integrating Community Resources into the Curriculum." Wigginton's ideas fit nicely into my progressive philosophy of teaching and suited the course topic to a tee, so this decision was not difficult. One big concern, however, was the nagging question, "Could I pull this whole thing off?" Self-doubt crept in as I recalled an earlier attempt at using the Foxfire method. Those previous students, in their course evaluations, gave me mixed reviews. Perhaps the class format, consisting of meeting two days a week for four weeks, was the problem. What would I do differently this time? How could I improve my approach and ultimately the students' feelings and their written evaluations? These were only two questions from a long list I asked myself as I prepared the new course syllabus.

What was this method all about anyway? I proposed a cultural journalism project which would involve my students with people and places in their local communities. As a group, they were asked to decide what the final product was to be and to plan the steps involved in producing it. I figured that my students, who were mostly seasoned teachers, probably would not have been taught this way before. Somehow they had to assume a sense of ownership by choosing what to do and how to do it. No longer were these decisions to come solely from me, as they had in the past. I wouldn't even dictate the content of their assignments or how long

each paper must be. I did list and distribute eleven possible course outcomes or goals to guide our journey along the Foxfire trail; however, I invited input from the students to modify or expand the list.

As a text, I chose *Sometimes a Shining Moment* (Wigginton, 1986) because of what the book had meant to me and because it contained the basic steps in Wigginton's approach. In three parts, he described his struggles and triumphs as he experimented with high school students; outlined some emerging educational principles labeled "overarching truths"; and showed how these ideas applied in a traditional public school English course, meeting for fifty-five minutes a day.

Before my first class session, I had more questions than answers. Was it supposed to be that way? (That was another one of my questions.) Would my students accept the challenge I naively offered or would they boldly rebel? How much control should I try to take? Could I keep my mouth shut when necessary? When should I step in to "teach" in the traditional sense of the word? Would the group come together as a unified whole or would communication snags persist to the end? What role did I have as a decision-maker in our class? Would my students take risks and try what they were learning with their own students? Would they view me as taking the easy way out by turning over important instructional decisions to them? Would my students accept my ignorance of computer word processing skills? Would they expect me to know the answers to all their questions? I could go on, but by now you may have the picture. This approach was more difficult than making all the course decisions myself and I was unsure about what would happen in class.

I knew that I wouldn't allow my questions and shaky confidence to scare me back into a traditional, teacher-centered straight jacket. I just *knew* this approach would work, or would it? I had little control over how my students would respond. If we were to feel successful on the last day of class, we would all have to trust the process and each other and work awfully hard, After thirty years of teaching at all educational levels, I was still taking risks, learning my craft, and feeling a mixture of excitement and anticipation before the first class. Once more, I asked myself the same basic question, but this time, slightly reworded, "Could *we* pull this whole thing off?"

Teaching the Course

Success with the Foxfire approach to teaching depends upon a positive and open climate for learning. We all must feel that we can trust each other and express our thoughts and feelings about how we learn best and what might be blocking us from learning. To begin the class, we shared the positive and memorable moments from our past school experiences. Then we analyzed the characteristics of meaningful learning and tried to figure out why we remembered what we did. With these thoughts in mind, we compared our responses to those listed in our textbook. These activities were the starting points for building a comfortable learning community designed to nurture decision making, problem solving, and creative thinking and writing.

Next, we brainstormed some possible projects. I suggested only three guidelines: the project had to deal with teaching and learning, involve all of us in investigating our local communities, and be completed within fourteen, three-hour sessions. I did request that everyone keep a personal journal to capture their insights as the course progressed. After slowly generating and carefully weighing several project alternatives (a recipe collection, a resource book on area volunteer programs, a "how to use" book describing local utility plants, community organizations, and other local services), we settled on a teachers' handbook that would illustrate how ordinary people and places could offer extraordinary learning opportunities for students at all grade levels. We could feel a sense of excitement and relief centering around this idea. We all seemed to know this was what we wanted to do. It had taken us almost two class sessions to begin to get to know each other and to arrive at this decision. Now we had to determine how to achieve this notable goal. I could almost hear the tension and doubt levels rise in their voices as the students asked questions and made comments. We took time to share our anxieties around working together in this way for the next few months. That seemed to help some. There were "only" twelve sessions left and so much still remained undone.

To provide some food for thought, we watched a videotape entitled, *Shining Moments,* produced by The Foxfire Fund, Inc. We watched teachers and administrators explain some of their joys and struggles with the Foxfire approach. Some of their comments already had a familiar ring to us. Feelings of fear cropped up in the teachers' words in the video. I guess our feelings of hesitation were more normal than unusual. Good teaching involves not only knowing certain strategies, but taking risks to overcome internal and external barriers.

We desperately needed some structure before writing the articles that would make up our final product. Where would that structure come from? Surely, not from me. We soon discovered we needed a written record of our good ideas and the areas of agreement so we could act on them later. Student volunteers emerged spontaneously to take notes and deliver them in polished and printed form the following week. After two more weeks of work, we produced two sets of writing guidelines entitled "General Limitations, Style Format" and "Format For 'Person' Article." Now we could begin writing...if we knew what to write about.

I had prepared and distributed a book of readings beforehand which, I had hoped, would fill some information gaps. These handouts were difficult to compile since I really didn't know where our Foxfire trail would lead. One of the readings was a transcribed and edited interview I had with Eliot Wigginton, completed a month earlier. Since only one of the students had ever interviewed someone and then transcribed and edited the results, my tape and article proved useful as a model. I felt good about anticipating this need. I freely shared how I had read Wigginton's book, prepared a list of possible questions, interviewed him, and then painstakingly typed, edited, and mailed the transcription back to Wigginton. When he returned the edited interview with his comments, I almost had a finished product. The students listened intently as I spoke from fresh experience. The one other experienced student spoke in glowing terms of the whole process. His enthusiasm inspired the class. I joked about him being a "plant," but he wasn't. We generated a list of core questions to ask each interviewee. We

groped for a way to get our "feet wet" and start writing. It just happened that one of our students asked to leave class a few minutes early each time to tell stories at the local library. Connecting this incident with our pressing need to begin, someone suggested that we interview him about storytelling and include that article in our resource guide. He was eager and somewhat flattered to share his "ordinary" story. We were relieved to discover an "extraordinary" guinea pig right under our noses to test the interviewing process.

The following week, we conducted the interview cooperatively and someone volunteered to transcribe the tape at home. To start the next session, our volunteer told us what she had learned and proudly produced an unedited, nine-page paper. We agreed to edit the work and reduce it to a manageable length. Two students rewrote and reorganized the original interview and read it aloud to us. Murmurs of approval filled the room after they read their work.

Next, someone offered to write an article about a place and let all of us edit it. The climate of trust was clearly building and his offer provided the modeling that would help to give others the courage to follow. I shared my editing suggestions of his article, "How To Find a Prairie," on overhead transparencies. We also developed a strategy of "round-robin" editing in which we passed our articles around the circle and scribbled our opinions in the margins. We reinforced the idea that the author always had the right to accept or reject these suggestions. Each writer was the final decision-maker, but it soon became clear that the articles belonged to all of us. This was "our" project now. Without consciously planning to use cooperative learning techniques, we were working as a team and feeling that individual successes were also group successes. The trust level seemed to grow before our eyes with each passing week. We would all volunteer our ideas for "next steps." The plans for each session seemed to grow naturally from what happened the previous week. We began to solve the problem of who to write about. "I want to talk to a balloonist." "I know an inventor." "I'm going for a centurion." "I want to interview a spelunker." The students were getting very animated. We still had the problem of where to go to find places to write about. Gradually, ideas about places began to emerge and tease their imaginations. "I know a landfill." "I'm going to a cave." "What about a hair salon?" "I'll explore the Chicago River." "I want the oldest building in town."

When we looked ahead and discussed the actual production stage of the project, several students investigated and reported on what they found. I can still recall the excitement expressed by one student as she shared her "homework" and told us about the projected cost to print the book. I didn't fully understand where her enthusiasm for numbers came from, but this was what ownership of an idea was all about. Learning had become fun because the assignment resulted from their felt need. A sense of accomplishment permeated the weekly reports and planning. As we gained momentum, the anxiety and doubts eased in the students and myself. The Foxfire approach was now more than a collection of words in a book or an idea from the mind of one teacher in Georgia. As the weeks passed, the students volunteered to read out loud from their personal journals. They spoke of their sometimes-shaky

attempts to use what we were learning with their own students. Someone remarked, "This is one of the first courses I can apply in my classes immediately."

We enjoyed sharing excerpts from *Sometimes a Shining Moment* (Wigginton, 1986). "Listen to this quote..." or "I really like the way he said this...," they would exclaim before reading their favorite parts. I could see they were reading the textbook without me assigning chapters for discussion. I shared parts of Studs Terkel's book, *Working* (1972), as another example of the power of the interview to communicate the thoughts and feelings of ordinary people.

One of the last steps in the production process was to figure out how to transform the ideas to words on the printed page. Someone asked permission to use the computer lab at their elementary school, so we agreed to meet there for an evening of word processing. Someone else offered the discs and program, and another told us that she had access to a laser printer. She proudly passed around two samples, one from an ordinary printer and the other from a laser printer. The "oohs" and "aahs" followed the papers around the room. The tone of helping each other emerged again and again as we acknowledged that we were at different levels of computer literacy.

Each student wrote one article about a person and one about a place. They painstakingly transformed their experiences into words on paper and felt the joys of success as well as the drudgery of hard work. It all resulted in a tangible final product we treasure: *Wow, I Never Thought of That: A Resource Guide for Learning Extraordinary Things from Ordinary People and Places.*

Summing It All Up

Was this group of teachers atypical? Did these special people come together just by chance? Or did the Foxfire approach flourish in a carefully constructed learning climate designed to help us feel a sense of community? I do know that our chemistry worked. We took our vision and developed it into this three-dimensional product. Along the way, we gained knowledge about each other, group dynamics, interviewing, editing and writing, the rich resources of local people and places, and the Foxfire approach to teaching. Some even had the opportunity to apply these "way out" methods with their students—the ultimate aim of an education course. There is no doubt in my mind that we are all different as a result. We are better teachers, learners, and human beings. We discovered that we *could* pull this whole thing off by risking, caring, trusting, believing in the process, and working awfully hard.

Note

I would like to extend my heartfelt gratitude to a wonderful group of students who helped to make this teaching experience meaningful. Thanks to: Martha Baldridge, John M. DiNovo, Claudia Geocaris, Wendy Habel, Matt Hermes, Debra Jezek, Mary Schultz, Shawna Sullivan, and Melanie A. Wulf.

Interactive Theatre as a Dramatic Resource

by Janet Salmons-Rue

A date ends in rape when "no" is understood as "yes."

A student fears that resistance to her professor's unwanted advances will jeopardize her grades.

Persistent inquiries into a co-worker's personal life yield unexpected information about her sexual preference.

An employer asks inappropriate (and illegal) questions on a job interview.

An emotionally withdrawn teenaged mother is more interested in soap operas than in the toddler she has locked in a bedroom.

Although incidents such as these usually take place behind closed doors, at Cornell University they take place in classrooms, workshops, and in-service training sessions for students, staff, faculty, and administrators. Although individuals involved in such situations may hold the experience in painful silence, here they respond to questions about what happened and why. These individuals are actors, the incidents are dramatizations, and this is interactive theatre.

For centuries, theater has engaged the minds and emotions of audience members. Through costumes, set, and script, the audience is drawn into a fictional reality. They identify with the characters and are thereby transported to other times, other places, and other life experiences. At the other end of the continuum is role play: sans costumes, set, or rehearsed script. The distance between the performer and audience member is erased: together they enter the fictional reality for the purpose of the exercise.

Although both theatre and role play are valuable, for the purposes of active learning both have limitations. Theater puts the audience members into a passive, receptive mode. However, portraying a person in a sensitive situation, and responding to an interaction in a way that accomplishes educational objectives, demands concentration and emotional characterization that role-play participants often lack.

Cornell Theatre Outreach draws elements from both ends of this continuum to develop interactive theatre techniques. Like traditional theatre, the audience is drawn into another reality where the problem at hand is brought to life. Original dramatizations illustrate the cognitive, affective, verbal, and non-verbal elements of the issue. But unlike traditional theatre, they are not passive onlookers. Like role play, participants take a role and bridge the distance between performer and audience member but, unlike role play, the actors guide the dialogue to reinforce learning goals and objectives. Depending on the goal of the program, participants may practice interviewing or counseling skills with the character, or they may discuss prevention or problem-solving strategies. The fiction of drama provides a safe, non-threatening environment where participants can explore the implications of actions and decisions, without having to live with the consequences.

People learn best from experience; however, there are some experiences we would hope to prevent. Child abuse and neglect, date rape, racism, sexism, and sexual harassment are such experiences that are explored in Cornell Theatre Outreach programs on college campuses and in community settings. Five- to ten-minute dramatizations, based on elements of actual cases or reports, bring the problem to life and give it a human face. In campus human relations training programs, for example, a racist joke is told with humorless results for a Black person present. Once the scene has been presented, the actors remain in character for discussion with the audience. Participants have the opportunity to confront the person who told the joke, to question her about what she had been thinking. They can question the other character about what he will do next, who he will talk with about this. This process provides a unique opportunity for participants to examine assumptions, develop skills, and begin to plan what they can do to make changes in themselves and in the world.

Chapter 11 Special Populations

Making No Apologies for Our Differences

by Jeff Moore

In so many ways, I hate to admit it—it makes me feel stupid—but Keith Strong is one of the most amazing people I know. No one has challenged me more to become a more caring and respectful person. Without even trying I am sure, but with unending patience and forgiveness, Keith, a man who was once deemed to be "severely mentally retarded," has helped me to learn so much.

Keith and I first met in the summer of 1976 when he was twenty and still living in the Mountainview Home, a remote and dreary provincial institution for people with intellectual handicaps. The doors were always locked and the yard was enclosed with a high wire fence.

Today, we live together in the university town of Wolfville, Nova Scotia, in a small intentional community called "Homefires." Keith is a real man about town even though he has significant intellectual limitations and he cannot speak. Still, he takes the local

Keith on the go with his spirited approach to life.

bus to work every morning at the sheltered workshop where he has proven to be a very capable and energetic worker. He goes downtown by himself for such things as a newspaper (which he loves to peruse even though he cannot read a word) or to have his hair cut. He enjoys going to a movie or bowling with friends. Every Wednesday evening, he goes out to dinner at a neighbor's home on his own. He is a confirmed member of the local United Church and regularly takes part in ushering and collecting the offering, a service he performs very well (after some practice). All in all, Keith has quite a full life.

Homefires is part of a widespread international network of homes for people with intellectual handicaps called L'Arche.[1] The philosophy of L'Arche is experiential in its very essence. It is, quite simply, to live with one another as friends. We share all aspects of life together—work, meals, play, friends, travel, etc. There is something very natural and honest about life in L'Arche, even if it is not always the most practical or efficient alternative.

Before becoming familiar with L'Arche, I was a social worker with years of experience working in government-run institutions and group homes. What most impressed me initially about L'Arche was the maturity of the people with intellectual handicaps—their responsibleness, their cooperativeness. I sensed there was something very different going on in L'Arche from what I had experienced in places where I had worked. The general atmosphere was also markedly different. In institutions and group homes, no matter how well-meaning the staff, there was always at least a tinge of sadness, a coldness, and an uneasiness. In L'Arche, I felt warmth and contentment. It was someone's home.

This was extremely paradoxical. Here was a situation with few, if any, professionals, and with little or no emphasis on the formal teaching of skills, and yet it appeared to be so much more conducive to learning. It lead me to rethink ideas that I had worked with for years.

This article represents my reflections on the underpinnings of L'Arche philosophy, which is based on experiential learning and on the notion of "celebrating our diversity," both for the handicapped and non-handicapped members of our community. Despite many similarities, it is an experiential learning process which differs in some ways from the more formalized and structured approaches of many experiential education programs which involve the intellectually handicapped. Hopefully, this article will raise questions and promote reflection among those who work with others who are very different than themselves.

Institutions and Normalization— Combating Differences

The story of Keith growing up in institutions is literally unbelievable to many people. It was the family doctor who suggested to Keith's family that he be sent to the old county "hospital" before he had reached the age of two. This was standard practice in North America at the time.[2]

As a learning environment for a child, such an institution could not have been much worse, with its lack of warm, stable relationships and its lack of opportunity for ordinary life experiences which facilitate language and concept development. Keith never did learn to talk, to trust in other people, or to take responsibility for himself. Keith's needs, beyond food and shelter, were virtually ignored. A cursory and rather chilling routine assessment by a staff psychiatrist concluded: "No change is recommended other than that this is no place for children." However, Keith lived in this setting until he was fifteen, then moved to a new and smaller institution for children for a few years, and then to the Mountainview Home until he was twenty. Throughout these years, Keith had virtually no contact with his family and very little contact with the community at large.

When I first met Keith, I was part of an effort to open one of the first group homes in North America for people who were classified as severely mentally retarded. The guiding principle behind such efforts was "normalization." When this approach was initially conceived in Scandinavia in the late 1960s, it was concerned with normalizing the general physical and social living conditions for people with intellectual handicaps. When it was reformulated by Wolf Wolfensberger (1972) for North America, the emphasis was changed from normalizing conditions to normalizing people, i.e., their behavior and appearance.[3] It was in essence changed from a progressive social reform movement to a rather conservative clinical procedure—a classic example of "blaming the victim" (Ryan, 1972).

Many of the young staff who came to work in this pilot project, including myself, were motivated by a keen idealism. They talked about creating a real home and building genuine friendships. However, the official plan was quite different—more of a human laboratory which would demonstrate the potential of behavior management technology to mold the behavior and skills of the residents in numerically significant ways. For all kinds of reasons—the large group size, low morale, high staff turnover, too much outside pressure—the experiment failed quite miserably for everyone involved.

I soon felt I had no choice but to leave and Keith subsequently moved on to a neighboring group home for higher functioning persons. He was somewhat desperately acclaimed as the first success. In this home, normalization was interpreted quite differently again, in part as a reaction to the laboratory approach of the previous home. The idea here went something like: "Everyone has the same rights I do and nobody can tell me what to do," with little regard for the ability of individuals to make decisions. With his lack of internal controls due to his institutional upbringing, this was not a good situation for Keith. His main activities at home were watching television and eating sandwiches.

During the two years Keith was living in this home, I married and started a family, but I kept in close contact with him. His energy and enthusiasm for most everything diminished with the exception of watching television. He was also mysteriously losing all of the hair on the top of his head. He became extremely overweight and was a sad young man.

Both my wife and I were professionals who were strongly advocating deinstitutionalization and normalization. There came a point, perhaps hastened by Keith's situation, that we felt challenged to practice what we preached. We asked Keith if he would like to come to live with us and he said he would—a decision that changed all of our lives quite dramatically.

Keith now had his own room for the first time in his life. This was something which he appreciated as he loved to keep his room and all his things very neatly organized. We helped him watch his diet and there were always lots of things to do and places to go. Keith became more and more active. And soon, Keith's bald spot, which the doctor was convinced was some form of scalp disease, started growing back. It became evident that in Keith's endless hours of watching television, he had literally pulled his hair out by twirling it for something to do.

Overcoming Our Differences

It was difficult to sort out our ideas about normalization. On the surface, it seemed simple and made so much sense—helping people who had been segregated to fit back into society.

From my experience, however, it seemed that people, and especially people who were handicapped, were too often taking a back seat to ideas, to the agendas of others. These agendas—to reform institutions, to rehabilitate individuals, to establish rights for the handicapped, to change society—were often well-meaning but misguided. They were not being carried out in a way that was responding to the basic needs and interests of the people involved. Living with Keith challenged my thinking on this. After spending many years figuring out how to normalize people, I was now living with a man who did not want to be my project or my cause. He wanted to be my friend. I had to get out of a deeply ingrained mind-set that had me constantly correcting and directing Keith,

sometimes only in thought, but too often in deed.

It became clear to me that normalization as it was commonly interpreted, was not doing justice to Keith, other people in his position, or me. The approach suggests that we cannot accept him the way he is and that he will only be accepted to the degree that he becomes "normal," which of course by our definitions he will never be. It was an impossible situation, a catch-22, not only for Keith, but for everyone involved with him. It creates a situation riddled with deception (rarely conscious), false hopes, and frustration. It also lets the community and social systems evade their responsibilities because there is a token mechanism for the reintegration of these people in place. It leaves all of the responsibility for change with those who are affected—it blames the victim. Normalization ends up rationalizing and excusing the exclusion and segregation of people rather than challenging it.

I wanted to be Keith's friend, but that was easier said than done. Keith is a man of unbelievable spirit. He does not always know exactly what to do with it but he certainly has it. He is totally irrepressible and seems absolutely convinced that he has every right to be who he is, to live where he lives, and say what he has to say, even if nobody understands a word of it.

While Keith understands most of what is said to him, his vocabulary is limited to a few words like "ma," "home," "out," "cow," and of all things, "big shit" (which he uses quite appropriately and fairly discreetly). However, Keith is very verbal, a natural politician, with what amounts to pretend talk, and given time he usually gets his point across. We have struggled with different speech therapists, alternative means of communication, and various forms of oppression to try to prevent embarrassing situations, but to no avail.

I have had to learn to accept Keith for who he is—to enjoy him for who he is. People now turn to me in hushed tones and ask, "What did he say?" and I usually have to say in an equally hushed voice, "I don't know." "Ohhhhh!?!?" they say, and it is okay. I no longer feel the constant need to apologize for the fact that Keith cannot talk.

In a sense, I have learned that being different is not Keith's problem; it is mine. The fact that he cannot talk but is more than willing to try to communicate with others, is a real gift. He has a lot to offer others, not only in spite of his differences, but indeed because of them. He teaches everyone he meets to go beyond superficial differences and appreciate our diversity, and more importantly our oneness.

L'Arche:[4] An Experiential Model of Community and Diversity

Outside observers tend to see L'Arche as merely quantitatively different—a good group home with a little more of this or that. In reality, it is qualitatively different. It has characteristics which are seldom, if ever, found in group homes or other rehabilitation programs, and many of these characteristics are a part of the experiential education approach (Joplin, 1981).

Unlike most rehabilitation services, including many experiential education programs, L'Arche is less formalized and starts from a basis of friendship, not service. We come together to live as friends and it is meant to involve two-way relationships in which each person has something to gain and something to give. It is my friendship and relationship with Keith that has in large part changed my perspective on working with others.

My mother, generally known as Granny Joe, is seventy-eight and lives at Homefires. She adds another element of diversity to our community and is a great reminder that it is good to both give and receive. With her waning strength and limited eyesight, Granny Joe is extremely appreciative of Keith's many gestures of kindness—always making sure she has a cup of coffee in the morning, a hug before he goes to work, and dropping in to share the news of the day. Granny Joe says it makes her feel important and it is clearly a two-way street. Keith and Granny Joe have a wonderful friendship.

When you start from the point of friendship, a lot of other things fall into place. I have often seen the aims and implications of ideal rehabilitation programs spelled out in great detail and have thought to myself that such enumeration would be unnecessary if you just started with natural, caring relationships. Granted, this is not always possible where you have large numbers, compartmentalization, hierarchies, shift changes, too much paperwork, and too much formalization. However, where there is a genuine caring about another person, it follows that there would naturally be enriched experience and reflection—you want what is best for them even if it means putting yourself out a bit. Efforts are directed toward meeting the real needs of people rather than those of third parties (agencies, government departments, professional groups, etc.). Efforts are evaluated in terms of how well people, individually and collectively, are benefiting.

In L'Arche, the idea is to keep the community small and flexible so we can adapt to people—rather than fitting people into preset programs. When we think about the next steps in developing our communities, we try to think about what people are asking for, even those who cannot express themselves very well. By the way they are behaving, someone may be asking for more quiet and less confusion; it might be more things to do outside; it might be more opportunities to go downtown.

There is also a desire to have everyone take as much responsibility for themselves and the well-being of the community as possible. Everyone is actively involved in choices and decisions affecting them. Most importantly, we try to give everyone the support and encouragement they need to take on ever increasing responsibilities and challenges. As friends, we do things with each other, sometimes for a purpose, sometimes just to be together. The experiences we share are real because living in L'Arche is not seen in terms of jobs that have to be done but more as a way of life which people choose. To live in L'Arche, you must choose to make an effort to overcome your differences and your ego in the interests of your friends who are handicapped. Just as children need their parents to work together, those with handicaps need those who take responsibility for them to work together so that they can live in peace and security.

As much as possible, each person is encouraged to make personal decisions for themselves. Where help is needed, an effort is made to be as discreet and respectful as possible. There are also times when you clearly must assume a parental role and set limits, enforce decisions, and enact consequences.

To make group decisions, we have a lot of meetings: weekly house meetings to divide up household responsibilities around cooking, cleaning, care of pets, etc.; regular individual review meetings involving work, family, professionals, etc.; weekly community meetings where all the houses get together for discussion, the planning of upcoming events, worship, and fun. Everyone is involved in determining what needs to be done, making decisions, making plans, and carrying them out. Where certain members of the community are unable to speak, we may use pictures or symbols to get them involved in the process.

Last, and possibly most important, friends need to have fun together. Most rehabilitation services I have been involved in take themselves far too seriously, one quality of which L'Arche could never be accused. We celebrate everything—birthdays, anniversaries, and any other special occasion. For example, on the anniversary date of a person coming to live in our community, they are first given breakfast in bed; then they choose their favorite supper and invite anyone they want; and after supper, we all sit around in a circle and tell the person all the gifts which they bring to the community. There are many such celebrations, large and small. We have regular Sunday evening get-togethers when we gather just to celebrate living together. These events loosen up the community and unite us. They help to melt away the difficulties that are inevitably experienced in any situation where people live together.

Our celebrations are simple but well prepared. We try to involve everybody to the greatest extent possible in food preparations, room decoration, skits, music, and games. Games, from charades to soccer, are adapted so everyone can be included. We often pair people up to help each other and we also prepare people beforehand, if necessary, so they can take more of a leadership role.

People are also always going off to their own activities, usually in groups of two to four—to movies, sporting events, fairs, or just a walk down to the local tavern for a beer and a game of shuffleboard. Such outings often have hitches but everything is reflected upon as a learning experience, and each person is provided with the guidance, support, or, if necessary, the limits which they seem to need.

There is also a strong spiritual dimension to life in L'Arche, and the communities across the world encompass all of the major religions, as well as nonbelievers. However, the thread that continues throughout all aspects of life in every L'Arche community is the spirit of hope, friendship, celebration, and forgiveness.

It is not all sacrifice. The benefits are many—more sharing of household and child-rearing responsibilities, more sharing of resources, more personal time, more support, more challenges, and an abundance of opportunities to learn, create, share, travel, and meet people from all over the world. However, there are also definite limitations to L'Arche. We are very small in practical terms. Worldwide, we only number in the thousands. The values espoused by L'Arche definitely go against the values prevailing in the world today—individualism, materialism, and the need to climb the ladder of success. It is not a life that many choose. Young and old, people seem to fear for their immediate and future security and see this coming from "the system." There is little doubt that you need strong social, political,

and/or spiritual convictions to come and remain in L'Arche.

To help people to grow in their understanding of L'Arche and its place in the world, everyone is encouraged to have personal accompaniment with someone more experienced in L'Arche. This is in addition to the supervision of your day-to-day responsibilities and deals more with your personal growth within the community. As well, we take time at our different community meetings to reflect on the gifts, as well as the challenges, of living in our community. Every assistant goes on at least two L'Arche retreats each year to reflect on life in L'Arche.

It is also difficult to stay in L'Arche because living a community lifestyle is not easy. So often, it would be such a relief to run away rather than face challenges to be more patient, more courageous, and more giving. When we were actually constructing our first community home, someone said to us that building the home was easy compared to building a community. One always has to be concerned about everyone—those living in the community, the board of directors, families, neighbors, friends, professionals—keeping all of them informed and involved. It would have been so much easier to have started a private boarding home but the differences would be profound. Without L'Arche, without the Board, without the many friends of our community, there would be few if any safeguards for the well-being of those who are handicapped. There would not be the security beyond the immediate circumstances, nor the quality of friendships, opportunities, and community involvement. It is the richness of this experience in the community that challenges each of us to continue to grow.

The ideas of L'Arche would seem to be widely applicable to other situations. It is basically living together as friends with those in need and this could be done with children, teenagers, people who have been involved in the mental health or correctional systems, or just people who want to live in a supportive community. Nor are the ideas limited to living situations. They have been used in educational and work settings as well. Here again, the emphasis would not be on efficiency, competition, and goal attainment, but rather on doing things together in a mutually supportive environment, and seeking fulfillment individually and collectively.

We are very fortunate in our community in that providing a good home is basically all that is expected of us by our funding sources.[5] So our chief purpose is simply to live well together.

Educational and vocational services are usually under pressure to plan, evaluate, and document the progress of individuals. People cannot just learn or work well together, they must accomplish specific goals.

That is not to say that life at Homefires is chaotic or without purpose. We do take the well-being and growth of the members of our community very seriously. Our life together is highly organized and decision-making processes are well thought out. It just centers on the needs of people as individuals and as a group, and not on artificial content and standards of achievement set down by a third party. Educational and work programs should also be situations where people as much as possible define their own needs and interests through learning and work experiences which are connected to the real world.

L'Arche is a community within a community. The network of friendships within the small community also extends to a network of friendships in the larger community. Everything else flows from this. It is important that the smaller community is not too large or segregated and that involvement in it is not time-limited. Many educational and vocational programs are time-limited or transitional. L'Arche is a long-term commitment—at least for many of us. However, it is also invigorating for the community to have people come for visits or shorter stays. But basically, people belong. It is their home. They make lasting friendships. They have some control.

We feel that the quality of what we have to offer is more important than quantity. L'Arche also poses questions and challenges to the larger society, as it did to me, about how we see others; how we see ourselves; and indeed, how we see the world and its future. It is our hope that ripples can go out from L'Arche to encourage others to be more honest, more caring, more socially responsible—more human. My relationship with Keith is but one ripple.

Notes

1. Homefires is part of a large network of similar communities called the International Federation of L'Arche. Each community is for the most part autonomous and has the responsibility to set up its own organization and arrange financing. It is the contributions from the individual communities, both financial and personnel, that support the larger network. In turn, the communities, divided into regions of three to five communities, and zones according to continents,

receive very substantial support of all kinds on both an ongoing and emergency basis.

2. In the first part of this century, the development of IQ tests and the science of genetics, along with great economic and social upheavals, led authorities to point to mental deficiency as being at the root of most of society's problems—poverty, illegitimacy, crime, alcoholism, etc. Although completely fallacious, this eugenic scare justified an almost universal campaign in Western society to remove people judged to be intellectually handicapped from schools, families, and communities, sending them to remote institutions.

3. From Wolfensberger (1972) "...The human manager will aspire to elicit and maintain behaviors and appearances that come as close to being normative as circumstances and the person's behavioral potential permit..." (pg. 28).

4. L'Arche was founded by Jean Vanier, a former professor of philosophy, along with his friend Père Thomas Phillippe, a Roman Catholic priest who was chaplain of an institution in the village of Trosly in northern France. Jean purchased a small home near this institution and welcomed two men who lived in the institution to come to live with him. There was no intention of going beyond this small home, but Vanier's example was so powerful that today L'Arche has almost one hundred communities, some as small as five or six people, some of one hundred or more, in every corner of the world.

5. In North America, communities are financed primarily through room and board payments for individuals by the state or provincial government. Additional funds are raised through donations. There can be very significant differences in terms of salaries and benefits paid to L'Arche assistants. This is worked out within each community according to their ideals of how community should be lived. Generally, there is a desire to be on a par with community members who are handicapped.

Growing Up Blind: Is There Anyone Like Me Who Can Help?

by Kennan Cole and Homer Page

Note: This article was originally published in 1986. For current information on the authors, please refer to the "Author Biographies" section at the end of this book.

The future is very uncertain for any young person. It is especially uncertain for a young blind person. There was a movie made for television entitled, "Up From Darkness." It told the story of a blind college student's struggle to be accepted by a medical school. One scene in the film came after the student had been rejected by over 200 medical programs. The young blind man had gone back to his parents' home for a holiday. In frustration, he had run out of their house into the yard. His father went out to talk with him. The blind student asked his father if he thought he could be a doctor. His father answered yes, that he thought he could, but he didn't think he would ever get the chance.

The self-doubt that rejection engenders and the hopelessness which follows in the wake of frustrating attempts to fulfill one's potential are well stated in this dramatic scene. Young blind persons need some direction in dealing with setting life goals, realistically assessing their own potential, and managing both socially imposed limitations and their response to those limitations. It is most important that they have the opportunity to interact with, and learn from, adult blind persons who can be effective role models for blind youth. The real life story upon which the film discussed above was based

had a happy ending. The student was admitted to a medical school as a special student. He graduated and is now a practicing psychologist. Youth need to know that adult blind persons do become successful.

In the following sections of this essay, the authors shall discuss the way in which one National Federation of the Blind program, The March on Washington, provides a context for blind youth and adults to interact, and for blind adults to model important behavior for the youth who are participating in the program. We shall also reflect on our own experiences with role models and identify some of the key aspects involved in effective role modeling. We are also concerned with the way in which the blind youth work with blind adults to achieve common goals.

Kennan Cole is 17 years old. He is a junior at Wasson High School in Colorado Springs, Colorado. He has been blind from birth. He has been a member of the National Federation of the Blind since 1983.

Homer Page is 44. He has been blind from birth. He currently teaches in the College of Education and directs the Office of Services to Disabled Students at the University of Colorado at Boulder. He is a member of the Boulder City Council, and he is First Vice

President of the National Federation of the Blind of Colorado.

I. The March on Washington

Over the last several years, the National Federation of the Blind has been increasingly concerned with the importance of bringing young blind people into contact with blind adults. Seminars have been held around the country sponsored by the NFB for the sighted parents of blind children, and a publication entitled Future Reflections has been established to aid parents of blind children. The NFB has established a Student Division which seeks to involve blind students in issues of importance to them. But the important activities that bring blind youth and adults together are the regular activities of the Federation. One of the programs which lends itself well to the involvement of youth with adults is the program that we call the March on Washington.

The National Federation of the Blind is a consumer organization. It was founded in 1940 to assist blind people achieve greater security, opportunity, and equality. It now has over 50,000 members. There are affiliates in each state, as well as the District of Columbia. The headquarters for the national organization is located in Baltimore, Maryland. The Federation actively lobbies with Congress and state legislatures around the nation. It also frequently becomes involved with court proceedings that affect blind people. It conducts a large public education program and operates a national jobs program for blind persons. The NFB has also long been involved with issues that affect the education and rehabilitation of the blind.

Each year in early February, the NFB organizes the March on Washington. Over 200 persons from 35-40 states gather in the nation's capital for several days to visit members of Congress and speak with them about issues of importance to NFB members and to the nation's blind population.

A briefing is held on Sunday evening prior to going to the Capitol. The issues that will be presented to the Congress are reviewed. Questions are asked and answered, and materials about the NFB and fact sheets which present relevant information concerning the issues under discussion are distributed.

Prior to the March, members from state delegations make appointments with their state Congressional delegation. After the briefing, each state delegation meets to review the schedule of appointments, assigns NFB members to meet with their representatives, and once again reviews the issues to ensure that each person has a good grasp of issues and procedures.

First-time delegates are paired with more experienced persons. Schedules are checked and travel directions are given. Often leaders of each state affiliate will speak individually with first-time delegates, and especially with youth, to help them feel more certain that they can communicate effectively with members of Congress and Congressional staff persons in the days ahead.

Early Monday morning of the week of the March, the NFB members spread out to the Senate and House office buildings to visit with the Congress. Blind persons have become a familiar site in the halls and offices of Congress. But for the first-time delegates, especially the very young delegate, this is an awesome experience. The young person experiences firsthand the sense of independence and competence associated with traveling with other blind persons through the city and Capitol complex, successfully locating Congressional offices, and carrying on discussions of importance with the members of the Congress.

After a day on the Hill, the delegates return to the hotel for an evening of debriefing. The events of the day are discussed, and participants are asked to make written reports about their visits with each Senator or Representative that they have seen.

This routine is repeated until all the members of Congress have been contacted. Data is then compiled. Those Congresspeople who are supporting legislation or who are willing to sponsor or co-sponsor NFB legislation are noted. Those who should be recontacted or provided additional information are identified. Assignments are made to those who should do this follow-up.

The March on Washington provides the context in which adult blind persons may act as role models for blind youth. We shall now turn to a discussion of why such role modeling is important, how we have personally experienced both positive and negative role modeling, and how the March on Washington actually functions to permit the interaction between adults and youth, which is needed for role modeling.

II. Kennan Cole: Blind Adults Can Help

I have been blind from birth. During the early years of my schooling, I attended the Kansas School for the Blind. But for most of the years of my education I have attended public school.

I did not know any adult blind people until I became active with the National Federation of the Blind. This occurred when I was 14 years old. It has been one of the most important things ever to happen to me. Before I met adult blind people, I knew that I was smart and that I could accomplish things in my life, if I would ever get the chance, but I had no idea of what I could really do. I thought about running a clothing store, but I didn't know what that meant. Now I know I would like to be active in public affairs. I would like to be a lobbyist or a director of governmental affairs for an organization seeking to affect public policy.

When I was in the seventh grade, I had a biology class. It had a lab. I wanted to participate in that lab, but the teacher didn't think that I could. I accepted her opinion, although I felt badly about it. The other kids told me I was lucky because I didn't have to do the work. Deep down inside, however, I knew that I was being left out and I wondered if my whole life would be like that. Later I had a chance to discuss this with blind adult members of the NFB. They told me that I should have participated in the lab. Some of them told me how they had taken a biology course, and done the lab work. The next year, I took a weight exercise course in Physical Education. The coach didn't want me to work out in the weight room. He was afraid I would get hurt. I talked with my friends in the NFB, and they told me I could take the class. That gave me the confidence that I needed; so I told the principal and the coach that I wanted to take the course, and that I intended to do it. They stopped trying to keep me out of it. I took it and, of course, I wasn't hurt. I really felt good about that. I felt that I could be like the other kids.

I have attended two Marches on Washington. I felt almost intimidated at first. There were so many people, and they were all talking about things I didn't understand very well. But they were nice to me, and told me just to listen and I would learn what to do. The first night, we went over the issues that would be discussed with the Congress the next day. I was assigned to a team which would be working together to visit with the Colorado Congressional representatives. I was a little scared, but my team leader made me feel at ease.

The next day we began our visits. I had never been very independent as a traveler. I would take help whenever it was offered by a sighted person. But these people traveled without help. They made me realize how important it was to be independent. I really learned a lot about the issues that were important to blind people, and I learned a lot about myself. I had wondered if blind people were very important, and if we were a little foolish going to Washington to ask for legislation. I had thought that we might be ignored or laughed at. But we were received with courtesy, and even sometimes with interest. I left Washington feeling that we had done a good job, and that I had a right to expect to be taken seriously.

I have thought a lot about what my involvement with the National Federation of the Blind has meant to me. I know I would not have done as well in school, or learned as much because I would not have demanded that I take part in everything. I know I wouldn't be as independent as I am now. I know that as I grow up, I will have to deal with discrimination, but I know that I can get help when I need it.

If it were not for the NFB I would not have met blind adults. I have never met one through school. I would be a lot worse off if I had not gotten to know the blind persons I now know. They have told me many things that I need to know. But it isn't what they have told me that is most important. The most important things have been what they have done, things such as traveling independently, working at interesting jobs, and standing up against discrimination, and having normal lives that give me a lot of hope for my future. I know my life won't be easy, but I believe I will be successful because I know other people who are leading successful lives as adults.

III. Role Modeling: The Meaning of Blindness: Homer Page

I am blind. I am now 44 years of age. I have been blind since birth.

Members of my family have been blind over several generations. I remember wondering if some curse hung over us. I rejected such thoughts at an early age, but for many blind persons the question, "Why me?" haunts them. The negative attitudes which they feel toward themselves, and that they experience from others, confirm the sense that their blindness represents some deep dark tragedy.

A few years ago I received a call from a guidance counselor who worked at a nearby junior high school. He told me that he had a blind student who was behaving difficultly. The student was experiencing a great deal of anger about his blindness which related to his inability to observe the sexual development of the young women, which was the predominant topic of conversation among his male peers.

It was my opinion that at the bottom of all this was a sincere feeling on the part of the blind student that he was not loveable, and that no woman would ever want him. My suggestion to the counselor was that he introduce the student to a family with an adult blind member so that the student could begin to learn that blind persons do lead normal adult lives. They have families, careers, and successful social and community involvements. Such insight can only come as young blind persons actually observe blind adults functioning in adult roles. This issue becomes more acute as mainstreaming places blind children in school settings where they do not come in contact with other blind persons, especially blind adults.

At the base of a blind person's struggle for self-actualization is a continuing need to affirm oneself against the hard wall of prejudice that is so very much a part of one's everyday life. It is this ignorant, condescending reality that saps the strength and warps the will of many blind persons. In some cases, a blind person may never be challenged to perform because those around him or her may have only the lowest expectations of his or her ability. When this situation occurs, the blind person may settle for a limited set of life accomplishments. He or she may accept the assessment of others that she or he can do little, and consequently never attempt to achieve standards of performance in her or his education, work, or social life that would apply if she or he were sighted.

The scenario is different for many other blind persons. These people refuse to accept the judgment that they are inferior. They rebel against that judgment. The struggle which they commit to is one that endures for a lifetime.

The first dimension of this struggle is the need to acknowledge and to accept the reality that, as a blind person, one must perform more effectively than one's sighted colleagues in order to achieve equal recognition, and the higher the goals of the blind individual, the more true is this axiom. No matter how successful the blind person may be, each new step upward requires one to prove all over again that he or she is competent. Too many people accept a lower level of success and quit trying to fulfill their potential. Blind and sighted alike are comfortable with the limited success that the blind person may achieve. It is so easy to believe that even the most mediocre level of success is "amazing," but the question nags at one, "If I were not blind, could I have done more?" The answer is always "yes." The question follows, "Did I quit too soon?" In the answer to this question lies one's integrity and hope for the future. For we all quit too soon, but some try again.

How can an adult blind person be an effective role model? In order to be an effective role model, an adult blind person must be able to acknowledge the reality of the prejudice and misconceptions that she or he has faced and will continue to face, and that the young blind person will confront. He or she must demonstrate how to concretely manage this reality in an effective and dignified way, while minimizing the personal psychic costs, and he or she must demonstrate that success is possible for someone who is blind even though real barriers do exist.

The March on Washington provides many opportunities for role modeling. The March is planned and conducted by blind persons. Its efficient operation, high-quality briefings, well-formulated position papers, and generally good reception from the members of Congress and their staffs demonstrate to the blind youth in no uncertain terms that blind persons can function as very effective adults.

The subject matter of the issues under discussion—protection from discrimination in the acquiring of insurance, inclusion under the Civil Rights coverage afforded other minority groups, and payment of minimum wage to blind persons employed in sheltered workshops—vividly remind the blind youth of the reality of the world that he or she must face. But the active, articulate presentation of these issues in the halls of Congress is also a reminder that there are effective strategies for combating these barriers. One need not passively accept a diminished life. One can actually play an important part in shaping one's own future, and can do it in an effective and dignified way.

Few issues are more important to a blind person than is independent travel. The Capitol complex, with its many levels, underground rail shuttle, changing office configurations, and large crowds, presents the blind person with ample opportunity to demonstrate his or her travel skills. In order to travel well, a blind person must have the confidence to move assertively in space. The independent travel of blind persons is probably the most unsettling behavior of blind persons for those who are sighted. They often worry about the safety of the blind individual. They will be overly helpful. This may create conflict between the blind person who wishes to be independent and the sighted person who wishes to be helpful. The situation is complicated by the genuine need which the blind traveler may have for information while moving around the Capitol complex.

The behavior which must be modeled by the blind adult from which the youth may learn requires confidence and maturity. When asking for information, the blind person must be direct, polite, and careful not to imply the need for more assistance than is being requested. Negotiating this interface with the sighted world in a dignified, polite, and effective manner provides the youth with a learning experience of great worth.

IV. Concluding Remarks

We treat young blind persons as if they would never grow up. I have heard parents and teachers say, "What will become of him or her?" The negative beliefs that are generally held about blindness and blind people make parents and teachers alike fearful for the future of the blind child. This fear is too often turned against the adult blind person who is viewed as a threat. The adult blind person is a reminder that the child will grow up, and will have to make a life on his/her own. The parent or teacher must let go. The child cannot be protected from the prejudice, the condescension, and the sighted world's evaluation of the worth of the child that awaits as she or he passes into adulthood.

Many blind children with ability, or even with just average intelligence, are told, "You are different. You are not like them. You do not need a cane nor do you need to learn braille. Those things will make you appear to be blind." We know well a blind youth who has very limited vision. His special education teacher had discouraged him from using a cane even though he would be a more effective traveler if he did. Adult blind persons convinced him that he should use a cane. When he went to his special education class carrying a cane, his teacher, a caring sincere person, told him that she had failed. In her eyes, he had slipped into the status of being blind. She had hoped to save him from that fate. But he was blind. That fate was already determined. What was not determined was how he would learn to accommodate to his blindness.

He needed to build a solid identity for himself as a blind person, and he needed to learn to use alternative techniques that would allow him to compete with his sighted peers. He is now a successful college student with a promising future in the computer field. This young person has also participated in the March on Washington, and has made important growth toward adulthood as the result of adult role models.

We know blind persons who were told that their rather average achievements were truly outstanding. This, too, is a form of overprotection. Those persons are now adrift in the world of adult responsibilities and realities. Such inappropriate feedback can be offset by contact with competent adults who can challenge young blind persons and can give honest, realistic feedback. This may be hard for the sighted parent or teacher who at bottom does not believe the youth can compete, and would protect him/her from

that brutal fact as long as possible. But the youth will grow up and the world will be hard, and those able to cope will survive, and those not able to cope will live lives of quiet desperation.

Finally, one last thing must be said. Many parents and teachers of blind children fear the conflict that blind persons introduce into the picture when they become involved. They do not want to be told how to raise their children. They do not want to lose them to a world of blind adults. They do not want to be reminded that their child is blind. And most of all, they do not want to challenge the education and rehabilitation establishment. The professional establishment promises that everything will be all right, and that they need not worry. Blind adults working through the National Federation of the Blind promise only sincere and competent support in a continuing struggle for selfhood in a world that will require much and give little.

Blind adults and blind youth are bound together in spite of efforts of parents, teachers, or even blind youths themselves to deny this reality. Programs which bring blind youth and adults together are of major importance to the future opportunities of these youth to live fulfilling, successful, and truly productive lives.

Families as Partners with Disabled Youth

by Christopher Roland, Timothy Dunham, Judith Hoyt, and Mark Havens

Every person, regardless of his or her particular situation and environment, is involved in a "family system." A type of family system which has recently received an increased amount of attention is the system with a member who is disabled. This paper focuses on the Dunham family from western Massachusetts which includes a sixteen-year-old son, Tim, who has a physical disability. The Dunhams are closely involved with the Family Challenge Program which is based at the Association for the Support of Human Services, Inc., in Westfield, Massachusetts. Through involvement in the Challenge Program, the entire family system, especially Mr. Dunham and Tim, have grown closer by improving communication, cooperation, and trust, thereby creating a partnership.

The Family System

Tim is one of 68 million persons in the United States with limiting or disabling conditions (Kraus, 1983). The onset of a physical disability does affect the entire family system as a working unit (DeLoch & Greer, 1981).

Knott (1979) points out in her work with parents of cerebral palsied children that the family unit must attend to issues of: understanding the primary causes and effects of cerebral palsy, finding and utilizing appropriate counseling services, obtaining effective educational and vocational programs, obtaining summer and after-school recreational activities, and soliciting employment

for their disabled family member. Additional stressors which have been observed include: obtaining appropriate child care for both able-bodied and disabled children, dealing with sibling jealousy, obtaining affordable housing that is most appropriate to the type of disability, and procuring special assistive devices.

One can also glean from the literature a general agreement between researchers concerning the following problems faced by the family system having a disabled family subsystem: excess strain due to demands on time, a tense home environment, and the pressure to do the right thing (be a "good" family) and to continually watch over the disabled child at all times (Knott, 1979; Tavormina, et al., 1981; Park, 1979; and De-Loch & Greer, 1981). This pressure faced by the family system seems to be a lifetime concern and can change at any time in the evolution of the unit, as explained by Minuchin (1974):

> ...increase of stress may occur when a child with a physical handicap...grows older. The family may have been able to adapt to the child's needs while he was young, but as the child grows older and experiences difficulties in interacting with an extrafamilial peer group that does not accept him, this stress may overload the family system. (p. 65)

The Role of the Professional

Allied health professionals and special educators are beginning to realize the importance of working with the entire family system, rather than isolating the disabled child for treatment and education. There remains a definite lack of practice in using this new concept, as is reported by DeLoch and Greer (1981): "...although a disabled child or adult creates stress within a family group, many professionals are excessively pessimistic and underestimate the families' abilities to eventually adjust to and cope with disability-related stress." (p. 59)

The Family Challenge Program

The Family Challenge Program was initially developed in 1981. Judith Hoyt, Program Director for the Association for the Support of Human Services, and parent of a non-speaking, quadriplegic son, spent a large percentage of her time coordinating and leading parent support groups. At this time, Judy was also a member of a Therapeutic Recreation Advisory Committee at Boston University. There she met some professionals who were involved with challenge education and adventure programming. After a few meetings, it was decided that some challenge activities, using a sequential approach (Roland & Havens, 1981), would be attempted with families from the Westfield, Massachusetts, area. The effort turned out to be an entire weekend experience, with five families coming together in a living environment for two-and-a-half days. Persons of all ages and abilities participated, including people who use wheelchairs. Challenge activities were integrated throughout the entire weekend.

From that time in 1981, the Family Challenge Program has expanded with more leaders, more families, as well as challenge equipment such as the Accessible Challenge Course—a "low ropes course" yet one that can challenge people of all abilities. In addition, specific techniques have been used in order to help with the entire learning process. One major technique is the Locus of Control. Roland and Hoyt (1983) explain:

> The entire skill of Locus of Control is merely developing an appreciation that there are really some important parts of one's life that he or she can control. Everyone has within them the power to control the outcome of their behavior. Once one begins to experience "internality," it becomes evident that everything one believes and wants is contingent upon one's own behavior, and not upon powerful others, chance or the social system. (p. 23)

The Dunham Family Profile

The Dunham family includes the mother, Elaine (occupation: nurse); the father, George (occupation: postal worker); Heather, an eleven-year-old daughter; and Tim. Tim, who is a Junior at West Springfield High School and is mainstreamed in all classes, has cerebral palsy which requires him to use crutches. Tim really dislikes the fact that his body does not always work as he would like it. Yet he wants to be as independent as possible and sometimes feels his parents won't let him. Due to this issue, there were often misunderstandings, a lack of trust and cooperation within the family system. At times, this has led to "triangulation." Minuchin (1974) explains:

> In triangulation, each parent demands that the child side with him against the other parent. Whenever the child sides with one, he is automatically defined as attacking the other. In this highly dysfunctional structure, the child is paralyzed. (p. 102)

In order to help the Dunhams better deal with their difficulties, they have often participated in the weekly, parent support group, while the entire family system has participated in the Family Challenge Weekend Program at least twice a year over the past five years. In addition, Mrs. Dunham was instrumental in organizing a "Mother's Challenge Weekend." Also, both parents were part of a parent weekend which was offered to professionals who wanted to openly experience the interaction with real family systems.

A Critical Incident

During a Family Challenge Program session in August 1985, a critical incident took place which at first placed some stress between Tim and his father, but later became a major learning step for both persons. The Dunham family was participating with other families on the Accessible Challenge Course. At the time, eight participants were negotiating the "Scoot Bridge." In the beginning, Tim and his father cooperated side-by-side by spotting and helping other participants negotiate the Bridge. Mr. Dunham and Tim commented how well one girl in particular responded to the challenge, especially with regard to the different ways she attempted the Scoot Bridge (on her back, straddling the side ropes, etc.)

However, when the time came for Tim to attempt a different challenge, the "Adjustable Inclined Balance Beams," the cooperation and communication between father and son quickly changed. Tim, with safety helmet secured and spotters ready, began the climb without his crutches. In the past, his father had the tendency to frequently give verbal suggestions, becoming in essence a "coach." Tim was aware of his father's coaching capabilities and was hoping he would remain quiet. But Mr. Dunham continued with his coaching strategy, constantly giving Tim suggestions on how to climb up the beams. At this point Tim became angry and refused to talk or even look at his father. Although Tim successfully completed the obstacle, with all the other spotters giving him encouragement and praise, Tim didn't say one word for the rest of the activity.

When the activity had been completed, a group debriefing was held. "Debriefing" is an open-ended interview conducted with the participants at the conclusion of outdoor challenge and adventure activities (Darst & Armstrong, 1980).

First, the event was recalled—who participated as spotters, who participated as climbers, and the feelings each participant had. When questioned by the Challenge Course Facilitator about how he and his father had worked together, Tim responded, "There's nothing to talk about—we've just had a little quarrel." He further explained to the facilitator that he sometimes doesn't need and want any help. "I'm not a kid anymore—please let me grow up! I want to make my own decisions!" At this point, the facilitator asked Tim not to direct his comments to her but to tell his father how he was feeling. Tim then directed his statements to his father. This was the beginning of a substantive dialogue concerning roles, responsibilities, and risk taking between father and son. Through the sequential challenge program of activities, Mr. Dunham began to realize that his teenaged cerebral palsy son could achieve some things on his own. Thus, father and son began to develop strong communication links.

After this critical incident, Tim and his father continued to improve their communication and cooperation. Although they are still learning from each other, the stressors on each member of the family system significantly decreased. Tim has acknowledged that he needs to share his feelings with his father. When he is uncomfortable with verbal communication, he is able to use nonverbal communication such as writing letters. Tim's father has acknowledged that he must be more open and allow Tim to make decisions as well as listen more carefully to what Tim has to say. Discussions continued at the next series of family weekends about how hard it is for parents of teens to "let go." The group setting gave the parents an opportunity to honestly discuss how they felt about allowing their handicapped son to make a decision on his own and to follow through on it. Parents agreed that without the challenging approach of the program, much of this discussion would never have taken place. Family members frequently commented how the Challenge Course is an excellent "tool" in which to learn. Tim said at one particular debriefing, "It's easier to talk about things at the Challenge Course than at the dinner table."

Another observation was made by Tim's father concerning professionals: too often professionals do not include the father in programs and meetings. Communication often revolves around other family members, especially the mother. Unfortunately, there is an alarming paucity of data regarding fathers of disabled children (Havens, 1983). The Family Challenge Program, on the other hand, encourages (almost demands) the father's participation. Facilitators realize how important a father's input and feedback can be. If families are to develop youth-adult partnerships, then the entire family system must be willing to take the initial risk of looking at themselves as an actual system and then begin working cooperatively.

Conclusion

The family with a disabled child has the same needs, wants, and concerns as any other family in our society. An individual's ability to grow within that family system is clearly affected by how the system interacts and functions as a whole. There are strong indications that the Family Challenge Program is a valuable tool that allows for a wonderful shared experience and, at the same time, enhances a family's communication, cooperation, and trust. However, it is critical that challenge activities be introduced slowly and sequentially. It is of equal importance that sufficient time be allowed for debriefing—both at the challenge site as well as during parent support groups and other family weekends.

Change in a family system, including the development of youth-adult partnerships, can be a slow process. Thus, any Family Challenge Program may need to span months, if not years. In order for the program to have a chance at being effective, professionals and family members must possess commitment, patience, and the desire to work and learn together. By working with a family like the Dunham's, a satisfying partnership is created between family members as well as between family members and professionals.

The authors would like to extend their sincerest appreciation to the Dunham family for their willingness to share their growth experiences with readers.

The Impact of the Americans with Disabilities Act on Adventure Education Programs

by Deb Sugerman

People with disabilities are moving into the mainstream of society. Chances are good that you know, work with, or have come into contact with someone who uses a wheelchair, has a visual or hearing impairment, or is mentally impaired. Being in the mainstream of society means having access to work environments, living situations, and recreational opportunities. In terms of recreation, many people with disabilities do not require or desire therapeutic activities in a segregated setting, which is the historical medical model. Many people simply want access to integrated recreational opportunities that they can share with family and friends. The Americans with Disabilities Act (ADA) legally provides that access. It also ensures that people with disabilities have opportunities that are similar to those of the rest of the population. For adventure education programs, this presents a unique challenge and opportunity. By providing programs for a broader spectrum of people, we will offer opportunities for individuals to begin to appreciate and value diversity, and in the end will serve all participants more effectively.

The ADA, which was signed into law on July 26, 1990, provides civil rights protections for persons with disabilities that are parallel to those that have been established by the Federal government for women and minorities. The intent of the law is to provide a clear and comprehensive national mandate for the elimination of discrimination against individuals with disabilities (Johnson, 1992) by providing access to critical areas of American life, such as education, employment, transportation, housing, and recreation.

According to the law, a person is considered disabled if he/she: 1) has a physical or mental impairment that substantially limits one or more major life activities, such as performing manual tasks, caring for oneself, walking, seeing, hearing, speaking, learning, or working; 2) has a record of such an impairment (for example, a person who has been in a psychiatric hospital); or 3), is regarded as having such an impairment (for example, a person who has severe facial burn scars). The law itself has five parts or Titles covering discrimination in employment and in services offered by state and local governments, and provisions for telecommunications services. Adventure education programs are covered under Title III, which prohibits discrimination in any business that invites the public to partake in its services.

According to the law, "no individual shall be discriminated against on the basis of disability in the full and equal enjoyment of the goods, services, facilities, privileges, advantages or accommodations of any place of public accommodation by any person who owns, leases (or leases to), or operates a place of public accommodation" (Johnson,

1992, p. 26). The law defines discrimination as: 1) imposing unnecessary eligibility requirements; 2) failing to ensure that no individual is segregated, or denied access to facilities or services; 3) failing to remove architectural and communication barriers; and 4), failing to make reasonable accommodations.

Eligibility Requirements

In developing eligibility or prerequisite skill requirements, programs cannot exclude qualified individuals with disabilities based solely on their disabilities. The prerequisite skills must be justifiable, have a clear tie-in with the activity, and be applied equally to all applicants. The provisions are intended to prohibit exclusion and segregation based on presumptions, patronizing attitudes, fears, and stereotypes. An example would be excluding a paraplegic person from rafting because he or she was unable to swim. Unless swimming ability was required for everyone on the trip, excluding that one particular person would be discrimination.

Integration

The law states that "the provision of goods and services in an integrated manner is a fundamental tenet of nondiscrimination on the basis of disability" (Johnson, 1992, p. 38). In other words, modified participation must be a choice, not a requirement. For example, you may offer two rock-climbing courses: one specifically for people with disabilities and the other an open enrollment course. A person who has a disability may decide to participate in the open course rather than the special course. You must give that person a choice and may not require that

he or she participate in the special session, which would be discrimination according to the ADA.

Physical Barriers

Physical barriers can include a lack of communication devices, transportation, and access to buildings and facilities. Phone systems, such as TDD (telecommunication device for the deaf), are not required by the ADA for adventure education programs, but many businesses are adding them to enhance their marketing capabilities. Accessible transportation systems are also not required for adventure education programs, but the intent of the law requires that programs make reasonable accommodations. For many organizations that transport participants during programs, inaccessible transportation systems would limit participation by people with disabilities. The people within these organizations need to be willing to work with participants with disabilities to find a means of providing transportation.

Many adventure education programs are not facility based, yet some program component parts may take place in a facility. ADA requires that physical barriers in existing facilities be removed or that alternative measures be provided. Examples of facility-based provisions are designated handicapped parking spaces and accessible buildings and bathrooms. If access is not possible, then reasonable alternative accommodations must be made, such as having group meetings on the first floor of a building rather than having participants negotiate a flight of stairs.

If ropes courses are part of an adventure program, the elements need to be accessible to people with disabilities. The concept that is currently in use is that of universal design, or designing buildings and products so that they can be used by everyone. In terms of ropes courses, this means designing elements that the entire group can use instead of having some elements designed exclusively for people with disabilities and some exclusively for non-disabled people. An excellent resource for information on accessible ropes courses is *Bridges to Accessibility* (Havens, 1992).

Reasonable Accommodations

Working together to find solutions is the essence of what ADA refers to as making reasonable accommodations. The addition of the phrase "We are willing to make reasonable accommodations for people with disabilities" in all marketing efforts is a first step. This addition eliminates the barrier of omission, in which a particular individual or group is overlooked or omitted from participation. Other areas in which accommodation might take place are transportation, facility access, program design, or equipment adaptation. Program managers and instructors do not necessarily have to possess all the newest adapted equipment, or know all the answers to providing access for disabled people, but they do need to be willing to work with them to provide the best possible accessibility.

Getting Down to Business

In order for the staff of adventure education programs to further understand the law and how it applies to them, administrators should take the initiative to become informed about the specific regulations of the law. The Office of the ADA will provide a copy of a technical assistance manual and will answer specific questions related to the law (see Resources at the end of this article).

To begin working with the new ADA regulations, brainstorm the ways in which your program could better accommodate people with disabilities in the areas of marketing, programming, policies, and procedures for administration and staff, and in dealing with structural barriers (e.g., access from the parking lot to the buildings, and access within buildings and restrooms). Invite a person with a disability who is knowledgeable about both accessibility and adventure education to your program site. Discuss with him or her the ideas that surfaced from the brainstorming session with staff, and go through your policies, procedures, and methods of operation so that he or she can suggest how to make your programs more accessible to people with disabilities. Keep asking, "How can I change things to make it better for you?" The responses, which may surprise you, encompass what is meant by "accommodation" in the ADA. After eliciting these suggestions, outline a detailed plan of how you will modify your program to accommodate people with disabilities.

The ADA is a vehicle to help bring persons with disabilities into the mainstream of American life. Because of ADA, adventure education programs should be working with a more diverse group of people. In programs that are currently working with integrated groups, the diversity can enable each person to utilize or appreciate his or her unique skills and abilities. Because the programs are based on success through group cooperation, individuals find that they have much in common. In addition, because stereotyping and emotional discomfort and separation are reduced, and often abandoned, integration enhances acceptance. The ADA demands a proactive approach in developing effective and integrated programs for the disabled. It also gives us increased opportunities to learn and make friends with a group of people who often have not had access to adventure education programs.

Resources

For information on ADA:
The Office of the Americans with Disabilities Act
Civil Rights Division
U.S. Department of Justice
P.O. Box 66118
Washington, DC 20035-6118
(202) 514-0301 (voice)
(202) 514-0383 (TDD)

Americans with Disabilities Act of 1990: Law and Explanation
Commerce Clearing House, Inc.
1-800-248-3248 to order and ask for catalogue #4998

Recreation...Access in the '90s
NRPA
3101 Park Center Drive
Alexandria, VA 22302

For information on standards for accessible facilities:
Specifications for Making Buildings and Facilities Accessible and Usable by Physically Handicapped People
American National Standards Institute
1430 Broadway
New York, NY 10018

A Guide to Designing Accessible Outdoor Recreation Facilities
Special Programs and Populations
National Park Service
Washington, DC 20240

Chapter 12

Experiential Activities

Cooperative Learning Techniques In the Classroom

by Scott C. Griffith

Can a conventional classroom be experiential? Some think that this is a very difficult proposition. But we need to take a look at the alternative learning options available and see how they might be "experientially" worked into the mainstream. One such possibility is cooperative learning.

Teachers who can successfully use cooperative learning techniques have the potential to make students responsible for their own learning, as well as allowing them to help others to master a particular topic. This kind of interaction can teach students the skills needed for life-long learning, Of course, these skills can also be acquired through other types of experiential programming, but cooperative learning can make it happen within the bounds of the conventional classroom. This article provides the rationale for cooperative learning techniques while describing specific techniques that can be applied immediately in the classroom.

Cooperative learning involves students working together in small groups (three to six persons) on a given task that has been clearly outlined by the teacher. It differs from other forms of small-group behavior in that a successful cooperative learning experience must possess two essential elements: a group goal and individual accountability (Slavin, 1988). These characteristics encourage students to work together to achieve optimal group output while at the same time increasing their own individual knowledge. Hence, students master content as well as gain important social skills.

Cooperative learning techniques can be utilized across the full spectrum of student populations regardless of age, cultural background, and ability level. Teachers can choose from a large breadth of techniques that can promote class unity, team building, social skill development, concept development, task specialization, and academic achievement (Kagan, 1989). Two techniques popular in secondary schools are the Jigsaw Strategy and Student Teams-Achievement Divisions.

The Jigsaw Strategy

This was originally developed by Elliott Aronson in order to promote academic achievement and positive social relations among students in recently desegregated schools (Myers & Lemon, 1988). Here's how it works:

1. Become an Expert (master the content). Students are assigned to groups where they will become *experts* on sub-topics which relate to a larger topic which the class as a whole is studying (Slavin, 1986). For example, a unit in Earth Science might be divided into content areas such that each group discusses a particular biome (i.e., alpine, grassland, coastal). The role of the teacher is to serve as an enabler to structure the learning activities so that they will be appropriate for the students, and to be a resource person and advice-giver.

2. Presentation (students become the teachers). Once the specific content is discussed in the expert groups, students form learning teams comprised of one member from each of the expert groups (see Fig.1). Students then teach their area of expertise to the other members of their learning team. In the Earth Science example, each member of the learning team would share what they learned in their expert groups about their particular biome.

3. Clarification (question and application time). Students are encouraged to ask questions and clarify the subject matter which their peers are teaching to them. This

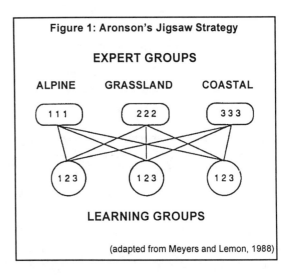

Figure 1: Aronson's Jigsaw Strategy

EXPERT GROUPS

ALPINE   GRASSLAND   COASTAL

LEARNING GROUPS

(adapted from Meyers and Lemon, 1988)

aspect of jigsaw learning is often the most difficult for students who have not had many opportunities to practice and articulate their higher-level thinking skills such as those outlined in Bloom's Taxonomy (Bloom, 1977). A student might ask, "How do the characteristics of grassland soils affect crop rotation?" or "Would you draw some distinctions between coastal and alpine birds?"

4. Evaluation of Learning (accountability). The class is tested in traditional ways; thus, the students are individually accountable for their own learning. However, acquiring the necessary information deemed important by the teacher requires all members to be actively involved in the teaching/learning process. Every student's contribution is critical for the success of all of them. In effect, they "sink or swim" together.

Students become active learners and generate feelings of ownership because they experience the role of the teacher and want to help the other members in their teams understand the concepts acquired in the expert groups.

Student Teams Achievement Division (STAD)

This activity is among the simplest and most adaptable of the cooperative learning methods. It can be used at any grade level from two to twelve in which there are single right answers, such as mathematics, language arts, foreign language, science, and much of the social studies (Slavin, 1986).

1. Assigning Students to Teams. Rank students on some measure of academic performance and divide the list into quarters. Put one student from each quarter on each team, making sure the teams are well balanced in gender and ethnicity.

2. Determine Individual Base Scores. Before beginning the activity, students' base scores can be determined by averaging their past three quiz/test scores or via this rough outline: A: 90pts. B: 80pts. C: 70pts. C-/D+: 65pts. D or F: 60pts.

3. Present the Lesson. Teach students the content in a style that is the most comfortable for the teacher, as the emphasis of this cooperative activity is placed on group discussion *after* students receive the information.

4. Team Study. During the team study (one or two class periods), the members' tasks are to master the material themselves and to make sure that their teammates have done so. Teachers should prepare worksheets that students can use to practice the skill being taught and to assess themselves and each other. Each team should only receive two copies of the worksheets as this will require students to work together. Emphasize that: they are not finished until they are sure all teammates will get a 100% on the quiz; worksheets are study guides and not to be handed in for grading; if there are ques-

tions, students should ask a teammate before asking the instructor. Circulate through the class, praising those who are working well, and sitting in on each of the groups (Slavin, 1986).

5. Evaluation. Once the students have had adequate time to study in their teams, distribute a quiz. Individual testing shows what each student has learned.

6. Determine Individual Improvement Scores. These scores should be determined as soon as possible after each quiz. Points are based on the degree to which their quiz scores *exceed* their base scores (see Table). These scores can be adjusted to adapt to differing student abilities and can be used in the computation of base scores for future STAD activities.

Scoring Criteria for STAD Teams

Quiz Score	Improvement Points
>10 pts. below base score	0
10-1 pts. below base score	10
1-10 pts. above base score	20
>10 pts. above base score	30
Perfect Paper (ignore base score)	30

7. Recognizing Team Accomplishments. Awards can be given to each team as they are not in competition with one another. "Your own enthusiasm about team scores and a communication that you value cooperation and success as a team are as important as any other factor in the success of STAD" (Slavin, 1986).

The ultimate reward is individual achievement, along with improved social relations among students who have learned to give and receive help from one another. It is evident that these characteristics of STAD parallel those associated with experiential theory. As a result, this and other cooperative learning techniques give teachers an avenue to make the conventional classroom experiential.

Support for Cooperative Learning

The effectiveness of cooperative-learning teaching strategies has been validated through a variety of research publications. Most research suggests that "good things" can and do happen when cooperative learning groups are used in the classroom (Vermette, 1988). These are a few of the most significant outcomes teachers might expect for their own students:

Academic Gains

"Cooperative learning promotes higher achievement than competitive and individualistic learning structures across all age levels, subject areas, and almost all tasks" (Kagan, 1989). This claim has been supported by a meta-analysis of over 122 studies by Johnson et al.(1981) and a cooperative learning review of 41 studies on student achievement (Slavin, 1983). This work also provides research evidence to reject the perspective that cooperative learning improves students' affective skills at the expense of academic mastery. The research indicates that the principle of individual accountability must be an integral component of any cooperative learning activity.

Attitudinal Changes

Cooperative learning research has also identified positive changes in students' attitudes toward each other. For example:

Slavin (1979) compared students who had friends from ethnic backgrounds other than their own in both traditional and cooperative classroom settings. The results showed that students from cooperative learning environments had over three times the number of friends of an ethnicity different than their own compared with students in the traditional classroom. (Kagan, 1989)

By creating learning groups that are balanced in gender, ability level, and ethnic background, students learn content in an environment that promotes positive, cross-cultural relations and value formation. This principle of face-to-face interaction is another key element of cooperative learning.

Social and Affective Development

Over two dozen studies have demonstrated that when students are allowed to work together, they experience an increase in self-esteem, self-direction, and role-taking abilities (Kagan, 1989). These outcomes of successful cooperative learning activities parallel those elements taught in most every type of experiential program. Whether students acquire this knowledge on a ropes course or in a classroom, they are learning through direct experience from the stimuli that surrounds them. Here are a few personal observations of cooperative learning in action:

- When I used a variation of the Jigsaw technique in an English-as-a-second-language class, students were less apprehensive about speaking English amongst their peers than they were when I asked them direct questions. Since they knew I would be testing them on what was shared in their groups, they had to communicate and rely on each other to clarify the information for which they were accountable. This principle of positive interdependence keeps the group working toward a common goal.

- A colleague uses cooperative learning in her social studies classes. Through debates, scored discussions, and case studies, students have the opportunity to work with their peers and experience a variety of roles, including those of teacher, recorder, and facilitator, This process can generate new perspectives on social issues.

- Cooperative learning was a major part of my teacher training program in a secondary methods class. Our teacher designed a good portion of the class using cooperative learning groups. We learned a number of techniques and experienced the roles students face when placed in similar settings. I was anxious in a couple of activities but was glad to have gained this experiential perspective on cooperative learning. It has been very beneficial for me when creating lesson plans.

Other situations where cooperative learning techniques have been used in the classroom have been validated through rigorous studies found in educational, social science, and psychological journals. This volume of research examines many variables, from student achievement to self-esteem.

The time is right for mainstream and experiential educators to begin to work together to provide students with the highest possible quality of education amidst the public outcry for reform of our troubled educational system. We need not re-invent the wheel, but can build on successful techniques that have already been tested. The mainstream classroom can become more experiential through cooperative learning techniques.

Most experiential educators rely heavily upon settings outside the classroom to run their programs. The approach of this discipline needs to be worked into the mainstream such that a majority of educators can come to understand and utilize learning by doing. After all, think of the endless possibilities for cooperative learning in a classroom. The challenge is there for all those who know the importance and positive results of learning through experience.

Using Initiative Games to Assess Group Cooperation

by Alan Warner

Experiential educators need to develop evaluation research measures which are an integral part of programming and provide practical information about key variables in the experiential learning process. Here is a specific technique involving initiative games that we have successfully used to assess the level of group cooperation among eleven- to thirteen-year-olds in a school setting. The basic approach would be applicable to any age group, but the specific tasks might have to be modified.

We developed a precise observational system for coding individuals' behavior in small groups of five to seven students while they tackled a series of initiative tasks.* The basic notion is that students who are able to work cooperatively will demonstrate a higher level of positive involvement on these tasks relative to students who are less cooperative.

The first step was to select an appropriate set of initiative tasks. We needed to come up with a series of roughly equivalent tasks because we wanted to assess changes in positive involvement within a group across time. Equivalent tasks are required because a problem cannot be repeated at a later date once participants are aware of the solution. We initially experimented with a large number of tasks before selecting nine tasks to pilot test intensively in order to standardize rules, adjust task difficulty, and examine behavior patterns.

Task difficulty had to be carefully monitored. If a task was too easy, the group would finish quickly and there would not be time for a sufficient number of observation periods. If a task was too difficult, the group would give up and complain. Task orientation was also a dimension which had an important impact on student behavior patterns. Some tasks have an individual orientation (e.g., Nitro Crossing, Electric Fence) in that participants typically complete the task one at a time to arrive at a group solution. Other tasks have a group orientation (e.g., Hanging Teeter Totter, Peanut Butter Bog, Points of Contact) in that the solution is reached only if the whole group is physically involved simultaneously. We ended up selecting the three group-oriented tasks identified above for our study and used them as pre-treatment, post-treatment, and follow-up tests.

The observational procedure required that an observer watch each group member during the task on a regular rotating basis. Each student was observed for five seconds and the observer then had five seconds to make a coding decision on a standard form. The observer had to decide whether the individual exhibited positive, passive, negative, or non-involvement with the task during the observation interval. Positive behavior was defined as physically or verbally doing something which contributed to the solution of the task. Negative behavior was saying or

Sample Observation Form

	Observation Cycle I								Observation Cycle II							
Student Name or Description																
Positive																
Negative																
Passive																
Non-involvement																
	Observation Cycle III								Observation Cycle IV							
Positive																
Negative																
Passive																
Non-involvement																

physically doing something which impeded progress toward the solution of the initiative task. Passive involvement consisted of a student focusing his or her eyes on the others in the group; whereas non-involvement was defined as staring away from the group. More precise definitions are available in the staff manual for those readers interested in duplicating this measurement technique in an accurate, reliable way.**

The observation and recording intervals were cued for the observer by a specially prepared tape, played through a cassette recorder with an earphone attachment. The tape defined ten cycles of observation periods with seven subjects per cycle. For smaller groups, the observer skipped the appropriate number of observation periods per cycle. Inter-observer reliability was checked by having two observers independently code behavior for the same group. Observers were able to attain a high level of agreement after a series of training sessions.

We successfully implemented the procedure with treatment and control groups and demonstrated that our experiential trips did significantly increase the level of positive involvement on the tasks. However, the potential applications for the methodology are more important than the specific results. The measure takes time and energy to develop, but it provides a practical assessment of cooperation which is compatible with a large number of programs.

*Detailed descriptions of a variety of initiative tasks are available in *Initiative Games*, by B. Simpson, available from the Colorado Outward Bound School, and *Cowstails and Cobras*, available from Project Adventure.

**Further details are available by writing to the author c/o Cornwallis House, Miller Hospital, Kentville, Nova Scotia, Canada B4N 1M7.

Some Simple Initiative Tasks

by Jeff Witman

The initiative tasks which follow have been successfully utilized with developmentally disabled individuals as a lead-up to more complex cooperative tasks. They've also proven effective as "ice-breakers" for programs combining disabled and non-disabled individuals.

1. **Rock Climb:** The challenge is to have every group member reach the top of or get up on a boulder.

2. **Trail Barriers:** The challenge is to move around/over/through barriers placed on a trail. Barriers could include: a brush pile, a fallen tree, a puddle.

3. **Jungle Co-op Meal:** Components of a meal or snack are hidden in various areas. The group is divided to search for the various objects (e.g., breakfast: a) cereal, b) eggs, c) silverware and utensils, d) milk and juice). Emphasis is placed upon the importance of each group's accomplishment of their task toward the success of the meal/snack.

4. **Creek-Cross:** The challenge is to utilize natural objects (e.g., branches, rocks) to form a bridge across a small stream.

5. **Total Silence:** A hunter is passing only a few yards away. The group (deer) must be completely silent and freeze until the hunter passes by.

6. **The King's Reward:** The king has offered a thousand gold coins to the group which can encircle the greatest number of trees. Begin with one and see how many you can enclose. To count, a tree must be taller than the tallest member of your group.

7. **Mother Nature's Revenge:** The challenge is to completely rid a picnic or other outdoor area of litter/debris for an inspection visit by Mother Nature, who's promised a 6-week delay of Spring if not completely satisfied.

8. **Guard the Treasure:** The group pairs up into twos. Each pair stands back to back. The treasure is placed between their backs. (Treasure is a ball or pillow.) Each pair has to get over a fallen tree and finally over a distance of twenty feet.

9. **The Bomb:** The bomb, a balloon, is thrown up among the group. The group has to keep the balloon up (not catching it) for as long as possible.

10. **Kick the Stick:** Assemble group in a line (using wide-open area) approximately five feet apart. First person kicks a stick to the second person and on until the stick reaches the opposite end of the line. (Divide by teams or time the event.)

11. **Bucket Brigade:** Object is to fill a container, using several smaller containers, by passing smaller containers from source of water to large container and back. Variation: put out campfire using a bucket brigade.

12. **Space Walk:** The challenge is for the entire group to remain in contact with the life line (a length of rope) during a hike.

Processing of the activities has worked particularly well when Polaroid photos of the sequence of an activity have been taken and reviewed.

The Idea Notebook

The "Idea Notebook" was a section of *The Journal of Experiential Education* designed to give readers an opportunity to share practical ideas that have worked for them.

An Initiative Problem and a "New Game"

Touch My Can
Object: For a group of about 10–12 students to make physical contact with a can while avoiding physical contact with one another.

The Rope Push
Halve your group and ask each half to stand on either side of a marker line (chalk line or rope). Hand them a 60- to 80-foot length of rope (any diameter or material) so that each side has an equal amount on their side of the marker line. Mark the center of the rope with a piece of tape. At this juncture they are probably ready for a good old Tug-of-War. BUT the object this time is, at the end of a one-minute time limit, to have more of your rope on their side than they have of the rope on your side! WHAT? That's right, this is a rope push, not pull. Here are a couple of rules to ease the transition from tradition to chaos:

- No one on either team is allowed to cross over and touch the other team's turf or person (no purposeful contact). Tugging on the rope is taboo—only push. Throwing the rope is not allowed.
- Judging this evenly is well nigh impossible, but who cares and a tie is usually well received by all except the most die-hard competitors. This confused melee is worth trying again, so suggest

taking a minute or two to develop team strategies and subterfuges of sneaky initiative ideas.

These ideas are taken from "Bag of Tricks," a quarterly newsletter with new ropes course, initiative, and game ideas, available from Karl Rohnke, P.O. Box 77, Hamilton, MA 01936.

Time Flies When You're Having Fun

Tom Herbert (Concord High School, Concord, New Hampshire) covers the clocks in his classroom and confiscates watches as his sociology class enters the room. As the students squirm, not knowing when the bell will ring, they come to realize our cultural dependence on scheduled and precise time.

Experiencing a Handicap

Gruffie Clough (Denver, Colorado) wanted her students to understand what it is like to be handicapped. Each student was greeted at the door one morning with a wheelchair in which the student had to remain for the entire school day. The wheelchairs were borrowed from a local agency such as Easter Seals.

Bridging the Generation Gap

As a homework assignment, students can be asked to interview their parents. They are to ask questions about a place or time which was important to their mother or father when he or she was a child, teenager, or young adult. The students return to class with their questions and answers, then brainstorm additional questions that they can ask their parents in order to get more details. (What songs were playing on that juke box in the soda shop? What kind of a car did you drive to get there?) As students interview their parents in some depth, the details usually begin to cluster around a special event or a typical time. Once they have collected enough details, students write a short story in the first person, telling the story through their parent's eyes. This assignment has the benefit of getting students to talk with their parents and also prepares them for later interviews with adults in the community.

Dave Bernstein and Greg Trimmer use this assignment with English and cultural journalism classes at Minnechaug Regional High School in Wilbraham, Massachusetts.

Simulating Literary Experiences

It is sometimes difficult to think of ways to include an experiential approach in the study of literature, which is a vicarious look into the lives of others. Two New Hampshire teachers try to simulate the problems and experiences of characters in the books.

One of Peggy Walker Stevens's classes reads *Dove,* an autobiographical account of a teenager who sails around the world alone. The greatest problem for the author was coping with loneliness during his trip. Students get a taste of this loneliness by being blindfolded at school and driven to an isolated wooded area where they are alone with only a notebook and pen until they are picked up

4 hours later. This "mini-solo" has a big impact on many younger teenagers who seldom spend any time alone. They can begin to understand what it is like for the author of *Dove* to have spent months by himself at sea.

Louise Hicky brings unfamiliar settings of books to life by having the students prepare meals similar to those eaten in that time period or in that region. Following the reading of *MacBeth,* students research the food of Shakespearean times and the traditional dishes of Scotland. They have prepared a feast of baked turkey (a whole boned turkey breast in a pie shell), Shrewsbury cakes, cider, and Scotch eggs (hard boiled eggs wrapped in sausage and deep fried).

Since most New Hampshire students are unfamiliar with the southern dishes described in *To Kill a Mockingbird,* students found recipes and prepared Smithfield ham, black-eyed peas, grits, and "Charlottes" (as served in *Mockingbird*).

Administrators are invited to the meals—a good way to gain support for creative ideas.

Got a Local Problem? Study It.

Branford, Connecticut, has a huge mountain of "trap rock," extruded waste material from the activity of Tilcon Tomasso, a local company that produces road-paving material. As a result of a recent Project Adventure Academic workshop, Joan Bailey of Branford became excited about using the "mountain" as a focus for an experiential unit. She approached the company and was received enthusiastically. As part of an interdisciplinary science-economics unit, students will study the plant operations, "mountain" composition, and local geology. The class will produce a contour model of the town and a slide tape of the company's operations. Ecological recommendations will be part of the slide tape.

The company has donated maps, chemicals, company assayist time, jeeps, drivers, film, and development costs.

This idea comes from Dick Prouty, a staff member of Project Adventure in Hamilton, Massachusetts.

Nothing Artificial

David C. Mellen

Photosynthesis or maple syrup—which would you prefer studying? Measurement, proportions, percentages, convection, boiling point, buoyancy, density, specific gravity, and precision should all be covered in science and math. Perhaps I can outline here how much sweeter they are to study through a maple sugaring project. To study this "industry" is also to study its people, for sugaring is richly steeped with culture. Taken as a whole, this project touches many topics and may motivate students toward everything from writing to physical labor.

Step One—the psych

Find a sugar house for a field trip. Write to the U.S. Department of Agriculture Forest Service or your state agricultural service for assistance. Take your class in late February or early March to see the operation in full swing. Arrange ahead for a complete tour—everything from tapping and collecting to testing the final product. Interview the people that do this yearly—why do they work so hard?

Step Two—the prep

In the fall, choose a site for your operation, identify the trees you will use, and prepare your boiling apparatus. Outdoors with even crude protection from wind and rain is preferable to indoors where the huge amounts of steam will produce more destruction than syrup. Sugar maples are the preferred tree, but red maples and even birch trees will make syrup.

A wood burning stove with flat top and large firebox will do fine in combination with an evaporating pan. The larger the pan the better and using a small second pan for the final step (indoors perhaps) is a good idea. You may not be able to copy the dividers and fins you will see in the professional evaporators on your tour and you may have trouble finding pans constructed from stainless steel or English tin. These are something to work toward for future years; use any old clean pan for now.

Step Three—tapping & collecting

Tap shortly after Washington's birthday (depending on your location) with a 7/16-in. bit, boring 7–8 cm. in to the tree at a slight slant for drainage. Tap height is not critical and one tap for every 25 cm. of tree diameter is allowable on a healthy tree. Do not plug the holes when you're through—they are small enough for the tree to close as it heals, and plugs retard the healing. Taps may be purchased, cut from tubing, or whittled from pithy branches like sumac (poke the soft center out to make them hollow). Plastic gallon jugs may be slit near the top and slipped onto the taps for collecting; tie them up by the handle to prevent the jugs from falling off the taps as they gain in weight. The jugs and any containers used to store the sap must be washed with diluted clorox before collecting and whenever cloudy, smelly sap is found growing—yes, growing! That is your bacteria and sanitation lesson. Sap must be stored in a cool place or used immediately. The sap looks like water but spill some inside and your custodian will surely join the lesson by pointing out the difference.

Students should be assigned a tree or trees. Many will bring sap from a tree at home. Don't miss this chance at data collecting and record keeping. Students may bargraph the amounts collected daily from their trees. A class high-low temperature graph plotted daily may be made on plastic. The horizontal axis should be marked off by the day in the same scale on both graphs so students may lay the plastic temperature graph over their bar graph and check for correlation. And of course—it's liters and Celsius now!

Step Four—"cauldron boil and cauldron bubble"

Syrup will sour if too thin and crystalize if too thick. How do you know when it is just right? This is an ideal question for students of science to wrestle with (even better since it has more than one good answer). The proper density is 1.32 kg/liter. To test density, students can measure the volume of a sample and put it on a balance. A 10-ml sample should be 13.2 g. They could then learn about specific gravity and try an even simpler test—a hydrometer should float in a sample at the 1.32 mark. Since expansion and contraction cause this to vary, taking syrup temperature and computing the adjustment is necessary if you wish to facilitate precision. If you're a social studies teacher full of compassion for students who cannot

handle this technical approach, send them out to interview an old-timer. With legwork and patience they will discover a technique worthy of Foxfire. It's so simple, science teachers will either groan or smile.

There is a lot to do during the boil-down process. Sap should constantly be added, scum should be skimmed, the fire needs continual stoking, and a cautious eye must always be on the foam and thermometer. Foaming over can be halted with a squirt of cream, and frequent temperature checks will warn you as the critical moment draws near. Inattention at this point spells disaster— scorched syrup and perhaps a ruined evaporating pan. One way to help prevent this is to make this a yearly project and revive the guild system. With a master, journeyman, and apprentice (or two) on hand at all times, you may self-perpetuate the project with high standards and guarantee success.

Boiling point is an important concept to understand for successful sugaring. The day you plan to finish off your syrup, check the boiling point of distilled water. It will vary with altitude and barometric pressure. Your syrup is ready for final testing when it boils at 4.1°C over the boiling point of pure water.

It may take anywhere from 32 to 60 l of sugar maple sap to boil down to 1 l of syrup. The average proportion is 1:40. Do your students understand the concept of percentage? What percentage of the sap is maple syrup? This percentage should be figured for every batch of syrup since it will vary considerably. As the season progresses, the ratio will generally increase until the buds begin to burst, the sap becomes cloudy, and the resulting "buddy" syrup is not worth the effort.

Sap contains more than sugar and water. Many of the minerals dissolved in sap will precipitate during boiling. Keep this secret at first and you may find students arguing over who threw sand in the syrup. This "sugar sand" is a combination of malate of lime or nitre and various other impurities. It should be removed immediately while the syrup is very hot and will filter most easily. Strain the hot syrup through a layer of wet white felt or multiple layers of cheese cloth.

Maple sugar candy might be the ultimate challenge for this project. With extreme care, the boiling process may be continued until the syrup is boiling at 10°C over the boiling point of pure water. Pour it into molds and it will crystalize into candies. It boils down fast at this point—you may end up with a burned mass of "caramel."

Step Five—ending with class

This may be the hardest logistic problem of the project, but if you can pull it off, it is unforgettable: a pancake breakfast with globs of grade A fancy, grade A, and, oh well, grade B maple syrup (hide the grade C).

Hindsight—why bother?

A maple sugaring project is a lot of work for everyone involved. The beautiful thing about it is that it combines hard work and fun while integrating learning. Most any old-timer will tell you that sugaring is a labor of love. Students who are intensely involved may discover a love of labor that could become the most valuable lesson they ever learned. A difficult, successful, and rewarding experience can carry great impact. With sugaring, the success is obvious and the reward is sweet.

Give Your Students a Leadership Course

by Nicholas Beer

They made a decision. They seem happy and are all working together! I never thought that finishing that project could be so easy. A week ago they barely knew each others' names. They are showing some leadership now!

Have you ever said this to yourself? Do you wonder how it happened? Did you do this on purpose? Teaching leadership means facilitating an experience through which students gain insight, increase understanding, and practice leadership. Many experiential educators teach leadership implicitly, and could easily adapt their program to explicitly provide a leadership learning experience.

Congruency between how a leadership program is run and what is taught is important. The collection of activities which they experience consciously and directly, is not the whole program. Indirectly, methods such as modeling what is taught and facilitating experiences sneak up behind the students and nudge them toward understanding. We are doing our best when the ways that we nudge are consistent with what we are putting consciously before them.

Lao Tzu reminds us:

Potent leadership is a matter of being aware of what is happening in the group and acting accordingly. Specific actions are less important than the leader's clarity or consciousness. That is why there are no exercises or formulas to ensure successful leadership. (Heider, 1985, p. 75)

Identifying the Idea of Leadership

In the context of an experiential education program, leadership is often about small groups working together efficiently and effectively. Many definitions and models of leadership exist, filling different circumstances and perspectives. Burns (1979, p.19) defines leadership as "...inducing followers to act for certain goals that represent the values and the motivations—the wants and needs, the aspirations and expectations—of both the leaders and followers."

The emphasis is on the group's process, not the leader, for our teaching work encompasses the role of the educator and other aspects such as vision and motivation.

Another perspective is given by distributed actions theory (Johnson & Johnson, 1987, p. 55). Leadership emerges from the group as different people, depending on their personal strengths and interests, share leadership functions. Group members are involved in a variety of tasks: completing itineraries, helping group members make personal decisions, running meetings, cooking meals, completing challenges, having fun together, learning together, etc. The group (sometimes unconsciously) selects different leaders for different needs and problems. There may be a head cook, a primary navigator, a lead spokesperson, a tension reliever, a best friend to all, a discussion leader, a cheerleader, and dozens of others all incorporated into a tiny group! The goals of the group at any one moment may require leadership that is visionary, managerial, maintenance-oriented, motivational, or task-oriented.

I define leadership as the process—within a person or group as a whole—which enhances the group's self-identity, cohesiveness, purpose, and/or effectiveness. This is what I teach when I offer a leadership course and has been the basis of my experience at Outward Bound where I developed the ideas in this paper. Imparting an understanding of leadership involves two interrelated variables: the educator as a leader (one's identity and methods), and the leadership curriculum.

The Educator as a Leader

The educator begins with awareness of his or her own motivations, teaching styles, knowledge, and abilities as a leader. Through the process of self-discovery, that leader will know what can be offered to the students. In the actual creation and fulfillment of a program, the educator may function as the program designer, role model, skills trainer, translator, group facilitator, and one-to-one counselor (Kalisch, 1979). In these functions there are leadership opportunities, and an awareness of the opportunities brings them to life.

Motivation to lead and to teach. The educator must be convinced that leadership is teachable. The educator's desire for a leadership course is essential because students sense sincerity or the lack of it. Without confidence and commitment to the experiential process, even an ideal curriculum may be ineffective.

Consciousness of leadership learning. In designing the program, the educator needs to ask questions such as: Why am I doing this particular activity? What is the benefit to the course as a whole? Is there something else that would better reach the overall goals? What are the overt and covert messages about leadership?

Understanding leadership in both a theoretical and practical sense. Leadership theories and models provide a context for interpreting and discussing our own experiences and those of others around us. Leadership is a part of any experience with a group of people, and a framework to use in thinking about it makes it more meaningful.

Using situational leadership. On a week-to-week, day-to-day, even minute-to-minute basis, activities can be designed and managed in a particular way for that particular moment. The term for this is "situational leadership" (Carew, Parisi-Carew, & Blanchard, 1986), which is a deliberate effort to match one's interaction style with the changing needs of the group. Two functions are involved: the accomplishment of tasks and goals; and the support of interpersonal relationships and motivation. Successful leaders, under differing circumstances, vary their leadership style. Facilitators of the entire learning process can also modify their interactions. The group's task may be climbing up a hill with heavy packs, deciding where to make camp, or discussing the successes and learnings of the day. The group may be very good at one task and not at another. The instructor's role will vary according to the group's immediate needs.

Not expecting every student to become a leader. Realistic expectations lead to success. Not every student wants to be a leader, or be a part of a leadership process, but they will likely gain a greater understanding of leadership.

Using a variety of tools to teach leadership. These include activities, initiatives, explanations, demonstrations, lessons, classes, discussions, and feedback. These are not necessarily different from any ordinary activity, but can be given a leadership "flavor" by the instructor. This diversity is a strength of experiential education programs. Integrating all of the various learning experiences makes leadership part of the program and not just the curriculum.

A Leadership Curriculum

A curriculum of leadership gives the program an overt agenda. It is the direct attempt to influence the students' knowledge and skills.

Teaching theories and models bring real-life examples to the students. Using models makes theory a part of curriculum. Models are maps which provide reference points and guidance for exploring unknown areas and orienting personal experiences.

Developing and using a vocabulary of leadership gives students the words and concepts to express, understand, and interpret their learning and experience. The goal is not to collect a glossary for its own sake, but to have resources for understanding what is happening in the group. Using and reinforcing this vocabulary turns unfamiliar jargon into everyday language.

Exposing myths about leadership (Bennis & Nanus, 1985, pp. 221-225) liberates students from stifling limitations. Here are some: (a) Only a few have the ability to become leaders. (b) Leaders are born and not

made. (c) Leaders are charismatic. (d) Leadership always comes from the top. (e) Leaders always direct and manipulate group members. These myths are perpetuated or challenged by our behavior, and can be fodder for discussions.

Actively analyzing leadership situations with the group brings these issues up for discussion. The facilitator can solicit feedback from the students so they become accustomed to looking at others' leadership and develop trust that they can say what is on their minds. At the end of an activity, one can ask: "What was my role? What was my leadership function?" It empowers the students and validates their own experience and perspectives, developing the norm that feedback and discussion are safe within the group.

Teaching skills and awareness of leadership through program elements gives the students skills such as: problem solving, decision making, giving feedback, clarifying values, communicating, managing, goal setting, serving others, and teamwork. Help the process by talking, reading aloud, brainstorming, making lists and diagrams, structuring initiatives, running role plays, doing awareness exercises, briefing and debriefing group processes, playing games, and having adventures. These activities are the tangible heart of a program.

Putting the Theory into Practice

Below are two examples of how to put the theory into practice. These are only small slices of a course and primarily demonstrate how an experiential education curriculum can be adapted to become a leadership curriculum. For example, initiatives and new games that teach certain lessons, e.g., the

Gordian Knot for problem solving, can be expanded to take on a new meaning, In the briefing session, the instructor simply states that "this is a leadership exercise" and continues with the presentation. In the debrief, the instructor raises leadership issues by asking key questions: How did you make decisions? Who was the leader? How did you know to follow that person's lead? Did the group make decisions or did one person? How involved were each of you in the problem-solving process?

Another example is a quick exercise to turn a daily camping chore into a leadership exercise. After students have learned to con-struct their tarps, ask them to divide into three groups. Each group uses a different leadership style to erect the tarp. One group must come to a consensus for every decision about the tarp. Another must vote on every aspect of the set-up, and the third will simply have an authoritative leader who will dictate exactly what is to be done. Afterward, talk about participants' reactions to the efficiency of each process, their investment in the actual outcome, and any other revelations or feelings. Go on to discuss when each style could be best applied to other circumstances. Give the students a leadership course!

What About the Young Child?

by Rita Yerkes

A glance at the 1987 Association of Experiential Education Conference Program reveals that both the practitioners' and researchers' primary focus seems to be experiential education for adolescents and adults. And yet as the membership gathered for major presentations, there was a noticeable increase in young children attending the proceedings. Perhaps it is due to the graying of the AEE membership. In any case, the Association has both the opportunity and challenge to rediscover the young child.

If we were to follow pre-school children through a day of early childhood education both in and out of the school setting, our observations may reveal children alienated from their own learning environment. In the kindergarten setting, emphasis is increasingly placed upon reading and writing developmental tasks, often using workbook drill, indoor games, and subtle computer manipulation. If we are concerned about young children, we must question the use of these teaching methods as seriously for this age group as we do for others and encourage the utilization of more experiential activities in the pre-school environment. It is not enough to model experiential education as parents; we must also seek other modes of experiences in the school setting to reinforce what children see at home.

It has always been a puzzle to me that in recreational settings, children are encouraged to get involved with play and their environment. However, in the formal, indoor classroom, children are discouraged from doing the same. The outdoor playground is usually of little interest to classroom teachers except when it is time for a classroom break or when used by them as a reward for good classroom behavior. This is not due to a lack of information. Early childhood educators and recreation professionals have been interested in and have conducted research on play and educational play environments for children for at least the past twenty-five years. The lack of interdisciplinary communication and cooperation between these two educational arenas that serve the young child is particularly striking.

Parents have increasingly sought after-school activities for their children or opted for day care at nursery schools, kindergarten, day camps, or recreational programs. They choose this option because of the increase in single-parent families and families where two parents work and because the parents want wholesome experiences for their children. This phenomenon has created greater challenges for early childhood centers to program experiences for their young charges.

The Need for Experiential Learning

Early childhood educators tell us that the business of childhood is experiential play (Yerkes, 1980). Play means free, spontaneous activity for its own sake. It means to be engaged in fantasy, exploration, and forms of creativity (all components of experiential education). Yet in their analyses of play by early childhood educators, one finds relatively little focus on outdoor play. Thus, the ever-present playground at nursery schools and day care centers remains a potentially powerful but neglected experiential educational tool. Early childhood teachers tend to think of the outdoor play area as merely external to more fundamental indoor activities. On the other hand, experiential educators are acutely aware of the positive influence that outdoor play activities can have on the cognitive and social development of children. In their professional literature, they emphasize the empowerment of well-planned experiential activities to reinforce and extend the aims of the educational curriculum (Yerkes, 1980). What is conspicuously absent from their discussions is the young child, that is, the child from ages 3-6. The problem seems to be an absence of programs with young children in the experiential education literature and the lack of professional training of early childhood teachers to prepare them to use outdoor experiential play as a method to develop the cognitive and affective domains in young children.

This paper will summarize educational experiments and research projects on outdoor experiential play for enhancing adventuresomeness, self-challenge, cognitive development, and socialization of young children. It will draw implications for further professional cooperation between early childhood educators and experiential educators to benefit young children and enrich their educational programs. Finally, the paper questions whether the Association of Experiential Education should take a greater role in early childhood education.

Research of Outdoor Play Environments

At first, the American "traditional playground" with slide, swings, and sandbox seemed to be the answer. However Hayward et al. (1974) discovered that the "traditional playground" affords children less cognitive and social play opportunities than "creative" or "adventure" playgrounds. What we now term the "adventure" and "creative" playgrounds are the result of 20 years of playground research in the specific areas of motor performance, socialization, playground preferences, and styles of adult playground leadership (Wuellner, 1970). These experiential play areas are different from the "traditional playground" in that they include forms, textures, and climbing structures of different heights arranged aesthetically in an outdoor setting. Manipulative materials such as cardboard boxes, toys, sand, and water are provided for the child's innate, manipulative curiosity. The play area components function to answer the child's need to explore and fantasize (Frost, et al., 1979). In 1980, a "creative-adventure" play area was developed, combining the concepts of exploration and creative pursuits, that permits children to develop their own ideas of play (Yerkes, 1980). It proved to be an effective setting for children to nurture and develop adventurous, explorative, risk-taking, and creative behavior.

M. J. Ellis, a renowned playground researcher, stated that "the essential characteristics for a playground is that it should elicit new responses from the children as they play, and that these responses increase as play proceeds" (1972, p. 4).

Gary Moore, after conducting a case study of the St. Francis Children's Activity and Achievement Center in Milwaukee, concluded that "graded challenge and paced alternatives assure the involvement of all children in play, motivate children to further development, and support a positive self-concept" (1980, p. 13).

To date, the most informative, empirical research on the value of these experiential play areas was conducted at Northern Illinois University in the Early Childhood Research Laboratory. The study was specifically designed to examine the effects of "creative-adventure" play area participation on development of visual-motor integration in 3- to 4 1/2-year-old pre-school boys and girls. Visual-motor integration is considered a fundamental skill to the level of the child's school readiness. This skill enables the child to distinguish an object from its background. A child cannot read or write without this ability. Visual-motor integration is recognized as a basic information-processing system and is accepted as a prerequisite for school readiness as evidenced by its systematic use in pre-school screening assessments, school readiness tests, and remedial programs.

The researchers, with the assistance of Big Toys Design Products, designed and constructed a "creative-adventure" playground. Building materials, toys, tools, sand, and water were added so that the children could change the environment or design their own ideas of play. The adult supervision ensured a safe play experience for each child independent of teacher domination. At the end of six weeks, teachers discovered that the children significantly increased their visual-motor integration skills. In addition,

teachers systematically noted behavior changes in the children regarding assertiveness, risk taking, and creativity. If young children can reliably achieve these skills through play, experiential educators and parents have the unique advantage of offering opportunities for both motor skill and academic readiness development in direct experience out-of-doors (Yerkes, 1980).

Eva Essa enhanced this experiential play study with her experiments in California on an early childhood, outdoor play area designed for the development of learning tasks. Having made numerous observations of children interacting with the play environment, she stated:

> So often pre-school teachers consider outdoor play as time for children to let off steam, a time away from work or learning, a time to exercise large muscles, and little else. But an outdoor environment can offer so much more, particularly if it is considered an extension of the inside classroom. (1981, p. 37)

One final factor should be noted. The image of adventuresome youth is that of boyhood. Although the playground participation in the Northern Illinois University study clearly helped all the children to improve, they were influenced differently according to gender. The group that made the largest gains were the girls who participated in the "creative-adventure" playground experience. Those girls who only had free play indoors or traditional playground experience made no significant gain in their test scores. They were the only group in the study that made no gain at all. The "creative-adventure" experiential play environment, therefore, may be particularly valuable to the physical and mental development of young girls whose opportunities for the development of visual-spatial skills seem to occur less frequently than for boys. In addition, adult models reinforce the idea that physical exploration and interaction with an experiential outdoor play environment is appropriate for both genders.

Children in a Bureaucratic World

Tom Sawyer, Huckleberry Finn, and Dorothy of *The Wizard of Oz* are among the most appealing images of childhood freedom and adventure that the American culture has created. If we are romantics at heart, we respond to these images as an expression of truth about the innate beauty of a carefree, independent childhood. Those of us who work in the out-of-doors, or with young children, keep alive the "child" in our own psyches, and try to help others to do the same. But this attitude has some troubling consequences for real children in our bureaucratic world of today. Believing that children need to have both freedom and safety to develop their own forms of play, we feel a little ambivalent about intruding upon and organizing their play experiences on the one hand, or exposing them to danger on the other. It is a striking contrast to see the enormous interest in new experiential programs for the elderly, minorities, and even corporate executives, all hoping to lead people to self-fulfillment in the world of nature. But what of the young child? It is easy to assume that children themselves "know" the things that we adults supposedly once knew and have forgotten. This comforting view, despite literary images, is untrue. Childhood is childhood in a particular culture, and it confers no

special or natural status safe from the tension of adult and social life. As adults, we have a responsibility to discover and provide the conditions for adventuresome and creative activities which enhance the full development of the child's capacity to create, explore, risk, and fantasize (Frost, et al., 1979). It is paramount that experiential education begin in early childhood.

Implications for Experiential Education and Parents

The implications of experiential play environments for experiential educators and parents are varied. First, evidence is offered that certain experiential play areas may be used as one type of outdoor resource center to the indoor classroom to reinforce fundamental learning tasks. Viewed as an extension of the classroom, teachers and parents can capitalize on the natural mode of children's learning, exploratory behavior, to enhance readiness for cognitive development. Viewed as an extension of outdoor adventure into the academic setting, it provides an effective preserve of childhood's creativity and daring. It also suggests that experiential education professionals should extend their interests to the educational programs of the young child and help teachers and parents develop these skills.

For early childhood educators, experiential education directors, and parents, child's play is a serious endeavor. Children learn from experiential play and what they learn can be enhanced by careful play environment design (Coursen, 1974). As Jeanette Stone, a playground advocate, once said, "If we are convinced of the importance of the early years of childhood, we must see outdoor play as a part of the educational process, not simply as a means for letting off steam, amusing oneself or passing time" (Ranzoni, 1970, p. 6). "Creative-adventure" experiential playgrounds provide these opportunities for the young child. But we must await more serious attention from ex-periential, early childhood educators and parents whose primary interests would be well served by further discussion, programming, and research in this area. Is experiential education only for adolescence and adulthood? What about the young child?

Section 4

Higher Education, Research, and Evaluation

Chapter 13

Experiential Higher Education and Teacher Education

The Student Teacher Who Wouldn't Go Away:

Learning From Failure

by J. Gary Knowles and Virginia B. Hoefler

In the field of traditional, pre-service teacher education, there are many opportunities for experiential learning. Entry-level education classes often require pre-service teachers to spend observation time in classrooms, to assist teachers in small group activities, to interview administrators and teachers, and to explore the context of education, teaching, and schooling. Finally, student teaching is regarded as the culminating experience of pre-service teacher education.

An implicit assumption of many teacher education programs is that pre-service teachers who enter student teaching will succeed. Some do not. Unfortunately, teacher education programs may not make provisions for the resolution of important personal issues that pre-service teachers experience during this last phase of learning to teach. Teacher education programs also may not consider the needs of those individuals who, for various reasons, fail student teaching. Further, the resolution of failure through reflection is not commonly encouraged by teacher educators.

This paper is about Angela's student teaching experience and the subsequent perplexing and enlightening events that evolved out of it. While it is about one type of experiential learning activity, there are many parallels with other experiential learning situations. Angela learned about teaching and about herself. The instructor also learned more about the needs of pre-service teachers, about aspects of the relationship between personal traits, experience, and teaching practice, and about how to resolve some of the problems associated with failure. Extensive reflection upon the circumstances surrounding the failure was a necessary component of what eventually turned out to be a valuable educational experience for Angela.

Some of the insights the instructor gleaned from Angela's experience have generic applications for other experiential education supervisors. Important questions arose about the program. Underlying the devastating experiences of failure for individuals like Angela is the need to assist them to examine their experience in light of their past behavior patterns and career choices. Particularly, it is important to support those who find the tasks difficult. In Angela's case, the hours spent discussing her experience were unavoidable and necessary. Supervisors who aspire to be caring and sensitive to the needs of their charges must commit ample time for dealing with those needs.

A petite and quiet mother of two children, Angela entered a pre-service teacher education program as a graduate student already possessing two undergraduate degrees and a variety of life experiences. Angela looked forward to being able to apply her knowledge and experiences in the field of education.

However, Angela's student teaching was not a success. She experienced an embarrassing and confusing failure that undermined her self-esteem. Failures in private are often of small consequence, but the failure of a student teacher is public knowledge (Ryan, 1986). While student-teaching peers may empathize, friends and family often ask embarrassing questions and display no knowledge about the difficulties of teaching. Lack of acceptance by family and friends, or more significantly by her peers and supervisors, could well have decimated Angela's perception of herself. To her credit, Angela overcame the obstacles resulting from the failure.

The line between Angela's experience being either constructive or destructive was very fine. According to Dewey (1938), educational experiences result in an individual's growth and the ability to obtain constructive meaning from that experience. A non-education experience is one that has no effect on the individual. Miseducational experiences are detrimental to the learner in that they inhibit further learning and prevent intelligent responses to a situation. In short, miseducation is destructive. For Angela, the fine line was between learning about herself and teaching, and losing confidence in herself and becoming bitter about the programmatic components of her training. Angela's goal after the failure was to ensure that she obtained constructive meaning from her student experience.

To describe how an unsuccessful student teaching experience became a successful learning experience, we use Angela's journal entries as illustrations and rely on the instructor's clinical notes for elaboration. In order to facilitate an understanding of the reflection process and to illustrate the generic implications for other experiential educators, we compare Angela's student teaching experience to the stages of a conceptual model of experiential education, and then discuss aspects of her experience from the perspective of the model.

Student Teaching and the Experiential Education Model

Joplin (1981) proposes a model of the experiential education process which consists of a continuous cycle of five stages: focus, challenging action, support, feedback, and debriefing. Joplin notes that, "Experience alone is insufficient to be called experiential education" (p. 17). Therefore, the model emphasizes the process of an "action-reflection" cycle in which components are deliberately planned, enacted, and reflected upon within a climate of support and feedback. In addition to the five stages, Joplin also identifies a number of characteristics typical of experiential education. Several which are pertinent to the student teaching setting include: the experience is *not* instructor-based; it is personal; it has both a product and a process orientation in which evaluation is important.

By comparing Joplin's stages with Angela's student teaching experience, we note where her experience could have become destructive, but did not. We feel that student teaching often falls short of the sort of outcomes sought by Joplin's experiential model, especially in support, feedback, and debriefing. Both Angela and the instructor put considerable effort into the processing of the experience—the failure—in much the same manner as advocated by Joplin in the last three stages of the model.

Focus

Focus is the first stage of the cycle. In this stage, the subject for study is defined and the student teacher prepares for the challenge. Angela was focused on becoming a classroom teacher. For many, the thought of student teaching conjures up feelings of either ecstasy or gloom (Ryan, 1986). Like a horse chafing at the bit, some pre-service teachers are rearing to get into the classroom while others are anxious, resistant, or worried. Angela was anxious, and her fears proved to be more substantial than was apparent at the beginning of the program.

The context of Angela's experience is significant. The Master of Education and Teacher Certification Program in which Angela participated encouraged close relationships with supervisors and cooperating teachers, had extensive field experiences, and encouraged the development of reflective and critical teachers. Early experiences in the year-long program sought familiarization with classrooms through fieldwork assignments. For the duration of her participation in the program, and afterwards, Angela maintained a journal, the basis for much of this analysis.

There were differences between Angela's views of schools and the views of the other pre-service teachers. Angela considered herself a "radical." She had read the works of educational reformers such as Holt and Illich, and she disagreed with the general social organization of schools. She was strongly oriented toward a "cognitive process" model of curriculum, learning, and teaching (see Eisner, 1979). Angela was eager to learn, as one of her early journal entries indicated:

> In the first few weeks of the class we discussed teaching from an intellectual approach. We analyzed rationales for teaching and discussed the ways choice of

rationale influence deeper consideration of the implications of teaching practice than I had previously considered. I thoroughly enjoyed these class discussions. (September 11)

Near the end of the first quarter, Angela began to express dissatisfaction with school structure. She was unhappy with a number of things she saw in the classroom and began to sense some of the incongruities between herself and the public school system. Part of her reactions stemmed from feelings about her own negative experience as a junior high student:

> I have long had philosophical problems with school organization—probably founded in past school experiences. But what I have seen here so far hasn't changed my mind about schools as places to *learn*. This looks to me like a situation that is counter-productive to learning. Students learn in spite of the setting. Teachers have to spend more time and effort maintaining some kind of order. Individual needs are impossible to address. I have some negative feelings about this school and class. Suddenly, I am back in eighth grade, in physical science, a class I didn't like. (November 10)

While Angela was focused on becoming a teacher, there were incongruities between her views of schools, her experiences, her own expectations, and those of the instructors and her peers. The focus stage serves to prepare the pre-service teacher for the next stage of challenging action. Though Angela satisfactorily completed the training provided in the first quarter of the program, she may not have been adequately prepared for the next stage, due to the discrepancies between her personal expectations and her prior experience.

Challenging Action

In the second stage of the cycle, challenging action, the increased responsibility placed upon the participant should not be beyond the capacity of the student, either as a result of background or innate disabilities. It is important that the situation is "appropriate to the learner and it is the teacher's responsibility to design it accordingly" (Joplin, 1981, pp. 18-19).

Early in the first quarter, Angela was placed in a medium-sized, urban, junior high school. She had an undergraduate major in Physical Geography and a minor in Environmental Studies, but because she lacked course preparation for secondary certification, she was advised to pursue a Middle School Teaching Certificate. As a result, her teaching subject areas were more general: Science and Social Studies instead of Environmental Studies and Physical Geography.

Angela's student teaching assignment did not "fit" her perceived needs and expectations. With trepidation she accepted the placement in Physical Science and Social Studies. She expressed anxiety in her journal:

> I have been assigned to a junior high, teaching Physical Science and American History (my two worst subjects). I don't know what to think about this! It seems pretty far off from the environmental studies and physical geography that I am prepared for. I should talk to someone about this, but I don't know what else to do. (October 15)

As a young student, Angela had experienced difficulties in a variety of educational settings. She had been intimidated by harsh teachers, troubled by inabilities to conform, and frustrated by the school environment.

She expressed a number of concerns as she reflected on her first day in the school where she would be student teaching:

> First visit to [the] assigned school. This is hard. Not only do I have to become acquainted with a foreign environment (junior high), but to a new city and driving on the freeway, too. I have lived in a rural area for so long that city traffic and freeways make me nervous. [I] arrived at the school early. I am awed by the numbers and the size of the students. The map of the school is confusing. I have trouble finding where I am supposed to be. I feel awkward and out of place here. The crowds and noise disoriented me for a while. I haven't been inside a junior high since I was 15—and I hated school then. I am reminded of all the "first days" of school as a kid, and how frightened I was then. (November 2)

Although reserved, Angela quickly made friends with her cooperating teachers. She initially felt good about her major cooperating teacher and admired his interest in "discovery" teaching:

> I enjoyed discussing ideas with him. He is all for me trying out whatever ideas I have. We both believe in presenting science in interesting and concrete ways, using laboratory experiments. His approach is to use a "discrepant event" to stimulate discussion and discovery by the students. (November 4)

The beginning of the second, ten-week quarter arrived, and Angela's instructor and cooperating teachers felt that she was academically prepared for her student teaching assignment. Angela, herself, still had some reservations, but was determined to "carry on." She had spent the end-of-quarter break doing extensive lesson plans. The cooperat-

ing teacher approved of her work: "He was impressed with the number of experiments I had planned to use," she noted (December 28). Despite her efforts, the first day of teaching came as a considerable shock:

> I found out really quickly that teaching wasn't what I'd thought it would be. Instead of being able to enjoy presenting an interesting lesson, I was sidetracked by administrative details, disruptive students, and a general unwillingness on the part of the students to take the class seriously. (January 5)

For the next few weeks Angela struggled with her Physical Science classes. Angela thought the classroom was too crowded, the students inattentive and disruptive, and the complexities of teaching highly demanding. She found herself overwhelmed by the task of relating to so many people at once. The instructor noticed Angela was having difficulties making her presence felt which meant that she could not get instructions across to students because they were not listening. Angela needed to broaden her focus in the classroom She concentrated on just a few students and seemed unaware of the rest. Her major problem appeared to be an inability to teach to the whole class.

Angela continued to look for ways to make the lesson materials interesting to the students but began to feel frustrated by her inability to capture their interest. She did have significant success with a few students, particularly those whom the cooperating teacher had not been able to reach. Her strengths in the classroom were her interest in individual students and her ability to encourage them on a one-to-one basis.

Angela appeared to be under a great deal of stress. The instructor felt Angela was exhausting herself, although she would not acknowledge it. But even though the experience in the classroom was increasingly taking its toll, she was able to muse over the situation: "It is looking like this job is really advanced baby-sitting, and I never liked beginning baby-sitting, or intermediate baby-sitting either" (January 24).

By the sixth week of student teaching, Angela felt considerable pressure. Her experiments and demonstrations were still well organized but her classroom presence had changed little. The vice principal was increasingly aware of her discipline problems and the principal predicted that parents would soon complain about her teaching. Considerable close support during this period was provided by the cooperating teacher, but because his management style was so similar to Angela's, he was not able to provide the concrete suggestions that she needed to remedy her discipline problems. Angela's journal entries reflected an increasing despondency:

> I realized that I'm not doing as well as a student teacher is expected. Controlling the students is much more difficult than I had imagined it could be. (February 6)

> I left class today feeling drained and dissatisfied.... I'm having to be so mean because of a few troublemakers. I'm afraid I'll lose the good students. Some of the kids are getting more "mouthy." I must look angry and frustrated. (February 11)

> Yuck! Some days I wonder "Why bother?" Managing these kids is an all-day fight.... I have to start over with them every day. They all did very poorly on the test. So if the kids are not here to learn, don't want to learn, and don't learn: why are they here? (February 13)

Angela's classes were observed several times during the sixth and seventh weeks. After a series of conferences with Angela, the cooperating teacher, and the vice-principal, the instructor suggested that Angela withdraw from student teaching. Her response was simply an uncertain: "I think that I agree" (February 16). Angela's uncertainty about the situation surfaced again several days later when she reflected on her interaction with the university instructor: "He is trying to be nice, but he says he is going to pull me out of the class. I don't know what to say. I guess he is right. We have tried everything" (February 19).

Angela withdrew from student teaching. The last day at the school was difficult for her:

> I finished up the lessons I had started. [The cooperating teachers] are reluctant to take back their classes. I still have the grades to do, and we have a few projects to finish that we were sharing. I guess I do feel relieved to not have to deal with the situation any more. But, I also feel let-down, cast adrift. I had a firm goal to be working toward, and now I am not at all sure of myself. I had given the impression that I would not quit, but would keep trying to succeed—and then I quit anyway. (February 20)

In challenging action stage of pre-service education, Angela was placed in a situation where the focused problem (in this case, classroom teaching) could not be avoided. Angela experienced difficulties in carrying out her teaching responsibilities. She soon noticed a number of incongruities between her expectations and the realities of public school teaching. To some extent, the anomaly of Angela's situation relates to the lack of satisfaction and "fit" that she felt with her student teaching assignment.

Support and Feedback

Support and feedback are intertwined and are the third and fourth stages of Joplin's model. Throughout the focusing and challenging action stages of the experience, the two stages of support and feedback are accomplished simultaneously. Angela had several layers of support and feedback. As in all student teaching situations, the cooperating teacher played an important and formative role in the development of the beginning teacher. Angela's teacher encouraged her to experiment with lesson designs and activities and regularly gave his perceptions of the classroom events. The school administrators supported her efforts and provided encouragement and advice.

Neither the teacher nor the vice principal were judgmental in their comments to Angela. The program facilitators did not intend to make a comparison with other student teachers or to make a summative evaluation of Angela's teaching; instead, they focused on defining and confronting problems in order to correct them. The university instructor's expressed aim was to provide formative comments on her performance. He sought ways in which her difficulties could be erased. As Angela's student teaching experience progressed, the instructor's feedback became more critical.

Another layer of formative support and feedback was provided by Angela's student-teaching peers who had the responsibility of observing one another. However, they tended to gloss over her difficulties, perhaps for fear of acknowledging their own similar problems. Still, Angela appreciated their

concern and the sense of camaraderie that counteracted the isolation student teachers sometimes experience.

Debriefing

Debriefing is the final stage of Joplin's model. The major element of this stage is reflection on the challenging action of the preceding phase. For learning to be educational, rather than miseducational, the learner must make connections between knowledge and experience. The student must seek meaning from the experience through reflection. To that end, Angela's extensive journal writing seemed to provide a platform for reflection and a vehicle for therapy (see Progoff, 1975). In potentially miseducational situations such as Angela's, the instructor's guidance is essential. The teacher education program had no provisions for dealing with failure and Angela's instructor felt he was ill prepared to help her. More importantly, the instructor had not anticipated the degree of support Angela required and the extensive period of time she would need to overcome her feelings of failure.

Angela and the instructor discussed issues of personality, her suitability for teaching, and her personal background on a number of occasions during this period. The question of Angela's suitability for teaching continued to concern the instructor. To what extent did Angela's personality—her personal style in the classroom—present difficulties for her in the teaching situation? Was her goal to become a teacher realistic? The instructor became aware of a need to develop methods for advanced recognition of personal predispositions, such as Angela's, that hinder preservice teachers. He also recognized the need for provisions within the program to specifically assist pre-service teachers to overcome negative aspects of their past experiences in the school, which resulted in their long period of observation in the classroom. This is the "apprenticeship of observation" mentioned by Lortie (1975) in his pivotal study of teacher socialization.

At this point, students who fail student teaching usually either fade from the scene and forget about education, set in motion an appeal, or initiate legal action. Angela was unwilling to drop out of the education scene. She was too involved and too successful in her other university studies to believe that failure in one area would mean failure in another. She did not feel that anyone was "at fault" or that anyone had "wronged" her. But she did feel distraught and confused, and in addition to humiliation, Angela felt profound disappointment. She had intended to make an important mid-life career change and now she did not know what to do. Her response was to seek advice and reassurance from her university instructor, for it was he who had first recognized her problems.

A few days after the withdrawal, Angela stormed into the office of her instructor. "You can't make me quit!" she exclaimed. She was going to cry, but she didn't. Surprised by this outburst and concerned about her failure, the instructor tried to help her reconcile the situation. As her supervisor, he felt responsible for her, and yet inadequate to address her frustration and disappointment. Not having any immediate solutions to the dilemma, they began simply by talking. That meeting was the beginning of the extensive debriefing.

The debriefing began as an attempt on Angela's part to readjust her expectations, plan for her academic career, overcome the disappointment and humiliation, and rid herself of the fears and anger she harbored. On the instructor's part, it was an attempt to placate a fearful and angry woman. Further, he was concerned for her well-being. He stated that "the extreme difficulties associated with the classroom 'failure' were not really failure. Instead, the event was a realization [that Angela had some] difficulties communicating with junior high students, and that perhaps she would feel more comfortable teaching another age group" (February 27). He suggested that she visit and observe classrooms of different grade levels, from elementary school through junior college, believing that she might feel more comfortable with other grades

Angela was critical of the lack of depth in which some of the foundational topics in education were treated in the university classroom:

> I don't think I was prepared for the real classroom. The university classes didn't provide the kinds of practical information that I need. I'm at a disadvantage now because you've expected me to know things that weren't part of the program. (March 4)

She felt that there was not enough focus on the practical aspects of teaching—which resulted in her not knowing how to implement the theories and philosophies of education in which she believed—and that she needed extensive help in discipline and classroom management. Later, she took steps in correcting this area of concern by enrolling in and completing a classroom management course.

It was the instructor's opinion that a number of personality traits and her personal experiences had contributed negatively to her teaching experience. "You are not assertive enough," he told her once. She agreed that becoming more assertive meant changing some personality traits, but she did not agree—and rightly so—that behaviors were "set in concrete":

> I don't believe you. The ability to teach is learned. People are not born with a teacher personality. They learn to be that way.... You have made me look at myself in a different way, though. I never realized how ineffectual my self-presentation was. I had thought being unassuming was polite and correct and I'd never considered whether or not it was appropriate in all situations. (March 4)

The instructor felt Angela evidenced patterns of thinking about schools, teaching, and education that had been established in childhood and during her school experiences as a student, and that those experiences affected her classroom actions (see Knowles, 1992). His comments to Angela focused on her view of herself-as-teacher:

> You have more conceptions of what you did *not* want to be, rather than what you want to be as a teacher. You have established those behaviors that you did not want to replicate, rather than those you want to implement. You think it's important not to be overly assertive; not to squelch creativity; not to act like most of the teachers you remember; not to be fault finding; and not to be insistent on conformity; in other words, not to be like most of the teachers you remember. Instead, you need to think of some positive examples of what you want to be. (March 15)

Angela had some difficulty with these assertions. On the one hand, she held some very strong views about education. On the other hand, she was not able to match her views with supporting actions in the classroom. The instructor's perspective challenged her assumptions and she began to question her impulse to become a teacher:

> Maybe you are right. I don't have the personality to be a teacher. I don't have the aptitude or the desire to become like other teachers—in things that I perceive to be negative and counter-productive to the learning process. (March 23)

Angela continued to work on the problem of her student teaching experience. She continued to question her motives, her assumptions, and her performance in the classroom. She observed other teachers and questioned them about their perceptions of their work. She continued to observe her peers. She tried to compare what she saw in other teachers with what she had observed in her own attempts at teaching. Eventually, Angela came to understand many more aspects of teaching, of schools, and of herself. By the end of the school year, Angela had come to view her student teaching as an important learning experience, even though it had not yielded the expected results. An entry in her journal indicated her new-found feelings: "Maybe I have learned things from this that I couldn't have learned otherwise—maybe I needed the shock treatment of returning to junior high school in order find myself!" (May 24).

Learning from Failure

Student teaching, when viewed as experiential learning, can be usefully analyzed with a model such as Joplin's. By looking at the experience in this way, certain weaknesses and strengths in the teacher education program become evident. Our sense is that the implications of Angela's experiences may be universal and that these weaknesses are common in other experiential education programs.

There were incongruities between the stages of the Joplin model and the characteristics of the program and of Angela's preparation for it. In the focus stage, discrepancies between the beliefs and expectations of Angela and the realities of public school teaching were evident. In the challenging action stage, we observed a lack of fit between Angela's placement and her capabilities and expectations. Ideally, her placement would have been exactly aligned to her subject area expertise, and her responsibilities in the classroom would have been more slowly and incrementally increased.

The two stages of support and feedback displayed some of the strengths of the program. Angela received considerable feedback and support from the university instructors, the cooperating teacher, the school administration, and her student teaching peers. But the strongest, and perhaps most unique, aspect of her experience was in the final debriefing stage—a stage that is absent in many programs—although Angela and the instructor did not think at the time about "debriefing." By the end of the academic year, they had discussed most of the significant areas of Angela's teaching practice in depth. Over six months, Angela and the instructor spent nearly 100 hours together as they reviewed aspects of her experience: the suitability of the placement; the incongruities of Angela's expectations with school realities; and the influences of her background on her personality and its

resultant effects on her teaching. Angela visited with the instructor several times a week for several weeks, then more irregularly as time passed. Often they talked for an hour or so, and sometimes over the telephone. Later, they spent long hours writing about the experience. The extended debriefing helped transform Angela's experience from one of potential miseducation to one of education.

To what degree is the student teaching experience the end of pre-service preparation? In one view, student teaching is the final stage. Either you pass or fail, and failed student teachers, for all intents and purposes, no longer exist! Our position is that student teaching is the challenging action phase in an experiential education model, and therefore it is *not* the end. The final stage is reflection upon the action. There was no structured program of "debriefing" included in the pre-service teacher education program. Angela and her instructor accidentally created an embryonic example of successful debriefing stage. In a structured debriefing stage, questions for reflection would be provided to the student teacher. A comprehensive consideration of all the strengths and weaknesses found in the classroom experience would be an integral component of the reflection. Instructors who are ill prepared to deal with the reflective requirements of an action-reflection experience will feel inadequate to deal with failed students. Students who are trained to reflect upon the focus and challenging actions stages of their experience will be better prepared to deal with the challenges—so that even failed student teaching experiences can be educative.

English in the Treetops

by Peter G. Beidler

"I can't do it. I just can't. Don't make me try. It's too far down. Please don't make me go across." The horizontal, 300-foot rope stretched in front of the waterfall and over the rocks a hundred feet below. It looked like a spider's filament, and Moji was scared.

I want to tell you about Moji, and about why she and eight other Lehigh University freshmen were with me in the woods in northern Pennsylvania on a chilly day in April 1985, looking at a Tyrolean Traverse stretched across Angel Falls.

Vacations and Bad Teaching

I teach English at Lehigh University. I have done so for twenty years. One of my favorite courses is the one I teach almost every semester: good old English I, the basic required composition course. I do not love grading papers, but I do love first-semester freshman students. Well, most of them.

The Spring, 1985, course was a particular challenge. For one thing, with 27 freshmen it was too big for one section but not big enough for a split into two. For another, it was an uncomfortable mix of students. Approximately a third of the students were first-semester freshmen who for one reason or another had not enrolled at Lehigh in the fall semester. Another third was transfer students, and the final third had failed the course at least once and were trying again.

Mojisola Shabi was one of these last. I later learned that Mojisola—who preferred to be called Moji—was born in Brooklyn to parents who had been born in Africa. She was an engineering student, and writing was *not* her favorite activity.

During the first week of classes I told my students my basic expectations in a freshman theme: a bold thesis, specific support for the thesis, and a clear organizational principle. Then in the second week I had my students write an in-class theme on one of several topics. The topic Moji chose to write on was "College: A Vacation from Home?" I reproduce the theme below, purged of the twenty-odd spelling and punctuation errors it contained:

College Is Not a Vacation

When entering college for the first time the college freshman is filled with anxiety, with exhilaration, and with anticipation.

And why not? He is about to embark on an experience which most likely will never occur again in his life. For the first time he is pretty much on his own. Even though mom and dad are a phone call away or a two-hour bus ride away, he is going to have to do things which he never had to do, i.e. the laundry, and make decisions he never had to make. The thought of all this is exciting so that it feels that one is on a vacation, on a break. Things like throwing out the garbage, walking the dog, or watching over the younger siblings are left ninety to a hundred miles away. One feels that this is the time for me and for me to do what I want.

A vacation, in my opinion, is a break; a break in a length of time or work. A vacation is used to relax, to enjoy, and most important to keep worries and problems out of one's mind. A vacation should be a selfish act in that it is a time for you and the ones you are with to pamper and enjoy themselves.

I'm sure most people would agree with me to a certain extent, from the busy executive to pressured student. But I feel college students, in particular, college freshmen, feel that the university is a "break" from the pressures and worries of home, but are rudely awakened by the fact that college is not quite a vacation and may present more problems than are at home.

But all this could be taken to an extreme. The freshman goes out every weekend and socializing and getting to know people become Priority One. He seems to forget why he is at college in the first and foremost place. But when finals and grades come around his memory is jolted if not kicked. This is the rude awakening. The freshman's retention in the university is at stake, which could trigger a chain reaction such as affect scholarships, future grants, and maybe his future in general

After first semester of freshmen year he realizes the vacation is over. In college one would probably have to deal with more pressure than he will ever experience after school. So in actuality life is going to be the vacation from college.

It was easy enough to see why Moji had failed English I the first time. Because she did not get around to stating a thesis until the end of her fourth paragraph ("college is not quite a vacation and may present more problems than are at home") and then quickly abandoned it, her theme never got very far. Because she offered no specific evidence or personal examples to support any thesis, her theme failed to be convincing or memorable. Because she had no organizational principle, her theme wandered with no apparent aim. Because she never decided on a single point of view, her "one's" and "me's" and "you's" and "he's" competed for control. Her logic was faulty (is doing one's laundry an activity usually associated with vacation time?). Her antecedents were vague (just what is "all this" that could be taken to an extreme?). Her thought processes were undeveloped (just why, in that last sentence, is "life," whatever that is, going to be a "vacation from college"?).

Moji had a problem.

As her English teacher, I had a problem, also. How was I to help her to improve her writing? How was I to take a young woman who had so little to say and help her to say it better?

With twenty years of experience behind me, I had some ideas about how to proceed. The comment I wrote on that first theme turned out to be longer than the theme itself. I explained how Moji must state a thesis earlier in the theme. I wrote a new introduction for her, one which contained both a thesis statement and an organizational plan. I explained how she should draw from specific experiences she had had last semester that showed how unwise it was to consider college as merely a vacation from home.

My comments were useful, I think, and Moji's revision on that theme as well as her next theme on "bad teaching" were somewhat better than her first effort. Still, something was missing. There was no fire to her writing. It was heartless, perfunctory, and mechanical.

After several weeks of having to read heartless, perfunctory, and mechanical writ-

Moji climbing to the high ropes course. "Now what?" (Tim Mayer)

ing from Moji and her classmates, I decided that at least part of the trouble was the writing assignments I was making. How much fire could I expect from those same old theme topics? We English teachers are all familiar with such topics: peer pressure; television; my favorite teacher; my roommate; racism; campus sports; the food in the freshman dining hall. In the hands of our better students, those topics yield pretty decent themes. Each can be dealt with in a couple of pages. Each can be approached in many different ways. Each encourages students to draw from personal experience.

But I was getting bored with reading about such topics, and I sensed that my students were getting bored with writing about them. I decided it was time for a change.

The Call of the Wild

As a result of a series of circumstances I cannot take the space to explain here, I had been invited to give a talk at the October, 1984, annual convention of the Association for Experiential Education at Lake Junaluska, North Carolina. While there, I talked with a number of people about what experiential education was all about. I learned about things called Outward Bound and wilderness treks and high ropes courses. Even then I found myself wondering if there might be ways to work experiential education into the freshman English curriculum.

I knew that students often did their best writing if they wrote about what they knew best—their own personal experiences. In practice, that usually meant having them draw from their memories.

Might it be a useful experiment, I wondered, if I provided experiences for my students that

they could then write about in their themes? If so, then there would be no need to rely on fuzzy recall of unmemorable experiences.

I decided to talk with some of the people I had met at the Association for Experiential Education in North Carolina. I got in touch with Bill Proudman, director of the Quest Program at Bloomsburg University in northern Pennsylvania. The Quest people routinely organized adventure education courses for Bloomsburg students. They also did contract courses for people not associated with Bloomsburg. I asked Bill if he could help me provide some memorable experiences for some Lehigh freshman English students.

Bill had heard my talk at Lake Junaluska and with very little ado said, "Sure."

Further talks with him and with his assistant, Heidi Hammel, resulted in our reaching agreement on a two-day, three-night, course just before Easter. We would take a two-hour bus trip from Bethlehem to Bloomsburg on Wednesday afternoon and, after some orientation and get-acquainted activities that night, sleep in the main lodge of an unused Girl Scout camp near Bloomsburg. Later we would split into two groups. Each group would complete a team-building "get the group over the log" exercise, a Trust Fall, a two-person tight-rope balance, a low-ropes course, a high-ropes course, a Tyrolean Traverse. We would also have some individual time alone in the woods, as well as camping experience. At the end of two days, the two groups would get together again to debrief, turn in their equipment, and leave Saturday morning. Bill Proudman would work with one group and Heidi Hammel with the other.

Having never done any of the activities Bill and Heidi described, I was not sure what

I was getting us into, but it sounded like fun and it sounded like the kind of experience that could make for some interesting writing. I asked a few questions about safety, then told Bill and Heidi that I needed two weeks to work on it at my end before I would let them know.

Working on it at my end meant two things: money and students. My first task was to convince my dean and provost that the $65 per student (including instruction, meals, equipment, lodging, and transportation) was something worth supporting. They replied quickly and affirmatively.

It was tricky business convincing my students that they should give up three days of their Easter break to join me in the woods to take part in some experiences seemingly irrelevant to freshman English. I think the worst moment came when I told them they would not be able to take a shower during the whole time. But, then, this trip was strictly voluntary and they were free to choose without reward or penalty. Those who opted for a traditional Easter vacation would return to a routine much as they had enjoyed since the beginning of the semester. For those who went to Bloomsburg I would cancel the next five regularly scheduled classes and see that they got credit for two themes from the experience: one would be for keeping a journal while at Bloomsburg; the other would be for writing a theme on something they learned there. Most of my students seemed interested but, at the same time were puzzled and hesitant. I called Heidi and told her about the puzzlement and the hesitation.

Heidi Hammel suggested that if it would help my students understand what to expect, she could visit Lehigh to show them some slides, to explain more about the program, and to answer any questions they might have. I was happy to accept her offer because I had never met Heidi and I had number of questions myself, the kinds of questions it is easier to ask face-to-face than over the phone.

She came to my class and we had a good session. Her slides were enticing but more than a little frightening. Heidi and I assured my students that none of them would be forced into any activity they preferred not to do.

In the end, two-thirds of my students joined the Bloomsburg expedition. Of those who did not, several had religious conflicts; others had sports conflicts; one or two were afraid.

Moji was afraid, but she went.

From Dusk to First Light.

The bus ride to Bloomsburg was depressing for all of us. At four o'clock that Wednesday afternoon most of the other Lehigh students were heading home to their families, and here we were—off to the wilds. Although we had met together three hours a week for two months in the classroom, we did not know each other well. I was the only one in the class who knew everyone's name. We were sullen and quiet as we dutifully ate the dry turkey sandwiches and the apples that were to be our supper. Looking through the windows of the Lehigh bus, we watched dark clouds gather over a misty dusk.

Upon our arrival in Bloomsburg two hours later, Heidi greeted us. Soon she, Bill, two interns, and eighteen shy Lehigh folk stepped into two vans with overnight bags and headed toward the Girl Scout lodge.

Once there, we played some ice-breaking games. While these made us feel silly at times and were a little threatening, we were pleased with our successes. Group members discovered that they had a lot in common.

Then we had a snack, unrolled sleeping bags and mattresses, and went to bed. We kept the lights on for an hour or so for those who wanted to begin writing in their journals.

Moji Keeps a Journal

Moji began writing that night, lying in her sleeping bag. I shall let her words tell most of her story, along with a few comments interspersed from me. Here is what Moji wrote that first night:

April 3. Hi there. I've decided to write my journal to someone. No one in particular, not even Prof. Beidler. But I think it will be easier for me to express myself if I think someone—anyone—will be reading this.

Well, I must say it has already been an interesting and thought-provoking start. The staff members, Bill, Heidi, Nancy, and Frances, are really nice people. They seem to have their act together emotionally and mentally. I mean, they seem very satisfied with what they are doing with their lives.

I can't say exactly how I feel about being here in Bloomsburg. Like Bill said, we could be worrying about the amount of work we have to do before school resumes. How do I feel about not being home and not *finally* seeing my friends from high school?

I feel excited. I've never done any kind of camping before. I can deal with sleeping on the floor, no shower or toilet, and no concept of time because it is like when my family and I go to Africa, where we live without any electricity at times.

The part that scares me is being able to handle the activities mentally and emotion-

ally. Will I crack up and chicken out? Will I ever realize and utilize my potential? Now that I think about it that is what I am really afraid of. I have been told that I have potential to go far and do great things, but I never seem to get past the average. I hope I get past it during this trip. My arm is getting tired so I'll talk to you later. Bye.

The next morning we split into two groups. One group went off with Bill. I was in Heidi's group. So was Moji. Heidi's group headed off to the low-ropes course. The low-ropes course involved several group activities. We had to help each other climb over a horizontal log, eight feet high. Then we did the Trust Fall in which each of us, in turn, stood on a four-foot-high stump, closed our eyes, and fell backwards into the arms of others in the group.

The most memorable event in the low-ropes course was the one we came to call "two on a tightrope." Two cables, three feet off the ground, were tied to a single tree at one end but to two different trees, some twelve feet apart, at the other end. The task was to start with a partner on separate cables at the apex of the "V" and gradually move outward. Moji and Christine were partners for this one, but had a hard time of it. When they fell off, Moji bruised her arm. Her second attempt with Tim was a little more successful.

Then we moved on to the high-ropes course. Our task was to shimmy up a steeply inclined log, climb some pegs to reach the proper level, then walk through a route in the treetops on steel cables. We were always secured by seat harnesses into safety cables so that if we fell off, we would dangle rather than crash to the ground. Almost all of us— me included—fell off at least one of the legs of the course. But we had been trained how to pull ourselves back up again. I followed Moji, and I could see how scared she was. She really did not want to be on the high ropes. But she was up there, and she completed the course. She wrote the following journal entry immediately after she reached the ground.

A sigh of relief is the only sound I can make. The feelings I was going through just now I only remember feeling when I was little under the age of 10. During that age period when I was told or saw something scary or frightening I would be terrified for lack of understanding or comprehension.

Later. I didn't finish my last entry because I was numb from the experience of the ropes course. Now I think I'm ready to write.

At times I feel stupid because I think everyone in my group must have done something similar to if not exactly like what we've been doing for the past couple of days. I mean, at one point during the ropes course I started to cry. I was terrified, even though I logically knew I was perfectly safe. I felt like a little child. I wanted to be safe on the ground hugging something like a tree or a stuffed bear or a person.

Later still. A lot of things that happened on the trip will stay with me for a while. One thing I realized was that it was all right to cry. I'm the type of person who will not cry no matter what. I probably feel it is a sign of weakness or that crying is a stereotypical characteristic of women. And I don't like to be classified. But when I was on the high ropes and had to change hands on the "hourglass" part I felt like I was going to die. I thought, this must be what

it feels like just before you die. That may seem a little harsh, but for some reason something told my mind that even though the high ropes course was probably 98.5% safe, I felt that 1.5% danger would appear when I was up in the trees.

All this sounds ridiculous considering I was perfectly safe, but I took the course as more than just a game or exercise. It was test, an aptitude test or personality test. As for failing or passing, I think I passed with flying colors.

That night we slept at the camp site across a stream. We were not in tents. Our only cover was a large orange tarp strung over a rope between two trees, open on all four sides. We stayed mostly dry when it rained a little, but most of us were uncomfortably cold, even in our goose-down sleeping bags.

The next morning we got up at first light again, had a hasty breakfast of oatmeal and hot chocolate, packed up our gear, and began the one-mile trek to Angel Falls. When we got there, we spotted the Tyrolean Traverse the other group had set up the previous day while we were on the ropes course. Moji panicked when she saw it. "I can't do it," she said.

April 4. My handwriting is messier than usual because I'm freezing. I just got off the traverse ten minutes ago. I am in shock. I'm shocked I actually went through with it and had a minimal amount of fear. I think I was more terrified on the high ropes course than on the traverse. The ropes course helped me deal with my fears.

I wish I wasn't so chicken. I'm not used to being a follower, but in this case I really have no choice. I guess one can't always be in the head. I don't think that anyone in my group thinks less of me because I am not the fastest or the strongest. If anything, they should be proud—no, I should be proud of myself—because I attempted and completed feats that I never really saw myself doing. I've always wanted to go camping and hiking and do almost dangerous things, but I just thought about doing them. "Someday I will," I said. But in the back of my mind I was really thinking, "Fat chance."

On the hike back from the Tyrolean Traverse, we did a Blind Man's Walk. Moji paired off with Christine again. Moji put on a blindfold, and Christine took her by the hand and led her some 20 yards through the woods to a certain tree or rock. Moji was to pay close enough attention with other senses—to the terrain, to the sounds, to the feel of the rock or tree—that after having been led back to the point of origin, she could remove the blindfold and set out to find that same tree or rock. After Moji had successfully performed the experiment, then Christine put on the blindfold and Moji led her to a different place in the woods.

One of the best parts of the trip was the "time alone." Heidi took each of us to a place off the main trail where we were to spend nearly two hours alone, out of sight of, and unable to hear, anyone else. We were to think or write or listen to the sounds of the woods. Moji used part of her time to write:

> I am now sitting all by myself in a clearing in the woods. Believe it or not, but I am not afraid. I like it a lot. I can talk out loud without anyone thinking I am crazy. I've been alone many times, for many reasons, but this is the first time I'm sincerely and truly enjoying it. I've always wanted to be alone in the woods and feel safe about it. There is something romantic and dramatic about just sitting and writing in the woods. It's like a scene from a movie or a play.

Friday night, the two groups got back together and we were all asked to respond orally to several questions: What had we learned? What was the high point of our experience? What did we like best about the person sitting to the right of us around the circle? Moji was impressed with what the group revealed and managed to say a few things beautifully herself. At the final meeting, she spoke with considerable eloquence about what the trip had meant to her. Some of that eloquence found its way into her journal:

> I found that when I am faced with an obstacle that makes me hesitant, if I work toward getting past, over, under, or through the obstacle, I surprise myself. I find I have qualities and abilities I never put to use. From the beginning of this trip I was worried about making a fool of myself, of looking like a wimp, of failing. But even in the things I did badly I realize I didn't fail, because each time I learned something. Example: two on a tightrope. I think the reason Christine and I didn't do well, even when I felt calm and balanced, was that there was this small part of me which didn't believe I could do it. Even though I was, with all my might, trying to concentrate on balancing, this little voice said, "You'll never make it." But later, when I did make it halfway with Tim, I only felt confident when I look in his eyes. He was smiling and that smile was louder than the little voice.

I shall quote no more from Moji's journal. That journal was of particular interest to me not only because of what it said, but also because Moji was writing differently in that journal than she had in any other writing she had done for me that semester. Most of the awkwardness was gone. She wrote with feeling and conviction about an experience that obviously meant something to her. Did she write with grace, feeling, and conviction because, for once, she had experienced something that did mean something to her? Or was it simply that, freed from the necessity to write a theme, that artificial exercise with a thesis, support, and an organizational pattern, Moji's writing style was able to flourish like a tulip released from the burden of a flat rock?

From Journal to Theme

Naturally I was curious to see whether Moji would write as well when she did her theme based on the Bloomsburg experience. For this theme, I asked my students to suggest several topics they would like to write on, and I would pick the one with which I thought they might best succeed with. Moji asked if she could write about her "internal metamorphosis." I told her I thought it would be a fine topic. Here is the theme she turned in.

Internal Metamorphosis

When Pete first mentioned the trip to Bloomsburg I was filled with excitement and anticipation because I had never been camping before. But as the day of the trip got closer my excitement lessened and I became worried. I was worried about what this trip might reveal about myself because after Heidi's slide presentation I began to think of the Quest program as a type of self-awareness program. So with that thought in my mind I began to worry whether I would come out of the three-day excursion with anything worthwhile or if I would actually learn something. Well, I must say I returned from Bloomsburg with a lot in tow. Aside from my luggage, I came back with stories of a new and excit-

ing experience, but most important I returned with a new me. No, it wasn't that I changed my hair or lost weight, but I was different inside. I was different in the way I acted, in how I felt, and in what I thought. Because of the trip I've returned to Lehigh with self-confidence, with a sense of appreciation of the things around me, and with a realization of my potential.

When the bus left the front of Lehigh's University Center on that Wednesday afternoon, I was a girl who was lacking in self-confidence and who constantly wondered what others thought of her. Now I am someone who cares very little what others may think of how I look, act, or dress. I think this new confidence in me came from the support I got from group in Bloomsburg. When I was on the high ropes course I was ready to stop in the middle of the course and turn back. But each time I hesitated to go on I found myself surrounded by people who for some reason had faith in my completing the course. At one point in the course I was scared to move and just felt like crying, yet from behind me I had Pete telling me to take my time. I also had Tim ahead of me advising on what to do and others on the ground yelling encouragement. At that moment I thought that here is a group of people who didn't even know me, yet were confident I could finish the course. I later realized that I couldn't always rely on others to tell me that I am capable. I had to tell myself. I had to develop the confidence.

After leaving Bloomsburg I became more deliberative. Instead of always looking as if I'm in a rush to be somewhere, I now take my time and am more observant. I'll stop and listen to birds or look more closely at clouds. This all may sound corny and not terribly profound, but the important thing is that I do stop to take notice. This probably grew from my blind walk in the woods because in that activity I had to be more aware of the little things in my surroundings, without sight. So when my blindfold was removed I had to find my way back to where I was previously led. In order to do so I had to recall things like bumps in the path and textures of bark. So now when I walk around campus my pace is less hurried and more leisurely.

I think the biggest change within me I've experienced is that I now realize my potential. For years, teachers and friends have told me I had such potential and that they could see me being famous and doing great things. Yet in school I only did a minimum amount of work and did well. And outside of the security of school I would hesitate in trying new things for fear of not being capable. But Quest helped me prove that I had capacities I had never used. The tyrolean traverse seemed impossible for me to attempt emotionally and physically. Yet when I was harnessed in and hooked on to the rope there was no turning back. I had no choice but to go forward. And when I finished exhaustedly I was amazed at how my terror before going across had turned had turned into an exhiliration of being 100 feet in the air next to a waterfall. I have to admit my realization of my potential was forced upon me in that I was put into situations in which I had no choice but to go on. But the fact that I did go on and sometimes succeeded showed me that in my past there was something mental stopping me from attempting challenging endeavors, whether physical, social, or academic.

How else can I conclude other than saying I had a great time and even though I didn't act like it when I was in Bloomsburg, I would go through the experience all over again. I am pleased with the new me and I hope I can continue to develop outside of Bloomsburg, Pennsylvania.

Moji's theme will not earn her a Nobel prize for freshman writing. There were still some spelling and punctuation errors (which I have corrected for her above). There are more serious problems, as well, which almost any reader and, certainly, all more polished writers would notice.

Still, Moji's writing in that theme was far and away the best she had done that year. She had a thesis, a point to make. She used personal examples to support that point. Her theme was organized, with a single point developed in each paragraph. Best of all, she wrote as if she believed in what she was saying, as if she cared, as if she wanted to tell the world—even the narrow world of her English professor—about an experience that was important to her.

Moji was pleased at the grade she got on that theme. "It doesn't seem fair," she told me, "I really sweated on those other ones and got those bad grades. This one was so *easy* and quick to write, and I got my best grade of the year."

Moji learned something about writing as a result of those days at Bloomsburg: that writing is easier if she has something she wants to say.

I learned something about the teaching of writing as a result of those days at Bloomsburg: that my job as a teacher of writing really extends beyond explaining the principles of writing, assigning topics, and commenting on the writing students do. Part of my job is to arrange experiences through which my students will learn enough about themselves or the world around them that they *want* to tell me about it in words they find are suddenly easy to write.

Thank you, Moji.

Experiential Components in Academic Courses

by G. Christian Jernstedt

Although there has been a tendency to separate academic and experiential learning, the two can be successfully integrated.

The Goals of Education

For what do we educate? The introductions of diverse college catalogues describe goals of higher education that are remarkably consensual. The purpose of education "is to free students to explore, for a lifetime, the possibilities and limits of the human intellect."[1] Toward this end, effective faculty "regard the mind...as a flame that is to be fed, as an active being that must be strengthened to think and feel...."[2] The mind, alight with learning, develops through "rigorous study and the acquisition of information and technique, on the one hand; and a sustained productive effort and vigorous personal expression on the other...."[3]

Aristotle alluded to this same dual nature of education in the fourth century, B.C.: "Their using the language of knowledge is no proof that they possess it...students who have just begun a subject reel off its formulae, though they do not yet know their meaning, for knowledge has to become part of the tissue of the mind...."[4] Thus, during the course of two millennia, we find an awareness that there are two elements to the state of being educated: the possession of skills and knowledge, and the expression of those abilities in intercourse with the world.

The Nature of Schooling

Cross-cultural studies of cognitive abilities suggest that certain unique attributes of Western schooling have had a profound effect on our use of language and, hence, on our modes of thought. The effect is quite complex, and involves a separation of language from its roots in everyday communication.[5] The advantage of such a formalization of language is its resultant power for deriving abstractions, rules, and general principles, and for logically manipulating facts and ideas. The danger in formalization and decontextualization of language is that knowledge may become separated from experience. Formal schooling may result in the development of skills appropriate to academic environments but ineffective in life situations. Comenius, Dewey, Piaget, and Bruner have all voiced a similar concern.[6]

The most dangerous response to this dilemma of Western schooling is to propose an unreserved emphasis on relevance in institutions of higher education. The goal of colleges and universities must remain the nurture of the life of the mind. But if the mind is to function in the complex world community of the present, it must be equipped with the ability to bring its abstract, intellectual skills to bear on the realities of secular existence. For the educated world citizen, intellectual ability must be inextricably linked with a testing of that ability through life experiences.

A serious problem with much of contemporary higher education is that students are tested on their acquisition of knowledge, with only the assumption that the use of that knowledge will follow its acquisition. What I propose is that we test our students' abilities to use their knowledge, realizing that successful use of knowledge proves the previous acquisition of that knowledge.[7] By training for knowledge and testing for use of knowledge, we simultaneously focus on the dual nature of education stated as early as Aristotle and as recently as this year's college catalogue.

Teaching Methods

Though institutions of higher education serve many functions, their initial and fundamental activity is teaching. Preeminent among teaching methods is didactics, the imparting of knowledge, principally through books and lectures. Teaching is not limited to didactics, finding expression also in heuristics, the use of problem-solving techniques, and philetics, the concern for the learner as person.[8] Yet comparisons of various teaching methods fail to find differential effectiveness. When educational outcome is measured by the average performance of students on final examinations, distinctly different teaching methods are found to produce similar scores.[9] We cannot, however, use these results to dismiss concern with teaching methods. Others have found that the grades which are based upon such examination performance do not predict

later adult competence and may, in fact, predict psychological immaturity in adulthood.[10] These data on teaching methods may best be interpreted as revealing that our attention should be focused on learning rather than teaching methods.[11] Apparently it is not what the teacher does, but what the teacher encourages or enables the student to do that determines what is learned.[12]

Learning Methods

Historically, memory researchers have focused their attention on the properties of the material to be learned more than on the actions of the learner. We must not forget, however, that active learning is more efficient than passive or highly directed learning.[13] Students who use information they are trying to learn, who challenge and grapple with their new knowledge, or who use it to solve new problems, tend to learn more effectively than students who passively read, memorize, or merely absorb that to which they have been exposed. Correspondingly, recent research on memory has shifted in attention from the material to be learned to the mental activities of the learner. We now know that learners remember not what they encounter while learning so much as what they do while learning.[14]

Furthermore, the research literature paints a surprisingly narrow picture of the impact of learning techniques on students. For a student to master a body of knowledge, the student must be trained in the task for which he or she wishes to use that knowledge. This conclusion is true for specific skills such as writing, for bodies of factual knowledge, and for such complex skills as problem solving. In each case, the most effective learning comes when the student, during the original learning, engages in the behavior which will later be used as test or example of the success of that learning.[15] Skills which are learned in classrooms may not simply transfer to life situations, whether those situations be the next course which the student takes or an event in his or her own life. The precise nature of the learning task is the determinant of the learning outcome. For example, reading and writing about material which one is learning produces different learning than reading about the material and studying for a test on it.[16] Neither method is better overall than the other; each produces particular benefits.

We see that the purpose and structure of learning activities guide the acquisition of knowledge. Operating in the domain of abstraction or pure knowledge may lead to an inability to use knowledge in situations other than those in which it was acquired. To move toward a state of being educated by studying in a purely academic environment may be most effective for future college and university faculty, but for few other students.

To describe education as a state may, in fact, be to obscure its meaning. The educated mind has not only acquired a structure but also developed a set of processes. This argues for the introduction of experience into the academic environment, as a means of reconnecting the structure of knowledge with the process of using knowledge. Research on learning methods supports the argument. Tying information to be learned to experience, even when the experience is purely hypothetical, can preserve that learning within the mind and prime the mind for new learning more effectively than other techniques.

A Proposal

In the context of what we now know about learning, we may formulate a proposal to meld the structures of knowledge with the processes of using knowledge. We must do this by retaining the accumulated strengths of classroom instruction and adding the breadth, mnemonic effectiveness, and active expression of life experiences.

By combining experiential components with academic courses, we may couple the acquisition of knowledge with the ability to use it. An experiential component is a part of a course which provides the student with what the dictionary defines as experience: "direct participation in events,...knowledge, skill, or practice derived from direct observation of or participation in events,...something personally encountered, undergone, or lived through...."[18]

I do not propose that we improve education simply by adding extensive practical or applied problem-solving experience. The life of the mind is nurtured by the study of abstract concepts, as well as by the application of those concepts to complex, lifelike situations. What we must do is increase the number and quality of ways in which the developing mind can encounter and grapple with the worldly embodiment of its expanding knowledge. The classroom is the traditional locus of education because it can be very effective. Our task is to redouble its effectiveness with experience.

Techniques

How shall we introduce this element of experience into the academic course; must we redesign the course first? I think not. I have examined the use of experiential components in many, different courses, where methods of teaching have varied from the traditional lecture-reading-examination format to the innovative, individualized style of each student following a unique path through the course materials.[19] Experiential components seem to be effective regardless of the format or style of the teaching methods. In exploring the use of experiential components, my attention has been directed at two domains of experiences. On the one hand, I have examined experiences which occur or are presented within the classroom. Techniques in this domain include examples, modeling, and demonstrations. On the other hand, I have ventured outside the formal classroom to develop experiences which may then be related back to the classroom. Here I have considered experiential laboratories and extended group-living experiences.

Experiences in the Classroom

Experience by Example

The previously cited advantage of active learning over passive learning argues for direct rather than vicarious experiences. However, a full understanding of the impact of experience on learning requires an awareness of its limits. Accordingly, I began by studying such vicarious experiences as examples of others' behavior.

Printed Handouts. The simplest and most direct way of integrating experiences into the academic course is through the use of printed examples. I have found that concepts which are taught with examples drawn from the natural environment are remembered more correctly and for a longer period of

time than are concepts taught without such referents. I gave a group of students a simple list of examples of concepts that had been covered in a lecture. This is certainly the extreme point on the continuum of experiential learning, but these students performed better on a later examination than did students who had not received the example list. Not only had the students with exposure to the list learned the basic concepts better, but they also were more proficient at using the concepts they had learned.[20]

Now, I do not propose that such a procedure is an ideal one; it was created to examine the limits of introducing experiential-like materials. But handouts work. What they seem to do is cause the students to transform and extrapolate the principles being learned, so as to relate them to the examples in the handouts, and these transformational activities refine the intellectual processes occurring within the students' minds.

Recalled Personal Experiences. It seems obvious, however, that reading another's examples should be less effective than using one's own. Consequently, I have used exercises in which students must take the concept being learned and apply it to an example from their own life. They are asked to describe a situation from their own experience to which the principle under study may be applied.[21] This is a more powerful and engaging activity than simply studying a list of examples. It, too, is very effective in enhancing learning, but it has a serious flaw which I have not been able to correct. The student must recall from memory the situation which is to be analyzed. Memory is imperfect and often acts to make our recollections more consistent with our desires than was the original situation. The often-distorted accuracy of these recollections is a serious impediment to their effective use. Since the instructor has available only the student's imperfect recall, we find a significant retardation in the learning of concepts when this method is compared with one in which there is a means of externally validating the information in the example. That is, the student's task is too simple. The original experience is recalled to fit the principles under study much more directly than true life situations fit. The result is a seriously limited ability to use the principle. To provide examples of real experiences but retain a means of externally validating the details of real experience, the instructor must provide the example.

Experiences in Novels. With instructor-supplied experiences, the goal is to provide each student with some form of life experience to which the concept being learned may be related. I have tried newspapers, magazines, novels, and films as resources for these experiences; novels are the most effective. A novel, if well chosen, provides the students with a stream of life-situation events and concomitant mental images. Though the experience is vicarious, it is powerful, realistic, and emotionally involving. Critical to its success is the fact that the instructor and student each have full access to the record of the experiences and can and must confront the experience in a factual, undistorted manner.

The novel is used to provide resource material for the students' learning activities. As with the recalled personal experiences described earlier, the student may be asked to find an instance of a particular concept in the novel or to take a scene in the novel and analyze it in terms of relevant course concepts. This use of vicarious, but realistic, life situations can improve homework activities, examination performance, and class discussions, as well as the ability to speak or write intelligently about what one has learned.

Instructor Modeling. A related use of vicarious experiences that is relatively unused in teaching, but which is powerful in its effect on learning, is modeling. I have found that modeling can bring not only improvement in learning but increased motivation to learn as well. Modeling involves having the instructor in the course actually engage in the behavior which the students are trying to learn. It resembles a test given to the instructor by the students.

Consider the following example. The instructor announces to the students that during the next class meeting he or she will accept problems from students and solve them in front of the class. The questions may range from requiring the writing of a paper on the blackboard to the solving of homework-like or exam-like problems. Critical to the success of this modeling is that the instructor does not know what he or she will be asked to do. In front of the students, the instructor then tries to prepare a good answer to the assignment. This may involve the use of resources such as the text or various heuristics, as well as false starts, incorrect solutions, and, usually, a successful solution.

An instructor needs a healthy sense of self-worth to engage in modeling. The results can be spectacular. Students who have languished with course materials can suddenly come alive. They have seen that their own weak attempts and wrong turns are not uncommon for even a skilled professional. Most importantly, they have a concrete expression of what it means to grapple intellectually with a difficult concept. (Do not forget for a moment that these student-provided questions will be tricky and difficult, though realistic.) I have measured a significant increase in student work level after such sessions and an increase in the quality of their thought about the course concepts. Once again, tying the mind to the reality of life enhances understanding and action.

Demonstrations. The most experiential of all the options for engaging students' minds within the classroom is the use of demonstrations or simulations. I once asked my students to come back a year after the course and tell me what they remembered of the course. This was a most revealing experience for me as a teacher. My students did not remember what I said to them in class, did not remember what they said in class, remembered very little of the textbook, but did remember the writing that they did. What they remembered best, and still remembered five years after the course, were the demonstrations. In other words, they remembered their experiences, the events which engaged their eyes, ears, and bodies along with their minds.

One of the best remembered demonstration experiences I have used may serve as a brief example. I was attempting to show my students that some strongly held beliefs about human behavior might be unfounded. My efforts at verbally convincing them of this proved futile. Eventually, I arranged an experiential proof of my point. The proof involved creating a situation in which obviously supernatural powers of a person were clearly and dramatically exhibited to the class. Later revelation of the deception involved in the situation served as a most compelling example of how easily we can confuse the intensity of a belief with its validity. One must personally hold an intense belief which is then discovered to be invalid before one can fully understand how ubiquitous these beliefs are. In other examples, what we find is that when students adopt the role of a senator in political science, when they try to write a short story as Hemingway would write, or when they try to authenticate a newly discovered document in history, they learn.

We have since studied the use of demonstrations in lecture courses and find it is not the demonstration, per se, that produces the enhanced learning. Courses in which lectures are supplemented with demonstrations are not necessarily better than those without. The critical element is the manner in which the demonstrations are chosen. Courses in which the instructor focuses on choosing demonstrations that are interesting and relevant do not produce the same learning as those in which the instructor focuses on the concepts to be taught and then finds demonstrations to fit those concepts.[22] The effectiveness of experiences for courses is a function of necessity for those experiences. Merely adding exciting or interesting experiences to a course does not lead to enhanced learning in our studies. All too often, we have found, instructors use demonstrations as motivating rather than intellectual devices. But the power of a demonstration to improve intellectual performance lies with its intellectual content and the necessity for the experience. The most effective procedure we have found for introducing demonstrations in a course is to have the instructor generate a list of ten most important concepts, the ten concepts which he or she wants the students to remember two years after the course. Then the instructor looks for the ten best, most interesting, and most enjoyable demonstrations which illustrate those ten concepts.

Experiences outside the Classroom

The Experiential Laboratory

It may be clear at this point that many of the procedures I have outlined thus far involve attempts to simulate direct experiences within the confines of the classroom. For almost no courses, however, are we confined to the classroom. One might propose that the truly effective experience should, as we have seen, be carefully designed by the instructor to fit with the concepts to be learned, and should, in addition, occur in a realistic life environment. In conjunction with the Dartmouth Outward Bound Center, we have developed the vehicle of the experiential laboratory to fulfill this purpose.[23]

Design. The experiential laboratory is a 2- to 4-day experience participated in by a small group of students, the course instructor, and a trained leader. The labs occur during the weekend, with occasional overlaps into the week. The labs are optional, and typically about one quarter of the students in a course opt for the lab. The labs may occur at any time during a course, though they usually take place early in the term. Some courses have as many as three labs, while others have only one. Each lab group is limited to 10 students. Often the instructor will not participate in all groups or labs. We normally provide specialized gear through the Outward Bound Center, but that is not necessary. The skilled group leaders, such as

are provided by Outward Bound, are absolutely necessary.

The purpose of the laboratory is to provide a planned experience in a prescribed environment that will serve as resource material for the intellectual content of the course. The small group nature of the labs provides for personal encounter and group interaction. The fact that the labs occur away from the classroom and the campus provides a sense of privacy and isolation in which the forces that are designed into the experience may operate. The novelty of the environment in which the labs occur provides a case study of the novel environments into which we all are placed throughout our lives. The short duration of the labs allows an intense focusing on the experience for each participant and an openness to exploration and experimentation with oneself and one's ideas. The typical presence of stress, uncertainty, and the need for problem solving and immediate judgment provides elements in the situation which are present at many important points in each of our lives.

The design of these laboratories is never casual; it typically takes a month to develop a new laboratory. Great cooperation and energy is required of both the instructor and the laboratory staff. The staff must know the concepts which the students are learning in the course. They normally read the texts or have taken the course. The instructor must understand the dynamics of group growth and individual development. Plans are usually quite detailed, often by the ten-minute block. The plans are not followed rigidly, but are absolutely necessary if the experience is be effective for the course.

The laboratories require great attention to safety and exceptional sensitivity to personal mental health principles. I would hesitate to design such a laboratory without the full involvement of a staff as highly and specially trained as those of the Dartmouth Outward Bound Center. The results of this care have been exceptional.

An Example. The best way to understand these experiential labs is to participate in them. In lieu of such direct experience, a description will explain their relationship to and impact on an academic course.

The most common lab is Rocks and Ropes. It is chosen by many instructors because it presents a novel, highly motivating, skill-requiring experience which relates well to a wide range of course materials. The lab requires one weekend. On a Friday afternoon, the participants engage in a variety of group initiative exercises designed to build interpersonal contact and trust. Retrieving the evening's food supply from a nearly inaccessible spot further develops this process and gradually introduces the feeling of isolation and privacy. The next day is spent in climbing and rappelling, climaxed by blindfolded climbs. On Sunday, a difficult ropes course is negotiated, involving both group-supported and individual efforts.

Course material is deliberately not discussed during the weekend. Journals are kept and individual reflective time is provided. With the exception of training for ropes, the instructors are present only to provide safety and challenges and see that the environment is structured to encourage the ultimate goal of the weekend. For this weekend, which is often used to introduce the laboratory idea and set the stage for later laboratories, the goals are simple.

The weekend raises the issues of why we must learn certain concepts and how the value of learning may only become apparent in the later expression of that learning. The climbing language is an excellent example of this. When first told of the series of commands and communications which climbers use, the group members feel self-conscious and awkward in using the language, especially while practicing on the ground. Learning of the language is typically minimal at this stage. When the group moves to the short cliff face used for intermediate training, the purpose of the language becomes clearer, but it is not yet needed and hence not fully learned. Finally, when climbing the steep rock face, when belayer is not visible to climber or when the climber is blindfolded, the full import of the language blossoms and it is learned. This example of a concept which cannot be understood fully until it is experienced serves well throughout the remainder of the course to illustrate the impact of motivation and action on the learning of knowledge and intellectual skills.

During the week after the experience, debriefing sessions are held. It is in these sessions that the direct connections to course materials are made. Here the students are asked to take the classroom materials and use them to describe, analyze, and predict their own behavior in the natural environment. The most obvious advantage of the experience that is revealed in these sessions is that students typically encounter in their courses only idealized examples of life situations. The natural complexity of the experiences in the labs make the application of course principles difficult and inexact, precisely the case when applying most abstract knowledge to natural situations. The most effective heuristic device which I have found to teach students the subtleties and complexities of translating academic knowledge to real world situations is this debriefing after the laboratory.

Representative Laboratory Themes. These laboratory experiences are not limited to courses which deal with psychology. We have designed and used a wide variety of laboratories in which concepts critical to courses from many disciplines may be presented. We have classified the laboratories according to their dominant theme.

One of the earliest themes we developed was that of novelty. For this theme, students are taken into the woods with sufficient gear for climbing and hiking and given 15 minutes to move their entire group into the trees for the duration of the weekend. Anything left from the group or anyone touching the ground after this period is removed. Establishing a community in the trees raises important questions about the skills which we have and can bring to new environments, about how easy or difficult we find it to change, and about what happens to individuals and groups when they are forced to make sudden modifications in their previously well-developed habits.

A related theme, which has led to the development of a very powerful laboratory, is uncertainty. There are times when nothing in our environment happens as we expect it to. In such a situation, as soon as we have decided how to act, the environment changes and the action is no longer appropriate. We create this situation in an experiential laboratory by issuing, first, an unusual equipment list to the students. They are required to bring with them sunglasses, swimming suits, a down jacket, a textbook to study, heavy work gloves, or other such gear. Upon departure, two small groups of students are put in two vans, with no outside view, and driven toward their destination. Along the way, they are required to select additional gear from that in the van, which includes snowshoes, an envelope of cash, climbing rope, a rubber life boat, and so forth. They have one hour to select about a third of what is available and to arrange to carry it all on their backs. Just when they have decided, the vans are stopped, and the groups are each split in half and rearranged in the vans. These new groups must then repeat the selection process since they do not agree. The groups continue traveling until they are suddenly told that in five minutes they will reach their destination. There they will have exactly 15 seconds to vacate the vans and be on their way, on their own. Anything not on someone's back or left in the van will be lost for the next two days. The vans then stop, the doors are thrown open, and the students burst forth with all manner of strange gear on their backs. They have been so intent on preparing for this moment that they have not listened to the sounds outside the van, and as the van roars off, they suddenly become dramatically aware of the fact that they are standing in the middle of a busy intersection in a large city. Their first task, left in an envelope, is to find and join up with the other group, which has been left somewhere else in the city. Their only restriction is that they may not move above ground. For the next hours, they travel on the subway, deciding on a strategy to locate the others, guessing the others' strategy, and collecting a list of items which their information packet requires that they present later for food and bedding, of which they have little. The list requires the names and birth places of thirty people on the subway, a surgeon's mask, sand from a local beach, a symphony ticket, a used ticket from the topless bar district, a pig's foot, and other such items. At two in the morning, when they have found each other and most of the items on the list, they are suddenly met by a leader and removed to the vans. An hour later, after being led blindfolded from the vans, they remove the blindfolds to see total darkness and discover that they are locked in a bomb shelter. The weekend continues.

As might be expected, this lab provides a full academic term's worth of experiences which are used in the course. Issues include the kinds of uncertainty which are most and least disruptive, the skills which can be carried from environment to environment, the nature of the adaptation process, the maintenance of stability in an uncertain world, and the assistance and comfort of others in times of stress. In fact, the urban environment has proven to be fully as effective as the wilderness for these experiences, though one typically does not think of programs like Outward Bound as providing an urban experience.

Equally powerful is a laboratory in the city in which many members of the group are handicapped, with limbs or senses immobilized for the weekend. With no food or money, the group must seek work. The job leads provided by the leaders before the experience are discovered to be difficult to develop due to the group's lack of training. When a dirty job cleaning the subway is found, and long hours spent working in the filth expecting a few dollars for food, the refusal of the employer to pay because of the "poor quality" of the work adds to the sense of frustration and helplessness. Courses in religion, history, economics, education, lit-

erature, and even technology may use this laboratory to enhance the learning of their students.

Even the designers of the laboratories are often surprised at the impact of these experiences on the intellectual growth of the students. One laboratory, in which students had to travel by bushwhacking through dense woods and make a variety of tools and implements to barter for food, motivated the students through the promise of a chicken banquet at the termination of the laboratory. The fact that the chickens were alive when the students arrived for the banquet provoked nearly half a day of discussion about food sources and ethics, about medicine and health, and most interestingly to the designers, about the law (is it legal to kill chickens?).

Evaluation. My evaluation of the laboratories has examined three points of their impact: the individual students who are attracted to the laboratories, the immediate outcomes from the labs, and the long-term results of the experience.

As might be expected, the students who are attracted to the laboratories are different from those who are not.[24] Those who sign up for this option in the courses I have examined have had more experience with outdoor adventure programs than their peers have had. They enter the course, even before they know about the laboratory option, expecting the course to be more flexible and less oriented toward factual content than do their peers. Once these students know about the lab option, their attitudes change compared to the attitudes of those who know that they are not participating in the labs. The participants-to-be expect the course to be more exciting than they did when they enrolled or than their peers do. They expect to develop more self-respect and self-confidence than do the other students. Their expectations also move toward a more interesting, valuable, and application-oriented course. The picture emerges of a participant who has used experiences for learning or simple pleasure in the past, and expects that they will enhance learning in the course.

Interestingly, the prior grade point averages of the lab participants are typically higher than those of the other students. I have since discovered that this is an artifact. There is no grade point difference between those who want and those who do not want to participate in the labs. The difference arises from the fact that among the initial applicants only those students who have relatively high grade point averages finally decide that they can afford the time for three weekends away from their other studies.

Students who have experienced the labs and their associated debriefings perform significantly better on later examinations than do their peers without the experiences, even when the differences in grade point average are controlled. This performance improvement is quite specific. The experiential students do not know more facts or principles; they understand concepts better. In situations in which they are asked to recognize instances of concepts or to choose and apply concepts correctly to complex situations, these students are superior.

The affective impact of the experiences at the end of the course depends, in part, on the teaching methodology used in the course.[25] To examine the worst case in which experiential laboratories might be used, we studied them in a course taught with the traditional lecture-text-examination format, and taught with no attempt on the instructor's part during the course to integrate the laboratory experiences with the course work. The only point of integration occurred during the one-hour debriefing sessions, in which the experiences were related to course material, following each of the three weekends. At the end of this course, the laboratory participants reported that the course was less difficult, less well integrated, less organized, less effective in teaching factual content, and less fair in grading than the other students reported. Interviews with the students suggested that these feelings derived from the contrast between the personal intensity and relevance of the laboratories and the more traditional nature of the course itself.

In traditionally taught courses and in courses with more innovative formats, when the labs are integrated with the course material by the instructor, this difference does not appear. In contrast, students in such courses who participate in the labs report feelings of better integration, organization, fairness, and so forth.

These differences between courses which integrate the laboratories and those which do not disappear by one year after the course. We questioned students 12 and 24 months after the courses, in order to observe how they felt after the experiences and the course materials had settled in their minds. Regardless of the nature of the teaching methods in the course, those students who had participated in the laboratories reported a greater interest in the course subject matter, a greater ability to approach new subject matter and use effective learning techniques, and a greater tendency to seek challenges in their lives as students. In addition, the laboratory participants reported the course, itself, to have been more challenging and more relevant than the other students reported it to have been.

Interviews again provided information to elaborate upon these findings. It appeared that the laboratory students, during the time since the course, had integrated the experiences with the course material and with their own lives. Their experiences in the laboratories had served as a bridge between the course content and their own experiences after the course. Because the laboratories were designed to illustrate course principles, and because the experiences of the labs had roots in common experiences in natural life situations, the labs aided the transfer of course learning to later life experience. It is important to realize that this transfer was accomplished by the students without the instructor, since it occurred after the course was over, but was apparent only for those students who had experienced the labs.

We are presently collecting information about the students' long-term retention of the course materials and about the actual behaviors in which they have engaged since the course. One early result suggests that laboratory participants are much more likely to engage in later experiential learning than are non-participants.

The same principle discovered with in-class demonstrations applies to the laboratories. They are only effective if the principles and concepts of the course are developed first and independently, and then experiences are designed to provide the necessary enhancement of the intellectual content.

Extensions of Experiential Components

Students who take an active role in the development of their own education and make aggressive use of the resources in their environment strengthen their cognitive and affective development and improve their intellectual disposition.[26] The success of the laboratories is due in part to their ability or tendency to attract active students and to their intensification of student-faculty interaction. A natural extension of these critical dimensions is field experience education, in which an entire course moves into the natural environment. Examples include internships and language study-abroad programs. Although the research literature on field experience education is methodologically weak, field experiences seem to attract different students than do more traditional courses, and to impact on their educational growth.[27]

A different manner of integrating life experiences with academic studies is that of the Living/Learning Term developed by the Dartmouth Outward Bound Center. Participants in this option combine a normal academic term with small-group living in a house on campus. The 10 to 12 participants organize and execute all logistics related to food, maintenance, and personal interaction. They take a full course load, sharing one course in common, and participate in all the elements of a standard Outward Bound course (initial expedition, rescue and service work, personal skill and fitness development, solo experience, and final expedition). The focus of the Living/Learning Term is neither on the content of a particular course, as is the focus of the laboratory experience, nor on a particular environment, as is the field experience course. Rather, its focus is on the integration of a series of life experiences with a spectrum of classroom-based courses. The impact of this long-range experiential program is complex and shares significant similarities with the laboratories and with field experience courses.[28]

Conclusion

What can we conclude about experiential components of academic courses? The techniques reported here are not radical. They make changes within the educational system as it now exists in institutions of higher education. It is obvious that the programs are more expensive than traditional teaching methods, but nearly all good, innovative methods require an increase in monetary or personal expenditures. These techniques are focused on two elements of learning which appear to be critical for the full development of the mind and the person: an active learner in interaction with his or her environment.

I have found that adding experiences, whether vicarious or direct, can lead to improvements in the learning which occurs in academic course. Experiential learning tends to make greater use of the whole person than does traditional academic learning. In doing so, it appears to produce more accurate and more persistent learning. The results can feel better and last longer than purely academic learning.

The success of experiential components in academic courses rests on the development first of the intellectual content of the courses. Experiences which are not necessary or important to the development of course concepts may provide increased student motivation, but do not appear to produce better learning.

Learning should be a lifelong process. Integrating the growth of the intellect in academic courses with life experiences can occur in college, improving the quality of education in the college years and building the foundation for an integrated style of learning in later life.

Notes

1. University of Chicago, <u>The College</u> (Chicago: University of Chicago, 1971), p. 9.

2. Williams College, <u>An Introduction</u> (Williamstown, MA: Williams College, 1979), p. 5.

3. Bennington College, <u>Catalog</u> (Bennington, VT: Bennington College, 1978), p. 5.

4. Aristotle, <u>Nichomachean Ethics</u>, in <u>The Philosophical Foundations of Education,</u> ed. Steven M. Cahn (New York: Harper & Row, 1970), p. 116.

5. Ann L. Brown, "Knowing When, Where, and How to Remember: A Problem of Metacognition." in <u>Advances in Instructional Psychology,</u> ed. Robert Glaser, (Hillsdale, NJ: Lawrence Earlbaum Associates, 1978), pp. 143–148.

6. David R. Olson, "The Languages of Instruction: The Literate Bias of Schooling," in <u>Schooling and the Acquisition of Knowledge,</u> ed. Richard C. Anderson, Rand J. Spiro, and William E. Montague (Hillsdale, NJ: Lawrence Earlbaum Associates, 1977), pp. 65–89.

7. G. Christian Jernstedt, "PSI/T: Personalized Instruction with Emphasis on Extra-classroom Transfer." Paper presented to the Conference on the Keller Plan Cambridge, MA, October, 1971.

8. H. S. Broudy, "Didactics, Heuristics, and Philetics," Educational Theory 22 (1972): pp. 251–261.

9. David C. Berliner and N. L. Gage, "The Psychology of Teaching Methods," in The Psychology of Teaching Methods, ed. N. L. Gage (Chicago: University of Chicago Press, 1976), pp. 15–19.

10. Douglas H. Heath, "Academic Predictors of Adult Maturity and Competence," Journal of Higher Education 48 (1977): pp. 613–632.

11. Donald Dansereau, "The Development of a Learning Strategies Curriculum," in Learning Strategies, ed. Harold F. O'Neil, Jr. (New York: Academic Press, 1978), pp. 1–29.

12. Christian Jernstedt and Wilfred K. Chow, "Lectures and Textual Materials as Sources of Information for Learning," Psychological Reports (under review).

13. W. J. McKeachie, "Research on Teaching at the College and University Level," in Handbook of Research on Teaching, ed. N. L. Gage (Chicago: Rand McNally, 1963), pp. 1118–1172.

14. Fergus I. M. Craik and Endel Tulving, "Depth of Processing and the Retention of Words in Episodic Memory," Journal of Experimental Psychology: General 104 (1975): pp. 268–294.

15. G. Christian Jernstedt, "The Relative Effectiveness of Individualized and Traditional Instruction Methods." The Journal of Educational Research 69 (1976): pp. 211–218.

16. Jernstedt, "The Relative Effectiveness of Individualized and Traditional Instruction Methods.

17. John D. Bransford, Kathleen E. Nitsch, and Jeffrey J. Franks, "Schooling and the Facilitation of Knowing," in Schooling and the Acquisition of Knowledge, ed. Richard C. Anderson, Rand J. Spiro, and William E. Montague (Hillsdale, NJ: Lawrence Earlbaum Associates, 1977), pp. 31–55.

18. Webster's New Collegiate Dictionary, 1975.

19. The evaluations of the programs described throughout this report have been carried out through the Experiential Learning in College Project at Dartmouth. Particular attention has been paid to the methodological and statistical validity of the evaluations. All results reported in this paper are significant. Full details cannot be included because of space limitations, but are available in reports from the author.

20. G. B. Northcraft and G. C. Jernstedt, "Comparison of Four Teaching Methodologies for Large Lecture Classes," Psychological Reports 36 (1975): pp. 599–606.

21. G. Christian Jernstedt, Learning: The Philosophy and Structure of a Course. (Hanover, NH: Dartmouth College, 1976), pp. 13–33.

22. Bruce Smoller, "Short and Long-Term Retention of Classroom Learning," Senior Fellow Dissertation, Dartmouth College, 1979, pp. 86–109.

23. G. Christian Jernstedt, "Learning about Learning: A Personal Guide," (Hanover, NH: Dartmouth College, 1977), pp. 15–16.

24. Amy Gillenson, Scott McGovern, and G. Christian Jernstedt, "Effects of Outward Bound Participation," (Hanover, NH: Experiential Learning in College Project, 1974), pp. 1–23.

25. Amy Gillenson, Scott McGovern, and G. Christian Jernstedt, "Effects of Outward Bound Participation," pp. 1–23.

26. Robert C. Wilson, Jerry G. Gaff, Evelyn R. Dienst, Lyn Wood, and James L. Bavry, College Professors and Their Impact on Students. (New York John Wiley, 1975), pp. 178–182.

27. Gregory J. McHugo and G. Christian Jernstedt, "The Affective Impact of Field Experience Education on College Students, Alternative Higher Education 3 (1979): pp. 188–206.

28. G. Christian Jernstedt and Gregory J. McHugo, "The Impact of Combined Experiential (Outward Bound) and Traditional Academic Programs on Personal Development," Alternative Higher Education, (under review).

A College-Level Experiential Learning Career Development Curriculum

by Michael J. Marshall, W. Patrick Haun, and Ronald G. Ramke

"Jim," like many college students, faced a sophomore's dilemma. He was eligible to declare a major, and felt he should, in order to plan his upper division coursework, but he still had no idea what major was best for him. He considered it a critical decision because, even though he attended a liberal arts college, his career opportunities would be influenced by his major, be it business, biology, psychology, or art. Even after a major is chosen, students in liberal arts programs may not recognize the relevance of classroom knowledge to their future careers, and more pragmatically, how to put their degrees to work after graduation (Osborne, 1987).

Our college has a career guidance center, but most students do not make adequate use of it. It is staffed by a career generalist who has little inside knowledge about the helping professions. In one college, only thirteen percent of juniors and seniors intending to achieve B.A. level employment sought help from the staff in the Career Planning and Placement Office (Osborne, 1987).

The faculty in our department feel that low student motivation levels, in large part, reflect a lack of maturity stemming from limited life experience (Shappell et al., 1970-71). Students sense this lack of experience in that behavioral science majors consider career preparation to be their greatest unmet need (Malin & Timmreck, 1979). We have chosen to address the needs of our students (identity and focus) by implementing a mandatory experiential curriculum component with a career preparation emphasis. This is intended to integrate classroom knowledge with real world experience. Most behavioral science departments offer formalized experiential learning in the form of practicums. However, they suffer from under-use and a lack of mission, according to a national survey of behavioral science departments (Vandecreek & Fleisher, 1984). Survey respondents did give the two highest endorsements for the purpose of practicums as "career development" and "to observe in action material taught in other courses."

Even though our mission is to provide a liberal arts education, we feel students should have the benefit of being able to explore career interests and test future employment options because of the pragmatic necessity of postbaccalaureate employment (Pinkus & Korn, 1973). Part of the maturation process associated with a liberal arts education involves the development of autonomy and a vocational identity (Heath, 1968).

Career Experiences as a Developmental Process

The goal of our program is to provide a structure that allows students to take responsibility for their futures. This program integrates the scattered career services available to students into a progressive framework of learning experiences within their major. The methods we chose to obtain this goal follow from three data-based assumptions. They are: 1) Transmitting information about the departmental curriculum to new students through retreats, colloquia, and a departmental handbook will help students formulate career goals (Ware, 1985). 2) Professional career experiences, as part of the curriculum, will help students acquire a professional career identity and improve classroom motivation and participation through the recognition of the interrelatedness of academic knowledge and the real world (Davis et al., 1987). 3) The process of identifying career interests and practicing job search skills will help students obtain satisfactory postbaccalaureate employment (Lunneborg, 1974-75).

The first career preparation experience occurs just prior to a student declaring a major in our department. Prospective majors must go through a screening process which requires: 1) filling out an application of intent describing why they want to major in our department; 2) meeting the GPA requirements; and 3), being interviewed by a departmental admissions committee made up of faculty. Upon acceptance, they receive a handbook describing departmental policy, options, and programs. The purpose of the screening process is to help students think more purposefully about how the department's curriculum is relevant to their interests.

Our career experiential learning program is designed as a required pass/fail series of one-unit courses. Students are required to take a one-unit course in the first semester of the sophomore year, both semesters of the junior year, and in the second semester of the senior year, for a total of four units.

The purpose of the sophomore class is to help students decided if they are in the right major and, if so, to get them thinking about career possibilities through direct experience. This is accomplished through a series of activities, fifteen hours in the classroom and thirty hours in community agencies. The Strong-Campbell Interest Inventory and SIGI PLUS (System of Interactive Guidance and Information) computerized career guidance programs are taken by students in the classroom component. These are intended to identify students' initial career interests and see if they are compatible with their choice of a major. Their career interests are then reality-tested through three experiences—a departmental weekend retreat, the career colloquium series, and an agency field observation period.

The first outside-class experiential activity is the departmental retreat. Students and faculty spend a weekend at a mountain YMCA camp. The purpose is to socially acclimate new majors to the department. The weekend's activities are designed to facilitate students getting to know each other and the faculty in an informal setting. The low-key atmosphere fosters the transmission of information about the major from faculty and veteran students to new departmental students.

Jim was one of the first students to enroll in the program. He attended the retreat which gave him ample opportunity to talk with the faculty about the possibilities available in our department. He realized he might be interested in the human services. The career interest inventories he took in the classroom component confirmed that his greatest interests were in working with people, supporting his decision to make human relations his major.

Students who cannot attend the weekend retreat have an option that involves interacting with professionals working in relevant career areas to their major through departmental colloquia. Students get to hear about and ask questions concerning what it is like to work in various careers.

The last sophomore-level experiential activity involves students spending thirty hours observing the work day of professionals in two agencies (fifteen hours each) consistent with their prospective career choices. Classroom time is used to discuss non-class activities, assessment results, and the text material.

Jim had the opportunity to test his interest in human services by doing his first field placement in a youth agency. He was very dissatisfied and decided for his next placement to try the personnel department at a local hospital. It turned out to be such a good experience for him that he encouraged other students to work there as volunteers.

The course objectives for the junior year are: to obtain and practice the skills necessary to secure satisfactory employment, to apply classroom learning to a career setting, and to acquire a professional career identity. Résumé writing, interview skills, and job hunting techniques are taught and practiced in the first semester. Students must put their knowledge to direct use by securing their own volunteer work experience (thirty hours) in an agency or organization of their choice. The work experience can increase students' class motivation and participation by providing a personal vehicle, a career-related agency, on which to hang intellectual course content (Jernstedt, 1980).

"Gail" was a junior education major who opted to enroll in the co-curricular program.

She knew she wanted to work with children but was dissatisfied with teaching after her practice teaching experience; thus, she chose to go to a volunteer youth agency for her work experience requirement. She found this area of human services to be very satisfying and she began to perk up in the classroom. She regularly challenged course content by claiming that theories taught in the classroom were inadequate to deal with the realities she encountered. She remarked that "without the co-curricular career program, I might have stayed in education and ended up as an unhappy teacher."

In the second semester of the junior year, students are required to attend a professional meeting (convention, seminar, etc.) in their career area. They then research a topic and prepare an in-house poster presentation. These activities are designed to help students build a professional career identity and explore relevant career topics, issues, and methods. The capstone experience occurs in the second semester of the senior year. Students put their career development skills and classroom knowledge to work by coordinating a department symposium and participating in it by presenting research papers.

Student Responses and Program Refinement

The program has been pilot tested and adjusted according to student feedback over four semesters. It is now ready for full implementation and its effectiveness will be evaluated with a pre-test/post-test, control-group research design (Cook & Campbell, 1975) using the Career Development Inventory (Thompson & Lindeman, 1981), My Vocational Situation (Holland et al., 1980), and a program-specific questionnaire (Ewert, 1987).

At this point, judging by their comments, students generally have favorable attitudes toward the program. However, there are some problems that must be addressed. Students enrolled in the senior component felt that preparing papers to present at the symposium was "one tremendous headache" due to the shortage of time. They also said that this program component needs to be better integrated with the first three components. The problems aside, perhaps "Brad's" comments about the program best represent our students' reactions to it: "I think it is very beneficial. It gives you a sense of direction. You can determine your interests and strengths, and test them while applying classroom knowledge at the same time. It is geared toward the type of learning I like best—experiential."

Chapter 14

Research and Evaluation of Experiential Learning

Research in Experiential Education: An Overview

by Alan Ewert

To me truth is precious....I should rather be right and stand alone than run with the multitude and be wrong....The holding of my beliefs has already won me the scorn and ridicule of some of my fellow scholars....But truth is truth, and though all the world reject it and turn against me, I will cling to truth still.

Charles deFord, 1931

For the experiential educator, dealing with colleagues, peers, and the public can often be described by the above quote. Experiential educators know the "truth" that combining experience with education is an effective way to learn. The problem lies in convincing other professionals and lay people. Before we move too far into the realm of self-righteousness, we would do well to remind ourselves that the above quote was from a booklet written by Charles de Ford in 1931 (Gardner, 1951, p. 12) in which he attempted to prove that the earth was FLAT.

In order to reach the "truth" and better understand experiential education, research and evaluation become very useful tools. More specifically, these tools help us explore the questions of *what* happened in an experiential education program, *how* it happened, and how the program can be altered to make "it" happen again, only *better*. While the terms research and evaluation are similar, research is generally associated with theory testing, and evaluation is more directly linked to information gathering for decision making in programs (Weiss, 1972). Both are vital links in the information chain of experiential education between the practitioner and researcher.

The purpose of this introduction is to outline some of the major issues surrounding research and evaluation in experiential education. These issues include the gap between the researcher and practitioner and current directions in research. Finally, some suggestions for addressing these and other concerns are provided so that future research efforts in experiential education might avoid the pursuit of a "FLAT" earth.

The Researcher/Practitioner Gap

> ...a tale told by an idiot, full of sound and fury, signifying nothing.
>
> Shakespeare

As illustrated by Shakespeare, one concern in experiential education is the separation of fact and fiction in examining research findings. Of equal concern is the distance between the researcher and practitioner with respect to areas of interest and types of information considered useful or valuable. Moreover, information that is acquired either by the practitioner or researcher is often not fully integrated into the other group. Reinharz (1979, p. 95) suggests that research is frequently conducted on the "rape model" where researchers take, hit, and run away with the information. All too often, research in experiential education becomes an exercise in data generation rather than the production of meaningful findings.

Part of this problem is structural in that practitioners and researchers are often faced with different concerns. For example, the practitioner may be interested in getting

information in order to facilitate making decisions about a program. Conversely, the researcher may be more concerned with theoretical relationships of little relevance to the practitioner. A sample of possible differences which can lead to misunderstandings is provided in Table 1.

Table 1. Differences Between Researchers and Practitioners

Researcher	Practitioner
Obligation to be critical	Doesn't like to criticize
Searching for truth	Needs to make decisions
Emotionally neutral	Emotionally involved
Information for theory development	Information for decisions
Limited by research design	Limited by cost
Working toward a perfect world	Making an imperfect world work

Modified from Ewert (1986).

These differences often result in criticism between practitioners and researchers, which is often justified and contributes to a lack of understanding and communication between the two groups. A portion of these criticisms is listed in Table 2.

This is not just a dilemma for the researcher. If practitioners want information which is both useful and specific, they must open their programs up to research and evaluation. A program with no allowance made for permitting research or evaluation will yield little in the way of new theoretical or developmental knowledge which could help the practitioner deliver a better product. While there are no repair manuals for fixing this situation, Hamilton (1979) suggests research and evaluation efforts that are cooperatively designed by researchers and practitioners. Practitioners should be afforded the opportunity for professional development in areas such as program evaluation or understanding research findings. These opportunities should be located at the workplace rather than the classroom and should focus on how-tos rather than strictly on theory. Lawson (1985) refers to this as recipe-knowledge and believes that it is an important part in the development of a profession.

Current Research Directions

One swallow does not make a summer; nor do two "strongly agrees," one "disagree" and an "I don't know" make an attitude or social value.

(Webb, et al., 1966, p. 172)

Experiential education is concerned with a variety of behavioral, educational, and affective components. These components are often complex, multifaceted, and difficult to observe. The issue is to determine what the researcher should study and how to study it. Too much of the research currently being done in experiential education is concerned with the outcome of the program (Shore, 1977; Burton, 1981). This is a problem, for while outcomes are often the sine qua non of experiential education, this type of research often does not provide an understanding as to *why* it happened or *how* it can be made to happen again. Without the ability to explain how and why an outcome (e.g., enhanced learning) is realized, we lose our ability to predict that outcome in differ-

ent situations or with different participants. Moreover, being able to explain how something works implies that it can be modified to become a better product. However, it should be remembered that this method of education places a strong emphasis on action and direct participation rather than passive verbalization. Not addressing the impact and effect of direct experience on an individual would ultimately do a disservice to the profession. A balance is needed, with research devoted to both outcome and process.

Table 2. Criticisms between Researchers and Practitioners

Criticisms Of Practitioners By Researchers	Criticisms Of Researchers By Practitioners
Never ask the right questions	Never get a straight answer
Pay little attention to advice	Too cautious, can never make generalizations
Want easy, black-and-white answers	Never have enough data or information
Not interested in objective truths	Retreat into research jargon
Reactive rather than proactive	"Could be" instead of "will be"
Looking for bargains	Crackpots versus capable—who can tell?
Do not comprehend the term "reliability"	Do not comprehend the term "meaningful"

Modified from Ewert (1986).

Another research area which has been neglected is program issues, such as the optimal mix of activities to place in a course and the most efficacious ways to market the activities and programs. Heath (1985) indicates that there is often too much concentration on statistical technique at the expense of conceptualizing a clear purpose or interpretation of the findings.

Obtaining these findings can involve using *qualitative* and *quantitative* research methods. Quantitative research is often associated with model testing, statistical treatments, prediction, and relationships between variables. Qualitative research has been termed naturalistic inquiry, participant observation, or ethnographic research, and involves phenomenology, field notes, self-descriptions, and open-ended interviewing. Both forms of research have an important role to play in experiential education, with no one method being intrinsically "better" than the other. The proper use of qualitative and quantitative research has always included the process of hypothesis testing, sound reasoning, and theory formation (Kirk & Miller, 1986). Qualitative work can provide theoretical insight, validate survey data, and help in the interpretive portion of a quantitative study. Quantitative research can be used to identify individuals or cases for further qualitative work (Fielding & Fielding, 1986).

Whatever style is used, any research and evaluation effort should be systematic, based on measurement and/or observation, explanatory as well as descriptive, replicable and explicit about the limitations. The importance of this research should not be underestimated as the future quality of our programs is dependent on the information presently being gained—or lost.

Implications and Suggestions

Wisdom came to earth and could find no dwelling place.

Enoch

Ultimately, the most important question asked of a research or evaluation study is what does it all mean. This is the critical link in the chain of knowledge in experiential education. A growing number of experiential educators have the statistical and research/evaluation design skills to conduct a variety of data collection projects. Research, however, is more than statistical analysis for it implies "meaning making" out of collected data. Finding relevant meaning out of a collection of information involves an interpretation of those data that often moves beyond the circumstances of their origin. Johnston and Pennypacker (1980, p. 395) refer to this as generality and suggest that generalizing research findings involves prediction with different subjects, settings, methods, and processes. What is suggested here is a refocusing of attention in the *interpretation phase* of research and evaluation. There may be some danger in this approach as researchers might formulate the wrong interpretations or draw incorrect pictures of reality. These errors can arise from inaccurate observation, illogical reasoning, ego involvement, and premature closure of inquiry (Babbie, 1983, pp. 10–15). While all these concerns are justified, to err is human and often worth the risk. By intensifying the interpretation phase of research, experiential education will gain valuable insight into the processes it promotes and the impact these methods might have on individuals.

What is needed is a *multimethod, multivariable approach* in which a number of variables are combined with a variety of methods. Research in experiential education is still too truncated, focusing mainly in the outdoor area. Work needs to be done in other arenas such as cross-cultural analysis, traditional education, and other social institutions that incorporate learning. Moreover, life is not so episodic that one event, even in experiential education, is unrelated to the other aspects of one's existence. There is a bonding between events and experiences which serves to provide a backdrop for the attitudes, behaviors, and abilities of an individual. Exploring this multivariable concept involves much more sophisticated research methods than are currently used in experiential education.

As research and evaluation in experiential education develops, the concern for ethical practices also increases. Bachrach (1981, p. 123) indicates that ethical research must contain the elements of informed consent, confidentiality, and acceptable procedures. With the increased emphasis in qualitative research methods, a number of ethical issues will develop. These issues include: role conflict between the participant and observer, observing people without their knowledge, and reporting on participants who are violating program policy. In addition, using research and evaluation to hide the reality of an ineffective program continues to plague this and other fields.

In sum, when compared to the more established disciplines of education or psychology, research in experiential education is still in an early stage of development. After all, it was only 13 years ago when experiential education became represented by a formal organization. Since that time, a substantial amount of research has been undertaken. Much of this research has pointed to the effectiveness and power of combining experience with education. To date, there are no indications that this trend will diminish, with research and evaluation continuing to play an important role in that process.

This Issue

This issue of the *Journal of Experiential Education* has been dedicated to research and evaluation. In a sense, it represents the "state of the art" in research within this field with respect to the topics covered and the problems encountered. Our research base is still very much focused on widely divergent outcomes with little in the way of building on the past work of others. Moreover, the research has consistently offered scant tidbits of practical information for people trying to make their programs work. Some of the research in this issue can be connected with that concern. What practical, usable advice the research community in experiential education can give the practitioner still remains an elusive mystery. Solving that mystery must remain one of the goals of future dialogues within the experiential education community.

A Note of Thanks

As is usually the case, an issue in the *Journal* is the compilation of the efforts of many. The Journal Advisory Board is to be congratulated for their foresight in making an issue available for the usually esoteric, often mundane topic of research. This was a refereed issue of the *Journal* in that manuscripts were anonymously reviewed. The reviewers came from a broad spectrum of backgrounds and included: Jenny Anderson, A.T. Easley, Steve Hollenhorst, Jasper Hunt, Kelly Kain, Rocky Kimball, Dean Kwasny, Cheryl Lane, Dennis Latess, Steve Proudman, Craig Rademacher, Dorna Schroeter, Mike Swiderski, Mike Wisnyai, and Rita Yerkes. Finally, a special thanks to the people who devoted the time and energy to submit a manuscript for review.

National Assessment of Experiential Education: Summary and Implications

By Dan Conrad and Diane Hedin

> *Experience is never limited, and it is never complete; it is an immense sensibility, a kind of huge spider's web of silken threads suspended in the chambers of consciousness and catching every airborne particle in its tissue.*

(Henry James, quoted in Pitchett, 1979, p. 3)

James's poetic characterization serves to put the Project and this report in perspective. As experience is too immense, too complex, illusive, even too mysterious a phenomenon to fully comprehend, so also is it the case with what is learned from it. There is no pretense in this report that its tables and numbers have miraculously captured that "sensibility" which has eternally eluded the poet. The report's more pedestrian aim has been to capture some small particles of experience, to reduce some part of the mystery to a size and form that can be grasped, understood, manipulated, and from which conclusions may be drawn and lessons learned.

Overview of Project

Case for Experiential Education

The arguments for experiential education are rooted in a concern for the total development of young people—social, psychological, and intellectual. This development is seen as jeopardized by a social milieu that increasingly isolates young people from the kinds of experiences, encounters, and challenges that form the basis for healthy development and that add purpose and meaning for formal education. The aim of social development—the development of active, concerned, involved citizens—is jeopardized by practices which isolate the young from adult society and deny them an active and valued role in it. The aim of sound psychological development—of persons who have a clear sense of who they are, what they believe, and what they can do—is jeopardized by lack of opportunity to demonstrate one's worth and to test, stretch, and challenge who one is and can be. The aims of intellectual development and academic learning are jeopardized by equating education with classroom instruction in an education process that produces graduates who are "information rich and action poor" (Coleman, 1974), who have had insufficient opportunity to test and apply that information, and who have not been prepared to continue learning from the experiences of everyday life outside of school.

More by default than desire or design, the schools have been left to play a central role in the total development of America's young people. Few educators have been at ease with the responsibility. Some have chosen to deny its broadest implications and to focus on the schools' more narrow and traditional aims of developing cognitive skills and transmitting the accumulated experience and wisdom of the society. Others have accepted a broader view—some from a sense of cultural necessity and some from a belief in the interrelationship of all dimensions of development—that no one aspect can be achieved in isolation from the others. Among the latter are numbered many of the advocates of experiential education.

Background of Project

While strong endorsements of experience-based education abound, there is relatively little "hard" evidence to demonstrate or document the impact of such programs on student participants. Little effort has been made to systematically test the assumptions underlying the endorsements or to investigate empirically which specific forms of experiential programs may be the most effective in realizing the hypothesized benefits.

The Evaluation of Experiential Education Project was undertaken to begin filling that gap—to assess the impact of experiential education programs on the psychological, social, and intellectual development of secondary school students. Equally importantly, it aimed at using this data to identify the program variables that are most effective in facilitating such development.

The project was initiated by the Commission on Educational Issues and co-sponsored by the National Association of Secondary School Principals, the National Association of Independent Schools, and the National Catholic Education Association. It evaluated 27 experiential programs in independent, public, and parochial schools around the country. Over 1,000 students participated in these programs. A preliminary study was also conducted, involving nearly 4,000 students in 33 programs.

Primary funding for the Project was provided by the Spencer and Rockefeller Foundations, with additional support from the General Mills Foundation. The Project operated out of the Center for Youth Development and Research, University of Minnesota, under the direction of Drs. Diane Hedin and Dan Conrad.

Defining Experiential Education

For purposes of this research effort, experiential programs are defined as "educational programs offered as an integral part of the general school curriculum, but taking place outside of the conventional classroom, where students are in new roles featuring significant tasks with real consequences, and where the emphasis is on learning by doing with associated reflection."

Selection of Programs

The programs included in the study are of four major types: volunteer service, career internships, outdoor adventure, and community study/political action.

Within each type, individual programs differ in terms of *length*—from four weeks to nine months; *intensity*—from 2–4 hours each week to full-time; nature of *reflective component*—from none to a daily seminar related to the field experience; *student characteristics*—from ages 12 to 19, from good students to poor, and from low income to highly affluent; its *voluntary or compulsory nature*—with nearly all programs being voluntary.

The school programs included in the study were not randomly selected, but chosen because of a demonstrated record of excellence—and as being representative of the major type of experiential programs. It seemed prudent to study only the most well conceptualized and established programs to discover the effects of experiential programs.

We assumed, in addition, that the teachers and administrators involved in exemplary projects would be the persons best able to define, articulate, and specify the fundamental outcomes for experiential education. Furthermore, this research effort was committed to an approach which was practical, understandable, and applicable to everyday life in schools. Thus, a "Panel of Practitioners" (the educators who ran the programs being studied), along with the research project co-directors, were responsible for defining the issues to be studied, for helping to select and develop assessment tools, for implementing the research design, and for helping to interpret the data collected. It would be impossible to overestimate the contribution of this Panel to the conceptualization and implementation of the research effort and the interpretation of the data collected. Such cooperation and counsel made this a shared effort throughout, one in which all felt a commitment to its success.

Selection of Issues

The first step of the research process was to survey the directors of 30 experiential programs. They were asked what they believed to be the actual effects of their programs on students, what each had directly experienced, seen, and heard.

There was a striking similarity in this "testimony of concerned observers." They described a core set of outcomes which each

of them had observed, whether they represented programs in small towns or large cities, work with low-income or affluent youth, or programs featuring outdoor adventure, service, internships, or political action. The important implication was that there are common threads that unite a variety of exemplars of experiential education.

Among the observed effects reported by the directors were 24 which appeared with high regularity. This list was redrawn as a questionnaire and in May 1978, administered to nearly 4,000 students in 33 programs. The students were asked which, if any, of the outcomes represented what they personally had gained from their program. A summary of the results of this survey is presented in Table 1 which is an abridgment of that found in Chapter Three of the final report. On 14 of the 24 items, there was an average agreement level of over 80% across all programs. The most frequently cited outcomes fit into three major categories—social, psychological, and intellectual growth. These became, then, the major areas of investigation for the project itself.

The Research Questions

In regard to *social development,* the research questions were as follows: to what extent do experiential programs have a positive impact on students': a) level of personal and social responsibility; b) attitudes toward others; c) attitudes toward active participation in the community; and d) involvement in career planning and exploration. In regard to *psychological development,* both general self-esteem and self-esteem in social situations were assessed, as was moral development. Finally, in regard to *intellectual and academic growth,* students were asked for

Table 1. What Students Learn in Experiential Learning —
Composite Profile of Students Responses from 30 Experiential Programs (N=4,000)
The first 10 and last 4 of 24 items

| | ITEM (in rank order) | PERCENTAGE OF RESPONSES | | |
		Agree*	Disagree*	Don't Know
1.	Concern for fellow human beings	93	4	3
2.	Ability to get things done and to work smoothly with others	93	4	3
3.	Realistic attitudes toward other people such as the elderly, handicapped, or government officials	88	4	8
4.	Self-motivation to learn, participate, achieve	88	7	5
5.	Self-concept (sense of confidence, sense of competence, self-awareness)	88	7	5
6.	Responsibility to the group or class	86	7	11
7.	Risk taking—openness to new experiences	86	7	8
8.	Sense of usefulness in relation to the community	85	8	6
9.	Problem solving	86	9	5
10.	Risk taking—being assertive and independent	86	9	5
21.	Use of leisure time	60	26	14
22.	Narrowing career choices	54	34	12
23.	To become an effective parent	52	29	19
24.	To become an effective consumer	46	32	22

*Strongly agree and agree are combined, and disagree and strongly disagree are combined.

self-reports on learning—were tested on problem solving and, as mentioned above, tested for levels of moral reasoning.

In addition to looking at the general effects of experiential education on student participants, we were also interested in determining the ways in which different program forms (community service, internships, political action, community study, and adventure education) and formats (length, intensity, characteristics of the individual field experience) affect student learning. For example, do short-term experiences of three to four weeks show any effect on attitudinal change? Does the intensity of the program—two hours versus ten hours per week—affect student outcomes? Are some types of programs, e.g., community service, more likely to promote a sense of social responsibility or interest in community participation? To what extent do the characteristics of each student's individual experience affect the results?

The Research Method

Test Instruments. The overall effects of social, psychological and intellectual development were operationally defined as scores on the test instruments and questionnaires employed in the study. The specific instruments used to measure psychological development were the Defining Issues Test (moral reasoning), the Janis-Field Feelings of Inadequacy Scale (self-esteem in social situations), and the Rosenberg Self-Esteem Scale. Social development was measured by the Social and Personal Responsibility Scale (social responsibility), three semantic differentials (attitudes toward others), and the Owens' Career Exploration Scale (career maturity). Intellectual development was investigated through the Problem-Solving Inventory and through self-reports of participants. The test battery included both standardized tests and adaptions of standardized tests. Two of the tests, the Social and Personal Responsibility Scale and the Problem-Solving Inventory were original instruments designated specifically for this study.

Because the outcomes being measured were elusive, triangulation of the data appeared to be the most reasonable approach. Each outcome was looked at from several different angles: paper-and-pencil tests; systematic observations of parents, teachers, and community supervisors; student journals and writing samples; case studies of individual students and programs; and a host of unobtrusive measures.

Design. All students were pre- and post-tested on or near the first and last days of the program. Six of the experimental groups (at least one in each program type cluster) also had comparisons. These were not random controls, but the students in each were comparable to those in their experimental pair in terms of age, grade in school, geography, grade point average, socio-economic status, classroom programs, and were tested pre- and post- at the same time as their experiential pairs.

Analysis. The data were analyzed in two phases. In the first, pre/post results were compared for each experimental and control group individually, by experimental and control groups combined, and by direct comparison between the four experimental/control pairs available for the study. In the second phase, specific features of the programs were examined to assess their influence on pre/post change scores. The specific elements investigated were: type, length, and intensity of the experience, existence of a reflective component, student demographic characteristics, and the specific characteristics of individual experiences (e.g., how interesting, how demanding of responsibility, etc.). The analytical tools employed included t-tests of significance, analysis of variance, and multiple regression.

Findings: Impact on Students

The results from the formal measures employed in this study demonstrated that the experiential programs did have a positive impact on the psychological, social, and intellectual development of the student participants. This conclusion, while true in general, masks significant patterns of effect and effectiveness which are summarized below.

Psychological Development

An important finding in research in schools is that studying the formal, academic curriculum does not automatically lead to personal and psychological growth. In fact, there is a body of research documenting the largely negative impact of schooling on such variables as self-esteem, interest in learning, and personal autonomy (Sprinthall & Sprinthall, 1977). Proponents of experiential education have argued that psychological growth is more likely to be achieved through their approach to learning. They believe that placing students in well-planned experiential confrontations with practical problems is an effective mode of promoting personal growth. In summary, psychological growth requires challenge, conflict, support, and significant experience.

Did the findings of this study corroborate this theoretical argument for experiential programs? The answer is clearly *yes* as discussed below.

Moral Reasoning. Students in two experience-based programs and one comparison group (from the same school) were administered the Defining Issues Test (DIT) pre- and post-. This is a paper-and-pencil test designed to measure levels of moral reasoning as detailed by Lawrence Kohlberg. All three groups received identical instructions in Kohlberg's theories, the only difference being that the two experiential groups were simultaneously involved in service activities in the community.

The test results showed that both experimental groups attained significant gains in their moral reasoning scores while the comparison group did not gain. This finding substantiated those of several other studies which have likewise shown the combination of significant role-taking experiences and active reflection to be an effective means of promoting growth in this aspect of development.

Self-Esteem. Students in experiential programs did show increases in self-esteem and to a degree slightly but consistently greater than those registered by comparable students in classroom-based programs.

On the Janis-Field Scale, which focuses on the confidence one feels in social situations (e.g., meeting new people, speaking in front of a class), 20 of the 27 experimental groups increased, 10 at a level of statistical significance (<.05). On the Rosenberg Scale, which deals with more general feelings of self-worth (e.g., "I feel I have a number of good qualities"), 23 of the 27 experimental groups increased, 9 at a level of statistical significance. Students in the comparison groups also registered some gain in self-esteem consistently on the Janis-Field Scale (3 of 6 groups increased, 2 significantly). In direct comparison, the experimental groups had greater increases on both scales, but this advantage was statistically significant only on the more stable Rosenberg Scale.

Among program types, the highest absolute levels of self-esteem, even on the pretest, were registered by students entering career internships. It may be that such programs attract students who are relatively more sure of themselves, at least enough to test themselves in adult career roles. The most consistent pre/post gains were registered by students in outdoor programs—both in comparison to other experiential programs and to their own gains on the social and intellectual dimensions of growth examined in the study. Since no other program category showed such consistent results, it suggests that intensive outdoor experience may have a particularly strong effect on self-esteem. This may result from the intensity and uniqueness of such experiences and/or from the fact that evidence of achievement is clearly seen by, matters to, and is immediately reinforced by both teacher and peers.

In summary, the results from the Defining Issues Test and the two measures of self-esteem lend support to the hypothesis that experiential programs can effectively promote the psychological development of adolescents and do so at least somewhat more effectively than classroom-based programs. The data further suggest that the impact is strongest when the experience is most intensive, most dissimilar from ordinary school activities, and, in the case of increased moral reasoning, when there is a combination of action and systematic reflection.

Social Development

In the past decade, there has been a great deal of public concern about the level of personal and social responsibility exhibited by teenagers. Charges of increased privatism, hedonism, and aimlessness among adolescents have become commonplace, along with findings that they feel a strong sense of powerlessness in relation to the larger society and no sense of having a significant role in it (Hedin, 1979). Experiential educators have argued that it is precisely this lack of a significant role in the community and society that has bred apathy, cynicism, and powerlessness. They counter by suggesting that placing students in responsible roles in which their actions affect others will help them develop more responsible attitudes and behaviors.

This section summarizes the findings relevant to this hypothesis: that responsible action in an experienced-based program would have a positive impact on students' levels of personal and social responsibility, have a positive influence on their attitudes toward adults and others, lead them to feel more inclined to participate in their communities, and, relatedly, help them to plan for and explore potential adult careers.

The results reported below clearly show that experience-based programs can have precisely those effects. Despite the inevitable differences between specific programs, there was a strong and consistent showing of positive impact among the experiential programs as a whole. Furthermore, these gains significantly discriminated between these programs and the comparison groups. The latter tended to decline or show no significant change on most of the scales and subscales relating to social development. These results are outlined below according to the specific scales employed.

Social and Personal Responsibility Scale (SPRS). The overall results from the total SPRS scale indicated general positive movement by the experimental groups and no change by the comparisons. The experimental groups combined had a mean increase of almost 2 full points (+1.92, P = <.0001) while the combined comparisons declined (-.09, P=NS). More precisely, 23 of 27 experimental groups increased, 13 by at least 1.50 mean points and at a level of statistical significance. Of the 4 groups which did not increase, 2 had the highest pre-test scores of any of the groups and were still among the highest on the post-test; the other 2 were very low-income groups who generally tended to do poorly on paper-and-pencil measures. In contrast to the above, 5 of the 6 comparison groups declined, 2 at a level of statistical significance.

There were some differences by program types. Career Internship programs showed the largest positive gains (an average of 2.58 points); Community Study/Action was next (1.77); followed by Service (.63) and Outdoor programs (.30).

SPRS Subscales. The SPRS contained five subscales relating to sense of *duty, social welfare* orientation, *social efficacy,* sense of *competence,* and assessment of *performance.* The combined total of all experimental groups showed significant positive change on all five subscales, while among the comparison groups (combined) there was no significant change on any subscale except Social Welfare—in which there was a statistically significant decrease. Nine of the experimental groups showed positive change on each subscale. There were only two instances of significant positive change among the comparison groups, both on the Competence subscale.

Overall, the strongest changes were toward taking responsible *action* as opposed to having more responsible *attitudes*; and, among attitudes, toward having more *personally* responsible attitudes as opposed to *socially* responsible attitudes. This finding is consistent with most research on attitudinal and behavioral change which suggests that changes in behavior tend to precede rather than follow changes in attitude. It also suggests that the traditional model in citizenship education, that instruction in proper attitudes about personal and social obligations will lead to responsible behavior, may need revision. While the evidence from this study can only be suggestive of that conclusion, it is further strengthened by the fact that most of the comparison students were in social studies classes which were deliberately, and apparently ineffectively, aimed at improving attitudes toward taking personal and social responsibility.

One further point from the Social and Personal Responsibility Scale data bears mention. Students in service programs had the highest pre-test scores on the SPRS followed by those in career internships, outdoor programs, and community study. The advantage for students in service programs was largely accounted for by their higher scores on the sense of duty and the social welfare subscales. This would be consistent with the fact that these students had volunteered for programs in which helping and serving others is the major task (in contrast, students in outdoor programs had the lowest social welfare pre-test and post-test scores). Students in Career Internships had the highest scores on the performance and competence subscales, which seems consistent with their choosing placements where they would be working independently with and as adults. It also coincides with their being the highest-ranked students on the two measures of self-esteem reported earlier.

Attitudes Toward Adults. A common critique of modern socialization practices is that young people are locked in an adolescent ghetto separated from meaningful interaction with adults. The implicit assumption is that separation breeds suspicion, if not hostility, and that greater contact with adults would promote more positive attitudes. This latter hypothesis was confirmed by the results of this study. Students in the experiential programs entered into collegial relationship with adults that are atypical of most school and work settings. These students tended to show large, consistent changes on the semantic differential scale toward more positive attitudes toward adults.

There was a positive change in 22 of the 27 experimental groups, and the combined mean change for all the experimentals was +1.45 which was statistically significant at P = <.0001. This mean change of near 1.5 was made on a scale of only 7 possible points. Students in comparison groups, conversely, showed an overall decline of -.74 mean points spread over 5 of the 6 groups.

It is clear, from the above, that the adolescents do not automatically think more highly of adults merely because they have moved a little closer to that status themselves. It depends on what they are doing during that time. Remaining in a classroom with an adult teacher appears not to be a situation which raises their esteem of adults. Associating with adults on a collegial basis outside the classroom does, however, seem to have such a positive effect.

Attitudes Toward Others. A further contention of the proponents of experiential/education is that when students are involved with persons they don't ordinarily encounter, they will come to value them more highly. The data, from a 10-item evaluative semantic differential scale, clearly indicates that community participation has a positive effect on students' evaluations of the people with whom they have been interacting. In the direct contrast between experimental/comparison pairs, each experimental group increased significantly while each of the comparison groups showed a decline. The difference was significant for the individual and the combined comparisons (the latter at <.001).

Considering specific groups or categories, students initially valued hospitals and little kids most highly, followed by old people, business persons, police, and, dead last, junior high kids. On the post-test, the ratings of all these categories had increased significantly—except for hospitals toward which there was a small increase and for business persons toward which there was a slight decrease in valuation.

The small increase in valuation of hospitals may reasonably be explained by the fact that the high pre-test rating (the highest of any category) left little room for positive change. The decrease in relations to business persons is less easily explained. Perhaps it is the nature of interaction, not interaction per se, that creates more positive attitudes. In the case of internships, students perhaps tended more to be observers than participants, a situation that could account for the lack of change.

In any case, the fundamental finding of this portion of the study is that students do tend to show increased appreciation for the people with whom they associate in their off-campus experiences.

Attitudes Toward Being Active in the Community. A further hypothesis of experiential educators is that direct participation in the community will lead students to value such activity more highly and increase the likelihood of their seeing themselves as accepting community responsibilities in the future. The first part of the hypothesis was tested through a semantic differential with pairs such as smart/dumb and useless/useful. The second was tested by single continuum from "something I will do" to "something I won't do." The results from both scales confirmed the hypothesis.

At the time of the pre-test, students in experiential classes valued the general notion of "being active in the community" less highly than did students in traditional classes. The highest rating was given by students in service programs, followed by the comparison group, and then students in community study, career internships, and outdoor programs. By the time of the post-test, the situation was reversed. All of the comparison groups decreased, while 20 of 27 experimental groups increased. The strongest gains were by students in community study and outdoor programs, and the least gain by students in career internships. It must further be noted that for 4 of the 6 comparison groups, the value and importance of community participation had been a deliberate (and seemingly unattained) emphasis of the in-school course.

A further question was whether students' evaluation of being active in the community carries over to an (at least reported) inclination to actually do it. The data here revealed that secondary students rather strongly assert that they will be active in their communities. However, from a position of virtual equality on the pre-test, the experimental students increased and the comparison students declined. A direct comparison between experimental and control groups showed the difference in change scores to be statistically significant.

Career Exploration. One common critique of adolescent socialization is the inability of many youth to make a smooth transition from school to work. Many teenagers appear to have very little information about the myriad careers available, and they fall into the trap of thinking that an interest in some activity implies a lifelong pursuit of one single occupation. An often-expressed goal of experiential learning programs is to increase a young person's knowledge about work and career options. To learn whether this goal was achieved, students were given the Career Exploration Scale.

The data from this scale show that 24 of 27 experimental groups registered a positive gain, 13 at a level of statistical significance. Measures were also registered by the six comparison groups, with 2 at a statistically significant level. The combined change scores for both experimental and comparison groups were significant, though the absolute level of increase was substantially greater for the experimental groups.

The Career Exploration Scale contains two subscales. The first measures Career Action, or the degree to which students have been actively engaged in exploring careers. The second asks about information they have gained about a career field. Analysis of these subscales revealed that the greater overall increase for experiential students was largely accounted for by greater gains on the Action subscale. All 27 experimental groups increased on the Action subscale, 16 significantly so. In contrast, no comparison groups showed significant gains on this subscale and 2 actually declined. The gains on the Information subscale were about equal for the experimental and comparison groups. Apparently, facts can be effectively conveyed either in or out of the classroom. But the experiential approach adds the dimension of active involvement in potential career choices.

Some interesting differences emerged from examining individual program scores. The highest pre-test mean was attained by affluent 12th-graders in an independent school and the lowest means by either junior high or low-income students. It does appear that active planning and exploring of careers is related to both age and income—with older and more affluent students having the advantage.

Among types of programs, those offering career internships did have the largest increases—most particularly a medical careers program for low-income, minority youth and a program featuring semester-long, full-time internship experiences. However, community study, service, and outdoor programs also showed strong increases even though they had almost no organized or explicit focus on careers. It may be that when young people want to learn about careers, they actively seek such information, on their own, in their field experiences.

In summary, the data discussed in this section support the hypothesis that participation in experiential programs does, or at least can, contribute to the social development of adolescents. Students in experiential programs increased significantly in social and personal responsibility, gained more positive attitudes toward adults and others with whom they worked, and felt more positively toward being active in the community. They also showed increased information about, and activity in, exploring careers. The data also show that such increases are not necessary and inevitable outcomes of any and all experiential programs. There were almost always exceptions to the general trends, suggesting there were dynamics operating within the programs that require closer analysis. Such analysis will be presented following the discussion of intellectual development.

Intellectual Development

Theorists of learning and intellectual development, from Aristotle through John Dewey to James Coleman, have stressed the necessary relation of experience and education. Experience serves both as the source of knowledge and as a process of knowing. Education is of, by, and for experience. The study examined this relation by looking both at academic learning and intellectual development.

Amount Learned. Because the programs varied widely regarding academic objectives, it was not practical to directly test the academic learning assumptions through any general test of facts or concepts. Instead, students were asked how much they felt they had learned in their experiential program compared to what they learned in an average class in school. Seventy-three percent of the students reported learning more (41%) or much more (32%) in their experiential program, with 25 of 27 programs having more responses that rounded of to 4 ("learned more") or higher. The mean responses of the other two were somewhat over 3 ("learned about the same"). Only 9% of the students reported learning less.

While all programs received high ratings on this dimension, there was a rather large spread between the higher and lower ranked programs which invited some speculation about the differences between them. Of the 12 highest ranked programs, 11 had a clearly defined seminar/reflective component, an element which characterized less than half (7) of the remaining 15 programs. Looked at from another perspective, 8 of the 12 programs with the highest ratings involved students who might be expected to have a low opinion of regular classes. Four were composed of students in special alternatives for economically and educationally disadvantaged students, and four others involved students who had opted out of regular school for a full semester (one year) to participate in an experience-based program. These factors did not characterize any of the lower ranked programs. Finally, the higher ranked programs were longer and more intensive than the lower programs.

The data indicate, therefore, that students tend to feel they learn more from experiential programs than from regular school classes and that this is most pronounced when the experiences are longer (at least 12 weeks), more intensive (at least 2 hours daily), include a formal reflective component, and, to a lesser extent, involve students who may be disenchanted with traditional classroom programs.

Problem Solving. The primary measure of intellectual development used in the study was the Problem-Solving Inventory. This Inventory presented students with 3 interpersonal problems and led them through the steps in problem solving outlined by John Dewey. Student responses were scored, pre- and post-, according to the number of alternatives listed, the degree to which they took responsibility for solving the problem, the degree to which they justified a decision according to its consequences, and the level of empathy and complexity of thought shown in the overall analysis of the problem.

On the whole, neither the experimental nor comparison students showed significant increases on the first three indices. This appeared, however, to be more a factor of test weariness than lack of program effect. Only one program showed significant increases in the alternatives and consequences indices, and this program was unique in the degree the students faced problems similar to those in the stimulus stories and to which problem solving per se was a central focus of their seminar sessions. One other finding of interest on these dimensions is that in nearly half of the cases (48%), students selected other than their first alternative listed as their "best choice." This suggests that the request for further alternatives did help elicit the best thinking of students and confirms the common sense notion that one's first impulse does not always represent one's best judgment.

The heart of the Problem-Solving Instrument is its Empathy/Complexity Index. This Index assesses the ability and/or inclination of the respondents to empathize with the key "other" in the story, the level of need upon which s/he focuses, and the complexity of analysis applied to the problem. The pre-test means were quite similar for all groups, with 27 of the 33 experimental and control groups having means that rounded off to level 4 (conventional, stereotyped thought and concern). On the post-test, there was general movement by experimental students toward level 5, a more complex pattern of thought with a focus on relational concerns. This is discussed more fully below.

The Complexity/Empathy Index did clearly discriminate between experimental and comparison groups and between types of experiential programs. In terms of mean changes, 21 of the 27 experimental groups increased, 8 increasing at least a one-third step on the seven-point scale. Five of the 6 comparison groups decreased, and one showed a non-significant increase.

Most interesting was the pattern between types of programs. To test a hypothesis, programs were divided according to the degree in which students were 1) directly confronted with interpersonal problems similar to those in the stimulus stores, and/or 2) where problem solving was a deliberate focus of accompanying seminar sessions. These turned out to be critical variables in promoting change in complexity/empathy. Programs which featured both conditions registered an average mean increase of .59 points. Programs in which all students had one condition and some (not all) had the other, showed an average increase of .22 points. Programs in which both conditions were only partially present showed an average mean gain of .17. Programs in which students had neither element showed an average decrease of -.15.

The data reported in this section suggest that experiential education programs can and do have a positive effect on student learning and intellectual development. This is most strongly the case when the program features a combination of direct experience and formal reflection on that experience.

Summary

To recapitulate what has been said thus far, the pre/post test data clearly show that experiential education programs can have a positive impact on students' psychological, social, and intellectual development. Students in experiential programs tended to increase significantly, both in absolute terms and in relation to students in classroom programs, in the major scales employed in this study. These included tests of moral reasoning, self-esteem, social and personal responsibility, attitudes toward adults and others, career exploration, and empathy/complexity of thought.

While the results were extremely positive on a general level, they were not invariably so. That is, on every scale there were important differences among the experiential programs. The discussion shifts, thus, toward examining the dynamics within individual programs that could account for the differences in obtained results.

Findings: Correlates of Effectiveness

The second major focus of the Evaluation of Experiential Learning Project was to identify the program practices which were most effective in facilitating development in students. The factors examined for effect were: 1) general *program features*: nature of off-campus experience, length, intensity, and reflective component; *student characteristics*: age, grade point average, and socio-economic status; and *characteristics of individual experiences*, including the degree of autonomy, amount of direction, how interesting and varied they seemed to participants, and the like.

The safest conclusion that can be drawn from the data is that no single practice or set of practices guarantees effectiveness from all students. Within every program and every type of program there were students who gained a great deal and others who did not. There were some clear patterns, however, patterns which suggest interesting hypotheses concerning the effective operations of experiential programs.

Program Features

As described earlier, there were four general types of programs in this study: service, outdoor adventure, career internships, and community study/action. In actual practice, however, few of these were pure types, with elements of one or more (e.g., service) being found in more than one category of program. It may have been this factor as much as anything that resulted in there being no discernible relation between program type and student growth. While service programs appeared to do somewhat better than others on rankings of programs on intellectual and social development, the advantage virtually disappeared in a regression analysis which controlled for other program and student characteristics. Other elements, however, did appear to make a difference.

Among other program features, the presence of a formal (and at least weekly) seminar proved to be the single strongest factor in explaining positive student change. This was particularly true on measures of social and intellectual development. Interestingly, there was no clear relationship between a seminar and growth in measures of personal growth such as self-esteem. Perhaps students can make personal meaning of their experiences on their own, but if this meaning is to affect their broader social attitudes and intellectual skills, systematic and directed reflection must be added.

Other factors which consistently related to positive student change were length and, to a lesser degree, intensity. Experiences lasting a full semester (18 weeks) were relatively stronger than shorter experiences, as were those in which students were in field placements 2 or more hours, 4–5 days per week. Of these two factors, that of length was stronger than intensity, though even in combination they were not as powerful predictors of change as was the presence of a seminar. It must be emphasized, however, that all of these factors collectively did not predict more than about 5% of the variance (by regression analysis) in pre/post change scores.

Student Characteristics

The student characteristics analyzed were age, grade point average, and socio-economic status. These were even less influential than program features, accounting for only about 3% of the variance between pre/post scores. Among the characteristics, only age showed any influence at all, with older students showing somewhat greater growth than younger students, especially on issues of social development. Neither student GPA nor socio-economic status were at all significant in predicting change. One other relevant fact which should be mentioned is that there did turn out to be a positive reaction between maturity (as measured by the Complexity/Empathy Scale) and the degree of approval given to an experience-based program.

The general finding of no strong relation between student demographic characteristics and program effectiveness does support one common contention of experiential education: that such experiences can benefit a wide variety, if not all kinds, of students.

Characteristics of Experience

One of the major problems in educational research and evaluation is that the assumption often has to be, or at least is, made that the program has been implemented as described and that all students participating in it have had the same experience. That neither is usually the case can be attested to by anyone closely associated with educational programs. Thus, it was an aim of this study to go beyond gross program descriptors and examine more directly the specific experiences of students within the programs. It proved to be a fruitful search.

Compared with program features and student characteristics, the specific characteristics of an individual's experience proved the more powerful predictors of pre/post gains. While the former two categories combined explained no more than 8% of the variance in change scores, the latter consistently accounted for from 15% to 20% of variance. The finding lends credence to the notion that individuals experience educational programs idiosyncratically and that this is especially likely to be true in experience-based programs. The specific pattern of impact is outlined below.

The first issue examined was the relation between characteristics of experience and general rating of the program. The characteristics contributing most strongly toward a student rating their program as "excellent" or "good" was that the experiences were rated as being "interesting" and that the student felt s/he was "appreciated for their work."

While feeling appreciated and doing interesting things contributed to favorable program ratings, these characteristics had little or nothing to do with whether students grew from their participation in a program. The factors which contributed most strongly to pre/post gains were, rather, a mixture of features describing a combination of autonomy (e.g., "did things myself") and a collegial relationship with adults (e.g., "discussed experiences with teachers"). The 13 characteristics which made any appreciable impact on student growth are listed, by rank, in Table 2.

Table 2. Relative Effect of Characteristics of Experiences on Mean Gain Scores for All Tests Combined

Rank	Characteristics of Experience
1.	Discussed experiences with teachers.
2.	Did things myself instead of observing.
3.	Adults did not criticize me or my work.
4.	Had adult responsibilities.
5.	Developed personal relations with someone on site.
6.	Had freedom to explore own interests.
7.	Discussed experiences with family and friends.
8.	Felt I made a contribution.
9.	Had a variety of tasks.
10.	Was free to develop/use own ideas.
11.	Got help when I needed.
12.	Made important decisions.
13.	Had challenging tasks.

It should be noted that the characteristics that the experiences were "interesting" did not make this list. Even more significantly, characteristics which describe a more typical student/adult relationship (esp., "given enough training to do my tasks" and "I was given clear directions") did not contribute to pre/post gains and, in fact, correlated negatively with them on several scales.

The characteristics of experience were further examined to see if certain ones contributed more to one kind of growth than another. In Table 3, the strongest contributors to social growth are listed next to the strongest influences on indices of personal development.

As evident from Table 3, it turned out that the characteristics suggesting autonomy (e.g., "free to develop and use own ideas")

Table 3. Relative Influence of Characteristics of Experience on Social and Personal Growth

Social Development	Rank	Personal Development
Discussed experiences with teachers	(1)	Did things myself instead of observing
Discussed experiences with family and friends	(2)	Free to develop and pursue own ideas
Adults did not criticize me or my work	(3)	Had challenging tasks
Had adult responsibilities	(4)	Developed personal relations with someone at site
Made important decisions	(5)	Free to explore my own interests
Felt I made a contribution	(6)	Discussed experience with teachers
Had a variety of tasks	(7)	Felt I made a contribution
Free to explore own interests	(8)	NS
Developed personal relations with someone at site	(9)	NS

were more influential in promoting personal growth (e.g., self-esteem) than in social growth (e.g., responsibility). Conversely, the characteristics suggesting a collegial relationship with, and even guidance by, adults, showed the opposite pattern of influence. In short, personal growth was stimulated most by dealing autonomously with challenging tasks, while social development accrued more from interaction with adults—as long as it was in a non-student role.

Analysis of student responses to an open-ended question asking them to explain why they rated their program as excellent or good revealed another interesting pattern. The majority of responses described personal benefits to the participant (e.g., "personal sense of improvement") while only a small minority cited more socially relevant gains (e.g., "affected another person," or "increased understanding of others' needs").

It goes only slightly beyond the data given to argue that the analysis suggests that students will rate a program highly if the experiences are interesting, if they're shown appreciation for their effort, and if they sense some personal gain from the experience. Similarly, students will make the strongest *personal* gain when they are given some autonomy to act on their own and to use their own ideas. In contrast, positive change in social attitudes and reasoning skills requires more interaction with adults—where the involvement is collegial, not patronizing, and when they can initiate the contact.

In summary, it was found that the most powerful predictors of growth were the *characteristics of the experiences* of individual students, with features suggesting auton-

omy being most productive of personal development and features suggesting a collegial relationship with adults and others being
most productive of social development.
Among *program* features, the most powerful
positive factor was the existence of a regular
seminar. Of somewhat less influence was
length of program (especially if 18 weeks or
longer); even less influential was intensity
(better if 2 or more hours 4–5 days a week).
There was a small positive relationship
between age and growth on social and intellectual measures. No significant relationship was found between student growth
and general type of program, on the characteristics of student GPA, or socio-economic status.

One final word may be the most significant of all. Ninety-five percent of the participants in experiential programs rated their
own program as either excellent (49%) or
good (46%). Perhaps no further comment is
needed.

Implications

It is not presumed that this study has defini-
tively answered the central questions of educators. Nonetheless, its findings, combined
with others reported within it, do contain
implications that merit consideration and application even before "all the facts are in."
Central among these are: 1) the demonstrated value of continuing and expanding
experiential programs; 2) the importance of
a developmental focus for education; 3) the
need for direct experience to meet developmental goals; 4) needed changes in teacher
education; and 5) the possibility and need for
simultaneously working toward personal
growth and social improvement.

Value of Experiential Education

The clearest and most significant conclusion
of this study is that experiential programs are
a powerful educational vehicle for promoting personal and intellectual development
and can do so more effectively than classroom instruction. The most important implication for secondary schools is that
experience-based programs should be
adopted and expanded. This is a significant
departure from the overwhelming trend in
public education to a return to "the basics."
The usual—and in our view—narrow meaning of "the basics" is classroom instruction
in symbolic representation of experience.
The consistent finding that classroom instruction in a traditional mode, as represented by the comparison groups, showed no
improvement in personal and intellectual development, in contrast to consistent, strong
growth for experiential programs, should
lead educators and the general public to
rethink the notion that only classroom instruction is legitimate and effective. The
strong positive showing of the experience-based programs do warrant schools
offering such experiences. At the very least,
experiential programs currently in existence
should be maintained. In many areas of the
country. declining enrollment and declining resources have led school systems to discontinue
all but the most traditional classroom instruction. This study indicates that dropping experiential programs is a serious mistake. On the
contrary, well-constructed programs, as those
in this study, warrant a significant and expanding role in secondary schools.

Development Focus for Education

The first implication—that experiential programs are effective in promoting develop-

ment and should be adopted by secondary schools—assumes that development is a legitimate aim of education.

It is through a peculiar misuse of the English language, or perhaps a symptom of something deeper, that the comprehension of symbols and the manipulation of mediated experience has come to be identified as learning the "basics." Such an interpretation of what is fundamental ignores the sources of learning (experience), the nature of the learner (especially development), and the purpose of learning (personal growth and social improvement). Theorists such as John Dewey (1902/1964) and Lawrence Kohlbert (1972) have made cogent arguments for considering development to be the aim of education; research on the effects of schooling (Heath, 1978; McClelland, 1973) has demonstrated the predictive power of personal development (in contrast to academic achievement) for adult success; the present study and others have shown the viability of promoting such development through deliberate educational interventions. It would seem more than reasonable for educators to act on this information. The aim and effect would not be the denigration of more traditional goals, but to imbue them with new vitality and purpose. For experiential educators as well, a focus on development can provide both a framework for organizing activities and a goal—that of promoting social, psychological, and intellectual development.

The Need for Experience

Educators who are serious about development as an aim of education may also have to be serious about adopting experiential methods for achieving that goal. Developmental theory, from the time of Dewey to the present, has stressed that development requires interaction, transaction, conflict, cognitive dissonance, consequential choices, and action on behalf of those choices. The more that children and adolescents are isolated from broad, varied, and significant experiences in the social environment, the more must schools encourage such involvement to successfully work toward facilitating development.

Furthermore, if significant experience is truly a critical element in development, it ought not be restricted to isolated doses in the later school years but be a central focus from the elementary years and on.

Finally, the provision of more meaningful participation cannot be met by the schools alone. The findings of this and other studies that experiential programs can promote development must not be overdramatized. It would be foolish to argue or believe that a change in school practice is enough to substantially counter the effects of impoverished experience and prolonged childhood and adolescence. Ways must be found to share the educational mission with the broader society and to provide opportunities for children and youth to be more seriously involved in their communities.

Changes in Teacher Education

Education through experience, and for human development, implies a new kind of teacher training. Needed is an emphasis on understanding adolescence and human development in contrast to the current emphasis on teaching a discipline. Needed also is increased knowledge of, and involvement in, the wider community by teachers themselves—partly for increasing their capacity to facilitate experiences within it, and partly for their own renewal and continued development.

Personal Growth and Social Improvement

> As the material of genuine development is that of human contacts and associations, so the end, the value that is the criterion and directing guide of educational work, is social. The acquisition of skills is not an end in itself. They are things to be put to use, and that use is their contribution to a common and shared life.
>
> (Dewey, 1934/1964, p. 11)

Americans have always had an enormous faith in education: that it would improve the individual and also make for a more prosperous, more just society. The above statement by John Dewey may serve as a gentle reminder that both goals are essential for either to be achieved. Perhaps one of the greatest strengths of experiential education is that it provides the opportunity to work on both goals simultaneously. As the individual grows from direct experience in the community, so may the community benefit, and not just in the long run, from the participation of youth in it. The study indicated that personal growth is a more automatic outcome of experiential education than is social development. To accomplish the dual goals of personal *and* social improvements, a new kind of relationship between student and teacher is necessary—a collegial mentorship.

There is much left to be learned about human development, about experiential education, and about how to bring about a better society. This study and the others cited within it do not tell us all we need to know. They provide a beginning and some idea of how to proceed. Again, John Dewey (1932) said it best:

> The sources of educational science are any portion of ascertained knowledge that enter into the heart, head and hands of educators, and which, by entering in, render the performance of the educational function more enlightened, more humane, more truly educational than it was before. But there is no way to discover what is "more truly educational" except by the continuation of the educational act itself. The discovery is never made, it is always making.
>
> (pp. 76–77)

Further Questions for Practice and Research

William Perry is fond of pointing out that people are bigger than the theories used to explain them. In like fashion, issues of education and human development are larger than can be contained in or investigated by one study. Therefore, it would be well to cite some important issues that require further examination.

Impact on Others and the Wider Community

If students are truly involved in significant experiences with real consequences, it should then be possible to detect the effects of their activities on others and on their communities, as well as on themselves. While the assertion is rather commonly made that experiential education programs can contribute to meeting the real economic, social, and educational needs of communities and the nation (National Commission on Resources for Youth, 1974), relatively little evidence has been assembled to date. An investigation into the social and economic impact of youth participation would seem particularly important as discussion of the utility of a national Youth Service Program grows more serious (Landrum, 1979).

Who Benefits?

Important questions remain concerning who benefits most from experience-based educational programs—and why. For example, to what degree is maturity, or advanced development, a cause or a consequence of learning through experience? If the exercise of autonomy leads to growth, is the demand for it a factor of the experience or setting itself, or do certain kinds of individuals carve out autonomous roles within the experiences made available to them? Is there a relation between cognitive style and ability or propensity to learn from experience? What are the specific skills and habits that enable a person to learn and grow from experience? Can these be isolated, and then taught and learned in the way that skills in learning from symbols have been? Such questions require a deeper, more focused examination of individuals and specific experiences than was possible or intended in this study.

How to Guide Experience and Reflection

As instructive as it may be to know that experience must be accompanied by reflection, it is not practically useful without more precise information on how best to structure, guide, and encourage such reflection. In addition, more information is needed to identify the kinds of off-campus activities which are most effective for achieving particular developmental and academic goals. One important issue, for example, is whether work-study (and other job experience) programs have effects similar to programs located in the general academic curriculum, such as were the focus of this study.

Effect on Academic Knowledge and Skills

The antidote to being information-rich and experience-poor is not to reverse the condition. More insight is needed to understand how direct experience and personal development may enhance the traditional academic aims of schooling—and vice versa.

Long-term Effects

The investigation of the impact of experience on development must be enriched by the study of, in Dewey's terms, "its influence upon later experience," the degree to which "they promote having desirable future experiences" (1938/1962, p. 27). Clearly it would be important to know if patterns established in the program—of learning from experience, of participating in the community, of exercising autonomy—were continued. Also of interest would be students' assessment of what aspects of their experiences seemed particularly valuable a year or two after, as opposed to during or immediately following, the experience.

Research Methods

An important problem in the investigation of experiential education has been the lack of appropriate methods and instruments. The Social and Personal Responsibility Scale and the Problem-Solving Inventory were developed to help fill this gap. The results indicate they were useful measures and merit further development and refinement.

Results from this study demonstrated that paper-and-pencil tests can be useful in detecting important effects of experiential education. They also demonstrated some of the limitations of this approach. Evidence from this and other studies suggests that such measures are less than satisfactory for some students, particularly those with a history of negative experiences with testing. In addition, such measures do not adequately capture the small individual changes, the critical incidents, the nuances, the sense and sensibility of experience. Thus, additional techniques must be developed and used. Interviews, observations, analyses of journals, ethnographies, and case studies could be used both to triangulate and to see beneath the findings from paper-and-pencil measures. Such measures could uncover, in Dewey's terms, "the qualitative characteristics of things as they are originally and 'naturally' observed" (1929/1960, p. 90).

Programs

An important aim of the study was to include schools that would represent a variety of program orientations (service, career internship, community study, outdoor adventure); of school types (independent, parochial, public); of geographic areas and types of community (urban, suburban, small town); of program structure (seminar/non-seminar, short and intermittent experience to long-term and intensive); and of student populations (poverty level to affluent, low to high grade point average).

Within these general guidelines, the chief criteria for inclusion in the study were that the program have a reputation for excellence, have been in operation for at least four years, that it be an integral part of its school's academic program, and that there be a local interest in being included. Potential participants were identified out of the project directors' working knowledge of experiential programs, nominations from the

sponsoring organizations (NAIS, NASSP, NCEA), and recommendations from the National Commission on Resources for Youth, Inc., and from the National Center for Service Learning. Of the schools finally contacted, only three chose not to be included. Of those who were included, three were unable to complete the testing (one independent, one parochial, and one public). The latter were replaced by schools which applied on their own initiative and met the criteria for inclusion.

The final roster of programs was as representative as might have been hoped for. The chief imbalances were an underrepresentation of schools from the West and South and of programs which had outdoor adventure (à la Outward Bound) as an exclusive program focus. By all other criteria, the programs were relatively balanced.

It must be noted, and cannot be too strongly emphasized, that any success achieved by this project was in no small measure due to the efforts of the individual program directors and administrators. They were responsible for identifying the key outcomes of experiential learning, defining the focus of the study, administering the tests themselves, and helping to interpret the data. Without such capable, willing, and energetic people, there is no possible way that a study of this scope could have been carried out, short of a twenty-fold increase in staff and budgets—and then it would have been doubtful.

———————

Schools included in the Project are: **Independent:** Dana Hall School, Wellesley, MA; Francis W. Parker School, Chicago, IL; Carolina Friends School, Durham, NC: Duluth Cathedral High School, Duluth, MN;

Parochial: St. Benedict's Preparatory School, Newark, NJ; Bellarmine High School, Tacoma, WA; Ward High School, Kansas City, KS; **Public:** Eisenhower High School, Hopkins, MN; Mitchell High School, Colorado Springs, CO: Minneapolis Public Schools; Allegheny Intermediate Unit, Pittsburgh; St. Paul Open School; South Brunswick High School, Monmouth Junction, NJ; Rochester, Minnesota Public Schools; Bartram School of Human Services, Philadelphia, PA; Beverly Hills High School; Ridgewood High School, Norridge, IL; Kirkwood High School, Kirkwood, MO; North Central High School, Indianapolis, IN.

Editor's Note: A preliminary report of the Evaluation of Experiential Learning Project was published earlier in *The Journal of Experiential Education* under the title: "Johnny Says He is Learning... Through Experience," Spring 1977, Vol. 2, No. 1. We are pleased to offer here the complete results of the study.

A summary of this study and/or the *Project Instrument and Scoring Guide* are available from the Center for Youth Development and Research, 48 McNeal Hall, University of Minnesota, St. Paul, MN 55108.

An Introduction to Research and Evaluation in Practice

by Richard Flor

Today, the educational climate is undergoing great change. "If experiential educators are to have an influence on the direction of public and private education in the closing years of this century, it is critical that we act now" (Kraft, 1984, p. 3). That "action" refers to broadening the impact experiential educators have on individuals in a variety of new settings, including more conventional education contexts. Paramount in efforts to integrate experiential education into more mainstream learning will be the ability to provide more concrete evidence as to program accomplishments. While experiential educators "know" the value of experience and reflection, the "problem lies in convincing other professionals and lay people" (Ewert, 1987, p. 4). Research and evaluation provide tools and methodologies which can help validate experiential education practice in order to gain greater credibility for the experiential learning process and a better understanding of it. This article is intended to dispel some of the mystery surrounding research and evaluation while providing basic definitions and discussing the benefits of these activities. In addition, readers are provided with some suggestions on how to begin a research and evaluation project.

While research and evaluation share many of the same methods and tools for gathering information, and consequently may be thought of as falling under the general heading of "disciplined inquiry," there are some fundamental differences which can be highlighted through a description of each process.

The Research Process

Research may be viewed as the foundation of disciplined inquiry. A researcher may want to investigate some phenomena to further his or her knowledge. Thus, questions or hypotheses about the phenomena are formulated as a means for focusing the search for information. Often, one begins the research process with a review of the literature on the topic. The review serves two main purposes: 1) to summarize the current state of knowledge about the topic, and 2) to minimize the chance that time will be needlessly spent investigating something which has previously been studied. In general, the review process helps the researcher further define the questions to be asked and the methods to be used in answering them.

Theories about concepts such as self-esteem, motivation, learning, behavioral and cognitive processes, socialization, and group dynamics all gain support through empirical studies. In efforts to understand more about experiential education, questions may be asked such as: 1) *How* are students affected? 2) *What* is affected? 3) *Why* does change take place? and 4) *When* is change most likely to occur? These questions may be answered by ongoing research in individual and social learning processes. Understanding such complex processes takes time, and no single study will "prove" why experiential education is effective.

There are two very different philosophical approaches to research which have been labeled rationalistic (positivist) and naturalistic (Klint & Priest, 1987). *Rationalistic research* is driven by questions aimed at "obtaining generalizable knowledge by testing relationships among variables or by describing generalizable phenomena" (Worthen & Sanders, 1987). Important here is the concept of a *variable*, which may fall into one of two broad categories.

Independent variables are factors which are manipulated or chosen by the experimenter (Howell, 1987), such as: program length and intensity, activities, teaching methods, age or sex of participants, and course components.

Dependent variables are those factors not directly under the researcher's control (Howell, 1987), and may be thought of as the "outcomes" of a program, such as: increased self-esteem, greater care and concern for the environment, better listening and communication skills, or more compassion for fellow beings. Thus, rationalistic research is interested in gaining an understanding of educational processes and hopes to discover causal relationships (Cook & Campbell, 1979).

The relationships between variables are sought to identify which dependent variables are influenced by which independent variables. One might ask, "Is self-esteem (dependent variable) related to the number of risk-taking activities (independent variable) engaged in during the course?" If a relationship is found, then there is new in-formation upon which new questions may be asked (e.g., Is there an optimal number of risk-taking activities for a certain course?). In this manner, research can be used as a means for increasing our understanding of human nature (or any phenomena for that matter). Questions with a broader or more abstract scope may guide researchers in theory building.

Naturalistic research takes an alternative philosophical approach, assuming that there is no one fixed, objective reality and no set of generalizable principles and theories that govern it (Rowley, 1987). This approach is not interested in searching for general cause-and-effect relationships between variables, but instead attempts to understand and describe the complex interactions of each setting. There may be the ability to transfer knowledge from setting to setting, but not to make universal generalizations across them. Each situation is different and there is not one reality (see Rowley, 1987, for further discussion of the differences between the two approaches).

Both approaches to research aim to generate knowledge and understanding of the educational experience through disciplined inquiry over the long term. But what about the short-term question of whether or not a program is really having an impact on participants? This is the role for evaluation.

The Evaluation Process

Evaluation asks questions about the worth or value of something and is concerned with gathering information which aids in making decisions about a program or product. Worthen and Sanders (1987) state, "In education, it is the formal determination of the quality, effectiveness, or value of a program, product, process, objective, or curriculum" (p. 22). There are two main types of evaluation which are most commonly recognized: formative (process), and summative (outcome) evaluation.

Formative evaluation is generally undertaken to provide information which is aimed at increasing the quality or effectiveness of a program; it is conducted during the operation or planning of a program (Worthen & Sanders, 1987). *Summative evaluation* is conducted at the end of the program and assesses outcomes or goals. A central question evaluators must keep in mind in either formative or summative evaluation focuses on who the decision makers are: from the instructor, program planner, and administrator, to the student who chooses which program to attend. Thus, a *stakeholder* is any individual or group that will be affected by or use evaluation results (Worthen & Sanders, 1987). For example, participants, parents, staff, funding agencies, and school districts, may ultimately be affected by the outcome of an evaluation. Stakeholders may be affected in different ways, depending on their relationship with the program, and whether they are actively involved in program decisions or passively affected by the outcomes of those decisions. Evaluation standards stress the importance of identifying all stakeholders and provide guidelines for how information is gathered and presented in responsible fashion (Joint Committee, 1981). In fact, it is often the stakeholder or audience for which the evaluation is being conducted that determines the type of evaluation.

Regardless of whether one decides to conduct a research-based project or an evaluation of a program, the issue of control and manipulation of variables needs to be addressed. The choice of naturalistic and rationalistic approaches requires one to make decisions about the generalizability of findings and how much the actual evaluation interferes with normal program operations. The notion of manipulating variables to determine which ones affect program quality is unsettling to many practitioners who would prefer a less intrusive approach. Ultimately, the purpose of the evaluation or research will determine the design options from which to choose.

Is There a Need for Research and Evaluation?

The answer to this question depends on one's perspective. One could just as well ask, "Do the students who participate in an experiential education program *need* to be there?" No, unless they have an interest in learning new skills or gaining personal insight. The same may be said for research and evaluation. No, it is not needed unless experiential educators hope to improve educational strategies and increase effectiveness, further justifying the growing profession! If there is an interest in program development or questions about learning outcomes for students, then the answer is YES. Programs that avoid research and evaluation will "yield little in the way of new theoretical or developmental knowledge which could help the practitioner deliver a better product (Ewert, 1987, p. 5). Of course, there may be a much more practical need for conducting program evaluation, much less esoteric than questions of why or how learning occurs: Program survival!

Imagine a program is up for review by the funding agency who supports it. The program has run for three years, but as budgets tighten, the funding agency wants to know just what is being done for three weeks in the woods. They want significant evidence of positive benefits, and ask for an evaluation of the program's effectiveness. What should be done? Where does one begin?

The bottom line is to improve the quality of learning which students experience as program participants. As experiential educators move into more varied educational settings and work with a greater diversity of individuals, it will be even more important to monitor effectiveness. Do the same learning outcomes happen in an urban classroom that take place in the wilderness? Are the same values stressed? Is there adequate opportunity for reflection and processing? Is there a distinct difference in the quality of experiences available in the urban environment as compared to the wilderness? Practitioners need to begin asking these types of questions in an effort to maintain and improve effectiveness as experiential programs become more integrated into conventional education settings.

There are many different reasons from a practitioner's perspective to conduct research and evaluation, but three are most prominent: gaining support and credibility, program improvement, and marketing.

Gaining Support and Credibility

Perhaps the greatest challenge facing the field of experiential education will be gaining acceptance in the established social systems. While many professionals in the education, health care, and criminal justice systems are looking for change, there is a natural skepticism toward anything labeled new or progressive. The status quo is often hard to change. Existing organizations and funding agencies will want to know the outcomes and benefits from incorporating experiential learning methods into their programs. More than anecdotes, they will want numbers supporting stated outcomes and results. In addition, experiential educators need to be certain that experiential methods are appropriate to new settings and different populations (Ewert, 1987). Research evaluation can help provide qualitative and quantitative findings which support the value and limits of experiential education.

Program Improvement

While gaining support for a program is certainly a valid reason for engaging in research and evaluation, maintaining program quality is an equally important factor. For many organizations this alone may provide the motivation for gathering information on the processes and outcomes of their program. In addition, stakeholders, especially those who hold power over whether or not a program exists (hardly a minor detail), will be curious about the quality control systems in place in the program.

In a sense, some form of disciplined inquiry should be a natural part of program development as a sort of organizational reflection and processing not unlike that in which students are engaged.

Marketing

There is a need to attract participants in addition to convincing funding agencies and administrators of the benefits of integrating experiential education into their programs. Certainly, positive outcomes identified through research and evaluation may be beneficial in selling a product to potential customers. Experiential educators may forget that a program exists within a broader economic environment, and to some funding agencies and administrators, financial stability is of primary importance. While this should be lower on a list for reasons to conduct program evaluation, it is nonetheless one way of utilizing information gained through disciplined inquiry. No program, however good it may be, can exist for long without students.

It is important to understand that there can be an overlap between research and evaluation efforts in these three areas; a good project may serve all three. The two guiding factors in performing either research or evaluation will be 1) the questions being asked, and 2) the audience and stakeholders for which the project is being conducted.

Where to Begin

First, one needs to identify the question to be explored. For example, what interpersonal skills do students gain from a two-week wilderness course? The next step is to determine the types of information needed to answer this question. It might be useful to ask students to write down what they learned, or observe them during their interactions with others on the course. It may be interesting to know whether the skills transfer to school or work settings. Friends and family members could be polled to assess whether the person has changed at home and

if the new skills are actually used. It is important to note that even a project asking relatively simple questions can involve the collection of a lot of information and require an investment of a wealth of resources.

Most administrators already have extensive data gathered on their programs, such as: number of participants, types of programs taught, program plans, students questionnaires and interviews, instructor notes, etc. These records may provide the foundation for program development through evaluation studies. Some programs already use this information as feedback to foster improvement. If not, or if one is interested in asking more complex questions by conducting some form of disciplined inquiry, guidance from an expert may be helpful.

Probably the best way to begin is by consulting someone who has experience or knowledge in research or evaluation. While many of the methods of gathering and analyzing data are relatively simple to perform, getting started on the right track can minimize problems later on. Often a cooperative effort between a practitioner and researcher can help in designing useful evaluations which promote greater knowledge and lead to program improvement (Hamilton, 1979). Colleges and universities are one source of expertise. Better yet, look to staff. There may be someone who could help in putting together an evaluation project.

The costs and benefits of performing research or evaluation need to be carefully weighed prior to conducting such a project. Without adequate time, energy, commitment, and expertise, the value of investing research and evaluation is questionable.

Conclusion

Experiential education has much to offer individuals in our changing society. Research and evaluation can play an important part in identifying the positive outcomes of experiential programs. In addition, program quality will improve as a greater understanding of the components and processes inherent in experiential learning develops.

Many people, in a variety of settings, can benefit from the process of experiential learning: quality experiences combined with personal reflection. As a profession interested in expanding its impact and integrating into more conventional social systems, the process of gaining credibility and acceptance will be crucial for the impact to be of a long-term nature. Yet programs must grow and develop through a reflective process similar to that which is so effective for students. The ability to look inside a program, to understand essential components, and to weed out that which does not foster growth and learning for students is needed. Just as learning for an individual is often preceded by personal questions, doubt, fear, and the need for understanding, so too can experiential education programs and practice benefit from inquiry into significant questions.

Meaningful Methods: Evaluation Without the Crunch
by Darl G. Kolb

To a small child with a hammer, everything looks like it needs a pounding. Likewise, program evaluation often becomes a method in search of a problem, rather than a variety of methods employed selectively to address a particular problem or interest. Experiential educators are not immune to this trend. It is possible that they entirely miss what they need to know about their programs by routinely administering questionnaires or standardized scales because they are the hammer of education measurement. It is odd that a discipline devoted to alternatives to conventional education relies so heavily upon conventional methods of inquiry when evaluating its work. As Ewert (1987, p. 5) puts it, "All too often research in experiential education becomes an exercise in data generation rather than the production of meaningful findings."

On the other hand, to continue with the metaphor, some experiential educators have thrown the hammer away, pretending that nothing needs a pounding. They reject conventional methodological approaches and assert as practitioners that some experiences are impossible to evaluate. They imply that experiential learning transcends all bounds of inquiry.

I suggest a third perspective in which the evaluation of experiential education programs and processes is considered a viable opportunity for increased understanding through more appropriate methods of inquiry. In short, there have been a limited number of approaches utilized within quite varied and complex educational contexts. The purpose of this article is to review some alternative methods of inquiry which can complement and/or replace the paper-and-pencil survey, achievement tests, personality assessments, and other commonly used measures of educational success.

Clarifications

A few caveats are in order. First, while the methods outlined below are qualitative, there is no intended inference that quantitative methods are "bad" or "wrong" in experiential education settings. There is a long-standing debate over the validity of qualitative versus quantitative measures and their underlying philosophical paradigms of research in the social sciences; however, it is not the subject of this article. For discussions of these issues as they relate to experiential education, see Chenery (1987), Klint and Priest (1987), and Rowley (1987). Moreover, some of the strategies featured here may involve what is known as "mixed methodology," approaches which use both types of methods (Greene, Caracelli, & Grahm, 1988).

Second, the techniques described may appear at first to be less "rigorous" than more conventional methods of inquiry. It may seem that information produced using these approaches is solely anecdotal and thus, unscientific. However, it should be pointed out that qualitative data analysis is a complex, laborious, and demanding set of procedures which does address the rigor and standards required of scientific inquiry. For more on qualitative date collection and analysis, see Lincoln and Guba (1985), Patton (1980), and Miles and Huberman (1984).

Third, for those who say that evaluation must be "objective," I contend, as do most evaluators, that totally bias-free social research using either quantitative or qualitative methods is impossible. Evaluators can choose to state their biases or not, and they can choose to reduce or address bias in their designs, but evaluators cannot eliminate all bias from their studies. While it is commonly recognized that the "human instrument," i.e., the interviewer or content analyst, gathering and analyzing qualitative data must account for her or his biases, it is far too often assumed that paper-and-pencil surveys and personality inventories provide bias-free measurements of social and/or psychological phenomena. Yet, a researcher's choice of subjects to investigate, questions to ask, question wording, the participants to include, and the amount of contextual data to collect represent biases which are no less present in quantitative designs than in qualitative designs (Lincoln & Guba, 1985).

Experiential educators might ask: "What are we accomplishing with our students/clients? Are we doing what we say we are doing? What could we be doing better?" These questions lead to discussions of how, and what type of, data can be collected (*meaningful methods*), how can the evaluation process be used to gain relevant information (*meaningful designs*), and how does evaluation fit within the educational process (*meaningful uses*).

Meaningful Methods

The following qualitative methods are not new, but are often overlooked in the evalu-

ation of experiential programs. These methods are particularly valuable in experiential settings where each learner has a unique response to the program. Methods which fail to capture individual differences miss the true depth and variance of experience.

Interviews

Since many experiential programs emphasize the verbal processing of experience, it is a natural extension of this process to interview individuals or groups to obtain data. Program staff may be excellent interviewers as they are generally good listeners, comfortable asking questions, and able to establish rapport with students. In other cases, openness within student groups is often extended to an outside evaluator and thus productive interviewing is possible even if the evaluator has not been present for the entire experience. A structured interview asks participants specific questions, usually pertaining to a limited set of themes. Semi-structured and open interviews give respondents options for personal interpretation of the themes or questions of interest. Interview data can be used to address many program evaluation questions. This method of data collection has the advantage of providing immediate feedback for program staff if they conduct the interview. Obviously, data on instructor performance and some organizational issues may be handled best by persons with some detachment from the organization or program being evaluated.

Participant Observation

This method harkens back to the field work of anthropologists, sociologists, and ethnographers. Participant observation has been used within the field of experiential education and, though relatively expensive, time-consuming, and exhausting for the evaluator, this method can yield tremendously rich data. In participant observation, the evaluator accompanies students into the field, classroom, or other settings in order to document the learning events and processes as they take place. Like the interview, participant observation attempts to provide a view of the activity through the eyes of participants, but the participant observer also has access to the setting, environmental factors, and group dynamics which influence participants' experiences. For more on participant observation, see Jorgensen (1989).

Journal Analysis

A relatively new and highly compatible data source for experiential programs is the personal journal or daily log. Written reflections are commonly incorporated into experiential learning approaches and represent a potential source of powerful data (Raffan & Barrett, 1989; Warner, 1984). The obvious concern is confidentiality. Certainly no personal journal should be utilized for any purpose, evaluation or otherwise, without the clear and expressed consent from the journal writer(s) who must have a full understanding of how their written entries will be used and for what purposes. One option is to have students keep two separate journals—one personal and one to be collected as data. Another tactic is to include evaluation questions on pull-out pages of students' personal course journals. These evaluation pages can be collected at the end of the course with no infringement upon the private portions of the students' journals. With the parameters of privacy carefully established, the day-to-day reflections of students can be useful

since they contain ongoing, progressive responses to the program—usually corresponding to each day's activities—and also represent participants' overall responses.

Journals may also be used to gather and track feedback from field staff. Information stored in staff journals can be analyzed or processed upon their return from the field. A recent innovative use of journaling involved research with classroom teachers to identify issues related to teaching. Rather than obtrusively observing classrooms, the researcher worked with teachers who recorded data regarding their teaching in journals, which were then collectively analyzed by the teachers and the researcher (Mathison, 1988). A similar process could be initiated between field staff and program directors in adventure-based programs.

Meaningful Designs

Case Studies

While it is tempting to eschew the case study in favor of large samples, comparability, or increased statistical power, it is important to recall the practicalities of this simple, yet effective design. First of all, case study designs go hand-in-hand with the qualitative methodologies outlined above. Since a case study is focused upon a single group of persons or a single program, it allows the evaluator the time necessary to collect and analyze detailed qualitative data. Second, the case study is wholly acceptable as a means of studying new phenomena, where theory and research hypotheses may not yet be in existence (Lincoln & Guba, 1985). Many of our experiential programs are fresh creations/adaptations and thus require some initial study before they can ultimately be tested for causal connections or outcomes. Case studies establish a base of knowledge and critical insight from which key programmatic factors and their interrelationships may be extracted for further research.

Finally, case studies, in and of themselves, can be meaningful and appropriate forms of evaluation (Cronbach, 1980; Lincoln & Guba, 1985). Indeed, causal inference and understanding, not merely descriptive analysis, is possible with a case study design. While we cannot generalize findings of the case to other settings or groups, the information obtained with this design is more useful in terms of transferability and applicability within the program or case in question. Cronbach (1980) would argue that such relevance to the actual setting or program is of paramount importance in evaluation. By his criteria, evaluators should be asked to defend the inclusion rather than the absence of a comparison group in their research designs. The point is that we should attempt to gain the most information possible from the program of interest, rather than allocating time and resources to the addition of control groups which seldom produce accurate comparisons for programs or groups anyway.

Participatory and Collaborative Evaluation

An important philosophical component of experiential education is the empowerment of students. Likewise, many evaluators share a concern over power dynamics in evaluation and have developed strategies which serve not only to inform administrators and staff, but also to empower staff and program participants via their involvement in the evaluation process. Participatory evaluation invites various stakeholders in the program to become involved in determining the evaluation agenda, foci, and priorities (Greene, 1987). The result is that the evaluation process itself is inherently more meaningful for program stakeholders as it addresses their information needs and concerns. Also, participatory evaluation mitigates against the final evaluation report being used by administrators to chastise unsuspecting staff, because they, the staff, are included throughout the evaluation process.

A step beyond participatory approaches is collaborative research wherein program staff and participants may actually become involved in the collection and analysis of data. Collaboration can enhance the validity of results since participants often have important insights and inherent rapport and trust with other program participants from whom data is being collected. Moreover, this strategy helps offset evaluation costs.

A collaborative design, for example, was used in a study in which teenage mothers were trained to interview other teenage mothers to improve the validity of data regarding life as a young mother (Whitmore, 1989). The study had the additional benefit of empowering the young interviewers as they collaborated with the researcher and sensed the importance of their role in the project. This manner of inquiry develops an experiential linkage between the study and those being studied. This linkage can become an important learning opportunity which is highly consonant with the goals of experiential learning.

Mixed Methods

Designs which reflect the need for more than one type of information or data are referred to as "mixed method" designs. Typically, these designs combine qualitative and quantitative data in response to differing evaluation needs and/or audiences. Some work has been done to coordinate the analysis and triangulation effect of using differing types of data, though generally combined analysis is new and still being developed (Greene, Caracelli, & Grahm, 1988). Mixed methods may serve experiential education well as the field struggles to integrate meaningful evaluation of unique programming with the legitimacy required by conventional or uninformed evaluation audiences, i.e., school boards, politicians, regulatory agencies, etc.

Meaningful Uses

Having looked at various tools and designs for evaluating experiential education programs, consider the question, "Why evaluate programs in the first place?" or "For what use should we employ these or any evaluation strategies?" Possible responses range from the practical to the provocative.

Utilization-Focused Evaluation

Patton (1986) makes a strong case for evaluations which are ultimately used by someone for some purpose! As simple as this seems, it is a reaction to program evaluations which, once completed, have no actual bearing upon program decisions or implementation. They just collect dust! The reasons for this vary from poor design or lack of focus to politics and power issues. Pragmatists and decision makers with small evaluation budgets can maximize the overall use of any evaluation plan by considering some of the issues of utili-

zation, i.e., who will use this and for what purpose? Of course, the evaluator's knowledge of the intended uses for the research may bring up ethical dilemmas, especially regarding the empowerment issues raised above. Generally, however, designs aimed at utilization have a greater impact upon programs than do designs which are merely in compliance with grant or contract mandates, or evaluations which are ultimately aimed at advancing basic research within a discipline rather than serving the program in question.

Explicating and Developing Program Theory

Some educators who use experiential techniques tend to regard evaluation as inadequate in capturing the "magic" of experiential processes. One way to break patterns of mystification is to identify the theories-in-use (Argyris & Schon, 1974) of experiential educators. Theories-in-use are the conceptual understandings and causal/relational information which practitioners carry in their minds regarding how they do their job and make sense of the world. In evaluation terminology, theories-in-use are also referred to as "program theory."

Experiential education researchers have underscored the necessity of theory development for program enhancement. Wichman (1983), in his review of research on experiential education, found that relatively little is known about how and why wilderness programs work. He suggests that future research look at the theories-in-use of experiential educators in order to address this gap in understanding. Warner (1984) calls for theory development as an important evaluation focus:

A second important research strategy is to alter our evaluation focus from producing general data on outcomes to providing specific information on *processes*. It is paradoxical that an educational movement which places so much emphasis on learning as a process focuses its research efforts on documenting products. It is both of practical and theoretical interest to begin to explore which components of programs produce particularly valuable learning experiences. (Warner, 1984, p. 41)

Evaluations with little emphasis on program theory have been called "black box" evaluations, wherein the program outcomes are measured with no understanding of what goes on inside the program. Without opening the black box, it is difficult to determine if a program's goals are being met or not, what parts of the program are most or least effective, and what useful changes might be possible to improve the program. Increased understanding of program theory serves not only the evaluator, but also the practitioner who can base programmatic improvements upon better articulated program theory as part of the evaluation process (Bickman, 1987; Chen, 1990). Articulating the theories-in-use of experiential programming may ultimately serve broader educational audiences by facilitating the incorporation of these experiential approaches within many school and societal contexts.

The Reflective Practitioner

According to Dewey, *Experience plus Reflection equals Education*. If reflection is taken seriously by the teacher as well as the student, one has what Schon (1983) calls the "reflective practitioner." The reflective practitioner processes information and feedback gathered from everyday work, continu-

ally developing and refining theories about how and why things work in a given way. Certainly, the amount practitioners learn themselves is associated with how much they look back, evaluate, and reflect upon what they do. Informally, the reflective process probably accounts for more growth and evolution within the experiential education field than any other form of professional training and development. Likewise, formal published evaluations represent the collective reflection of practitioners and scholars within the field. As Warner (1984, p. 40) states, "Reflection is a key ingredient in learning through experience—it is time that experiential educators embrace this basic principle as it applies to program development through evaluation research." Programs and practitioners who cease to evaluate their progress, who treat their teaching as magic—too precious to scrutinize—stop learning and begin to pay the price of stagnation. A commitment to reflective practice, both formal and informal, is essential if we value our own learning as part of the process of teaching others.

Advocacy

While experiential educators must look critically at their endeavors in order to enhance them, and though it is important to identify biases as part of the research process, there are those evaluators who suggest that advocating a certain position or perspective is not necessarily out of bounds for the overall evaluation process. In effect, it is argued that issues related to social injustice, such as sexism, racism, or classism, justify the use of evaluation findings to promote social change, educational alternatives, or other societal reforms. These approaches are sometimes referred to as "critical theory" or "advocacy" research paradigms. They illustrate another alternative perspective on the evaluation process. Indeed, evaluators often discover overarching issues of social need and inequity. Confronting such issues with information gained through systematic evaluation may be quite legitimate as a means of enhancing the social dialogue surrounding the issues. More specifically, evaluators of experiential education programs do not need to rid themselves of all belief in learning through experience. In fact, whenever possible, evaluation should proceed in the interest of improving that which is being evaluated.

Conclusions

For years, educational evaluation and research has been perceived as number crunching. Indeed, the power of statistical analysis has in many cases led to a tyranny of method. The crunch of numbers has unfortunately produced a crunch in thinking about evaluation and its role as a feedback mechanism for practitioners. While the first crunch encourages us to consider meaningful alternatives to conventional methods of inquiry, the second crunch must likewise be overcome if experiential educators are to continue learning by reflecting upon—evaluating—what they do.

Returning to the original metaphor, it is fitting that the hammer is held by a child, a humble and developing creature, because evaluation, especially in the forms suggested here, is a humbling process. For every question answered, there are more and deeper questions to be raised.

Notes

I would like to thank Alan Warner and two anonymous reviewers for their helpful input in bringing this article to its final form.

Conducting Research in Experience-Based Training and Development Programs: Passkeys to Locked Doors

by Simon Priest, Aram Attarian, and Sabine Schubert

Experience-based training and development (EBTD) or corporate adventure training (CAT) is a form of learning which employs challenging experiences and adventurous activities as vehicles for employees to improve interpersonal and intrapersonal workplace skills. The experiences and activities involve placing individual employees and/or intact work groups in unusual or unfamiliar settings. They are challenged to come up with creative solutions and to make decisions regarding problems or tasks with uncertain outcomes. CAT programs assist employees by providing learning opportunities which are metaphorically transferable back to the business world (Bank, 1985; Gass, Goldman, & Priest, 1992). For this reason, CAT is evolving to be one of the most dynamic educational tools available for organizational learning. The growing number of outdoor adventure providers and the increasing number of companies getting involved with this form of management education are two strong indications of its popularity (Latteier, 1989).

Every year, American corporations invest billions of dollars in general training and development programs for management (Lawler, 1988). However, very little is known about the effectiveness or success of these general programs attended by managers (Rice, 1979, 1988). Saari, Johnson, McLaughlin, and Zimmerle (1988) have reported that many of the companies sending their managers to training workshops, seminars, or courses rarely attempt to evaluate the effectiveness of these programs. This is especially true of those that use adventure training (Roland, 1985). Information that does exist in this arena is mostly anecdotal (Long, 1984; Willis, 1985; Gall, 1987; Forester, 1987; Stolzenburg, 1987). Despite rapid growth in the industry of CAT, most human resource professionals have little information regarding its usefulness (Hogg, 1988; Darby, 1989).

Research is the "passkey" to opening these "locked doors" of CAT program effectiveness. At several recent conferences held by the Association for Experiential Training and Development (AETD) and by the Experience-based Training and Development (EBTD) professional group of the Association for Experiential Education (AEE), presenters have attempted to address the need for further research, but the response by academicians and practitioners is slow in coming.

Research is a means to establishing much-needed professional credibility in this field. In an effort to encourage deeper investigation and to generate an awareness for the related pitfalls, this article begins by reviewing the activities and benefits associated with corporate adventure training (in other words, the things that researchers examine). It then summarizes those few studies which have been conducted to date on the efficacy of CAT programs, outlines the need for further inquiry, and discusses the barriers to producing meaningful research. Readers interested in conducting research of their own are directed to past issues of *The Journal of Experiential Education* for some excellent treatments of this topic (Rowley, 1987; Braverman, Brenner, Fretz, & Desmond, 1990; Flor, 1991; Kolb,1991).

GENERAL	SPECIFIC	SAMPLES AND EXAMPLES	PRINCIPLE PURPOSES
CLIENT VISITATIONS	Diagnostic interview	Open-ended questions focus on client dysfunction	Needs assessment & group observation
	Follow-up report	Formal report presented to sponsor & client groups	Present training outcomes & overall results
CLASSROOM SESSIONS	Goal setting	Discussion of benefits & presentation of theories	Goal setting & understanding basic concepts
	Action planning	Solo reflection time & open sharing of action plans	Action planning & personally pledging to change
SOCIALIZATION GAMES	Familiarization	Name Toss, Group Juggling, Two Truths & A Lie	Getting to know other's names & needs
	Deinhibitization	Gordian Knots, Blindfolded Walks in Pairs, Lap Sits	Comfortable touching & working together
GROUP INITIATIVES	Team Tools	Trust Falls, Trolleys, Non-verbal Line-ups	Trust, cooperation, & effective communication
	Team tasks	Nitro Crossing, Spider's Web, Traffic Jam	Problem Solving & empowered decision making
ROPES COURSES	Low (spotted)	Tension Traverse, Swinging Log, Mohawk Walk	Group support, asking for & giving help
	High (belayed)	Burma Bridge, Pamper Pole, Beam Walk	Risk Taking, dealing with fear, stress, & anxiety
OUTDOOR PURSUITS	Activity-based	Climbing, Kayaking, Caving, Orienteering, Rafting	Confidence, coping with change & uncertainty
	Wilderness-based	Expedition-style Backpacking & Canoe Tripping	Leadership, conflict resolution, & judgment
OTHER ADVENTURES	Simulated	Flying Starship Factory & Gold of the Desert Kings	Able to see the bigger picture & time management
	Non-traditional	Firewalking, Bungee Jumping, Pit Crew/Car Racing	Motivation, commitment, & leadership of teams

Figure 1: Chart of EBTD/CAT activities arranged by General and Specific Categories.

Activities

The activities which constitute CAT programming can be arranged in seven general categories: client visitations, classroom sessions, socialization games, group initiatives, ropes courses, outdoor pursuits, and other adventures (see Figure 1). By understanding what activities constitute CAT programming, researchers will be better able to discern appropriate treatments to study. For example, the latter category of "Other Adventures" (simulated and non-traditional) would likely be considered by the majority of CAT providers not to be a part of their programming repertoire. Furthermore, some providers may not involve themselves with the two categories of client visitations or classroom sessions, preferring to utilize an educational mix of pure adventure: socialization games, group initiatives, ropes courses, and outdoor pursuits. The beneficial outcomes obtained have a lot to do with the activities chosen by careful and competent CAT providers. Uninitiated researchers, on the other hand, may lump all these activities together, mistakenly making generalizations about benefits or not adequately distinguishing one activity from another.

Benefits

Corporate adventure training can benefit the individual employee, the management work unit, and the parent organization (Mossman, 1982). Figure 2 depicts a triangle which lists the common areas of application for CAT programs: cultural development, individual development, group development, and the interaction of all three (Ehrhardt, 1991).

Benefits to the individual include developments in self-confidence, leadership style,

risk-taking propensity, dealing with fear and stress, decision making, and personal inspiration and commitment (Willams, 1988; Beeby & Rathborn, 1983; Gahin & Chesteen, 1988). The work unit benefits from improvements in goal setting, team building, time management, conflict resolution, group problem solving, collaboration, and cooperation (Creswick & Williams, 1979; Long, 1987; Kadel, 1988). Benefits for the organization may involve an enhancement of systems, structure, values and ethics, vision and mission, corporate climate, and motivational atmosphere, which results in the bottom line of increased productivity, decreased absenteeism, and greater profits (Brathay Hall Trust, 1985; Fleming, 1987). Lastly, an interaction of the other three developmental areas (cultural, personal, and group) can lead to empowerment, trust and integrity, effective communication, environmental safety, judgment based on experience, and coping with change and uncertainty, as these benefits are shared among all aspects of the corporate organization, individuals, and work units (Mossman, 1982). These benefits are the mainstay claims of CAT programming. What evidence exists to substantiate them?

Previous Research

Very little research has been conducted on the efficacy of CAT programs. A few minor unpublished studies were conducted in the 1980s and are described below. Roland (1981) is credited with one of the earliest studies in this field, which attempted to measure the impact of adventure training with 58 middle managers from two companies engaged in a 3-day outdoor program focusing on team building and group

Cultural Development of the
ORGANIZATION
Systems, Structures, Values & Ethics, Vision & Mission,
Corporate Climate, Motivational Atmosphere

ALL
Empowerment,
Trust & Integrity,
Environmental Safety,
Effective Communication,
Judgment based on Experience,
Coping with Change & Uncertainty

Personal Development of the
INDIVIDUAL
Self-Confidence, Leadership Style,
Risk-Taking Propensity, Dealing with Fear & Stress,
Individual Decision Making,
Personal Inspiration & Commitment

Group Development of the
WORK UNIT
Goal Setting, Team Building,
Time Management, Conflict Resolution
Group Problem Solving, Cooperation & Collaboration

Figure 2: The CAT Triangle.

problem solving through a ropes course experience. During Roland's study, three questionnaires measured managerial change in the participants as perceived by themselves, and as perceived by their 68 subordinates and 37 superiors. A fourth questionnaire measured participant learning. Subjects were pre-tested and post-tested with an average of 71 days between tests. Findings indicated that change took place on

a number of managerial constructs, including: time, planning, suggestions, human relations, trust, goals, group process, supervision, and feedback. Changes were speculated to have resulted from high levels of participant commitment and emotional involvement.

King and Harmon (1983) evaluated an early adventure course for an aerospace company. The purpose was to analyze personal beliefs, behaviors, and professional attitudes of employees as a result of participating in the program. Graduates of a two-day, in-house course called "Managing Personal Growth" (MPG) attended a 4-day Outward Bound (OB) course.

Interviews were conducted with 33 employees selected from a stratified random sample of MPG graduates who attended the OB course. The researchers concluded that three major benefits were evident: greater self-confidence, increase in morale, and an enhanced sense of teamwork, friendship, and respect for co-workers in the company. A major finding indicated that those who attended both the MPG and OB courses had lower turnover rates (1.7%) when compared to MPG-only turnover rates (6.0%) and company-wide turnover rates (8.4%).

A few years later, Isenhart (1983) administered a 22-item questionnaire to 350 Outward Bound program graduates. Of these, 140 (40%) were returned with findings that revealed that participants felt their personal behavior had changed (76.4%), their work behavior had improved as a result of having participated in their course (78.6%), and they were better able to handle work responsibilities as a result of their participation (88.6%). A more recent survey (Colorado Outward Bound School, 1988) of 274 alumni of the course, contacted to determine the effectiveness of their experience, suggested that a positive impact on professional and personal aspects of the participants were obtained. Responses concluded that the program was valuable in team building (96%), gave new insights into leadership (86%), and participants gained increased closeness to teammates (92%).

Personal gains were evidenced in the areas of personal growth (92%) and extension of one's personal limits (86%). The program also was found to have value in building professional relationships (80%) and providing a fuller understanding of self (80%).

Current Research

Some studies, published in the early 1990s, have looked at specific benefits within the three areas mentioned earlier: personal development of the individual, group development of the work unit (or team), and cultural development of the organization. The following abstracted studies are arranged under these headings.

Personal Development of the Individual

Galpin (1989) implemented a study to investigate the effects of a 3-day Outward Bound course for managers on a number of self-perceptions, including self-concept, hardiness, trust of others, and involvement in group process. Sixty-four middle-level managers from a large hospital completed an impact survey and the "Personal Views Survey." Data were gathered one month prior to the course, immediately at the start, upon completion, and one month after the course. Analysis of data revealed that participation in the adventure training program had a positive impact on the manager's self-concept and hardiness, with females impacted to a greater degree that males, and with older managers affected more than younger ones. Changes were maintained during the follow-up month, with females retaining changes to a greater extent than males.

A recent study (Goldman & Priest, 1990) examined the transfer of risk-taking behaviors from adventure training to the work-place for 27 financial managers involved in the one-day, risk-taking exercise of rappel-ling (the controlled descent of a cliff face by using ropes and rock-climbing equipment). The hypothesis being tested was whether a brief, but powerful, adventure training session would alter the work-related perceptions of risk and propensity to take risks for these managers. The results of the study showed that the session did indeed positively affect employees' risk-taking be-haviors in the business setting. Managers remarked that they felt supported by their peers and more willing to risk as a result of their "belay and backup." The terms used during the adventure session were being used in the culture of the organization to describe work situations which were meta-phoric representations of the adventure.

Attarian (1992) examined the effects of adventure training on the risk-taking pro-pensity of corporate managers. A total of 57 managers representing service, manufactur-ing, and retail distributing companies par-ticipated in three, 5-day management training courses administered by OB. Sub-jects completed the "Choice Dilemmas Questionnaire" immediately before partici-pation and 30 days after completion of the training program with 87.6% returned. Data were subjected to product moment correla-tions in order to examine the relationships between a manager's age, experience, and risk-taking propensity; and to "Analysis of Covariance" (pre-test as the covariant) to determine outcome differences across gen-der, management level, company type, and job role. The following were concluded: (a) A manager's age, years of employment, and risk-taking propensity were not highly cor-

related; (b) make and female managers did not differ in risk-taking propensity; (c) no differences in risk-taking propensity were evident among any management levels; and (d) no significant differences in risk-taking propensity were observed between the serv-ice company, manufacturing concern, and retail organization. Overall, subjects showed greater risk-taking propensity through mean score comparisons; however, difference were not statistically significant at the .05 level of probability.

Group Development of the Work Unit

Baldwin, Wagner, and Roland (1991) con-ducted an evaluation on the effects of an outdoor challenge training program. The program included a series of group problem-solving initiatives common to most adven-ture-based training programs. Subjects in this study included 458 civilian employees and 13 supervisors from a military base. Two questionnaires were developed to col-lect relevant data on a variety of group and individual measures. Findings from the study suggested that outdoor challenge training had a moderate effect on group awareness and effectiveness and individual problem solving, as measured three months after the training. No significant changes were observed in trust or self-concept.

Dutkiewicz and Chase (1991) undertook a study of MBA students to empirically measure the changes that participants un-dergo following participation in an out-door-based, leadership training experience. A control group of 43 students and an experi-mental group of 41 students participated in the study with the experimental group re-ceiving treatment. Results indicated that the MBA students exhibited change in the domains of trust, confidence in peers, group clarity, group cohesiveness, group awareness, and group homogeneity. Lesser changes were noted in the measures of self-assessment and problem solving.

Bronson, Gibson, Kichar, and Priest (1992), compared two intact work groups from an aerospace company. A control group of 11 managers received no treatment, while an experimental group of 17 underwent a three-day, off-site, adventure training program composed mostly of challenge course events and group initiative activities. Both groups completed a survey (designed to measure team development behaviors) about two months before and two months after the three days of training. Statistical analysis of responses to the surveys showed that both groups were reasonably equivalent before the training program began, but were significantly different after. While the control group showed no change over the study period, the experimental group improved on teamwork items related to group goals, genuine concern, effective listening, decision making, respect for diversity, high standards, recognition of ideas, and encouragement for feedback. No improvements were noted for conflict resolution or offering assistance. The comments of the managers supported the conclusion that team developments were due to the adventure training program and recommended further study to examine trends in team development which take place over time during a program, and research into the effectiveness of transfer in corporate adventure training.

Cultural Development of the Organization

A study concerned with changes in the corporate culture and motivational climate of a organization choosing total employee involvement in adventure training was recently completed with an Australian company. Eighty-three out of 100 randomly selected managers responded to several surveys: six months before the training program began, in the middle of the program, and six months after it was completed. The adventure training program was five days in duration and consisted of sequenced events, including socialization exercises, group initiative activities, high ropes course, personal reflection and solo time, lectures, and action planning. Responses of 83 managers, from all areas and levels of the organization, indicated that this particular company improved its planning utility, structure flexibility, systems functioning, sensible and supportive roles, positive relationships, excessive delays in work flow, reflection time, and mission and goal clarity during the first year. Concern for getting the job done (rather than accounting for time and cost), alignment, marketplace impact, and profit versus growth decreased over the same period, although decreases were not seen as necessarily detrimental in this case, since the company moved through a desired period of much-needed readjustment. During the second year, reflection time decreased, but work enjoyment improved, even though workloads increased over both years as a result of necessary readjustment. The experiential training program was attributed by company executives to have positively resulted in these outcomes. Furthermore, the organization became more flexible around rules, more willing to embrace or accept chaos as a valuable catalyst for change, more concerned with the needs or well-being of employees, and more relaxed around the concept of empowerment of individuals and teams. To some extent, the organization became open around the disclosure of information or opinions, and employees became comfortable around the idea of interacting with one another. Overall, managers perceived the company to have undergone dramatic changes, resulting in a new and completely different way of motivating its employees.

In summary, before the training program, this company was characterized as an organization motivated by "control-expert influence" and "control-dependency" orientations. After the one year of corporate adventure training, in which all employees participated, those descriptors had shifted to "achievement-affiliation" and "achievement-extension" orientations. The company was transformed from an autocratic bureaucracy where rules reigned supreme to an empowered and team-oriented environment where people were valued. This was both the desire and intent of the company executives when they undertook the CAT program. Although the entire transformation cannot be attributed solely to the adventure training (change may have been driven by environmental factors and financial necessity), the executives were convinced that the program was a powerful and supportive adjunct to their own efforts at making cultural changes (Priest, 1992).

Need for Further Inquiry

To paraphrase Ewert (1983), CAT programs are like electricity; we're certain that they work, but we really don't know how or why. The challenge for researchers is to determine the how and why of CAT programming.

However, before one can claim to know precisely where the future of CAT research should be headed, a map of the opportunities and a full understanding of where the research has already been is necessary. The map is supplied in the form of a pyramid as in Figure 3.

The "Question of Research" pyramid (Priest, 1991) rank-orders the type of questions researchers commonly ask in attempting to understand a phenomenon such as CAT. First, they seek to describe the phenomenon: What is IT or what does IT appear to be? Second, they attempt to differentiate the phenomenon: What is IT like, similar to, or different from? Third, they try to relate the phenomenon to other variables: What is IT associated with? Fourth, they begin to determine the influence of these associations: What is IT affected by? Fifth, they become interested in discriminating its occurrence: Can IT be predicted? Sixth, they experiment with causality: Can IT be controlled?

To better understand this model, consider the recent appearance of the disease known as AIDS. In the past, doctors described the disease and compared or contrasted it to other maladies. In the present, medical experts explore the conditions associated with AIDS and determine the factors which cause or contribute to AIDS. In the future, health researchers will work on predicting and controlling the occurrence of this modern disease.

However, before they could look for a cure at Level Six, these researchers had to conduct a great many studies in the five levels below. A basic premise of designing research proposals is that each should be founded on the results of earlier studies. This disciplined patience, coupled with systematic

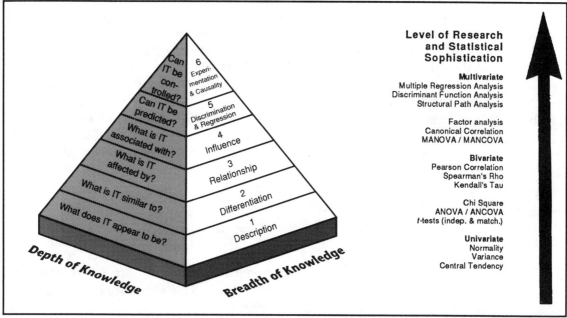

Figure 3: A question of research.

rigor, is a common hallmark for most researchers; however, it appears to be lacking in many of those who research CAT.

Most work on corporate adventure training has been conducted at Level One: description. The vast majority of writings have taken the anecdotal or testimonial approach by describing what the programs are composed of and what they appear to achieve. Very few studies have been conducted at Levels Two and Three: some of the research results mentioned earlier are examples of differentiation and association. However, these studies appear to have been designed with the shotgun approach in mind: ready, fire, and then aim! A clear or coordinated direction is not immediately obvious; hence, outcomes are scattered and relatively ungeneralizable.

Future research needs to be more sequential. For example, the construct of team building seems to be the most common goal of CAT programs. Studies on team building need to initially determine and describe whether team performance does improve as a result of CAT and how the improvement compares with several other forms of training, including a control group with no training. Then, and only then, studies need to identify what components of the CAT program cause or contribute to these improvements (considering type of activity, length of training, residential or not, etc.). Next, studies need to address the concern of whether these key components can be used to predict improvements and control the amount of improvement in team performance during a CAT program.

Once the efficacy of CAT programs has been established, the next issue of concern will be that of transference: we know it works, but does it last? Three ways exist to provide strong evidence of the transfer from the "artificial" adventure environment to the "real" world of management. The first is qualitative and the other two are quantitative. In a qualitative approach, subjects may be observed during the training program and may be interviewed after. Observations and interview questions might focus on what was learned and how it was applied on the job. A report written in descriptive language leaves interpretation of results to the reader. Specific examples and substantiation from co-workers adds to the credibility of qualitative findings.

One of the two quantitative designs requires the use of two groups. One group (experimental) receives the CAT program treatment, while the other does not (control group). Both groups are surveyed or measured on some construct (such as cooperative behavior) before and after the treatment and several months later while back in the office. If the experimental group shows an increase in cooperation from before to after training, and the control group does not, then the increase can likely be attributed to training (other uncontrolled variables may also bring about such changes). If the levels of cooperation remain elevated in the experimental group back at the office, but the control group remains the same, then the training may have transferred effectively. If levels for both groups alter in some way, a closer comparison must be made before such a claim is valid.

If a control group is not available, since matching subjects, structure, or function is simply not possible, then an alternative approach using a time-series design may be an appropriate substitute. With only one experimental group, multiple measurements must be taken before and after the CAT program treatment to establish base-line values. If these prior values are not statistically different from one another, and if the post values are also not different from one another, then the average before and the average after can be compared for differences with the base-lines acting as a sort of self-control. Once again, multiple measurements back at the office help to establish the effectiveness of transfer.

Barriers to Overcome

A consensus has existed for some time, among researchers and practitioners alike, to move beyond the anecdotes and testimonies, and to provide data-based evidence (Keslake & Radcliff, 1980). However, several barriers have existed to make this difficult, and most still exist today.

First, participation in adventure training is strictly voluntary, since credible providers operate under an ethic of "challenge by choice" (Hunt, 1991) where clients are not forced to participate in an adventure. This means that subjects will volunteer for the most part, as the risk-averse and the skeptical likely avoid participation. Hence, quasi-experimentation (without random selection or assignment of subjects) is likely to be the type of research conducted, as opposed to true experimentation (with randomization). This means that the credibility of studies will be slightly compromised to begin with.

Second, because, in order to maximize the experience and optimize the learning, adventure training typically takes place in small groups of eight to twelve participants, sample sizes under study will often be quite small. Small sample sizes mean that the distribution of survey answers will likely not fit within the normal curve. Without normality (usually present on groups of 15 or more) certain statistics known as parametric procedures cannot be used and the less popular nonparametric analyses must be substituted. Since nonparametric statistics are considered in the eyes of most researchers to be less believable than parametric ones, the credibility of studies in CAT will be further compromised.

Third, the sample-size problem cannot be easily overcome by combining small groups with similar training programs, since adventure training must be customized to meet the particular needs of each client group and its individual members. If the training is altered to include by coercion larger groups or identically standardized treatments, it is no longer corporate adventure training by definition; hence, the research is being conducted on some other type of training and the results have limited usefulness. In summary, constancy over all research will prove difficult and any results obtained will, therefore, have limited generalizability.

Fourth, exerting control over research design is also very difficult. Any control group (selected from within the same company as the experimental group) is going to experience a "spill over" contamination effect as experimental groups return from their treatment training and interact with other employees as part of their daily work. The new enthusiasm and excitement of returning subjects will likely confound the control group, either elevating or depressing levels of whatever variables are measured in the study, leading to biased results. Selecting a control group from outside the company being studied invalidates the research, since the purpose of the control group is to be influenced by the same environmental variables which effect the experimental group so that any changes can be attributed to the treatment. Choosing a control group from within the company, but outside the normal interaction of the experimental group is most difficult since a good control group is matched in structure and content. Groups with identical function and membership in the same company are highly unlikely.

Fifth, quantitative research in CAT is currently hampered by a lack of good instrumentation to measure the constructs of primary interest, such as conflict resolution, goal setting, time management, leadership, problem solving, decision making, and organizational ethics. Although steps are being taken by researchers to remedy this situation, valid and reliable instruments are a long way off. The alternative of using "homemade" surveys gives little guarantee that the data collected will really represent what the study is about. Trustworthy instruments are a necessary component of quantitative research in CAT.

Sixth, these latter concerns point to the possible usefulness of qualitative methods as an alternative or even enhancement to the more accepted quantitative designs. Qualitative inquiries are likely to get around some of these barriers and generate useful findings, provided the interviews and observations are performed in a rigorous and scholarly manner. Unfortunately, a great deal of prejudice exists toward the paradigm or philosophical view under which most qualitative research takes place. Naturalistic inquiry, as it is known, makes some fundamental assumptions about knowledge and reality which many positivistic scientists have trouble understanding, let alone agreeing with. Using qualitative methods outside the governing paradigm jeopardizes the effectiveness of the techniques.

Seventh, the gap between producer and consumer of research is a wide one. A few researchers fail to follow established and widely accepted ethical guidelines for conducting studies. Their disclosure of information (such as company names, even with permission), and their claiming greater applications of findings than are possible given the flaws present in all research, give all researchers a bad reputation. As a result, some consumers distrust every study; while others, perhaps eager for any "proof" or ignorant of the subtle nuances of research, gobble up any study and believe it to be the final word! This makes some credible researchers reluctant to claim any outcomes from their study, for fear these will be exaggerated out of proportion. Better communication between researchers (who produce studies) and practitioners (clients or the media who consume them) is the answer to bridging this gap.

Lastly, companies sending large numbers of employees through these programs are often reluctant to permit research to be undertaken since some are concerned that they may not like the findings if the research indicates the program is poor and perhaps money has been wasted. Furthermore, business organizations and governmental agencies are not interested in research about corporate adventure training because of the additional time commitments and expense (Cacioppe & Adamson, 1988). For this same reason, training and development, in general, is one of the least researched areas in top business funding priorities (Rice, 1979).

Some Hope through Collaboration

Despite these barriers, some hope seems evident through the collaboration of the two associations (AEE and AETD) which represent the industry. The AEE professional group for EBTD has set up a research alliance of approximately 50 CAT providers who will collect team development data on their programs and submit these data to a central clearinghouse for analysis. Since the programs and subjects will likely differ among providers (some drastically), these analyses will have limited generalizability. Nevertheless, a technique known as meta-analysis will be applied to examine the individual studies (rather than subjects). If the outcomes are mostly positive across a majority of programs, then this technique may permit wider application of the team development findings.

The research task force of the Association for Experiential Training and Development (AETD) has begun work on selecting or developing instruments for measuring constructs other than team building, such as communication, interpersonal trust, risk taking, and motivational climate within a corporate culture. These instruments will also be available for use by the research alliance. These two groups are working collaboratively in a win-win situation to address the credibility needs of a very diverse industry.

Conclusion

Corporate adventure training is special for several reasons (Gass, Goldman, & Priest, 1992). First, it is experiential: people learn best by doing. Activities utilize perceived risk and yet are quite safe. Second, it is dramatic: the excitement and emotional nature of these activities focus attention and sharpen minds. People remember what they learn. Third, it is novel: because of the unique context and uncertainty of outcome for these activities, no one in the group is considered to be an expert. Adventures tend to equalize people and breakdown the hierarchical barriers and apprehensions which often exist in large companies. Fourth, it is consequential: errors have potential ramifications in adventures (getting wet in a canoe or falling on a rope), unlike in a classroom simulation (where play money is lost). Furthermore, success and failure is supported by those who really matter (co-workers and oneself). Fifth, it is metaphoric: adventures are a microcosm of the requirements needed and changes taking place in the business world. The behaviors demonstrated by individuals and groups during these activities are parallel representations of the way they act and what happens in the office. As such, new learning (skills, coping strategies, and bonding among personnel) can be analogously applied toward future efforts on the job. Finally, it is transferable: testimonials by past participants support the utility of adventure training and limited research studies substantiate that new learning does indeed show up in the workplace. People refer back to their experiences and approach their tasks from a fresh perspective.

Attarian (1992) adds that the unique characteristics of corporate adventure training are the importance placed on the setting or natural environment, the use of experiential-learning methodology, the importance of effective instruction, and debriefing the experience through feedback or reflection. Miner (1994) explains that corporate adven-ture training is holistic, involving all the senses and accommodating a variety of learning styles, with clear and simple goals providing immediate feedback on performance, regardless of success or setback. Unlike simulated games, CAT programs offer concrete experiences which are task oriented, just like work, and are intriguing, so that everyone desires to get involved. The activities are new, fun, and invigorating; they provide opportunities to experiment with new behaviors and skills in a safe environment which encourages risk taking of all kinds.

The whole idea of corporate adventure training may be a hard concept to accept. As a "new" discipline, CAT has had a brief opportunity to grow and demonstrate its effectiveness as a development tool for contemporary companies. As with any new product, technique, or innovation, problems are bound to arise. CAT, with its unique approach, is no exception. The most visible concerns are the lack of adequate and reliable research and evaluation (Rice, 1979, 1988; Darby, 1989); a lack of "quality control" coupled with a consequential concern for safety (Garvey, 1989; Miner, 1991); questionable qualifications of instructors (Knecht, 1983); and some skepticism (Zemke, 1988; Falvey, 1988).

The greatest concern for the proponents of corporate adventure training lies in substantiating claims that the training is valid and reliable. Plenty of testimonial and anecdotal evidence can be found in the literature, but in these days of the tighter development dollar, a definite need exists for further research to generate hard data on the utility and efficacy of this training. To ensure the growth and reputation of adventure as a method of management education, these issues (and the other concerns elucidated above) need to be discussed and resolved. It is only then that the high-impact programs of corporate adventure training will become commonly accepted adjuncts and alternatives to more traditional organizational learning schemes. Research is one passkey capable of opening these locked doors and establishing professional credibility.

Appendix

1

References

**Chapter One:
Experiential Educational Theory**

**What Constitutes Experience? Rethinking
Theoretical Assumption
by Martha Bell**

Dewey, J. (1938). Experience and education. New York: Collier.

Ewert, A. W. (1987). Research in outdoor adventure: Overview and analysis. Bradford Papers Annual, II, 15-28.

Freire, P. (1985). The politics of education: Culture, power and liberation. South Hadley, MA: Bergin & Garvey.

Friedrich, M., & Priest, S. (1992). Developing androgynous individuals through outdoor adventure experiences. Journal of Adventure Education and Outdoor Leadership, 9(3), 11-12.

Gass, M. (1992). Theory and practice. Journal of Experiential Education, 15(2), 6-7.

Henderson, K. A. (1989). The need for critical theory in the study of leisure and minority groups. Leisure Information Quarterly, 15(3), 1-3.

Joplin, L. (1981). On defining experiential education. Journal of Experiential Education, 4(1), 17-20.

Knapp, C. E. (1985). Escaping the gender trap: The ultimate challenge for experiential educators. Journal of Experiential Education, 8(2), 16-19.

Kolb, D.A. (1984). Experiential learning: Experience as the source of learning and development. Englewood Cliffs, NJ: Prentice-Hall.

MacNeill, M. (1988). Active women, media representations and ideology. In J. Harvey & H. Cantelon (Eds.), Not just a game: Essays in Canadian sport sociology (pp. 195-211). Ottawa: University of Ottawa Press.

McDermott, J. J. (Ed.). (1973/1981). The philosophy of John Dewey: Two volumes. Chicago: University of Chicago Press.

Mitten, D. (1986). Meeting the unknown: Group dynamics in the wilderness. Minneapolis: Woodswomen.

Phipps, M. (1991). Group dynamics in the outdoors: A model for teaching outdoor leaders. In D. Cockrell (Ed.), The wilderness educator: The wilderness education association curriculum guide (pp. 35-64). Merrillville: ICS Books.

Smith, D. E. (1984). Textually mediated social organization. International Social Science Journal, 36(1), 59-75.

Warren, K. (1985). Women's outdoor adventures: Myth and reality. Journal of Experiential Education, 8(2), 10-14.

Experiential Education:
A Search for Common Roots
by Greg Druian, Tom Owens, and
Sharon Owen

Buckman, R. B. (1976). The impact of EBCE—An evaluation viewpoint. Illinois Career Education Journal, 33(3).

Crowe, M. R., & Adams, K. A. (1979). The current status of assessing experiential education programs. National Center for Research in Vocational Education, Ohio.

Hagans, R. W. (1976). What is experience-based career education? Illinois Career Education Journal, 33(3).

McBee, D. (1979). Finding yourself in the wilderness. Passages (magazine of Northwest Orient Airlines, 10(11).

Reynolds, S. (1979). Golden hindsight, homespun, lagniappe, et al. Teacher, 96(7).

Rice, B. (1979). Going to the mountain. Psychology Today, 13(7).

Shore, A. (1977). Outward Bound: A reference volume. Greenwich, CT: Outward Bound.

Wigginton, E. (1975). Moments: The Foxfire experience. Kennebunk, ME: Star Press.

The Future of Experiential Education as a Profession
by Paul Michalec

Becher, T. (1989). Academic tribes and territories. The Society for Research into Higher Education. Open University Press.

Clifford, G., & Gutherie, J. (1988). Ed school. Chicago: University of Chicago Press.

Denzin, N. (1978). The research act: A theoretical introduction to sociological methods. New York: McGraw Hill.

Dewey, J. (1938). Experience and education. New York: Collier Books.

Eisenhart, M., & Borko, H. (1993). Designing classroom research: Themes, issues, and struggles. Boston: Allyn & Bacon.

Eisenhart, M., & Howe, K. (1992). Validity in qualitative research. In M. LeCompte, W. Millroy, and J. Preissle (Eds.), The handbook of qualitative research in education. San Diego: Academic Press.

Feiman-Nemser, S. (1990). Teacher preparation: Structural and conceptual alternatives. In R. Houston (Ed.), Handbook of research on teacher education. New York: Macmillan.

Gass, M. (1992). Theory and practice. Journal of Experiential Education, 15(2), 6-7.

Gillis, L. (1992). Therapeutic uses of adventure-challenge-outdoor-wilderness: Theory and research. Keynote presentation for the coalition for education in the outdoors symposium. Bradford Woods, Indiana University: Bloomington, IN.

Hanna, G. (1992). Ripples in the water: Reflections on experiential education research designs. In G. Hanna (Ed.), Celebrating our traditions, charting our future. Proceedings of the 1992 Association for Experiential Education 20th International Conference. AEE: Boulder, Co.

Khun, T. (1962). The structure of scientific revolutions. Chicago: University of Chicago Press.

Lave, J., & Wenger, E. (1991). Situated learning: Legitimate peripheral participation. New York: Cambridge University Press.

Marcus, G., & Fisher, M. (1986). Anthropology as cultural critique. Chicago: University of Chicago Press.

Schon, D. (1983). The reflective practitioner. New York: Basic Books.

Shuttenberg, E., & Poppenhagen, B. (1980). Current theory and research in experiential learning for adults. Journal of Experiential Education, 3(1), 27-31.

Toulmin, S. (1972). Human understanding. Princeton: Princeton University Press.

Wichmann, T. (1983). Evaluating Outward Bound for delinquent youth. Journal of Experiential Education, 5(3), 106-16.

Chapter Two:
The National Reports and Educational Reform: A Contemporary and Historical View

School Reform for the Nineties: Opportunities and Obstacles for Experiential Educators
by Joel Westheimer, Joseph Kahne, and Amy Gerstein

Bloom, A. (1987). The closing of the American mind. New York: Simon & Schuster.

Conrad, D., and Hedin, D. (1981). National assessment of experiential education: Summary and implications. Journal of Experiential Education, 4(2), 6–20.

Cuban, L. (1984). How teachers taught: Constancy and change in American classrooms, 1890–1980. New York: Longman.

Dewey, J. (1916). Democracy and education. New York: The Free Press.

Dewey, J. (1938). Experience and education. New York: Collier.

Dryfoos, J. (1990). Adolescents at risk: Prevalence and prevention. New York: Oxford University Press.

Fine, M. (1991). Framing dropouts: Notes on the politics of an urban public high school. Albany: State University of New York Press.

Gardner, H. (1989). Multiple intelligences go to school: Educational implications of the theory of multiple intelligences. Educational Researcher, 18(8), 4–9.

Gerstein, A., Kahne J., and Westheimer, J. (1992). An evaluation of Pacific Crest Outward Bound's Bay Area Urban Youth Program. Unpublished paper, Stanford University, Stanford, California.

Goodlad, J. (1984). A place called school. New York: McGraw Hill.

Hamilton, S. (1980). Experiential learning programs for youth. American Journal of Education, February (2).

Hirsch, E. D. (1987). Cultural literacy: What every American needs to know. Boston: Houghton Mifflin.

Ianni, F. (1989). The search for structure: A report on American youth today. New York: Free Press.

Kielsmeier, J. (1989). Growing with the times: A challenge for experiential education. Journal of Experiential Education, 14(1), 40–44.

Kirst, M. W. (1984). Who controls our schools? American values in conflict. Stanford, CA: Stanford Alumni Association.

Kozol, J. (1991). Savage inequalities: Children in America's schools. New York: Crown.

McLaughlin, M. W., & Talbert, J., with Kahne, J., & Powell, J. (1990). Constructing a personalized school environment. Phi Delta Kappan, 72(3), 230–35.

National Commission for Excellence in Education. (1983). A nation at risk: The imperative for educational reform. Washington: U.S. Department of Education.

Powell, A. G., Farrar, E., & Cohen D. K. (1985). The shopping mall high school: Winners and losers in the educational marketplace. Boston: Houghton Mifflin.

Ravitch, D., & Finn, C. (1987). What do our 17-year-olds know? A report on the first national assessment of history and literature. New York: Harper & Row.

Sakofs, M., et al. (1988). The Cooperstown Outward Bound Summer Program: An informal look at the program's impact on the lives of students. Greenwich, CT: Outward Bound.

Sarason, S. B. (1971). The culture of the school and the problem of change. Boston: Allyn & Bacon.

Sarason, S. B. (1990). The predictable failure of educational reform: Can we change course before it's too late. San Francisco: Jossey- Bass.

Shepard, L. (1991). Interview on assessment issues with Lorrie Shepard. Educational Researcher, 20(2), 21–23.

Shore, A. (Ed.), (1977). Outward Bound: A reference volume. Portland, OR: Northwest Outward Bound School.

Sizer, T. (1985). Horace's compromise: The dilemma of the American high school. Boston: Houghton Mifflin.

Sizer, T. (1992). Horace's school: Redesigning the American high school. Boston: Houghton Mifflin.

Smith, M. L. (1976). Experiential study of the effects of Outward Bound. Final report. Boulder, CO: Bureau of Educational Field Services, Colorado University.

Taini, R. (1992). Keynote address at the 1992 West Regional Conference of the Association for Experiential Education.

Udall, D. (Ed.). (1991). Lessons from our classrooms: A guide for experiential educators. New York: New York City Outward Bound Center.

Wehlage, G. G., Rutter, R. A., Smith, G. A., Lesko, N., & Fernandez, R. R. (1988). Reducing the risk: Schools as communities of support. London: Falmer Press.

Wigginton, E. (1986). Sometimes a shining moment: The Foxfire experience. Garden City, NY: Anchor Press/Doubleday Books.

A Summary of the Educational Reform Reports in the 1980s
by Richard J. Kraft

Academic preparation for college: What students need to know and be able to do. (1983). New York: College Entrance Examination Board.

Action for excellence: A comprehensive plan to improve our nation's schools. (1983). Denver, CO: Task Force on Education for Economic Growth, Education Commission of the States.

Adler, M. J. (1982). The Paideia proposal. New York: Macmillan.

America's competitive challenge: The need for a national response. (1983). Washington, DC: Business-Higher Education Forum.

An Education of Value. (1984). Washington, DC: National Academy of Education.

Boyer, E. L. (1983). High school: A report on secondary education in America. New York: Harper & Row.

A celebration of teaching: High school in the 1980s. (1984). Washington, DC: National Association of Secondary School Principals and the National Association of Independent Schools.

Computerized factory automation: Employment, education and the workplace. (1984). Washington, DC: Joint Economic Committee of the U.S. Congress.

Educating Americans for the 21st century. (1983). Washington, DC: National Science Foundation.

Education, character, and the American schools. (1983). Syracuse, NY: National Institute of Education and The Ford Foundation, Good Schools Project.

Goal-based education program. (1983). Portland, OR: Northwest Regional Educational Laboratory.

Goodlad, J. I. (1983). A place called school: Prospects for the future. New York: McGraw-Hill.

Kennedy, D. (1985). The study of Stanford and the schools. Palo Alto: Stanford University.

Meeting the need for quality: Action in the South. (1983). Atlanta, GA: Southern Regional Education Board.

A nation at risk: The imperative for educational reform. (1983). Washington, DC: National Commission on Excellence in Education, Government Printing Office.

Redefining general education in the American high school. (1983). Washington, DC: Association for Supervision and Curriculum Development.

Task force on federal elementary and secondary education policy. (1983). New York: Twentieth Century Fund.

Chapter Three:
Service Learning

Developing a Service Ethic
by Anthony Richards

Achjani, A. (1978). Guidelines for carrying out Kuliah Kerja Nyata (KKN). Department of Education and Culture.

Dickson, A. (1976). In M. Dickson (Ed.), A chance to serve. London: Dobson Books.

Dickson, A. (Not dated). Study Service in Hong Kong and Elsewhere. Youth Call. Maidstone: Royal British Legion Press.

Dickson, A. (Not dated). West Germany's Zivildienst. Youth Call. Maidstone: Royal British Legion Press.

Glenn, H. S., & Warner, J. W. (1982). Developing capable young people. Texas: Humansphere.

Koesnadi, H. (1982). Study service as a subsystem in Indonesia higher education. Jakarta: PN Balai Pustaka.

Naisbett, J. (1982). Megatrends. New York: Warner Books.

Richards, A., & Scrutton, E. (1980). Progress report to Halifax School Board, Nova Scotia.

Richards, A. (1987). Study service: An Indonesian case study. Paper presented to the Second International Camping Conference, Washington.

UNESCO. (1981). Youth in the 1980s. Paris: UNESCO.

The Social, Psychological, Moral, and Cognitive Effects of Service Learning
by Richard J. Kraft

Alexander, R. (1977). A moral education curriculum on prejudice. Unpublished doctoral dissertation, Boston University.

Bontempo, B. (1979). A study of experience based learning in alternative public high schools: Implications for a new role for educators. Unpublished doctoral dissertation, Indiana University.

Bourgeois, M. (1978). Experiential citizen education for early adolescents: A model. Unpublished doctoral dissertation, University of North Carolina, Greensboro.

Braza, G. (1974). A comparison of experiential and classroom learning models in teaching health problems of the poor. Unpublished doctoral dissertation, University of Utah.

Broudy, H. (1977). Moral citizenship education: Potentials and limitations. Occasional paper No. 3. Washington: National Institute of Education.

Calabrese, R., & Schumer, H. (1986). The effects of service activities on adolescent alienation. Adolescence, 21, 675–687.

Clayman, C. (1968). Experiencing the role of teacher as liaison: Case study of the training of pre-service teachers through direct community experiences. Unpublished doctoral dissertation, Boston University.

Conrad, D. (1979). The differential impact of experiential learning programs on secondary school students. Unpublished doctoral dissertation, University of Minnesota.

Conrad, D., & Hedin, D. (1982). The impact of experiential education on adolescent development. In Conrad, D., & Hedin, D., Youth participation and experiential education. Child and Youth Services, 4:3/4, 57–76.

Corbett, R. (1977). The community involvement program: Social service as a factor in adolescent moral and psychological development. Unpublished doctoral dissertation, University of Toronto.

Edwards, C. (1974). The effect of experiences on moral development: Results from Kenya. Unpublished doctoral dissertation, Howard University.

Ellington, J. (1978). The effects of three curriculum strategies upon high school seniors' attitudes toward the elderly. Unpublished doctoral dissertation. University of California.

Exum, H. (1978). Cross age and peer teaching: A deliberate psychological education program for junior college students. Unpublished doctoral dissertation, University of Minnesota.

Glass, J., & Trent, C. (1979). The impact of a series of learning experiences on ninth grade students' attitudes toward the aged: Summary and lesson plans. Raleigh, NC: North Carolina University.

Hamilton, S., & Zeldin, R. (1987). Learning civics in community. Curriculum Inquiry, 17, 407–420.

Harrison, C. (1987). Student service: The new Carnegie unit. Princeton: The Carnegie Foundation for the Advancement of Teaching.

Hedin, D. (1987). Students as teachers: A tool for improving school climate and productivity. Social Policy, 17(3), 42–47.

Houser, V. (1974). Effects of student-aide experience on tutors' self-concept and reading skills. Unpublished doctoral dissertation, Brigham Young University.

Hunt, D., & Hardt, R. (1969). The effect of upward bound programs on the attitudes, motivation and academic achievement of Negro students. Journal of Social Issues, 25, 117–129.

Kazunga, D. (1978). A youth program in the local community's context: The case of the young farmers of Uganda program. Unpublished doctoral dissertation, University of Wisconsin.

Keene, P. (1975). Social problems analysis through community experience: An experimental study of high school seniors toward race and poverty. Unpublished doctoral dissertation, Pennsylvania State University.

Kelly, H. (1989). The effect of the helping experience upon the self-concept of the helper. Unpublished doctoral dissertation, University of Pittsburgh.

Kraft, R. J., Goldwasser, M., Swadener, M., & Timmons, M. (1993). First annual report: Preliminary evaluation: Service-learning Colorado. Denver: Colorado Department of Education. Boulder: University of Colorado.

Krug, J. (1991). Select changes in high school students' self-esteem and attitudes toward their school and community by their participation in service learning activities at a Rocky Mountain high school. An unpublished doctoral dissertation, University of Colorado-Boulder.

Lewis, J. (1977). What is learned in expository learning and learning by doing? Unpublished doctoral dissertation, University of Minnesota.

Luchs, K. (1981). Selected changes in urban high school students after participation in community based learning and service activities. An unpublished doctoral dissertation, University of Maryland.

Markus, G., Howard, J., & King, D. (1993). Integrating community service and classroom instruction enhances learning: Results from an experiment. Educational Evaluation and Policy Analysis, 15(4), 410–419.

Marsh, D. (1973). Education for political involvement: A pilot study of twelfth graders. Unpublished doctoral dissertation, University of Wisconsin.

Mosher, R. (1977). Theory and practice: A new E.R.A.? Theory Into Practice, 16(2), 166–184.

Newman, R. (1978). The effects of informational experiential activities on the attitudes of regular classroom students toward severely handicapped children and youth. Unpublished doctoral dissertation, University of Kansas.

Newmann, F., & Rutter, R. (1986). A profile of high school community service programs. Educational Leadership, 43(4), 65–71.

Owens, A. (1979). The effects of experiential learning on student attitudes. Unpublished doctoral dissertation, Temple University.

Reck, C. (1978). A study of the relationship between participation in school service programs and moral development. Unpublished doctoral dissertation, Saint Louis University.

Riechen, H. (1952). The volunteer work camp: A psychological evaluation. Cambridge: Addison-Wesley.

Rutter, R., & Newmann, F. (1989). The potential of community service to enhance civic responsibility. Social Education, 53(6), 371–374.

Sager, W. (1973). A study of changes in attitudes, values, and self-concepts of senior high youth while working as full-time volunteers with institutionally mentally retarded people. Unpublished doctoral dissertation, United States International University.

Saunders, L. (1976). An analysis of attitude changes toward school, school attendance, self-concept and reading of secondary school students involved in a cross age tutoring experience. Unpublished doctoral dissertation, United States International University.

Shoup, B. (1978). Living and learning for credit. Bloomington, IN: Phi Delta Kappa.

Smith, M. (1966). Explanation in competence: A study of peace corps teachers in Ghana. American Psychology, 21, 555–566.

Soat, D. (1974). Cognitive style, self-concept, and expressed willingness to help others. Unpublished doctoral dissertation, Marquette University.

Sprinthall, R., & Sprinthall, N. (1977). Educational psychology: A developmental approach (2nd ed.). Reading, MA: Addison-Wesley.

Stockhaus, S. (1976). The effects of a community involvement program on adolescent students' citizenship attitudes. Unpublished doctoral dissertation, University of Minnesota.

Tobler, N. (1986). Meta-Analysis of 143 adolescent drug prevention programs: Quantitative outcome results of program participants compared to a control or comparison group. Journal of Drug Issues, 16(4), 537–567.

Wilson, T. (1974). An alternative community based secondary school program and student political development. Unpublished doctoral dissertation, University of Southern California.

Chapter Four:
Outdoor and Environmental Education

Tasting the Berries: Deep Ecology and Experiential Learning
by Bert Horwood

Bly, R. (1990). Iron John: A book about men. New York: Addison-Wesley.

Henley, T. (1989). Rediscovery. Vancouver: Western Canada Wilderness Committee.

Henley, T. (1990). Rainforest universities. Journal of Experiential Education, 13(3), 6–11.

Horwood, B., & Raffan, J. (1988a). Recreation and education in the outdoors: Exploring the boundaries. CAPHER Journal, 54(3), 7–9.

Horwood, B. (1988b). Canoe trips: Doors to the primitive. In J. Raffan & B. Horwood (Eds.), Canexus. The canoe in Canadian culture. Toronto: Betelgeuse Books.

LaChapelle, D. (1991). Educating for deep ecology. Journal of Experiential Education, 14(3), 18–22.

Meeker, J. (1980). The comedy of survival. In search of an environmental ethic. Los Angeles: Guild of Tutors Press.

Naess, A. (1985). Identification as a source of deep ecological attitudes. In M. Tobias (Ed.), Deep ecology. San Diego: Avant Books.

Snyder, G. (1977). The old ways. San Francisco: City Lights Bookstore.

Van Matre, S. (1990). Earth education. A new beginning. Warrenville, IL: The Institute for Earth Education.

Wilderness Keeping by Wilderness Educators
by John C. Miles

Cordell, K. H., and Hendee, J. C. (1980). Renewable resources recreation in the United States; supply, demand, and the critical policy issues. Washington, DC: American Forest Association.

Fazio, J. R. (1979). Communicating with the wilderness user. Bulletin 28, College of Forestry, Wildlife and Range Sciences, University of Idaho, Moscow, Idaho.

Hammitt, W. E., and Cole, D. N. (1987). Wildland recreation: Ecology and management. New York: John Wiley and Sons.

Hampton, B., and Cole, D. (1988). Soft paths. Stockpole Books.

Miles, J. C. (1987). Wilderness as a learning place. Journal of Environmental Education, 10(3), 33–40.

Miles, J. C. (1988). Environmental issues and outdoor recreation: The privilege and the obligations. In John Cedarquist, (Ed.), Proceedings of the 1986 Conference on Outdoor Recreation. Salt Lake City, UT: University of Utah.

Miner, J. L. (1964). Is our youth going soft? Princeton Alumni Weekly, XLIV, 14.

Stremba, R. (1989). Reflection: A process to learn about self through outdoor adventure. Journal of Experiential Education, 12(2), 7–9.

United States, 88th Congress, 3 September 1964. Public Law 88–577: Wilderness Act, Section 2(a).

The Failed Curriculum
by James Raffan

Bloom, B. (Ed.). (1956). Taxonomy of educational objectives: The classification of educational goals. New York: David McKay.

Caldicott, H. (1990) Physician to the planet. Education Forum, Summer, 30–34.

Cundiff, B. (1989). Reading, writing and the environment. Seasons, Autumn, 16–19.

Defenders of the planet. (1990, April 23). Time, 58–60.

Gardner, H. (1983). Frames of mind: A theory of multiple intelligences.

Hines, J. M., et al. (1986–87). Analysis and synthesis of research on responsible environmental behavior: A meta-analysis. Journal of Environmental Education, 18(2), 1–8.

Ludlow, R. (1989, October 4). When industry and government speak, no one listens. Ottawa Citizen, p. B1.

McDonald, N. (1990, March 4). Peter Dundas: citizen and guardian of Earth. Kingston Whig Standard, 27.

Minsky, M. (1985). The society of mind. New York: Simon & Schuster.

Raffan, J. (1986). Dilemma in outdoor education. Outdoor Recreation Research Journal, 1 (Winter), 31–40.

Reid, A. (1990, March 13). Canadians want more wilderness protected and are willing to pay, poll says. Canadian Nature Federation Press Release.

Schafer, R. (1979). The dung heap syndrome. Journal of Environmental Education, 11(1), 5.

Sia, A. P., et al. (1986). Selected predictors of responsible environmental behavior: An analysis. Journal of Environmental Education, 17(2), 31–40.

Suzuki, D. (1990, May 12). Greenhouse gases a reckless gamble. Vancouver Sun, p. A8.

Tognacci, L. M., Weigel, R. H., Wideen, M. F., & Vernon, T. A. (1972). Environmental quality: How universal is public concern? Environment and Behaviour, March, 73–86.

Who made a difference. (1989). Outdoor Canada, Winter, 57–79.

Williams, A. T. (1979). The new environmentalism—a meaningless epithet. Journal of Environmental Education, 10(4), 4.

Williams, T. (1988). Why Johnny shoots stop signs. Audubon, September, 112–114.

The Experience of Place: Exploring Land as Teacher
by James Raffan

Barnes, T. J., & Duncan, J. S. (Eds.). (1992). Writing worlds: Discourse, text and metaphor in the representation of landscape. London and New York: Routledge.

Berger, J. (1980). About looking. New York: Pantheon Books.

Bookchin, M. (1990). The philosophy of social ecology: Essays on dialectical naturalism. New York: Black Rose Books.

Clifford, J., & Marcus, G. E. (Eds.). (1986). Writing culture: The poetics and politics of ethnography. Berkeley: University of California Press.

Cosgrove, D., and Daniels, S. (1988). The iconography of landscape. Cambridge: Cambridge University Press.

Dansereau, P. (1975). Inscape and landscape: The human perception of environment. New York: Columbia University Press.

Geertz, C. (1988). Works and lives: The anthropologist as author. Stanford, CA: Stanford University Press.

Hay, R. B. (1988). Toward a theory of sense of place. Trumpeter, 5(4) Fall, 159–164.

Jackson, P. (1989). Maps of meaning: An introduction to cultural geography. London: Unwin Hyman.

Moss, J. (1991). Imagining the arctic: From Frankenstein to Farley Mowat, words turn the arctic landscape into unreality. Arctic Circle March/April, 32–40.

Porteous, J. D. (1990). Landscapes of the mind: Worlds of sense and metaphor. Toronto: University of Toronto Press.

Raffan, J. (1992). Frontier, homeland and sacred space: A collaborative investigation into cross-cultural perceptions of place in the Thelon Game Sanctuary, Northwest Territories. Doctoral dissertation, Queen's University, Kingston, Ontario. E.R.I. C. RCO19102.

Tuan, Y. F. (1990). Realism and fantasy in art, history, and geography. Annals of the Association of American Geographers, 80(3), 435–446.

Tuan, Y. F. (1991). Language and the making of place: A narrative descriptive approach. Annals of the Association of American Geographers, 81(4), 684–696.

Chapter Six:
Cross-Cultural Settings

Closed Classrooms, High Mountains, and Strange Lands: An Inquiry into Culture and Caring
by Richard J. Kraft

A nation at risk. (1983). Washington, DC: U.S. Government Printing Office.

Adler, P. S. (1975). The transitional experience: An alternative view of culture shock. Journal of Humanistic Psychology, 15, 13–23.

Bochner, S. (1982). Cultures in contact: Studies in cross-cultural interaction. Oxford: Pergamon.

Bochner, S., Lin, A., & McLeod, B. M. (1980). Anticipated role conflict of returning overseas students. Journal of Social Psychology, 110, 265–72.

Church, A. T. (1982). Sojourner adjustment. Psychological Bulletin, 91, 540–72.

Fuller, B. (1989). Third world school quality. Educational Researcher, 18(2), 12–19.

Furnham, A., & Bochner, S. (1986). Culture shock. London: Routledge.

Guthrie, G. M. (1975). A behavioral analysis of culture learning. In R. W. Brisling, S. Bochner, and W. J. Lonner (Eds.), Cross-cultural perspectives on learning. New York: Wiley.

Guthrie, G. M. (1981). What you need is continuity. In S. Bochner (Ed.), The mediating person: Bridges between cultures. Boston: Schenkman.

Goodlad, J. (1984). A place called school. New York: McGraw-Hill.

Harris, J. G., Jr. (1973). A science of the South Pacific: Analysis of the character structure of the Peace Corps Volunteer. American Psychologist, 28, 232–47.

Jacobson, E. H. (1963). Sojourn research: A definition of the field. Journal of Social Issues, 19(3), 123–9.

Lopez, B. (1989). Mapping the real geography. Harpers, 279, 19–24.

McLuhan, M. (1964). Understanding media: The extensions of man. New York: McGraw-Hill.

Oberg, K. (1960). Cultural Schock: Adjustment to new cultural environments. Practical Anthropology, 7, 177–82.

Resnick, L. (1987). Learning in school and out. Educational Researcher, 16(9), 13–20.

Torbiorn, I. (1982). Living abroad: Personal adjustment and personnel policy in the overseas setting. Chichester: Wiley.

Walsh, V., & Golins, G. (1976). The exploration of the Outward Bound process. Denver, CO: Colorado Outward Bound School.

How Inclusive are You? Ten Ways to Limit or Empower Members of Oppressed Groups
by Mary McClintock

Hardiman, R. (1980). Ten ways to make a third world person lose effectiveness in an organization. Unpublished manuscript.

Hardiman, R., & Rauscher, L. (1986). Counseling students with disabilities: Ten ways to be effective. Unpublished manuscript.

Palmer, J. D. (1978). Ten ways to make a woman lose effectiveness in an organization. Unpublished manuscript.

Young, V. (1985). Ten ways to limit a member of a subordinate social group. Unpublished manuscript.

The Power of Stories: Learning from the Lives of Young People
by Denis Udall

Garrod, A., & Howard, R. W. (1991). Making moral youth. Harvard Education Review, 60, 513–526.

Youth Take the Lead: Cherokee Nation's Approach to Leadership
by McClellan Hall and James Kielsmeier

Allen, R., & Bread, J. Johnson-O'Malley Program, Youth Leadership Conference Curriculum Design. May 26, 1993.

Conrad, D. Evaluation Report of the National Leadership Conference, Camp Pin Oak, Missouri and Camp Miniwanca. Michigan, June, July 1982. Center for Youth Development and Research, University of Minnesota, October 1982.

Conrad, D. Evaluation Report of the National Leadership Conference, Bradford Woods, Indiana and Lake of the Ozarks, Missouri. Missouri, July, August 1983. Center for Youth Development and Research, University of Minnesota, November 1983.

Conrad, D. Evaluation Report of the Indian Youth Leadership Conference, Camp Lutherhoma, Tahlequah, Oklahoma. June 1–8, 1983. Center for Youth Development and Research, University of Minnesota, August 1983.

LaClair, M. Developing student leadership skills. Indian Education Act Resource and Evaluation Center Five, Tulsa, Oklahoma, 1984.

Chapter Seven:
Experiential Learning

The Midwife Teacher: Engaging Students in the Experiential Education Process
by Karen Warren

Beidler, P. (1986). A turn down the harbor. In R. Kraft & J. Kielsmeier (Eds.), Experiential education and the schools (pp. 118–126), Boulder, CO: Association for Experiential Education.

Belenky, M. F., Clincy, B. M., Goldberger, N. R., & Tarule, J. M. (1986). Women's ways of knowing. New York: Basic Books.

Dewey, J. (1938). Experience & education. New York: Collier.

Freire, P. (1984). Pedagogy of the oppressed. New York: Continuum.

Heider, J. (1986). The tao of leadership. New York: Bantam.

Horwood, B. (1986). Are good teachers born or made: A Canadian attempt at teacher midwifery. In R. Kraft & J. Kielsmeier (Eds.), Experiential education and the schools (pp. 331–333). Boulder, CO: Association for Experiential Education.

Hunt, J. (1990). Ethical issues in experiential education. Boulder, CO: Association for Experiential Education.

Jensen, M. (1979). Application of small group theory to adventure programs. Journal of Experiential Education, 2(2), 39–42.

Kramarae, C., & Treichler, P. (1991). Feminist dictionary. Champaign, IL: University of Illinois Press.

Lazarus, R. S., & Launier, R. (1978). Stress-related transactions between person and environment. Perspectives in Interactional Psychology, 287–327.

Rich, A. (1979). On lies, secrets, and silence. New York: W. W. Norton.

Rogers, C. (1969). Freedom to learn. Columbus, OH: Charles E. Merrill.

Shor, I. (1986). Equality is excellence: Transforming teacher education and the learning process. Harvard Educational Review, 56(4), 406–422.

Shrewsbury, C. (1987). What is feminist pedagogy? Women's Studies Quarterly, XV:3 & 4 (Fall/Winter), 6–13.

Solomon, N. K., & McLean, M. (1991). The traditional midwife. Midwifery Today, 19, 30–32.

Tippett, S. (1988). Small group development. Unpublished manuscript.

Warren, K. (1988). The student directed classroom: A model for teaching experiential education theory. Journal of Experiential Education, 11(1), 4–9.

Warren, K., & Tippett, S. (1988). Teaching consensus decision making. Journal of Experiential Education. 11(3), 38–39.

Weber, R. (1982). The group: A cycle from birth to death. NLT reading book for human relations training. National Training Laboratories Institute.

Wigginton, E. (1985). Sometimes a shining moment: The Foxfire experience. New York: Anchor Press/Doubleday.

Willis, S. (1991). The traditional midwife. Midwifery Today, 19, 28–30.

Reflections on Reflection
by Bert Horwood

Schoel, J., Prouty, D., & Radcliffe, P. (1988). Islands of healing: A guide to adventure based counseling. Hamilton, MA: Project Adventure.

Schon, D. (1982). The reflective practitioner: How professions think in action. New York: Basic Books.

Schon, D. (1987). Educating the reflective practitioner: Toward a new design for teaching and learning in the professions. San Francisco: Jossey-Bass.

Chapter Nine:
Experiencing Mathematics and Science

Eureka! A Yurt! Integrating Mathematics, Cooperative Learning and Community Service
by Jo Anna Woo Allen

Kagan, S. (1989). Cooperative learning: Resources for teachers. San Juan Capistrano, CA: Spencer Kagan.

The Gunpowder River Project: Experiential Education in a Large Public School System
by Jo Anna Woo Allen

Conrad, D., & Hedin, D. (1986). National assessment of experiential education: Summary and implications. In R. Kraft and J. Kielsmeier (Eds.), Experiential education and the schools (pp. 229–243). Boulder, CO: Association for Experiential Education.

Gunpowder River School Action Project: A Chesapeake Bay tributary. (1986). Curriculum Guide of Baltimore County Public Schools, Towson, MD 21204.

Maslow, A. (1954). Motivation and personality. New York: Harper & Brothers.

Peters, T. J., & Waterman, R. H., Jr. (1982). In Search of Excellence. New York: Warner Books.

Chapter Ten:
Experiencing the Language Arts

Time, Place, & Community: Ingredients for Good Writing
by Ian Sykes

Calkins, L. M. (1983). Lessons from a child. Melbourne: Heinemann.

Dewey, J. (1963). Experience and education. New York: Collier

Goodman, K. S. (1986). What's whole in whole language. Richmond Hill: Scholastics.

Harste, J., Woodward, V., & Burke, C. (1984). Language stories and literacy lessons. Portsmouth, NH: Heinemann.

Joplin, L. (1985). On defining experiential education. In R. Kraft & M. Sakofs (Eds.), Theory of experiential education. Boulder, CO: Association for Experiential Education.

Murray, D. M. (1982). Learning by teaching. Upper Montclair, NJ: Boynton/Cook Publishers.

Storytelling Tips for Experiential Educators
by Lana S. Leonard

Baker, A., and Greene, E. (1987). Storytelling: Art and technique. New York: R. R. Bowker.

Bettelheim, B. (1976). The uses of enchantment, the meaning and importance of fairy tales. New York: Alfred A. Knopf.

Breneman, L., & Breneman, B. (1987). Once upon a time: A storytelling handbook. Chicago, IL: Nelson Hall.

Bruner, J. (1986). Actual minds, possible worlds. Cambridge, MA: Harvard University Press.

Egan, K. (1988). Teaching as storytelling. London, England: Routledge Press.

Livo, N., & Reitz, S. (1986). Storytelling: Process and practice. Littleton, CO: Libraries Unlimited.

Pellowski, A. (1977). The world of storytelling. New York: Bowker.

Sawyer, R. (1977). The way of the storyteller. New York: Penguin.

Putting Principles into Practice: Traveling the Foxfire Trail in Graduate School
by Clifford E. Knapp

Jennings, W. B. (Ed.). (1990, Fall). Other "brain compatible" networks. The Brain Based Education Networker, p. 6.

Terkel, S. (1972). Working, New York: Ballantine.

Wigginton, E. (1986). Sometimes a shining moment. New York: Anchor Press/Doubleday.

Interactive Theatre as a Dramatic Resource
by Janet Salmons-Rue

Johnson, L., & O'Neill, C. (1984). Dorothy Heathcote: Collected writings on education and drama. London: Hutchinson.

McCaslin, N. (1984). Creative drama in the classroom. New York: Longman.

McCaslin, N. (1987). Creative drama in the intermediate grades. New York: Longman.

McCaslin, N. (1987). Creative drama in the primary grades. New York: Longman.

Spolin, V. (1986). Theater games for the classroom. Illinois: Northwestern University Press.

Chapter Eleven:
Special Populations

Making No Apologies for Our Differences
by Jeff Moore

Joplin, L. (1981). On defining experiential education. Journal of Experiential Education, 4(1), 17–20.

Ryan, W. (1972). Blaming the victim. New York: Vintage.

Wolfensberger, W. (1972). Normalization. Toronto: National Institute of Mental Retardation.

The Impact of the Americans With Disabilities Act on Adventure Education Programs
by Deb Sugerman

Havens, M. S. (1992). Bridges to accessibility. Iowa: Kendall/Hunt.

Johnson, M. (Ed.). (1992). People with disabilities explain it all for you. Kentucky: The Advocado Press.

The LIFE resource manual. (1988). (Available from Curriculum in Leisure Studies and Recreation Administration, 207 Pettigrew Hall, CB #3185, University of North Carolina - CH, Chapel Hill, NC 27514.)

Weber, A., & Zeller, J. (1990). Canoeing and kayaking for persons with physical disabilities. Virginia: American Canoe Association.

Chapter Twelve:
Experiential Activities

Cooperative Learning Techniques in the Classroom
by Scott C. Griffith

Bloom, B., & Krathwohl, D. (1977). Taxonomy of educational objectives. In Handbook 1: Cognitive domain. New York: Longman.

Johnson, D. W., Johnson, R. T., & Holbec, E. J. (1986). Circles of learning: Cooperation in the classroom (rev. ed.). Englewood Cliffs, NJ: Prentice Hall.

Johnson, D. W., Maruyama, G., Johnson, R., Nelson D., & Skon, L. (1981). Effects of cooperative, competitive, and individualistic goal structure on achievement: A meta-analysis. Psychological Bulletin, 89(1), 47–62.

Kagan, S. (1989). Cooperative learning: Resources for teachers. Riverside, CA: University of California.

Myers, J., & Lemon, C. (1988). The jigsaw strategy: Cooperative learning in the social studies. History and the Social Science Teacher, 24(1), 18–22.

Slavin, R. E. (1983). Cooperative learning, New York: Longman.

Slavin, R. E. (1986). Learning together. American Educator, 12(1), 6–13.

Slavin, R. E. (1988). Cooperative learning and student achievement. Educational Leadership, 46(2), 31–33.

Vermette, P. J. (1988). Cooperative grouping in the classroom: Turning students into active learners. The Social Studies, 79(6), 271–273.

Give Your Students a Leadership Course
by Nicholas Beer

Bennis, W., & Nanus, B. (1985). Leaders. New York, NY: Harper & Row.

Burns, J. M. (1979). Leadership. New York, NY: Harper & Row.

Carew, D. K., Parisi-Carew, E., & Blanchard, K. H. (1986). Situational leadership. Training and Development Journal. June.

Heider, J. (1985). The tao of leadership. New York, NY: Harper & Row.

Johnson, D. W., & Johnson, F. P. (1987). Joining together - group theory and group skills. Englewood Cliffs, NJ: Prentice Hall.

Kalisch, K. R. (1979). The role of the instructor in the Outward Bound educational process. Wisconsin: Wheaton College.

What About the Young Child?
by Rita Yerkes

Berry, K. (1967). Developmental test of visual-motor integration administration and scoring manual. Chicago. Follett.

Coursen, D. (1974). Playground facilities and equipment. NAESP School Leadership Digest Series, number nine, ERIC/CEM Research Analysis Series, number eleven. Washington, DC: (ERIC Document Reproductive Service No. 099952)

Ellis, M. J. (1972). Play: theory and research. In W. J. Mitchell (Ed.), Environmental Design: Research and Practice, Vol. 1, Los Angeles: University of California School of Architecture and Urban Planning.

Essa, Eva. (1981). An outdoor play area designed for learning. Day Care and Early Childhood Education, 9, 37–42.

Frost, J. (1978). The American playground movement. Childhood Education, 54, 176–182.

Hayward, D. G., et al. (1974). Children's play and urban play environments: A comparison of traditional, contemporary and adventure playground types. Environment and Behavior, 6 131–168.

Moore, G. T. (1980). The design of therapeutic play environments. In W. M. Cruickshank (Ed.), Crossroads to Learning. Syracuse, NY: Syracuse University Press.

Ranzoni, P. (1973). Considerations in developing an outside area for schools/centers for young children. (ERIC Document Reproduction Service No. ED 100018)

Wuellner, L. (1970). The present status of research on playgrounds. Educational Product Report, 3, 8–15.

Yerkes, R. (1980). The effects of creative-adventure playground participation on the development of visual-motor integration of young children. Doctoral dissertation, Northern Illinois University.

Chapter Thirteen:
Experiential Higher Education and Teacher Education

The Student Teacher Who Wouldn't Go Away: Learning from Failure
by J. Gary Knowles and Virginia B. Hoefler

Eisner, E. W. (1979). The educational imagination. New York, NY: Macmillan.

Dewey, J. (1938). Education and experience. New York, NY: Macmillan.

Joplin, L. (1981). On defining experiential education. Journal of Experiential Education, 4(1), 17–20.

Knowles, J. G. (1992). Models for understanding pre-service and beginning teachers' biographies: Illustrations from case studies. In I. F. Goodson (Ed.), Studying teachers' lives,(pp. 99–152). London & New York: Rutlidge.

Lortie, D. (1975). School teacher: A sociological study. Chicago, IL: The University of Chicago Press.

Progoff, I. (1975). At a journal workshop. New York: Dialogue House.

Ryan, K. (1986). The induction of new teachers. Bloomington, IN: Phi Delta Kappa Educational Foundation.

Experiential Components in Academic Courses
by G. Christian Jernstedt

Johnson, B. T., & Jernstedt, G. C. (1975). The effects of long term groups on their participants. Experiential Learning in College Project, 1–30. Hanover, NH.

McHugo, G. J. (1979). A multivariate analysis of self-selection and change due to college experience, 1–627. Dissertation. Dartmouth College.

A College-Level Experiential Learning Career Development Curriculum
by Michael J. Marshall, W. Patrick Haun, and Ronald G. Ramke

Cook, T. D., & Campbell, D. T. (1979). Quasi-experimentation: Design and analysis for field settings. Chicago: Rand McNally.

Davis, J., Steen, T., & Rubin S. (1987). A study of the internship experience. Journal of Experiential Education, 10(2), 22–26.

Ewert, A. (1987). Research in experiential education: An overview. Journal of Experiential Education, 10(2), 4–7.

Heath, D. H. (1968). Growing up in college. San Francisco: Jossey-Bass.

Holland, J. L., Daiger, D. C., & Power, P. G. (1980). My Vocational Situation. Palo Alto, CA: Consulting Psychologists Press.

Jernstedt, G. C. (1980). Experiential components in academic courses. Journal of Experiential Education, 3(2), 11–19.

Lunneborg, P. W. (1974-75). Can college graduates in psychology find employment in their field? Vocational Guidance Quarterly, 23, 159–166.

Malin, J. J., & Timmreck, C. (1979). Student goals and the undergraduate curriculum. Teaching of Psychology, 6, 136–139.

Osborne, G. L. (1987). A case study of career preparation by psychology majors: Implications for career development at the departmental level. Paper presented at the meeting of the Southeastern Psychological Association, Atlanta, GA.

Pinkus, R., & Korn, J. (1973). The preprofessional option: An alternative to graduate work in psychology. American Psychologist, 28, 710–718.

Shappell, D. L., Lacy, G. H., & Tarrier, R. B. (1970-71). School motivation and occupation orientation. Vocational Guidance Quarterly, 19, 97–103.

Thompson, A. S., & Lindeman, R. H. (1981). Career Development Inventory. Palo Alto, CA: Consulting Psychologists Press.

Vandecreek, L., & Fleischer, M. (1984). The role of the practicum in the undergraduate psychology curriculum. Teaching of Psychology, 11, 9–14.

Ware, M. E. (1985). Assessing a career development course for upper-level college students. Journal of College Student Personnel, 26, 152–155.

Chapter Fourteen
Research and Evaluation of Experiential Learning

Research in Experiential Education: An Overview
by Alan Ewert

Babbie, E. (1983). The practice of social research (3rd ed.). Belmont, CA: Wadsworth Publishing.

Bachrach, A. (1981). Psychological research: An introduction. New York: Random House.

Burton, L. (1981). A critical analysis and review of the research on Outward Bound and related programs. Doctoral dissertation. Rutgers University, The State University of New Jersey.

Ewert, A. (1986). What research doesn't tell the practitioner. Parks and Recreation, 21(3), 46–49.

Fielding, N., and Fielding, J. (1986). Linking data. Sage University Paper series on Qualitative Research Methods (Vol. 4). Beverly Hills, CA: Sage.

Gardner, M. (1957). Fads and fallacies in the name of science. New York: Dover Publications.

Hamilton, S. (1979). Evaluating experiential learning programs. Paper presented at the Annual Meeting of the American Educational Research Association. April.

Heath, D. (1985). Teaching for adult effectiveness. In R. Kraft and M. Sakofs (Eds.), The theory of experiential education. Boulder, CO: Association for Experiential Education.

Johnston, J., and Pennypacker, H. (1980). Strategies and tactics of human behavioral research. Hillsdale, NJ: Lawrence Erlbaum Associates.

Kirk, J., and Miller, M. (1986). Reliability and validity in qualitative research. Sage University Paper series on Qualitative Research Methods (Vol.1). Beverly Hills, CA: Sage.

Lawson, J. (1985). Challenges to graduate education. Journal of Physical Education and Recreation, 44, 23–25.

Reinharz, S. (1979). Social science. San Francisco: Jossey-Bass.

Shore, A. (1977). Outward Bound: A reference volume. New York: Topp Litho.

Webb, E., Campbell, D., Schwartz, R., & Sechrest, L (1966). Unobtrusive measure: Nonreactive research in the social sciences. Chicago: Rand McNally.

Weiss, C. (1972). Evaluation research: Methods of assessing program effectiveness. Englewood Cliffs, NJ: Prentice-Hall.

An Introduction to Research and Evaluation in Practice
by Richard Flor

Cook, T. D., & Campbell, D. T. (1979). Quasi-experimentation design & analysis for field settings. Boston: Houghton Mifflin.

Ewert, A. (1987). Research in experiential education: An overview. Journal of Experiential Education, 10(2), 4–7.

Hamilton, S. (1979, April). Evaluating experiential learning programs. Paper presented at the Annual Meeting of the American Educational Research Association.

Howell, D. C. (1987). Statistical methods for psychology (2nd ed.). Boston: PWS Publishers.

Joint Committee on Standards for Educational Evaluation (1981). Standards for evaluations of educational programs, projects, and materials. New York: McGraw-Hill.

Klint, K., & Priest, S. (1987). Letters to the editor. Journal of Experiential Education, 10(3), 50–51.

Kraft, R. J. (1984). 1984: The Orwellian year of educational politics and reform. Journal of Experiential Education, 7(1), 3–4.

Rowley, J. (1987). Adventure education and qualitative research. Journal of Experiential Education, 10(2), 8–12.

Worthen, B. R., & Sanders, J. R. (1987). Educational evaluation. White Plains, NY: Longman.

Meaningful Methods: Evaluation Without the Crunch
by Darl G. Kolb

Argyris, C., & Schon, D. (1974). Theory in practice: Increasing professional effectiveness. San Francisco: Jossey- Bass.

Bickman, L. (Ed.). (1987). Using program theory in evaluation. San Francisco: Jossey-Bass.

Chen, H. T. (1990). Theory-driven evaluations. Beverly Hills: Sage.

Chenery, M. F. (1987). A sampler of qualitative research in organized camping. Journal of Experiential Education, 10(2), 13–16.

Cronbach, L. (1980). Toward reform of program evaluation. San Francisco: Jossey-Bass.

Ewert, A. (1987). Research in experiential education: An overview. Journal of Experiential Education, 10(2), 4–7.

Greene, J. C. (1987). Stakeholder participation in evaluation design. Is it worth the effort? Evaluation and Program Planning, 10 379–394.

Greene, J. C., Caracelli, V. J., & Grahm, W. F. (1988). Toward a conceptual framework for mixed-method evaluation designs. Panel presentation to the Annual Meeting of the American Evaluation Association, New Orleans.

Jorgensen, D. L. (1989). Participant observation: A methodology for human studies. Beverly Hills, CA: Sage.

Klint, K., & Priest, S. (1987). Letter to the editor. Journal of Experiential Education, 10(3), 50–51.

Lincoln, Y. S., & Guba, E. G. (1985). Naturalistic inquiry. Beverly Hills: Sage.

Mathison, S. (1988). Collaborative research with classroom teachers at S.U.N.Y., Albany. Seminar presentation, Cornell evaluation group.

Miles, M. B., & Huberman, A. M. (1984). Qualitative data analysis: A sourcebook of new methods. Beverly Hills: Sage.

Patton, M. Q. (1980). Qualitative research methods. Beverly Hills: Sage.

Patton, M. Q. (1986). Utilization-focused evaluation. Beverly Hills, Sge.

Raffan, J., & Barrett, M. J. (1989). Sharing the path: Reflections on journals from an expedition. Journal of Experiential Education, 12(2), 29–36.

Rowley, J. (1987). Adventure education and qualitative research. Journal of Experiential Education, 10(2), 8–12.

Schon, D. A. (1983). The reflective practitioner. New York: Basic Books.

Warner, A. (1984). How to creatively evaluate programs. Journal of Experiential Education, 7(2), 38–43.

Whitmore, E. (1989). Collaborative evaluation methods with a teenage parenting programme in Nova Scotia. Presentation to the annual Cornell program evaluation conference.

Conducting Research in Experience-Based Training and Development Programs: Passkeys to Locked Doors
by Simon Priest, Aram Attarian , and Sabine Schubert

Attarian, A. (1992). The effects of Outward Bound training on the risk-taking propensity of corporate managers. Unpublished doctoral dissertation, University of Oregon, Eugene, OR.

Baldwin, T. T., Wagner, R. J., & Roland, C. C. (1991). Effects of outdoor challenge training on group and individual outcomes. Unpublished manuscript. Indiana University, School of Business: Bloomington.

Bank, J. (1985). Outdoor development for managers. London: Gower.

Beeby, M., & Rathborn, S. (1983). Development training: Using the outdoors in management development. Management Education and Development, 14(3), 170–181.

Brathay Hall Trust. (1985). Leadership and development training. Promotional brochure.

Braverman, M., Brenner, J., Fretz, P., & Desmond, D. (1990). Three approaches to evaluation: A ropes course illustration. Journal of Experiential Education, 13(1), 23–30.

Bronson, J., Gibson, S., Kichar, R., & Priest, S. (1992). Evaluation of team development in a corporate adventure training program. Journal of Experiential Education, 15(2), 50–53.

Cacioppe, R., & Adamson, P. (1988, November). Stepping over the edge: Outdoor development and programs for management and staff. Human Resource Management Australia, 77–91.

Colorado Outward Bound School. (1988). Survey of professional development program participants, 1988. Unpublished manuscript. Denver, CO.

Creswick, C., & Williams, R. (1979). Using the outdoors for management development and team building. Unpublished manuscript. The Food, Drink and Tobacco I.T.B.

Darby, M. (1989, June). Adventure training. Australian Institute of Training and Development, 8.

Dutkiewicz, J. S., & Chase, D. B. (1991, October). Behavioral impact of outdoor based leadership training on University of Denver's MBA students: 1990–1991. Paper presented at the International Assoc. for Experiential Education Conference, Lake Junaluska, NC.

Ehrhardt, S. (1991, December 5-8). Paper presented at the Research Symposium in EBTD, Pecos River Ranch, Santa Fe, NM.

Ewert, A. (1983). Outdoor adventure and self-concept: A research analysis. Center for Leisure Studies, University of Oregon, Eugene, OR.

Falvey, J. (1988, October 3). Before spending $3 million on leadership, read this. Wall Street Journal.

Fleming, J. (1987, September). Roughing it in the bush. Business Magazine, 40–48.

Flor, R. (1991). an introduction to research and evaluation in practice. Journal of Experiential Education, 14(1), 36–39.

Forrester, R. A. (1987, September/October). How Outward Bound can lead to better buying. Retail and Distribution Management, 21–23.

Gahin, F. S., & Chesteen, S. A. (1988). Executives contemplate the call of the wild. Risk Management, 35(1), 44–51.

Gall, A. (1987). You can take the manager out of the woods, but.... Training and Development Journal, 41, 54–58.

Galpin, T. J. (1989). The impact of a three-day outdoor management development course on selected self-perceptions of the participants. Unpublished doctoral dissertation, University of California at Los Angeles.

Garvey, D. (1989). The corporate connection: From bowlines to bowties. Journal of Experiential Education, 12(1), 13–15.

Gass, M., Goldman, K., & Priest, S. (1992). Constructing effective corporate adventure training programs. Journal of Experiential Education, 15(1), 35–42.

Goldman, K., & Priest, S. (1990). Risk taking transfer in development training. Journal of Adventure Education and Outdoor Leadership, 7(4), 32–35.

Hogg, C. (1988). Outdoor training. Personnel Management, 22.

Hunt, J. (1991). Ethics and experiential education as professional practice. Journal of Experiential Education, 14(2), 14–18.

Isenhart, M. W. (1983). Report to the Colorado Outward Bound School. Denver, CO.

Kadel, S. (1988, May 3). Executives grasp goals, teamwork in outdoors. The Business Journal, 3.

Keslake, P. S., & Radcliff, P. J. (1980). Inward bound—A new direction for Outward Bound: Towards a holistic approach to management development. In J. Beck & C. Cox (Eds.), Advances in management education (pp. 41–54). Chichester: John Wiley & Sons.

King, D., & Harmon, P. (1983). Evaluation of the Colorado Outward Bound School's career development course offered in collaboration with the training, education, and employee development department of Martin-Marietta Aerospace. Boulder: Colorado Outward Bound School.

Knecht, G. B. (1983, July). Executives go Outward Bound. Dun's Business Month, 56–58.

Kolb, D. (1991). Meaningful methods: Evaluation without the crunch. Journal of Experiential Education, 14(1), 40–44.

Latteier, C. (1989). Learning to lead. United States Air Magazine.

Lawler, E. E. (1988, January). Human resources management: Meeting the challenges. Personnel, 22–27.

Long, J. (1984). The wilderness lab. Training and Development Journal, 38(5), 58–69.

Long, J. W. (1987). The wilderness lab comes of age. Training and Development Journal, 41(3), 30–39.

Miner, T. A. (1991). A descriptive analysis of the experience-based training and development field. In C. Birmingham (Ed.), Association for Experiential Education: 1991 conference proceedings and workshop summaries book (pp. 59–66). Boulder, CO: Association for Experiential Education.

Miner, T. (1994). Adventure training. In W. Tracey (Ed.), Human Resources Management & Development Handbook (2nd ed.), (pp. 879–886). New York: American Management Association.

Mossman, A. (1982). Management training for real. Unpublished manuscript.

Priest, S. (1991). Research in Outward Bound for the 1990s. Paper presented at the 50th Anniversary and 4th International Outward Bound Conference, Aberdovey, Meirionnydd, Snowdonia, Wales, June 25, 1991.

Priest, S. (1992). The impact of total employee participation in an experiential training and development program or corporate adventure training program on the corporate work climate. In K. A. Henderson (Ed.), Coalition for Education in the Outdoors Research Symposium Proceedings (pp. 103–104). Bradford Woods, Martinsville, IN: Coalition for Education in the Outdoors.

Rice, B. (1979). Going to the mountain. Psychology Today, 13(7), 65–81.

Rice, B. (1988). Work or Perk? Psychology Today, 22(6), 26–28.

Roland, C. C. (1981). The transfer of an outdoor managerial training program to the workplace. Unpublished doctoral dissertation, Boston University.

Roland, C. C. (1985). Outdoor managerial training programs: Do they work? Bradford Papers, 5, 69–77.

Rowley, J. (1987). Adventure education and qualitative research. Journal of Experiential Education, 10(2), 8–12.

Saari, L. M., Johnson, T. R., McLaughlin, S. D., & Zimmerle, D. M. (1988). A survey of management training and education programs in US companies. Personnel Psychology, 41(4), 731–742.

Smith, R., & Priest, S. (1991). CATI staff training manual. Brock University Press, St. Catharines, ON.

Stolzenburg, L. (1987, May). Tell your managers to go climb a rock. Colorado Business Magazine, 28–31.

Williams, D. H. (1988). Adventure with a purpose. The Training Officer, 16(10), 259–261.

Willis, R. (1985). Peak experience: Managers in the mountains. Management Review, 74, 18–23.

Zemke, R. (1988, April). Raiders of the lost metaphor. Training, 8.

Appendix 2

Author Biographies

Allen, Jo Anna Woo, Ph.D. Jo Anna Woo Allen, Ph.D., is a Home/Hospital teacher with the Baltimore County Public Schools in Towson, Maryland, USA.

Attarian, Aram. Aram Attarian is an assistant professor with the Department of Physical Education at North Carolina State University in Raleigh, North Carolina, USA. He is also a consultant with various adventure-based programs.

Beer, W. Nicholas. W. Nicholas Beer is chief instructor at the Pacific Crest Outward Bound School in Portland, Oregon, USA.

Beidler, Peter G. Peter G. Beidler is a professor of English at Lehigh University in Bethlehem, Pennsylvania, USA. He was named National Professor of the Year by the Council for Advancement and Support of Education.

Bell, Martha. Martha Bell is a lecturer in Outdoor Education at the University of Otago in Dunedin, New Zealand.

Bernstein David. David Bernstein is the co-director of Project Blueberry at Minnechaug Regional High School in Wilbraham, Massachusetts, USA.

Brown, Jim. Jim Brown is a professor of History at Samford University in Birmingham, Alabama, USA.

Burkhardt, Robert. Robert Burkhardt is the Head of School at Eagle Rock School and Professional Development Center in Estes Park, Colorado, USA.

Clough, Gruffie. No current information available.

Cole, Kennan. No current information available.

Conrad, Dan. Dan Conrad is Director of Community Involvement at Hopkins High School in Hopkins, Minnesota, USA.

Crew, Dr. Adolph B. Dr. Adolph B. Crew is Professor Emeritus at the University of Alabama and the director of the Learning Center for Tannehill Historical State Park, Tuscaloosa, Alabama, USA.

Druian, Greg. No current information available.

Dunham, Timothy. No current information available.

Ewert, Alan W. Alan W. Ewert is Professor and Programme Chair at the University of Northern British Columbia, Prince George, British Columbia, Canada.

Flor, Richard. Richard Flor is an assistant professor of Leadership and Human Development at the University of Wyoming in Laramie, Wyoming, USA.

Gerth, Tom. No current information available.

Gerstein, Amy. Amy Gerstein is the associate director of the Bay Area Region Coalition of Essential Schools in Redwood City, California, USA. She is also a doctoral candidate at Stanford University.

Griffith, Scott C. Scott C. Griffith is a social studies teacher with the Boulder Valley School District, Boulder, Colorado, USA. He holds a Master's Degree in Experiential Education from the University of Colorado at Boulder.

Hall, McClellan. McClellan Hall is the founder/director of the National Indian Youth Leadership Project Based in Gallup, New Mexico, USA. His tribal affiliation is Cherokee/Pawnee.

Haun, W. Patrick. W. Patrick Haun is an assistant professor of Human Relations at High Point University in High Point, North Carolina, USA.

Havens, Mark, Ed.D., C.T.R.S. Dr. Mark Havens works as a consultant to agencies, organizations, and corporations in adventure- and experience-based training. He currently resides in Sisters, Oregon, USA.

Hedin, Diane. Diane Hedin (1943-1991) was a professor in the Center for Youth Development and Research, University of Minnesota, Minneapolis, Minnesota, USA.

Heneveld, Ward. Ward Heneveld is a senior education specialist for The World Bank in Washington, D.C., USA.

Herbert, Tom. Tom Herbert is a teacher at Concord High School in Concord, New Hampshire, USA. He has been a teacher for 23 years, including 20 years with R.O.P.E.

Hoefler, Virginia. No current information available.

Horwood, Bert. Bert Horwood is Professor Emeritus for the Faculty of Education at Queen's University, Kingston, Ontario, Canada. He is also currently a director of the Institute for Earth Education (Canada).

Hoyt, Judith A. Judith A. Hoyt is a Family Challenge Consultant with ASLAN/ Eagle and Associates in Oxford, Massachusetts, USA.

Jernstedt, G. Christian. No current information available.

Johnson, Bruce. Bruce Johnson is the International Program Coordinator for the Institute for Earth Education in Greenville, West Virginia, USA.

Kahne, Joseph. Joseph Kahne is an assistant professor of Education at the University of Illinois at Chicago, Chicago, Illinois, USA.

Kielsmeier, James. James Kielsmeier is the president and chief executive officer of the National Youth Leadership Council in St. Paul, Minnesota, USA. He is a former president of AEE and Kurt Hahn Award recipient.

Knapp, Clifford E. Cliff Knapp is a professor of Outdoor Teacher Education at Northern Illinois University, Taft Field Campus, in Oregon, Illinois, USA.

Knowles, J. Gary. J. Gary Knowles is an assistant professor of Education at the University of Michigan in Ann Arbor, Michigan, USA.

Kolb, Darl G., Ph.D. Darl G. Kolb, PhD., is a lecturer in Organisational Development and Management in the School of Commerce and Economics at the University of Auckland, New Zealand. He has been involved in adventure and experiential education since 1979.

Kraft, Richard J. Richard J. Kraft is a professor of Education at the University of Colorado in Boulder, Colorado, USA. He is former executive director of AEE and a Kurt Hahn Award recipient.

Lackie, Joyce C. Joyce C. Lackie is a professor of English at the University of Northern Colorado, in Greeley, Colorado, USA.

Leonard, Lana S. No current information available.

Luckmann, Charles W. Charles W. Luckmann is the education director for the North Cascades Institute in Bellingham, Washington, USA, and the editor of the *Journal of Experiential Education* for AEE. He has a long history with Outward Bound (1972-83) and was a high school teacher for 8 years in Seattle, Washington.

Marshall, Michael J., Ph.D. Michael J. Marshall, Ph. D., is an associate professor of Psychology at West Liberty State College in West Liberty, West Virginia, USA.

Marty, Roger H. Roger H. Marty is an associate professor of Mathematics at Cleveland State University in Cleveland, Ohio, USA.

McClintock, Mary. Mary McClintock is the administrative coordinator for the National Association for Mediation in Education (NAME) in Amherst, Massachusetts, USA.

Mellen, David. No current information available.

Michalec, Paul. Paul Michalec is a doctoral student in Experiential Education at the University of Colorado at Boulder, Boulder, Colorado, USA.

Miles, John C. John C. Miles is a professor of Environmental Studies at Huxley College, Western Washington University, in Bellingham, Washington, USA.

Moore, Jeff. No current information available.

Muessig, Raymond H. Raymond H. Muessig is a professor of Humanities Education at the Ohio State University in Columbus, Ohio, USA.

Nathan, Joe. Joe Nathan is the director of the Center for School Change at the Humphrey Institute, University of Minnesota, in Minneapolis, Minnesota, USA.

Owen, Sharon K., Ph.D. Sharon K. Owen, Ph.D., is a senior research analyst for the Multnomah County Sheriff's Office in Portland, Oregon, USA.

Owens, Thomas R. Thomas R. Owens is the associate director of the Education and Work Program for the Northwest Regional Education Laboratory in Portland, Oregon, USA

Page, Homer. Homer Page is the Boulder County Commissioner, Boulder, Colorado, USA, and the president of the National Federation of the Blind of Colorado.

Priest, Dr. Simon. Dr. Simon Priest is a full professor and director of CATI at Brock University in St. Catharines, Ontario, Canada.

Prouty, Dick. Dick Prouty is the executive director of Project Adventure, Hamilton, Massachusetts, USA.

Raffan, James. James Raffan is the coordinator of Outdoor and Experiential Education at Queen's University in Kingston, Ontario, Canada.

Ramke, Ronald G. Ronald G. Ramke is a professor of Sociology and the chair of the Department of Behavioral Sciences at High Point University in High Point, North Carolina, USA.

Ramsey Chandross, Kathryn. No current information available.

Richards, Dr. Anthony. Dr. Anthony Richards is a professor at Dalhousie University in Halifax, Nova Scotia, Canada.

Rohnke, Karl. Karl Rohnke works with Project Adventure, Inc., in Wenham, Massachusetts, USA.

Roland, Dr. Christopher C. Dr. Christopher C. Roland is managing partner of Roland/Diamond Associates, Inc., in Keene, New Hampshire, USA. He has 7 years of experience as a teacher, university professor, and planning & training specialist.

Salmons-Rue, Janet. Janet Salmons-Rue is the training and services director for MAGIC ME AMERICA: Learning to Serve...Serving to Learn, in Baltimore, Maryland, USA.

Schubert, Sabine. No current information available.

Silcox, Harry C. No current information available.

Stanton, Timothy K., Ph.D. Timothy K. Stanton, Ph.D., is the director of the Haas Center for Public Service at Stanford University in Stanford, California, USA.

Sugerman, Deborah, Ph.D. Deborah Sugerman, Ph.D., is an associate professor of Outdoor Recreation at Unity College in Unity, Maine, USA.

Sweeney, Shawn. No current information available.

Sykes, Ian. Ian Sykes is the vice principal at Silver Springs Elementary School for the Calgary Board of Education in Calgary, Alberta, Canada.

Timmer, Greg. Greg Timmer is an English teacher at Minnechaug Regional High School in Wilbraham, Massachusetts, USA.

Udall, Denis. Denis Udall is a school design specialist at Expeditionary Learning/Outward Bound of the New American Schools Development Corporation in Cambridge, Massachusetts, USA.

Walker Stevens, Peggy. Peggy Walker Stevens is the program director for the Education Development Center in Newton, Massachusetts, USA. She is also a past president of AEE and a former editor of the *Journal of Experiential Education*.

Warner, Alan. No current information available.

Warren, Karen. Karen Warren is an instructor with the Outdoors Program and Recreational Athletics at Hampshire College in Amherst, Massachusetts, USA.

Westheimer, Joel. Joel Westheimer is an acting assistant professor and director of the Experiential Curricula Project at Stanford University School of Education in Stanford, California, USA.

Williamson, John E. (Jed). Jed Williamson is a consultant for Education and Outdoor Pursuits in Hanover, New Hampshire, USA. He is also a former Outward Bound School Director and a faculty member at the University of New Hampshire.

Wilson, David A. David A. Wilson is the vice president of Educational Services for EcoGroup, Inc., in St. Louis, Missouri, USA.

Yerkes, Rita. Rita Yerkes is associate dean of the George Williams College and the chairperson for the Recreation Administration Department at Aurora University in Aurora, Illinois, USA. She is a also a past president of AEE.

Appendix 3 Index of Original Publication Dates

Unless otherwise noted, all articles were originally published in *The Journal of Experiential Education (JEE)*, published by the Association for Experiential Education. The issue and date of publication are listed after each title. A complete listing of all articles published in the *JEE* since 1978 can be found in the *Journal Index,* available from the Association for Experiential Education, 2885 Aurora Avenue #28, Boulder, Colorado 80303, USA, (303) 440-8844.

Section One: Theoretical Underpinnings of Experiential Learning

Chapter One: Experiential Educational Theory

The Association for Experiential Education (AEE)

The Association for Experiential Education (AEE) is a not-for-profit, international, professional organization committed to furthering experiental-based teaching and learning in a culture that is increasingly "information-rich but experience-poor." AEE sponsors local, regional, and international conferences and publishes the *Journal of Experiential Education,* the *Jobs Clearinghouse*, directories of programs and services, and a wide variety of books and periodicals to support educators, trainers, practitioners, students and advocates.

To receive additional information about the Association for Experiential Education, call or write: AEE, 2305 Canyon Blvd., Ste. #100, Boulder, Colorado, USA 80302-5651, (303) 440-8844, (303) 440-9541 (FAX).

Please send information on the following:

- ☐ Membership in AEE
- ☐ Program Accreditation Services
- ☐ Conferences
- ☐ Publications List

Please send the following AEE-K/H books:

Qty.	ISBN#	Author & Title	AEE Member	Non-Member	Total
	0-7872-2222-4	Finch/*The K.E.Y. Group*	16.00	21.95	
	0-8403-8272-3	Gass/*Adventure Therapy*	23.00	29.95	
	0-7872-0306-8	Gass/*Book of Metaphors*, Volume II	23.00	29.95	
	0-8403-9038-6	Hunt/*Ethical Issues in Experiential Education,* Second Edition	16.00	23.00	
	0-7872-1596-1	Horwood/*Experience and the Curriculum*	24.00	29.95	
	0-7872-0183-9	Kraft & Kielsmeir/*Experiential Learning in Schools and Higher Education*	30.00	38.00	
	0-7872-0262-2	Warren et al/ *The Theory of Experiential Education*, Third Edition	24.00	35.95	
	0-7872-2059-0	Warren/*Women's Voices in Experiential Education*	19.00	23.95	
AL, AZ, CA, CO, FL, GA, IA, IL, KY, LA, MA, MD, MI, NJ, NY, PA, TN, TX, & WI orders, please add your appropriate sales tax.				Tax:	
Please add $4.00 shipping and handling for the first book. Add $.50 for each additional book ordered. International customers—call for estimate.				Shipping:	
				Total:	

Ship To:

Name _____

Address _____

City_____ State_____ Zip _____

Phone (___) _____

AEE Membership number _____

Payment:

- ☐ Check enclosed ☐ Purchase Order

Charge to: ☐ Am. Express ☐ Visa ☐ MasterCard

Card # _____

Name as it appears on card: _____

Signature _____

(Signature required for all charge orders.)

Copy or detach this form and either:

Mail: Kendall/Hunt Publishing Company
Customer Service
4050 Westmark Drive
P.O. Box 1840
Dubuque, IA 52004-1840, USA

Toll-Free FAX: 1-800-772-9165
(24 hours a day/7 days a week)
International FAX: 1-319-589-1046
For a complete listing of available AEE publications and member information, please contact AEE at the phone number or address listed above

About the Association for Experiential Education

The Association for Experiential Education (AEE) is a not-for-profit, international, professional organization with roots in adventure education, committed to the development, practice, and evaluation of experiential learning in all settings.

AEE sponsors local, regional, and international conferences, projects, seminars, and institutes, and publishes the *Journal of Experiential Education*, the *Jobs Clearinghouse*, directories of programs and services, and a wide variety of books and periodicals to support educators, trainers, practitioners, students, and advocates.

AEE's diverse membership consists of individuals and organizations with affiliations in education, recreation, outdoor adventure programming, mental health, youth service, physical education, management development training, corrections, programming for people with disabilities, and environmental education.

To receive additional information about the Association for Experiential Education call or write:

AEE
2885 Aurora Avenue #28
Boulder, CO USA 80303-2252
(303) 440-8844
(303) 440-9581 (fax)